Law and The Christian Tradition in Scandinavia

This book presents a comprehensive history of law and religion in the Nordic context.

The entwinement of law and religion in Scandinavia encompasses an unusual history, not widely known yet important for its impact on contemporary political and international relations in the region. The volume provides a holistic picture from the first written legal sources of the twelfth century to the law of the present secular welfare states. It recounts this history through biographical case studies. Taking the point of view of major influential figures in church, politics, university, and law, it thus presents the principal actors who served as catalysts in ecclesiastical and secular law through the centuries. This refreshing approach to legal history contributes to a new trend in historiography, particularly articulated by the younger generation of experienced Nordic scholars whose work is featured prominently in this volume.

The collection will be a valuable resource for academics and researchers working in the areas of Legal History and Law and Religion.

Kjell Å Modéer is Professor Emeritus of Legal History at Lund University, Sweden.

Helle Vogt holds the Chair in Legal History at the Faculty of Law, University of Copenhagen, Denmark.

Law and Religion

The practice of religion by individuals and groups, the rise of religious diversity, and the fear of religious extremism, raise profound questions for the interaction between law and religion in society. The regulatory systems involved, the religion laws of secular government (national and international) and the religious laws of faith communities, are valuable tools for our understanding of the dynamics of mutual accommodation and the analysis and resolution of issues in such areas as: religious freedom; discrimination; the autonomy of religious organisations; doctrine, worship and religious symbols; the property and finances of religion; religion, education and public institutions; and religion, marriage and children. In this series, scholars at the forefront of law and religion contribute to the debates in this area. The books in the series are analytical with a key target audience of scholars and practitioners, including lawyers, religious leaders, and others with an interest in this rapidly developing discipline.

Titles in this series include:

Christianity and Criminal Law
Edited by Mark Hill QC, Norman Doe, R. H. Helmholz and John Witte Jr.

Law and the Christian Tradition in Italy
The Legacy of the Great Jurists
Edited by Rafael Domingo and Orazio Condorelli

Church Laws and Ecumenism
A New Path for Christian Unity
Edited by Norman Doe

For more information about this series, please visit: www.routledge.com/Law-and-Religion/book-series/LAWRELIG

Law and The Christian Tradition in Scandinavia

The Writings of Great Nordic Jurists

Edited by
Kjell Å Modéer and Helle Vogt

Produced by the Center for the Study of Law and Religion, Emory University

Routledge
Taylor & Francis Group
LONDON AND NEW YORK

First published 2021
by Routledge
2 Park Square, Milton Park, Abingdon, Oxon OX14 4RN

and by Routledge
605 Third Avenue, New York, NY 10017

First issued in paperback 2022

Routledge is an imprint of the Taylor & Francis Group, an informa business

Publisher's Note
The publisher has gone to great lengths to ensure the quality of this reprint but points out that some imperfections in the original copies may be apparent.

British Library Cataloguing-in-Publication Data
A catalogue record for this book is available from the British Library

Library of Congress Cataloging-in-Publication Data
A catalog record has been requested for this book

ISBN: 978-0-367-56357-8 (pbk)
ISBN: 978-0-367-85824-7 (hbk)
ISBN: 978-1-003-01525-3 (ebk)

DOI: 10.4324/9781003015253

Typeset in Galliard
by codeMantra

Contents

Contributors

Per Andersen, Professor of Law, Vice-Dean for Education, Aarhus BSS – Aarhus University

Lisbet Christoffersen, Professor of Law and Religion, Roskilde University

Niels Henrik Gregersen, Professor of Systematic Theology, University of Copenhagen

Anders Jarlert, Senior Professor in Church History, Centre for Theology and Religious Studies, Lund University

Morten Kjær, Associate Professor, Department of Law, University of Southern Denmark

Sören Koch, Professor of Legal History and comparative law, Faculty of Law, Bergen University

Mia Korpiola, Professor of Legal History, Faculty of Law, Turku University

Torgeir Landro, Associate Professor, NLA University College Bergen

Alexander Maurits, Assistant Professor in Church History, Centre for Theology and Religious Studies, Lund University

Kristian Mejrup, PhD in church history, independent researcher

Kjell Å Modéer, Professor emeritus of Legal History, Faculty of Law, Lund University

Egil Morland, Professor of Theology (Homiletics and Ecclesial Law), NLA University College, Bergen, Norway

Bertil Nilsson, Professor emeritus in Church History, Gothenburg University

Heikki Pihlajamäki, Professor of Comparative Legal History, Faculty of Law, University of Helsinki

Jussi Sallila, PhD in legal history, editor of the Law section of the Helsinki Term Bank for the Arts and Sciences

Mattias Skat Sommer, Postdoc in Church History, University of Göttingen

Stina Fallberg Sundmark, Associate Professor in Ecclesiology, Faculty of Theology, Uppsala University

Helle Vogt, Professor of Legal History, Faculty of Law, University of Copenhagen

John Witte, Jr., Director, Center for the Study of Law and Religion, Emory University

Foreword

A decade ago, distinguished Swedish legal historian Kjell Å Modéer helped lead a team of Scandinavian scholars in the publication of a pathbreaking study titled *Law & Religion in the 21st Century—Nordic Perspectives.* That welcome volume introduced the English-speaking world to the richness and diversity of current Scandinavian understandings of church and state, society and politics, faith and freedom, religion and rights, family and education, and more. It was a surprise for some readers to learn about the growing disestablishment of Lutheranism and the growing separation of church and state in several of these Scandinavian lands. It was also a surprise to learn that this region—long known as Europe's leader in cultural secularization, social experimentation, and institutional innovation—was now blossoming with new legal life "growing in the ruins" of traditional Christian ideas and institutions.

While that first volume presciently mapped the future of law and religion in Scandinavia in the third millennium, this new volume expertly maps the interaction of law and religion in the second millennium. Here, the focus is not on the new green shoots of law and legal theory sprouting among the ruins of Christian monuments. The focus is on the monumental growth of the public, private, penal, and procedural law and legal theory that emerged when Christianity ruled Scandinavia as the established religion, and church and state cooperated in the governance of Christian realms.

In this volume, Professor Modéer has teamed up with Denmark's top legal historian, Helle Vogt, in leading two dozen distinguished scholars in a fresh interdisciplinary study of some of the greatest Scandinavian architects of law and Christianity, from the twelfth through the twentieth centuries. The editors have judiciously commissioned case studies of a score of Catholics and Lutherans, canonists and civilians, Pietists and Romantics, churchmen and statesmen, theologians and jurists, and natural lawyers and historical schoolmen whose lives and work collectively shaped and reshaped the interaction of law and religion in Nordic history.

Much of this material will be new to Anglophone readers. A few Reformation specialists will recognize the names of such Lutheran pioneers as Bugenhagen, the Petris, and Hemmingsen. A few constitutional historians might know the groundbreaking legal and political work of Grundtvig, Taranger, and Castberg.

But many other figures who come to light and life in these pages deserve to be better known. For example, though I know a bit about the history of criminal law, I was chastened to learn for the first time about the remarkable reforms of criminal law initiated on overt Christian terms by Karl Gustav Ehrström. While I knew something of Bonhoeffer and other German Lutheran resistance writers against Nazism, the extraordinary and sacrificial work of Eivind Berggrav was a special revelation. Though the work of famous Nordic legal realist Alf Ross was standard reading when I was in law school, I had never heard of Göran Göransson, whose work seems so much more creative and sustaining. This volume is the first such comprehensive history of law and religion in a Scandinavian context, and other readers will enjoy finding similar treasures and discoveries in these pages.

This volume is part of an ongoing project on Great Christian Jurists in World History. This project is directed by the Center for the Study of Law and Religion at Emory University, where Professors Modéer and Vogt are nonresidential senior fellows. Each volume in this series focuses on a specific country, region, or era and samples the life and work of a score or more of its greatest legal minds over the centuries. These legal minds include not only civil and canon lawyers and judges but also theologians, philosophers, and church leaders who contributed decisively to legal ideas and institutions or helped create landmark statutes, canons, or cases. Thus, familiar jurists like Gratian, Grotius, Blackstone, Kuttner, and Scalia appear in this series, but so do theologians and churchmen like Augustine, Isidore, Aquinas, Calvin, Barth, and Romero. This biographical approach is not intended to deprecate institutional, doctrinal, social, or intellectual histories of law, nor will it devolve into a new form of hagiography or hero worship of dead white males. It is instead designed to offer a simple method and common heuristic to study the interaction of law and Christianity around the world over the past two millennia. In due course, we hope to produce some fifty volumes and one thousand biographical case studies, all told.

Columbia University Press opened this series in 2006 by publishing a three-volume work titled *Modern Christian Teachings on Law, Politics, and Human Nature*, divided into case studies of nearly thirty modern Catholic, Protestant, and Orthodox Christian figures. Cambridge University Press has in print or in press newly commissioned studies on great Christian jurists in the first millennium as well as in English, Spanish, French, Lowlands, and American history. Routledge will publish major new volumes on great Christian jurists in Italian, Russian, Welsh, and Latin American history. Mohr Siebeck is taking up the German story; Federation Press is taking up the Australian story. In due course, the Center for the Study of Law and Religion aims to commission similar studies for other parts of the world, particularly countries in Eastern Europe and Eurasia, and discrete regions and eras in the Middle East, Africa, and the Pacific Rim.

This volume was made possible by a generous grant from the McDonald Agape Foundation, which supported the work of the editors and contributors, and underwrote round-table conferences at Lund University and Emory, where the editors and contributors hammered out the parameters of this volume and critiqued preliminary draft chapters. On behalf of the editors and my colleagues in the Center for the Study of Law and Religion, we express our deep thanks to the late Ambassador Alonzo McDonald, Ms. Suzie McDonald, Mr. Peter McDonald, and the other members of the foundation board for their generous support for this and many other related volumes on law and Christianity. We give thanks as well to The Royal Society of Letters at Lund for further underwriting a second workshop at Lund University.

We are deeply grateful to Dr. Gary S. Hauk, senior editor in our Center, for sharing his superb editorial talents so generously in copyediting this manuscript. We also express our warmest thanks to our Center colleagues Ms. Amy Wheeler and Ms. Anita Mann for their skillful administration of this and other scholarly projects, and for their organization of the Emory conference.

It was a joy for me to work with Professors Modéer and Vogt, and the wonderful group of scholars from throughout Scandinavia who contributed to this volume. I learned much from these experts while enjoying the wonders of Nordic hospitality and culture. Several Scandinavian universities are doing powerful and innovative work in legal history and church history, most notably at Lund and Copenhagen, where Professors Modéer and Vogt are leading their colleagues.

It is a delight to publish this volume and several others in the distinguished Law and Religion series, edited by one of the world's preeminent scholars of law and religion, Professor Norman Doe. Professor Doe and his many colleagues in the Cardiff Centre for Law and Religion have been vital trans-Atlantic allies with the Emory Center for the Study of Law and Religion. We give thanks for their leadership in this expanding global field of interdisciplinary legal study and for their partnership with us in publishing this and parallel volumes on law and Christianity.

Finally, the editors and I express our warm thanks to Alison Kirk and her colleagues at Routledge in taking on this volume and applying their usual standards of excellence in their editing, production, and marketing.

John Witte, Jr.
Director, Center for the Study of Law and Religion
Emory University

Introduction

Kjell Å Modéer and Helle Vogt

This book fills a gap in the literature of modern law and religion. The connection between law and religion is different in Scandinavia than in many other regions of Europe because of the lack of university-trained lawyers in the Nordic countries up to the eighteenth century. This meant that individual scholars and legal thinkers shaped the law and legal development, while theologians had an essential role in lawmaking. To arrive at a holistic picture of the relation among law, religion, and the historical figures presented here, the book covers the whole of Scandinavian legal history, from the first written legal sources that appear in the twelfth century to the present secular welfare states.

This volume takes first of all the point of view of the actors in the history, and it thus contributes to a new trend of presenting the foremost catalysts in ecclesiastical law as well as secular law. The book also presents this field of Scandinavian law in an international context. Thus the book presents Nordic intellectual history as manifested in current scholarly work in the relationship between law and religion.

We have chosen a number of jurists or legal thinkers who have had an important role in shaping church law or implementing Christian doctrines in secular law. It will become apparent to the reader that the actors described in this volume achieved their greatness through their interactions with other important contemporaries. One phenomenon that becomes evident is that the cognitive structures of theologians and jurists are not identical but parallel and intertwined.

It has not been an easy task to select these great Christian jurists. One challenge has been that being a jurist in the Nordic context has played out differently in different legal cultures and national territories, so it is difficult to sum up and outline a monolithic, common Nordic history of Christian jurisprudence. The contexts have differed not only across national legal cultures and religious traditions but also across time, including different interpretations of texts produced by the great theologians and jurists throughout the centuries. Thus, tracing the birth of a Nordic legal culture and jurisprudence and outlining a common Nordic history of Christian jurisprudence are made difficult by the often asynchronous historical development in the Nordic countries and the mere fact that there were far fewer jurists—especially those studying or writing about Christendom and law—in the Nordic countries than in many of the neighboring countries to the south, east, and west.

Moreover, many Nordic jurists were not trained in law in a modern sense. Most of the Nordic thinkers on Christian law *were* learned and *had* studied at a European university at some time, but most of them studied theology, not connecting it with legal studies, as happened in many other regions of Europe. The Nordic legal tradition was and is not a tradition of highly theoretical law, neither in the past nor today. Admittedly, there was and has always been a learned legal environment which sprang from Christian thinking and the teaching of law at the universities in southern Europe. But this environment included only a few Scandinavian individuals from time to time—never numerous enough to establish the direction of or a pivotal influence on the more practical (pragmatic) tradition taking root and developing in the Nordic countries from the Middle Ages on. From the beginning, the Christian legal environment in Scandinavia included very few active thinkers and writers, which makes it difficult to talk about a scientific discipline as such, in either a modern or a contemporary sense. During the various historical periods, there were too few to form a scientific environment, and they contributed too little to legal learning to influence the legal tradition in a decisive, learned, and theoretical direction.

This is not to say that jurists have played no role in the development of the Nordic Christian legal tradition—not at all. They *have* played a role—just not in the foreground, but rather indirectly legitimizing the moral and ethical—or even learned, legal, technical—background of law as it was put forward by pragmatically orientated, power-seeking kings and other legal actors throughout history. The Nordic legal tradition is first of all pragmatic, developed on a very distinct, practice-focused foundation rooted in old, nonlearned traditions. Like many other legal traditions, however, the Nordic tradition from time to time has needed to be legitimized by more than just pragmatism and the internal rationale of the laws or legal thinking. Many Nordic jurists today are unaware of the Christian influence of the Nordic tradition or the jurists who played a decisive role in it. Thus, the aim of this volume is to present a choice of the great jurists from the Nordic countries, that, is, those representative figures who shaped the theological as well as legal cognitive structures in which they lived.

Identity and culture in a Nordic context

Within comparative law, the Nordic countries are regarded as a harmonious region, as a homogeneous "legal family" within Western civilization. As implied above, there is much merit in this interpretation on a general level, but there are many local differences among the Nordic countries as well, which will become clear throughout the biographies presented in this volume. To talk about "the Nordic tradition" or "the Nordic legal family" is a generalizing construct that leaves out a lot of the differences among the different countries. But after all, it does make some sense—as also implied above—when one wants to describe a historical development, even though there are sometimes few sources to rely on. Therefore the "Nordic" forms a reasonable and suitable frame for the presentations that follow.

However, one must be aware of a competing frame. Since the end of the Cold War and the breakdown of the Soviet Union, the construct of a Nordic legal family has received competition from the Baltic region, especially when it comes to the legal tradition of the early modern period—a period characterized by the increased importance of science, technological breakthroughs, gradual secularization of the political sphere, commerce, and the emergence of capitalist economies, all while the territorial state becomes the dominant political entity. Traditionally, the Baltic Sea has been regarded as a *Mare lutheranum*, where most of the inhabitants have belonged to either Lutheran folk churches or important Lutheran minorities formed and acting in the early modern period following the Reformation in the beginning of the sixteenth century. In this sense, the Baltic region and traditions fit well into a broader concept of a Nordic legal tradition or "family" when it comes to the early modern period. Thus, this broader geopolitical entity could have been defended in terms of legal history for inclusion in this volume on law and religion. We have decided, however, to exclude Iceland and the Baltic states, limiting the figures included to those active in the Nordic mainland.

The reasons for excluding Iceland are twofold. First, since the Old Covenant subjugated Iceland to Norway in 1262–64, Iceland remained part of other Nordic countries until after World War II—first as part of Norway, then as part of the Danish kingdom, receiving sovereignty under Danish rule in 1918 but declaring its independence from Denmark only in 1944. Therefore, it would be an incorrect construction to handle any historical Icelandic jurist as Icelandic in any independent sense. Second, no Icelandic jurists have risen to a level of greatness to merit inclusion in the dual context of law and religion.

The reason for excluding the Baltic states is the same as for Iceland: history and the absence of what one could call great Christian jurists with a connection to the Nordic countries. In Viking times, the Baltic region was populated by several different peoples (Esters, Livonians, Latvians, Lithuanians, Prussians, et al.) who had close contacts with people from the Nordic area. But as a result of the German eastward expansion in the twelfth and thirteenth centuries, the Balts came under German influence, followed by a union between the Lithuanians and Poland. After the Reformation, all the Baltic peoples became Lutheran, but once again the political and cultural influence was tipped when the area was divided between Sweden and Poland following the Livonian War in 1558–83. Finally, in the eighteenth century, all the Baltic countries were united under one ruler—but once again not a Baltic ruler, rather the Russian tsar. Only in 1918–20 did the Baltics gain independence. In 1940–41 and again after 1945, they were incorporated into the Soviet Union, once more with no possibility to have or develop their own legal culture and legal literature until independence after the end of the Cold War.

Excluding Iceland and the Baltic region makes it easier to maintain the idea of a more or less homogeneous Nordic legal culture. Not only within law but also in religion, the Nordic countries appear to have a common—though diverse—history in relation to the rest of Europe. But the Nordic region is not in opposition to the European, not at all. This volume will demonstrate that the theologians and jurists presented here as great figures in ecclesiastical or church law have two or more identities. They are part of a common European intellectual paradigm, but they are simultaneously acting in different national legal cultures throughout the history of shifting political borders.

Structure of the book

The book is divided into five sections: the medieval period; the early modern period, focusing on legal changes resulting from the Lutheran Reformation; the eighteenth century, when the Enlightenment and Pietism led to changes in Lutheran orthodoxy; the nineteenth century, when democracy and the struggle for freedom rights challenged the state-dominated theology; and finally modernity, the twentieth century, with the creation of the secular Scandinavian welfare states and the state churches. Each section begins with a general introduction to the period focusing on law and political matters, and then a number of legal thinkers from the period are presented.

Part 1

The Middle Ages

1 Introduction

The Middle Ages

Bertil Nilsson and Helle Vogt

The first jurist in this volume is Archbishop Absalon of Lund, who lived in the second half of the twelfth century, when the legal order based on written laws emerged in the Scandinavian kingdoms. Hence, legal thinkers became important.

Big differences in economic and social structures existed among the Scandinavian kingdoms. With regard to the linguistic and political scene, however, there were common features. The kingdoms were linked by a common linguistic understanding, *dönsk tunga* (lit. "Danish tongue"), yet one should not imagine that it was one language. Rather, the northwest (where Old Norse prevailed) and the southeast (where Old Danish and Old Swedish predominated) were connected by the similarities of these languages. The political power was divided between the king and his council, comprising the best men of the realm, i.e., the most powerful secular lords and the bishops.[1] Originally, Iceland was an independent unit, but in 1262–64 the Icelanders came under the Norwegian crown. In 1380, Norway and Denmark were united, and in 1397, they entered into a union with Sweden—the Kalmar Union, named after the town in Sweden where the agreement was reached. In principle, each kingdom upheld its own council, but the same king ruled them all. Denmark was the leading player in the union, whereas the Swedes rebelled several times in the fifteenth century, finally breaking away in 1523. Norway and Denmark remained united until 1814.[2]

Beginning in the twelfth century, the Scandinavian church provinces consisted of slightly more than twenty episcopal sees. The metropolitans/archbishops resided in Lund (Denmark since 1103/4), Trondheim/Nidaros (Norway since 1153), and Uppsala (Sweden since 1164). The church provinces in Denmark included today's Swedish provinces of Scania, Blekinge, and Halland, and in Norway, they included Iceland and Greenland as well as the Norse islands in the Western Ocean. The Swedish church province also comprised today's Finland, which was part of the Swedish kingdom until 1809. The province of Jämtland (today in Sweden) belonged politically to Norway but ecclesiastically to the archdiocese of Uppsala. Today's Swedish provinces of Härjedalen and Bohuslän belonged to Norway. Episcopal sees were successively established from the early Middle Ages on, at first in Denmark from the middle of the tenth century, and a little bit later in Norway and Sweden. The vast majority of the sees existed throughout the whole of the Middle Ages, although some were moved, and others ceased to exist.[3]

Although politically the kingdoms shared some common features, Scandinavia is geographically and economically very diverse. Denmark and parts of southern Sweden were dominated by rich agricultural land and villages. Hence, grain production was the main source of income. Further north, the landscape was rockier and more forested. Especially in Norway, agricultural land was scarce, and the countryside was dominated by mountains and large valleys of great political and economic importance. Norwegian farms were not centered in villages but spread over the countryside. Here income derived largely from fishing, sheep herding, fur production, and forestry.[4]

The chosen legal thinkers and the source situation

The legal circumstances in the Scandinavian countries meant that it was not until the early modern period that secular lawyers started to receive formal legal training. Before that, jurists with formal training were all ecclesial. There is a very rational basis for our choice of jurists from the medieval period: They all belong to the quite small number of jurists about whom we actually know something more than just their names, although this also means that they are not necessarily the most representative. When studying the Scandinavian medieval jurists, the greatest difficulty lies in dealing with sources. The few narrative texts preserved deal primarily with political matters; therefore, when jurists are mentioned, mainly their political and legal functions are described. In addition to the law texts, which can inform about legal knowledge in general but very seldom about individual jurists, the most important sources are charters, where we get glimpses of legal practice.

Unfortunately, the evidence gained from Scandinavian charters appears rather poor when compared to those from other parts of Europe. The number of extant charters is limited. Very few originals are preserved, the vast majority of the copies or summaries found in late medieval monastic cartularies. Many archival records were of course lost during the early modern period because of war, fires, accidents, and so on, while others seem to have been discarded by medieval monastic archivists.[5]

The languages of Scandinavian charters are divided between an eastern and a western Nordic tradition. In Denmark and Sweden, all charters were drawn up in Latin until the later Middle Ages, when the use of vernacular was introduced in the second half of the fourteenth century (Sweden) and the early fifteenth century (Denmark).[6] In Norway, the picture is more complicated. Among ecclesiastical institutions, the standard language was Latin, but charters issued by kings or other laypeople were written in the vernacular at least from the 1170s and probably even earlier.[7]

The legal foundation[8]

All the Scandinavian kingdoms were divided into legal provinces, each with its own provincial assembly (*thing*) and most with their own law. Sweden consisted of eight main provinces, Norway four, and Denmark three. Owing to very limited source material, precious little is known about law and legal practice in the eleventh and twelfth centuries. However, it seems that the commitment of laws to writing started in Norway and Iceland in the twelfth century, in Denmark from the late twelfth century, and in Sweden from the mid-thirteenth century.[9]

There are both national—and, for Sweden and Norway, regional—differences among the laws in terms of style and contents. A large portion of the laws concerned procedure. They cover areas such as inheritance, donations, regulation of the household and partnerships, property transfer, sale, mortgage, and contracts compensation. Other parts contain what we today call penal law and, in the Danish and Swedish laws, village and agricultural matters. The Danish laws differed in style among themselves, but the contents were quite uniform. This might be the reason why Denmark, unlike Norway (1274) and Sweden (c. 1350), did not develop a national law covering the whole kingdom before 1683. All the laws were written in the vernacular. When comparing the older and newer laws, it becomes clear how a legal language gradually was created.[10]

The main secular institution for the administration of justice in medieval Scandinavia was the *thing* (*placitum, curis secularis,* or just *ius*), a public assembly of all free men within a province or a certain jurisdictional district. The *thing* was not a court of law in the narrow sense. It had no judges, scribes, or legal officials of its own, and it had no executive power. Rather, it was a multifunctional venue for discussion and determination of any matter of communal concern, such as public announcements, calling of the military levy, publication of social status, settling of disputes, and the like. The proceedings of the *thing* took place at regular intervals in the open air at fixed sites protected by the peace.[11]

There existed different levels of assemblies, from relatively local ones dealing primarily with local matters, to big main assemblies covering a whole province. Eventually, royal courts also appeared. In the later Middle Ages, an appeal system started to develop, probably inspired by the system found at ecclesiastical courts.

Geography and infrastructure were also important for the administration of justice. The size of the legal units and the frequency of the assemblies' meetings were determined by the size of an area's population and how long and difficult the journey to the assembly was. In Denmark, for instance, the local assemblies met every week. With the exception of the districts in the wooded areas in the Scanian province, it never took more than a couple of hours on horseback to get to the assembly. Even to reach the provincial assemblies, more than a day or two of transport was very rare. In Norway and large parts of Sweden, the legal units were much larger, and traveling even short distances was difficult because of mountains and forests. Here the assemblies met more seldom, and the provincial assemblies especially were summoned only a few times each year, during the traveling seasons, which for the coastal areas and the fjords was the summertime, whereas in the interior parts the traveling season was the wintertime, when snow evened out the countryside for sleighs. These assemblies lasted much longer than the regular Danish ones.

The provincial laws of Denmark contain no rules regulating religious issues. At the time the laws were written down, the authority of canon law and the ecclesiastical courts seems to have been fully accepted.[12] In this respect, Denmark differs from Norway and Sweden, where all the provincial laws began with a section of church law. On the other hand, separate church laws existed for Zealand and Scania. They were not officially part of the provincial laws, but in practice, they are often found in the provincial-law manuscripts. The sections of church law regulated parishioners' rights and obligations—for instance, in matters of religious practice, church buildings, and the functions of the priest. In both Norway and Sweden, however, ecclesiastical courts were often located at a great distance from the parties' homes. In that case, lawsuits involving church law were pursued at the local secular assembly. In Norway, this practice of mixed jurisdiction was maintained throughout the Middle Ages.

Together with the bishop, the cathedral chapters played a decisive role in implementing canon law in the different dioceses as well as in maintaining liturgical unity within them.[13] The earliest cathedral chapters were regular—i.e., their members, the canons, lived according to a rule similar to those prevalent in monasteries. This type of chapter was not established at every cathedral in the Scandinavian church provinces and seems rather to have been rare. Gradually, the regular chapters, almost without exception, were replaced by secular ones. At cathedrals without regular chapters, secular ones were organized. The secular canons lived in the "world," holding an office in the diocese for their maintenance, and they were obliged to stay regularly in the cathedral city. By and by, the canons to a greater extent were supported by donations, i.e., by prebends. In this respect, however, there was no uniformity. The leading canons of the chapter, the prelates, usually had received a higher education at a university, in either theology or canon law or both. Therefore, many of them were well prepared to handle legal issues for the whole of the diocese and its clergy. Several of them were appointed bishops.[14]

In Denmark, a number of regular cathedral chapters are known from the end of the eleventh century and around the year 1100; possibly there were two in Sweden during the twelfth century and the first decades of the thirteenth century. In the Norwegian church province, no regular chapters seem to have existed. Seemingly, during the latter part of the thirteenth century, almost all Nordic cathedrals had secular chapters, except in Iceland, where probably only one chapter existed. In the Norse islands in the Western Ocean, only the cathedral on the Orkneys had one.[15]

The number of canons varied from one cathedral to another. As self-governed ecclesiastical societies, the cathedral chapters had their own right of decision. For this purpose, successive written statutes were issued regulating the relations between the chapter and the bishop, on one hand, and the chapter's internal conditions and activities on the other. Such statutes are preserved in all three church provinces, though not from every cathedral chapter. These were supplemented by choir statutes (Sw. *korstadga*) giving prescriptions with regard to the services in the cathedral. The most important legally founded external tasks of the chapter were to vote at episcopal elections and to be the bishop's adviser. The bishop had to ask for the chapter's advice regarding all important matters. When the episcopacy became vacant, the chapter took charge of the bishop's judicial and administrative power, his *potestas iurisdictionis.* Nothing indicates that there were considerable differences within the three Nordic church provinces, or among them, in these respects, albeit there were variations in the practice and among individual cases.[16]

As means for implementing valid canon law in the church provinces, the Western church used the papal legate system, on one hand, and the provincial councils on the other. According to a decree issued at the Fourth Lateran Council, in 1215, which confirmed several hundred years of practice, the archbishop should convoke all his subordinate bishops (the suffragans) in the church province, as well as advisers such as abbots and representatives of the cathedral chapters, to a provincial council every year. In 1425, this rule was changed to every third year. Neither the first nor the second frequency was maintained in the Nordic church provinces, in several cases owing to the climate in combination with the long distances and the geography. Provincial councils were held in different places, not necessarily and not even normally in the cathedral city where the archbishop resided. Papal legates summoned and chaired a number of provincial councils, though not many. At the councils, a number of legal ecclesiastical matters of varying importance were treated, and sometimes fundamental and comprehensive statutes were promulgated. Slightly more than ten provincial statutes are known from Norway; in Denmark and Sweden, the number is slightly fewer.[17]

To further disseminate the legal ideals, yearly meetings with the priesthood (diocesan or bishop's synods) would be held in each diocese. In the presence of the clergy, and after advisory participation by the members of the cathedral chapter and a number of synodal witnesses consisting of some of the priests present, the bishop issued diocesan statutes. These dealt not least with the priests' liturgical duties but could also contain prescriptions relevant for every adult parishioner in the diocese—as, for instance, concerning the sacrament of penance.[18]

In Sweden, prescriptions from the late Middle Ages imply that the provincial statutes should be put up on the church's door and read by every parish priest in his church. Furthermore, all the provincial statutes—not only the latest ones—should be studied at the diocesan synods. Diocesan statutes are preserved to a greater extent than provincial statutes, yet with differences between the church provinces. In Sweden, in contrast to the other two church provinces, a compilation of statutes was put together during the first half of the 1440s at the order of the archbishop of Uppsala, after an inventory made in the different dioceses. The compilation, known as *Compendium statutorum Upsalensis prouincie,* comprises a great number of paragraphs and was valid in the whole of the church province.[19]

One of the most important duties of the cathedral chapter was to instruct those who would become clerics in the diocese. This was done in the cathedral schools, which were provided with important libraries that in time comprised fundamental sources of canon law and legal commentaries. The earliest cathedral school in Scandinavia was established in Lund, Denmark, possibly as a consequence of a royal letter of donation as early as 1085. Since universities were founded in Scandinavia only in 1477 (Uppsala) and 1479 (Copenhagen), clerics who wanted to reach higher positions in the church studied abroad. These clerics were supported by, among others, the cathedral chapter through direct allowances or loans. In the beginning, Paris was the principal place of study for young men from Scandinavia, and its university was of great importance for Scandinavian theological erudition. The figures are uncertain and can be calculated only sporadically, but, for example, perhaps 40–50 Swedish young men studied in Paris during the 1310s and 1320s. By this time, a change had occurred that cannot be unambiguously explained, but from then on students from Scandinavia increasingly studied at the university in Prague. After foreign students more or less were forced to leave Prague in 1409, for reasons that had to do with church politics, other universities became increasingly significant for students from Scandinavia. These universities included, above all, those in Erfurt, Cologne, Leipzig, Rostock, and Vienna.[20]

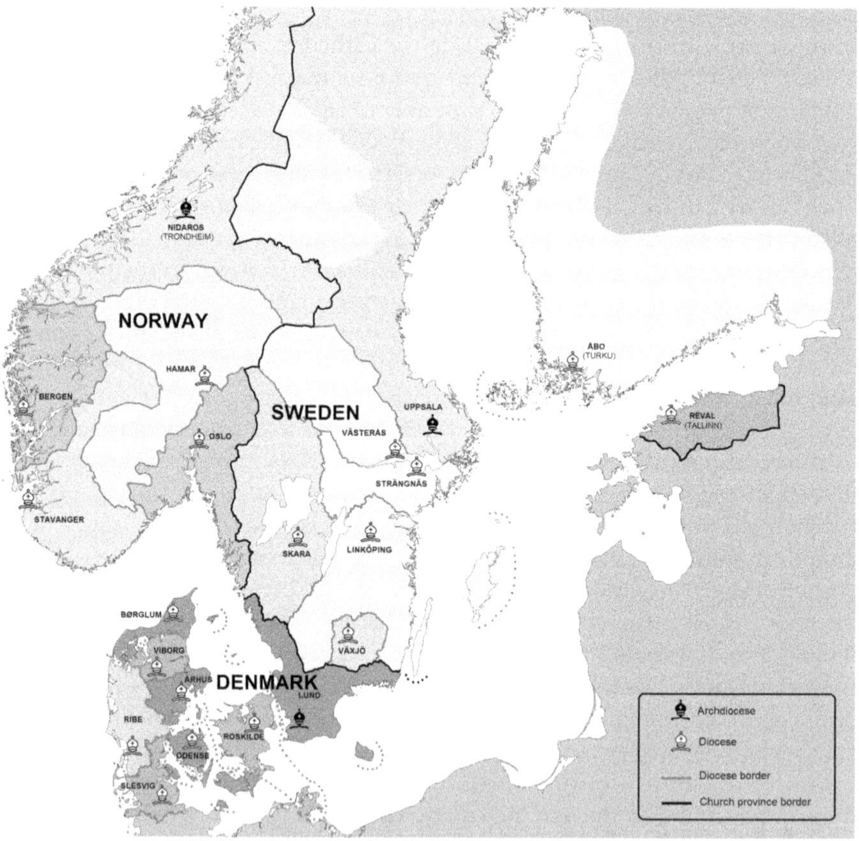

Illustration Dioceses in Scandinavia in the Middle Ages. The map is drawn by Johnny Grandjean Gøgsig Jakobsen

Notes

1 The gathering was called *hof* in Old Danish, translated into Latin as *parlamentum*: *parlamentum, quod hof dicitur. Den danske rigslovgivning indtil 1400*, ed. Erik Kroman (Copenhagen: Munksgaard, 1971), text 1, § 1:75. A similar institution was known in Norway from the second half of the twelfth century (Knut Helle, *Konge og gode menn i norsk riksstyring ca. 1150–1319* (Bergen/Oslo/Tromsø: Universitetsforlaget, 1972)). In Sweden, the institution was first formalized around 1350 by Magnus Eriksson's National Law, but the institution must be older.

2 For a general historical introduction in English, see Birgit Sawyer and Peter Sawyer, *Medieval Scandinavia: From Conversion to Reformation, Circa 800–1500* (Minneapolis: University of Minnesota Press, 1993) and "Early Political Organisation," *The Cambridge History of Scandinavia. Vol. 1: Prehistory to 1520*, ed. Knut Helle, (Cambridge: Cambridge University Press, 2003), 160–234.

3 Eljas Orrman, "Church and Society," *The Cambridge History of Scandinavia*, ed. Knud Helle, 426–31; Bertil Nilsson, "Scandinavian Church," *The Oxford Dictionary of the Middle Ages*, Vol. 4, ed. Robert E. Bjork (Oxford: Oxford University Press, 2010), 1482–83.

4 On the material resources in Scandinavia, see Bjørn Poulsen, Jon Vidar Sigurdssen, and Helle Vogt, eds. *Nordic Elites in Transformation, Vol. 1. Material Resources* (New York: Routledge, 2019). Specifically for Denmark, see Nils Hybel and Bjørn Poulsen, *The Danish Resources c. 1000–1550: Growth and Recession* (Leiden/Boston, MA: Brill, 2007).

5 Brian P. McGuire, *The Cistercians in Denmark: Their Attitudes, Roles, and Function in Medieval Society* (Kalamazoo, MI: Cistercian Publications, 1982), 202–03.

6 Anders Leegaard Knudsen, "Testimonia Placiti—Private Charters as Public Instruments: A Study in Medieval Danish Diplomatics," *Archiv für Diplomatik* 57 (2011): 147–79.

7 Sverre Bagge, *From Viking Stronghold to Christian Kingdom: State Formation in Norway, c. 900–1350* (Copenhagen: Museum Tusculanum Press, 2010), 243–47.

8 For a general English introduction to the Nordic provincial laws, see Helle Vogt, *The Function of Kinship in Medieval Nordic Legislation* (Leiden: Brill, 2010); for the Danish, see Per Andersen, *Legal Procedure and Practice in Medieval Denmark* (Leiden: Brill, 2011).

9 The dating of most of the laws is very uncertain, but roughly they can be dated as follows. In Denmark, the church laws of Scania and Zealand date to the 1170s; the Law of Scania, 1202–16; Valdemar's Law of Zealand, the 1220s; the Law of Jutland, 1241; and Erik's Law of Zealand, the 1240s. The Danish laws are printed in *Danmarks gamle Landskabslove med Kirkelovene*, vols. I–VIII + supplement to vol. IV, eds. Johs. Brøndum-Nielsen and Poul Johs. Jørgensen (Copenhagen: Det Danske Sprog- og Litteraturselskab, 1933–61). The laws are translated into English in Ditlev Tamm and Helle Vogt, eds. *The Danish Medieval Laws: The Laws of Scania, Zealand and Jutland* (New York: Routledge, 2016). In Norway, the Gulathing Law and Frostathing Law are from the middle of the twelfth century onwards, redacted several times; the laws from the two other Norwegian provinces are, with the exception of the sections of the church law, not preserved. The Norwegian laws are printed in *Norges gamle Love indtil 1387*, vols. 1–2, eds. R. Keyser and P.A. Munch (Christiania: Gröndahl, 1846–48). The Gulathing and Frostathing laws are translated into English in *The Earliest Norwegian Laws Being the Gulathing Law and the Frostathing Law*, trans. Laurence M. Larson (New York: Columbia University Press, 1935). In Sweden, the laws were written down much later than in the other countries. The oldest Västgöta Law might be as early as the 1220s, whereas all the other laws in the version we know date from the 1290s to the 1330s. The Swedish laws are printed in *Corpus Iuris Sueo-Gotorum Antiqui*, vols. 1–6, eds. H.S. Collins and C.J. Schlyter (Stockholm/Lund, 1827–44). On the

writing of the Nordic laws, see Helle Vogt, *The Function of Kinship in Medieval Nordic Legislation* (Leiden: Brill, 2005), 27–110; and Per Norseng, "Law Codes as a Source for Nordic History in the Early Middle Ages," *Scandinavian Journal for History* 16/3 (1991): 137–66. For the dating of the Swedish laws, see Bertil Nilsson, "The Swedish Ecclesiastical Legislation and the Question of Its Nordic Character," in *How Nordic are the Nordic Medieval Laws? – Ten Years after. Proceedings of the Tenth Carlsberg Academy Conference on Medieval Legal History 2013*, eds., Per Andersen, Kirsi Salonen, Helle Sigh, and Helle Vogt (Copenhagen: DJØF Publishing, 2014), 81–112.

10 Carl-Ivar Ståhle, *Syntaktiska och stilistiska studier i fornnordiskt lagspråk* (Lund: Carl Blom, 1958); Hans-Peter Naumann, *Sprachstil und Textkonstitution. Untersuchungen zur altwestnordischen Rechtssprache* (Basel/Stuttgart: Helbing & Lichtenhahn, 1979); Nils Jørgensen, *Studier över syntax och textstruktur i nordiska medeltidslagar* (Uppsala, 1987); Rune Røsstad, *A tveim tungum. Om stil og stilvariation i norrønt lovmål,* KULTs skriftserie nr. 73 (Oslo: Noregs Forskingsråd, 1997); Ditlev Tamm and Helle Vogt, "Creating a Danish Legal Language: Legal Terminology in the Medieval Law of Scania," *Historical Research* LXXXVI/233 (2013): 505–14.

11 For a further explanation, see Kim Esmark and Helle Vogt, "Introduction to Part Two: Local Disputes: Property, Justice, and Social Transaction," in *Disputing Strategies in Medieval Scandinavia*, eds. Kim Esmark, Lars Hermanson, Hans Jacob Orning, and Helle Vogt (Leiden: Brill, 2013), 143–60.

12 In Norway, church jurisdiction in Christian matters was recognized by the second half of the twelfth century, although it is difficult to establish what that meant in practice. (Sverre Bagge, "Kirkens jurisdiksjon i kristenrettssaker for 1277," *Historisk Tidsskrift (Norway)* 60 (1981): 144–45). In Sweden, efficient ecclesiastical legal control was not established in many areas before the thirteenth century, and there were probably variations among the provinces.

13 On the formation of cathedral chapters in the Nordic countries in general, see Anna Minara Ciardi, *On the Formation of Cathedral Chapters and Cathedral Culture. Lund, Denmark, and Scandinavia, c. 1060–1225*, Bibliotheca Historico-Ecclesiastica 60 (Lund: Lund University, 2016), 18–34, and cited literature.

14 Kauko Pirinen, "Domkapitel," *Kulturhistoriskt lexikon för nordisk medeltid* 3, cols. 185–95.

15 Ibid.; Lars Hamre, "Domkapitel, Norge," *Kulturhistoriskt lexikon för nordisk medeltid* 3, cols. 195–98; Magnús Már Lárusson, "Domkapitel, Island," *Kulturhistoriskt lexikon för nordisk medeltid* 3, cols. 198–201.

16 Pirinen, "Domkapitel," cols. 185–95.

17 The Norwegian provincial statutes are printed in *Norges gamle Love indtil 1387*, vol. 3, eds. R. Keyser and P.A. Munch (Christiania, 1849), 229–306; see also Vegard Skånland, "Provinsialkonsil," *Kulturhistoriskt lexikon för nordisk medeltid* 13, cols. 527–29; the Swedish provincial statutes are printed in *Statuta synodalia veteris ecclesiae sveogothicae*, ed. Henrik Reuterdahl (Lundae, 1841); *Statuter från svenska medeltida provinsialkonsilier (Upsaliensis prouincie statutorum prouincialium). Enligt Ragvaldus Ingemundi 1506. Linköpings stifts- och landsbibliotek, cod. J 73)*, ed. Sigurd Kroon, Scripta ecclesiologica minora 13 (Skellefteå: Artos bokförlag, 2010); the Danish provincial statutes are mainly printed in different volumes of the *Diplomatarium Danicum*; see Erik Buus, "Statuter, Danmark," *Kulturhistoriskt lexikon för nordisk medeltid* 17, cols. 59–63.

18 On the Norwegian diocesan statutes, see Lars Hamre, "Statuter, Norge," *Kulturhistoriskt lexikon för nordisk medeltid* 17, col. 70; Swedish diocesan statutes are printed in *Statuta synodalia. . .* 1841; *Synodalstatuter och andra kyrkorättsliga aktstycken från den svenska medeltidskyrkan*, ed. Jaakko Gummerus (Stockholm: Skrifter utg. af kyrkohistoriska föreningen, 1902); Danish diocesan statutes are mainly printed in different volumes of the *Diplomatarium Danicum*; see Buus, "Statuter, Danmark," cols.

63–65; Icelandic diocesan statutes are printed in *Diplomatarium Islandicum*; see Jakob Benediktsson, "Statuter, Island," *Kulturhistoriskt lexikon för nordisk medeltid* 17, cols. 70–71.

19 *Statuta synodalia veteris ecclesiæ sveogothicæ*, ed. Henrik Reuterdahl (Lundae, 1841), 128–64; *Statuter från svenska medeltida provinsialkoncilier. (Upsaliensis prouincie statutorum prouincialium. Enligt Ragvaldus Ingemundi 1506.(Linköpings stifts- och landsbibliotek, cod J 73).* Addendum: *Compendium statutorum provincialium, Upsaliensis provinciæ Nicholai Archi-Episcopi. Efter 1525 års tryck. (Utg. Av Chr. Nettelbladt i "Schwedische Bibliothec" vol. 2, 1728*), ed. Sigurd Kroon, Scripta ecclesiologica minora 13 (Skellefteå: Artos, 2010).

20 Sverre Bagge, "Nordic Students at Foreign Universities," *Scandinavian Journal of History* 9 (1984): 1–17; Roger Andersson, "Undervisning och utbildning," *Sveriges kyrkohistoria. 2: Hög- och senmedeltid*, ed. Sven-Erik Pernler (Stockholm: Verbum, 1999), 221–31; Bertil Nilsson, "Kyrka och lärdom," *Signums svenska kulturhistoria. Medeltiden*, ed. Jakob Christensson (Lund: Bokförlaget Signum, 2004), 103–07, 169–71, and cited literature; Olle Ferm and Erika Kihlman, eds. *Swedish Students at the University of Vienna in the Middle Ages: Careers, Books and Preaching* (Stockholm: Sällskapet Runica et Mediævalia. Scripta Minora 20, 2011); Olle Ferm and Sara Risberg, eds. *Swedish Students at the University of Leipzig in the Middle Ages: Careers, Books, and Teaching* (Stockholm: Sällskapet Runica et Mediævalia. Scripta Minora 21, 2014).

Bibliography

Andersen, Per, *Legal Procedure and Practice in Medieval Denmark* (Leiden: Brill, 2011).

Andersson, Roger, "Undervisning och utbildning," Sven-Erik Pernler, ed., *Sveriges kyrkohistoria. 2: Hög- och senmedeltid* (Stockholm: Verbum, 1999), 221–31.

Bagge, Sverre, "Kirkens jurisdiksjon i kristenrettssaker for 1277," *Historisk Tidsskrift* (*Norway*) 60 (1981): 144–45.

Bagge, Sverre, "Nordic Students at Foreign Universities," *Scandinavian Journal of History* 9 (1984): 1–17.

Bagge, Sverre, *From Viking Stronghold to Christian Kingdom: State Formation in Norway, c. 900–1350* (Copenhagen: Museum Tusculanum Press, 2010).

Buus, Erik, "Statuter, Danmark," *Kulturhistoriskt lexikon för nordisk medeltid* 17, cols 59–63.

Ciardi, Anna Minara, *On the Formation of Cathedral Chapters and Cathedral Culture. Lund, Denmark, and Scandinavia, c. 1060–1225*, Bibliotheca Historico-Ecclesiastica 60 (Lund: Lund University, 2016).

Compendium statutorum provincialium, Upsaliensis provinciæ Nicholai Archi-Episcopi. Efter 1525 års tryck. (Utg. Av Chr. Nettelbladt i "Schwedische Bibliothec" vol. 2, 1728), Sigurd Kroon, ed. Scripta ecclesiologica minora 13 (Skellefteå: Artos, 2010).

Corpus Iuris Sueo-Gotorum Antiqui, vols 1–6, H.S. Collins and C.J. Schlyter, eds. (Stockholm/Lund, 1827–44).

Danmarks gamle Landskabslove med Kirkelovene, vols I–VIII + supplement to vol. IV, Johs. Brøndum-Nielsen and Poul Johs. Jørgensen, eds. (Copenhagen: Det Danske Sprog- og Litteraturselskab, 1933–61).

Den danske rigslovgivning indtil 1400, Kroman, Erik, ed. (Copenhagen: Munksgaard, 1971).

Diplomatarium Danicum, various eds. (Copenhagen: Det danske Sprog- og Litteraturselskab, 1938–).

Diplomatarium Islandicum, vols I–IVI, Jón Sigurðsson and Jón Þorkelsson et al. eds., (Reykjavík, 1857–1976).

Esmark, Kim and Helle Vogt, "Introduction to Part Two: Local Disputes: Property, Justice, and Social Transaction," Kim Esmark, Lars Hermanson, Hans Jacob Orning, and Helle Vogt, eds., *Disputing Strategies in Medieval Scandinavia* (Leiden: Brill, 2013), 143–60.

Ferm, Olle and Erika Kihlman, eds., *Swedish Students at the University of Vienna in the Middle Ages: Careers, Books and Preaching* (Stockholm: Sällskapet Runica et Mediævalia. Scripta Minora 20, 2011).

Ferm, Olle and Sara Risberg, *Swedish Students at the University of Leipzig in the Middle Ages: Careers, Books, and Teaching* (Stockholm: Sällskapet Runica et Mediævalia. Scripta Minora 21, 2014).

Hamre, Lars, "Domkapitel, Norge," *Kulturhistoriskt lexikon för nordisk medeltid* 3, cols 195–98.

Hamre, Lars, "Statuter, Norge," *Kulturhistoriskt lexikon för nordisk medeltid* 17, col. 70.

Hybel, Nils and Bjørn Poulsen, *The Danish Resources c. 1000–1550: Growth and Recession* (Leiden/Boston, MA: Brill, 2007).

Jakob Benediktsson, "Statuter, Island," *Kulturhistoriskt lexikon för nordisk medeltid* 17, cols 70–71.

Jørgensen, Nils, *Studier över syntax och textstruktur i nordiska medeltidslagar* (Uppsala: Svenska Fornskriftsällskapet, 1987).

Knudsen, Anders Leegaard, "Testimonia Placiti—Private Charters as Public Instruments: A Study in Medieval Danish Diplomatics," *Archiv für Diplomatik* 57 (2011): 147–79.

Knut Helle, *Konge og gode menn i norsk riksstyring ca. 1150–1319* (Bergen/Oslo/Tromsø: Universitetsforlaget, 1972).

Magnús Már Lárusson, "Domkapitel, Island," *Kulturhistoriskt lexikon för nordisk medeltid* 3, cols 198–201.

McGuire, Brian P., *The Cistercians in Denmark: Their Attitudes, Roles, and Function in Medieval Society* (Kalamazoo, MI: Cistercian Publications, 1982).

Naumann, Hans-Peter, *Sprachstil und Textkonstitution. Untersuchungen zur altwestnordischen Rechtssprache* (Basel/Stuttgart: Helbing & Lichtenhahn, 1979).

Nilsson, Bertil, "Kyrka och lärdom," Jakob Christensson, ed., *Signums svenska kulturhistoria. Medeltiden* (Lund: Bokförlaget Signum, 2004).

Nilsson, Bertil, "Scandinavian Church," Robert E. Bjork, ed., *The Oxford Dictionary of the Middle Ages*, Vol. 4 (Oxford: Oxford University Press, 2010), 1482–83.

Nilsson, Bertil, "The Swedish Ecclesiastical Legislation and the Question of Its Nordic Character," in Per Andersen, Kirsi Salonen, Helle Sigh, and Helle Vogt, eds., *How Nordic Are the Nordic Medieval Laws? – Ten Years After. Proceedings of the Tenth Carlsberg Academy Conference on Medieval Legal History 2013* (Copenhagen: DJØF publishing, 2014), 81–112.

Norges gamle Love indtil 1387, vols 1–2, R. Keyser and P.A. Munch, eds. (Christiania: Gröndahl, 1846–48).

Norseng, Per, "Law Codes as a Source for Nordic History in the Early Middle Ages," *Scandinavian Journal for History* 16/3 (1991): 137–66.

Orrman, Eljas, "Church and Society," Knud Helle, ed., *The Cambridge History of Scandinavia* (Cambridge: Cambridge University Press, 2008), 426–31.

Pirinen, Kauko, "Domkapitel," *Kulturhistoriskt lexikon för nordisk medeltid* 3, cols 185–95.

Poulsen, Bjørn, Jon Vidar Sigurdssen, and Helle Vogt, eds., *Nordic Elites in Transformation, vol. 1. Material Resources* (New York: Routledge, 2019).

Røsstad, *Rune, A tveim tungum. Om stil og stilvariation i norrønt lovmål,* KULTs skriftserie nr. 73 (Oslo: Noregs Forskingsråd, 1997).

Sawyer, Birgit and Peter Sawyer, *Medieval Scandinavia: From Conversion to Reformation, Circa 800–1500* (Minneapolis: University of Minnesota Press, 1993).

Sawyer, Birgit and Peter Sawyer, "Early Political Organisation," Knut Helle, ed., *The Cambridge History of Scandinavia. Vol.1: Prehistory to 1520* (Cambridge: Cambridge University Press, 2003), 160–234.

Skånland, Vegard, "Provinsialkonsil," *Kulturhistoriskt lexikon för nordisk medeltid* 13, cols. 527–29.

Statuta synodalia veteris ecclesiae sveogothicae, Henrik Reuterdahl, ed. (Lundae, 1841).

Statuter från svenska medeltida provinsialkonsilier (Upsaliensis prouincie statutorum prouincialium). Enligt Ragvaldus Ingemundi 1506. Linköpings stifts- och landsbibliotek, cod. J 73), Sigurd Kroon, ed., Scripta ecclesiologica minora 13 (Skellefteå: Artos bokförlag, 2010).

Ståhle, Carl-Ivar, *Syntaktiska och stilistiska studier i fornnordiskt lagspråk* (Lund: Carl Blom, 1958).

Synodalstatuter och andra kyrkorättsliga aktstycken från den svenska medeltidskyrkan, Jaakko Gummerus, ed. (Stockholm: Skrifter utg. af kyrkohistoriska föreningen, 1902).

Tamm, Ditlev and Helle Vogt, "Creating a Danish Legal Language: Legal Terminology in the Medieval Law of Scania," *Historical Research* LXXXVI/233 (2013): 505–14.

Tamm, Ditlev and Helle Vogt, eds. *The Danish Medieval Laws: The Laws of Scania, Zealand and Jutland* (New York: Routledge, 2016).

The Earliest Norwegian Laws Being the Gulathing Law and the Frostathing Law, trans. Laurence M. Larson (New York: Columbia University Press, 1935).

Vogt, Helle, *The Function of Kinship in Medieval Nordic Legislation* (Leiden: Brill, 2010).

2 Legal reforms around 1200 in Denmark

Archbishops Absalon (1128–1201) and Anders Sunesen (d. 1228)

Per Andersen and Helle Vogt

Introduction

This chapter is about two Danish archbishops, Absalon and Anders Sunesen, who between them served as bishops from 1158 to 1223. It may seem quite strange that the first chapter in a book on the writings of Nordic jurists is about two men who were not jurists in the traditional sense. Neither of them had a law degree. It is unlikely that Absalon studied law in a systematic way, and while Anders probably studied law in Bologna, it was only for a limited period, making it possible for him to gain a basic understanding of law but not enough to become an expert. That they were great Christians, however (and Anders Sunesen a great theologian), there is no doubt. More important, during their reign over the Danish church, the foundation of the Danish legal order was laid—an order that in many respects lasted until the nineteenth century, when the influence of the German historical school finally led to major changes in the Danish legal tradition. Both Absalon and Anders Sunesen played a crucial role in defining the early Danish legal order and its long-lived tradition.[1]

There are several reasons for treating the two men in the same chapter. First, they came from the same social and political background, as they were related; one not only succeeded the other as archbishop, but in many ways they had a similar story. Second, several of the legal initiatives perhaps begun by Absalon were further developed by Anders Sunesen, and owing to the limited number of sources, it is sometimes impossible to say whether a particular initiative came from one or the other. Third, the scarcity of historical sources also means that our knowledge of the two archbishops is limited, but by writing about them in the same chapter, we can bring together the limited source material to create a coherent story.

The position of the church in twelfth-century Denmark

During the eleventh century, the Danish church changed structure from a mission church to a permanent established organization, culminating in 1103/04, when the pope created an archbishopric in Lund and made the Danish archbishop primate over all the Nordic bishoprics. As the church became better organized, its wealth also increased, and the bishops came from the most influential families in the realm. Through donations, the bishops became huge landholders, and the wealth of the bishoprics increased further thanks to extensive royal gifts. For instance, the bishops received some of the royal privileges in the church's land, and in return, they swore allegiance to the king and were obligated to participate in royal warfare. Thus, the bishops bore a double responsibility: they should be faithful towards the king and towards the church at the same time.

From the mid-thirteenth century on, this double responsibility and the inherent conflict as to which authority would be higher—the king or the church—led to ongoing clashes between the bishops and the king. In the days of Absalon and Anders Sunesen, however, everything was going well. Thanks to the close personal relationship between the two bishops and the king, the interests of the two powers coincided, resulting in the creation of a strong Christian kingdom with a strong, well-founded church order. Thus, the period in which Absalon and Anders Sunesen acted as heads of the Danish church is known as the Waldemarian period, after the kings who brought peace and prosperity to the Danish realm and laid the foundation for the legal order built on written laws. But behind every strong medieval king is a strong bishop—and in the late twelfth and early thirteenth centuries in Denmark, these were Absalon and Anders Sunesen.

Biographical background

The Danish source material from the High Middle Ages is quite limited, and the narrative sources often depend on each other. Absalon is the hero in Saxo Grammaticus's *Res Gesta Danorum*,[2] a history written in the most beautiful silver-age Latin about the deeds of the Danes from ancient times until 1186. Through this history, Saxo demonstrates how Denmark had always been a great nation that could easily stand in comparison with the Roman and German empires. About one-third of the manuscript, which is over eight hundred pages long, is dedicated to Absalon and his deeds. This is hardly surprising since Absalon was the promotor of the book and, thus, Saxo's employer. For Saxo, it was Absalon as an adviser, a politician, a military leader, and a crusader who was interesting, whereas his legislation and church reforms are hardly mentioned.

The same picture of Absalon is depicted in the Knytlinge Saga, written by an anonymous Icelandic skald in the mid-thirteenth century. It is a short history of the Danish kings from Harald Bluetooth (r. c. 957–86) to Knud VI (r. 1182–1202). Here Absalon is portrayed as the king's closest adviser and the commander of the Danish fleet. Another and more nuanced description of Absalon comes from Abbot Arnold of the Order of St. John of Jerusalem abbey, in Lübeck's *Chronicle of the Slavs* (Chronica Slavorum), dating to around 1210. According to Abbot Arnold, Absalon tried to reform and purify the Danish church; besides this, he should be remembered as a great mediator and, not the least, as a big donor to the church.[3]

Unlike Absalon, Anders Sunesen has no major narratives depicting his life and deeds. The life of Absalon's successor has to be pieced together from a lot of scattered information in chronicles, yearbooks, and more than one hundred charters and papal letters that mention his deeds as bishop or archbishop.[4] In his introduction to *Gesta Danorum*, Saxo praises Anders Sunesen as a learned and educated man. Unlike Absalon, who did not leave any writings to posterity, Anders Sunesen has left, as far as the manuscripts reveal, two works, namely, the Latin poem "Hexaëmeron" and a Latin explanation of the Law of Scania (known as Liber Legis Scaniæ).[5] In addition, he is thought to have written a now lost poem about the seven sacraments. But it is "Hexaëmeron" that steals the show for posterity since it is unique in the Danish medieval context.

"Hexaëmeron" is a comprehensive theological didactic poem of 8,040 hexameters in twelve books. It starts by describing the Creation followed by the Fall into sin and its consequences. In broad terms, the Ten Commandments are described and the interaction between the written law and the divine natural law discussed. Then the Christian virtues follow, with teachings about sin and mercy, before "Hexaëmeron" gives a thorough account of Christology, including the personal incarnation of the image of God in a human being. The poem concludes with a description of the resurrection of the dead on Judgment Day. Some parts of "Hexaëmeron" are quite standardized, as the poem follows Peter Lombard's systematic presentation of dogmatics, is reminiscent of Alanus ab Insulis's and Bernhard's writings and mysticism, and is connected to the Chartres school's humanism. Some parts of the poem, however, present a personal interpretation of the relationship between sin and mercy, and thus they show Anders Sunesen's interest in and understanding of the legal aspect of the relationship in theory and practice.

Both Absalon and Anders Sunesen belonged to the rich and powerful Hvide family, who owned large parts of the Danish main island Zealand and had close ties with the kings. We do not know when either of them was born, only that they must have been at least thirty years old when they were elected bishops. Both King Valdemar I (r. 1157–82) and his father grew up at the estate belonging to Absalon's grandparents and parents. Absalon's father and Anders Sunesen's grandfather were brothers; hence, Absalon was Anders Sunesen's first cousin once removed.

Both being the younger sons in the family, they were predetermined for a career in the church, and as young men they were both sent to Paris to study. Hardly anything is known of their time in Paris, but Absalon probably studied with the Victorines in Saint Victor or the canons at Sainte Geneviéve. At Sainte Geneviéve, he in all probability met the canon (and later saint) Wilhelm, whom Absalon years later invited to Denmark as abbot of the newly founded Paraclete Abbey.[6]

Compared to the more ecclesiastically educated Absalon, Anders Sunesen probably studied at secular schools in Paris as well as studying law in Bologna, and according to Saxo he also studied in England. After finishing these studies, he returned to Paris, where as a master he took part in teaching. The details of this thorough and many-sided education are unknown, apart from the traces they have left both in his literary works and in his partially known book collection, which he donated to the chapter in Lund. In Paris and Bologna, Anders Sunesen had the same teachers as his somewhat older contemporary, the later Pope Innocent III (1198–1216).[7]

In 1156 or 1157, Absalon returned to Denmark and entered the political scene, where he is mentioned as one of Valdemar's supporters in the struggle for the crown that ended with Valdemar's definitive victory in 1157. The year following, Absalon was appointed bishop of Roskilde by the king;[8] next to the Danish archbishopric in Lund, Roskilde was the wealthiest of the Danish bishoprics. In 1177, the archbishopric became vacant, and Absalon was elected archbishop. Saxo tells that he declined the election because he would not leave the bishopric of Roskilde. He finally accepted when the pope granted him dispensation to be bishop of both bishoprics. He held both positions until 1191, when Peter Sunesen, Anders Sunesen's older brother, reached the age of thirty, the age required to become a bishop. Besides his ecclesiastical titles, Absalon was also one of the king's councilors, a position he held after Valdemar I died in 1182, leaving the crown to his 19-year-old son, Knut VI.

When Absalon died in 1201, his successor was Anders Sunesen, who continued the close cooperation with the king on Absalon's legal reforms, among other subjects. To judge from the scarce sources, Anders Sunesen must have returned to Denmark in the early 1190s, becoming dean of the chapter of Roskilde and chancellor to the king of Denmark, an office he held when he was elected archbishop following the death of Absalon.

Neither Absalon nor Anders Sunesen was merely a desk adviser. On the contrary, they both played active parts in the crusades that were an important part of the politics of securing and expanding the Danish realm. Thus, Saxo pictures Absalon's influence by writing,

> No sooner was he elected bishop than he began to act as much like a sea rover as a spiritual father, for he thought little of protecting the church within if he allowed it to be endangered from without. Driving off the enemies of the state religion is just as important a part of priestly duties as safeguarding its ceremonies. . . . He was a parent as much as a pontiff of his country, striking for his brilliant combination of soldiering and priesthood.[9]

The reason for this characterization is the merit Absalon earned for himself in the battles with one of the West-Slavonic peoples in the northern part of today's Germany and Poland. During the civil wars that ended with Valdemar I's victory in 1157, the Wends had had free reign to plunder the Danish coasts. The Wends were a pagan people, having their political and religious center at the island of Rügen. After Valdemar I came to power, he started a number of raids against the Wends, and if we are to believe Saxo, Absalon was the de facto strategist for the Danish fleet. That a prince of the church was next to the king as leader of the army is not surprising, since Pope Eugen III in 1147 had issued the papal bull *Divini dispensation*, which gave those who fought the pagans in Northern Europe the same privileges, both spiritual and temporal, as those who fought for the liberation of Jerusalem.[10] The papal bull meant that the Danes could give the warfare a double legitimacy, both securing the Danish coasts and doing God's will.

The warfare culminated in 1168 with the conquest of Rügen and the conversion of the Wends.[11] The pope approved the conquest in 1169 in a papal letter to Absalon, in which the pope placed Rügen under the Roskilde see.[12] The crusades did not stop with the conquest of Rügen, as the Danes continued their crusading warfare with Absalon as their prime mover during the next two decades, sometimes as allies with, sometimes as rivals to, the Saxon and other German princes who wanted to expand their territory to the east as well.

When, in 1177, Absalon was elected archbishop, he was not only the unquestioned leader of the Danish church but also the leader of the Danish crusading strategy—a strategy that brought great wealth to the Danish church and to the Danish king.[13]

Compared to his predecessor, Anders Sunesen was just as devoted to the conversion of pagans as Absalon, and he too led several expeditions against them, mainly the Estonians. In 1204, Pope Innocent III appointed him papal legate and, hence, the leader of the papal crusading policy in the Baltic Sea. This explains his often independent political activity in the area. It culminated in 1218, when the Germans and the Danes joined forces under the command of Valdemar II (r. 1202–41), who had papal permission to annex all the conquered land under the Danish crown. The result was the conquest of Estonia in 1219.

While he made a strong impact on forming the boundaries of the Danish realm, strengthening the royal position, and enhancing cooperation among the secular, ecclesiastical, and royal powers, Anders Sunesen's health was not strong. The archbishop suffered from a rheumatoid disease that ended up crippling him. In 1221, he asked the pope for permission to resign from office, and this permission was granted the next year. Anders Sunesen died on 24 June 1228.

Both the bishops/archbishops were very generous toward the church by giving big donations to their bishoprics. Like his parents and siblings, Absalon was buried at the Cistercian abbey in Sorø founded by his father and uncles, whereas Anders Sunesen was entombed in Lund Cathedral. Absalon's will is preserved as one of the oldest known wills in Denmark,[14] and as mentioned above, Anders Sunesen donated his book collection to the chapter in Lund. If the books in one's possession say something about his scholarly attainment, then Anders Sunesen seems much more intellectual than Absalon: Absalon's will makes no mention of personal books, and his personal belonging—which he left to family, friends, and clerics—were instead weapons, horses, fur, clothes, silver tableware, and jewels.

The Danish crusades against the Wends and later the Estonians are good examples of how secular and ecclesiastical interests coincided. The kings needed bishops like Absalon and Anders Sunesen, not only because of their personal skills but because they and the church could preach the crusades and provide the kings with theological legitimacy for war—not to mention the financial support through donations and crusading taxes. Last, but not least, Absalon and Anders

Sunesen belonged to the wealthiest and most powerful family in Denmark and hence could provide the kings with both military and political support from their relatives.

Legislation

The available information about the legal activities at the time of Valdemar I is, in brief, very sporadic, as is true for the rest of the twelfth century. There is no evidence that laws in the modern sense existed in the Danish territory before The Book of Inheritance, which probably can be dated to 1170.[15] In that year, the *Ryd Chronicle* states in the annals that "the laws of the Danes were issued" (*Leges Danorum edite sunt*).[16] This information indicates that in the early formative phase of the Danish realm, attempt was made to introduce a law for the entire kingdom and not just for a single province. The attempt to issue such legislation seems to have been abandoned later, introducing—or reintroducing—the idea of provincial legislation. The only source discussing legal activity in this early period is Saxo, who in relation to an assembly consisting of the king, the bishops, and the most prominent men on the island of Samsø in 1184, reports that they were assembled to issue the civil laws, *iuris civilis emendandi*.[17] Probably Absalon was the one taking the initiative to convene the meeting, maybe to secure the support of the influential members of the elite to legal reforms within the property or inheritance law,[18] as suggested by the mentioning of the *ius civilis*.

In the thirteenth century, however, the process of putting the laws into writing sped up. In 1200, King Knut VI issued an ordinance on homicide and other crimes. This was re-edited during the reign of his brother Valdemar II, probably in the period 1202–16. In addition, the ordeal by red-hot iron was abolished in Denmark in 1216 or shortly afterward by royal legislation. The ordeal was replaced by boards of nominated men who investigated cases following the Roman-canonical legal procedure as a direct consequence of the abolition of clerical participation in the ordeals issued at the Fourth Lateran Council in 1215.[19] The royal ordinances were all issued for the eastern province of Scania, and it was here that the first Danish collected law book, the Law of Scania, written in vernacular, saw the light of day. The law dates to between 1202 and 1216.[20] The Lund chapter—and hence Anders Sunesen—was probably one of the leading forces behind the writing of the law, which appears as a compromise among the king, the secular elite, and the church, as suggested by formulations like "the king wishes it to be law" and "this some men now want to be law."[21] That Anders Sunesen had strong opinions about legal matters and was highly interested in the legal development is also evident in the fact that he wrote *Liber Legis Scaniæ*, which gives the impression of a learned introduction to the law in Scania.

The following sections focus on three areas where the two bishops played an important role on the legal scene: (1) peace regulation, (2) church laws and the recognition of canon law in Denmark, and (3) property, inheritance, and donations.

Peace regulation

Upholding and strengthening the peace was an important factor in the legislative process, especially in the archdiocese around 1200. It is not surprising that bishops would try to strengthen the peace in society. To be a peacemaker was an ideal the church shared with kings. One of the many obligations laid on a Christian king was to be the protector and creator of peace since peace was instituted by God in the Garden of Eden but destroyed through the Fall into sin. The right kind of peace could be found only in Heaven; hence, the earthly ruler must seek to maintain public order and at least ensure some kind of regulation against disorder and violence.

Ideals were one thing; reality, however, was another. Even though the power of the Danish king was increasing in the second part of the twelfth century, it was still very difficult to regulate violence at a local level. The king simply did not have the necessary power. One way to regulate the violence was to encourage that conflicts be settled peacefully—and to develop methods for doing so. It seems that Absalon was very active in this process, at least according to Saxo, who wrote that "the Zealanders perceived how beneficial was the aid of his eloquence; by its tempering effect local assemblies, which were disputatious to the point of breeding violence and brawls, were induced by his guidance to a more peaceful frame of mind."[22] In addition, Arnold of Lübeck regretted the death of Absalon by saying, "All Denmark mourned his death deeply and remembered how many conflicts he had led to peace and reconciliation."[23]

Both quotes mention Absalon as a peacemaker, and Saxo underscores that he made the local courts focus more on peacemaking than on vengeance. How he did this, Saxo does not say, but looking at the legislation regulating the payment of wergild, or compensation, from the year 1200, we might find a clue. According to the provincial laws, the backbone of the Danish criminal sanctions was the compensation that the kin of a person committing homicide had to pay collectively to the dead person's kin. The first time we find legislation regulating the payment of this compensation[24] is in the Ordinance of Homicide for the province of Scania. According to the ordinance, the king, "mindful of the duty conferred on us by divine grace," recognized

> that we are obligated towards all our subjects who love justice to further progress for all, both singularly and in general. But being, as we are, concerned for your true welfare and peace, we have heard from complaints by esteemed men in your province and also from general testimony that your province, more than other parts of our realm, is vexed by crimes of homicide.[25]

The prologue of the ordinance continues by explaining that the lack of strict regulation of paying and receiving man's compensation, as well as requirements for exchanging vows of peace and reconciliation, was the reason why Scania was so troubled by homicides.

Saxo's writing about Absalon's influence on the local assemblies can be interpreted to suggest that Absalon had tried to get more of the Zealanders to pay and accept man's compensation, and it is most likely that he continued his efforts in Scania after becoming archbishop. The Ordinance of Homicide was in many ways the culmination of a process in which collective payment of man's compensation had become the most common sanction, but one in which problems could arise from the collective liability (for instance, the need to ensure that the kin paying the compensation would not face vengeance after paying, or that the killer, having collected the compensation, would not flee or spend it and thereby force his kin to pay twice). The sources do not say whether similar ordinances were made for the other provinces, but the same rules that are in the Ordinance for Scania are found in all the provincial laws.

The ordinance was promulgated by the king as a secular piece of legislation with the consent of the best men of the province, including the archbishop. It is commonly accepted that the person who wrote the ordinance must have been a cleric with good knowledge of Latin, theology, and canon law, and likewise had a good knowledge of how conflicts were handled at the secular assemblies. Hence, the arrow points in the direction of Absalon, both because of what Saxo and Arnold of Lübeck wrote and because—when the sources become more frequent during Anders Sunesen's time as archbishop—it becomes clear that the archbishopric played an important part in the legislative process.[26] Moreover, the ordinance laid the foundation for the man's compensation procedure and was implemented in the Law of Scania together with much more detailed rules.

Church law and canon law

While one can make only a qualified guess that Absalon was the architect behind the ordinance, there is no doubt about his crucial role in the making of the Church Laws for Scania and Zeeland from the early 1170s on.[27] The contexts of the laws are almost alike, and the reason for giving the laws is mentioned in the prologues and postscript:

> This is the law that was laid down after deliberation at a meeting in Ringsted by Archbishop Absalon at the request of all Zealanders, as the law between bishop and householders[28] had previously been too harsh.

"In return for this law, the householders gave the bishop one third of the tithes of all their grain."[29] The Church Laws regulated, among other things, donations, violence against clerics and relatives, annulment of marriages, and consecration of churches—all areas in the grey zone between canon and secular law because containing elements of both. For instance, concerning the annulment of marriages due to consanguinity or affinity, the limits were decided by canon law, but the procedure to establish the degrees of kinship resided with local boards of kinsmen. The same is true for the building and consecration of churches since how and why a church should be consecrated or reconsecrated were defined by canon law, but how the bishop should be paid for his services, the size of his revenue, and who should be held responsible if a church was violated were regulated in the Church Laws.

It is quite interesting that even though the prologues state that the laws are a moderation of previous laws between bishop and householders, nothing of consequence in the laws conflicted with canon law. The Church Laws regulated primarily payment for ecclesiastical service, church buildings, elections of priests, and the kind of procedure and oaths to be used in specific cases, together with the size of the fees to the bishop for his services. One can imagine that the fees were made lower as a way of getting the householders to accept the bishop's tithe.

Strikingly, when the provincial laws were written down in the first half of the thirteenth century, they did not cover the areas regulated by canon law. It is difficult not to interpret this as a proof of the secular power recognizing the church's judicial authority and canon law in the legal subjects covered by canon law. Before there could be any meaning in recognizing that the *causae spiritualis* belonged to the church's jurisdiction, it was necessary for the church to have a well-educated administration and trained lawyers, or at least canons, who had a solid knowledge of canon law. During Absalon's and Anders Sunesen's terms of offices, we can see an increasing number of Danish students not only in Paris, but more importantly in Bologna.[30] Most of these young men were destined for a career in one of the bishoprics, which also was a steppingstone to the royal chancery. Yet the coin also had a flipside. To claim complete spiritual supremacy over the lay population put pressure on the clerics to hold the moral high ground and live in celibacy, and in this effort, Absalon and Anders Sunesen were met with a lot of hard resistance in their attempts to get the clerics to respect celibacy. Arnold of Lübeck wrote about Absalon that besides all the good he did, he

> had to endure much and hard contradiction, because he, like the apostle, was jealous for them with a godly jealousy,[31] and both with convictions and conjunctions and punishing words did he train them [the clerics] to guard over their chastity.[32]

Anders Sunesen also was praised for his chastity, being an eager reformist.[33] Of the one hundred diplomas that mention his name, ten are papal letters concerned with legal questions that Anders had addressed to the curia.[34] Several of the letters deal with subjects concerning clerical celibacy, i.e., concubines, ordination of priests' sons, and even a priest killed by a husband who caught his wife and the priest in adultery. Other subjects in the letters concern annulment of marriage, and laypersons' penance for sexual crimes and violent acts.

We know very little about how Absalon implemented church reforms and strengthened church discipline in Denmark, but from Anders Sunesen's period in office we find some synod statutes, which are unique for Danish conditions. Anders Sunesen promulgated the statutes in 1206 as a result of a synod in which all the Danish bishops participated. The statutes established the penance for a long line of criminal acts, and hence show that church discipline started to be recognized. The cases brought forward included parents who by accident suffocated infants or children while they slept, abortion, cutting off limbs, rape, killing, violation of churches, and incest. The statutes also regulated blessings, ordination of clerics, and regulation of where to celebrate services and holy days.[35] In the statutes we see a glimpse of Anders Sunesen's legal and humane thinking, when he explains the reason for why a mother, whose child died through her negligence, should only be inflicted with a relatively mild penance, "since the punishment may be more noticeable for the mother in her severe [emotional] pain than in her sense of guilt."[36] More examples of his understanding of how emotions should be reflected in the law are found in several places in *Liber legis Scaniæ*. One is in Chapter 21, where he explains how it happens that even though paternal kin in general have precedence over maternal kin in cases of guardianship for fatherless children, exceptions are possible: "A maternal grandfather, however, because he is believed to have greater affection for his grandson, takes precedence over a paternal uncle, even though he is related on the father's side."[37]

Property, inheritance, and donations

It is hardly a coincidence that the oldest written Danish legislation we know is the Book of Inheritance, which, among other things, regulated inheritance and donations. When the provincial laws were written down in the thirteenth century, they also began with chapters on inheritance.

Firm rules for how inheritance should be divided were an important tool in securing the peace in medieval society. Many of the conflicts known to us arose from disputes about who had the right to the family property. Such disputes arose both between kin and between the deceased's family and representatives of the church, often leading to a situation where the donation to a religious party was disputed or renegotiated. The same discussion could arise over long-completed sales, and hence, regulation of how and how much could be transferred outside the kin group was asked for. Such discussions took a lot of time and were very resource-consuming for both the ecclesiastical and the lay parties, and therefore both sides were interested in rules about transfer of property to a third party.

This is not the place to go into the details of Danish inheritance and donation law, but the system did build on the parentela principle privileging blood relatives. All children were entitled to inherit from their parents, but sons received twice as much as daughters, and the free share that could be donated to a third party was the same size as a daughter's share.[38]

The fixing of these provisions took place between 1170 and 1220, i.e., during Absalon's and Anders Sunesen's time in office. This of course indicates a connection between Christian doctrines and Danish inheritance and donation law. The connection cannot be defined exactly since the legislative history of the act and the considerations behind the provision are not known. However, it is hardly a coincidence that the right to receive inheritance followed the canonical degrees of kinship, and that the donation rules were structured after the Augustine principle of making Christ co-heir.[39]

In the Danish provincial laws, we find only elements of canon law and theological thinking, not rules pointing directly towards learned law. But this is not the same as postulating that (many of) the apparently local rules and ideas in the laws had origins beyond learned law. Many of the local legal traditions and ideas and ways of thinking about law were transferred into a system that was coherent with Christian doctrines and structures, even though this was not obvious to the unlearned Danes. A good example of this is rules governing the conveyance of landed property. In the Book of Inheritance, there were no rules regulating land transactions, except how much could be donated to the church. It was clearly a problem that no strict procedure for conveyance was found in the law, and the customary way of conveyance could be questioned. To solve this problem, Absalon wrote to Pope Innocent III to get his opinion. Absalon's letter is not preserved, but we know what the pope replied in a letter from 1198. The letter reproduces the information that Absalon provided concerning the normal procedure of conveyance of donations to ecclesiastical institutions:

> The procedure at such donations is usually to take some earth and put it either at the extreme end of the altar cloth, which the bishop or another prelate holds in his hand, or you envelope earth in a small piece of cloth and place it humbly on the altar, while the attestation of the spectators and listeners follows the procedure for the form of gift giving which in the vernacular is called 'scotatio.' But . . . you [Absalon] claim that such a gift is questioned wickedly by certain quibblers.[40]

The *cauillotores*, or quibblers, Innocent prescribed should be subject to ecclesiastical punishment, though just how, he did not state more precisely. For Absalon, it was probably not a solution that could have been carried out if the legal side of the contestation had been valid according to the Book of Inheritance. Thus Absalon had to make sure that the legal procedure became a part of the legislation to make it more difficult to challenge a donation.

A procedure for conveyance very close to what Absalon had described—with the important difference that it also covered conveyance between laypeople—is found in the Law of Scania, and here it is explained in the same way as in the papal letter.[41] Even though the law, as we know it, was written down after Absalon's death, it is very convincing that the sketch for these paragraphs was made at Absalon's request, and that the reason for informing the pope was to make sure that the conveyance procedure would not conflict with canon law.

Summing up

At the end of the twelfth and the beginning of the thirteenth centuries, many developments combined in decisive ways to change formal law. The church and the royal powers of Europe underwent a previously unseen institutionalization, both in real power politics and in ideology. Learning blossomed across the Continent as universities developed out of existing cathedral schools or were founded in towns that had become centers of financial and intellectual interaction. There had been a sustained increase in social stratification because of a growing population and increased economic activity. All this developed alongside a distinctive common European understanding of the nature of law and how law should reach its decisions. The starting point for the learned understanding of law was this period's symbiosis of the old formalistic Roman law and a canon law focused on morals and ethics.

The new power politics and ideological currents meant that law developed quickly, informed by new scientific learning at universities and the church's wish for a more objective, and thus more just, law following the ideas and doctrines of canon law. This should be the case not only when questions arose in the church's own jurisdiction but also when it came to legal questions raised in what was normally defined as the secular sphere. Thus, the period from the end of the twelfth century to the mid-thirteenth century was characterized by the church's outspoken interest in cooperation with the rising territorial powers of kings—kings who at the same time needed the instruments of learned, written law to develop and secure their newly institutionalized positions.

The persons succeeding in bringing the Danish part of the Christian church and the secular power of the Danish kings under the same arch of ideology and legal thinking were the two archbishops Absalon and Anders Sunesen. They succeeded in framing local law into a Christian structure according to fundamental Christian doctrines, but they did so without creating tension between the local way of practicing the law and Christian ideology. They both succeeded because they continuously were in contact with their secular families, maintaining the idea of connecting the secular and the Christian legal thinking within a Christian frame. Compromises were better than being rigidly doctrinal in order to develop a firm and grounded foundation for a Christian ideology of law. Thus, they met more critics from the ecclesiastical ranks than from the secular environment. Absalon and Anders Sunesen were reformers of the Danish local law and ways of thinking about law, and they left a mental foundation that lasted through centuries, not fundamentally secularized until the nineteenth century.

Notes

1 Absalon and Anders Sunesen had a Norwegian equivalent, Archbishop Eystein of Nideros († 1188). Like the two Danish archbishops, he had studied in Paris and was closely connected to the Victorines and founded two Victorine monasteries in Norway. In the 1160s, Norway witnessed a wave of legal activities with regard to both secular law and the sections of church law that were included in the secular laws. Eystein seems to have played a crucial part in that process. On Eystein, see: Tore Iversen, ed., *Archbishop Eystein as Legislator: The European Connection,* Rosta–Trondheim Studies in History (Trondheim: Tapir Academic Press, 2011). Where literature in English or German languages exists, it is used in the references.

2 For more information on Saxo and his chronicle, see Per Andersen and Thomas Heebøll-Holm, eds., *Saxo som samtidshistoriker* (Aarhus: Aarhus University Press, 2011); Inge Skovgaard-Petersen, *Da tidernes herre var nær: Studier i Saxos historiesyn* (Copenhagen: Den danske historiske forening, 1987); for literature in English, see: Karsten Friis-Jensen, "Saxo Grammaticus's Portrait of Archbishop Absalon" and Inge Skovgaard-Petersen, "Saxo, the *clericus* of Absalon," in *Archbishop Absalon of Lund and His World*, Karsten Friis-Jensen and Inge Skovgaard-Petersen, eds. (Roskilde: Roskilde Museum, 2000), 159–79 and 181–93, respectively.

3 Monumenta Germaniae Historica, *Arnoldi Chronica Slavorum*, Liber Quintus, 18, p. 173 (Hanover, 1878). http://bsbdmgh.bsb.lrz-muenchen.de/dmgh_new/app/web?action=loadBook&bookId=00000766

4 The sources for his early life are found in the introduction of Sten Ebbesen and Lars B. Mortensen, eds., *Andreae Sunonis filii Hexaemeron*, Corpus Philosophorum Danicorum Medii Aevi X.1-2 (Copenhagen, 1985–88).

5 *Danmarks gamle Landskabslove med Kirkelovene*, vol. I; 2. Svend Aakjær and Erik Kroman, eds. (Copenhagen: Det Danske Sprog- og Litteraturselskab, 1933).

6 On Absalon's education, see, for instance: Birger Munk Olsen, "Absalons studier i Paris," *Absalon fædrelandets fader*, Inge Skovgaard-Petersen, Frank Birkebæk, and Tom Christensen, eds. (Roskilde: Roskilde Museums Forlag, 1960), 57–72. On Wilhelm, see, for instance, Anthony Perron, "Fugitives from the Cloister: Law and Order in William of Æbelholt's Denmark," *Law and Learning in the Middle Ages: Proceedings of the Second Carlsberg Academy Conference on Medieval Legal History 2005*, Helle Vogt and Mia Münster-Swendsen, eds. (Copenhagen: DJØF Publishing, 2006), 123–36.

7 Torben K. Nielsen, *Cølibat og kirketugt. Studier i forholdet mellem Innocens III og Anders Sunesen, 1198–1120* (Aarhus: Afhandlinger fra Aarhus Universitet, 1993), 36–37.

8 Saxo, who had a good knowledge of canon law (Helle Vogt, "Saxo og kanonisk ret," *Saxo som samtidshistoriker*, Per Andersen and Thomas Heebøll-Holm, eds. (Aarhus: Aarhus University Press, 2011), tried in his chronicle to disguise the fact that Absalon was appointed by the king and not the canons by describing the election as being according to canon law and by making it appear merely a coincidence that Valdemar at the same time was in Roskilde with a great army. Saxo14.21.2: "Now in a calm mood Valdemar at once entered Roskilde and went into the presbytery belonging to the priests who served the cathedral of the Trinity, where he meant to give his backing to their votes of a new bishop. Although he appeared qualified to exercise certain rights in a church which had been founded and endowed by his ancestors, he said that he would not attempt to infringe their prerogatives with illegal steps or violation of usage; he knew that under ecclesiastical law it was stipulated that the clergy's special powers of election should not be subject to any royal directive. His presence would in no way inhibit the electors from abiding by their independent judgements when they voted. The clergy then acknowledged his just and scrupulous conduct with expressions of deepest gratitude and came away from the meeting of the chapter to their choice with some care. They had been considering the merits of three men, all of proven reputation, and added a fourth, Absalon, on account of his excellent character, intent on taking the most able of this group; . . . . The result was that all their signatures concurred in one decision, and it was decreed that Absalon should hold the supreme office." See *Saxo Grammaticus: Gesta Danorum: The History of the Danes*, vol. 2, K. Friis-Jensen, ed., P. Fisher, transl. (Oxford: Clarendon Press, 2015), 1117.

9 Saxo 14.21.3, vol. 2, 1116: *Qui mox antistes creatus non minus piratam se quam pontificem gessit, parui estimans intus religionem tueri, se foris eam periclitari pareretur. Neque enim minus sacrorum attinet cultui publice religionis hostes repellere quam cerimoniarum tutele uacare. . . . conuulsos patrie penates erexit.*

10 11 April, *Patrologiae cursus completus. Series Latina*, dir. J.P. Minge (Paris: Garnier Fratres, 1857–66), vol. 180, cols. 1203–04.
11 John H. Lind, Carsten Selch Jensen, Kurt Villads Jensen, and Ane L. Bysted, eds., *Danske korstog – Krig og mission i Østersøen* (Copenhagen: Høst & Søn, 2004), 77.
12 *Diplomatarium Danicum* (herafter cited as DD), various eds. and publishers (Copenhagen: Det danske Sprog- og Litteraturselskab, 1938–), ser. 1, vol. 2 (4 November 1169), no. 189.
13 Lind et al., *Danske korstog*, 92.
14 DD., vol. 1, ser. 4, 1201, no. 32.
15 For the dating of the laws, see Michael H. Gelting, "Pope Alexander III and the Danish Law of Inheritance," *How Nordic Are the Nordic Medieval Laws? Proceedings of the First Carlsberg Conference on Medieval Legal History*, 2nd edition, Per Andersen, Ditlev Tamm, and Helle Vogt, eds. (Copenhagen: DJØF, 2011), 86–115; Helle Vogt, *The Function of Kinship in Medieval Nordic Legislation* (Leiden and Boston, MA: Brill, 2010), 64–73; and Per Andersen, *Legal Procedure and Practice in Medieval Denmark* (Leiden and Boston, MA: Brill, 2011), 71–83.
16 Erik Kroman, ed., *Danmarks middelalderlige annaler*, Selskabet for Udgivelse af Kilder til dansk Historie (Copenhagen, 1980), 166.
17 Saxo, *Gesta Danorum*, 16:4:2, 520.
18 Inger Dübeck, "Skånske Lov og den europæiske baggrund," *Historie/Jyske Samlinger*, ny række, vol. 18, 1989, 419.
19 Andersen, *Legal Procedure and Practice*, 84–191.
20 Erik Kroman and Stig Iuul, eds., *Danmarks gamle Love paa nutidsdansk*, vol. 1, (Copenhagen: G.E.C. Gad, 1945), ix.
21 The translation is taken from Ditlev Tamm and Helle Vogt, eds., *The Danish Medieval Laws. The Laws of Scania, Zealand and Jutland* (London and New York: Routledge, 2016), ch. 80, p. 69, and ch. 125, p. 77, see *Danmarks gamle Landskabslove med Kirkelovene*, vol. I, 1. Johannes Brøndum-Nielsen and Svend Aakjær, eds. (Copenhagen: Det Danske Sprog-og Litteraturselskab, Gyldendal, 1933), chs. 78, 80, 125.
22 Saxo 14.21.3, 1117–19: *Eloquentie quoque wius presidia Sialandenses salutaria senserunt. Nam domesticas conciones ad uim et rixam usque litigiosas moderatione sua ad pacatiorem habitum perduxit.*
23 *Arnoldi Chronica Slavorum*, Liber Quintus, 18, 173–74.
24 In Danish, *manbot* and in English, often referred to as "wergild."
25 DD, 1. serie, vol. 4, no. 24, 45. The translation is taken from Tamm and Vogt, *The Danish Medieval Laws*, 98.
26 Dübeck, "Skånske Lov og den europæiske baggrund."
27 On the dating of the church laws, see: Per Andersen, "Dating the Laws of Medieval Denmark: Studies of the Manuscripts of the Danish Church Laws," *Denmark and Europe in the Middle Ages, c.1000–1525: Essays in Honour of Professor Michael H. Gelting*, Kerstin Hundahl, Lars Kjær, and Niels Lund, eds. (Farnham, Surrey and Burlington, VT: Ashgate Publishing Company, 2014), 183–201. The Church Law of Scania is translated into English in *The Danish Medieval Laws*, 52–55.
28 The Old Danish word is *bonde*, literally translated as "a resident person," i.e., someone who had his own household.
29 *Danmarks gamle Landskabslove*, vol. VIII, ch. 1, 445.
30 About the Danish students in Bologna and Paris, see: Åke Sällström, *Bologna och Norden, intill Avignon påvedömets tid*, Bibliotheca Historica Lundensis 5 (Lund: Glerup, 1957); and Sverre Bagge, "Nordic Students at Foreign Universities," *Scandinavian Journal of History*, vol. IX (1984): 1–29.
31 2 Corinthians 11:2.

32 Arnold of Lübeck, "Arnoldi Chronica Slavorum," *Monumenta Germaniae Historica* (Hanover, 1878), 3, 5 http://bsbdmgh.bsb.lrz-muenchen.de/dmgh_new/app/web?action=loadBook&bookId=00000766.
33 Ibid., 5, 18.
34 Nielsen, *Cølibat og kirketugt*, 37.
35 DD, vol. 1, ser. 4, no. 65.
36 Ibid.
37 *Danmarks gamle Love*, vol. I, 2, ch. 21.
38 For further reading, see Stig Iuul, *Fællig og Hovedlod: Studier over Formueforholdet mellem Ægtefæller i Tiden før Christian V's Danske Lov* (Copenhagen: Nyt nordisk Forlag – Arnold Busck), 194. For an English overview, see Vogt, *The Function of Kinship.*
39 On the connection between canon law and Danish inheritance law, see Vogt, *The Function of Kinship.* On the Augustinian principle, see Charles Reid, "The Jurisprudence of the Forced Share: The High and Late Middle Ages," *Donations, Inheritance and Property in the Nordic and Western World from Late Antiquity until Today*, Ole-Albert Rønning, Helle Sigh, and Helle Vogt, eds. (London and New York: Routledge, 2017), 80–81 (64–114).
40 [A]ut in extremitate pallii quod manu episcope uel cuiuslibet alterius prelati ecclesie sustinetur. aut super ipsum altare aliquot inuolutum panniculo cum debita humilitate ponendum sub testimonio uidentium et audientium forma donationis huiusmodi subsequente que scotatio uulgariter appellatur. Uerum quia huiusmodi donatio maliciose a quibusdam cauillatoribus sicut asseris impeditur. *DD*, 1. serie., 3. vol., no. 238.
41 *Danmarks gamle Love*, vol. I, 1, Law of Scania, ch. 78, vol. I, 2, Liber legis Scaniæ, ch. 38.

Bibliography

Andersen, Per, *Legal Procedure and Practice in Medieval Denmark* (Leiden and Boston, MA: Brill, 2011).

Andersen, Per and Thomas Heebøll-Holm, eds., *Saxo som samtidshistoriker* (Aarhus: Aarhus University Press, 2011).

Andersen, Per, "Dating the Laws of Medieval Denmark: Studies of the Manuscripts of the Danish Church Laws," *Denmark and Europe in the Middle Ages, c.1000–1525: Essays in Honour of Professor Michael H. Gelting*, Kerstin Hundahl, Lars Kjær, and Niels Lund, eds. (Farnham, Surrey/Burlington: Ashgate Publishing, 2014), 183–201.

Arnold of Lübeck, "Arnoldi Chronica Slavorum," *Monumenta Germaniae Historica* (Hanover, 1878) http://bsbdmgh.bsb.lrz-muenchen.de/dmgh_new/app/web?action=loadBook&bookId=00000766

Bagge, Sverre, "Nordic Students at Foreign Universities," *Scandinavian Journal of History*, vol. IX (1984), 1–29.

Ebbesen, Sten and Lars B. Mortensen, eds., *Andreae Sunonis filii Hexaemeron*, Corpus Philosophorum Danicorum Medii Aevi XI.1-2 (Copenhagen: Det danske Sprog- og Litteraturselskab, 1985–88).

Danmarks gamle Landskabslove med Kirkelovene, Det Danske Sprog-og Litteraturselskab Johannes Brøndum-Nielsen and Svend Aakjær, eds. (Copenhagen: Gyldendal, 1933–61).

Diplomatarium Danicum, various eds. (Copenhagen: Det danske Sprog- og Litteraturselskab, 1938–).

Dübeck, Inger, "Skånske Lov og den europæiske baggrund," *Historie/Jyske Samlinger*, ny række, vol. 18, 1989, 396–420.

Friis-Jensen, Karsten, "Saxo Grammaticus's Portrait of Archbishop Absalon," Karsten Friis-Jensen and Inge Skovgaard-Petersen, eds., *Archbishop Absalon of Lund and His World*, (Roskilde: Roskilde Museum, 2000), 159–79.

Gelting, Michael H., "Pope Alexander III and the Danish Law of Inheritance," Per Andersen, Ditlev Tamm, and Helle Vogt, eds., *How Nordic Are the Nordic Medieval Laws? Proceedings of the First Carlsberg Conference on Medieval Legal History,* 2nd ed. (Copenhagen: DJØF, 2011), 86–115.

Iversen, Tore, ed., *Archbishop Eystein as Legislator: The European Connection,* Rosta–Trondheim Studies in History (Trondheim: Tapir Academic Press, 2011).

Iuul, Stig, *Fællig og Hovedlod: Studier over Formueforholdet mellem Ægtefæller i Tiden før Christian V's Danske Lov* (Copenhagen: Nyt nordisk Forlag – Arnold Busck, 1940).

Kroman, Erik, ed., *Danmarks middelalderlige annaler*, Selskabet for Udgivelse af Kilder til dansk Historie (Copenhagen, 1980).

Kroman, Erik and Stig Iuul, eds., *Danmarks gamle Love paa nutidsdansk*, vol. 1–3 (Copenhagen: G.E.C. Gad, 1945–48).

Lind, John H., Carsten Selch Jensen, Kurt Villads Jensen, Ane L. Bysted, eds., *Danske korstog – Krig og mission i Østersøen* (Copenhagen: Høst & Søn, 2004).

Nielsen, Torben K., *Cølibat og kirketugt. Studier i forholdet mellem Innocens III og Anders Sunesen, 1198–1120* (Aarhus: Afhandlinger fra Aarhus Universitet, 1993).

Olsen, Birger Munk, "Absalons studier i Paris," Inge Skovgaard-Petersen, Frank Birkebæk, and Tom Christensen, eds., *Absalon fædrelandets fader* (Roskilde: Roskilde Museums Forlag, 1960), 57–72.

Patrologiae cursus completus. Series Latina, 161 vol., dir. J.P. Minge (Paris: Garnier Fratres, 1857–66).

Perron, Anthony, "Fugitives from the Cloister: Law and Order in William of Æbelholt's Denmark," Helle Vogt and Mia Münster-Swendsen, eds., *Law and Learning in the Middle Ages: Proceedings of the Second Carlsberg Academy Conference on Medieval Legal History 2005* (Copenhagen: DJØF Publishing, 2006), 123–36.

Reid, Charles, "The Jurisprudence of the Forced Share: The High and Late Middle Ages," Ole-Albert Rønning, Helle Sigh, and Helle Vogt, eds., *Donations, Inheritance and Property in the Nordic and Western World from Late Antiquity until Today* (London/New York: Routledge, 2017), 64–114.

Saxo Grammaticus: Gesta Danorum: The History of the Danes, vol. 2, ed. Karsten Friis-Jensen, transl. Peter Fisher (Oxford: Clarendon Press, 2015).

Sällström, Åke, *Bologna och Norden, intill Avignon påvedömets tid*, Bibliotheca Historica Lundensis 5 (Lund: Glerup, 1957).

Skovgaard-Petersen, Inge, *Da tidernes herre var nær: Studier i Saxos historiesyn* (Copenhagen: Den danske historiske forening, 1987).

Skovgaard-Petersen, Inge, "Saxo, the *clericus* of Absalon," Karsten Friis-Jensen and Inge Skovgaard-Petersen, eds., *Archbishop Absalon of Lund and His World* (Roskilde: Roskilde Museum, 2000), 181–93.

Tamm, Ditlev and Helle Vogt, eds., *The Danish Medieval Laws. The Laws of Scania, Zealand and Jutland* (London/New York: Routledge, 2016).

Vogt, Helle, *The Function of Kinship in Medieval Nordic Legislation* (Leiden and Boston, MA: Brill, 2010).

Vogt, Helle, "Saxo og kanonisk ret," Per Andersen and Thomas Heebøll-Holm, eds., *Saxo som samtidshistoriker* (Aarhus: Aarhus University Press, 2011), 35–50.

3 Swedish Church Law around 1300

Andreas And, Brynolf Algotsson, and Laurentius Olavi

Bertil Nilsson and Stina Fallberg Sundmark

Introduction

The preserved legal source material regarding the three Christian jurists treated in this chapter belongs to different spheres of normativity, thus mirroring their positions within the ecclesiastical hierarchy. Among the three, Brynolf Algotsson had the highest rank as bishop of Skara from 1278 until his death in 1317. From him originated a number of diocesan statutes as well as a couple of other statutes, mainly relevant for internal ecclesiastical considerations, such as the services in the parish churches and in the cathedral of Skara, and thus for the priests' practice of their ministry. The bishop also took part in the revision of the Västgöta Law, finalized during his time of office. The section on church law (Swedish *kyrkobalk*) regularized the relations between the church—i.e., the bishop and the clergy—on the one hand and the parishioners in the diocese on the other hand. This section was part of the secular legislation negotiated between representatives of the laypeople and the church.

The second person treated here took part in the commission that worked out the Uppland Law, ratified by a royal letter in 1296. He was the Uppsala provost Andreas And, whose activities within the field of church law otherwise are little known. Andreas was the provost during two periods—1278–1299 and then from 1302 until his death in 1317. It may be assumed, however, that as the only representative of the church in the law commission, he had considerable influence on the wording of the law's section on church law, even if no specific provisions can be attributed to his fundamental theological opinions since those are unknown. Still, his position in the cathedral chapter in Uppsala and his membership in the law commission account for his place in this chapter.

The third person treated here, Laurentius Olavi—or in Swedish, Lars Olofsson, and often Laurentius of Vaksala—was a canon at the cathedral of Uppsala at least from 1289, and also dean from around 1300. He died in 1332. His lasting contribution as Christian jurist consists of two preserved writings (he also wrote a third, which is lost) aiming at spreading further knowledge of canon law among the clergy in the Swedish church province.

These three jurists lived during a decisive period of the Swedish history of law when the majority of the provincial laws took their final form and were written down. Each provincial law contained a section on church law. Regarding the oldest, the Older Västgöta Law, the editing might have taken place as early as the 1220s, while the most recent, the Hälsinge Law, was edited perhaps as late as 1350. It should be observed, however, that the exact dating of the editing of all provincial laws remains uncertain, with the exception of the Uppland Law.[1]

In Sweden, the latter part of the thirteenth century as well as the early fourteenth century were characterized both ecclesiastically and secularly by important changes and political turbulence, especially towards the end of the period. In 1248, the papal legate Cardinal Bishop William of Sabina summoned and chaired a provincial council in the town of Skänninge, in the province of Östergötland and the diocese of Linköping, in the presence of the worldly dignitaries of the realm, chief among them the earl Birger Magnusson (normally called *Birger jarl*). He was the highest leader of the realm besides the king and is supposed to have influenced the council's decisions in some parts.[2] In 1279, the archbishop of Uppsala and the suffragan bishops of the Swedish church province gathered in a provincial council in what is now Södertälje, in the province of Södermanland and the diocese of Strängnäs. They issued the most comprehensive statutes preserved from any council in the Swedish church during the Middle Ages.[3]

The decrees promulgated by the cardinal legate in 1248 concerned fundamental, yet at the same time controversial, topics with regard to the church's legal constitution—for instance, the question of clerical celibacy, the right of priests' children to inherit from them, and the bishops' rights to compensation for visitations and other journeys *ex officio* in the diocese and for obtaining supplies. The decrees of 1279 once again called attention first of all to disobedience among the clergy regarding the requirement for celibacy. Furthermore, some other prescriptions from 1248 were repeated, and some new ones regarding the clerics' rights and obligations were added, among others the requirement for *privilegium canonis*.

Consequently, those engaged in the wording and content of the ecclesiastical prescriptions of the provincial laws had a lot of authoritative decisions to start out from, made within the borders of the church province. In the case of the Skänninge council of 1248, the decrees had direct papal assent as a consequence of William of Sabina's position as a *legatus a latere*. Furthermore, the cardinal legate had ordered every bishop in the church province to procure the *Liber Extra* from 1234 within one year.

During the period concerned, four different kings reigned in Sweden. The first two, Valdemar (r. 1250–75) and Magnus (r. 1275–90), were the sons of the earl *Birger jarl*. He had an immense political influence from around 1250 until his death in October 1266 and may be considered the person who gave the Swedish royal power a marked strength and contributed to Sweden's formation into a medieval state.[4]

King Magnus, often called *Magnus Ladulås* (Barnlock), issued a comprehensive letter of privileges for the church in 1281. Right up to the Reformation, the letter constituted a legal text to which representatives of the church could refer questions concerning exemption from taxes and charges, as well as to whom specific fines should pertain.[5]

After the death of King Magnus, in 1290, the times were characterized by bloody battles for power among his three sons, out of whom the eldest came of age and began to rule formally only in 1298. As a consequence, the *marsk* (lord high constable) Torgils Knutsson had actual political influence over Sweden even until 1305, when he was imprisoned and soon executed. The struggle among the three royal brothers led to the realm once again being without a ruling king of age until the three-year-old boy Magnus Eriksson, elected king in 1319, came of age in 1332.[6] Under these external circumstances, the three jurists made their contributions to Swedish ecclesiastical and secular law.

Brynolf Algotsson

Biography

Brynolf Algotsson probably was born at the end of the 1240s into the family of an influential and wealthy great man in the diocese of Skara, in the province of Västergötland. Beginning in 1270, his father was the provincial lawspeaker (Swedish *lagman*), an official unique to Scandinavia, responsible for memorizing the law and reciting it to the governing assembly, or *Thing*, which the lawspeaker also helped administer. Brynolf had six brothers, of whom certainly one, or maybe a couple, played an important role in his ecclesiastical career.[7]

A hundred years after Brynolf's death, the process to canonize him[8] was begun, leading to his beatification by Pope Innocent VIII (1484–92) on August 16, 1492. A biography from this process is preserved, *Vita S. Brynolphi*, along with the documents of the process.[9] These texts, presented in Skara in 1417 with permission of the Council of Constance,[10] provide some basic information about Brynolf's life. Furthermore, in connection with the beatification in 1492, a *legenda* was composed for the *officium* on his feast day on August 16.[11] In the *Vita* and the *legenda*, respectively, one finds that he studied in Paris for 18 years, first philosophy and then theology.[12]

The *legenda* notes that Brynolf 'in a remarkable way improved and corrected the land's [i.e., the province of Västergötland] laws.'[13] Likewise, the *legenda* records that he 'supplemented his church's [i.e., that of Skara] statutes and regulations, so that they did not diverge from the Lord's law and the decrees of the holy fathers.'[14] According to the *legenda*, Brynolf also brought about miracles already during his lifetime.[15] In 1317 'he passed away peacefully, full of years' and was interred in the cathedral of Skara.[16]

On July 25, 1278, Bishop Erik of Skara died.[17] On August 20 that same year, the cathedral chapter of Skara informed the archbishop of Uppsala that an episcopal election had taken place and wished the archbishop to give his confirmation.[18] The elected was 'our co-canon and dean in Linköping,' Brynolf Algotsson. On May 15, 1279, Brynolf for the first time in preserved records is mentioned as bishop of Skara, and thus in all likelihood should be regarded as consecrated bishop by that date, although we do not know where and when the consecration took place.[19] In the letter to the archbishop, Brynolf was described as born within wedlock, sufficiently learned, suitable, and known by many people for his way of living and good morals.

Apart from his contributions in the field of ecclesiastical law, his liturgical writing should be mentioned especially—though without any further examination here, since there has been considerable discussion in Swedish research concerning the attribution to Brynolf.[20] It consists of four rhymed offices to (1) St. Elin of Skövde, (2) St. Eskil, (3) the Virgin Mary, and (4) a thorn of Christ's crown of thorns,[21] which Brynolf somehow[22] received as a gift from the Norwegian king Håkon Magnusson and brought to the cathedral of Skara.

On March 19, 1317, the cathedral chapter of Skara informed the archbishop of Uppsala and the cathedral chapter there that a new bishop had been elected after Brynolf, 'once our bishop, remembered with gratitude.'[23]

With relevance for his legal activity and esteemed position, it should be mentioned that in statutes, valid in the diocese of Skara and promulgated in 1411 and 1472, respectively, reference was made only to Bishop Brynolf and his diocesan statutes; no other bishop of Skara was quoted with regard to activities in the field of ecclesiastical law.[24]

Legal activities

Bishop Brynolf's legal activities resulted in two texts that can be attributed to him without doubt: (1) a number of diocesan statutes issued on July 7, 1280 and (2) the *Biskop Brynolfs stadga* (Bishop Brynolf's statute) from 1281. In addition, there is (3) a choir statute intended for the services in the cathedral of Skara and usually ascribed to Bishop Brynolf by the name of *Notulae Brynolphi*.[25] On uncertain bases, it was earlier presumed that he was the author also of (4) diocesan statutes issued after 1280 and probably intended for the diocese of Skara (see below). Finally, his legal activities included participation in (5) the revision and re-editing of the Västgöta Law, resulting in the Younger Västgöta Law and its section on church law, eventually revised and written down most likely between 1310 and 1315.[26]

First, as regards the internal ecclesiastical prescriptions and statutes from 1280, preserved in a manuscript from the middle of the fifteenth century—according to Jaakko Gummerus's investigation of 1902, nothing speaks against their authenticity and thus—as the heading and preamble in the manuscript maintain—issued by Bishop Brynolf.[27] No one has questioned Gummerus's conclusions in this case.

According to the text's introduction, the statutes were intended for all categories of clergy in the diocese of Skara. The aim was to carry through necessary reforms among the clerics and laity entrusted to the bishop, 'to Our Savior's praise'[28] and 'to the benefit of our souls.'[29] Thus, it was a superior church representative with official responsibility who addressed himself to his subordinates. In all likelihood, the statutes were issued by the bishop in connection with the diocesan synod in Skara in the summer of 1280, although this is not expressly stated in the text.[30] The year before, Bishop Brynolf participated in the provincial council in (Söder)Tälje,[31] which resulted in comprehensive statutes regarding the bishops as well as the clergy, with additional consequences for the laity. It was presupposed that the prescriptions should be implemented in the different dioceses, and they were characterized by the internationally valid ideals of canon law, at this time most clearly expressed in Pope Gregory IX's decretals, the *Liber Extra*, with related doctrine.

According to the text, Bishop Brynolf's statutes had come into being through the counsel and approval of the cathedral chapter of Skara. They contained decrees on the Easter obligation, administering the sacrament of the altar to sick people, celebrating the mass, weddings after the required banns, the priest's bination, and the church's properties. Further decrees addressed the washing of liturgical utensils and priests' vestments, the priest's action during mass in case of accidental occurrences (for instance, the priest forgetting to pour wine into the chalice before the consecration or spilling consecrated wine, or a fly or spider ending up in the wine). Jaakko Gummerus and others after him have shown that parts of the statutes have clear similarities with French models, and they have surmised that this might have had to do with Brynolf's studies in Paris.[32]

Thus, the statutes were mainly internal to the church and concerned the clergy, except for three matters that also concerned the laity, namely, the Easter obligation, weddings, and parish property. The last topic and its related decree have been taken as a pretext for parish self-governance in economic matters, i.e., in opposition to the dictate of canon law that the bishop alone had power to decide economic questions.[33]

There are also more comprehensive statutes, but they are anonymous and undated. Nowadays, however, they are regarded as issued by Bishop Brynolf and consequently intended for the diocese of Skara. According to the latest research, Brynolf issued these statutes after his counsel with the yearly diocesan synods simultaneously with the revision of the Västgöta Law.[34] Research by Göran B. Nilsson confirms the attribution so surely that there should no longer be any doubt about Bishop Brynolf's authorship.[35] These statutes are found in a manuscript from the first half of the fifteenth century in the Uppsala University Library and comprise thirty-two paragraphs.[36] Their compilation is complicated, and there are difficulties in trying to establish their predecessors with regard to content.[37] The decrees first and foremost address internal church concerns like those in the statutes of 1280. In this case, however, they are more precise and comprise more matters. On one hand, they are prescriptions related to the priests and their obligation to hear confession. On the other hand, they are prescriptions related to secular law, not least concerning the economic reality, as for instance the obligation to pay tithes and charges for the priest's service for weddings and funerals. In these cases, the priest was not allowed to charge anything beforehand, in accordance with canon law.

Some of the decrees should be specifically highlighted here. One of them has been regarded as an example of how Bishop Brynolf 'made a daring and strong move' to implement the requirements of canon law.[38] In the fifteenth paragraph, the text says that the bishop's consent was required—under threat of excommunication—when selling or lending the church's income and property. This was contrary to the statutes from 1280, according to which the priest and two reliable parishioners should administer the church's property but take nothing from it without the consent of the parishioners. Furthermore, it is worth mentioning that a layman could impose the *excommunicatio minor*, provided that he had the bishop's permission to do so [§ 22].

Moreover, two of the paragraphs (29 and 30) dealt with a very important issue at that time, namely, the question of how or whether the church should prevail in the law of marriage. Traditionally, marriage was regarded as a secular matter, and attempts by leaders of the church to maintain influence in this matter had so far turned out unsuccessfully. Thus, the statutes required that a layman who did not want to either repudiate or marry his concubine should pay a three-mark fine to the bishop. And if those who had married did not want to have a church blessing, they should be deprived of the right to receive the body of Christ during mass.

Finally, paragraphs 23 and 24 prescribe that the bishop should receive what was called *ius regum,* i.e., the fines that normally went to the king. These should go to the bishop when a priest, deacon, or subdeacon—i.e., those in major orders of the ecclesiastical hierarchy living in a church property—committed a crime. These requirements should be regarded as part of Bishop Brynolf's way of trying to maintain the church's demand for *privilegium fori*, i.e., the requirement that the church's men (and women) should be sentenced before the bishop's court, not at secular courts.

As already mentioned, Bishop Brynolf in all likelihood issued a choir statute (Swedish *korstadga*) intended for the services in the cathedral of Skara. This statute is preserved in a manuscript from the fifteenth century in the university library in Uppsala.[39] The statute contains very detailed prescriptions for how different parts of the prayers at the canonical hours should be carried out under different circumstances and on different days and periods during the ecclesiastical year. The statute had hardly any interest outside the cathedral or for laypeople, but it constituted an important contribution to the legal regulation of the liturgical life of prayer among those who served in Skara.

Bishop Brynolf's participation in legal matters in the relation between the church and the secular power becomes evident at the earliest in the *Biskop Brynolfs stadga*.[40] The coming into being of the statute seems a bit peculiar, as is obvious already by its wording. It starts by establishing that King Magnus (*Ladulås*), having consulted the cathedral chapter of Skara, issued decrees concerning the existing disunity between clerics and laypeople with regard to the rights of the church. At the end of this record, the bishop, with the canons' counsel, ratifies the king's decrees. It may be regarded as unusual that a bishop ratifies royal decrees, albeit with the chapter as supporting instance, and probably this bears witness to the strong position and influence (maybe as a consequence of his education abroad) that Bishop Brynolf had in relation to the secular authority. The statute contains five points, mainly intended for laypeople, not clerics.

They concern (1) payment of crop tithes and tithes from the living and punishments for those who did not pay; (2) capital tithes that should be paid from the whole of the capital, real as well as movable property, at special occasions, such as division of an estate, marriage, and the consecration of the parish church; (3) manslaughter and injury of another, along with applicable punishment if such crimes were committed, for instance, in places and on feast days especially important for the diocese of Skara (the fines should go to the bishop); (4) breaking the holy day by working on specifically mentioned feast days—in these cases, too, the fines should go to the bishop; (5) fines that should go to the bishop if people 'committed sins' by having illegal sexual relations, which were specified; among those mentioned are homosexual love-affairs, although the term is not used.[41]

So far, Bishop Brynolf's direct and indirect influence regarding ecclesiastical as well as secular legal matters is relatively clear and obvious. Considerably more difficult to point out is his role in secular legislation during his episcopacy. That work was about improving and revising the Västgöta Law, which was written down for the first time perhaps during the 1220s,[42] the result of the revision being the Younger Västgöta Law. With the help of the documents presented here, Göran B. Nilsson, in his research, showed that Brynolf actively participated and was the driving force behind the revision of the law, especially its section on church law. Contrary to older research, Nilsson called attention to the fact that 'the Skara church [mainly] got the secular society's approval and support in its ambition to clericalize the social life in the spirit of canon law in quite a different way than the Older [Västgöta Law].'[43] He demonstrated this convincingly with prescriptions from the Younger Law's section on church law concerning the fines to the bishop from those who (a) swore oaths during forbidden periods: for instance, Advent and Lent; (b) broke the church mass peace, i.e., the special peace that should prevail in the whole parish on a church's consecration day; (c) broke the fast on prescribed fasting days without a valid reason; and (d) repudiated a concubine officially but continued to have sex with her.

Consequently, thanks to Nilsson's thorough study, Bishop Brynolf stands out as a very important lawgiver, to say the least, within both the ecclesiastical and the secular spheres. He seems to have dedicated almost the whole of his episcopacy, except possibly the very last years, to working within the sphere of ecclesiastical law, which to a great extent was also relevant for secular legislation. In these cases, he always tried to maintain the church's rights and demands in accordance with canon law. In many respects, he seems to have been successful in relation to the representatives of the secular authority. Therefore, he should be regarded as one of the most influential Christian jurists in the medieval Swedish church.

Andreas And

Biography

When and where Andreas Andersson (And)[44]—normally called just Andreas And—was born are unknown, but an informed guess is around 1250, probably on an estate just to the west of Uppsala called Lårsta, in the parish of Giresta. Archbishops as well as lawspeakers were among his relatives. His parents were Anders Andersson (And) and a daughter of a lawspeaker called Israel. Andreas had one brother, who in time became both a knight and a lawspeaker. At his death on March 27, 1317, Andreas had been the provost in Uppsala during two periods, 1278–99 and 1302–17.[45]

When Andreas first appears in written documents, he is mentioned as witness to King Magnus's (*Ladulås*) letter of sale to the Cistercian nuns in Skokloster on September 21, 1276. His title is *magister*, and he is a canon in the cathedral chapter of his relative Archbishop Folke Johansson's (Ängel).[46] Some scholars regard the title *magister* as justification for the assumption that he had studied in Paris.[47] Andreas is referred to as provost in Uppsala for the first time around 1279/1280,[48] when he was present in a legal context, albeit a secular one, namely, when King Magnus promulgated the *Alsnö stadga* (the Alsnö statute), a letter of privilege and protection whereby the Swedish secular nobility came into existence.[49]

At the end of 1290, the provost of Uppsala cathedral was excommunicated, and the chapter was suspended by the archbishop of Lund, Jens Grand, due to conflicts concerning Lund's primacy over Uppsala. The conflict was not brought to an end until 1294 when a settlement was issued between the Uppsala chapter and those parties which originally had turned to the archbishop of Lund. Through this whole process, Andreas as provost played an important role. This was partly due to the fact that in reality he was the leader of the Uppsala church after archbishop-elect Johannes died in September 1291 on his way to Orvieto, where the pope resided, and the successor, Nils (Allesson) did not take office until May 1296.[50] Andreas's role in secular matters at this time is evident from a royal letter of 1288. He was then a member of the king's board[51] and reappeared in this capacity a couple of times in the beginning of the fourteenth century.[52]

Andreas And's distinguished position in the church as well as in secular society is evident from the fact that the lawspeaker of Uppland, Birger Persson, when making his last will, appointed Andreas, together with Duke Erik (Magnusson), son of King Magnus (*Ladulås*), to be the guardian of his children as well as the executor of his will.[53]

Legal activities

Our knowledge about Andreas's legal activities is very scarce. As is evident from a number of records, as provost he was constantly involved in different types of administration of justice in the broad sense of the term—for instance, concerning economic matters. In addition, however, he exercised some influence in the elaboration of the Uppland Law. This was ratified by a royal letter on January 2, 1296, even though King Birger (Magnusson) (r. 1290–1318) still had not come of age at that time. In practice, the realm was governed by the *marsk* Torgils Knutsson, the leading person of the regency.[54] The royal letter is the only record expressly stating that Andreas was part of the efforts at working out the law.

Thus, scholars have asked what kind of influence he had regarding its contents, especially the section on church law, and how this section relates to the demands of international canon law by that time. One point of departure has been the possibility that he received his education and the title *magister* in Paris. On one hand, this assumption rests only on his title and the fact that as provost he evidently supported students from the diocese of Uppsala who were in Paris. On the other hand, nothing indicates that he took his degree at any other university.

In Paris, he most likely took the courses necessary for a clergyman, namely, those on the holy scriptures, and participated in the lectures on Peter Lombard's *Sentences*,[55] which constituted the compulsory textbook together with the Bible. Our knowledge of how the theological faculty in Paris was organized in Andreas's day is poor, so guesses about it have been made by using statutes from the fourteenth century and from other universities.[56] Whether Andreas also studied canon law in Paris remains unclear, especially since the University of Paris was particularly concentrated on teaching philosophy and theology. Considerably less important was the faculty of canon law. If you wanted to take jurisprudence at this time, you actually still had to set out for the universities in southern Europe.[57]

In the letter of ratification of the Uppland Law,[58] the king maintained that on several occasions he had been asked to remedy the fact that the laws of the three *folkland* (i.e., the smaller regions or districts of the province) in Uppland were scattered in different collections. He emphasized, however, that he had remained uncommitted since he did not want to change old law 'without urgent reasons' and would not institute new laws 'of no use.' Considering the wording of the letter, scholars have assumed that these laws actually were written down,[59] not just orally transmitted, but this cannot be substantiated.

Furthermore, the letter makes it clear that the task of leading the commission elaborating the Uppland Law was given to the lawspeaker in Uppland, Birger Persson. The royal instructions implied that he should decide what was old law and what ought to be inserted into it and decreed in a new law. As associates, he appointed a 'twelve-man commission' consisting of fifteen[60] people from the three *folkland* in Uppland, representing the church, the knights, the farmers, and the jurists. Four were knights, one was a lawspeaker, two were judges, and most of the others were representatives of the peasantry. Provost Andreas was the only representative of the church. Judging from the wording of the letter of ratification,[61] the law, after being completed, was approved in a common assembly (Swedish *ting*) for all three *folkland*. By way of introduction, the royal letter also stressed, as a sort of basic principle and fundamental reflection about the compiling of laws, that people's social intercourse with each other [changes]; because during the course of time many new cases can come about, and, furthermore there is a good deal in old law which is mentioned only with a few words and not as clearly as required. In these cases, changes are made both with regard to ecclesiastical and civil traditions of law, so that some part is abolished, some part is provided with additions, and some part consists of totally new regulations.

The question remains as to which contribution to the Uppland Law[62] Andreas And may have made. In the biography of Andreas in *Svenskt biografiskt lexikon*,

K.B. Westman presupposed that 'A's influence obviously was great,' asserting that 'his erudition in canon law is clearly observable' in the law.[63] In reality, this cannot be substantiated, and there is no method to detect what was actually Andreas's contribution.[64] Westman's opinion takes for granted that it is possible to determine what was new in the Uppland Law, especially in the section on church law. However, as we have seen, the royal letter of ratification already presupposed that there were older laws, whose content is inaccessible to us. How much of them was comprised of canon law? The question is legitimate since international canon law was not at all unknown in Sweden when the commission started to work. As mentioned, according to the decrees of the provincial council of Skänninge in 1248, every Swedish bishop was obliged to acquire the *Liber Extra* within one year.[65] Furthermore, since the latter part of the twelfth century, there were already a number of papal letters to the Swedish kings and bishops containing fundamental and normative prescriptions from canon law.[66] In addition, a provincial council in 1279, held in (Söder)Tälje, resulted in comprehensive statutes.[67] Perhaps Andreas was even present at the council, though this cannot be proven. Internationally, however, no new collection of canon law was promulgated until 1298 with the *Liber Sextus*.

Thus, there was a lot of material to use for those who compiled the Uppland Law, material which did not necessarily have anything to do with Andreas And's alleged education in canon law. Despite that, we may assume that his contributions to the discussions on the contents of the section on church law were important and were regarded as such by his contemporaries.

It is incorrect for scholars to describe the work with the legislation concerning the church as a conflict between ecclesiastical and secular interests, or at least as problematic in the way that laypeople in the commission opposed a considerable number of ecclesiastical requirements. The legally skilled laypeople should be regarded as familiar with those prescriptions from canon law which already were valid in their respective law districts. Besides, it is not self-evident that Andreas in all cases kept to the supranational ecclesiastical line; he might have had opinions of his own which not always and necessarily agreed with the requirements coming from the popes and the general councils, at least if he was not alone holding them. Otherwise he probably would have been excommunicated. Furthermore, he had grown up with and was educated in the Swedish church province's legal traditions. Therefore, Andreas should not be regarded as a lonely fighter against fifteen laymen, including the commission's chairman.

Even if his influence cannot be mapped out in particular, still, something can be said about the extent to which the section on church law in the Uppland Law is characterized by canon law, or the cases in which the requirements of canon law had no effect during the legislative process in Uppland. One should also keep in mind that this legislation concerned the absolute fundamental level of the society: the prescriptions applied to the overwhelming majority of inhabitants, i.e., the farmers living in the parishes throughout the province of Uppland.

In at least four important matters affecting almost all male parishioners (Swedish *sockenmän*)—with the stress on *mature male* parishioners—one can observe divergences between the ecclesiastical ideal and the reality in Uppland. The first matter concerned the strong influence that (male) parishioners (farmers) were granted in relation to the bishop regarding the appointment of parish priests (UL Kk 5).[68] Second, regarding last wills, farmers were required to have the consent of their heirs before bequeathing property to churches or monasteries as gift for the soul or for the church's *mensa* or *fabrica*, except that one-tenth of inherited land could be willed away (UL Kk 14). Third, laymen who offended against a cleric were to be brought before a secular court, not that of the church; this was valid also in disputes between the church and farmers over land (UL Kk 20). Fourth, farmers had the right to appeal the bishop's judgment to secular authority, i.e., to the king (UL Kk 20). As already noted, it is not possible to discern Andreas's position in these matters during his work on the law commission.

Finally, it should be mentioned that Andreas And as provost closely participated in the work of Archbishop Nils (Allesson) concerning the promulgation of diocesan statutes and rules for the canons regarding the services in the cathedral.[69] In at least the rules for canons in Uppsala Cathedral, in 1298, the archbishop underscored that they had come into being with the counsel and approval of the chapter,[70] in which Andreas And played an important role for a number of decades.

Laurentius Olavi

Biography

Laurentius Olavi (d. 1332)—in Swedish called Lars Olofsson and in the sources often called Laurentius de Vaxald, after the parish related to that prebendary bound to the dean at Uppsala Cathedral—was one of the most prominent representatives of canon law in medieval Sweden. He hailed from a wealthy landowning family, probably near the town of Enköping, southwest of Uppsala.[71] He is mentioned for the first time in the sources in 1289, as canon at Uppsala Cathedral; around 1300, he was appointed dean. In 1289, he was also called *magister.*[72] During the thirteenth and fourteenth centuries, Paris was the principal town for higher education for students from the Nordic countries. Supposedly, Laurentius had thus taken the degree of *magister artium* from that university and would by that time have been around the age of thirty, which means that he was born around 1260.[73]

In 1310, Laurentius willed, for his and his parents' souls, his farm (*curia*) with all buildings, tools, and animals, together with a piece of ground close to St. Peter's church in Uppsala, with the aim of funding a prebendary in the choir of St. Peter and St. Paul in Uppsala Cathedral.[74]

During his last years, Laurentius entered the Dominican convent in Sigtuna. He donated his collection of books on canon law, theology, and homiletics to the convent, together with his house in Uppsala and a boathouse in Enköping.[75] According to a note in a preserved collection of sermons in the Uppsala University Library (UUB C 18) that Laurentius donated to the friars in Sigtuna, he died in 1332.[76]

Laurentius's works

Studying and gaining his degree in Paris during the late thirteenth century, Laurentius received education in the scholastic theology during its high point and in its most prominent milieu. Using scholarly arguments and strict distinctions, the most distinguished scholastic theologians sought to structure, systematize, define, and analyze the traditional Catholic dogmatics. The argumentation was gathered into *summæ*, such as the *Summa theologiæ* by Thomas Aquinas (c. 1225–74). The philosophical works by the scholastics are built on their academic study of the Bible. But exegetic as well as systematic theology aimed to benefit preaching. As a result, works of pastoral character also were produced at the universities by this time.[77]

Laurentius is the author of three works. Two of these are preserved: *Suffragium curatorum* (Guide for Ministers) and *Summa de ministris et sacramentis ecclesiasticis* (On the Ministers and Sacraments of the Church), usually known as *Summula. Suffragium curatorum* is a handbook for confessors.[78] *Summula* is a manual with prescriptions for the priest's lifestyle and duties towards God and parishioners.[79] The third work, according to a will from 1360, is called *Vocabuletum decani*.[80] All three works are systematically written, in the scholastic tradition. It is plausible that they were all used for training priests.

The purpose of *Suffragium curatorum* and *Summula* was to make canon law better known to Swedish clergy in general. Canon law was given a comprehensive form, so that the ordinary parish priest, without any full and varied education—poor and simple priests they are called in the introduction to *Summula*—would be able to understand canon law without access to the extensive commentary literature. The content is not unique for its time; it reflects the common Western view of the priest and his part in the church. These two works are based on the international canon law and expositions of the great theologians.

Summula

Summula has been preserved in four almost complete copies and four fragments. It is fairly uncommon to find a medieval Swedish work from the early fourteenth century retained in so many copies. *Summula* is mentioned in some other sources, such as wills and inventories—an indication that it had a high position and was widely used.[81] This fact also points to Laurentius Olavi as an important transmitter of canon law to the church province.

The *Summula* is divided into twenty chapters. The first ten contain detailed rules and theological commentaries on clerical ministry and way of life.[82] Hierarchy and ordinations to different holy orders are treated, as is the duty of following canon law. A larger part of this section of the book includes rules for the life and reputation of the clergy. The clergy should live an honest and worthy life, in chastity and moderation, with wisdom, hospitality, and sobriety.[83] The following ten chapters treat the duties of the priestly ministry, such as education and preaching, prayer, divine service, and administration of the sacraments.[84] This second part of the work gives directions about the Catholic faith and how to perform the mass and holy office, baptism and confirmation, penance, communion for the sick, extreme unction, and holy orders. There are also explanations of the regulations on the sacraments according to canon law and theological interpretations.[85]

Laurentius's aim was not to write down his own views on these matters but to synthesize canon law and theological expositions of central themes, and to do so in a pedagogical, well-arranged, and lucid way suitable for parish priests. Without any international model, Laurentius produced an original work with a conscious selection of directions that he found necessary for the clergy.[86]

Suffragium curatorum

Suffragium curatorum presents a summary of what the church taught on the sacrament of penance according to canon law and pastoral guidelines. It is written from the perspective of the ordinary parish priest in his role as confessor. The work has survived to its full extent only in one copy (UUB C 69) and one extract (UUB C 582). Taking canon law as his point of departure, Laurentius gives a concise account of the prescriptions regarding the sacrament of penance. He opens by categorizing the different kinds of sins. Then he deals with the importance of the priest being pure in body and soul when celebrating the Eucharist. He follows this with a statement about the sacrament of penance consisting of remorse, confession, and acts of penance. The rules concerning the parish priest's giving of absolution and penance are explained. An extensive part of the work is dedicated to the regulation on excommunication. One part deals with the result of sincere penance. *Suffragium curatorum* ends with counsels to the confessor.[87]

Laurentius and canon law

In the introduction to *Summula*, Laurentius states that the aim of the work is to introduce and implement international canon law among Swedish clergy, especially those not well educated and without the use of the extensive commentaries on canon law (*maxime pauperum et simplicium sacerdotum, qui copiam canonum vel doctorum habere nequeunt*).[88] He builds his work on canon law and the tradition from the church Fathers.[89] The main sources are different collections of canon law—for instance, *Decretum Gratiani* (1140), the decretals by Gregory IX, also called *Liber Extra* (1234) and the sixth book of these, called *Liber Sextus* (1298).[90] The scriptures and the great theologians' interpretations and exegesis play a central part in Laurentius's works, as he repeatedly refers to certain parts of scripture and to Fathers like Augustine (354–430), Gregory the Great (ca. 540–604), Isidor of Seville (ca. 560–636), the Venerable Bede (672/673–735), Hrabanus Maurus (780–856), and Hostiensis/Henricus of Segusia (d. 1270).[91] The *summa* genre was well established in Europe at this time. Nevertheless, Laurentius has compiled his sources and studied them independently. There is no direct model in the international literature.[92]

When he entered the Dominican convent in Sigtuna, he donated his collection of literature in canon law and theology. The list of works gives an impression of the kind of literature Laurentius probably used when working on *Summula* and *Suffragium curatorum*, literature of his own possession. The literature he donated was:

> *Decretum meum. Decretales cum glosa ordinaria. vincencium in duobus uoluminibus. bibliam vnam. & duo volumina de dictis originalibus doctorum diuersorum.*[93]

We see here that Laurentius owned a Bible and what seem to be texts by different theologians collected in two volumes. The other books are mostly different works of canon law, such as the comprehensive work of *Decretum Gratiani*. The *decretales* mentioned is the decretals of Gregory IX. *Decretum Gratiani* was provided by commentaries and explanations through glosses—notes between the lines or in the margins. What is mentioned as *decretales cum glosa ordinaria* is *Apparatus* by Bernhard of Parma (d. 1266), a work that gained status as *glossa ordinaria*. Laurentius also owned a copy of a work by Vincent of Beauvais (c. 1190–1264) in two volumes, perhaps the whole or parts of the comprehensive encyclopedia *Speculum maius*. Apart from this literature, Laurentius might have used the library of Uppsala Cathedral.[94] Laurentius consciously chose what sources would form the basis of his works. In all likelihood, he chose what he found was useful for the domestic priests.

Laurentius does not claim to have produced anything distinctive and original, but he states that he builds on canon law and the tradition of the Fathers.[95] Perhaps this circumstance, that his works contain what was regarded as the universal canon law, contributed to the spread of his works. Laurentius used the *summa* genre, and through that he connected to those works produced in the same genre on the Continent, thereby placing himself in a well-established tradition of education and culture. In this way, he also connected the peripheral church province of Uppsala to the Continental Catholic Church. This counts to his great merit.

Summula and *Suffragium curatorum* do not relate specifically to Swedish circumstances and do not always correspond with the domestic statutes. Perhaps this was already well known and relatively easily accessible for the Swedish clergy while Laurentius realized the need of transmitting other, more detailed and supplemental, prescriptions.[96] His aim was to introduce elementary knowledge of canon law and theology in a pedagogical, focused, and comprehensible way to give clergy a necessary guiding rule for a good way of life and a correct practice of office. Through increased knowledge in this field, Laurentius's works made international canon law more accessible and influential, tying priests closer to the universal church instead of the developing national state in a way regarded as positive in the eyes of the leaders of the church province of Uppsala.[97]

Conclusion

Our analysis shows how the bishop Brynolf Algotsson, the provost Andreas And, and the dean Laurentius Olavi at the end of the thirteenth century and the beginning of the fourteenth contributed to the implementation of international canon law in Sweden through their written works as well as their participation in legal activities. All their work related to the different levels in the ecclesiastical organization, i.e., the parishes, the dioceses, and the church province. The bishops as well as the parish priests, the secular leaders as well as the farmers, were all in different ways and with regard to different aspects influenced by these leaders' contributions in the sphere of church law. Their efforts at spreading and inventing ecclesiastical decrees and prescriptions had long-lasting consequences for the church in Sweden and were sometimes relevant for the rest of the Middle Ages until the Reformation changed the foundations for church law—in fact, in some cases even after that. Therefore, when trying to write Swedish medieval church history, historians must take into account all three legal thinkers.

Notes

1 See Bertil Nilsson, 'The Swedish Ecclesiastical Legislation and the Question of Its Nordic Character', *How Nordic Are the Nordic Medieval Laws?—Ten Years After. Proceedings of the Tenth Carlsberg Academy Conference on Medieval Legal History 2013,* Per Andersen, Kirsi Salonen, Helle Sigh, and Helle Vogt, eds, (Copenhagen: DJØF Publishing, 2014), 81–112, especially 86–94.

2 *Diplomatarium Suecanum* (henceforth DS) 359 = *Svenskt diplomatariums huvudkartotek,* https://riksarkivet.se/sdhk (henceforth SDHK) 613. — On the council, see Åke Ljungfors, 'Mötet i Skänninge 1248', *Kyrkohistorisk årsskrift* 50 (1950), 1–32; Bertil Nilsson, 'The Provincial Council of Skänninge, Sweden, 1248', *Annuarium Historiae Conciliorum* 38 (2006), 115–46. On legal demands to the Swedish church province proclaimed by papal letters during the twelfth and thirteenth centuries before the council, see an overview in Nilsson, 'The Provincial Council', 116–22.

3 DS 692 (SDHK 1070); L.M. Bååth, *Bidrag till den kanoniska rättens historia i Sverige* (Stockholm: O.L. Svanbäcks boktryckeri, 1905), 191–95; Yngve Brilioth, *Svenska kyrkans historia. 2: Den senare medeltiden 1274–1521* (Stockholm: Svenska kyrkans diakonistyrelses bokförlag, 1941), 24–29; Britt Hedberg, *Uppsala stifts herdaminne. Från missionstid till år 1366,* Uppsala stifts herdaminne. Serie IV Missionstid, medeltid, reformationstid, IV:1 (Uppsala: Stiftshistoriska kommittén i Uppsala, 2007), 203–07.

4 Dick Harrison, *Sveriges historia 600–1350* (Stockholm: Norstedts, 2009), 254–59.

5 See Sven-Erik Pernler, *Sveriges kyrkohistoria 2: Hög- och senmedeltid* (Stockholm: Verbum, 1999), 50.

6 Harrison, *Sveriges historia,* 264–67.

7 On Brynolf's ancestors and his contemporary relatives, see Bo J. Theutenberg, 'Västergötlands lagmän—Algotsöner och folkungar. Om biskop Brynolf Algotssons anfäder och samtida släktingar', *Biskopen och törntaggen*, Johnny Hagberg, ed. (Skara: Skara stiftshistoriska sällskap, 2004), 245–322.

8 On this, see Anders Fröjmark, 'Brynolf Algotssons kanonisationsprocess', *Brynolf Algotsson—scenen, mannen, rollen*, Karl-Erik Tysk, ed. (Skara: Viktoria Bokförlag, 1995), 137–49, especially 137–41.

9 'Vita S. Brynolphi episc. Scarensis cum processu eius canonizationis', *Scriptores rerum svecicarum medii aevi* (henceforth SRSMA) III:2, Claudius Annerstedt, ed. (Upsaliae, 1871 & 1876), 138–85; translation into Swedish in Sven Blomgren, *Den helige biskop Brynolfs av Skara levnad jämte hans kanonisationsprocess* (Skara: Föreningen för Västgötalitteratur, 1998).

10 See the preface of 'Vita S. Brynolphi' in SRSMA, 139–41; Blomgren, *Den helige biskop Brynolfs,* 9–15.

11 The *legenda* was edited and translated into Swedish in Tryggve Lundén, 'Sankt Brynolf, biskop av Skara. II. Hans eftermäle', *Credo. Katolsk tidskrift* 27 (1946): 14–39.

On both of these texts, the *Vita* and the *legenda*, see also Fredrik Öberg, 'Den liturgiska Brynolfsbilden', *Biskopen och törntaggen*, 149–70; Öberg made a thorough comparison of the texts.

12 See Tryggve Lundén, 'Sankt Brynolf, biskop av Skara. I. Hans liv och författarskap', *Credo. Katolsk tidskrift* 26 (1945), 185; reading 3 and 4 in Lundén, 'Sankt Brynolf' (1946), 28–29; 'Vita S. Brynolphi', SRSMA, 141.

13 Reading 5 in Lundén (1946), 30.

14 Ibid.

15 Reading 7 and 8 in Lundén (1946), 31–32.

16 Reading 9 in Lundén (1946), 33.

17 DS 650 (SDHK 1060).

18 Ibid.

19 DS 670 (SDHK 1086); Sven-Erik Pernler, 'Brynolf Algotsson, lagmanssonen som blev biskop', Tysk, *Brynolf Algotsson*, 87–104, especially 91–92.

20 For a most thorough study of the research tradition in this case, see Dagmar Lagerberg, *Författartradition Brynolf. En granskning av diskussionen kring de liturgiska verk som tillskrivits biskop Brynolf av Skara jämte transkription av de s.k. Notule Brynolphi och deras förlaga* (Stockholm: Instant Book, 2016).

21 On Brynolf's liturgical writing, see Tryggve Lundén, '*Brynolf Algotssons* samlade diktverk (Helenaofficiet, Eskilsofficiet, Sigfridsofficiet, Jungfru Marias lördagsofficium, Törnekronans officium)', *Credo. Katolsk tidskrift* 27 (1946): 73–124; Alf Härdelin, 'Mysteriets metaforer. Om bildspråk och tankemönster i Brynolf Algotssons (?) liturgiska "hystorior"', *Brynolf Algotsson*, 105–20; Anders Piltz, 'Brynolf och den liturgiska författarrollen', *Brynolf Algotsson*, 121–36; Lagerberg, *Författartradition Brynolf* (2016).

22 Incompatible information on how it happened can be found in the office for the crown of thorns and the *Vita*, respectively; see reading 6 in Lundén, 'Sankt Brynolf' (1946), 30–31; reading 1 in Lundén, 'Brynolf Algotssons samlade diktverk' (1946), 112; 'Vita S. Brynolphi', SRSMA, 142. See further Pernler, 'Brynolf Algotsson, lagmanssonen som blev biskop', 96–97; Rune Ekre, 'Pilgrimsvägarna genom Lödöse och törntaggens färd till Skara', *Biskopen och törntaggen*, 45–68, especially 53–62.

23 DS 2100 (SDHK 2796).

24 See Jaakko Gummerus, ed., *Synodalstatuter och andra kyrkorättsliga aktstycken från den svenska medeltidskyrkan* (Upsala: Norstedt, 1902), 18 and cited sources.

25 On the *Notulae* with an edition, see Lagerberg, *Författartradition Brynolf*, 216–73.

26 See Göran B. Nilsson, *Nytt ljus över Yngre Västgötalagen. Den bestickande teorin om en medeltida lagstiftningsprocess*. Rättshistoriskt bibliotek 69. (Stockholm: Institutet för rättshistorisk forskning, 2012), passim, but especially 29–100, 178–94.

27 Gummerus, *Synodalstatuter och andra kyrkorättsliga aktstycken*, 12, 14f.; the statutes are edited in ibid., 57–61. See also Nilsson, *Nytt ljus över Yngre Västgötalagen*, 75–78.

28 Gummerus, *Synodalstatuter och andra kyrkorättsliga aktstycken*, 57.

29 Ibid.

30 See Sigurd Kroon, *Det svenska prästmötet under medeltiden. Dess uppkomst och ställning i samhälle och kyrka* (Stockholm: Svenska diakonistyrelsens bokförlag, 1948), 57–58.

31 See DS 692 (SDHK 1070).

32 Nilsson, *Nytt ljus över Yngre Västgötalagen*, 77 and cited literature.

33 Ibid.

34 Ibid., 190.

35 Ibid., 79–88.

36 See Gummerus, *Synodalstatuter och andra kyrkorättsliga aktstycken*, 15–17; the statutes are edited in ibid., 61–65.

37 See Nilsson, *Nytt ljus över Yngre Västgötalagen*, 79–87.
38 Nilsson, *Nytt ljus över Yngre Västgötalagen*, 78.
39 Gummerus, *Synodalstatuter och andra kyrkorättsliga aktstycken*, 13–14; the statute is edited in ibid., 46–57.
40 DS 709 (SDHK 1160). The statute is translated into Swedish in Åke Holmbäck and Elias Wessén, *Svenska landskapslagar. Tolkade och förklarade för nutidens svenskar. Femte serien* (Stockholm: Hugo Gebers förlag, 1946), 224–25; Lundén, 'Sankt Brynolf, biskop av Skara', 183–215 especially 191–92; see also Nilsson, *Nytt ljus över Yngre Västgötalagen*, 72–75.
41 It may be debated whether homosexuality is meant by the expression "crime against nature," but it seems feasible. Another possible interpretation is bestiality; see further Nilsson, *Nytt ljus över Yngre Västgötalagen*, 74 note 52 and cited literature.
42 See Nilsson, 'The Swedish Ecclesiastical Legislation', 81–112, especially 89.
43 Nilsson, *Nytt ljus över Yngre Västgötalagen*, 188; see also Nilsson, 'The Swedish Ecclesiastical Legislation', 91–92.
44 On the And family, see K.B. Westman, 'And', *Svenskt biografiskt lexikon* vol 1 (Stockholm: Bonnier, 1918–), 647–51.
45 Westman, 'And', 648–51; Hedberg, *Uppsala stifts herdaminne*, 306–07.
46 DS 618 (SDHK 1008).
47 See H. Schück, 'Svenska Pariserstudier under medeltiden', *Kyrkohistorisk årsskrift* 1 (1900), 9–78, especially 44–46; Westman, 'And', 648; Brilioth, *Svenska kyrkans historia*, 164.
48 On the dating of the statute, see SDHK 1122; Harrison, *Sveriges historia*, 397.
49 DS 799 (SDHK 1122); on the statute and its contents, see Harrison, *Sveriges historia*, 397–401.
50 See Westman, 'And', 648–49.
51 See DS 975 (SDHK 1421).
52 Westman, 'And', 650.
53 DS 2008 (SDHK 2669).
54 Harrison, *Sveriges historia*, 264–65.
55 *Sententiarum libri quattuor*, written during the years 1148–51.
56 René Kieffer, 'Parisuniversitetet på Brynolfs tid', *Brynolf Algotsson*, 71–86, especially 74–75.
57 J. Verger, 'Universität', *Lexikon des Mittelalters* 8 (München: Lexma Verlag, 1997), 1249–55; and J. Verger, 'Paris, Schulen und Universität', *Lexikon des Mittelalters* 6 (München und Zürich: Artemis & Winkler Verlag), 1993, 1718–21.
58 DS 1154 (SDHK 1684, 1685); translation into modern Swedish with explanations in Åke Holmbäck and Elias Wessén, *Svenska landskapslagar. Tolkade och förklarade för nutidens svenskar. Första serien* (Stockholm: Hugo Gebers förlag, 1933), 5–6, 8–10.
59 See Holmbäck and Wessén, *Svenska landskapslagar*, 1933, 9, note 8.
60 No one seems to have been able to clarify in a satisfactory way why the letter at this point obviously contains contradictory information regarding the number of members; see Holmbäck and Wessén, *Svenska landskapslagar*, 1933, 9f., note 11.
61 See Holmbäck and Wessén, *Svenska landskapslagar* 1933, 10, note 12.
62 On the Uppland Law as a whole, see Dieter Strauch, *Mittelalterliches nordisches Recht bis ca. 1500. Eine Quellenkunde.* 2., völlig neu bearbeitete und erweiterte Auflage (Berlin/Boston, MA: De Gruyter, 2016), 422–44; especially on the process of its creation, see Sam. Henning, 'Upplandslagens redigering och dess handskrifter. En studie kring 1607 års edition', *Arkiv för nordisk filologi 48* (1932), 121–55, especially 130–36.
63 Westman, 'And', 649.
64 However, see Henning, 'Upplandslagens redigering', 134–35, who has made a short attempt, though building entirely on guesses.
65 See Nilsson, 'The Provincial Council of Skänninge', 142.

66 See Nilsson, 'The Swedich Ecclesiastical Legislation', 82–86.
67 DS 692 (SDHK 1070).
68 To that, see also Bertil Nilsson, 'The Church Law of Scania on the Consecration of Churches and the Appointment of Parish Priests: International Canon Law and that of Scania', *Denmark and Europe in the Middle Ages, c. 1000–1525. Essays in Honour of Professor Michael H. Gelting*, Kerstin Hundahl, Lars Kjær, and Niels Lund, eds. (Burlington, VT: Ashgate Farnham, 2014), 157–82, especially 177–81.
69 See further Hedberg, *Uppsala stifts herdaminne*, 223–24, 544–50; see also DS 1187 (SDHK 1727).
70 DS 1235 (SDHK 1791).
71 Olle Ferm, 'Varifrån var Lars av Vaksala?', *Personhistorisk tidskrift* (1987), 99–100; Göran Dahlbäck, *Uppsala domkyrkas godsinnehav med särskild hänsyn till perioden 1344–1527*, Studier till Det medeltida Sverige 2 (Stockholm: Almqvist och Wiksell), 60, 83–84.
72 DS 995 (SDHK 1455), DS 3835 (SDHK 5055), DS 3835 (SDHK 5055), DS 995 (SDHK 1455). See also Ferm, 'Varifrån var', 99; Olle Ferm, 'Laurentius Olavi de Vaksala', *Medieval Nordic Literature in Latin*, Stephan Borgehammar, ed. (forthcoming).
73 Yngve Brilioth, *Svenska kyrkans historia* 163–76; Olle Ferm, 'Universitet och högskolor', *Norden og Europa i middelalderen*. Rapporter til Det 24. Nordiske Historikermøde 1 (Århus, 2001), 104–06; Ferm, 'Varifrån var', 99.
74 DS 1683 (SDHK 2367). See also Dahlbäck, *Uppsala domkyrkas godsinnehav*, 156–57; Göran Dahlbäck, Olle Ferm and Sigurd Rahmqvist, *Det medeltida Sverige, 1 Uppland, 2 Tiundaland, Ulleråker, Vaksala, Uppsala stad* (Stockholm: Riksantikvarieämbetet, 1984), 215. On this choir, see Christian Lovén and Herman Bengtsson, 'Domkyrkans kor och altaren under medeltiden', *Uppsala domkyrka. 3 Byggnadsbeskrivning, byggnadshistoria, domkyrkans konsthistoriska ställning*, Sveriges kyrkor 229, Christian Lovén, Herman Bengtsson, and Markus Dahlberg, eds. (Uppsala: Upplandsmuseet, 2010), 245–55.
75 DS 2672 (SDHK 3550); DS 2673 (SDHK 3549); DS 2776 (SDHK 3711). See also Dahlbäck, Ferm, and Rahmqvist, *Det medeltida Sverige* 317. On Laurentius's book collection, see Brilioth, *Svenska kyrkans historia*, 161–62; Toni Schmid, 'Om Sigtunabrödernas böcker och böner', *Sigtuna Mariakyrka 1247–1947*, H. Arbman, ed. (Sigtuna: Sigtuna fornhems förlag, 1947), 79; Tönnes Kleberg, *Medeltida Uppsalabibliotek, 2 Bidrag till deras historia fram till år 1389*, Acta Universitatis Upsaliensis. Skrifter rörande Uppsala universitet. C. Organisation och historia (Uppsala: Almqvist & Wiksell, 1972), 53–54.
76 *Iste liber est fratrum predicatorum conuentus siktunensis quem dedit eis reuerendus pater dominus laurencius olaui decanus vpsalensis qui eciam postea in ordine professus obiit anno domini M°CCC°XXX°II tercio kalendas marcij.* UUB C 18, fol. 198v. See also Jarl Gallén, *La province de Dacie de l'ordre des frères prêcheurs, 1 Histoire générale jusqu'au grand schisme* (Helsinki: Söderström, 1946), 149; Schmid, *Om Sigtunabrödernas böcker*, 52, 54.
77 See, e.g., Thomas F. O'Meara, 'Paris as a Cultural Milieu of Thomas Aquinas's Thought', *The Thomist* 38:4 (1974); Marie-Dominique Chenu, *La théologie au douzième siècle*, Études de philosophie médiévale 45: (Paris: J. Vrin, 1957); Marie-Dominique Chenu, *Das Werk des hl. Thomas von Aquin*. Vom Verf. durchges. und verb. deutsche Ausg. Die deutsche Thomas-Ausgabe 2 (Heidelberg: Kerle, 1960); Alf Härdelin, *Världen som yta och fönster. Spiritualitet i medeltidens Sverige*, Scripta minora 1 (Stockholm: Sällskapet Runica et Mediævalia, 2005), 16–17, 19–20, 221, 317, 442; Alf Härdelin, 'Jean Gerson. En senmedeltida praktisk teolog', *Jean Gersons Ars moriendi, Om konsten att dö*, Markus Hagberg, ed., Skara stiftshistoriska sällskaps skriftserie 45 (Skara, 2009).
78 For an edition and commentary on *Suffragium curatorum*, see Berit Gustavsson, 'Laurentius av Vaksala. Suffragium curatorum. En textkritisk utgåva med inledning och indices', unpubl., 2007.

79 *Summula* is analyzed from the perspective of salvation history with lengthy quotations from the work in the footnotes in Stina Fallberg Sundmark, *Teologi för praktiskt bruk. Frälsningshistoriska perspektiv på Summula av Laurentius av Vaksala*, Bibliotheca Theologiæ Practicæ 95 (Skellefteå, 2014).

80 The *Vocabuletum decani* is given by the archdean Ringvid Nilsson to the school at the chapel of St. Erik in Uppsala. DS 6357 (SDHK 7842).

81 Fallberg Sundmark, *Teologi för praktiskt bruk*, 18–20, 32.

82 *Capitulum I De distinccione ordinum et officiorum ecclesiasticorum* 1r–5v
Capitulum II De obseruancia canonum 5v–10v
Capitulum III De vita et honestate clericorum 10v–13r
Capitulum IV De sanctimonia clericorum 13r–17r
Capitulum V De castitate clericorum 17r–29r
Capitulum VI De temperancia clericorum 29v–33v
Capitulum VII De ornatu clericorum 33v–43r
Capitulum VIII De prudencia clericorum 43r–45v
Capitulum IX De hospitalitate clericorum 45v–47r
Capitulum X De sobrietate clericorum 47r–49v.

83 The chapter on the hospitality of the clergy is analyzed in Stina Fallberg Sundmark, 'En handbok för fattiga och enkla präster – Summula av Laurentius av Vaksala från svenskt 1300-tal', *Kyrka, kultur, historia – en festskrift till Johnny Hagberg*, Markus Hagberg, Lena Maria Olsson, and Sven-Erik Pernler eds., Skara stiftshistoriska sällskaps skriftserie 69 (Skara, 2012).

84 *Capitulum XI De fide catholica et eius articulis* 49v–56r
Capitulum XII De horis canonicis et impedimentis circa eas contingentibus 56r–107r
Capitulum XIII De baptismo 107r–123v
Capitulum XIV De confirmacione quae fit per episcopum 123v–127v
Capitulum XV De penitencia clericorum 128r–197r
Capitulum XVI De viatico 197r–203v
Capitulum XVII De extrema unctione 203v–207r
Capitulum XVIII De ordine clericali 207r–209v
Capitulum XIX De matrimonio 209v–222r
Capitulum XX De curatis et eorum doctrina 222r–230v

85 For studies on certain chapters on the sacraments, see Carl-Gustaf Andrén, 'Laurentius' av Vaxala Summula och den kanoniska rätten', *Kyrkohistorisk årsskrift* 55 (1955); Bengt Ingmar Kilström, 'Två förlagor till botkapitlet i Laurentius' av Vaxala Summula', *Kyrkohistorisk årsskrift* 56 (1956); Carl-Gustaf Andrén, *Konfirmationen i Sverige under medeltid och reformationstid*, Bibliotheca Theologiæ Practicæ 1: (Lund, 1957); Bengt Ingmar Kilström, *Den kateketiska undervisningen i Sverige under medeltiden*, Bibliotheca Theologiæ Practicæ 8 (Uppsala, 1958); Mia Korpiola, 'The Two Husbands of Helleka Horn: Interpreting the Canonical Law of Marriage in Late Medieval Sweden' , *Panta rei. Studi dedicati a Manlio Bellomo* 3 (Rome, 2004); Stina Fallberg Sundmark, *Sjukbesök och dödsberedelse. Sockenbudet i svensk medeltida och reformatorisk tradition*, Bibliotheca Theologiæ Practicæ 84 (Skellefteå: Artos, 2008); Fallberg Sundmark, *Teologi för praktiskt bruk.*

86 Fallberg Sundmark, *Teologi för praktiskt bruk*, 16–18.

87 Gustavsson, 'Suffragium curatorum'.

88 UUB C 64 fol. 1 r. For an overview of the canonic literature used in the Nordic region, see, e.g., Toni Schmid, 'Kanonistisk litteratur', *Kulturhistoriskt lexikon för nordisk medeltid* 8 (1963), 229–32; Jan Brunius, *From Manuscripts to Wrappers. Medieval Book Fragments in the Swedish National Archives*, Skrifter utgivna av Riksarkivet 35 (Stockholm 2013), 169–72.

89 UUB C 64 fol. 1r.

90 Jaakko Gummerus, *Beiträge zur Geschichte des Buss- und Beichtwesens in der schwedischen Kirche des Mittelalters* (Uppsala, 1900), xlvii; Andrén, 'Laurentius' av Vaxala', 18–30; Andrén, *Konfirmationen i Sverige*, 37–38.

91 Andrén, 'Laurentius' av Vaxala', 20.
92 Ibid., 18.
93 DS 2672 (SDHK 3550).
94 DS 2673 (SDHK 3550). Kleberg, *Medeltida Uppsalabibliotek*, 53–54, 119–20.
95 *Summula* fol. 1r.
96 For instance, see prescriptions concerning communion and extreme unction. Fallberg Sundmark, *Sjukbesök och dödsberedelse*, 104–05, 174, 206, 208, 217–18.
97 For discussions on Laurentius' aim in his works, see Andrén, 'Laurentius av Vaxala', 27–29.

Bibliography

Andrén, Carl-Gustaf, 'Laurentius' av Vaxala Summula och den kanoniska rätten', *Kyrkohistorisk årsskrift* 55 (1955), 9–41.

Andrén, Carl-Gustaf, *Konfirmationen i Sverige under medeltid och reformationstid*, Bibliotheca Theologiæ Practicæ 1 (Lund: Gleerups forlag, 1957).

Bååth, L.M., *Bidrag till den kanoniska rättens historia i Sverige* (Stockholm: O.L. Svanbäcks boktryckeri, 1905).

Biskopen och törntaggen, Johnny Hagberg, ed. (Skara: Skara stiftshistoriska sällskap, 2004).

Blomgren, Sven, *Den helige biskop Brynolfs av Skara levnad jämte hans kanonisationsprocess* (Skara: Föreningen för Västgötalitteratur, 1998).

Brilioth, Yngve, *Svenska kyrkans historia. 2: Den senare medeltiden 1274–1521* (Stockholm: Svenska kyrkans diakonistyrelses bokförlag, 1941).

Brunius, Jan, *From Manuscripts to Wrappers. Medieval Book Fragments in the Swedish National Archives*, Skrifter utgivna av Riksarkivet 35 (Stockholm: Riksarkivet, 2013).

Brynolf Algotsson—scenen, mannen, rollen, Karl-Erik Tysk, ed. (Skara: Viktoria Bokförlag, 1995).

Chenu, Marie-Dominique, *La théologie au douzième siècle*, Études de philosophie médiévale 45, (Paris: J. Vrin, 1957).

Chenu, Marie-Dominique, *Das Werk des hl. Thomas von Aquin*. Vom Verf. durchges. und verb. deutsche Ausg. Die deutsche Thomas-Ausgabe 2 (Heidelberg: Kerle, 1960).

Dahlbäck, Göran, *Uppsala domkyrkas godsinnehav med särskild hänsyn till perioden 1344–1527*, Studier till Det medeltida Sverige 2 (Stockholm: Almqvist och Wiksell).

Dahlbäck, Göran, Olle Ferm, and Sigurd Rahmqvist, *Det medeltida Sverige, 1 Uppland, 2 Tiundaland, Ulleråker, Vaksala, Uppsala stad* (Stockholm: Riksantikvarieämbetet, 1984).

DS = *Diplomatarium Suecanum*, vol. 1- , (Stockholm: different publishers, 1829-).

Ekre, Rune, 'Pilgrimsvägarna genom Lödöse och törntaggens färd till Skara', *Biskopen och törntaggen*, Johnny Hagberg, ed. (Skara: Skara stiftshistoriska sällskap, 2004), 45–68.

Ferm, Olle, 'Varifrån var Lars av Vaksala?', *Personhistorisk tidskrift* (1987), 99–100.

Ferm, Olle, 'Universitet och högskolor', *Norden og Europa i middelalderen*. Rapporter til Det 24. Nordiske Historikermøde 1 (Århus, 2001), 104–06.

Ferm, Olle, 'Laurentius Olavi de Vaksala', *Medieval Nordic Literature in Latin*, Stephan Borgehammar ed. (forthcoming).

Fröjmark, Anders, 'Brynolf Algotssons kanonisationsprocess', *Brynolf Algotsson*, 137–49.

Gallén, Jarl, *La province de Dacie de l'ordre des frères prêcheurs, 1 Histoire générale jusqu'au grand schisme* (Helsinki: Söderström, 1946).

Gummerus, Jaakko, *Beiträge zur Geschichte des Buss- und Beichtwesens in der schwedischen Kirche des Mittelalters* (Uppsala, 1900).

Gummerus, Jaakko, ed., *Synodalstatuter och andra kyrkorättsliga aktstycken från den svenska medeltidskyrkan* (Upsala: Norstedt, 1902).

Gustavsson, Berit, 'Laurentius av Vaksala. Suffragium curatorum. En textkritisk utgåva med inledning och indices', unpubl., 2007.

Harrison, Dick, *Sveriges historia 600–1350* (Stockholm: Norstedts, 2009).

Hedberg, Britt, *Uppsala stifts herdaminne. Från missionstid till år 1366,* Uppsala stifts herdaminne. Serie IV Missionstid, medeltid, reformationstid, IV:1 (Uppsala: Stiftshistoriska kommittén i Uppsala, 2007).

Henning, Sam., 'Upplandslagens redigering och dess handskrifter. En studie kring 1607 års edition', *Arkiv för nordisk filologi* 48 (1932), 121–55.

Holmbäck, Åke and Wessén Elias, *Svenska landskapslagar. Tolkade och förklarade för nutidens svenskar. Första serien* (Stockholm: Hugo Gebers förlag, 1933).

Holmbäck, Åke and Wessén, Elias, *Svenska landskapslagar. Tolkade och förklarade för nutidens svenskar. Femte serien* (Stockholm: Hugo Gebers förlag 1946).

Härdelin, Alf, 'Mysteriets metaforer. Om bildspråk och tankemönster i Brynolf Algotssons (?) liturgiska "hystorior"', *Brynolf Algotsson - scenen, mannen, rollen,* Karl Erik Tysk, ed. (Viktoria bokförlag), 105–20.

Härdelin, Alf, *Världen som yta och fönster. Spiritualitet i medeltidens Sverige,* Scripta minora 1 (Stockholm: Sällskapet Runica et Mediævalia, 2005).

Härdelin, Alf, 'Jean Gerson. En senmedeltida praktisk teolog', *Jean Gersons Ars moriendi, Om konsten att dö,* Markus Hagberg, ed., Skara stiftshistoriska sällskaps skriftserie 45 (Skara: Skara stiftshistoriska sällskap, 2009).

Kieffer, René, 'Parisuniversitetet på Brynolfs tid', *Brynolf Algotsson- scenen, mannen, rollen,* Karl Erik Tysk, ed. (Viktoria bokförlag), 71–86.

Kilström, Bengt Ingmar, 'Två förlagor till botkapitlet i Laurentius' av Vaxala Summula,' *Kyrkohistorisk årsskrift* 56 (1956), 30–48.

Kilström, Bengt Ingmar, *Den kateketiska undervisningen i Sverige under medeltiden,* Bibliotheca Theologiæ Practicæ 8 (Uppsala: CWK Gleerup, 1958).

Kleberg, Tönnes, *Medeltida Uppsalabibliotek,* 2 *Bidrag till deras historia fram till år 1389,* Acta Universitatis Upsaliensis. Skrifter rörande Uppsala universitet. C. Organisation och historia (Uppsala: Almqvist & Wiksell, 1972).

Korpiola, Mia, 'The Two Husbands of Helleka Horn: Interpreting the Canonical Law of Marriage in Late Medieval Sweden,' *Panta rei. Studi dedicati a Manlio Bellomo* 3 (Rome. 2004), 153–81.

Kroon, Sigurd, *Det svenska prästmötet under medeltiden. Dess uppkomst och ställning i samhälle och kyrka* (Stockholm: Svenska diakonistyrelsens bokförlag, 1948).

Lagerberg, Dagmar, *Författartradition Brynolf. En granskning av diskussionen kring de liturgiska verk som tillskrivits biskop Brynolf av Skara jämte transkription av de s.k. Notule Brynolphi och deras förlaga* (Stockholm: Instant Book, 2016).

Ljungfors, Åke, 'Mötet i Skänninge 1248', *Kyrkohistorisk årsskrift* 50 (1950), 1–32.

Lovén, Christian and Bengtsson, Herman, 'Domkyrkans kor och altaren under medeltiden', *Uppsala domkyrka. 3 Byggnadsbeskrivning, byggnadshistoria, domkyrkans konsthistoriska ställning,* Sveriges kyrkor 229, C. Lovén, H. Bengtsson, and M. Dahlberg, eds. (Uppsala: Upplandsmuseet, 2010), 252–67.

Lundén, Tryggve, 'Sankt Brynolf, biskop av Skara. I. Hans liv och författarskap', *Credo. Katolsk tidskrift* 26 (1945), 183–215.

Lundén, Tryggve, '*Brynolf Algotssons* samlade diktverk (Helenaofficiet, Eskilsofficiet, Sigfridsofficiet, Jungfru Marias lördagsofficium, Törnekronans officium)', *Credo. Katolsk tidskrift* 27 (1946), 73–124.

Lundén, Tryggve, 'Sankt Brynolf, biskop av Skara. II. Hans eftermäle', *Credo. Katolsk tidskrift* 27 (1946), 14–39.

Nilsson, Bertil, 'The Provincial Council of Skänninge, Sweden, 1248', *Annuarium Historiae Conciliorum* 38 (2006), 115–46.

Nilsson, Bertil, 'The Church Law of Scania on the Consecration of Churches and the Appointment of Parish Priests: International Canon Law and that of Scania', *Denmark and Europe in the Middle Ages, c. 1000-1525. Essays in Honour of Professor Michael H. Gelting*, Kerstin Hundahl, Lars Kjær, and Niels Lund, eds. (Burlington, VT: Ashgate Farnham, 2014), 157–82.

Nilsson, Bertil, 'The Swedish Ecclesiastical Legislation and the Question of Its Nordic Character', *How Nordic are the Nordic Medieval Laws?—Ten Years After. Proceedings of the Tenth Carlsberg Academy Conference on Medieval Legal History 2013,* Per Andersen, Kirsi Salonen, Helle Sigh, and Helle Vogt, eds. (Copenhagen: DJØF Publishing, 2014), 81–112.

Nilsson, Göran B., *Nytt ljus över Yngre Västgötalagen. Den bestickande teorin om en medeltida lagstiftningsprocess.* Rättshistoriskt bibliotek 69. (Stockholm: Institutet för rättshistorisk forskning, 2012).

Öberg, Fredrik, 'Den liturgiska Brynolfsbilden', *Biskopen och törntaggen*, Johnny Hagberg, ed. (Skara: Skara stiftshistoriska sällskap, 2004), 149–70.

O'Meara, Thomas F., 'Paris as a Cultural Milieu of Thomas Aquinas's Thought', *The Thomist* 38:4 (1974), 689–722.

Pernler, Sven-Erik, *Sveriges kyrkohistoria 2: Hög- och senmedeltid* (Stockholm: Verbum, 1999).

Pernler, Sven-Erik, 'Brynolf Algotsson, lagmanssonen som blev biskop', *Brynolf Algotsson - scenen, mannen, rollen,* Karl Erik Tysk, ed. (Viktoria bokförlag), 87–104.

Piltz, Anders, 'Brynolf och den liturgiska författarrollen', *Brynolf Algotsson - scenen, mannen, rollen,* Karl Erik Tysk, ed. (Viktoria bokförlag), 121–36.

Schmid, Toni 'Om Sigtunabrödernas böcker och böner', *Sigtuna Mariakyrka 1247–1947,* H. Arbman, ed. (Sigtuna: Sigtuna fornhems förlag, 1947), 45–82.

Schmid, Toni, 'Kanonistisk litteratur', *Kulturhistoriskt lexikon för nordisk medeltid* 8 (1963), 229–32.

Schück, H., 'Svenska Pariserstudier under medeltiden', *Kyrkohistorisk årsskrift* 1 (1900), 9–78.

SDHK = *Svenskt diplomatariums huvudkartotek,* https://riksarkivet.se/sdhk

SRSMA = *Scriptores rerum svecicarum medii aevi,* various eds., vol. 1–3 (Uppsala: Zeibel och Palmblad, 1818–1876).

Strauch, Dieter, *Mittelalterliches nordisches Recht bis ca. 1500. Eine Quellenkunde.* 2., völlig neu bearbeitete und erweiterte Auflage (Berlin/Boston, MA: De Gruyter, 2016).

Sundmark, Stina Fallberg, *Sjukbesök och dödsberedelse. Sockenbudet i svensk medeltida och reformatorisk tradition,* Bibliotheca Theologiæ Practicæ 84 (Skellefteå: Artos, 2008).

Sundmark, Stina Fallberg, 'En handbok för fattiga och enkla präster – Summula av Laurentius av Vaksala från svenskt 1300-tal', *Kyrka, kultur, historia – en festskrift till Johnny Hagberg,* Markus Hagberg, Lena Maria Olsson, and Sven-Erik Pernler eds., Skara stiftshistoriska sällskaps skriftserie 69 (Skara: Skara stiftshistoriska sällskap, 2012), 129–44.

Sundmark, Stina Fallberg, *Teologi för praktiskt bruk. Frälsningshistoriska perspektiv på Summula av Laurentius av Vaksala,* Bibliotheca Theologiæ Practicæ 95 (Skellefteå: Artos Norma Bokförlag, 2014).

Svenskt diplomatariums huvudkartotek, https://riksarkivet.se/sdhk

Theutenberg, Bo J., 'Västergötlands lagmän—Algotsöner och folkungar. Om biskop Brynolf Algotssons anfäder och samtida släktingar', *Biskopen och törntaggen*, Johnny Hagberg, ed. (Skara: Skara stiftshistoriska sällskap, 2004), 245–322.

Verger, J., 'Paris, Schulen und Universität', *Lexikon des Mittelalters* 6 (München und Zürich: Artemis & Winkler Verlag), 1993, 1718–21.

Verger, J., 'Universität', *Lexikon des Mittelalters* 8 (München: Lexma Verlag, 1997), 1249–55.

'Vita S. Brynolphi episc. Scarensis cum processu eius canonizationis', *Scriptores rerum svecicarum medii aevi*, III:2, Claudius Annerstedt, ed. (Upsaliae, 1871 & 1876), 138–85.

Westman, K.B., 'And,' *Svenskt biografiskt lexikon* 1 (Stockholm: Bonnier, 1918), 647–51.

Part 2

Reformation and early modern times

4 Introduction

Reformation and early modern times

Mia Korpiola and Heikki Pihlajamäki

Main trends

In Scandinavia, the early modern period brought significant transformation in law by way of the Reformation of the 1520s and 1530s, and dynastic change in Denmark-Norway and Sweden. The Kalmar Union under one (Danish) king was dissolved by war in the 1520s. After this, Sweden (including present-day Finland), moved from elective to hereditary succession to the throne, consolidating royal power.

During this period, Scandinavia more generally experienced a centralization of royal power and thereby more effective governance. In Sweden, this change was especially connected with—and a precondition for—its rise to become a great European power through warfare and territorial expansion in the seventeenth century. In both Sweden and Denmark-Norway, royal authority increased with the Reformation, although in Denmark-Norway it soon diminished in favor of the aristocracy.[1] By the seventeenth century, both Scandinavian kingdoms had developed into estate societies, though different from those in other parts of Europe. From a European perspective, both countries had a small noble class. Many Swedish and Norwegian peasants owned their land, and these countries both had a sizeable class of landowning yeomen-farmers, whereas a significant proportion of Danish peasants were and became increasingly tied to turf. Yet feudalism never grew to the proportions in Denmark that it did in most other parts of Europe. In Sweden, the militarized seventeenth century brought with it an upsurge of feudalistic features, but the zenith of the feudal period was short-lived. In Sweden, the peasant estate was represented at the Diet, which helped to turn the feudal apotheosis quickly to destruction by the Great Reduction of 1680, which revoked a large part of the previous land grants from the crown to aristocrats, military officers, and government officials. Moreover, due to the growing Swedish bureaucracy and recurrent warfare, the Swedish noble estate experienced flux through constant ennoblements, while the Danish nobility remained to a larger extent closed and smaller.

Warfare and the failures of the aristocracy played into the hands of the kings. After 1660, Denmark-Norway became one of the most absolutist states in Europe, largely until 1848. By contrast, in Sweden—where financing of wars required more regular meetings of the Estates—the royal absolutist period was shorter (1680–1718). This period was followed by a counter-reaction, the so-called Age of Liberty (1718–1772), during which political power lay mostly in the hands of the Estates and the Diet.

Reformation, confessionalization, and Lutheran orthodoxy

While Sweden was the first monarchy outside the German lands to embrace Protestantism, Denmark-Norway quickly followed. In both countries, the religious upheaval coincided with political revolution. The secular ruler's position now became based on his role as the mediator between his subjects and God, insofar as the "earthly kingdom" was concerned. As *executor divinarum et suarum legum*, "executor of laws both divine and his own," the prince had to enact laws which secured the observance of both tables of the Ten Commandments. As guardian of the first table, the prince needed to ensure that the first three commandments (regarding idolatry, blasphemy, and keeping of the Sabbath) were observed, that "pure doctrine" was not violated, and that the obstinate were punished. The second table of the Decalogue—the other seven Commandments—had to do with the relations between the subjects. These commandments also needed to be implemented through secular legislation: thus, punishments for adultery, theft, homicide, perjury, and a whole range of crimes now drew their legitimacy from the second table of the Decalogue. It is not that these crimes would have gone unpunished in the Middle Ages, but they were now transferred exclusively to the ruler's competence in the Lutheran lands.[2]

In Denmark, the decisive turn to the Reformation is usually dated to the year 1536, although the evangelical movement had spread to urban areas already in the 1520s. The Danish Reformation was more of a movement from below than the Swedish Reformation, especially as the towns on both sides of the Sound were influenced first by humanist thinking and then by reforming preachers.

The Danish Reformation was more directly influenced than the Swedish Reformation by German reformers, most notably Johannes Bugenhagen (1485–558, see article in this volume). At the invitation of King Christian III (r. 1534–59), Bugenhagen stayed in Denmark in 1537–39 and 1542. He also authored the Lutheran Church Ordinance of 1537 according to German models. In Norway, Catholicism persisted until the second half of the sixteenth century, and the Danish church ordinance regulated Norwegian ecclesiastical matters until 1607, when the local church ordinance was given.[3]

The changes that the Lutheran Reformation in Germany produced in law left their mark also in Scandinavia, a strong bastion of Lutheranism. In Sweden, more than in Denmark-Norway, the Reformation was motivated by political concerns and consequently was more of a top-down process. In Sweden, the 1520s proved a decisive decade in terms of both politics and church reform. King Gustav I Vasa (r. 1523–60) took power in 1521 and was elected king in 1523, after which he severed relations with the Roman Catholic Church. The Diet of Västerås (1527) is traditionally considered the decisive turning point in the Swedish Reformation. Not particularly given to theological finesse, the king was primarily motivated by political concerns and the property of the church. It took time, however, for the Lutheran faith to gain final acceptance and for the evangelical theological doctrine to become established. With the Synod of Uppsala of 1536, the Reformation was fully introduced. Yet the first Church Ordinance was not issued until 1571 by Archbishop Laurentius Petri (1499–573, see article in this volume).

The impact of the Reformation on Lutheran legal orders was considerable. Ecclesiastical courts did not completely disappear, but they now fell under the state's authority and lost the international dimension they had had as part of the Catholic Church. Parts of their jurisdiction were transferred to the secular courts. The Scandinavian models came to differ from each other to some extent. In Denmark, for example, special marriage courts were introduced, while Sweden largely preserved its cathedral chapters (*domkapitel*).

Sweden offers an example of the changes in the judicial system,[4] as ecclesiastical courts lost their independence vis-à-vis the secular ruler but did not completely disappear. After a brief interim period following the outbreak of Reformation in Sweden in the 1520s, the rural dean's assizes reassumed their functions and continued operating until the late sixteenth century.

The Reformation had wide repercussion on criminal law.[5] As elsewhere in Lutheran lands, biblical or Mosaic law (and for Denmark-Norway, in particular, fear of the wrath of God)[6] became important sources of criminal law in Scandinavia. In 1608 King Charles IX of Sweden, while confirming that King Christopher's Law of the Land (1442) would continue in force, declared that "in capital and other serious crimes one should observe God's law as it is written in the Holy Scripture." The law's famous appendix contained a list of legal rules taken from the Pentateuch. Among other crimes, swearing, violence against one's own parents, extramarital intercourse, and perjury were now punishable by death.[7]

The Lutheran understanding of marriage as a secular institution—a "*weltlich Ding*," as Luther had put it—was incorporated into Scandinavian statutory law. The Danish marriage ordinance (*Ægteskapsordinansen*) of 1582, heavily influenced by the work of the second-generation Danish reformer Niels Hemmingsen (1513–600, see chapter in this volume) allowed for divorce in cases of unfaithfulness and *desertio malitiosa*, or when one of the partners had left the common home without reason. Divorce was also possible if impotence was proven at the beginning of the marriage, and when a marriage partner was sentenced to deportation or a long prison term for a crime. The Code of 1683 then confirmed these norms.

In Sweden, a similar marriage law found its way into legal practice and was then codified in the church ordinances of 1571 and 1686, and finally in the 1734 code. The Swedish reformers were cautious, however, when it came to reforming marriage laws. Clerical marriage was introduced rather quickly after the Reformation, although it took some decades for it to become firmly established. The law of marriage impediments changed little, and marriage formation showed much more continuity to the medieval canon law; a marriage contracted against parents' wishes could normally not be annulled. If sexual intercourse occurred after the exchange of conjugal promises, a marital bond was formed. For the Lutheran church, it was just as difficult as it had been for the Catholic Church to demand public solemnization of marriages: in Sweden, the ecclesiastical marriage ceremony did not become obligatory until the Code of 1734. Divorce became possible in Sweden; in fact, the courts allowed divorce on more grounds than those expressly stated in the church ordinance of 1571.[8]

In both Denmark and Sweden in the sixteenth century, reformers had to position themselves vis-à-vis the kin marriages of the ruling monarchs. Both Laurentius Petri and Nils Hemmingsen were required to write statements on the lawfulness of the unions of King Gustav Vasa of Sweden and King Frederick II (r. 1559–88) of Denmark-Norway, respectively. In Sweden, the clerics defied King Gustav, who married his late wife's niece regardless of the protests of the clergy, but in Denmark, Niels Hemmingsen argued for the permissibility of marriage between first cousins. By contrast, in Sweden Laurentius Petri absolutely forbade such unions, writing a treatise against them.

Legal scholarship and universities

Legal learning in the form of university-trained lawyers had reached its peak in the Scandinavian kingdoms shortly before the Reformation. For example, high Swedish clerics had never been more learned in law than during the decades preceding the Reformation. We know of at least fourteen doctors of canon law, three doctors of both laws (canon and Roman), three licentiates in canon law, and several baccalaureates in canon law in Sweden after 1437.[9] In contrast, the level of legal learning among Swedish, Danish, and Norwegian clerics plummeted after the Reformation. No post-Reformation Swedish cleric is known to have had a law degree,[10] and more generally, the number of doctors of law in the pre-Reformation century was not surpassed until the nineteenth century in Sweden.

The first Scandinavian university was established in Uppsala in 1477 and the second in Copenhagen two years later (1479). Both mainly trained priests, and the theology students also got some elementary training in canon law and Roman law. However, the scanty sources would indicate that while law teaching probably disappeared in Uppsala in the early 1500s, the faculty of law was more robustly based in Copenhagen, and law was taught there until the onset of the Reformation.[11]

As the Reformation wreaked havoc on the funding and staff of the universities of Uppsala and Copenhagen, both ceased to function by the 1530s. The University of Copenhagen resumed its activity in 1537, but its law faculty—founded in 1539—continued providing training to theology students. The upheaval was more profound in Sweden, where the University of Uppsala—reopened in 1593 to ensure the training of priests in accordance with the Lutheran creed after the important Synod of Uppsala—started *de facto* legal education only in 1620.

Both law faculties were small, consisting of only one to three professors throughout the period. The teaching at the sixteenth-century University of Copenhagen, as elsewhere in Europe, concentrated exclusively on Roman law.

The Swedish development took a slightly different path as, since the 1620s, the Uppsala faculty's second professor began to teach Swedish law also, comparing it with Roman law, whereas Roman law remained the other professor's main area of teaching.[12] In Sweden, new universities were founded in Turku (Sw. Åbo, 1640) for the Finnish provinces, Tartu (Sw. Dorpat, 1632) for the Baltic provinces, and Lund (1666) for the formerly Danish provinces newly annexed after the Peace of Roskilde in 1658. During the second half of the century, the position of natural law gained strength in the law curricula. Nordic legal science first appeared in the seventeenth century as the German-born professor Johannes Loccenius (1579–636) was the first in Scandinavia to write scholarly legal commentary (*Synopsis iuris ad leges Sueticas accommodata*, 1648).

Sources of law

An important characteristic of Scandinavian law was that it was largely based on statutory law from early on. This is understandable in view of the social setting of these remote European regions. Even during the later Middle Ages, although all three Scandinavian kingdoms were under the same (Danish) ruler during the Kalmar Union, there had been almost no standardization of law among the three kingdoms. At the beginning of the early modern period, the status of the town laws reflected the status of law elsewhere in each country: the town laws in Norway had been much unified in the late thirteenth century and in Sweden in the mid-fourteenth century, immediately after the "national" laws for the countryside had been finished. By contrast, Danish towns had their own individual laws, which were not as comprehensive as their Norwegian and Swedish counterparts.[13]

Roman law, recycled over again in European legal scholarship and *ius commune* since the Middle Ages, existed in the Nordic kingdoms as well, albeit as a thinner layer. The spreading of learned law was crucially dependent on a university-trained legal profession, and one cannot talk of such a profession before the seventeenth century in Sweden. Only during the later seventeenth century did Swedish appellate court judges increasingly have legal training, something that happened in Denmark-Norway in the following century. Although what counted as legal training was interpreted rather liberally, some high court judges had solid training from the best European universities.[14] This enabled the appellate courts to apply *ius commune* in their decisions, a practice that appears clearly, for instance, in criminal and procedural law and in the different fields of private law, such as the law of obligations and inheritance. But even while the legal professional largely predominated in many parts of Europe, this was not so in Scandinavia. There, lawyers in courts were unheard of, except in some larger town courts, and most lower court judges were seldom trained in law until the late seventeenth century. Thus, the leading Swedish reformer Olaus

Petri (1493–552, see also chapter in this volume), who acted as the town clerk of Stockholm in the 1520s after studies at Wittenberg, was an unusually learned court official. Later, he also authored the so-called "Judge's Rules," a collection of *brocardica*, or legal maxims. Nevertheless, the general lack of learned judges meant that learned law needed to adapt to the local conditions—in other words, be simplified.

Thus, basically all major bodies of European law—customary law, feudal and manorial law, town law, and Roman law—existed in Sweden and Denmark-Norway as well. Despite differences among the Scandinavian realms, all of these bodies of law emerged weaker in Scandinavia than in the more southerly parts of the Continent. The combination of legal sources was a zero-sum game, in which the weakness of some of the sources meant a stronger position for others. In Scandinavia, statutory law was the one legal source that started to expand considerably from early on. Statutory laws gained ascendance in Denmark-Norway and Sweden from the Middle Ages and received further impetus in the sixteenth and seventeenth centuries.[15]

Growing royal powers over the court system and the early modern law codes

Not only did the Reformation change legal norms, but the church's disciplinary powers became a central instrument of social control. While growing Swedish military power depended on internal peace and social coherence, the new "modern," centralized state was still all too weak to administer locally effective social control by itself. Crown and church thus acted as partners in social control, and the alliance was beneficial not only for the crown but also for the church. The discipline that the church was able to enforce by way of delegation from the secular power restored much of the prestige that the Catholic Church had enjoyed in the Middle Ages and that had been lost in the Reformation. The Protestant church thus remained an important factor in social life throughout the seventeenth and eighteenth centuries. According to the precepts of Lutheran social theory, the church functioned as the *brachium seculare*, or secular arm, of the state when it came to worldly matters entrusted to the church. Priests monitored the morality of the people in matters of sexual discipline, but they were also in charge of educating the people. From the theological perspective of Luther's two-kingdom theory, salvation was the ultimate end of the alliance between the crown and the church and their common efforts at efficient social control.[16]

The amount of royal legislation rapidly increased in both Denmark and Sweden from the late Middle Ages onwards. The preparations for Denmark's law code (*Danske Lov*) started almost immediately after the new absolutist form of government of 1660 had entered into force. The Code of 1683 unified Danish law, which until then had consisted of provincial laws. [17] The Norwegian Code of 1687 was practically identical to the Danish one. The Swedish code, although it appears newer than the other two, is actually a product of much the same period. Its preparations started already in the 1680s, although almost half a century passed before the law's completion.

The Scandinavian law codes were all in some ways products of the centralized state with weak estates. They wiped out the competing sources of law, which had begun to rise like mushrooms in the sixteenth and seventeenth centuries. The law codes were royal legislation and accepted by the estates. They left little room for customary law, town laws, patrimonial courts, or Roman law.

The law codes were based on similar sources: medieval legislation and, to an extent, learned Roman law. Seventeenth-century products and thus older than the Swedish Code, the Danish and Norwegian laws are based on learned law to a lesser extent than the Swedish law. Danish (and Norwegian) legal literature had not yet emerged when the laws were drafted; neither had Danish legal practice absorbed as much influence of learned law as Swedish law by the beginning of the eighteenth century. The Danish Code probably exerted influence on the Swedish one, although less in the details than in the concept of a complete code. However, because the Danish and Norwegian laws were older, they also became antiquated earlier. New piecemeal legislation appeared beside them, and legal practice in many cases—criminal law, for instance—distanced itself from the letter of the law. In Sweden, legal literature emerged earlier and had more time to influence the Code of 1734. Also in Sweden, of course, new statutes were written after 1734, and legal practice departed from the letter of the law less than in Denmark-Norway.

All of the Scandinavian early modern codes were products of the period preceding the Enlightenment, which is why they have not usually been taken as "true" codifications. The biggest difference between the Nordic codes and the Enlightenment codes is that the latter built on the systematization efforts of natural law philosophers such as Christian Wolff. The Scandinavian codes, in turn, were organized on principles derived from medieval provincial laws. Other than that, the differences are of gradation only.

To be sure, some important areas of law were left out of these compilations, such as administration, financial, and commercial regulation—all the areas of law which at the time were grouped under the heading of *ius politiae* or *Policeyrecht*—"police law," a term that encompassed a broad sphere of social regulations governing economics, religion, and moral behavior. As heads of developing modern states, Danish and Swedish kings had taken advantage of this modern legislative tool. As elsewhere in Europe and the Americas, the Scandinavian early modern police regulations covered a wide range of administrative and economic affairs.[18] The early modern Scandinavian law codes contained only such rules as were thought to be immutable, leaving no room for police regulations in them.

Notes

1 See Ylikangas, "The Crown and the Aristocracy", 101–32.
2 Witte, *Law and Protestantism*, 134–35.
3 On the Danish, Icelandic, and Norwegian Reformations, see Grell, "The Reformation", 44–59.
4 Although minor differences abound, the Danish changes are similar enough to render repetition superfluous. For the history of Danish church discipline after the Reformation, see Lausten, *Christian den 3. og kirken*, 178–207.

5 For a detailed treatment of Lutheran church penalties, see Pihlajamäki, "*Executor divinarum et suarum legume*", 194–202.
6 Kjær, *Guds og øvrigheds straf – centralmagt og sædelighed.*
7 See Takala, *Lex Dei – Lex Politica Dei*; and Sundin, *För Gud, staten och folket.*
8 Korpiola, "Lutheran Marriage Norms in Action", 131–69.
9 E.g., Malmström, *Juridiska fakulteten i Uppsala*, 42–47.
10 On Brask, see, e.g., Sjödin, "Hans Brask"; and Mia Korpiola, "Lutheran Marriage Law".
11 Norvin, *Københavns Universitet i Middelalderen*, esp. 77–81, 99, 204–07; Tamm,"-Juraen på Københavns Universitet 1479-2005," esp. 8–12.
12 Almquist, *Svensk juridisk litteraturhistoria*, 187, 199; Jørgensen, "Retsundervisningen og Retsvidenskaben", 11–114 and 529–35; Klinge, *Helsingin yliopiston historia 1640–1990*, 524.
13 E.g., Korpiola, "High- and Late-medieval Scandinavia".
14 For Sweden, see, Vasara-Aaltonen, "From Well-travelled 'Jacks-of-all-Trades' to Domestic Lawyers".
15 For overviews on the early modern legal systems of Scandinavia and Sweden more particularly, Pihlajamäki, "Scandinavian Law in the Early Modern Period"; and Korpiola, "Legal Diversity".
16 Aalto, *Kirkko ja* kruunu, 140–41.
17 For the preparations of the Danish Law of Realm, see Iuul, *Kodifikation eller kompilation?*
18 For police regulations in Sweden, see Kotkas, *Royal Police Ordinances*; and for Denmark, Tamm, "Gute Sitte und Ordnung".

Bibliography

Aalto, Seppo, *Kirkko ja kruunu siveellisyyden vartijoina: Seksuaalirikollisuus, esivalta ja yhteisö Porvoon kihlakunnassa 1621–1700* (Helsinki: Suomen Historiallinen seura, 1996).

Almquist, Jan Eric, *Svensk juridisk litteraturhistoria* (Stockholm: Norstedt, 1946).

Grell, Ole Peter, "The Reformation in Denmark, Norway and Iceland," *The Cambridge History of Scandinavia*, E. I. Kouri and Jens E. Olesen, eds. (Cambridge: Cambridge University Press, 2016), 44–59.

Juul, Stig, *Kodifikation eller kompilation? Christian V's Danske Lov på baggrund af ældre ret* (Copenhagen: Bianco Lunos, 1954).

Jørgensen, Poul Johs., "Retsundervisningen og Retsvidenskaben ved Københavns Universitet, 1537–1736," *Festskrift i Anledning af Tohundrede Aars Dagen af Indførelsen af Juridisk Eksamen ved Københavns Universitet*, Erik Reitzel-Nielsen and Carl Popp-Madsen, eds. (Copenhagen: Københavns Universitet, 1936), 11–114 and 529–35.

Kjær, Morten, *Guds og øvrigheds straf – centralmagt og sædelighed i Danmark-Norge* (Copenhagen: Ex Tuto Publishing, 2017).

Klinge, Matti, et al., *Helsingin yliopiston historia 1640–1990, I: Kuninkaallinen Turun Akatemia 1640–1808* (Keuruu: Helsingin yliopisto, 1987).

Korpiola, Mia, "High- and Late-medieval Scandinavia: Codified Vernacular Law and Learned Legal Influences," *Oxford Handbook on European Legal History*, Heikki Pihlajamäki, Mark Godfrey, and Markus D. Dubber, eds. (Oxford: Oxford University Press, 2018), 378–403.

Korpiola, Mia, "Legal Diversity—Or the Relative Lack of It—In Early Modern Sweden," *Law and Diversity: Pre-Modern Europe and India in Comparison (12th to 17th Centuries)*, Thomas Ertl and Gijs Kruijtzer, eds. (Berlin, Boston, MA: De Gruyter, 2017), 142–65.

Korpiola, Mia, "Lutheran Marriage Law in Sixteenth- and Early Seventeenth-Century Sweden: Authorities and Sources of Law," *Law and Religion: The Legal Teachings of the Catholic and Protestant Reformations*. Refo500 Academic Studies, vol. 20, Wim Decock, Jordan J. Ballor, Michael Germann, and Laurent Waelkens, eds. (Vandenhoeck & Ruprecht: Göttingen, 2014), 107–32.

Korpiola, Mia, "Lutheran Marriage Norms in Action: The Example of Post-Reformation Sweden, 1520–1600," *Lutheran Reformation and the Law*, Virpi Mäkinen, ed. 13 (Leiden: Brill, 2006), 131–69.

Kotkas, Toomas, *Royal Police Ordinances in Early Modern Sweden: Emergence of Voluntaristic Understanding of Law* (Leiden: Brill, 2014).

Lausten, Martin, *Christian den 3. og kirken 1537–1559* (Copenhagen: Akademisk Forlag, 1987).

Malmström, Åke, *Juridiska fakulteten i Uppsala: Studier till fakultetens historia 1: Den medeltida fakulteten och dess historiska bakgrund*. Acta Universitatis Upsaliensis – Skrifter rörande Uppsala universitet C:34 (Uppsala: University of Uppsala, 1976).

Norvin, William, *Københavns Universitet i Middelalderen* (Copenhagen: G.E.C. Gads Forlag, 1929).

Pihlajamäki, Heikki, "*Executor divinarum et suarum legum*: Criminal Law and the Lutheran Reformation," *Lutheran Reformation and the* Law, Virpi Mäkinen, ed., (Leiden: Brill, 2006), 194–202.

Pihlajamäki, Heikki, "Scandinavian Law in the Early Modern Period," *Oxford Handbook on European Legal History*, Heikki Pihlajamäki, Mark Godfrey, and Markus D. Dubber, eds., 806–29.

Sjödin, L., "Hans Brask," *Svenskt Biografiskt Lexikon 6*. (Stockholm, 1926).

Sundin, Jan, *För Gud, staten och folket: Brott och rättskipning i Sverige 1600–1840* (Lund: Institutet för rättshistorisk forskning, 1991).

Takala, Martti, *Lex Dei – Lex Politica Dei: Lex Politica Dei –teos ja Kaarle IX:n lainsäädäntö* (Helsinki: Suomen Kirkkohistoriallinen Seura, 1993).

Tamm, Ditlev, "Gute Sitte und Ordnung: Zur Entwicklung und Funktion der Polizeigesetzgebung in Dänemark," *Policey im Europa der Frühen Neuzeit*, Michael Stolleis, ed. (Frankfurt am Main: Vittorio Klostermann, 1996), 509–30.

Tamm, Ditlev et al., "Juraen på Københavns Universitet 1479-2005," *Københavns Universitet 1479–1979 6:1: Det rets- og statsvidenskabelige fakultet 1*, Ditlev Tamm and Ejvind Slottved, eds. (Copenhagen: University of Copenhagen, 2005), xvii–45.

Vasara-Aaltonen, Marianne, "From Well-Travelled 'Jacks-of-all-Trades' to Domestic Lawyers: The Educational and Career Backgrounds of Svea Court of Appeal Judges 1614–1809," *The Svea Court of Appeal in the Early Modern Period: Historical Reinterpretations and New Perspectives*, Mia Korpiola, ed. (Stockholm: Institutet för rättshistorisk forskning grundat av Gustav och Carin Olin, 2014), 301–54.

Witte, John Jr., *Law and Protestantism: The Legal Teachings of the Lutheran Reformation* (Cambridge: Cambridge University Press, 2002).

Ylikangas, Heikki, "The Crown and the Aristocracy in Co-operation in Denmark and Sweden (the 'Aristocratic regime')," *The Cambridge History of Scandinavia, Vol. 2: 1520–1870*, E. I. Kouri and Jens E. Olesen, eds. (Cambridge: Cambridge University Press, 2013), 101–32.

5 The architect of the Danish-Norwegian reformation

Johannes Bugenhagen (1485–1558)

Morten Kjær and Mattias Skat Sommer

Introduction

> Here nothing else is treated but the clean and pure gospel, the sacraments according to Christ's institution, singing and sacred lessons, an honest gathering at the sermon, and the distribution of the Holy Sacrament; how the youth ought to be disciplined after the book and the liberal arts, to the word of God and the sacred scripture; how the servants of the holy church may be provided for and the schools maintained; how the poor be tended; and how the catechism may prevail in all houses.[1]

With these words from the 1537/1539 Danish church ordinance, Johannes Bugenhagen (1485–1558) outlined the core of Christianity. According to Bugenhagen, it is the duty of the king to establish a sound framework in which Christianity's core may flourish, in terms of preaching and worship, education of young people, payment of pastors and other church staff, poor relief, and general knowledge of doctrine among commoners. As the church organizer of the Wittenberg Reformation, which developed during the 1520s, Bugenhagen became obliged to assist princes and cities in introducing "Reformations" of doctrine and life.

As a German, Bugenhagen cannot strictly be considered a *Nordic* Christian jurist. However, he resided in Denmark-Norway during the middle 1530s, acting as a consultant to King Christian III (r. 1534–59), who in 1536–37 introduced a princely Reformation in his realm.[2] Indeed, Bugenhagen was not the first Wittenberg theologian to come to Scandinavia and support the royal attempts of Reformation; in the early 1520s, Andreas Bodenstein von Karlstadt (1486–1541) temporarily stayed in Copenhagen, invited by King Christian II (r. 1513–23), who, inspired by the rumors of Luther from the south, was avid for legal, political, and theological reform in his dominions. Neither Karlstadt nor Christian II had much success: Karlstadt was soon sent back to Saxony by the king—the brother-in-law of Emperor Charles V (r. 1519–56)—who suddenly found it less attractive to turn Lutheran after the 1521 Diet of Worms, and in 1523 Christian himself was forced to flee to the Low Countries. On the other hand, Bugenhagen became far more influential, as we are going to show.

In this chapter, we first focus on Bugenhagen's biography and theology. Second, we analyze Bugenhagen's work in Denmark-Norway during the 1530s, focusing on the 1537 church ordinance that entailed a certain understanding of the royal *ius reformandi*, and on his treatise on marriage, dedicated to Christian III. Bugenhagen's seminal writings thus belong to the legal teachings of the Danish Reformation.

Bugenhagen's life and thought in context

Bugenhagen in Pomerania

The son of a burgomaster, Bugenhagen was born on 24 June 1485 on the Pomeranian island of Wollin (present-day Poland) in the Baltic Sea, just off the coast. He was named after John the Baptist, who was commemorated on that day in the ecclesiastical year.[3] He probably received his primary education in the Stettin Latin school before enrolling in the University of Greifswald (founded in 1456) in January 1502. As was customary, he began with studies in the faculty of arts. At the turn of the century, German universities began to exchange the various scholasticisms with new methods drawn from pan-European humanism.[4] In Greifswald Bugenhagen may have delved into the humanist curriculum of mastering proper Latin style, perusing the ancient *auctores* (both Christian and pagan), living according to a civic, this-worldly ethic, and studying scripture. He never enrolled in the higher faculties at the university, leaving Greifswald after little more than two years of study, and it is uncertain whether he completed his studies by formally receiving the master of arts degree.

In 1504 Bugenhagen was appointed rector of the Latin school in the city of Treptow an der Rega, where he disseminated the humanist learning he had encountered in Greifswald. While lecturing to his students on Latin grammar and patristics authors, Bugenhagen proceeded with his own studies, engaging deeply with theology and the Bible. The rector's interest in theological matters quickly was reflected in his teaching, as he began to offer catechetical instruction of the youth, based on the creed and the Decalogue, and to give additional lectures on the exegesis of Biblical books. Clearly, Bugenhagen expressed the humanist ideal of the merger of *eloquentia* with *pietas*.[5] Students from all over the Baltic area were attracted by Bugenhagen's teaching, and even some of the Treptow burghers and the Premonstratensian monks from nearby Belbug monastery—founded in the late twelfth century by Danish clerics from Lund—came to attend the young rector's lectures. As a rector appointed by the Belbug abbot, Bugenhagen also performed duties of ecclesiastical polity, acting as a notary and as a juridical secretary of the monastery.

Early visions of reform

Bugenhagen enjoyed good relations with the various Premonstratensian abbots throughout his years as a rector. He was called to the office by the abbot Joachim (who is likely to have had good contacts with the university in Greifswald, Bugenhagen's alma mater), and in the spring of 1509 he was ordained a vicar at the St. Mary's collegiate church in Treptow by the prelate of Pomerania—even before his twenty-fourth birthday, which was the minimum age for priests according to canon law, and even without formal theological education. Bugenhagen did not join the Premonstratensian order, but while evidence is scant, there is good reason to believe his ordination relied on his good connections within the ecclesiastical network of Treptow. When, in 1517, Bugenhagen was installed as a lecturer of scripture and patristics in the monastic school of Belbug by the monastery's newly appointed abbot, Johannes Boldewan (c. 1485–c. 1529)—a Greifswald fellow student—he now seized the opportunity to influence the Belbug brethren's theology (still without any theological education himself).[6] Following the publication of the Ninety-Five Theses in late 1517, Augustinian friar Martin Luther (1483–1546) of Wittenberg, Saxony, became the subject for discussion all over Germany. It was during these years that Bugenhagen developed an interest in ecclesiastical and spiritual reform, eager to sanitize church life and Christian living. Bugenhagen was not unique in this; the demand for reform was audible across Europe, and it was only from the early 1520s, when Bugenhagen came to Wittenberg, that he turned distinctively Lutheran.

The Pomeranian's early vision of reform was influenced by Erasmus of Rotterdam. Bugenhagen was reluctant to challenge what Luther and others would see as the abuses of the church, but instead was content with emphasizing the need to study scripture and to make this the guide of one's living as a Christian. Probably in 1519 or 1520, Bugenhagen delivered a sermon on 29 June, the day of commemoration for St. Peter and St. Paul. In the sermon, Bugenhagen highlighted the need for Christians only to seek the well-being of their fellow human beings. And, as he admonished his clerical listeners, this also applied to priests. Instead of "feasting, drinking, fornicating, bowling, and gambling," they should serve God by diligently performing their duties.[7] In another early writing, Bugenhagen's 1518 chronicle *Pomerania*, he noticed that corrupt clerics were "ignorant of holy scriptures and the teachings of Christ." The way to solve this problem is to educate, instruct, and catechize the clergy, as the experience in Belbug shows, Bugenhagen wrote.[8] Thus, during the late 1510s, Bugenhagen managed to make Belbug the center of reform in Pomerania.

Bugenhagen in Wittenberg

Bugenhagen, however, soon abandoned his early Erasmian vision of reform. Books by Luther reached the cities along the coast and the wider Baltic area. Different sources tell the story of Bugenhagen's "conversion" during 1520, when he read Luther's *Babylonian Captivity of the Church.* Apparently, Bugenhagen was so excited about Luther's criticism of the Roman Church's sacramental "misuses" that he wrote a letter to the reformer, keen on learning more, especially about the relationship of faith and good works. Luther accepted Bugenhagen's letter and his wish to explore the scriptural outlines for true Christian living, and in return he sent him his treatise *Freedom of a Christian* and a note that advised

Bugenhagen not to seek moral guidelines as such in theology, but to follow what the Spirit wills; good works flow freely from faith, as Luther claimed in the treatise.[9] Ignited by the Lutheran message, Bugenhagen gathered a circle of like-minded believers in Treptow, only to leave Pomerania for Wittenberg in the early spring of 1521. The electoral city on the River Elbe would remain Bugenhagen's home for the rest of his life. Luther and Bugenhagen did not spend much time together, however, as the former was summoned to appear before the estates at the Diet of Worms and left Wittenberg on 2 April. Instead, Bugenhagen studied theology—his very reason for coming to Wittenberg—with Andreas Karlstadt and Philipp Melanchthon (1497–1560), while Luther was away. Karlstadt had been a professor of theology in Wittenberg since 1510, and Melanchthon had held the chair of Greek since 1518.

Bugenhagen's intention to study theology was soon met with another reality. By the time he enrolled at the Leucorea, he already had a name in Pomerania, and those of his compatriots who studied in Wittenberg encouraged him to teach there. So he began to lecture on the Psalms, initially only privately, but the members of the theological faculty asked Bugenhagen to do so publicly. Although Bugenhagen held no doctorate and therefore formally was not allowed to give university lectures, he acted as an unofficial member of the faculty. It was only in 1533 that he was promoted to doctor and his faculty status was recognized; in 1535 he was finally awarded a chair in the Wittenberg faculty of theology.

To be sure, Luther did not return to Wittenberg before March 1522, as he was kept safe in the elector's Wartburg castle in western Thuringia following the diet's edict on the obliteration of Luther's movement. With Luther away, it was up to Karlstadt and Melanchthon to spearhead the Wittenberg reform movement, which had been built up since 1517. Karlstadt would soon take the lead. He advocated a radical reform of church life in Wittenberg, canceling the use of Latin as an ecclesiastical language, replacing Holy Mass with distribution of bread and wine to laypeople, proposing iconoclasm, and even marrying (Karlstadt was an archdeacon at the Wittenberg All Saints' Church, and as a member of the clergy, he was not allowed by canon law to marry). Karlstadt also sought to convince the city council that a social reform was needed in addition to an ecclesiastical one.[10]

Bugenhagen, however, did not agree with Karlstadt on the course of reform. In the same vein that Luther would show after his return from the Wartburg, Bugenhagen was lenient, and he saw in Karlstadt's attempts to reform nothing less than rebellion against divine order and disdain for Christ's sacraments. As he wrote in 1525 in a letter to Silesian reformer Johann Hess (1490–1547), Karlstadt was erroneous in believing that with the institutional words of the sacrament "this is my body" (Matt. 26:26–28), Christ signified only his presence.[11] Bugenhagen would later state, promoting the doctrine of real presence,

> [s]piritual and sacramental eating and drinking should be inseperable among true Christians in the reception of the sacrament, as Christ's command also sounds forth, that we should proclaim the death of the Lord there, not with hypocrisy but from the heart, that is, in faith.[12]

His disagreements with Karlstadt notwithstanding, Bugenhagen followed the example of his coreformer and entered the estate of marriage, wedding Walpurga (we do not know her maiden name) on October 13, 1522. Still a student, he was secured an income to provide for his wife and children in 1523, when the city council of Wittenberg elected Bugenhagen as their new pastor to serve at St. Mary's church. Moreover, as a city pastor, Bugenhagen would become Luther's personal spiritual counselor.

When Luther returned from the Wartburg in the spring of 1522, Karlstadt's radical reform came to an end. With the so-called *Invocavit* sermons, Luther, having electoral support, sought to retract Karlstadt's reforms, for example by restoring Holy Mass. Although Karlstadt and Luther had been working closely together since Luther settled in Wittenberg in the early 1510s, Karlstadt's actions during Luther's absence did not nurture future collaborations between the two theologians. Instead, a new team gathered around Luther, constituting the "Wittenberg Circle."[13] Besides Bugenhagen, the Wittenberg Circle consisted of Melanchthon, Justus Jonas (1493–1556), and Caspar Cruciger (1504–48). Together, these men spoke for the model of the "Wittenberg Reformation," which spread across Northern Europe beginning in the 1520s and favored a gradual, not a radical, reform. While Luther was bound to remain within the territories of the Saxon elector, and Melanchthon took care of the relationship of the Wittenberg Reformation with other reformations and Protestantism evolving during the late 1520s, Bugenhagen emerged as the church organizer of the nascent Lutheran confession. The Wittenberg Circle constituted a corporate identity, and, especially from the late 1530s onwards, the electoral government consulted its members (including professors from the faculty of law) when in need of expert opinions, *Gutachten*, on confessional, political, and social matters (e.g., marriage), commonly shorthanded as *gute policey*.[14] The understanding of university professors as "experts" and consultants to the rulers was to be applied to outstanding effect in the Scandinavian reformations and contributed to the formation of strong and centralized states.[15]

Early evidence testifies to the common effort of the Wittenberg Circle. In 1524 Bugenhagen's *A Beautiful Revelation of the Antichrist* was anonymously translated into German from the Latin and published as an appendix to Melanchthon's Latin *Opinion on Luther*. Defending his colleague against Rome, Melanchthon wrote that Luther never advocated an abolition of all ecclesiastical ceremonies—only those that impeded Christian faith. In the appendix, Bugenhagen stated that papal jurisdiction and Roman law were signs of the Antichrist and therefore did not apply to Christians. The empire of the pope constituted the same danger to present-day Christians as did the Roman Empire to the contemporaries of St. Paul. Yet the papal reign of the Antichrist cannot be subverted, Bugenhagen claimed, with fleshly weapons, but only with the preaching of the Gospel.[16] Bugenhagen is in concord with the early Wittenberg view, fueled by Karlstadt's attempts of reform in Wittenberg, that armed resistance was problematic. It was only after 1530 that the Wittenberg reformers, and even Luther, began to change their minds.[17]

Following the Wittenberg reformers, Bugenhagen believed that worldly order was an essential part of Christian doctrine, and that the gospel could not sound properly and Christian society could not exist without strategies for education and poor relief. Consequently, in 1524 Bugenhagen reorganized the school system in Wittenberg, and in 1527 he established a poor chest to support the city's impoverished residents.[18] Both education and poor relief would go on to constitute integral parts of the various church ordinances drafted by Bugenhagen from the 1520s through the 1540s.[19]

Bugenhagen as church organizer

Even if Bugenhagen clearly distinguished between law and gospel, he was convinced (as were the other members of the Wittenberg Circle) that human beings were in distress without law and order, simply because justification only justified the sinner but did not eradicate sin.[20] Time and again, Christians were to be taught how they should live. Otherwise, chaos would reign. Also, the events in Wittenberg during Luther's stay at the Wartburg clearly indicated that other reformations were possible. For those leaning towards conservative, slow reform, it became the natural choice to call on the expertise of the Wittenberg theologians, especially Bugenhagen, who mastered the Low German dialect prevalent in the northern parts of the empire and in Scandinavia.[21]

The first to send for Bugenhagen was the St. Nicholas congregation in the Hanseatic city of Hamburg, in late 1524. The congregation wanted Bugenhagen to come and oversee the establishment of a stable, ecclesiastical organization. Bugenhagen was granted a leave of absence from the Wittenberg congregation, but eventually the Hamburg city council prevented him from coming to the north of the empire, as the council was concerned about transgressing the edict of Worms by opening the gates to a Lutheran. Bugenhagen reluctantly accepted the council's decision and declined the invitation of the congregation, yet not without warning the council members that they misused their authority to oppose divine will.

Instead, Bugenhagen, together with Luther and Melanchthon, organized a general visitation to be carried out in electoral Saxony; the results—Luther's catechisms (1529) and the Wittenberg group's text *Instructions for the Visitors of Parish Pastors in Electoral Saxony* (1528)—became important guidelines for reform. Bugenhagen, however, did not act as a visitor in Saxony, since he was sent for by the city of Braunschweig. This city, in the northern part of the empire, was marked by tensions among the church, the city council, and the Roman Catholic duke, on one hand, and a Lutheran faction around the preacher Gottschalk Kruse (c. 1499–1540), on the other. The Lutheran party had the wind at its back, but inner divisions were beginning to appear. Bugenhagen came and succeeded in introducing a Wittenberg-style reformation in the city. In the church ordinance drafted during his stay in Braunschweig, Bugenhagen stated that to reform meant,

> first, to establish good schools for the children; secondly, to appoint preachers who explain God's word purely to the people and also provide Latin lectures and interpretations of Holy Scripture for the educated; thirdly, to establish common chests with church properties and other gifts out of which such and other ecclesiastical offices are supported and the need of the poor is addressed.[22]

Braunschweig wanted Bugenhagen as the city's first superintendent, but Saxon elector Johann (r. 1525–32) refused their request, and Bugenhagen resumed his reforming activities, now in the Hanseatic cities of Hamburg and Lübeck, close to the Danish king's sphere of interest. Evidence suggests that Bugenhagen saw his organizational activities as missionary work: to him, the act of reforming church and society was a dramatic act of the end times, when God would fight against the Devil, who for his part was perpetually seeking to suppress the power of the Gospel.[23] Therefore, Bugenhagen and the other Wittenberg reformers advocated post baptismal exorcism, as a Lübeck correspondence among Bugenhagen, Luther, Jonas, and Melanchthon shows.[24] This perspective highlights that to Bugenhagen, establishing order was not just an enterprise secondary to "proper" theology. On the contrary, it was a matter of pastoral concern and counseling of believers' souls.

Bugenhagen and Denmark-Norway

The Danish reform movement of the 1520s

Across the Baltic Sea, in Christian II's Denmark, thoughts akin to Bugenhagen's early vision of reform were advanced. Danish humanists were particularly active in the towns of Copenhagen, Malmø, and Elsinore, all situated at the narrow Øresund, the strait that connected them with the Baltic Sea. Thoughts of reform were also present in the 1521–22 law for the towns and countryside, in which Christian II on one hand highlighted the need of clerics to preach scripture and perform pastoral care, and on the other hand limited the legal rights and privileges of the church as stipulated in canon law, by aiming at a centralized state with civil servants loyal only to the king.[25] The discourse of reform was, however, turned down, when Christian was forced into exile by the nobility, and as a symbolic act, the tomes of the Body of Law were thrown into the fire.[26] On seizing power from his nephew in 1523, Frederik I (r. 1523–33) was presented with a coronation charter that urged him to suppress the vision and theology flourishing during Christian's reign and to eradicate Lutheranism from the territories. Nevertheless, Frederik broke with the Church of Rome: in 1526 the parliament that met in the city of Odense decided that annates should revert to the crown rather than Rome, and at another parliament in Odense, in 1527, the king himself refused to choose sides in the quarrel between Roman Catholics and Lutherans. Yet he issued royal letters of protection for non-Roman preachers so that, the Reformation could spread without impediments. Until the eventual introduction of a princely reformation in 1537, there thus was a "reformation from below," since the major towns now embarked on a course of reform by the initiative of magistrates and preachers. It was only with the intervention of Christian III and the assistance of Bugenhagen that the Danish-Norwegian Reformation turned distinctively "Wittenbergian."[27]

The Lutheran reformation and Christian III

Before he eventually went to Denmark in 1537, Bugenhagen temporarily resided in his native Pomerania in 1534–35 and produced a church ordinance for that territory, and in 1536 he was elevated to the newly created office of general superintendent in electoral Saxony, which gave him responsibility for supervising both pastors and congregation throughout the territory. In the same year, the young Danish king, Christian III, continued the efforts of his father, Frederik I, to reform church and society. As a duke of the fiefs of Haderslev and Tønning, in northern Schleswig, Christian had already introduced a princely reformation during 1526, and because of the Roman Catholic majority among its members, the council of the realm was reluctant to elect Christian as the new king of Denmark-Norway after Frederik's death in 1533. Civil war broke out, lasting until the summer of 1536, when Christian entered the besieged city of Copenhagen. Although Evangelical congregations had emerged in various towns since the late 1520s, the victorious Christian was determined to control the course of the Reformation.

One of his first official acts was to issue a statute that stipulated the design of his reformation and reordering of the realm: in order to overcome all sorts of "hate, envy, enmity, and suspicion," which had instigated the civil war, the Catholic bishops—the sole persons responsible for the war—were to be dismissed from their posts, excluded from the council of the realm, and imprisoned.[28] In their stead, "Christian bishops and superintendents" were to be installed.[29] Moreover, monks were free to leave their monasteries, and "extraordinary wise and learned men" ought to see to it that the pastors preached the gospel, the hospitals cared for the sick, and only those genuinely deserving poor relief received it.[30] For the sustenance of the king and the benefit of the realm, the diocesan properties and revenues were henceforward to accrue to the crown. The statute was issued on the same day as the coronation charter of Christian III, which replaced the obligation to protect the privileges of the (Catholic) church with a personal obligation of the monarch to the Christian faith. Together they mark the legal implementation in the Danish part of the twin monarchy, which a year later was extended to Norway. In general, the statute is marked by tendencies towards royal supremacy over church life, public welfare, and laws. While absolutism was not achieved until 1660, the statute declared in article 10 that the highest office of the realm was imposed on the king, and it reflects the idea that the king as a *pater patriae* and a *principium membrum ecclesiae* is responsible for the material and spiritual welfare of his citizens.[31] To successfully carry out his plans, Christian now sent for the Wittenberg Circle.

Since 1521, when Christian saw Luther at the Diet of Worms, he had been a passionate advocate for reform. His connections to Wittenberg were good, and he wanted the Reformation in his realm to progress along the lines of the reform in Saxony. In August 1536, after he had raised the siege of Copenhagen, he wrote to Johann Friedrich (r. 1532–47), asking the elector to "lend" him Bugenhagen and Melanchthon for the sake of advancing God's honor and establishing Christian order in Denmark. The elector initially refused, but after a new letter from the king in April 1537, Johann Friedrich agreed to send Bugenhagen and his family to Copenhagen; they arrived in the summer.[32] During these months, the king had a commission prepare a draft for a church ordinance, but it was eventually Bugenhagen who came to write the final document, the so-called *Kirkeordinansen*. Bugenhagen stayed in Copenhagen until 1539, and he played a central role in the public staging of the princely reformation of Christian III during 1537, crowning the royal couple in Our Lady's Church on August 12, ordaining the superintendents mentioned in the 1536 statute on September 2, and taking part in the reopening of the University of Copenhagen on September 9. During the civil war, lectures had been suspended, but now the university was refashioned in a way similar to the Leucorea, in fact constituting a vocational school that trained future Danish pastors and civil servants.

After Bugenhagen returned to Wittenberg in 1539, Christian continued to employ the Pomeranian's services. In 1541, the bishopric of Schleswig became vacant, and the king would have liked Bugenhagen to accept the position. He declined, but the next year the king had Bugenhagen travel to the duchies, organizing the ecclesiastical structures and preparing a church ordinance for these territories. Occasionally helping various German territories with Reformation matters, Bugenhagen lived the rest of his life in Wittenberg, where he continued to minister at St. Mary's and lecture at the university. He often experienced hard times because of the theological and political quarrels within Lutheranism following Luther's death in 1546, yet he remained adamant in his beliefs that the pastoral and organizational work was needed all the more since it could counsel and console believers' souls.[33] Until his death, Bugenhagen kept in touch with Christian III, seeing eye to eye with the king on the necessity of maintaining unity and concord within Lutheran Christendom.[34]

The Church Ordinance of 1537/39

> Then we asked … [to] send us beloved Johannes Bugenhagen of Pomerania, a doctor of the holy scripture, and by the help and advice of the same learned man, we, together with our council, have finished this holy ordinance.[35]

The Church Ordinance of 1537/39 marks the culmination of the legal implementation of the Reformation in Denmark-Norway and the efforts—especially of Christian III—to create a Lutheran church controlled by the secular authority. It is also the crowning achievement of Bugenhagen's work as a reformer in Denmark-Norway.

Shortly after the events of 1536, the work began to formulate a church ordinance providing the new Lutheran church with a substantial legal framework. A draft was sent to Wittenberg for the approval of Luther, especially, and at the request of the king, Johannes Bugenhagen arrived in Copenhagen on July 5, 1537. With Bugenhagen's arrival, the work could be finalized. The ordinance was finished in September and was published on December 12 in an edition supervised by Bugenhagen and titled *Ordinatio Ecclesiastica Regnorum Daniæ et Norwgiæ et Ducatuum Sleswicensis Holtsatiæ etcet. Anno Domini M.D. XXXVII.* In 1539, this work was translated into Danish and slightly revised, and this final version of the ordinance was issued in a printed version in 1542. Because of the close relationship between the Latin and the Danish ordinance, they are often referred to as one, the Church Ordinance of 1537/1539.[36]

The church ordinance opened with a royal letter in which Christian III explained and legitimized the Reformation and the ordinance itself. Because of its style and theological content, the royal letter is believed to have been written by Bugenhagen.[37] In the 1539 Danish version, the royal letter was supplemented with a preamble by the king and council similar to preambles found in most legislation during this period. In accordance with the church order of Braunschweig, the Danish ordinance highlights what it considers the most essential part of any church ordinance: teachings; ceremonies and sermons; schools; providing for the poor and for the church, the superintendents, and the rural deans; and finally, books.[38]

The inclusion of school reform in the ordinance was a continuation of the reformers' work for general educational reform. *Instructions for the Visitors of Parish Pastors in Electoral Saxony* contained a detailed program for school reforms, and Bugenhagen's church order of Braunschweig had a very strong emphasis on schools, highlighted in the first sentence in his prefatory letter: "In this order good schools are established."[39] A similar strong emphasis on schools is somewhat lacking in the royal letter included in the church ordinance in Denmark-Norway, and while schools were mentioned first in the list of necessary content in the church order of Braunschweig, they had been delegated to third place in the church ordinance of Denmark-Norway. Both ordinances rested, however, on the same foundation provided in *Instructions for the Visitors of Parish Pastors in Electoral Saxony*,[40] and the arguments for the necessity of including schools in the church order were similar. Education was necessary for the youth and served both the kingdom of heaven and earth. Schools should foster knowledge of the gospel and virtues among the youth and, at the same time, "keep and protect a good civil and secular authority."[41] In the church order of Braunschweig, Bugenhagen summarized the need for schools in this way:

> in time there will emerge good schoolmasters; good preachers; good lawyers, good medical doctors; good, God-fearing, capable, honest, upright, obedient, friendly, learned, peaceful, not wild but joyful burghers who will also take care of their children in the best possible manner in the future, and so on from generation to generation.[42]

While the church ordinance did not contain a specific reference to a confession, the list of recommended books shows its dependence on works by Luther and Melanchthon. Among others, the list included Luther's Small Catechism, Melanchthon's *Loci communes* and Apology of the Augsburg Confession, and the *Instructions for the Visitors of Parish Pastors in Electoral Saxony*, which Bugenhagen translated into Latin in 1538 for use by Danish pastors.[43] While this list did not include works by Bugenhagen, the ordinance appended his *Pia et vere catholica* (1535) especially for the canons of the cathedral chapters.[44] Moreover, the ordinance stipulated that Bugenhagen's compilation of the passion of Christ from the synoptic gospels should be read out loud on Good Friday.[45]

The royal letter has been subject to much scholarly discussion, especially with regard to its view of the Wittenberg reformers' position on the relationship between secular authority and the church.[46] In our view, the royal letter can best be interpreted as legitimizing the church ordinance as a secular law issued by the secular authority to establish a Lutheran princely church. To this end, the letter emphasized the aid of the Danish theologians and priests, the approval from Wittenberg (especially by Luther), and the help from Bugenhagen noted above. His help was needed "in order that such divine deed could be achieved in a better way."[47] The letter continued to cite the core of Christianity, quoted at the beginning of this chapter. In overall terms, the royal letter of the ordinance relied on Bugenhagen's understanding that it was a royal duty to establish a sound framework for the newly reformed Lutheran church. This becomes evident in the part of the letter where the king stressed that he also had been given some insight into the gospel and therefore would like to add his opinion on the ordinance. The king then distinguished between the ordinance of God and the ordinance of the king: The ordinance of God contains matters relating to the word of God, the sacraments, the instruction of children, and provision for the clergy, the schools, and the poor; later on, the ordinance of God is equated to the content of the first three commandments. In describing the ordinance of God, the letter contains an uncompromising attack on the state of the Roman Catholic Church reflecting the position of Bugenhagen, who denounces the Roman Church as "the Antichristian party" and "the Devil's teachings," which, fortunately, are being returned to the Devil by the Reformation and this ordinance.[48] While the ordinance of God must not be violated by any human being, there is also the king's ordinance, according to which the king can regulate what may be termed the more practical matters of the church, such as rules concerning time and place of worship, singing, ceremonies, and visitations.

While the royal letter distinguished between the ordinance of God and that of the king, the ordinance indeed sought to regulate both ecclesiastical and state matters. By doing so, Christian III assumed the responsibility for establishing a Lutheran church in Denmark-Norway. The king acted as the "guardian of both tables of the Decalogue" while reforming the church so that it might correspond with the ordinance of God, as found in the first three commandments. The ideal of princely ecclesiastical governance was a commonplace among the Wittenberg Circle. While Luther argued that the prince could act as an emergency bishop and thus carry out reform when the (spiritual) leadership of the church failed, Melanchthon stressed that the prince as the guardian of the Decalogue was obliged to carry out a Lutheran reform. As the royal letter of the church ordinance shows, Bugenhagen obviously shared the beliefs of his colleagues. While the rhetoric and the framing of the reformers may be different, their results are essentially the same: the approval of a reform carried out by the prince—as in the case of the Reformation in Denmark-Norway.[49]

As a secular law issued by the secular authority, the church ordinance effectively established a Lutheran prince's church in Denmark-Norway aided by Bugenhagen. This is also evident from the ordinance's procedure for amendment, which could be done only by the king and council after consultation with theologians. Even though it prohibited any changes contrary to the gospel and God (God's ordinance), it once again placed ecclesiastical polity with the secular authority in Denmark-Norway.[50] In this regard, the king played a significant role and even had the final authority to confirm appointments of both pastors and superintendents, who, in turn, were required to begin their oaths by promising loyalty to the king.[51]

In his farewell address to the church in 1539 at the end of his two years in Denmark-Norway, Bugenhagen stressed that the aim of the ordinance was securing peace within the realm.[52] As the architect of the Reformation, Bugenhagen had been crucial to ending the religious and political turmoil in favor of creating a lasting Lutheran princely church. The ordinance stood on a strong foundation of the theology of Wittenberg, so when leaving Denmark-Norway, Bugenhagen was optimistic about the future of the Reformation:

> You agree on the teachings on justification or forgiveness of sins, on the sacrament of Christ, on love or the good fruits, on the cross, on authority, on human traditions, and other things included in our confession or apology [the Augsburg Confession] and in the instructions for the visitors of Saxony, which I have given you in Latin. Glory to Christ in eternity!"[53]

On marriage matters

> I wrote this tract to serve Your Royal Majesty and to instruct those who need such counsel, especially the authorities and marriage judges.[54]

Like many of his colleagues, Bugenhagen was called on for advice on various legal matters. In the minds of the rulers, the counsel of theologians was necessary to legitimize their policies (even if it could be ignored). As the Wittenberg Circle's organizational and legal expert par excellence, with a close relationship to the king, Bugenhagen naturally found Christian III turning to him for advice in legal matters.[55]

Bugenhagen's 1540 book on marriage constitutes one important example of his role as a legal consultant.[56] While writing about marriage was common among Protestant reformers, Bugenhagen's tract was closely linked to his role as a legal adviser to Christian III. The book originated in Danish marriage cases from 1539, in which the authorities had to decide whether to grant divorce in a case of desertion (*desertio*): was leaving a spouse without valid reason a ground for divorce, and, if so, in which cases? In the first instance, Bugenhagen's guidance was not called on, but afterwards the king turned to the Pomeranian for advice about divorce on grounds of adultery and desertion. It turned out to be necessary advice.

Prior to the Reformation, marriage law in Denmark-Norway had been subject to canon law and was adjudicated by the church. The church ordinance stipulated, however, that jurisdiction over marital cases be transferred to the secular sphere, while it contained only a few substantial rules on marriage and was completely silent as to the question of divorce.[57] Beginning in Copenhagen and finalizing his work in the royal castle in Nyborg with a dedication to Christian III, Bugenhagen wrote a tract on marriage legislation. In 1540, it was published along with Luther's *Vom Ehesachen* and Melanchthon's *De Arbore Consangunitatis & affinitatis siue de gradibus*, an overview of the forbidden degrees of relationship in incest.[58] Bugenhagen not only intended the tract for the king but also, in his farewell address to the church, recommended it to the superintendents and preachers.[59] While the tract of course is an important contribution to the reformers' discussion on the law of marriage, our main interest in this chapter is Bugenhagen's reflections on his role as a legal adviser and his use of legal sources.

Bugenhagen initially approached his role as a legal adviser to the king with humility and some irony. Immediately after the dedication to the king, Bugenhagen referred to the many writings on marriage throughout time, especially in "the jurisdiction of the Roman papal chair," that is, canon law, which has "no end to laws, writings, and counsels." While himself adding to these writings and counsels by the other reformers, Bugenhagen hoped to be able to "address the matter which concerns" the king.[60] In his capacity as an adviser, Bugenhagen was keen to stress that when marriage cases dissolve into disputes, they belong to "the temporal authorities." In such cases, the temporal authority might well ask preachers such as Bugenhagen for advice:

> If we preachers are asked by the authorities, we are obliged to answer what is proper on the basis of God's word or to give our good counsel that conforms to God's word according to justice or Christian love.[61]

It is an old truth that an answer depends on the person being asked, and when Protestant reformers such as Bugenhagen were asked for advice, they naturally based their answers on their interpretation of the Bible. While declaring himself ready to answer every question from his superiors, Bugenhagen both wisely and humbly suggested that the authority might solve the problem in a better way, and that some in fact only ask with a view to criticizing the answers. The prime counsel for Bugenhagen and the other reformers accorded with Romans 13 (that the secular authority protects the innocent and punishes the evil).[62] Whereas these initial reflections suggest a very humble approach—at least officially—Bugenhagen in another paragraph sighed that authorities often refused to use good counsel. While arguing in favor of divorce for the innocent party and harsh penalty for adultery and desertion, Bugenhagen carefully tried to be balanced in order not to be accused of advocating these things. Yet he could not hide his frustration with secular authorities in general. Addressing the question of how to deal with a deserting spouse, Bugenhagen sighed:

> We would gladly counsel something good, especially if we are asked. On the other hand, we shout rightfully against the temporal authority that it should punish such shame and wantonness and help the miserable party . . . and it will answer to God for such negligence.[63]

While this paragraph was not directly addressed to the king, it could also apply to the law in Denmark-Norway. Bugenhagen preferred that adultery be punished by death, and in fact such a punishment was prescribed in the law of 1537 issued by king and council. However, the punishment was mitigated after complaints from the subjects in 1539, and thus the death penalty was only to be applied if one committed adultery for a third time.[64]

Addressing the law of marriage, Bugenhagen was faced with the general problem of the Reformation on how to view the existing sources of law—especially canon law.[65] Bugenhagen presupposed as a matter of course that canon law is not a binding source of law, and he then evaluated canon law against natural law, which he identified as God's law. When rules in canon law contradicted natural law, Bugenhagen quickly denounced them using classical Protestant rhetoric such as "Devil's laws," "demonic laws," "unjust laws," "their twisted papal law," and ultimately—with regards to the pope's demand for "absolute power in heaven and on earth"—as "good antichristian law." Bugenhagen recognized, however, the existence of some useful laws and practices in canon law and from papal marriage judges. Toward the end of the book, he even tolerated the use of canon law at marriage courts, with the exception of "some unjust laws," including, of course, the rules on adultery and desertion.[66] This position on canon law illustrates the general development after the Lutheran Reformation in the German principalities. While the reformers never hesitated to denounce canon law—and in Luther's case even burn it—canon law principles played an important part in shaping the new Protestant legislation. When canon law was not believed to be contrary to the word of God—as interpreted by the reformers—its principles could continue to be applied.[67] In contrast to his mixed position on canon law, Bugenhagen sported a very positive view on Roman law (*Keiserlichen Rechten*), including classical Roman law and the law of the Holy Roman Empire, which he believed to originate in natural law. While referring to the marriage court instituted in Lübeck during his stay in that Hanseatic city, he underscored that one of the court's seven judges knew Roman law in order to use it in their case law.[68]

Bugenhagen only briefly touched on the national legislation in Denmark-Norway, when he referred to the prohibition of incest in the paragraph on marriage in the church ordinance. Canon law prohibited incest in the first four degrees of consanguinity and affinity, and affinity was created both by marriage and fornication. This concept was supplemented by the idea of spiritual kinship, which arose from Christian ceremonies such as baptism. The ordinance limited this prohibition to the first three degrees but did not mention spiritual kinship.[69] In Bugenhagen's short discussion of the question, he mentioned that the degrees are fixed in the church ordinance; therefore, he left the matter as it is. He then added, however, that spiritual kinship "is the work of fools" and therefore invalid. Being in accordance with the other Wittenberg reformers' criticism, Bugenhagen thus tried to make sure that no one would interpret the church ordinance as rubber-stamping this prohibition.[70] While national legislation according to Bugenhagen's view obviously was subordinate to God's law, in this instance he avoided a potential conflict through interpretation.

Bugenhagen's view of the legal sources can thus be summarized in the following table:

Source of law	*German terminology*[71]	*Binding*	*Inspiration*
Natural law/ God's law	*Natürliches Recht / Gottes Recht*	Yes	–
National law	–	Subordinate to God's law Must be interpreted in light of God's law	–
Roman law	*Keiserlichen Rechten*	Based on natural law	Yes
Canon law	*Papstrecht*	–	Yes

Bugenhagen's book on marriage highlights its author's reflection on his own role as a legal adviser to the secular authority in general and to Christian III in particular. It also shows his reflections on the legal basis for the new Protestant marriage law. Perhaps it also was a contributing factor in the institution of the new marriage courts in 1542, when jurisdiction was transferred from the regular court to a special marriage court consisting of the members of the cathedral chapters and a royal official.[72] Even if he abstained from addressing the question directly, Bugenhagen noted the necessity of a court to deal with marriage cases and highlighted the use of "wise people" in such cases. His marriage tract was a response to the wish for theological and legal guidance in marriage cases, and with the new marriage court begun in 1542, the use of learned theologians from the cathedral chapters became a permanent feature of marriage law in Denmark-Norway. Bugenhagen's impact on the substantial law of marriage is tangible since adultery and desertion would become valid reasons for divorce. It was only in 1582, however, that legislation was issued. Rather than building on Bugenhagen's work, the legislation was founded on the work of another influential theologian, Niels Hemmingsen (see chapter 8).

Conclusion

Perhaps as the legal expert par excellence among the members of the Wittenberg Circle, Bugenhagen was the key theological figure in the legal implementation of the Reformation in Denmark-Norway, which culminated in the Church Ordinance of 1537/39 and his work as legal adviser to Christian III. Bugenhagen himself was aware of the important (and not always easy) position of a legal adviser to the king and carefully tried to balance the tasks of giving advice, criticizing legal practice, and respecting secular authority. While both his ecclesiology and his understanding of marriage reflect a clear break with the Roman Catholic Church and canon law, he did not completely abandon all elements of canon law. Indeed, canon law could continue to be used in many cases, when it was not contrary to God.

The church ordinance and Bugenhagen's work as a reformer and legal expert in general in Denmark-Norway are testimonies to his function as the architect of the Danish-Norwegian Reformation. During the Reformation, the ordinance was highly influential. As is evident from the title, the ordinance should apply in Denmark, Norway, and the German principalities of Schleswig and Holstein, which were ruled by the Danish-Norwegian king. In 1542, however, the principalities received their own church ordinance, once again with the aid of Bugenhagen. With the completion of the Reformation in Iceland in 1551, the ordinance was applied there as well. To accommodate the specific need in Norway, a Norwegian church ordinance was issued in 1607 and extended to Iceland in 1622, yet while it contained several changes, it still closely followed the 1537/39 Danish pattern, as this was the specific wish of the king and council. The regulation of the church in the Danish Code of 1683 and the Norwegian Code of 1687 was, in turn, closely modeled after the ordinances of 1537/39 and 1607.[73]

The ordinance reflected Bugenhagen's view of Christianity's core and of the king's duty to provide a sound legal framework in which Christianity could flourish. This entailed that the king be a protector of preaching and worship, education of the youth, payment of pastors and other church staff, poor relief, and the general knowledge of Christian doctrine among the commoners. Whether fashioned as a *Notbischof* or *summus episcopus*, Bugenhagen in the church ordinance followed the thought of Luther and Melanchthon and provided the Danish-Norwegian Reformation with a robust theological and legal understanding of the ecclesiastical duties incumbent on the person holding the royal office.

The legal heritage of Bugenhagen and the Reformation is still present in Scandinavian legal thought. According to the constitutions of Denmark and Norway, the sovereigns must profess Lutheranism. In Denmark, which has perhaps adhered more closely than other Nordic countries to the original prince-state model promoted by Bugenhagen, the Lutheran church is still the established church and is supported by the state.[74]

Notes

1 Martin Schwarz Lausten, ed., *Kirkeordinansen 1537/39* (Copenhagen: Akademisk Forlag, 1989), 151.

> Effterdi her tracteres dog intet andet end det rene oc kalre Euangelium. Desligeste Sacramenterne effter Christi eygen indskickelse, Sang oc hellige lectier, om en erlig samquem til predicken oc det hellige Sacramentes tildelelse, Huorledes wngdommen maa optuctis y bogen oc gode konster, til Guds hellige ord oc den hellige schrifft, Huorleddis tiennerne wdi den hellige kircke maa bliffue wel forsørgede och Scholerne holdes wed mact, De fattuge haffue deres røct, At Børnelerdommen maa wære vdi alle huse.

2 "Denmark-Norway" is used colloquially to refer to the realm of the early modern Danish kings, consisting of the kingdoms of Denmark and Norway, the duchies of Schleswig and Holstein, and the North Atlantic Norwegian appanages of Greenland, Iceland, and the Faroe Islands.

3 Regarding Bugenhagen's biography, see Kurt K. Hendel, "Bugenhagen, Johannes," in *Encyclopedia of Martin Luther and the Reformation*, vol. 1, ed. Mark A. Lamport (Lanham, MD: Rowman & Littlefield, 2017), 94–96; Kurt K. Hendel, "Johannes Bugenhagen: Reformer beyond the Limelight," in *Johannes Bugenhagen: Selected Writings* (hereafter: SW), vol. I, ed. and trans. Kurt K. Hendel (Minneapolis, MN: Fortress Press, 2015), 1–75; and Wolf-Dieter Hauschild, "Bugenhagen, Johannes," in *Oxford Encyclopedia of the Reformation*, vol. I, ed. Hans J. Hillerbrand (New York: Oxford University Press, 1996), 226–27.

4 Lewis W. Spitz, "The Impact of the Reformation on the Universities," in *University and Reformation*, ed. Leif Grane (Leiden: Brill, 1981), 9–31, esp. 15–17.

5 Regarding this, see, e.g., Erasmus of Rotterdam's (1466–1536) prefatory letter to his *Copia* (1512), in which the Dutch humanist lauds English scholar John Colet (1467–1519), not only for "bringing Christ into the hearts of [his] countrymen by means of continual preaching and by holy instruction," but also for founding a school "that far excels the rest in beauty and splendour, so that the youth of England, under carefully chosen and highly reputed teachers, might there absorb Christian principles together with an excellent literary education from their earliest years." In *Collected Works of Erasmus*, vol. 24, ed. and trans. Craig R. Thompson (Toronto: University of Toronto Press, 1978), 284.

6 Hans-Günter Leder, "'Sacerdos Christi, Ludimagister Treptovii:' Johannes Bugenhagen in Treptow bis zu seinem Anschluß an den Schul- und Bibelhumanismus (1504 bis ca. 1515)," in *Johannes Bugenhagen Pomeranus – Vom Reformer zum Reformator: Studien zur Biographie* (Frankfurt am Main: Peter Lang, 2002), 95–121.

7 Johannes Bugenhagen, *Belbucker Klosterpredigt*, in *Johannes Bugenhagen: Reformatorische Schriften (1515/16–1524)*, ed. Anneliese Bieber-Wallmann (Göttingen: Vandenhoeck & Ruprecht, 2013), 59. Bugenhagen's Latin words of the sermon are rendered by Hendel, "Johannes Bugenhagen," 11.

8 Johannes Bugenhagen, *Pomerania, in qvatuor libros divisa*, ed. Jacob Heinrich Balthasar (Greifswald: Jac. Löfler, 1728), 116–18.

9 Luther stated, "[s]ince each and every person thus thrives through their own faith—so that all other works and the sum total of life flows out from this very faith—by these works each may serve and benefit the neighbor with willing benevolence." In *The Annotated Luther*, vol. 1: The Roots of Reform, ed. Timothy J. Wengert (Minneapolis, MN: Fortress Press, 2015), 521.

10 Amy Nelson Burnett, *Karlstadt and the Origins of the Eucharistic Controversy: A Study in the Circulation of Ideas* (New York: Oxford University Press, 2011), 15–30.

11 Johannes Bugenhagen, *An Open Letter against the New Error Concerning the Sacrament of the Body and Blood of our Lord Jesus Christ*, in SW I, 492.

12 Johannes Bugenhagen, *Against the Thieves of the Cup* (1532), in SW I, 617.
13 Timothy J. Wengert, "The Wittenberg Circle," in *The Oxford Handbook of Martin Luther's Theology*, ed. Robert Kolb, Irene Dingel, and L'ubomír Batka (Oxford: Oxford University Press, 2014), 491–501.
14 Armin Kohnle, "Wittenberger Autorität: Die Gemeinschaftsgutachten der Wittenberger Theologen als Typus," in *Die Theologische Fakultät Wittenberg 1502 bis 1602*, ed. Irene Dingel and Günther Wartenberg (Leipzig: Evangelische Verlagsanstalt, 2002), 189–200.
15 Thomas Kaufmann, "Lutheran Academic Culture in Early Modernity – Some Remarks," in *Lutheran Theology and the Shaping of Society: The Danish Monarchy as Example*, ed. Bo K. Holm and Nina J. Koefoed (Göttingen: Vandenhoeck & Ruprecht, forthcoming).
16 Johannes Bugenhagen, *Annotationes in decem epistolas Pauli/Ain schoene offenbarung des Endchrists*, in *Johannes Bugenhagen: Reformatorische Schriften (1515/16–1524)*, 740–65 (English translation in SW II, 777–95).
17 Cynthia Grant Shoenberger, "The Development of the Lutheran Theory of Resistance: 1523–1530," *The Sixteenth Century Journal* 8/1 (1977): 61–76.
18 Hendel, "Johannes Bugenhagen," 23–24.
19 Regarding poor relief, see Tim Lorentzen, *Johannes Bugenhagen als Reformator der öffentlichen Fürsorge* (Tübingen: Mohr Siebeck, 2008), *passim* and esp. 210–327.
20 In his *Concerning the Marriage of Bishops and Deacons* (1525), Bugenhagen contrasted law and gospel, saying that preaching of the law "is the voice from heaven like a great water and like a great thunder" which condemns all human works as sin, while preaching of the gospel "creates new people through the Spirit where the old Adam is driven out." Johannes Bugenhagen, *Concerning the Marriage of Bishops and Deacons*, in SW II, 870; regarding Bugenhagen's theology, see Volker Gummelt, *Lex et Evangelium: Untersuchungen zur Jesajavorlesung von Johannes Bugenhagen* (Berlin: Walter de Gruyter, 1994), 138–46.
21 Hendel, "Johannes Bugenhagen," 29–70.
22 Johannes Bugenhagen, *The Christian Order of the Honorable City of Braunschweig*, in SW II, 1185–86. Cf. Bugenhagen's formulations in the Danish church ordinance below.
23 See also the royal prefatory letter of Bugenhagen's Danish church ordinance: "Out of his clemency and compassion God has re-sent (in these last days) the holy and pure gospel of Christ." Lausten, *Kirkeordinansen 1537/39*, 150.
24 See Bugenhagen's letter to the Wittenberg Circle in *D. Martin Luthers Werke, Briefwechsel*, vol. 5 (Weimar: Hermann Böhlaus Nachfolger, 1934), 668–74 (no. 1744). Regarding this, see Timothy J. Wengert and Philip D.W. Krey, "A June 1546 Exorcism in Wittenberg as a Pastoral Act," *Archiv für Reformationsgeschichte* 98 (2007): 71–83 (79–80).
25 Regarding the king's Body of Law, see Christina Lysbjerg Mogensen, "Christian II's land- og bylov: En acceleration af centraliseringen," *Temp – tidsskrift for historie* 9 (2014): 5–22.
26 Ibid., 8.
27 Ole Peter Grell, "From Popular, Evangelical Movement to Lutheran Reformation in Denmark. A Case of Two Reformations," *Archiv für Reformationsgeschichte* 102 (2011): 33–58; Niels Knud Andersen, *Confessio Hafniensis: Den københavnske Bekendelse af 1530. Studier i den begyndende Reformation* (Copenhagen: G.E.C. Gad, 1954).
28 Recess of 1536, in *Den Danske Rigslovgivning 1523–1558*, ed. Aage Andersen (Copenhagen: Det Danske Sprog- og Litteraturselskab & Selskabet for Udgivelse af Kilder til Danmarks Historie, 2015), 178–93: "had, niid, affuend och mystancke."
29 Ibid. § 3: "christelige biscoper och superattendenter."
30 Ibid. § 8: "merckelige, wiise och lærde mend."

31 Ibid. §10: "thet høgeste regementte vdi riiget henger mest paa koningens persoen." See also Ditlev Tamm, "Law and Protestantism in Denmark," *Zeitschrift der Savigny-Stiftung für Rechtsgeschichte: Kanonistische Abteilung* 102 (2016): 406–18 (409); and Svend Andersen and Morten Kjær, "The Legal Framework of Lutheran Churches," in *On Secular Governance: Lutheran Perspectives on Contemporary Legal Issues*, ed. Ronald W. Duty and Marie A. Failinger (Grand Rapids, MI: William B. Eerdmans Publishing Company, 2016), 247–65 (249–51).
32 Christian III to Johann Friedrich, 23 August 1536, and Johann Friedrich to Christian III, 16 May 1537, in *Entdecktes Staats-Cabinet*, vol. IV, ed. Johann Joachim Müller (Jena: Christian Pohl, 1716), 318–20, 337–44.
33 Regarding Bugenhagen's theology during the late years, see Martin J. Lohrmann, *Bugenhagen's Jonah: Biblical Interpretation As Public Theology* (Minneapolis, MN: Lutheran University Press, 2012).
34 Hendel, "Johannes Bugenhagen," 64–75.
35 Lausten, *Kirkeordiansen 1537/39*, 151 and 93:

> Da haffue wy begiered . . . [at] sende oss elskelig Hans Bugenhagen aff Pomern, en Doctor y den Hellige schrifft, huess same høglerde mands raad oc tilhielp wy med wortt Raad haffue brugt till att fult giøre denne helige Ordinantz.

36 Lausten, *Kirkeordinansen 1537/39*, 9–37. The Latin version is found at pp. 93–149 and the Danish at pp. 150–243.
37 Ibid., 27; Martin Schwarz Lausten, *Johann Bugenhagen – Luthersk reformator i Tyskland og Danmark* (Copenhagen: Anis, 2011), 124. The letter is printed in Lausten, *Kirkeordinansen 1537/39*, 93–96 and 150–56.
38 Lausten, *Kirkeordinansen 1537/39*, 98 and 157–58.
39 Bugenhagen, *The Christian Order of the Honorable City of Braunschweig*, 1181. Regarding the Protestant Reformation of Schools, see John Witte Jr., *Law and Protestantism: The Legal Teachings of the Lutheran Reformation* (Cambridge: Cambridge University Press, 2002), 257–92.
40 Bugenhagen, *The Christian Order of the Honorable City of Braunschweig*, 1221; Lausten, *Kirkeordinansen 1537/39*, 202 including n. 160; Witte, *Law and Protestantism*, 279–80.
41 Lausten, *Kirkeordinansen 1537/39*, 120 and 202: "opholde oc beuare et got Ciuile oc werdzlig Regimente." Cf. Bugenhagen, *The Christian Order of the Honorable City of Braunschweig*, 1181–82 and 1214–15.
42 Bugenhagen, *The Christian Order of the Honorable City of Braunschweig*, 1215.
43 Lausten, *Kirkeordinansen 1537/39*, 136 and 230–31, including note 229.
44 Ibid., 138 and 234–35, including note 236.
45 Ibid., 107 and 178.
46 See, e.g., the articles in the two Scandinavian anthologies: Carl Gustaf Andrén, ed., *Reformationen i Norden. Kontinuitet och förnyelse* (Lund: G.W.K. Gleerup Bokförlag, 1973), and Ingmar Brohed, ed, *Reformationens konsolidering i de nordiska länderne 1540–1610* (Oslo: Universitetsforlaget, 1990).
47 Lausten, *Kirkeordinansen 1537/39*, 151: "Men paa dett saadan en gudelig handell motte gaa dess rettere till."
48 Lausten, *Kirkeordinansen 1537/39*, 153–54: "den Antichristelig parthi," "Dieffuelsens lerdom."
49 Witte, *Law and Protestantism*, 131–32: Lausten, *Johann Bugenhagen*, 82 and 125–26; Martin Schwarz Lausten, *Christian d. 3. og kirken (1537–1559)* (Copenhagen: Akademisk Forlag, 1987), 13–15 and 46–47; and especially James M. Estes, *Peace, Order and the Glory of God: Secular Authority and the Church in the Thought of Luther and Melanchthon 1518–1559* (Leiden: Brill, 2005), 205.
50 Lausten, *Kirkeordinansen 1537/39*, 243.

51 Ibid., 189, 227–29, and 238–39; cf. Andersen and Kjær, "The Legal Framework of Lutheran Churches," 255–56.
52 The address is published in Holger Fr. Rørdam, "Et nyt Bidrag til Oplysning om Dr. Johan Bugenhagens Virksomhed i Danmark," *Ny Kirkehistoriske Samlinger* III (1864–66): 469–82, 477.
53 Ibid., 471:

> De doctrina iustificationis siue remissionis peccatorum, de sacramentis Christi, de caritate siue bonis operibus, de cruce, de magistratu, de traditionibus humanis et alijs, quae sunt in confessione et apologia nostra et in visitatione Saxonica, quam vobis Latinam dedi, inter vos conuenit, sit Christo gloria in æternum.

54 Johannes Bugenhagen, *Marriage Matters*, in SW II, 1105–57 (1154).
55 See, in general, Lausten, *Johann Bugenhagen*, 207–19.
56 German title: *Vom Ehebruch und Heimlichen weglauffen* (*on adultery and desertion*), Wittenberg, 1540.
57 Lausten, *Kirkeordinansen 1537/39*, 111 and 187.
58 Lausten, *Johann Bugenhagen*, 213; Bugenhagen, *Marriage Matters*, 1107, 1154, and 1157.
59 Rørdam, "Et nyt Bidrag," 477.
60 Bugenhagen, *Marriage Matters*, 1106–07.
61 Ibid., 1108.
62 Ibid.
63 Ibid., 1119.
64 Ibid., 1107, cf. Morten Kjær, *Guds og øvrigheds straf. Centralmagt og sædelighed i Danmark-Norge 1536–1648* (Copenhagen: Ex Tuto, 2017), 142–46 and 365.
65 Regarding Bugenhagen's use of legal sources, see Heiner Lück, "'Recht' und 'Gesetz' in den Kirchenordnungen Johannes Bugenhagens," in *Der späte Bugenhagen*, ed. Irene Dingel and Stefan Rhein (Leipzig: Evangelische Verlagsanstalt, 2011), 177–95. Cf. the chapter on Hemmingsen, who was faced with the same problem of a legal hierarchy after the Reformation.
66 Bugenhagen, *Marriage Matters*, 1107, 1124, 1138–39, and 1155–56.
67 Witte, *Law and Protestantism*, 10–11, 16, 22–23, and in particular 53–85; Harold J. Berman, *Law and Revolution: II, The Impact of the Protestant Reformations on the Western Legal Traditions* (Cambridge, MA: The Belknap Press of Harvard University Press, 2003), 64.
68 Bugenhagen, *Marriage Matters*, 1156.
69 Richard H. Helmholz, *Marriage Litigation in Medieval England* (Cambridge: Cambridge University Press, 1974), 78; Lausten, *Kirkeordinansen 1537/39*, 111 and 187.
70 Bugenhagen, *Marriage Matters*, 1110–11; Witte, *Law and Protestantism*, 241–42.
71 Bugenhagen, *Vom Ehebruch und Heimlichen weglauffen*, 4, 169 and 170.
72 Lausten, *Johann Bugenhagen*, 215–16; Andersen and Kjær, "The Legal Framework of Lutheran Churches," 257.
73 Lausten, *Johann Bugenhagen*, 208; Kjær, *Guds og øvrigheds straf*, 119 and 245.
74 *Danmarks Riges Grundlov*, §§ 4 and 6; *Kongeriket Norges Grundlov*, §4; Andersen and Kjær, "The Legal Framework of Lutheran Churches," 247 and 264–65.

Bibliography

Andersen, Niels Knud, *Confessio Hafniensis: Den københavnske Bekendelse af 1530. Studier i den begyndende Reformation* (Copenhagen: G.E.C. Gad, 1954).

Andersen, Svend and Kjær, Morten, "The Legal Framework of Lutheran Churches," *On Secular Governance: Lutheran Perspectives on Contemporary Legal Issues*, Ronald W.

Duty and Marie A. Failinger, eds. (Grand Rapids, MI: William B. Eerdmans Publishing Company, 2016), 247–65.

Andrén, Carl Gustaf, ed., *Reformationen i Norden. Kontinuitet och förnyelse* (Lund: G.W.K. Gleerup Bokförlag, 1973).

Berman, Harold J., *Law and Revolution: II, The Impact of the Protestant Reformations on the Western Legal Traditions* (Cambridge, MA: The Belknap Press of Harvard University Press, 2003).

Brohed, Ingmar, ed., *Reformationens konsolidering i de nordiska länderne 1540–1610* (Oslo: Universitetsforlaget, 1990).

Bugenhagen, Johannes, *Annotationes in decem epistolas Pauli/Ain schöne offenbarung des Endchrists*, in *Johannes Bugenhagen: Reformatorische Schriften (1515/16–1524)*, 740–65 (English translation in SW II, 777–95).

Bugenhagen, Johannes, *Belbucker Klosterpredigt*, in *Johannes Bugenhagen: Reformatorische Schriften (1515/16–1524)*, Anneliese Bieber-Wallmann, ed. (Göttingen: Vandenhoeck & Ruprecht, 2013).

Bugenhagen, Johannes, *The Christian Order of the Honorable City of Braunschweig*, in SW II, 1181–1400.

Bugenhagen, Johannes, *Concerning the Marriage of Bishops and Deacons*, in SW II, 843–986.

Bugenhagen, Johannes, *Marriage Matters*, in SW II, 1105–57.

Bugenhagen, Johannes, *Against the Thieves of the Cup* (1532), in SW I, 589–754.

Bugenhagen, Johannes, *An Open Letter against the New Error Concerning the Sacrament of the Body and Blood of our Lord Jesus Christ*, in SW I, 492–499.

Bugenhagen, Johannes, *Pomerania, in qvatuor libros divisa*, Jacob Heinrich Balthasar, ed. (Greifswald: Jac. Löfler, 1728).

Bugenhagen, Johannes, *Vom Ehebruch und Heimlichen weglauffen* (Wittenberg, 1540).

Burnett, Amy Nelson, *Karlstadt and the Origins of the Eucharistic Controversy: A Study in the Circulation of Ideas* (New York: Oxford University Press, 2011).

Collected Works of Erasmus, vol. 24, Craig R. Thompson, ed. and trans. (Toronto: University of Toronto Press, 1978).

D. Martin Luthers Werke, Briefwechsel, vol. 5 (Weimar: Hermann Böhlaus Nachfolger, 1934).

Den Danske Rigslovgivning 1523–1558, Aage Andersen, ed. (Copenhagen: Det Danske Sprog- og Litteraturselskab & Selskabet for Udgivelse af Kilder til Danmarks Historie, 2015).

Entdecktes Staats-Cabinet, vol. IV, Johann Joachim Müller, ed. (Jena: Christian Pohl, 1716).

Estes, James M., *Peace, Order and the Glory of God: Secular Authority and the Church in the Thought of Luther and Melanchthon 1518–1559* (Leiden: Brill, 2005).

Grell, Ole Peter, "From Popular, Evangelical Movement to Lutheran Reformation in Denmark. A Case of Two Reformations," *Archiv für Reformationsgeschichte* 102 (2011): 33–58.

Gummelt, Volker, *Lex et Evangelium: Untersuchungen zur Jesajavorlesung von Johannes Bugenhagen* (Berlin: Walter de Gruyter, 1994).

Hauschild, Wolf-Dieter, "Bugenhagen, Johannes," in *Oxford Encyclopedia of the Reformation*, vol. I, Hans J. Hillerbrand, ed. (New York: Oxford University Press, 1996), 226–27.

Helmholz, *Marriage Litigation in Medieval England* (Cambridge: Cambridge University Press, 1974).

Hendel, Kurt K., "Bugenhagen, Johannes," in *Encyclopedia of Martin Luther and the Reformation*, vol. 1, Mark A. Lamport, ed. (Lanham, MD: Rowman & Littlefield, 2017), 94–96.

Hendel, Kurt K. "Johannes Bugenhagen: Reformer beyond the Limelight," in SW I, 1–75.

Johannes Bugenhagen. Selected Writings, vol I–II (SW), Kurt K. Hendel, ed. and trands. (Minneapolis, MN: Fortress Press, 2015).

Kaufmann, Thomas, "Lutheran Academic Culture in Early Modernity – Some Remarks," in *Lutheran Theology and the Shaping of Society: The Danish Monarchy as Example*, Bo K. Holm and Nina J. Koefoed, eds. (Göttingen: Vandenhoeck & Ruprecht, 2018), 151–68.

Kirkeordinansen 1537/39, Martin Schwarz Lausten, ed. (Copenhagen: Akademisk Forlag, 1989).

Kjær, Morten, *Guds og øvrigheds straf. Centralmagt og sædelighed i Danmark-Norge 1536–1648* (Copenhagen: Ex Tuto, 2017).

Kohnle, Armin, "Wittenberger Autorität: Die Gemeinschaftsgutachten der Wittenberger Theologen als Typus," *Die Theologische Fakultät Wittenberg 1502 bis 1602*, Irene Dingel and Günther Wartenberg, eds. (Leipzig: Evangelische Verlagsanstalt, 2002), 189–200.

Lausten, Martin Schwarz, *Christian d. 3. og kirken (1537–1559)* (Copenhagen: Akademisk Forlag, 1987).

Lausten, Martin Schwarz, *Johann Bugenhagen – Luthersk reformator i Tyskland og Danmark* (Copenhagen: Anis, 2011).

Leder, Hans-Günter, "'Sacerdos Christi, Ludimagister Treptovii:' Johannes Bugenhagen in Treptow bis zu seinem Anschluß an den Schul- und Bibelhumanismus (1504 bis ca. 1515)," *Johannes Bugenhagen Pomeranus – Vom Reformer zum Reformator: Studien zur Biographie* (Frankfurt am Main: Peter Lang, 2002), 95–121.

Lohrmann, Martin J., *Bugenhagen's Jonah: Biblical Interpretation As Public Theology* (Minneapolis, MN: Lutheran University Press, 2012).

Lorentzen, Tim, *Johannes Bugenhagen als Reformator der öffentlichen Fürsorge* (Tübingen: Mohr Siebeck, 2008).

Lück, Heiner, "'Recht' und 'Gesetz' in den Kirchenordnungen Johannes Bugenhagens," *Der späte Bugenhagen*, Irene Dingel and Stefan Rhein, eds. (Leipzig: Evangelische Verlagsanstalt, 2011), 177–95.

Mogensen, Christina Lysbjerg, "Christian II's land- og bylov: En acceleration af centraliseringen," *Temp – tidsskrift for historie* 9 (2014): 5–22.

Rørdam, Holger Fr., "Et nyt Bidrag til Oplysning om Dr. Johan Bugenhagens Virksomhed i Danmark," *Ny Kirhehistoriske Samlinger* III (1864–66): 469–82.

Shoenberger, Cynthia Grant, "The Development of the Lutheran Theory of Resistance: 1523–1530," *The Sixteenth Century Journal* 8/1 (1977): 61–76.

Spitz, Lewis W., "The Impact of the Reformation on the Universities," *University and Reformation*, Leif Grane, ed. (Leiden: Brill, 1981), 9–31.

Tamm, Ditlev, "Law and Protestantism in Denmark," *Zeitschrift der Savigny-Stiftung für Rechtsgeschichte: Kanonistische Abteilung* 102 (2016): 406–18.

The Annotated Luther, vol. 1: The Roots of Reform, Timothy J. Wengert, ed. (Minneapolis, MN: Fortress Press, 2015).

Wengert, Timothy J. and Krey, Philip D.W., "A June 1546 Exorcism in Wittenberg as a Pastoral Act," *Archiv für Reformationsgeschichte* 98 (2007): 71–83.

Wengert, Timothy J., "The Wittenberg Circle," *The Oxford Handbook of Martin Luther's Theology*, Robert Kolb, Irene Dingel, and L'ubomír Batka, eds. (Oxford: Oxford University Press, 2014), 491–501.

Witte Jr., John, *Law and Protestantism: The Legal Teachings of the Lutheran Reformation* (Cambridge: Cambridge University Press, 2002).

6 Olavus Petri (1493–1552)

Transplanting foreign law in Reformation Sweden

Heikki Pihlajamäki

Introduction

Olavus Petri is mainly known for his major contribution to the Protestant Reformation in Sweden. In the Finnish and Swedish national legal pantheons, however, Olavus Petri stands among the greatest. The *Instructions* of Olavus Petri are printed in the semiofficial law books of Finland and Sweden. Sweden's law book, *Sveriges rikes lag*, has appeared in its present form since 1861, and the *Instructions* have been printed in all of its editions since 1734. In Finland, the *Instructions* appeared already in the first statute collection beginning in 1881. They were left out of two editions in 1920 and 1932, but otherwise they have remained in the Finnish laws books ever since. I will try to explain why this is the case, what Olavus Petri did to gain such recognition, and how legal historians raised Olavus Petri to such an eminent place among the two nations' leading legal figures.

This chapter starts with a brief account of Olavus Petri's life. With the help of Olavus Petri's writings, the chapter then shows what kind of novelties he wished to introduce into the Swedish legal life of the sixteenth century, and how he modified foreign legal ideas and instruments while transplanting them. This section approaches the question of how Olavus Petri's writing influenced practical legal life. Here the chapter surveys Olavus Petri's writings on law thematically, beginning with his thoughts on political theology—the power relationship between God and the earthly ruler. The section then turns to Olavus Petri's thinking on legal interpretation and evidentiary law, with frequent allusions to the writings of Philipp Melanchthon, whose influence on Olavus Petri's legal thinking was probably greater than anyone else's. We do not know how well and whether Olavus Petri new the preceptor of Germany personally, as older Swedish historiography suggested, but at least Petri must have been influenced by his scholarship while in Germany.

Olavus Petri was, above all, a clever importer of legal transplants. His primary concern was to reform the medieval Swedish legal heritage along the lines of European legal learning. As a realist, he took pains to transform these transplants so that they could be adjusted to the realities of the Swedish legal landscape. Despite this, Olavus Petri's reform project was not particularly successful. This was because it lacked the institutional support that had helped to carry through similar reforms in other countries.

The last section of the chapter focuses on emerging legal histories of Finland and Sweden and will explain how a place in those histories was cleared for Olavus Petri. Here, the essential argument is that the story of Olavus Petri as a national legal reformer who represented the "true" Swedish and Finnish values was invented in the early twentieth century.

The life of Olavus Petri

Olavus Petri was probably born on 6 January in 1493 or 1497. He went to school in Örebro and continued at the University of Uppsala, where one of his academic teachers was the theologian Peder Galle, who later became his opponent. As was customary, Olavus Petri continued his studies in Germany, probably first in Rostock, but certainly after 1516 in Leipzig. That same year, he transferred to Wittenberg and graduated in 1518. It is not known whether he formed any kind of personal relationship with Martin Luther or Philipp Melanchthon, but at least he clearly identified himself as Luther's student.[1]

On his return to Sweden in 1518, Olavus Petri was appointed chancellor of the bishop of Strängnäs, Matthias Gregor, who also ordained Olavus Petri as deacon. In November 1520, the last union king of Denmark, Christian II, organized a bloodbath in Stockholm, and among others, the bishop was executed. Olavus Petri lost his position but attained another job as teacher in the cathedral school of Strängnäs, where he was allowed to preach in the cathedral. Olavus Petri could thus spread the word of Lutheranism, which the bishop of Linköping, Hans Brask, attempted to prevent. Olavus Petri was supported, however, by his supervisor, Archdeacon Laurentius Andreae. In 1523, Gustav Vasa was elected king, and Laurentius Andreae became his chancellor. In 1524, the king helped Olavus Petri become the secretary of the Stockholm city council. His *Commentary on the Town Law* and *A Little Clarification on Some Old Words That Are in the Law Books but No Longer in Daily Use*[2] probably date to this period. Olavus Petri married Christina on Septuagesima Sunday in 1525. The public marriage was the first for a cleric who had taken higher orders (*diaconus*) in Sweden and was certainly intended to provoke. As Olavus Petri himself later commented, all "papists" had protested his marriage.[3]

In the following years, he attacked many of the teachings and practices of the Catholic Church in several writings, and he translated the New Testament into the vernacular. In 1527, the king convened the Diet to Västerås, where the Swedish Reformation started. In 1528, Gustav Vasa was crowned king, with Olavus Petri delivering the coronation sermon. In this sermon, Olavus Petri not only lauded the king's person but also explicated his own understanding of the crown as God's tool. The Finnish historian Heikki Ylikangas has surmised that the sermon may have contained the seeds of the conflict between the king and Olavus Petri.[4]

Olavus Petri continued translating and writing, and in 1531 he was appointed the chancellor of the realm. His relations to the king, however, soon deteriorated, and he has deposed in 1533. He continued preaching in the Church of

Saint Nicholas in Stockholm, frequently criticizing the king in his sermons. In 1536, a group of German burghers was caught plotting against the king (the so-called Gunpowder Plot). Olavus Petri and Laurentius Andreae pleaded for lenient punishment and were active, for instance, in consoling the family members of the plotters. In the late 1530s, the opposition against the king's tough ecclesiastical and internal policies grew. In the mid-1530s, Olavus Petri wrote *A Little Introduction to the Law Book,* and a few years later the famous *Instructions for the Judge*. In 1539, he was ordained priest.[5]

In late 1539 and early 1540, Olavus Petri and Laurentius Andreae had to stand for criminal charges at the nobility meeting of Örebro. Olavus Petri was blamed for many of Gustav Vasa's political problems and mutinies against him. Both of the accused were sentenced to death "in order to warn others." The City of Stockholm offered, however, to pay a large sum of money in fines if Olavus Petri were pardoned. He was indeed pardoned, but his ecclesiastical career was for all practical purposes over. In 1543, he was appointed vicar of the Church of St. Nicholas, but his relations to the king never returned to what they had been. Olavus Petri died in 1552.

As a legal figure, Olavus Petri is mostly known for his *Instructions for the Judge*. Technically, the *Instructions* belong to the medieval *brocarda* (or *brocardica*) tradition. The *brocarda* was meant as procedural advice for jurists and used as a pedagogical tool.[6] Even in Sweden, the *Instructions* had predecessors: the oldest manuscript of the Provincial Law of Western Gothia (14th c.) contains rules for judges and was subsequently copied to many manuscripts. The *Instructions* themselves show influence from this manuscript.[7]

As far as the contents are concerned, the *Instructions* represent the transition from medieval Swedish law to a legal order in which the influence of European *ius commune* is visible. Olavus Petri acted as a bridge between the learned German circles that he had acquainted himself with, on one hand, and the unlearned Swedish law. The reform spirit of his *Instructions* is far from radical. Instead, Olavus Petri was realistic in not even attempting to introduce procedural ideas in the form to which they had developed in contemporary European and German legal scholarship. The *brocarda* was an ideal way of presenting some of the central ideas of procedural legal scholarship in an abbreviated and simplified form, understandable to lay judges of sixteenth-century Sweden.

The *Instructions* soon came to form part of legal manuscripts that Swedish judges and their substitutes, the so-called law readers, routinely used as handbooks. In this way, the *Instructions* acquired normative force, some of which they have retained until today. Much of the *Instructions* soon, of course, became outdated, and they were formally acknowledged as a legal source. A formal acknowledgment of legal sources is, on the other hand, a modern concern.[8]

Olavus Petri was a great writer and a Christian, but was he a jurist? The instinctive answer would be of course not, he was a theologian. In his famous charge against Olavus Petri, King Gustav Vasa indeed said that "the good master Olavus Petri had experience in almost all liberal arts and faculties, namely theology, in divine and civil law, in medicine, and many others," but that he was unable to dictate or draw documents properly. Therefore, he was about as suitable for a chancellor "as a donkey for a lute player." Based on this evidence, Jan Eric Almquist concludes that Olavus Petri was an autodidact as a jurist, and not a particularly good one at that.[9] Gunnar Westin, however, disagrees, stressing that Gustav Vasa's utterances need to be understood in the context of a bitter political strife between the two men, and that they prove nothing about Olavus Petri's training.[10]

Most of Olavus Petri's oeuvre was indeed theological, but following the medieval tradition, the link between theology and law continued strong, and thus the legal angle can already be seen in many of his primarily theological works. Another point to be taken into account is that early sixteenth-century Sweden was practically void of jurists in the modern sense of the word—if a jurist is defined as a professional with a university degree in law. Since the Middle Ages, the church had financed legal studies of young men, who then returned the favor by serving in the ecclesiastical bureaucracy. Gustav Vasa brought legal expertise from Germany to serve the needs of his administrative and judicial reforms and diplomacy.[11]

In the sixteenth century, however, jurists did not still figure in the mundane jobs of the administration or judiciary, nor were there any professional advocates in the country. It is telling that when the Swedish high courts were founded in the seventeenth century, half a year of legal studies sometimes sufficed to qualify one for a judgeship within the quota of judges with legal training. In other words, being a jurist was loosely defined in early sixteenth-century Sweden. If anyone was a jurist, by contemporary standards and from the point of view of this book, Olavus Petri certainly was.

Importing legal ideas from center to periphery

Lutheran political theology

In his "Sermon Against the Oath," Olavus Petri made clear that he supported the Lutheran concept of political theology. The secular authority ("*överhet*") was "God's servant and bore the sword." God had created the secular authority and had not given it great powers in vain: it was the authority's duty to see that God was respected, to prevent the opposite, and to punish those who failed to respect God.

> The overlord, who is God's servant and bears the sword, should take this thing seriously and henceforth punish for such atrocious perjury and blasphemy, for his office requires this, because God has for this reason founded the overlordship and given it large powers, so that he might further His honor, and resist and prevent that which is against Him.[12]

Should the secular authority not succeed in keeping its flock under control, God's wrath would fall upon the land. Here Olavus Petri—as probably the first in Sweden—joins the medieval rhetorical tradition of God's wrath, which came to play an important role in the Protestant criminal-law discourse of the sixteenth and seventeenth centuries. In connection to the German Peasants' War of 1524–25, Martin Luther himself had written:

> For in this case a prince and lord must remember that according to Romans 13 [:4], he is God's minister and the *servant of his wrath*, and the sword has been given to him to use against such people. If he does not fulfill the duties of his office by punishing some and protecting others, he commits as great a sin before God as when someone who has not been given the sword commits murder. If he is able to punish and does not do it—even though he would have had to kill someone or shed blood—he becomes guilty of all the murder and evil that these people commit. For by deliberately disregarding God's command, he permits such rascals to go about their wicked business, even though he was able to prevent it and it was his duty to do so. This is not a time to sleep. And there is no place for patience or mercy. *This is the time of the sword, not the day of grace.*[13]

If the secular *Obrigkeit* thus failed, according to Luther, to guarantee social peace, he committed a sin himself. The question of legal sources was important because it was by way of laws that the secular authority was to guide people into the right path. In one of his early writings, Olavus Petri borrowed his theory of legal sources from Melanchthon, distinguishing between natural law, Mosaic law, and secular laws. "Good custom" (*god sedvänja*) was equal to law whenever no written law existed.[14]

The king's will was law if supported by reasons (*med skäl*).[15] Olavus Petri does not further elaborate on what these reasons for law-giving might be, but his listing of sources suggests that he simply followed the medieval theory that was still mainstream in the early sixteenth century. Late medieval canonists and lawyers had already built safeguards to limit the legislative power of the prince, and these limitations remained the mainstream political theology of the sixteenth century. Three factors thus limited the legislative power of the prince. The laws needed to be in accordance with the natural law and with God's law, and they needed to enhance the common good (*bonum commune*). The theory may have begun with Panormitanus, and it was alive and well in the writings of Jean Bodin.[16] The French political theorist formulates the idea this way:

> For if we define [absolute power as being] freed from all laws, no prince anywhere possesses sovereignty (*iura maiestatis*), since divine law, the law of nature, the common law of the people, which is established separately from divine and natural law, binds all princes.[17]

In the *Instructions*, Olavus Petri then also refers to the concept of *bonum commune*: "The best law is to the benefit of the common people; therefore, whatever is seen to be beneficial for the common people should be deemed law, even though the words of the written law would seem to command otherwise" (Instruction 13).

Without engaging here the complicated questions concerning customary law and common law, or *ius commune,* it is interesting that Olavus Petri, like Bodin, refers to the "law of the people." Bodin, however, clearly refers to learned *ius commune*, as the thirteenth-century canonist Hostiensis had as well.[18] Olavus Petri's context, however, was different. Because of the scarcity of learned jurists and the corresponding heavy lay domination in Sweden, the question of customary law must have been important to Olavus Petri. The writings of Luther and Melanchthon did not offer much help here, because they were not concerned with customary law at all. If anything, both Luther and Melanchthon strongly favored Roman law, which was strongly juxtaposed to customary law in the legal landscape of early sixteenth-century Germany and its peasant uprisings.[19]

Olavus Petri, with his "good custom," thus refers to customary law. Customary law figures in the *Instructions* as well: "The custom of the land, if it is not unfair, should be reckoned as the law, according to which judgments ought to be made" (Instruction 14). As Roy Garré has shown, late medieval jurists had "tamed" the "wild" customary law of the early Middle Ages. Legal customs had to be based on the will of the people (*voluntas populi*), but beginning in the twelfth century, the acceptance of the prince (*permissio* or *patientia principiis*) played an increasing role. From the sixteenth century onwards, Italian jurisprudence developed additional criteria to match political absolutism. To be acceptable, customary law now had to fulfill criteria that were even more strictly defined and emphasized the role of the judiciary in defining customary law. Customs, in order to qualify as customary law, had to be used in courts with a certain minimum frequency (*frequentia actuum*) during a certain minimum period (*diutirnitas temporis*). They needed to be rational (*rationalitas*)—of which Instruction 14 cited above is a clear adaptation—and proven (*probatio consuetudinis*), and they still had to be founded on a "tacit popular consensus" (*tacitus consensus populi*). According to the medieval ideology still prevalent, old customs were always better than "arbitrary" statutory law.[20]

Whether Olavus Petri is referring specifically to one of these legal theories when he says that, to be accepted, the custom must be "good" and should not be "unfair," cannot be ascertained, but it is highly probable. His brief remarks need to be read in their context, which in this case is Olavus Petri's training in Germany, where the idea of customary law as important but theoretically defined and restricted was the order of the day.

It is thus interesting that in his political theology, Olavus Petri largely followed medieval canonists and lawyers who had constructed the prevailing theory of limitations to princely power. Instead of taking note of these limitations, previous research has concentrated solely on Olavus Petri's contribution to strengthening that power. This side of his thinking is, no doubt, highly significant as well. The Lutheran conception of the secular authority's duties and prerogatives suited the emerging strong kingship of Gustav Vasa, which Olavus Petri still supported in the 1530s. The Reformation and Olavus Petri in its front line importantly contributed to Sweden's becoming probably the most centralized of the early modern states.

Legal interpretation

Equity (*epieikeia, aequitas*) was a central concept in Melanchthon's theory of legal interpretation. As he stated his negative definition of what a rightful legal interpretation at least was not, "rigor of law is not the same as calumnious interpretation of law" (*summum ius non est calumniosa interpretatio iuris*). Interpretation was "calumnious" when a strict law was applied without mitigation, even if circumstances would allow departing from the strict interpretation. An example is when a young thief is condemned to death, even though he has stolen out of necessity and not bad will. Equity was, however, not to be used carelessly, and never against natural law or God's law. [21]

Following Melanchthon, Olavus Petri writes on equity as well, identifying it as a way of considering particular circumstances of the legal case.[22] Olavus Petri says that law should not be wrenched out of its rightful meaning,

> which often seems to happen, especially by jurists, who study in order to be able to take a wrongful case and decorate it with one paragraph of law from here and another from there, and set many glosses thereupon, against the law's rightful meaning.[23]

One of the most cited passages of the *Instructions* also represents the idea of equity (Rule 9): "What is not just and fair cannot be law either; for it is on account of the fairness which dwells in the law that the law is accepted."

It may be difficult to understand that Olavus Petri would have despised jurists since, in early sixteenth-century Sweden, few existed and none were trained. The most probable explanation for his attitude is simple, however: he followed the example of Luther, a notorious jurist-hater. Not surprisingly, the jurist theme does not develop further than this in Olavus Petri's works.

Evidentiary law

Medieval canon law considerably influenced criminal procedure. Most importantly, inquisitorial procedure emerged during the late twelfth century. The new mode of procedure allowed ecclesiastical authorities to initiate investigations themselves instead of relying on accusations from below. After the principles of the inquisitorial procedure were confirmed in the constitutions of the Fourth Lateran Council of 1215, the law of proof also changed. The Lateran Council prohibited churchmen from participating in the administration of ordeals, which until then had been in frequent use. An alternative approach to evidence, the so-called statutory theory of proof, soon developed to replace ordeals. Closely linked to this new package of criminal control was judicial torture, which could be used to extract confession under determined circumstances. If no one had seen the crime, and the suspect refused to confess, confession could be wrung out with the help of torture if a sufficient amount of circumstantial evidence was at hand. The legal prerequisites for torture were, however, stringently defined in legal literature. By the early modern period, the inquisitorial principles came largely to dominate the Continental criminal procedure of the secular sphere as well.[24]

In the medieval statutory or Roman-canon theory of proof, judicial torture was thus designed to produce confessions in cases of serious crime in which "full proof" in the form of confession or two eyewitnesses was needed to convict. Not surprisingly, judicial torture was a theme that preoccupied Olavus Petri. He wanted criminal verdicts to be based on eyewitness statements and confessions, as the inquisitorial procedure had it, and no longer on oaths and compurgators—that is, sworn witnesses to the innocence or good character of an accused person. Olavus Petri was not sure what to think of torture, however. In Rule 38, and after some critical comments, he finally accepts it in cases of treason and homicide. In Rule 31, on the other hand, he seems to condemn judicial torture categorically. He mentions and condemns certain "bailiffs," implying torture, undoubtedly referring to the practice in the Stockholm town court. Judicial torture indeed managed to gain a narrow bridgehead in Sweden, as it came to be used, for instance, in King Eric XIV's high court (*Höga nämnd*) in the 1560s. Torture was, however, never accepted as a general means of fact-finding in Sweden. By the mid-seventeenth century, the last vestiges of torture were rooted out.[25]

Why was Olavus Petri not successful in introducing judicial torture in Sweden? First, judicial torture mixed poorly with the system of oaths and compurgators, which was still in place in sixteenth-century Sweden. Swedish criminal procedure was accusatorial, not inquisitorial, and it was dominated by laymen not knowledgeable or trained in the nuances of legal scholarship. Second, the procedures were public and oral, and judicial torture combined poorly with such a procedure. It is indeed difficult to see how local jurors could have tortured their peers. If they had nevertheless been willing to act as torturers, they certainly were not permitted to. If local courts had been allowed to torture, safeguards against misuse of such a power would have been necessary. The only safeguards available were doctrinal, however, and they could not be mastered without legal expertise.[26]

Criminal law

The idea of individualized criminal guilt appears already in the works of decretists (commentators on Gratian's *Decretum*), such as Rufinus (d. 1192), Huguccio (d. 1210), and Stephen of Tournai (1135–203). Building on Peter Abelard's (1079–142) distinction between sin and crime, these canonists moved further toward seeing crime and punishment from the point of view of individual guilt. They built on the voluntaristic supposition that, in a normal situation, the human being could freely choose whether or not to commit crimes or sins. The human being was then also responsible for these choices. The decretists used expressions such as "knowledge" (*scientia*), "knowingly" (*sciens*), and "deliberation" (*deliberatio*) to describe the relationship between doer and deed. They also discussed whether the intention, *mens rea*, should be determined in terms of the objective probability of the harmful consequence of the deed or according to the subjective conception of the doer.[27]

In the thirteenth century, penance as a theological instrument developed strongly. As one of the byproducts of penance, Raymond of Penyafort and other canonists refined the concept of individual guilt. Penitential literature, the literature of the *forum internum*, then influenced criminal law in general. More than likely, a relation existed between the law of penance and the actual canon criminal law of the external forum. Guilt, the central idea of canonist criminal law, was reflected in the work of the late medieval jurists. These ideas were then adopted by the leading *ius commune* authors of the sixteenth century—for instance, by the prominent Italian sixteenth-century criminal law scholars Julius Clarus and Tiberius Decianus (1509–82) and the Frenchman Andreas Tiraquellus (1488–558).[28]

Following medieval canonists and the *ius commune* criminal-law theory,[29] Olavus Petri introduced the principle of individual guilt in Rule 35:

> When judging a deed, it must be beheld what the doer's intention was, whether a deed was wrought with malice aforethought or not. And therefore, he who stealthily takes from another cannot on every occasion be found guilty of theft, because it may happen that he took something by accident and imagined that the goods which were not his own belonged to him, or some other similar case; or that one person might steal out of malice while another might steal out of dire penury. No one is to be deemed guilty of theft if he did not knowingly or with stealth take from another that which belonged to the other man. And so it is in all other cases that intention and state of mind are to be looked at rather than the deed itself.

The principle of *rei publicae interest, ne crimina remaneant impunita* (crimes shall not remain unpunished) was of canonist origin as well. The canonists of the twelfth and thirteenth centuries developed the principle, which was closely connected to the growth of the inquisitorial procedure and the new theory of evidence.[30] The idea was that crime should be punished regardless of whether a statute or custom existed to condemn it. The principle was thus the virtual opposite of the later legality principle. *Ne crimina remaneant impunita* is found in the *Instructions*, 11 and 18:

> The law does not countenance all that may go unpunished because the law book cannot contain all the kinds of crimes (Rule 11).

The principle of *ne crimina remaneant impunita* obviously suited well the growing absolutism and concentration of powers in Olavus Petri's Sweden, just as it had served the power aspirations of the Catholic Church in the twelfth and thirteenth centuries. The Swedish reformer speaks also, this time following Melanchthon's theory of punishment, of the need to use punishment as betterment.

The reception and influence of Olavus Petri

It is now worth asking how well Olavus Petri's legal thinking succeeded in his own time, and whether at least some parts of his legal thinking had more lasting effect on Swedish law. As far as his legal philosophy is concerned, it left little mark on Swedish legal thinking. The actual Swedish legal literature appeared in the seventeenth century, a whole century after Olavus Petri, and was by nature too pragmatic to include philosophical ponderings. Thus, his thoughts on customary law—embryonic, to be sure—were not developed further in the seventeenth or eighteenth centuries, and the same can be said of his teachings about legal interpretation.

The *ius commune* theory of evidentiary law, Olavus Petri's major import, fared much better. The statutory theory of proof slowly replaced the medieval oath procedures during the seventeenth century. However, this process probably had little to do with the writings of our Reformer and much more with the introduction of *ius commune* through universities, both foreign and domestic. Again, a gap of several decades separates Olavus Petri and the acceptance of new evidentiary law. Olavus Petri's partial and reserved acceptance of judicial torture gained ground somewhat earlier, in the late sixteenth- and early seventeenth-century Swedish legal practice. However, the practice of judicial torture was rooted out during the second half of the seventeenth century. As for criminal law, the principles of individual guilt and *ne crimina remaneant impunita* were accepted in legal practice after Olavus Petri. Again, however, it is difficult to ascertain whether this happened because of Olavus Petri's writings. To sum up, there must be other reasons for Olavus Petri's revered place in the legal mythology of Finland and Sweden than his influence on law and legal thinking.

The present-day esteem that Olavus Petri's work enjoys is, more than anything, based on his *Instructions for the Judge*. As already noted, the *Instructions* were used as a legal source in the early modern period. Ample evidence from sixteenth- and seventeenth-century court records shows this. We also know that the *Instructions* were customarily copied into the law manuscripts that judges needed to have with them while sitting court. The *Instructions* were thus law, "although they were never promulgated," as Henrik Munktell puts it.[31]

In older Swedish legal literature, such as Johan Stiernhöök's historical treatise *De jure sveonum et gothorum vetusto* (1672), we find no traces of admiration towards Olavus Petri. At the end of nineteenth century, however, the admiration begins to grow. Henrik Schück, in his history of Swedish literature (1890), coined the term "Reformator of Sweden" for Olavus Petri. At Schück's proposal, a statue of Olavus Petri was raised outside one of Stockholm's main churches (Storkyrkan) in 1898.[32] In 1914–17, Bengt Hesselman and Knut B. Westman published an edition of Olavus Petri's collected works.[33]

In the period preceding legal positivism, the fact that the *Instructions* were not officially sanctioned was not a problem; the Bible and natural law were used as sources as well. The official position of the *Instructions* only became a problem once legal positivism had been entrenched. Law, in the positivist ideology of the late nineteenth and twentieth centuries, was only written law approved by a competent lawgiver (and customary law, the importance of which was rapidly waning as statutory law gained ground).

Simultaneously, however, as positivism gained ground, legal history as an independent legal discipline was taking shape. The early part of the twentieth century was the golden period of Swedish legal history with giants such as Åke Holmbäck, Jan Eric Almquist, and Henrik Munktell building a discipline through meticulous source studies. These men, and legal history such as it now emerged—modernized—"saved" the *Instructions* and gave them a new position in Swedish legal culture: no longer as part of its normative system but as part of Swedish legal heritage and culture.

Schück already had said about the *Instructions* that they represent "a terse, genuine Swedish legal style. Exactly so, and not in any other [style], should these sentences [be written]."[34] According to Åke Holmbäck, "in few places does the Swedish language sound so manly and proud as in the sentences of the *Instructions for Judges*."[35] Olavus Petri was depicted as a representative of a true Swedish legal culture: always on the side of the common person. The leading idea of the *Instructions* was to protect the common person from arbitrariness and hardness of the law and to ensure that the innocent are not punished for crimes they have not committed. Munktell, in 1944, was wondering why the *Instructions* had exerted such great influence in Sweden. It was because, "[t]he simple and sound rules have been easily understood by the common man . . . their contents have been in harmony with the character of Swedish law in general."[36] Almquist (1940), in turn, called the *Instructions* "an important unifying link between ancient and modern Swedish legal life."[37] Göran Inger's widely distributed legal history textbook from the 1980s repeats the same phrases.[38]

In Finland, the adoration followed suit a little later. In 1951, Aatos Alanen wrote that the *Instructions* "created an independent and responsible judiciary. The Finnish judges have aimed at the common good, the high principle of justice and equity."[39] Even though Alanen's view became dominant, in 1968 criticism was voiced as well. According to Erik Castrén, "The *Instructions* were so out of time, that they should be removed or at least heavily edited."[40] This, however, did not happen.

Olavus Petri as a representative of "true Swedish legal culture" is, however, a myth. He did not aim at conserving the Swedish medieval legal legacy in any way. He wanted to get rid of the archaic law of proof and replace it with learned theory of proof as far as this was realistically possible in a country with so little legal learning as sixteenth-century Sweden had. Influenced by canon law, Olavus Petri introduced the principle of individual guilt. He was critical of jurists, not because they would have been a real nuisance in sixteenth-century Sweden, but because he had learned the critical attitude from his theologian colleagues in

Germany. *Aequitas*, equity, which Olavus Petri emphasizes in many of writings and in the *Instructions*, many have identified as the cornerstone of his thinking. But, of course, *aequitas* was no Swedish invention but part of the package Olavus Petri brought with him from the German universities.

Olavus Petri did not consider his main task to be faithfully describing and preserving Swedish legal culture. In fact, he despised many of its features deeply. Instead, Petri ran an import agency of legal ideas. He was well aware, however, that the products he imported needed to be tailored carefully to fit the Swedish market.

But myths—such as Olavus Petri's position as the grand figure of Swedish and Finnish legal culture—are not necessarily true or false. Myths exist in their own right. They are construed for a reason, and they have a life of their own. As myths always do, this is one is partially built on elements that stand the test of closer inspection. One element in Swedish legal culture that he took seriously (although probably not with real respect) was its practical, lay-oriented nature. Olavus Petri wanted to ensure that his *Instructions* had a practical impact: therefore, much of the *Instructions* is based on norms already in force ("oath shall not go against oath," "unlawful acquisition is no acquisition," "he who does not have cattle shall pay fines with his body"). In the poor northern periphery that Sweden was, there was no alternative for this, and these features have persisted in many ways until the twenty-first century. At the time of national conscience building, the late nineteenth and early twentieth centuries, when legal historians such as Holmbäck, Munktell, and Almquist hacked and hammered a Swedish national legal history out of ingredients at hand, the only Swedish legally trained scholar from the sixteenth century came in handy. Practical solutions instead of legal theories, more laypersons and fewer jurists in charge of running the legal system—these became the hallmarks of Swedish and Finnish legal cultures, hallmarks of which we have been trained to be proud.

Notes

1 Schmidt, *Richterregeln*.
2 *En liten uttydning på några gamla ord som finnas i lagböckerna och äro nu icke i dagliga brukning*.
3 Westin, "Olavus Petri"; Korpiola, "Lutheran Marriage Norms", 137.
4 Ylikangas, *Olavus Petrin tuomarinohjeet*.
5 For an English translation by Jarkko Tontti and Linda Augustine, see http://www.jarkkotontti.net/blog/tieteilya-ja-filosofiaa/Olavus Petri-petri-and-the-rules-for-judges-associations). Although some writings may have been falsely attributed to Olavus Petri, such as *Een liten boock om sacramenten* [A Small Book on the Sacraments] from 1528, most probably a work of Laurentius Andreae, the *Instructions* was most certainly Olavus Petri's.
6 Erler and Kaufmann, "Brocarda".
7 Schück, *Svensk litteraturihistoria*, 493.
8 On the influence of the *Instructions* on legal practice, see Munktell, *Domarereglerna*.
9 Almquist, "Domarregler", 8.
10 Westin, *Historieskrivaren Olavus Petri*, 240–41.
11 See Korpiola, "Desperately Needing Lawyers".

12 "Öfverheten, som Guds tjänare är och bär svärdet, skulle taga denna saken allvarligen för och härledigen näpsa och straffa sådana gräsliga eder och gudshädelser för ty hennes ämbete kräver det, efter det Gud hafver för den skull stiftat öfverheten och gifvit henne stora makt, att hon skulle förordra hans ära och pris och avvärja och förhindra det, som honom är emot" (translation from Swedish to English, HP). See Holmquist, *Svenska kyrkanns historia,* 175–76.

13 Luther, "Against the Robbing". For the original German text, see Luther, *D. Martin Luthers Werke*, 360: "Wider die räuberischen und mörderischen Rotten der Bauern [1525]," WA 18, 360.

> Denn eyn Fuerst und herr mus hie dencken, wie er Gotte amptman [röm 13,4] und *seyns zorns diner* is Ro. 13, dem das schwerd uber solche buben befolhen ist. Und sich eben so hoch für Gott versundigt, wo er nicht strafft und weret und seyn ampt nicht volfuret, als wenn eyner moerdet, dem das schwerd nicht befohlen ist, Denn wo er kann und strafft nicht, es sey durch mord odder blutvergiessen, so ist er schuldig an allem mord und ubel, das solche buben begehen, als der da mutwilliglich durch nachlassen seyns Goettlichen befehls zu lesst solchen buben, yhre bosheit zu uben, so ers wol weren kan und schuldig ist, Darumb ist hie nicht zu schlaffen. Es gillt auch nicht hie gedult odder barmherztigkeyt. Es ist des *schwerds und zorns zeyt* hie und nicht der gnaden zeyt. (emphasis HP)

Luther's text here is very much due to the particular circumstances of the Peasants' War, but he used similar rhetoric on other occasions as well.

14 "Swar vppå jtt ochristelighit sendebreff." Petri, *Samlade skrifter I,* 196. This "Answer to an un-Christian decree" from 1527 was directed towards the Catholic attacks on Luther. See Almquist, "Tvenne förut otryckta juridiska skrifter," 132.

15 Petri, *Samlade skrifter* IV, 304.

16 Pennington, *The Prince,* 232–36.

17 Quoted and translated by Pennington, *The Prince*, 8.

18 See Pennington, *The Prince*, who cites Hostiensis at 52.

19 The tension between Roman law and customary law remained for centuries, despite the fact that customary law in its written form was essentially a creation of jurists. See Watson, *The Evolution*, 65–85; and Whitman, *The Legacy*, 17.

20 Garré, *Consuetudo,* 83–84, 278–80. See also Strauss, *Law*, 98–102.

21 Kisch, *Melanchthons*,, 170–84.

22 Petri, "Kommentar," 318

23 Petri"Kommentar," 317.

24 Pihlajamäki and Korpiola, "Medieval Canon Law".

25 Pihlajamäki, "Painful Question".

26 Pihlajamäki, "Painful Question," 577–78.

27 Kuttner, *Kanonistische Schuldlehre*; Engelmann.

28 Pihlajamäki and Korpiola, "Medieval Canon Law," 201–24.

29 *Ibid.*

30 Fraher, *The Theoretical Justification.*

31 Munktell, *Domarreglerna.*

32 Westin, *Olavus Petri, Peder Svart och Gustav Vasa,* 51.

33 Hesselman and Westman, *Olavus Petri.*

34 Schück, *Svensk litteraturhistoria*, 493.

35 Holmbäck, "Domarregler," 266.

36 Munktell, *Rättsarvet,* 172.

37 Almquist, "Domarreglernas slutord".

38 Inger, *Svensk rättshistoria*, 65–66.

39 Alanen, "Tuomarinohjeiden peruslinjat," 12.

40 Castrén, "Mietteitä".

Bibliography

Alanen, Aatos, "Tuomarinohjeiden peruslinjat," *Valvoja* (1951). 8–12.

Almquist, Jan Eric, "Domarereglernas slutord," *Svensk juristtidning* 21 (1936). 186–94.

Almquist, Jan Eric, "Tvenne förut otryckta juridiska skrifter av Olavus Petri," *Lychnos* (1937). 130–36.

Castrén, Erik, "Eräitä 'tuomarinohjeisiin' liittyviä mietteitä," *Juhlajulkaisu Tauno Tirkkosen 70-vuotisjuhlapäivänä*, Tauno Ellilä, Jouko Halila, and Jorma S. Aalto, eds., (Vammala: Suomalainen Lakimiesyhdistys, 1969), 44–50.

Engelmann, Woldemar, *Die Schuldlehre der Postglossatoren und ihre Fortentwicklung: eine historisch-dogmatische Darstellung der kriminellen Schuldlehre der italianischen Juristen des Mittelalters seit Accursius* (Aalen: Scientia Verlag, 1965).

Erler, Adalbert and Kaufmann, Ekkehard, "Brocarda," in Wolfgang Stammler (ed.), *Handwörterbuch zur Deutschen Rechtsgeschichte I*, (Berlin: Erich Schmidt, 1964), 519–520.

Fraher, Richard M., *The Theoretical Justification for the New Criminal Law of the High Middle Ages: Rei Publicae Interest, Ne Crimina Remaneant Impunita* (Champaign: University of Illinois Law Review, 1984), 577–96.

Garré, Roy, *Consuetudo: Das Gewohnheitsrecht in der Rechtsquellen- und Methodenlehre des späten ius commune in Italien (16.-18. Jahrhundert)* (Frankfurt am Main: Klostermann, 2005).

Hesselman, Bengt and Westman, Knut B. (eds.), *Olavus Petri samlade verk* (Stockholm: Sveriges Kristliga Studentrörelse, 1914–17).

Holmbäck, Åke, "Våra domarregler," *Festskrift tillägnad Axel Hägerström* (Uppsala: Almquist & Wiksell, 1928), 265–79.

Holmquist, Hjalmar, *Svenska kyrkans historia 3. Reformationstidevarvet 1521–1611* (Stockholm: Svenska Kyrkans Diakonistyrelses Bokførlag, 1933–46).

Inger, Göran, *Svensk rättshistoria*, (Malmö: Liber ekonomi cop., 1997).

Kisch, Guido, *Melanchthons Rechts- und Soziallehre* (Berlin: de Gruyter, 1967).

Korpiola, Mia, "Desperately Needing Lawyers: Contacts in the Baltic Sea Region and the Rise of Diplomacy in Reformation Sweden," *Migration und Kulturtransfer im Ostseeraum während der Frühen Neuzeit*, Otfried Czaika and Heinrich Holze eds. (Stockholm: Kungliga biblioteket, 2012), 101–20.

Korpiola, Mia, "Lutheran Marriage Norms in Action: The Example of Post-Reformation Sweden," *Lutheran Reformation and the Law*, Virpi Mäkinen ed. (Leiden: Brill, 2007), 131–70.

Kuttner, Stephan, *Kanonistische Schuldlehre von Gratian bis auf die Dekretalen Gregors IX systematisch auf Grund der handschriftlichen Quellen dargestellt* (Rome: Vatican City, 1935).

Luther, Martin, *D. Martin Luthers Werke: kritische Gesamtausgabe. 18. Bd* (Weimar: Böhlau, 1908).

Luther, Martin, "Against the Robbing and Murdering Hoards of Peasants," in Robert C. Schulz (ed.), *Luther's Works, vol. 46: The Christian in Society III* (Philadelphia: Fortress Press, 1967), 52–53.

Munktell, Henrik, *Det svenska rättsarvet* (Stockholm: Bonniers, 1944).

Munktell, Henrik, *Domarereglerna i praxis fore 1734 års lag* (Svensk Juristtidning 1939).

Pennington, Kenneth, *The Prince and the Law, 1200–1600: Sovereignty and Rights in the Western Legal Tradition* (Berkeley: University of California Press, 1993).

Petri, Olavus, "Kommentar till stadslagen," *Samlade skrifter af Olavus Petri IV* (Uppsala: Sveriges Kristliga Studentrörelse, 1917), 315–46.

Petri, Olavus, *Samlade skrifter I* (Uppsala: Sveriges Kristliga Studentrörelse, 1914).
Petri, Olavus, *Samlade skrifter IV* (Uppsala: Sveriges Kristliga Studentrörelse, 1917).
Pihlajamäki, Heikki and Korpiola, Mia, "Medieval Canon Law: At the Origins of Modern Criminal Law," *The Oxford Handbook of Criminal Law*, Tatjana Hörnle and Markus Dubber, eds. (Oxford: Oxford University Press, 2014), 201–27.
Pihlajamäki, Heikki, "The Painful Question: The Fate of Judicial Torture in Early Modern Sweden," *Law and History Review* 25:3 (2007). 577–92.
Schmidt, Gerhard, *Die Richterregeln des Olavus Petri: ihre Bedeutung im allgemeinen und für die Entwicklung des schwedischen Strafprozessrechts vom 14. bis 16. Jahrhundert*, (Göttingen: Vandenhoeck & Ruprecht, 1966).
Schück, Henrik, *Svensk litteraturhistoria: Första bandet, Medeltiden och reformationen* (Stockholm: Hugo Geber, 1890).
Strauss, Gerald, *Law, Resistance, and the State: The Opposition to Roman Law in Reformation Germany* (Princeton: Princeton University Press, 1986).
Tontti, Jarkko and Augustine, Linda, "Olaus Petri and the Rules for Judges," *Associations. Journal for Social and Legal Theory* 4:1 (2000). 113–28.
Watson, Alan, *The Evolution of Law* (Baltimore, MD: Johns Hopkins University Press, 1985).
Westin, Gunnar T., *Historieskrivaren Olavus Petri: Svenska krönikans källor och krönikeförfattarens metod* (Lund: Lund University, 1946).
Westin, Gunnar T., *Olavus Petri, Peder Svart och Gustav Vasa: Religion, politik och historieskrivning i början av 1500-talet* (Stockholm: Runica et Mediaevalia, 2002).
Westin, Gunnar T., "Olavus Petri," *Svenskt biografiskt lexikon*, Band 28 (1992–94). 151–66.
Whitman, James Q., *The Legacy of Roman Law in the German Romantic Era: Historical Vision and Legal Changes Germany* (Princeton: Princeton University Press, 1990).
Garré, Roy, *Consuetudo. Das Gewohnheitsrecht in der Rechtsquellen- und Methodenlehre des späten ius commune in Italien (16. –18. Jahrhundert)* (Frankfurt am Main: Klostermann, 2005).
Ylikangas, Heikki: *Olaus Petrin tuomarinohjeet* (Helsinki: Markkinointi-instituutti, 1982).

7 Archbishop Laurentius Petri (1499–1573)

The respected authority of the Swedish reformation

Mia Korpiola

Introduction

Laurentius Petri (1499–1573), also known as Laurentius Petri Nericius after his home province of Närke to distinguish him from his namesakes with the same name and patronym, was the first Lutheran archbishop of Uppsala from 1531 until his death. Thus, he occupied a central position in the Swedish evangelical Church during its first four decades, and he could establish the tone and tenets of the Lutheran Reformation in Sweden during many turbulent phases.

Regardless of his fundamental role in the Swedish Reformation and his political survival during three kings, Laurentius Petri has been overshadowed by his older brother, the famous Swedish Reformer, Olavus Petri. Olavus Petri's collected works were published a century ago (1914–17), and his legal thinking is analyzed by Heikki Pihlajamäki in this volume. Laurentius Petri has been called "one of the Stars of the Reformation"[1]—not merely of the Swedish Reformation, but the Reformation in general. Yet many of his writings existed only as manuscripts at the time of his death, and today, these are mostly scattered as sixteenth-century prints, later source editions or sparse manuscripts.[2]

We have certainly no evidence that Laurentius Petri had studied law whilst in Wittenberg, and unlike his brother Olavus, he wrote no actual legal works. Despite this, as archbishop, Laurentius Petri participated in judging both in ecclesiastical courts (the Chapter of Uppsala presided by himself and other *ad hoc* panels, e.g., at ecclesiastical synods),[3] and as a secular judge in *ad hoc* panels, e.g., apparently as one of the judges sentencing his brother Olavus to death in January 1540.[4] Thus, especially Laurentius Petri represents well the Swedish post-Reformation prelate who had apparently no formal studies of law, who certainly had no university degree in Roman or canon law and who hardly ever referred to (canon) law. In itself, this is unremarkable as the Swedish secular legal culture had always relied on laymen as judges and legislators and this situation was only slowly changing from the seventeenth century on.

In this chapter, I will first consider Laurentius Petri's life and works as well as discuss him as a theologian, before turning to more "legal" issues for investigating some of his perceptions highlighting his thinking as a Reformation jurist in a broad sense. These works are particularly the explanations of the Ordinance of

Västerås,[5] the Church Ordinance of 1571,[6] his introduction to the Old Testament[7] and his tractate on ecclesiastical statutes and ceremonies (1566).[8] In this short presentation, I will be investigating especially his views on ecclesiastical and secular jurisdiction as well as law and mercy.

Short biography: the highlights of Laurentius Petri's career and works

Born in Örebro as the son of Peder Olofsson, a smith, and Kristina Larsdotter, Laurentius Petri was able to pursue some studies in Wittenberg since 1527 thanks to both a scholarship and a letter of recommendation to Martin Luther (1483–1546) from King Gustav Vasa (r. 1523–60).[9] After his return, he was nominated to the post of schoolmaster of the cathedral school of Uppsala in 1530.[10] In August 1531, he was elected archbishop at the meeting of the clerical estate in Stockholm, convened by the king. This represented a departure from the medieval tradition, sanctioned by canon law, that the cathedral chapter elects the next bishop/archbishop. Apparently, at the meeting about 170 clerics were present, and the overwhelming majority was behind Laurentius Petri.[11] As Eric W. Yelverton has observed,

> [i]t cannot have happened often in the history of the Church that a young priest of thirty-two years has been preferred to the dignity of an archbishopric and the primacy of a national Church [...] without having had the experience of a diocesan bishop or even a parish priest [...].[12]

Gustav Vasa was in some haste to appoint a new archbishop to solemnize the marriage between himself and his bride, Catherine (Katarina) of Saxony-Lauenburg (1513–35), in September 1531. Yet the apostolic succession was preserved as Petrus Magni, bishop of Västerås (ep. 1524–34), probably consecrated the new archbishop two days before the King's wedding.[13]

Unlike his brother Olavus Petri and some other clerics, Laurentius Petri did not pertain to the first wave of Swedish Reformers who committed themselves to the new faith by clerical marriage before clerical celibacy was officially abolished in 1536. However, by 1548, he had wedded Elisabet Didriksdotter (d. ca. 1594–97) whose German father was Master of the Royal Mint in Uppsala and whose aristocratic mother Birgitta Kristiernsdotter [Vasa] (ca. 1485~1490-d. after 1566) was a cousin of King Gustav. Laurentius Petri was ennobled by King Erik XIV (r. 1560–68) in 1562.[14] This would have benefitted his sons especially, but the pestilence struck Laurentius Petri's family of seven children cruelly in 1566. Four children succumbed and perished, including the adolescent son Petrus Laurentii, for whom Laurentius Petri Gothus (archep. 1574–79) wrote a published funerary Latin elegy lamenting the youth's premature passing.[15] The epidemy raged hard and the sense of crisis was so acute in the country that Laurentius Petri—possibly after the blows his own family had suffered albeit the chronology is unclear—issued a long, almost pamphlet-length circular on the wrath of God to the diocese of Uppsala on October 20, 1566.[16]

Yet, through his surviving daughters, Laurentius Petri established an archepiscopal dynasty. His daughter Margareta married two subsequent archbishops: first Laurentius Petri Gothus, his father-in-law's immediate future successor, and in her second union she became the second wife of Gothus's successor Andreas Laurentii Björnram (archep. 1583–91). In turn, Laurentius Petri's daughter Magdalena had married Björnram's successor Abraham Angermannus (archep. 1593–99), while his daughter Kristina's second husband was Olaus Jonae Luth (d. 1580), professor of theology in Uppsala.[17]

Laurentius Petri has been described as basically loyal to the ruler, who in 1527 had become the supreme head of the Swedish Church. King Gustav Vasa exhibited a suspicious attitude against bishops, whose powers he attempted to reduce by establishing superintendents (royal ecclesiastical officials) to administer dioceses or parts of them. Yet "there was generally a good relationship between the archbishop and the king during the entire reign of the latter."[18] Despite his acceptance of the supremacy of the king in most fields, Archbishop Laurentius Petri—and with him the Swedish clergy—also stood his ground on important points, including the forbidden degrees of consanguinity and affinity. When King Gustav Vasa wanted in 1552 to contract his third marriage in the first and second degrees of affinity, i.e., with Katarina Stenbock (1535–1621), the niece of his second wife, the Swedish clergy—headed by the Archbishop—refused to grant a dispensation. Apparently as a result of this conflict, Gustav Vasa's third wedding was the only one that Laurentius Petri did not perform even if he assisted at the coronation of the new queen the following day.

During the reign of Erik XIV and John III (r. 1568–92), Laurentius Petri had more space of action. [19] Yet Erik XIV did not accept Laurentius Petri's draft for a church ordinance of 1561 and not until the reign of John III was the archbishop successful in finally having the newest draft of the Church Ordinance[20] first approved and printed by the king in 1571. It was accepted by the convened clergy at a church council in Uppsala the following year. [21] The end result of some three decades of reforms and drafting, it enjoyed great longevity forming the basis of Swedish Lutheran canon law until the Church Law of 1686. Indeed, it has called "the culmination of Laurentius Petri's life's work in the service of the Swedish Reformation."[22]

However, it is worth observing that the Swedish post-Reformation ecclesiastical church statutes, including the Church Ordinance of 1571, were not very "legal" in the sense that for example marriage law was not detailedly regulated. Moreover, very little was said about the procedure of the church courts. As Färnström has described the Church Ordinance of 1571,

> it is not a Church Law with clearly defined laws and norms that have a juridical character. As such it would be far too diffuse and incomplete. It is rather to be seen as an investigating and clarifying treatise – one could say a textbook in practical theology in which certain leading principles are

> decided on and norms are given for the Church's activities in the fields of preaching, liturgy, ecclesiastical rites, pastoral care and lay-teaching as well as education.[23]

Thus, in comparison to Germany, for example, the Swedish Protestant canon law remained underdeveloped, and for example in matrimonial cases, there seems to have been a tacit reliance on German ecclesiastical law with much continuity vis-à-vis medieval canon law.[24] It has also been correctly observed that the Swedish Church Ordinance "concerns itself mainly with the internal affairs of the Church" and assiduously avoids any potential bones of contention between the secular and ecclesiastical powers.[25]

Not only occupied by his political and pastoral duties including occasional visitation trips (e.g. to Norrland in 1534), Archbishop Laurentius Petri was a prolific writer and translator. As mentioned above, he wrote an explanation of the Recess and Ordinance of Västerås in 1533 even if these remained unprinted.[26] Under his auspices, the Bible (1541) was translated in full into Swedish—his brother Olavus Petri did not know Hebrew. The Bible translation included the apocrypha which was explained by observing that although not part of the Hebrew Bible, the apocrypha were still included as being useful to read.[27] Apparently, some Bible translations stemmed from Laurentius Petri's own pen, and the Hebrew original and the Vulgate are among his sources.[28] In general, Laurentius Petri considered it important that the clergy know Latin even if it was not to have any special privileged position as the vernacular Swedish was to be used in divine services.[29] Another indication of this is that some of his earlier church statutes, such as the 1566 *Hypotiposes*, are in Latin.[30] It is also possible that he wrote some of the psalms published in the psalm book of 1536. In 1573, the archbishop's sermons on the suffering and death of Jesus Christ also appeared in print.[31]

Unfortunately, neither do not know what books Laurentius Petri had in his library. We know that he had borrowed some works from Georg Norman when he translated the New Testament into Swedish, while King Gustav Vasa wished, in turn, to borrow Laurentius's Danish history written by Saxo Grammaticus.[32] However, no book inventory has been preserved after him. His library was presumably largely a mixture of theology and books related to a general humanist education. In 1588, his son-in-law Abraham Angermannus accused Petrus Michaelis Fecht (d. 1576), the secretary of Johan III and father of his Catholicizing liturgical reforms, of secretly ransacking the archbishop's private library and taking books away in the nighttime before it came to the hands of the lawful heirs. According to Abraham, the Cathedral library of Uppsala had also been emptied of Luther's works by the Jesuit Johannes Herbst.[33] The rest of Laurentius Petri's library was probably divided between his daughters as his three sons-in-law would have had use of its contents.

Two main works of Laurentius Petri were edited only posthumously by his exiled son-in-law Abraham Angermannus in Germany. "On Church Statutes and Ceremonies" [Sw. *Om Kyrkio Stadgar och Ceremonier*, 1566] was printed in

1587 in Wittenberg.[34] The Latin controversy *Refutatio erroris Herbesti* against Johannes Herbst, the Catholic chaplain of Queen Catherine Jagellonica (1526–83), from 1572 was published in Hamburg in 1588. Abraham Angermannus explained in his preface why the text of Laurentius Petri, his "dear father-in-law" (*soceri mei charissimi*), was still topical to fend against "the occult machinations" of Herbst, other Jesuits, and Petrus Michaelis Fecht (d. 1576).[35] The foundation of this work is scriptural and few Church fathers are referred to or cited - partly because Herbst is criticized for his reliance on Church Fathers rather than the Bible. Laurentius Petri argued that the tradition was Christ's slave (*seruus Christi*) and the value of tradition was dependent on this ultimate function of subjection to Christ.[36]

Archbishop Laurentius Petri was also a translator, publishing the *Postil* [Sw. Postilla, 1555], a collection of German sermons, Luther's pamphlet on the Eucharist as *Een liten vnderwijsning, huru Christet folk må warda förmanat til Sacramentet*, published in Stockholm in 1558, and possibly also the 1567 Catechism [Sw. *Catechismus*].[37] The German reformer Justus Menius's (1499–1558) *Vom Exorcismus... bei der Taufe* (1551) became known in Laurentius Petri's Swedish rendering as "Explanation on Exorcism in Baptism") in 1562.[38] Certain translated works were meant for a wider audience, for example, "Against drunkenness" [Sw. *Emoot Dryckenskap*, 1557] by Matthäus Friderich of Görlitz, (1510–59, German original first publ. 1552).[39] Laurentius Petri's *Oeconomia Christiana* (1559), is a Swedish rendering of the homonymous work (1529) by the German reformer Justus Menius (1499–1558).[40] Laurentius Petri's own "A Sermon Against Homicide" [Sw. *Een Predican emoot mandråp*, 1562] was also intended for a lay audience. [41] He authored circulars, some expressly intended for the clergy of his archdiocese of Uppsala, others for a mixed public of laymen and clerics. The former can be represented by a circular exhorting public prayer for victory against the enemies of the Realm (in practice, mainly Denmark) after the outbreak of the Nordic Seven Years' War (1563–70) in 1563, [42] and the latter by "An Exhortation to Penance and Repentance" [Sw. *Förmaning till Clerkerijt samt medh menige man om Boot och bättring och almenneliga böner*, 1558].[43]

During his work (1546–71) on various versions of the Swedish Church Ordinances, he used a number of German church ordinances as sources for his drafts and the final 1571 Swedish Church Ordinance.[44] According to Emil Färnström and Hjalmar Holmquist, the draft Church Ordinance of 1546 was influenced by the church ordinances of Wittenberg, Brandenburg-Nuremberg and Mark Brandenburg. As for the final Swedish Church Ordinance of 1571, particularly the church ordinance of Württemberg, but also of Mecklenburg and Pfalz have been recognized as some of its additional sources. Some sections have been translated almost verbatim, while others have been freely adapted to Swedish circumstances.[45] Laurentius Petri also used Justus Menius's *Von Exorcismo* (1551) and Bishop Erik Falck of Skara's (1510s–1570) *Een kort vnderwijsning* from 1558 that, in turn, was a free translation of Johannes Spangenberg's (1484–1550) *Margarita theologica* (1540).[46]

Laurentius Petri as a theologian: the example of the sacramentary controversies

The Swedish reformers—echoing Luther and others—called for a return to the Bible. However, what this meant in practice was disputable. As Laurentius Petri wrote, Christians were to act in everything in accordance with God's Word and Commandment as expressed in the Bible, while any human laws that curtailed Christian liberty were to be avoided. The true (and Biblical) tradition was essential for salvation and one had to purify all ceremonies and elements from the statutes that were not in accord with the Bible and Apostolic teaching. [47] In "An Explanation on Holy Water" [Sw. *En forclarning om Wijgdawatn*, 1538], one of his early works, he dismisses holy water as a useless and superstitious fraud, a human invention that was completely unbiblical. To its representing a long tradition in Church, he countered that "new health was to be preferred to old illnesses."[48]

After translating Luther's work on the Eucharist into Swedish, Laurentius Petri continued on the topic in his "On some points Regarding Our Lord Jesus Christ's Communion" [Sw. *Om Någor stycker wårs HERras Jesu Christi Nattward anrörandes*, 1562], written as a dialogue between two men: Christophorus, apparently his alter ego, and Georgius. The book—a response to King Erik XIV's questions on the sacrament raised at the diet of 1562—discussed opinions held by Sacramentarians, Anabaptists, and Catholics. It defended the sacramental union through the real presence of the body and blood of Christ in the Lord's Supper.[49] However, Swedish Sacramentarian controversies were only about to surface in the 1560s as part of what have traditionally been seen as Calvinist influences. This controversy came to center around the possible use of water, mead, apple juice, or other beverages in lieu of wine (hence Sw. *likvorister*), and it was partially triggered by the trade embargo during the Nordic Seven Years' War causing a lack of wine in Sweden.[50]

Laurentius Petri had to instruct his clergy how to act in case of a lack of wine in his printed pastoral letter from 1564. He considered the lack of wine a general divine punishment of the Realm of Sweden caused by the many grave sins of its inhabitants. As such, the affliction had to be borne patiently. No other beverage could replace the wine, as the Archbishop demonstrated with the authority of the Bible and Church Fathers. Thus, the Eucharist had to be canceled if no wine (or somewhat watered-down wine) was available. Neither could bread be replaced by apples, pears, or other comestibles. In this eventuality, the dying, whose salvation was not dependent on the Sacrament, were to be comforted by the Word of God.[51] King Erik XIV consulted the bishops of Strängnäs and Västerås as well as Laurentius Petri concerning the implications of the lack of wine, and wine was delivered from the royal cellars for sacramental use.[52] Yet the debate continued with Bishop Johannes Nicolai Ofeegh of Västerås (ep. 1562–74), who, while adhering to the archiepiscopal policy, cited Augustine, Martin Luther, Lucas Lossius (1508–82), Erasmus of Rotterdam (1466–1536) and David Chytræus (1530–1600) suggesting that if there was no wine, other liquids could be used. Ofeegh justified his position by his conviction that it was better to give communion in water than wholly omit the sacrament, the solace of the believers, in the time of war and calamity. However, he stressed that he was suggesting the use of watered-down wine, not water, but that the type of wine or bread (wheat or rye) was irrelevant for the sacrament.[53]

In his turn, Laurentius Petri emphasized that the Bible and the word of Christ plainly spoke about bread and wine, and that no right-minded Christian was to act against the Divine Order. He quoted Church Fathers and observed that those who used water had been condemned as heretics already in Antiquity. He also accused Ofeegh in no uncertain terms of shamelessly distorting the words of Chytræus and Lossius in his "ungrounded and frivolous writing" [i.e. first circular], and suggested that his opinions had a tinge of heresy.[54] In the aftermath of the dispute, Laurentius Petri had the Swedish leading clergy, including the bishops, demonstrate their unity in the issue by having them sign the 1565 "*fundamenta fidei de sanguinis dominici partipacione*," defining the position of the Swedish Church on the topic and backed up by quotations from a list of ancient and modern authorities. Moreover, the question of the sacrament was made one of the main topics of the synod of Uppsala.[55] However, it has been assessed that as a thinker, Laurentius Petri was not "a speculative theologian." Rather, he did not dwell further on sacramental or Christological questions than he needed because of his polemicists' arguments.[56]

Generally, in addition to Martin Luther, Laurentius Petri regarded Philipp Melanchthon (1497–1560) and Johannes Brenz (1499–1570) as leading Reformation authorities (or *scriptores recentiores*).[57] For example, in his *Hypotiposes*, church statutes of 1566, Laurentius Petri referred many times to the authority of Luther and occasionally Melanchthon, while Andreas Bodenstein of Karlstadt's (1486–1541) tumultuous iconoclasm was expressly condemned.[58] Yet he has been assessed as more closely Lutheran than Melanchthonian or Brenzian, even if he demonstrated an independent mind towards even the notions of the former.[59]

Secular and ecclesiastical jurisdiction: Laurentius Petri and the two regiments

King Gustav Vasa was keen to keep the progress of the Reformation in his own hands. In 1533, he wrote Laurentius Petri, forbidding the archbishop to "pursue Reformation in any way" without consulting the King in advance about what the archbishop wanted reformed and how. The King observed that hasty "reformations" tended to cause scandal which was why any reforms had to be well considered and discussed in advance.[60] King Gustav repeated this to the Archbishop even more sharply in 1539: no reformation was to take place thereafter without the king's prior knowledge and consent nor was any printed matter to be published without prior royal authorization.[61] The king also expressly observed that Christ had meant clerics to be preachers and not lords. He stated that he would not permit bishops to regain the sword, i.e. power in other matters than spiritual ones.[62] In itself, this was in line with Laurentius Petri's thinking. He wrote that the two different offices (*embete*), the secular authorities and the servants of the Church, that had so strictly been kept apart in the Bible, had been mixed during the papacy. This was not to be.[63] Laurentius Petri held that the clerical estate was instituted solely because of sin to teach people what was sinful and reconcile sinners with God. Consequently, the clergy was not authorized to involve in temporal governance (*lekamlighit Regement*) or the management of worldly property.[64]

Again, in accordance with Luther and his followers, Laurentius Petri held that marriage matters belonged to the secular jurisdiction, and all difficult cases that could not be decided without its "sentence and authority" were to be referred to it.[65] The right to dispense justice belonged to the secular ruler: here, the Swedish king and his appointees. However, they had not adjudicated in marriage matters for a long time as only ecclesiastical judges had had them in their exclusive jurisdiction. As a result, secular judges were unexperienced in matrimonial causes, which why bishops were allowed to continue to judge cases revolving around the validity of a marriage and grant divorces until secular judges had learning and experience in such cases. [66] This also what happened in practice, and the king gave sentences and was consulted in marriage cases.[67]

Laurentius Petri considered that "God's written Law" and second to it, the Church Ordinance, provided regulations in matrimonial causes.[68] The lack of preserved records prevents a deep-going analysis of Laurentius Petri's activities as an ecclesiastical judge. However, there are some indications suggesting that even here he referred to the Bible. A case from 1571 involved the validity of the subsequent marriage of former lovers and the legitimation of their offspring thereby. Swedish secular law unequivocally authorized this and there was also long medieval canonical practice confirming the rule of legitimation by subsequent marriage. Yet, instead of referring to secular law, canon law, or the long practice of the Swedish Church, Laurentius Petri observed in his sentence that the marriage to one's former concubine was not against the Holy Scripture and God's Word and therefore was to be regarded as valid.[69]

King Gustav was intent on curtailing episcopal power and submitting the clerical estate to his authority. Consequently, he nominated Georg Norman as the superior (*ordinator och superattendent*) over bishops, prelates, and all clerics on December 8, 1539. He also appointed ordinaries (*ordinarius*), royal officials, to oversee dioceses, such as Skara in 1544.[70] In order to reduce episcopal power, dioceses were also divided into smaller entities between ordinaries and bishops. This hardly represented Archbishop Laurentius Petri's notions of an ideal ecclesiastical administrative structure, but he submitted to this, too, until the traditional dioceses under bishops were restored in the early 1570s.[71]

Laurentius Petri defended the Crown's takeover of ecclesiastical property and income by observing that the royal office required a bigger income than the episcopal office as the tasks of the latter were "performed by the word of God and not power."[72] The bishop did not need much when traveling with his retinue around his diocese to do his duty, to teach the laity and deal with the clergy, whereas royal administration required power and great expense. As both these offices were to be maintained by the consent of the common people, one was to take from the office that was lavishly provided for and to add to the one that did not have enough. Thereby, both could do their duty: the bishop to teach the Word of God and the king to punish and combat injustice, violence, and breaches of peace.[73] Secular rulers were to guarantee that the clerical estate could "freely and unhindered" preach and teach God's Word and the Gospel.[74] Canons could also concentrate only on God's Word instead of giving so much attention to "jurisdiction, hearing causes and governance" (*Jurisdiction, Sakehörelsse och Regementhe*).[75] Human statutes and decrees, constituted by the secular powers, could "often be useful and good." Yet they could also relatively frequently be lacking and against God's commandments, causing more damage than gain.[76]

Indeed, in Laurentius Petri's works, God's Word is the paramount and absolute authority.[77] For Laurentius Petri, tradition and canon law formed the battleground between God and the Devil, while the Bible and Christ acted as the beacons, or in modern terms, a litmus test, in helping to distinguish false and true traditions from each other.[78] In the 1571 Church Ordinance, Laurentius Petri argued that Swedes had not abandoned the Roman Church's statutes and ceremonies "out of ignorance in many respects".

> Rather, in truth, it was forced upon us because the papal ecclesiastical statutes, the Decrete and the Decretals, have to a large extent departed from the simplicity that is in Christ, and that anyone wanting to have and keep the right and pure Evangelical Doctrine must forsake and discard such statutes and other matters that are hindering and outrageous.[79]

According to Laurentius Petri, Catholic canon law consisted of "statutes, decretals, canons, decretals etc.," i.e. human statutes. Even if these were neither based on Holy Scripture nor express God's Commandments, prelates had considered them to be necessary and accepted them in councils and synods.[80] He stressed that Christians were first and foremost to obey God's Word and Commandments as expressed in the Bible. Christians were also to avoid human statutes that "offended one's Christian liberty." Secular and ecclesiastical statutes that were contrary to God's Commandments were not valid.[81] No "right-minded Christian congregation" could with a good conscience follow such "abominable and unchristian laws or customs."[82] After listing some of the false customs of the Catholic Church (e.g., saints, indulgences, and monastic orders) in the 1571 Church Ordinance, he queried how right-minded Christians could accept such "abominations" included in the papal canon law.[83]

However, despite his criticism of medieval canon law, Laurentius Petri considered statutes and ordinances necessary even for the spiritual regiment. Such ordinances and statutes that helped to promote "honesty, discipline and good customs" in a Christian congregation. Christian freedom and a good conscience were important, and righteous Christians happily submitted to norms based on

"God's own written law and commandments. As long as people were of flesh and blood, living in this temporal world, they needed norms".[84] Precisely because of human frailty, the Church needed statutes in order to maintain "good and proper" ecclesiastical order, discipline, and manners.[85]

Nevertheless, some old laws and ceremonies were necessary and beneficial, pertaining to a good Christian ecclesiastical governance, discipline and honesty. They also contributed to the building of the congregation in the true religion as well as to order, unity, and harmony within the Church.[86] The acceptance of such norms and ceremonies were to be discussed and investigated by the whole congregation or its appointed and ablest representatives at a general council. Thereafter, it was to be obeyed for the maintenance of good Christian governance just like towns and countries necessitated their own laws and statutes for secular governance. Those "arrogant peacocks and wayward minds" who refused to accept ecclesiastical norms and rules, abused Christian liberty. They were to be forced to obey the Church Ordinance consented to by the whole congregation both through ecclesiastical censure and secular punishment.[87]

As for the spiritual sphere, even if the secular ruler had the authority to intervene, such interference was to be exceptional as it would have encroached on the domain of the spiritual regiment. Thus, while upholding the dominance of the secular authorities, Laurentius Petri advocated and defended the independence of the spiritual sphere and the clergy. Indeed, this has been perceived as being "in marked contrast with [...] contemporary German Church Orders, which seem to assume that the secular Government will have the decisive control of the Church."[88]

The secular ruler took care of adjudication and he was also responsible for "external punishment," while bishops were only to punish with the Word of God.[89] As the secular authorities or the king had been given the sword, i.e., the power of "external punishment" over everyone without exception, explained Laurentius Petri, this meant that the clergy was to have no special *privilegium fori*. Instead they were to sue and be sued—both in person and on behalf of the Church—in ordinary courts in secular matters such as land disputes, crime, or commercial cases. Clerics could only be accused at an ecclesiastical court for spiritual matters involving the clergy, for example when accused of dereliction of duty. Because the king had the power to punish, he was also entitled to all fines for any wrongdoings.[90] Yet, as bishops and rural deans had so long collected fines, they were allowed to do so for the time being provided the fines were given to the King's use. When the custom had spread that the King was entitled to them and the royal officials had become more experienced in how such matters were dealt with, this was to change.[91]

As for secular and ecclesiastical legislation, Laurentius Petri explained that God had authorized the leaders of both the spiritual and the "worldly regiments" to enact such laws "that necessity demanded" provided these were founded on justice and truth and did not in any way go against God's Word. "Just, sensible and pious authorities" decreed such norms that served to create "good, just and proper governance for the use and good of the subjects, for discipline and honest customs, for peace and calm, for law and justice."[92]

Laurentius Petri on law and mercy, the old and new testament

In his preface to the Swedish translation of the New Testament, Laurentius Petri addressed the reader for the first time directly in the 2. singular (*må tu see til*) when he admonished the reader not to make Christ into Moses and make "a law-book out of the Gospels" as Laurentius Petri claimed his contemporaries were doing.[93] Laurentius Petri explained that people needed law since sin and death had appeared after the Fall, because of the evil of the Devil and Adam's fall. After that, the world had become so wild that people no longer knew what sin was or why there was death. Consequently, God had given Moses the law by which to instruct the world and reveal sins to the people.[94] But whereas Moses was a "law-writer and -driver" (*Laghscriffuare och driffuare*) "driving, forcing, compelling, hitting and punishing severely" in his books, according to Laurentius Petri, "Christ was your own with all his life, teaching, deeds, death, resurrection and all that he is, has, does and can do." [95]

The authorities—and all people—were bound by both the tables of the Law of Moses that were the commandments God himself had given. The secular ruler was the custodian of God's law.[96] As God authorized secular rulers (*Öffuerhet*) to adjudicate in his place and gave them "the sword in their hand as to punish the wicked and protect the good," this carried responsibilities with it. Neither were the authorities themselves permitted to sin against God's Commandments.[97] The sword was not only symbolic but meant to actually eliminate those who committed serious and scandalous crimes such as homicides, thieves and adulterers. However, God had given the spiritual authorities the word, and the disobedient were to be considered heathens and as such outside the congregation, until penance had been performed.[98]

God's law existed alongside secular law such as the Roman law (*Keysarelagh*)—Laurentius Petri probably mentioned it because of German models rather than its relevance in Sweden at the time—mostly to discipline and restrain the wicked. "This is why such law is more of a law of prohibitions rather that a law of teaching." For example, according to Laurentius Petri, is was secular law when Moses gave a letter of divorce to a wife.[99] However, both kinds of laws were measured and tempered by the law of faith and love.[100] The teaching of the decalogue was intensified during the period, and penitents were also to recite the Ten Commandments each morning and evening together with Our Father and the creed.[101] The Old Testament was a book of law, teaching people what to do and permit, while the New Testament was a book of grace and mercy.[102]

Laurentius Petri felt that those who administered justice were not

> always to insist on the law in the extreme, but occasionally temper somewhat the strictness as the conditions of the time and circumstances of the case could require. When this did not take place, the saying "supreme law is supreme injustice"[103] and this law, that otherwise is reasonable, becomes unfairly applied because of them who administered it unequitably.[104]

Furthermore, Laurentius Petri observed that the situation became even worse when laws were out-and-out misused and interpreted in another way than intended to serve the injustice of those who were supposed to apply them. Therefore, as had been said: "people were better governed by good men than good law." Unless those who applied law were pious, sensible and honest, people would not be governed well by law as it could always be distorted and misinterpreted. However, honest men would not do this.[105] Laurentius Petri seems to have been influenced by Greek philosophy here (e.g. Plato).

Even if Christ occasionally taught and gave commandments, this was not his main and true calling and reason for coming to the world. Christ did not force or compel, but persuaded kindly using expressions like "Blessed are the poor." Similarly, the apostles used expressions like "I ask" and "I exhort." The Gospels were first and foremost a sermon or proclamation of the good deeds of Christ that he had proven and dedicated to the people [us] if they [we] believe.[106] At the end, Christ gave no other commandment than love. It is through love one recognized His disciples and true Christians: where love and deeds did not appear, and follow each other, there was no true faith.[107]

Reading Laurentius Petri's texts, one gets the impression that his emphasis vacillated between God's justice and wrath and divine mercy. He answered the question why preachers claimed that God was mild, merciful, and forgiving of sins if criminals (such as homicides) were treated severely and were not to be pardoned their crimes. According to him, there was no contradiction here. The Bible was full of examples of God's mercy but it was only to be preached after Divine Justice. God's wrath and "petty corporeal sternness" did not hinder God's ever-lasting clemency: while God forbade homicides their worldly life, he did not deny them eternal life as long as they had a heartfelt regret of their sins and believed in His mercy. The example of the robber on the cross demonstrated this.[108] Moreover, worldly death for homicide was not even an act of severity, argued Laurentius Petri, but rather a great act of God's mercy towards themselves and others. In addition, by the execution of homicides and other criminals, God provided people with a warning example to fight against evil and be peaceful themselves.[109]

Even if Laurentius Petri at times stressed the wrath of God and how God hated sin, "punishing this wicked and disobedient world with scourges such as famine, pestilence and war," his message was essentially of mercy.[110] In Laurentius Petri's booklet on General Days of Prayer, he stressed that after the clergy had taught people about "God's wrath and cruelty over sin" and some trepidation had been awakened in them, they were to be taught of his mildness. While God hated sin and became irate because of it, he was by nature good and gentle. When God punished the most, he only wanted people to repent, and when this occurred, God let the punishment altogether fall or made it "light and bearable." God did not want to destroy any repentant sinner, but pardon him. While it was easy to find examples of divine wrath in the Bible, the archbishop claimed instances of God's mercy were even more plentiful. Yet God's charity was not to be used as a pretext for sinning more freely, but rather as a remedy for despair.[111]

Laurentius Petri stressed the message of the Reformation: Christ had conquered sin, death and hell for all those who believed in him and saved them, but not through human deeds, but through his own deeds, torment and death.[112] According to him:

> [N]othing could ever be more comforting for a poor person who is burdened with sin, death and hell than to hear such a precious and sweet message of Christ. Thus, her heart must delight and rejoice greatly thereof if she believes that it is the truth.[113]

While Christ's suffering and death on the cross had atoned for people's sins, they kept sinning through human frailty and the devil's inciting. Yet the gate of mercy was always open for those who repented from their heart and wanted to perform "true Christian penance."[114] Performed penance could never completely atone for sins which Christ's death alone had done. Instead, public penance served the same function as punishments in the secular court—a deterrent for the sinner and others. Moreover, it was a public demonstration of obedience and true repentance as well as an act of reconciliation with the congregation that had been scandalized by the offense.[115] Thus, the shameful and potentially painful public penalty or execution was an offered gateway to divine life through the sacrifice of Christ, repentance, and divine grace. Yet, based on a comparison between the version of 1561, the final Church Ordinance of 1571 and certain other texts, Laurentius Petri's attitudes towards penance had become harder and the sanctions more severe with time.[116]

Conclusion

It is also easy to concur with Yelverton on his assessment of Laurentius Petri's 42-year career as the first Reformation Archbishop of Sweden that he "fulfilled the duties of his high office with conspicuous courage and success in an age of kaleidoscopic change."[117] It has rightly pointed out that one cannot expect a "complete and elaborated Christian doctrine" in the work of Laurentius Petri. He was, after all, a practical clergyman and archbishop in charge of arranging the Church of the whole country in turbulent times.[118] Indeed, because of Laurentius Petri's "interests in the practically religious and the cult," he has been compared to Archbishop Thomas Cranmer (1489–1556) even if he himself may have considered Johannes Brenz to be a kindred spirit.[119] Several of his writings were prompted by topical incidents and debates in Sweden, and they became authoritative statements for the Swedish Church and society.

Laurentius Petri formulated the groundwork of the institutional and normative principles that the Swedish Lutheran Church was built upon for the following century through the 1571 Church Ordinance and his many other texts. His own family came to set the example of the new priestly model family for the Swedish clergy. Moreover, through the matrimonial alliances of his daughters, he has been identified as establishing "a dynastic system of relationships in the

Swedish episcopate" in which it has upheld "a conservative continuity" until Modernity.[120]

While Laurentius Petri has been called traditional and conservative, it makes sense to see the first Reformation decades are dogmatically somewhat fluid. During debates against various theological opponents, different themes were elaborated using slightly varying sets of authorities. In this sense, without such anachronistic labels, his perceptions have been interpreted as adhering closely to those of the German Reformers displaying mere variations of common themes. Bo Ahlberg has observed that Laurentius Petri saw that the "right tradition" was waging a two-front war against both Catholics and other Protestant thinkers, necessitating quite different strategies. His flexibility was caused by this, and consequently, he saw tradition in a consequent albeit complex way.[121] According to Remi Kick, Laurentius Petri reiterated common and fundamental Reformation tenets, but without losing his originality in the process.[122] Admittedly, Laurentius Petri was no radical Reformer and the Swedish Lutheran Church maintained many old practices and structures. Yet an adherence to scripture is first and foremost in Laurentius Petri's thinking.

When the sword and the word were separated after the Reformation, both the secular and ecclesiastical authorities had to ensure that their office was taken care of in accordance with God's word. The secular magistrates had to use the sword justly and righteously obeying God's Commandments—and Laurentius Petri insisted that the secular authorities use the death penalty for heinous crimes—while clergy was to preach penitence and divine mercy. The wrath of God was a recurring theme in Laurentius Petri's pastoral texts. All temporal scourges were caused by people's disobedience and sinfulness, and divine anger was to be placated with patience, prayer, and penance. Even when the life of the sinner had to be exterminated in accordance with God's commandment, God always extended his grace and eternal life to the genuinely repentant believer as Christ had promised the penitent thief on the cross.

It is also worth emphasizing that unlike Luther and Bugenhagen, Laurentius Petri was no university professor. Instead, his practical duties did not allow him to write many thorough treatises.[123] In addition, he was the foreman of the clergy of a vast kingdom in which centralization was only then taking place. Archbishop Laurentius Petri was first and foremost an Evangelical practical theologian who preferred justifying things with the Bible rather than law and legal sources. This is nowhere more clearly visible than in the one lonely reference to classical canon law in the treatise on consanguinity and affinity that gives the impression of being second hand. Laurentius Petri's devotion to the scripture above church law is visible in his written works as well as practical activities, as has been analyzed here. Yet he stressed that secular and ecclesiastical statutes were required to maintain a well-ordered society. He himself was responsible for creating such norms for the Swedish people during several decades using the Bible as his guiding principle in the interests of the Christian commonweal and obeying God's commands. Consequently, Swedish Protestant Church law came to be less "legal" and procedural than medieval canon law had been or German

Protestant canon law was to become. Even if Laurentius Petri was less a practical lawyer than his brother Olavus Petri and less of a *ius commune jurisperitus* than many of the Swedish clerics of the generation preceding him, he can rightfully be called one of the main "Christian jurists" of post-Reformation Sweden.

Notes

1 Eric W. Yelverton, *An Archbishop of the Reformation: Laurentius Petri Nericius, Archbishop of Uppsala, 1531–73 – A Study of His Liturgical Projects* (London: The Epworth Press, 1958), viii.

2 See, e.g. Remi Kick, *Tel un navire sur la mer déchaînée: La communauté chrétienne dans l'œuvre de Laurentius Petri, archevêque d'Uppsala (1531–1573)*, Studia Theologica Lundensia 52 (Lund: Lund University Press, 1997), 3–7. For a bibliography of Laurentius Petri's works, see ibid. 391–419.

3 The records of the Cathedral Chapter of Uppsala have not survived from this period. Nevertheless, for example, manuscript N 1908 at the Uppsala University Library contains a later transcript of a marriage sentence, dated in Uppsala on the feast of St. James (*S. Jacobi dagh*) 1571 by Archbishop Laurentius Petri. It was a relatively straightforward case in which the Archbishop confirmed the validity of the marriage of a man to his former lover with whom he had had children prior to his marriage with another woman. After his wife's death, the man proceeded to marry his ex-lover and thereby also legitimized their children—precisely according to Swedish law. This was obviously related to an inheritance dispute as the other heirs contested this sentence after the Archbishop's death making the counter-claim that the couple had had sex during the wife's lifetime rendering the union adulterous. However, Laurentius Petri's successor, Archbishop Laurentius Petri Gothus, observed that there was no evidence of this, and confirmed the earlier sentence in 1574, UUB, N 1908, fol. 55.

4 Hjalmar Holmquist, *Svenska kyrkans historia 3: Reformationstidevarvet 1521–1611*, vol. 1 (Stockholm: Svenska Kyrkans Diakonistyrelses Bokförlag, 1933), 274–75, 296; Nils Edling, ed., *Uppländska konungsdomar från Vasatiden intill Svea Hovrätts inrättande* (Uppsala: Almqvist & Wiksell, 1933), 4.5.1541, 115–18. He sat also in a royal mixed panel of judges sentencing the recalcitrant peasants of Alunda (Uppland) to a collective 4,000 mark fine for defending a pilgrimage crucifix.

5 Laurentius Petri, "Förklaring på Ordinantien som och i Westeråhrs giordes på samme tidh," *Handlingar til Sverges reformations- och kyrkohistoria under Konung Gustaf I* [hereafter *HSRKH*], vol. 1, P.E. Thyselius, ed. (Stockholm: C. A. Bagges Förlag, 1841), 84–101.

6 Emil Färnström, ed., *Laurentius Petris Kyrkoordning av år 1571* (Stockholm: Samfundet Pro fide et Christianismo, 1932).

7 Laurentius Petri, "Förspråk på thet Gamla Testamentet," *Biblia sacra, thet är All then hellgha scrifft på swensko* (Uppsala, 1541).

8 Laurentius Petri, *Om Kyrkio Stadgar och Ceremonier, Hurudana och huilka Man vthi een Christeligh församling bruka må eller ey* (Wittenberg: M. Simon Cronenberg, 1587 [1566]).

9 Olle Hellström, "Laurentius Petri," *Svenskt biografiskt lexikon* [hereafter *SBL*], vol. 22 (Stockholm: Albert Bonniers Förlag, 1979), 376–85, here 376; Gottfrid Carlsson, "Vår förste lutherske ärkebiskops Wittenbergstudier," *Kyrkohistorisk Årsskrift*, vol. 16 (1915), 42–46; Herman Lundström, "Efterskrift," *Kyrkohistorisk Årsskrift*, vol. 16 (1915), 47–49.

10 Hellström, "Laurentius Petri," 376. Cf. Yelverton (*An Archbishop*, 4) calls this "a professorship at the University of Uppsala". However, the University of Uppsala had in practice ceased to exist already in the 1510s.

11 Holmquist, *Svenska kyrkans historia 3:1*, 217–18; Peder Swart, *Konung Gustaf I:s krönika*, Nils Edén, ed. (Stockholm: Aktiebolaget Ljus, 1912), 146–47; Yelverton, *An Archbishop*, 5.
12 Yelverton, *An Archbishop*, vii.
13 Hellström, "Laurentius Petri," 376; Holmquist, *Svenska kyrkans historia 3:1*, 218; Peder Swart, *Konung Gustaf I:s krönika*, 147.
14 Hellström, "Laurentius Petri," 376. On the abolition of clerical celibacy in Sweden, see Holmquist, *Svenska kyrkans historia 3:1*, 246; Mia Korpiola, "Lutheran Marriage Norms in Action: The Example of Post-Reformation Sweden, 1520–1600," *Lutheran Reformation and the Law*, Virpi Mäkinen, ed., Medieval & Early Modern Studies 112 (Leiden: E. J. Brill, 2006), 131–69, here 136–43.
15 Laurentius Petri Gothus, *Epicoedivm in fvnere optimi adolescentis, Petri Laurentij, filij Reuerend[i] viri D. Archi[e]piscopi Vpsalensis, scriptum a L. P. Gotho* (Stockholm: 1566); Hellström, "Laurentius Petri," 376.
16 Circular to the diocese of Uppsala 20 Oct. 1566, printed in *Skrifter Och Handlingar, Til Uplysning i Swenska Kyrko och Reformations Historien* [hereafter *SHSKRH*], vol. 3, Uno von Troil, ed. (Uppsala: Tryckt hos Direct. Johan Edmans Enka, 1791), 202–30.
17 Ivan Svalenius, "Laurentius Petri Gothus," *SBL*, vol. 22 (Stockholm: Albert Bonniers Förlag, 1979), 385–87, here 385–86; N. Ahnlund, "Andreas Laurentii (Björnram)," *SBL*, vol. 4 (Stockholm: Albert Bonniers Förlag, 1924), 661–68, here 661; E. Hildebrand, "Abrahamus Andreæ Angermannus," ibid., 24–37, here 24; Hans Gillingstam, "Luth, släkter," *SBL*, vol. 24 (Stockholm: Riksarkivet, 1982–84), 440–15, here 411.
18 Hellström, "Laurentius Petri," 379.
19 Holmquist, *Svenska kyrkans historia 3:1*, 381–82.
20 Called by Yelverton (*An Archbishop*, xiii), "Church Order". However, I have chosen to call it an "ordinance".
21 Sven Kjöllerström, *Svenska förarbeten till kyrkoordningen av år 1571*, Samlingar och studier till svenska kyrkans historia 2 (Stockholm: Svenska kyrkans diakonistyrelses bokförlag, 1940), 30–34.
22 Emil Färnström, "Inledning," *Laurentius Petris Kyrkoordning av år 1571*, Emil Färnström, ed. (Stockholm: Samfundet Pro fide et Christianismo, 1932), ix–xxxi, here xi.
23 Färnström, "Inledning,"xiv.
24 For Germany, see e.g., Anneliese Sprengler-Ruppenthal, "Zur Rezeption des Römischen Rechts im Eherecht der Reformatoren," *ZRG*, KA, vol. 68 (1982), 363–418, esp. 384–92; Wilhelm Maurer, "Reste des Kanonischen Rechtes im Frühprotestantismus," *Zeitschrift der Savigny-Stiftung für Rechtsgeschichte* [hereafter *ZRG*], Kanonistische Abteilung [hereafter KA], vol. 51 (1965), 190–253; Udo Wolter, "Die Fortgeltung des kanonischen Rechts und die Haltung des protestantischen Juristen zum kanonischen Recht in Deutschland bis in die Mitte des 18. Jahrhunderts" and John Witte, Jr., "The Plight of Canon Law in the Early Dutch Republic," both in *Canon Law in Protestant Lands*, Richard H. Helmholz, ed. (Berlin: Duncker & Humblot, 1992), 13–48 and 135–64. For Sweden, see e.g. Mia Korpiola, "Kerstin Oxenstierna's Lost Maidenhead: Honour, Sin and Matrimonial Law in Late Sixteenth-Century Sweden," *Inter amicos: Liber amicorum Monique Vleeschouwers-van Melkebeek*, Michiel Decaluwé, Véronique Lambert and Dirk Heirbaut, eds., Iuris scripta historica XXVI (Brussels: Wetenschappelijk comite voor rechtsgeschiedenis, Koninklijke Vlaamse academie van België voor wetenschappen en kunsten, 2011), 243–68; Korpiola, "Lutheran Marriage Law," esp. 132–33, 160–64.
25 Färnström, "Inledning," xvi–xvii. Translation and quotation in Yelverton, *An Archbishop*, 10.

26 Holmquist, *Svenska kyrkans historia 3:1*, 231.
27 E.g., Letter of L.P. to Georg Norman, *HSRKH* 2, ed. Thyselius, 240–42; Holmquist, *Svenska kyrkans historia 3:1*, 382; *Apocry/pha./ Thet äro Böker som icke fin/nas i then Ebreiska Biblien, och äro för then/ skul icke lijka reknadha widh the andra böker i then/ helgha Scrifft, Doch nyttigha til at läsa./* (Uppsala: 1541). The apocryphical books included were: *Judith, Wijsheten; Tobias; Syrach; Baruch; Maccabeorum; Stycker aff Esther; Stycker aff Daniel.*
28 Isak Collijn, *Sveriges bibliografi intill år 1600*, vol. 2 (Uppsala: Svenska Litteratursällskapet, 1927–31), 267, 316–17.
29 E.g., Yelverton, *An Archbishop*, 24, 26; Bo Ahlberg, *Laurentius Petris nattvardsuppfattning*, Studia Theologica Lundensia 26 (Lund: Teologiska fakulteten i Lund, 1964), 96–102.
30 Laurentius Petri, "Hypotiposes, sive breves subiectiones, pro formandi moribus monistrorum Verbi Dei" *SHSKRH* 4, ed. von Troil, 221–68.
31 Laurentius Petri, *Öffuer Histo-/rien om wårs HER-/RAS Jesu Christi werdigha/ Pino och Dödh, någhra eenfalli/gha Sermoner eller Predi-/caner. Lau. Vp./ 1572* (Stockholm: Amund Laurentzson, 1573); Collijn, *Sveriges bibliografi intill år 1600*, vol. 2, 425–26.
32 Archbishop Laurentius Petri to Georg Norman, 12 Nov. 1540 and King Gustav I Vasa to Archbishop Laurentius Petri, 17 Mar. 1558, both in *HSRKH* 2, ed. Thyselius, 240–42, 406–07.
33 "Cathedralem Vpsalensem Bibliotheca*m* Herbestus Lutheri scriptis euacuauit; [...] Defuncti Archiepiscopi priuatam librariam, Fechtenius bis perlustratam antequam in manus haeredum venisset, praestantissimis lucubrationibus, & nonnullis alijs libris nudauit," Abraham Andreae Angermannus, Unpaginated preface, *Refvtatio erroris Herbesti de consecratione sacramenti evcharistici, solis Papisticis Sacerdotibus commendata. Et, quod ipsum Papisticum Sacerdotium sit Chimera & res plane ficticia: firma probatio. L. P. Vpsal. Præfixa est vna cvm praefatione historia litvrgica, seu Tractatus de Imposturis Iesuitarum [...]*, ed. Abraham Andreae Angermannus. *Authore A. A. A. Hamburgi, in officina Henrici Binderi*, 1588. On Fecht, see Bengt Hildebrand, "Petrus Michaelis Fecht," *Svenskt biografiskt lexikon*, vol. 15 (Stockholm: Albert Bonniers Förlag, 1956), 436–42.
34 Laurentius Petri, *Om Kyrkio Stadgar.*
35 Abraham Andreae Angermannus, *Refvtatio erroris Herbesti de consecratione sacramenti evcharistici* (Hamburg: Henricus B. Ginderus, 1588), unpaginated preface.
36 Bo Ahlberg, "Laurentius Petri och traditionen," *Kyrkohistorisk Årsskrift*, vol. 63 (1963), 145–97, here 179–82.
37 Laurentius Petri, *Een liten vnder/wijsning, huru Chri-/stet folk må warda förma-/nat til Sacramentet eller wårs/ HERras Jesu Christi/ Nattward./ Doc. Mar. Lut./ Vtsatt aff Tydzkon/ på Swensko./ L.P.* (Stockholm: Amund Laurentzson, 1558); Collijn, *Sveriges bibliografi intill år 1600*, vol. 2, 216–20, 239–41, 345–53.
38 Laurentius Petri, *At thet är Rett och Christelighit, bruke Exorcismum widh Döpelsen, såsom alment och aff ålder j Christenhetenne haffuer waret, och vthi wåra Församblingar än nw är plägsed. Justi Menij Förklaring, Förswenskat aff. Lau. Vp.* (Stockholm, 1562), also printed in *SHSKRH* 5, ed. Uno von Troil (Uppsala: Tryckt hos Direct. Johan Edmans Enka, 1791), 84–127.
39 Laurentius Petri, *Emoot Dryckenskap: Några wigtiga orsaker, hwarföre alla menniskior sigh wachta skola för dryckenskap. Item, Några Insagor, som Drinckare plägha förebära, och swar ther uppå. Aff Tydszkon vthsatt på Swensko. L. Up.* (Stockholm: Amund Laurentzson, 1560), also printed in *SHSKRH* 5, ed. von Troil, 27–81; Collijn, *Sveriges bibliografi intill år 1600*, vol. 2, 216–20, 232–33.
40 Laurentius Petri, "Oeconomia Christiana: Om Cristeligit Husholdh och huadh huario person eientligh effter gudz befolningh i huusholl tilkommer," *SHSKRH* 5, ed. von Troil, 27–81.

41 Laurentius Petri, *Een Predican emoot mandråp, Stelt öffuer thet femte Bodhordet, Tu skalt icke dräpa* (Stockholm: Amund Laurentzson, 1562); Collijn, *Sveriges bibliografi intill år 1600,* vol. 2, 300.

42 Collijn, *Sveriges bibliografi intill år 1600,* vol. 2, 316. For other examples of such circulars, see ibid., 335–36; Circular to the diocese of Uppsala 24 Apr. 1573, printed in *SHSKRH* 5, ed. von Troil, 243–50.

43 Laurentius Petri, *Förmaning til Clerkerijt samt medh menige man om Boot och bättring och almenneligha böner* (Uppsala, 1558), also printed in *SHSKRH* 5, ed. von Troil, 1–18; Collijn, *Sveriges bibliografi intill år 1600,* vol. 2, 241–43.

44 Färnström, "Inledning," xi. For a summary in English of the Swedish Church Ordinance of 1571, see Yelverton, *An Archbishop,* 53–94.

45 Färnström, Emil, *Om källorna till 1571 års kyrkoordning särskilt med hänsyn till tyska kyrkoordningar.* (Uppsala: Almqvist & Wiksell, 1935), esp. 7–8, 280–82; Färnström, "Inledning," xii–xiii; Holmquist, *Svenska kyrkans historia 3:1,* 211.

46 Sven Kjöllerström, *Striden kring kalvinismen i Sverige under Erik XIV: En kyrkohistorisk studie,* Lund universitetets årsskrift, N. F. Avd. 1, 31:5 (Lund: Lund University, 1935), esp. 45, 129; Holmquist, *Svenska kyrkans historia 3:1,* 358.

47 E.g. Laurentius Petri, *Om Kyrkio Stadgar,* 3–6.

48 Laurentius Petri, "En forclarning om Wijgdawatn," *SHSKRH* 4, ed. von Troil, 113–48, esp. 115–16, 148; Collijn, *Sveriges bibliografi intill år 1600,* vol. 2, 60–61.

49 Laurentius Petri, *Om Någor stycker wårs HERras Jesu Christi Nattward anrörandes* (Stockholm: Amund Laurentzson, 1562), see Collijn, *Sveriges bibliografi intill år 1600,* vol. 2, 299. Printed in *SHSKRH* 4, ed. von Troil, 149–220; Ahlberg, *Laurentius Petris nattvardsuppfattning,* 88–90, 118–30, also ibid., 174–87, 214–32; Kjöllerström, *Striden kring kalvinismen,* esp. 86–91.

50 Kjöllerström, *Striden kring kalvinismen,* esp. 197–252; Ahlberg, *Laurentius Petris nattvardsuppfattning,* 53–79.

51 Archbishop Laurentius Petri's letter to the clergy of the diocese of Uppsala, 14 Feb. 1564, *SHSKRH* 3, ed. von Troil, 173–90, esp. 181–88; Collijn, *Sveriges bibliografi intill år 1600,* vol. 2, 320. On comforting the sick in the Swedish tradition, see Stina Fallberg Sundmark, *Sjukbesök och dödsförberedelse: sockenbudet i svensk medeltida och reformatorisk tradition.* Bibliotheca theologiae practicae 84 (Skellefteå: Artos, 2008).

52 Kjöllerström, *Striden kring kalvinismen,* 201–25.

53 The two circulars of Ofeegh are printed in *SHSKRH* 3, ed. von Troil, 191–95 and 224–42, see esp. 193–95, 239–37.

54 Archbishop Laurentius Petri, 8 July 1564, printed in *SHSKRH* 3, ed. von Troil, 195–224, esp. 198–202, 207, 224.

55 Both printed in *SHSKRH* 3, ed. von Troil, 248–77.

56 Ahlberg, *Laurentius Petris nattvardsuppfattning,* 250.

57 E.g., Ahlberg, *Laurentius Petris nattvardsuppfattning,* 157–61.

58 Laurentius Petri, "Hypotiposes", e.g. 228, 238, 257.

59 Holmquist, *Svenska kyrkans historia 3:1,* 227; Ahlberg, *Laurentius Petris nattvardsuppfattning,* 236–54.

60 Gustav I Vasa's open letter to Archbishop Laurentius Petri, 11 Nov. 1533, *HSRKH* 2, ed. Thyselius, 40–42, here 42.

61 Gustav I Vasa's letter to Archbishop Laurentius Petri, 24 Apr. 1539, *HSRKH* 2, ed. Thyselius, 113–18, here 117.

62 Gustav I Vasa's letter to Archbishop Laurentius Petri, 24 Apr. 1539, *HSRKH* 2, ed. Thyselius, 113–18, here 115: "*thet wij skulle lathe kommat ther till, ath Bisperne schole återfå swerdett igen, thet behöffue i jnthet tenckie.*"

63 "Til läsaren," *Laurentius Petris kyrkoordning,* ed. Färnström, 19; Laurentius Petri, *Een Christeligh Predican om werdzligh öffwerheet* (Stockholm: Amund Laurensson, 1561), Bij[v].

64 Laurentius Petri, "Förspråk på thet Gamla Testamentet," fol. Aij^{v}.
65 Laurentius Petri, *Om förbudhen skylskap och swågerskap Een liten vnderwijsning Ther aff gott Christet folck och må haffua förwarning at the icke byggia ächtenskap vthi förbodhna ledher* (Uppsala, 1572), fol. Dviij.
66 Laurentius Petri, "Förklaring på Ordinantien," 88.
67 See, e.g., Korpiola, "Lutheran Marriage Law," 134–45.
68 Laurentius Petri, *Om förbudhen skylskap*, fol. Dviij.
69 UUB, N 1908, fol. 55: "*icke ähr emot then helghe skrifft och Gudz ord, och moste för then skull wara godt och gilt*". For the Swedish law and practice, see Mia Korpiola, "The Deathbed Marriage of Karl Knutsson Bonde: Legitimation by Subsequent Marriage, Property and Family Strategies in Late Medieval Sweden," *Tijdschrift voor Rechtsgeschiedenis*, vol. 80 (2012), 129–55.
70 Gustav I Vasa's authorization, 8 Dec. 1539, *HSRKH* 2, ed. Thyselius, 122–26, here 124.
71 E.g., Gustav I Vasa's authorization, 26 Feb. 1544, *HSRKH* 2, ed. Thyselius, 199–202; Hjalmar Holmquist, *Svenska kyrkans historia 3: Reformationstidevarvet 1521–1611*, vol. 2 (Stockholm: Svenska Kyrkans Diakonistyrelses Bokförlag, 1933), 7–10.
72 Laurentius Petri, "Een forklaring och Uthtydelse på Westeråhrs Recess, aff hwadt orsaak och Grund, han giord war," *HSRKH* 1, ed. Thyselius, 69–83, here 72: "*ty Biskopz embetter drijfues medh Gudz ordh, och icke medh wälde.*"
73 Laurentius Petri, "Een forklaring och Uthtydelse på Westeråhrs Recess," 73.
74 "Til läsaren," *Laurentius Petris kyrkoordning*, ed. Färnström, 19. On Laurentius Petri's notions on the duties of the ecclesiastical and secular authorities, see also Kick, *Tel un navire*, 347–65 and passim.
75 Laurentius Petri, "Een forklaring och Uthtydelse på Westeråhrs Recess," 75.
76 Laurentius Petri, *Om Kyrkio Stadgar*, 6–7.
77 Ahlberg, *Laurentius Petris nattvardsuppfattning*, 29.
78 Ahlberg, "Laurentius Petri och traditionen," 192. On the Devil in Laurentius Petri's works, see, e.g. Kick, *Tel un navire*, 68, 72–73, 76, 114–15, 121–23, 140–41, 143, 146, 148, 153–54.
79 "Til läsaren," *Laurentius Petris kyrkoordning*, ed. Färnström, 6.
80 Laurentius Petri, *Om Kyrkio Stadgar*, 7.
81 E.g. Laurentius Petri, *Om Kyrkio Stadgar*, 9–10, 12–13, 15v–16.
82 Laurentius Petri, *Om Kyrkio Stadgar*, 65v–66.
83 "Til läsaren," *Laurentius Petris kyrkoordning*, ed. Färnström, 7. See also Laurentius Petri, *Om Kyrkio Stadgar*, 67–87v.
84 "Til läsaren," *Laurentius Petris kyrkoordning*, ed. Färnström, 10.
85 Laurentius Petri, *Om Kyrkio Stadgar*, 88
86 Laurentius Petri, *Om Kyrkio Stadgar*, 15–16, 17–18, 20–21: "*nödhtorfftiga and helsosamma Stadgar och Ceremonier som höra til itt Christeligit gott kyrkio Regement, och hielpa till församblingennes vpbyggekse vthi sanskylliga Religion*" (quotation on 15).
87 Laurentius Petri, *Om Kyrkio Stadgar*, 15–16, 17–18, 20–21, 30–30v, quotation on 15.
88 Hellström, "Laurentius Petri," 377; Yelverton, *An Archbishop*, 10.
89 Laurentius Petri, "Förklaring på Ordinantien," 90.
90 Laurentius Petri, "Förklaring på Ordinantien," 86–92, 97.
91 Laurentius Petri, "Förklaring på Ordinantien," 86–92, 97.
92 Kjöllerström, *Striden kring kalvinismen*, xvii; Hellström, "Laurentius Petri," 377; Yelverton, *An Archbishop*, 10.
93 Laurentius Petri, "Förspråk på thet Nyia Testamentet," in *Biblia sacra, thet är All then hellgha scrifft på swensko* (Uppsala, 1541), fol. Aij^{v}.
94 Laurentius Petri, "Förspråk på thet Gamla Testamentet," fol. Aij^{v}.
95 Laurentius Petri, "Förspråk på thet Nyia Testamentet," fol. Aiij.

96 "Til läsaren," *Laurentius Petris kyrkoordning*, ed. Färnström, 17.
97 Laurentius Petri, *Een Predican emoot mandråp*, Aiiij.
98 See, e.g. Kick, *Tel un navire*, 268.
99 Laurentius Petri, "Förspråk på thet Gamla Testamentet," fol. Aiii^{v}.
100 Laurentius Petri, "Förspråk på thet Gamla Testamentet," fol. Aiii^{v}: "*all annor Lagh skola och moste haffua sijn reglo och mått aff troonne och kärlekenim.*"
101 Kick, *Tel un navire*, 264–65.
102 Laurentius Petri, "Förspråk på thet Gamla Testamentet," fol. Aij-Aij^{v}.
103 Here Laurentius Petri referred to the famous saying "*Summum ius, summa iniuria*" of Cicero (*De Officiis*, I, 10).
104 Laurentius Petri, "Förklaring på Ordinantien," 99–100.
105 Laurentius Petri, "Förklaring på Ordinantien," 100.
106 Laurentius Petri, "Förspråk på thet Nyia Testamentet," fol. Aiij.
107 Laurentius Petri, "Förspråk på thet Nyia Testamentet," fol. Aiij.
108 Indeed, the example of the salvation of the penitent and believing robber on the cross was mentioned many times in various Laurentius Petri's texts, see e.g. Kick, *Tel un navire*, 73–80, 238.
109 Laurentius Petri, *Een Predican emoot mandråp*, Gviij^{v}.
110 Laurentius Petri, *Förmaning til Clerkerijt samt medh menige man*, 5.
111 Laurentius Petri, *Förmaning til Clerkerijt samt medh menige man*, 8–10.
112 Laurentius Petri, "Förspråk på thet Nyia Testamentet," fol. Aij^{v}
113 Laurentius Petri, "Förspråk på thet Nyia Testamentet," Aij: "*Så kan jw nu een fattigh menniskia, som medh syndenne, dödhen och heluetet bekayat är, intet tröstelighare någhon tijdh få höra, än sådana dyrbar, och ljuffligħit bodhskap om Christo, Ty moste ock hennes hierta stoorligha fröghdas och glädhias ther öffuer, om hon ellies troor, at så j sanning är.*"
114 "Om syndaboot och scriffermål," *Laurentius Petris kyrkoordning*, ed. Färnström, 65–66. On penance in Laurentius Petri's writings, see also Kick, *Tel un navire*, esp. 210–87.
115 E.g. "Om vppenbara scrifft," *Laurentius Petris kyrkoordning*, ed. Färnström, 78–79.
116 E.g. Kick, *Tel un navire*, 280–81.
117 Yelverton, *An Archbishop of the Reformation*, vii.
118 Ahlberg, *Laurentius Petris nattvardsuppfattning*, 11.
119 Holmquist, *Svenska kyrkans historia 3:1*, 227–28, 390.
120 Yelverton, *An Archbishop*, 18.
121 Ahlberg, "Laurentius Petri och traditionen," 183, 191, 193.
122 Kick, *Tel un navire*, 376–77.
123 Kick, *Tel un navire*, 377.

Manuscripts

UUB [Uppsala University Library, Uppsala, Sweden], N 1908.

Sources

Angermannus, Abraham Andreae, *Refvtatio erroris Herbesti de consecratione sacramenti evcharistici* (Hamburg: Henricus Ginderus, 1588).

Apocrypha. Thet äro Böker som icke finnas i then Ebreiska Biblien, och äro för then skul icke lijka reknadha widh the andra böker i then helgha Scrifft, Doch nyttigha til at läsa. (Uppsala, 1541).

Edling, Nils, ed., *Uppländska konungsdomar från Vasatiden intill Svea Hovrätts inrättande* (Uppsala: Almqvist & Wiksell, 1933).

Färnström, Emil, ed., *Laurentius Petris Kyrkoordning av år 1571* (Stockholm: Samfundet Pro fide et Christianismo, 1932).

Petri, Laurentius, *At thet är Rett och Christelighit, bruke Exorcismum widh Döpelsen, såsom alment och aff ålder j Christenhetenne haffuer waret, och vthi wåra Församblingar än nw är plägsed. Justi Menij Förklaring, Förswenskat aff. Lau. Vp.* (Stockholm: 1562).

Petri, Laurentius, *Een Christeligh Predican om werdzligh öffwerheet* (Stockholm: Amund Laurensson, 1561).

Petri, Laurentius, "Een forklaring och Uthtydelse på Westeråhrs Recess, aff hwadt orsaak och Grund, han giord war," *Handlingar til Sverges reformations- och kyrkohistoria under Konung Gustaf I*, vol. 1, P.E. Thyselius, ed. (Stockholm: C. A. Bagges Förlag, 1841), 69–83.

Petri, Laurentius, *Een liten vnder/wijsning, huru Chri-/stet folk må warda förma-/nat til Sacramentet eller wårs/ HERras Jesu Christi/ Nattward./ Doc. Mar. Lut./ Vtsatt aff Tydzkon/ på Swensko./ L.P.* (Stockholm: Amund Laurentzson, 1558).

Petri, Laurentius, *Een Predican emoot mandråp, Stelt öffuer thet femte Bodhordet, Tu skalt icke dräpa* (Stockholm: Amund Laurentzson, 1562).

Petri, Laurentius, *Emoot Dryckenskap. Några wigtiga orsaker, hwarföre alla menniskior sigh wachta skola för dryckenskap. Item, Några Insagor, som Drinckare plägha förebära, och swar ther uppå. Aff Tydszkon vthsatt på Swensko. L. Up.* (Stockholm: Amund Laurentzson, 1560).

Petri, Laurentius, "En forclarning om Wijgdawatn," *Skrifter Och Handlingar, Til Uplysning i Swenska Kyrko och Reformations Historien*, vol. 4, Uno von Troil, ed. (Uppsala: Tryckt hos Direct. Johan Edmans Enka, 1791), 113–48.

Petri, Laurentius, "Förklaring på Ordinantien som och i Westeråhrs giordes på samme tidh," *Handlingar til Sverges reformations- och kyrkohistoria under Konung Gustaf I*, vol. 1, P.E. Thyselius, ed. (Stockholm: C. A. Bagges Förlag, 1841), 84–101.

Petri, Laurentius, *Förmaning til Clerkerijt samt medh menige man om Boot och bättring och almenneligha böner* (Uppsala: 1558).

Petri, Laurentius, "Förspråk på thet Gamla Testamentet," in *Biblia sacra, thet är All then hellgha scrifft på swensko* (Uppsala: 1541).

Petri, Laurentius, "Förspråk på thet Nyia Testamentet," in *Biblia sacra, thet är All then hellgha scrifft på swensko* (Uppsala: 1541).

Petri, Laurentius, "Hypotiposes, sive breves subiectiones, pro formandi moribus monistrorum Verbi Dei," *Skrifter Och Handlingar, Til Uplysning i Swenska Kyrko och Reformations Historien*, vol. 4, Uno von Troil, ed. (Uppsala: Tryckt hos Direct. Johan Edmans Enka, 1791), 221–68.

Petri, Laurentius, "Oeconomia Christiana: Om Cristeligit Husholdh och huadh huario person eientligh effter gudz befolningh i huusholl tilkommer," *Skrifter Och Handlingar, Til Uplysning i Swenska Kyrko och Reformations Historien*, vol. 5, Uno von Troil, ed. (Uppsala: Tryckt hos Direct. Johan Edmans Enka, 1791), 27–81.

Petri, Laurentius, *Om förbudhen skylskap och swågerskap Een liten vnderwijsning Ther aff gott Christet folck och må haffua förwarning at the icke byggia ächtenskap vthi förbodhna ledher* (Uppsala: 1572).

Petri, Laurentius, *Om Kyrkio Stadgar och Ceremonier, Hurudana och huilka Man vthi een Christeligh församling bruka må eller ey* (Wittenberg: M. Simon Cronenberg, 1587 [1566]).

Petri, Laurentius, *Om Någor stycker wårs HERras Jesu Christi Nattward anrörandes* (Stockholm: Amund Laurentzson, 1562).

Petri, Laurentius, *Öffuer Historien om wårs HERRAS Jesu Christi werdigha Pino och Dödh, någhra eenfalligha Sermoner eller Predicaner. Lau. Vp. 1572* (Stockholm: Amund Laurentzson, 1573).

Petri Gothus, Laurentius, *Epicoedivm in fvnere optimi adolescentis, Petri Laurentij, filij Reuerend[i] viri D. Archi[e]piscopi Vpsalensis, scriptum a L. P. Gotho* (Stockholm, 1566).

Swart, Peder, *Konung Gustaf I:s krönika*, Nils Edén, ed. (Stockholm: Aktiebolaget Ljus, 1912).

Thyselius, P.E., ed., *Handlingar til Sverges reformations- och kyrkohistoria under Konung Gustaf I*, vol. 2 (Stockholm: C. A. Bagges Förlag, 1844–45).

von Troil, Uno, ed., *Skrifter Och Handlingar, Til Uplysning i Swenska Kyrko och Reformations Historien*, vol. 3 (Uppsala: Tryckt hos Direct. Johan Edmans Enka, 1791).

von Troil, Uno, ed., *Skrifter Och Handlingar, Til Uplysning i Swenska Kyrko och Reformations Historien*, vol. 5 (Uppsala: Tryckt hos Direct. Johan Edmans Enka, 1791).

Literature

Ahlberg, Bo, "Laurentius Petri och traditionen," *Kyrkohistorisk Årsskrift*, vol. 63 (1963), 145–97.

Ahlberg, Bo, *Laurentius Petris nattvardsuppfattning*, Studia Theologica Lundensia 26 (Lund: Teologiska fakulteten i Lund, 1964).

Ahnlund, N., "Andreas Laurentii (Björnram)," *Svenskt biografiskt lexikon*, vol. 4 (Stockholm: Albert Bonniers Förlag, 1924), 661–68.

Carlsson, Gottfrid, "Vår förste lutherske ärkebiskops Wittenbergstudier," *Kyrkohistorisk Årsskrift*, vol. 16 (1915), 42–46.

Collijn, Isak, *Sveriges bibliografi intill år 1600*, vol. 2 (Uppsala: Svenska Litteratursällskapet, 1927–31).

Färnström, Emil, "Inledning," *Laurentius Petris Kyrkoordning av år 1571*, Emil Färnström, ed. (Stockholm: Samfundet Pro fide et Christianismo, 1932), ix–xxxi.

Färnström, Emil, *Om källorna till 1571 års kyrkoordning särskilt med hänsyn till tyska kyrkoordningar* (Uppsala: Almqvist & Wiksell, 1935).

Gillingstam, Hans, "Luth, släkter," *Svenskt biografiskt lexikon*, vol. 24 (Stockholm: Riksarkivet, 1982–84), 440–15.

Hellström, Olle, "Laurentius Petri," *Svenskt biografiskt lexikon*, vol. 22 (Stockholm: Albert Bonniers Förlag, 1979), 376–85.

Hildebrand, Bengt, "Petrus Michaelis Fecht," *Svenskt biografiskt lexikon*, vol. 15 (Stockholm: Albert Bonniers Förlag, 1956), 436–42.

Hildebrand, E., "Abrahamus Andreæ Angermannus," *Svenskt biografiskt lexikon*, vol. 4 (Stockholm: Albert Bonniers Förlag, 1924), 24–37.

Holmquist, Hjalmar, *Svenska kyrkans historia 3: Reformationstidevarvet 1521–1611*, vol. 1–2 (Stockholm: Svenska Kyrkans Diakonistyrelses Bokförlag, 1933).

Kick, Remi, *Tel un navire sur la mer déchaînée: La communauté chrétienne dans l'œuvre de Laurentius Petri, archevêque d'Uppsala (1531–1573)*, Studia Theologica Lundensia 52 (Lund: Lund University Press, 1997).

Kjöllerström, Sven, *Striden kring kalvinismen i Sverige under Erik XIV: En kyrkohistorisk studie,* Lund universitetets årsskrift, N. F. Avd. 1, 31:5 (Lund: Lund University, 1935).

Kjöllerström, Sven, *Svenska förarbeten till kyrkoordningen av år 1571*, Samlingar och studier till svenska kyrkans historia 2 (Stockholm: Svenska kyrkans diakonistyrelses bokförlag, 1940).

Korpiola, Mia, "Kerstin Oxenstierna's Lost Maidenhead: Honour, Sin and Matrimonial Law in Late Sixteenth-Century Sweden," *Inter amicos: Liber amicorum Monique Vleeschouwers-van Melkebeek*, Michiel Decaluwé, Véronique Lambert and Dirk Heirbaut, eds., Iuris scripta historica XXVI (Brussels: Wetenschappelijk comite voor rechtsgeschiedenis, Koninklijke Vlaamse academie van België voor wetenschappen en kunsten, 2011), 243–68.

Korpiola, Mia, "Lutheran Marriage Norms in Action: The Example of Post-Reformation Sweden, 1520–1600," *Lutheran Reformation and the Law*, Virpi Mäkinen, ed., Medieval & Early Modern Studies 112 (Leiden: E. J. Brill, 2006), 131–69.

Korpiola, Mia, "The Deathbed Marriage of Karl Knutsson Bonde: Legitimation by Subsequent Marriage, Property and Family Strategies in Late Medieval Sweden," *Tijdschrift voor Rechtsgeschiedenis*, vol. 80 (2012), 129–55.

Lundström, Herman, "Efterskrift," *Kyrkohistorisk Årsskrift*, vol. 16 (1915), 47–49.

Maurer, Wilhelm, "Reste des Kanonischen Rechtes im Frühprotestantismus," *Zeitschrift der Savigny-Stiftung für Rechtsgeschichte*, Kanonistische Abteilung, vol. 51 (1965), 190–253.

Sprengler-Ruppenthal, Anneliese, "Zur Rezeption des Römischen Rechts im Eherecht der Reformatoren," *Zeitschrift der Savigny-Stiftung für Rechtsgeschichte*, Kanonistische Abteilung, vol. 68 (1982), 363–418.

Sundmark, Stina Fallberg, *Sjukbesök och dödsförberedelse: sockenbudet i svensk medeltida och reformatorisk tradition.* Bibliotheca theologiae practicae 84 (Skellefteå: Artos, 2008).

Svalenius, Ivan, "Laurentius Petri Gothus," *Svenskt biografiskt lexikon,* vol. 22 (Stockholm: Albert Bonniers Förlag, 1979), 385–87.

Witte, John, Jr., "The Plight of Canon Law in the Early Dutch Republic," *Canon Law in Protestant Lands*, Richard H. Helmholz, ed. (Berlin: Duncker & Humblot, 1992), 135–64.

Wolter, Udo, "Die Fortgeltung des kanonischen Rechts und die Haltung des protestantischen Juristen zum kanonischen Recht in Deutschland bis in die Mitte des 18. Jahrhunderts," *Canon Law in Protestant Lands*, Richard H. Helmholz, ed. (Berlin: Duncker & Humblot, 1992), 13–48.

Yelverton, Eric W., *An Archbishop of the Reformation: Laurentius Petri Nericius, Archbishop of Uppsala, 1531-73 – A Study of His Liturgical Projects* (London: The Epworth Press, 1958).

8 The Christian jurisprudence of Niels Hemmingsen (1513–1600)

Mattias Skat Sommer and Morten Kjær

Introduction

Niels Hemmingsen stands out as the single-most important figure among the second generation of Danish reformers. A student at the Wittenberg *Leucorea* in the 1530s, he did not participate in the king's introduction of a Wittenberg-style reformation in Denmark in 1536, sanctioned by the Wittenberg circle and overseen by Johannes Bugenhagen (1485–1558). However, he returned to his native Denmark in the early 1540s to take up a professorship of arts in Copenhagen. Obtaining degrees in theology at Copenhagen, he was transferred to the Faculty of Theology in the 1550s. Until his eventual suspension from office in 1579, Hemmingsen not only expounded the Bible for future Lutheran pastors in the university but also was a close adviser to the kings of Denmark-Norway (Christian III, r. 1534–59, and Frederik II, r. 1559–88) in matters legal and moral.

Noting that Hemmingsen did not abandon either medieval provincial laws or canon law as sources of law, this chapter argues that for the rulers to govern and pursue their confessionalizing policies, they could not completely break from the legal tradition that Luther himself called un-Evangelical or even Antichrist. They needed scholars with legal competency. In this chapter, we focus on Hemmingsen as one of these scholars. First, we outline Hemmingsen's biography and the general characteristics of his theology. Second, we discuss Hemmingsen's understanding of natural law and of Martin Luther's so-called teaching of the three estates—pivotal elements in the Danish reformer's vision of ordering post-Reformation Danish-Norwegian society. This part deals with Hemmingsen's view of the basic elements of society. Third, we focus on Hemmingsen's view of marriage law, centering on his understanding of the legal hierarchy and on the impact of the 1582 Ordinance of Marriage.

Hemmingsen's life and thought in context

Early life and student years

Niels Hemmingsen was born in 1513, probably on June 4, near the village Errindlev, situated on Lolland, a Danish island in the Baltic Sea.[1] Not much is known of his adolescence. His parents died when he was a young boy, so he was raised by other family members. After he had attended grammar schools in the towns of Nakskov, Nykøbing, and Slagelse, he was enrolled at the chapel school at the Cathedral of Roskilde during the early 1530s, before he eventually became a pupil at the chapel school at Lund, the Danish archbishopric. During these years, a Lutheran reformation in the Danish-Norwegian realm was in the pipeline.

However, at the time of the introduction of the princely reformation from above in the territories of Christian III during 1536–37, Hemmingsen left his native country. Provided with financial resources from a noble family, Hemmingsen enrolled at the Wittenberg *Leucorea* in the winter term of 1537–38, as many of his compatriots had done before him. He resided in the town until the early 1540s, and during his stay, he may have heard Martin Luther's exegesis of the Book of Genesis, in which the Reformer profoundly expounded the teaching of the so-called three estates. Between 1535 and 1545, Luther lectured on the Bible's first book, though often interrupted by outbreaks of plague and political and theological negotiations. Hemmingsen resided in Wittenberg until 1542, which means that he would have listened to Luther's elucidations of Genesis 17–28.[2] Luther had begun to develop his social teachings in the early 1520s, but it was only during the late 1530s that they reached their mature shape. According to Luther, God in creation had structured the world in such a way that it was to be governed by three *Stände* (estates), namely *ecclesia*, *politia*, and *oeconomia*—the church, secular authority, and the household. When Luther expounded upon Genesis 27:28–29 (Jacob receiving the blessing from his father, Isaac), he stated that God's blessing took a threefold shape, namely, the three "hierarchies" of home, state, and church. According to Luther's understanding, the structure of the divine blessing becomes the pattern for the vocation imposed by God on all human beings, who must respond to the call by which God bids them to act in the world.[3]

During Hemmingsen's stay in Saxony, a theological controversy regarding Christian living broke out in Wittenberg. The Eisleben schoolmaster Johann Agricola (1492–1556) came to Wittenberg and there taught his understanding of Luther's basic theology: that only the gospel and not the law was the ethical guiding light for a Christian life. Luther, however, disagreed with Agricola, stressing not only in the Genesis lectures but also in publications like *Wider die Antinomer* (1539) that the law was an essential element of doctrine because it taught human beings the fear of God. Works could never merit salvation, but they were nevertheless pleasant to God and crucial for the maintenance of a good, public order. Thus, it was necessary that pastors preach the law along with the gospel since the church was a body of sinners and righteous alike. Luther also claimed, as he had done already in *On Secular Authority* (1523), that the law applied to all human beings, regardless of whether they were Christians or not. Philipp Melanchthon (1497–1560) agreed with Luther, and in the 1535 reworking of his dogmatic textbook *Loci Communes* (first printed in 1521), he advocated—as did John Calvin (1509–64) throughout the various versions of his *Institutes* from 1536 onwards—a threefold use of the law: civil, theological, and pedagogical, pertaining, respectively, to creating discipline in society, to convicting human conscience of sin and pointing towards the gospel, and to making justified Christians do good works.[4]

As Melanchthon wrote, the first use coerces human nature to discipline, the second use highlights sin, and the third use teaches human beings what good works are and how they please God.[5] He would even refine Luther's argument and claim, "natural law is knowledge of divine law, which is engrafted in the human nature. Nothing is better and more beautiful . . . than the fact that God has imprinted his effigy and image of his sapience in the human mind."[6] Drawing on humans' prelapsarian conditions and God as creator, Melanchthon considered the mind to have a remnant of the divine effigy and thus to hold the ability to do good and shun evil. This is the sum of the natural law, and even if the ancient, pagan philosophers taught its precepts, it finds the pithiest expression in the Decalogue. In a 1537 sermon on John 1:18, delivered when Luther stood in for Bugenhagen, who was residing in Denmark, the Reformer followed Melanchthon's understanding and distinguished between two kinds of knowledge of God: one guided by the gospel towards divine grace, and one guided by reason, which knows God "according to natural law and Moses, because the law is inscribed in our hearts."[7]

Melanchthon, however, did not adopt Luther's estates teaching, and likewise, Luther did not teach *triplex usus legis*. Nevertheless, they shared the opinion that natural law—what Melanchthon and Calvin saw in the "first use" and what Luther saw in the three estates—functioned as a pattern for the formulation of the positive laws of a Christian society; thus their teachings contained the possibility that the theological concept of law could be transformed into a legal one. Furthermore, the reformers believed that it was the duty of the magistracy, as the servant of the church, to implement this transformation, though they framed it in different terms.[8] Driven by the assumption that it was possible to organize a Christian society by use of the natural law, the estates teaching served as a discursive regulator when early modern Lutheran jurists and theologians pondered social order.[9] The "Christian" society envisioned by the Lutherans did not first and foremost pertain to the citizens who inhabited it; they might, after all, be labeled Christians simply because they lived in a territory in which Christianity was the prevailing and only legitimate religious practice, and not because of their personal piety. Rather, the term pertained to the notion that religious reform should affect all aspects of social life, not only ecclesiastical practice. As we are going to show, these seeds sown at Wittenberg had a lasting impact on Hemmingsen and his work in Denmark-Norway.

Hemmingsen as a professor and policy adviser

After he had concluded his studies in Wittenberg by receiving a master's degree in arts, Hemmingsen returned to Denmark in 1542 and was installed as a professor of Greek in Copenhagen. Prior to his return, the university had been reformed according to Bugenhagen's measures and after the Wittenberg statutes, functioning as a vocational school for future Danish-Norwegian pastors and civil servants. Hemmingsen himself was not yet formally a theologian, and even though he ministered to the congregation at the Church of the Holy Ghost beginning in 1547, it was only after his acquisition of a bachelor's degree in theology in 1553 (to which he added a doctorate in 1557) that he became eligible to give lectures in the theological faculty. In the year in which he obtained the doctoral degree by a public defense attended by Christian III and his brother-in-law, the Saxon elector August (r. 1553–86), he also received a canonry at the Cathedral of Roskilde. Holding this office enjoined him to act as a legal judge in matrimonial cases since the cathedral chapters together with the local royal official functioned after 1542 as matrimonial courts.[10] Four times, he was elected university rector, and during 1572, he also acted as the university's vice-chancellor.

The duties incumbent on the university rector and vice-chancellor entailed that Hemmingsen govern the property and estates of the university and preside at disputations and business meetings of the university senate. As a professor, he was responsible for pastoral training, and beginning in the mid-1550s he published a number of textbooks and sermon collections intended for students of theology and for pastors, covering not only the areas of exegesis and doctrine but also jurisprudence. In accord with the ecclesiastical tradition of the Middle Ages, theology was not conceived of as independent from jurisprudence, economics, and politics; consequently, Hemmingsen's theological works are full of references to questions about social life, as shown below. Even as a theology professor, Hemmingsen had to deal with secular matters, and in this regard, the Reformation did not bring an end to medieval jurisprudence.[11] He exerted enormous influence on students: for example, some of his pupils would translate his Latin books into Danish for general readers; records from visitations show that the superintendents recommended that pastors follow Hemmingsen's theology; and his sermon collections were used as a model for pastors' preparations of their own sermons. The 1561 outline to a new church ordinance for the realm (which, however, failed) even stipulated that copies of Hemmingsen's sermon collection and his *Enchiridion*, the handbook of doctrine, were to be included in every pastor's library.[12]

His works were printed not only in Copenhagen. A great many of his books were published by Lutheran printers in the German empire and, from the 1570s onwards, by non-Lutheran Protestants around Europe, most remarkably in England, the Swiss Confederation, and the Low Countries. Hemmingsen soon became one of the leading figures among European divines and one whom both Lutheran and non-Lutheran scholars would cite.[13]

To Hemmingsen, the work of a professor of theology was one of building up the church of God. This meant that a professor was to secure "consensus in doctrine and faith," that is, "the pristine gospel," which is the "very fundament."[14] The idea of consensus in doctrine and faith was central to the Danish-Norwegian religious policies during Hemmingsen's years, and as a professor, he was one of those who were to ensure the consensus, for example by censorship of books. Bugenhagen's Danish church ordinance made it crystal clear that no books could be printed in the king's realm without the approval of the university professors and the superintendents.[15] The theological polemics and discord of German Lutheranism that followed in the wake of Luther's death in 1546 were regarded with suspicion by Christian III and his son and successor, Frederik II. According to them, nothing was more harmful to the gospel and Christian society than religious strife, which therefore had to be eschewed by all means.

Contrary to the history of German Lutheranism during the latter half of the sixteenth century, Danish-Norwegian Lutheranism was predominantly characterized by religious concord, owing not least to the theologians' acceptance and furtherance of the royal irenic policies. The ideology of peace drove the kings to deliberately ignore differences between Luther's and Melanchthon's approaches, and the situation of "confessional competition" witnessed in the empire was effectively avoided by allowing only the Lutheran confession in the Danish-Norwegian territories. This policy notwithstanding, Danish-Norwegian academia in the latter part of the sixteenth century was quite liberal, and the king did not show any particular interest in imposing confessional regimentation on the scientific and intellectual milieu.[16] For example, despite strict regulations on censure, books by Hemmingsen and other Danish-Norwegian authors were still seen into print, even when they espoused doctrines quite close to Reformed doctrine.

The politics concerning adherents of foreign confessions was different from that concerning the king's own scholars: in 1553, Marian refugees from the Dutch Reformed Church in London, headed by Jan Łaski (1499–1560), arrived in Kolding and Copenhagen, but owing to their non-Lutheran beliefs about the Eucharist, at the behest of Christian III and with the blessing of his theologians, they were not granted residence.[17] Some years later, Hemmingsen was the key driver behind two attempts during the reign of Frederik II to secure confessional uniformity. With the 1561 *Confessio precipuorum doctrine ac fidei ecclesiarum danicarum* and *Ordinatio ministerii ecclesiastici in inclyto regno Daniæ*, Hemmingsen endeavored to replace Bugenhagen's church ordinance, not least driven by Frederik II's wish to imitate the German Lutheran princes' struggle to establish unity in religion at the Naumburg diet, which convened in the same year.[18] This attempt failed; the 1537/39 church ordinance was kept in force (only to be replaced by the Danish National Law in 1683). But the confessional document shows an affinity towards Melanchthonite Lutheranism, for example by stressing a threefold use of the law, not mentioning Christ's ubiquity in the understanding of the Eucharist, and specifically addressing the question of sanctification.[19] Confronted with the rising number of Dutch, English, and Scottish immigrants to Danish towns, which—according to the king—caused doctrinal and ceremonial quarrels, Frederik ordered Hemmingsen to draft the *Twenty-Five Articles on Religion*, or *Strangers' Articles*, in 1569; these were subsequently printed in Danish, German, and Latin and made law.[20] Like the 1561 *Confessio*, the *Strangers' Articles* ventilated Hemmingsen's Melanchthonite sentiment. If foreigners failed to subscribe to and let themselves be examined on the articles (plus the ancient creeds and the Augsburg Confession), they would face banishment from the realm; moreover, Frederik's preamble ruled that a refusal to go into exile or a subsequent breach of the articles would result in not only forfeiture of property but also capital punishment.

Ironically, Hemmingsen himself ultimately fell victim to religious policy. Even though he executed the king's wish to implement religious regimentation in the realm, he corresponded with leading figures in Reformed Protestantism, and beginning in the 1570s, he adopted some of their sentiments in his theology of the Lord's Supper and stressed his basic Melanchthonite criticism of the doctrine of ubiquity. In Lutheran Saxony, Hemmingsen's books were still used frequently, but the electorate did not look favorably on the developments in Copenhagen. In a bitter fight between the two parties that came into existence after Luther's death (the so-called Gnesio-Lutherans and Philippists), Elector August tried to eradicate all tendencies towards Reformed doctrine, whose proponents were looked on as fifth columnists. He called on his brother-in-law to take remedial action, but eventually Hemmingsen only slightly changed his position and adhered to his basic Melanchthonite attitude of the *variata* version of the Ausgburg Confession, which relaxed the notion of Christ's bodily real presence in the Eucharist. In 1579, Hemmingsen was suspended and transferred to his canonry in Roskilde, where he lived for the remainder of his life.[21] Neither Frederik nor his successors on the throne, however, joined the party of conservative Lutheranism evolving around 1580, and the Book of Concord was never (and still is not) received as one of Danish and Norwegian Lutheranism's confessional documents, unlike in neighboring Sweden.

Indeed, various evidence suggests that despite the suspension, Hemmingsen never fell from grace at court. His Melanchthonite Lutheranism would come to characterize the theological climate for the rest of the century, and after his passing his body was even interred in the Cathedral of Roskilde, which Frederik II had made the sepulchral church of his line. An internationally renowned academic, Hemmingsen was cherished as a "highly deserving man," as his slab reads, and in the funeral sermon, Bishop Peder Winstrup (1549–1614) commended him as the "Light of Denmark."[22]

Hemmingsen's social theology: natural law and three estates

Hemmingsen's various offices established him as a public theologian and jurist, that is, an agent active in the state building of early modern Denmark-Norway—not as a politician but as one who theologically and legally underpinned the confessional policies of the Danish-Norwegian Reformation kings. One should not be too eager to interpret the policies as mere expressions of the will to power in the kings, in that "confessionalization" was more than a set of political decisions. Confessionalization entailed a certain discourse and certain agents who propounded such discourse.[23] In the case of early modern Denmark-Norway, Hemmingsen's discourse of confessionalization was informed by natural law and the three estates.

In 1562 Hemmingsen published his synthesis of natural law, the *De lege naturae*. Introducing the topic on the law, Melanchthon had written in his 1521 *Loci*: "With regards to the natural laws, I have not yet seen anything worthily written, neither by the theologians nor the lawyers."[24] One could say that with his synthesis of natural law, Hemmingsen tried exactly to fill this gap detected by his old teacher. To be sure, there is also something truly Melanchthonite about Hemmingsen's statement that God has impressed in human beings a "firm knowledge of the principles of cognition and action." Reason uses these principles to the "governance of human life, so that the human being may know, want, choose, and do the right things and avoid the opposite." According to Hemmingsen, the cogitative principles are rooted in the conscience. Because of its universality, natural law was a resource to which all people had access. Therefore, it could function as a legal basis when human beings wrote their own laws, since it pertains to justice, "which sustains the homes, the cities, the provinces, and the realm."[25] In Hemmingsen's view, a prudent ruler kept this in mind. Some years after he had published the *De lege naturae*, he prefaced court chaplain Niels Nielsen Kolding's (1525–78) *The Most Extraordinary Stories, Sentences, and Examples*—a book that lauded the prudent rule of Frederik II and collected Bible passages regarding secular authority. Here, Hemmingsen pondered natural law and established its connections to all sorts of offices in the world, in a way similar to what Max Weber aptly noted as the core of the "Protestant ethic":

> It is expedient that everybody who has been called to an office (whether in house, church, or secular authority) knows the rule by which he shall conduct himself, and that he sees before his eyes the examples by which the said rule is painted, as it were, and expressed. Thus, he does not only understand by means of the rule what he ought to do, but sees by means of the examples how he should do so. Rule therefore gives *Sapientiam*, that is, wisdom of what is right and what is wrong. Example gives *Prudentiam*, that is, cautiousness and reason, so that he heeds when and where he does the right things and averts the wrong.[26]

To Hemmingsen, each person had to follow his or her conscience, onto which natural law was engrafted. In short, one's Christian living had certain inherent moral standards. This means that in Hemmingsen's vision of a Christian society, one's dealings were to conform to Christian doctrine. In concord with Melanchthon's *Loci*, Hemmingsen taught that Christians—being justified by their faith in Christ—were sanctified, "the human heart is softened, and the natural stubbornness (which comes from original sin) is put away. The human being sets itself to be obedient towards God according to reason, which has been infused in the heart by the Holy Spirit."[27]

Hemmingsen's 1563 exegetical commentary on the Letter of James establishes a relationship between these moral standards and social life by discussing a critical challenge most people encountered, namely the use and abuse of money. Hemmingsen dealt with this problem in his discussion of James 5, which contains, in Hemmingsen's words, an indictment of the wealthy, a request for patience toward the poor, a prohibition of thoughtless oaths, a casuistic doctrine, and a praise of various offices. Verses 1–6 belong to the first theme, the accusation of the wealthy. According to Hemmingsen, however, the warning does not refer to all wealthy people, but only to those who, as he wrote, treat the poor inhumanely by misusing their fortunes or spending them on pleasures and delights.[28] Hemmingsen judges such behavior as unlawful, contrasting these self-serving practices with the lawful ones instituted by God, of which there are only three, namely, the political, the economical, and the ecclesiastical, as determined in the First and the Fourth Commandments of the Decalogue. These three offices open up a variety of callings—pastors, civil servants, paterfamilias, domestic workers, traders, and bankers. The only criterion for these vocations is that they should serve the church of God, the house, or the political order. This makes both the vocations themselves and the office holders lawful.[29] According to Hemmingsen, everyone is free to choose a way of life, but a distinction between public and private offices is to be observed. The public office requires a so-called ordinary authority; one must be lawfully called by the authorities to hold a public office, whereas one can choose for oneself a private office, for example, the office of a merchant.[30] In executing an office, faith and love (*fides et caritas*) should be ruling principles, so that God will not be offended, and so that no person will be treated with injustice. The reality, however, proves different, since the majority uses wealth badly. Yet there were some good men—prudent rulers—who understood to use their fortunes for the public good: namely, David, Josiah, and Hezekiah; and, outside biblical history, Roman emperors Constantine (r. 306–37) and Theodosius I (r. 379–95); Johann Friedrich, Duke of Saxony (r. 1547–54); and finally, Christian III, King of Denmark-Norway. They all worked to glorify God by preserving schools and godly teachers.[31]

Hemmingsen's Christian jurisprudence

The reformation and the law of marriage

One of the most important areas of law affected by the Reformation in 1536 was the law of marriage. Prior to the Reformation, marriage had been regulated by canon law, but with the abolition of canon law in 1536 a new law of marriage was needed in Denmark-Norway. The church ordinance contained only a few substantial rules on marriage, and it was not until 1582 that the Ordinance of Marriage of Frederik II provided a substantial legal framework on the law of marriage. Until then, advice on the law of marriage was needed. While Johannes Bugenhagen provided such advice in his 1540 treatise on marriage, the most influential piece of advice was to come from Niels Hemmingsen. He elaborately discussed the matter in his 1557 *Enchiridion*, but we are going to concentrate on two of his weightier publications. While his treatment in the *Enchiridion* was largely informed by theological discourse, his later publications on the subject included substantial legal reflections as well.[32]

As a judge in the matrimonial court, Hemmingsen had firsthand knowledge of marriage law, and in 1572 he published two books on marriage—one in Danish and one in Latin. The Danish book was published first and was a more general book on marriage. Hemmingsen had three principal purposes for the book: namely, (1) to educate people on marriage in general, (2) to encourage all people to honor marriage, and (3) to make both secular and spiritual authorities punish sexual offenses more severely. The book thus contained rules concerning marriage, betrothal, and divorce along with arguments in favor of harsher punishments and more general advice on married life. Hemmingsen concluded the book with an address to each of the three estates on how to promote and defend marriage.[33]

The Latin book was a judicial dissertation on the law of marriage and was aimed at the judges of the marital courts. This was apparent from the title of the book: "A little book on marriage, broken betrothals, and divorce to help those brothers who are judges in marriage cases in the realms of Denmark and Norway."[34] Both books became very popular and were published in five editions, the last dating from the mid-seventeenth century.[35]

A Protestant legal hierarchy

The abolition of canon law led to the important question as to which legal sources the new law of marriage should be based upon. Hemmingsen gave an initial response in the beginning of his Latin book, rejecting the definitions of marriage offered by Roman law and canon law, and pointing instead to the definition given by Moses in the Bible.[36] The foundation of the law of marriage must thus be found in the Bible and not in the legal sources of *ius commune.* Hemmingsen later returned at length, however, to the subject of a legal hierarchy in both the Danish and Latin book. He did so in relation to his discussion of incest.[37] This question was pressing in the king's territories in 1572 because Frederik II was about to—and later that year did—marry his cousin. Such a marriage was contrary to canon law, which prohibited incest in the first four degrees and supplemented this prohibition with a ban on spiritual kinship. The marriage was also contrary to the law in Denmark-Norway, in that the 1537/39 church ordinance limited the prohibition to the first three degrees and abolished the prohibition of spiritual kinship (as demonstrated in the chapter on Bugenhagen herein). In his books, Hemmingsen was thus confronted with the challenge of defending the possible marriage of the king, and in doing so he outlined what can be called a Protestant legal hierarchy. In the Danish book, he did this with a clear reference to the possible marriage of Frederik II, while in his Latin book, he discussed the problem in more general terms.[38] In his discussion of a Protestant legal hierarchy, Hemmingsen distinguished between divine law and human law. The starting point for Hemmingsen is divine law—God's law—and then he discusses three different sources of human law, namely, canon law, Roman law, and national law.

God's law is binding, and the king is not allowed to make exceptions to the rules therein. For incest, God's law can be found in Leviticus 18, and

Hemmingsen stated that this prohibition applied not only to the Israelites but to all humankind, because of its status as natural law. This was a common view among the Protestant reformers and lawyers.[39] In this case, Hemmingsen used natural law as an argument for the binding nature of a rule in Mosaic law and its status as part of God's law. Throughout his books, Hemmingsen was very keen to stress that the demands of God's law and natural law are identical, and this explains why Hemmingsen does not include natural law as a separate source of law in his legal hierarchy.[40]

With regard to Mosaic law, however, it is less clear to what extent Hemmingsen believed it to be binding as natural or divine law. In his books, Hemmingsen often argued in favor of the rules in Mosaic law, but it is not always clear whether he did so because he believed them to be binding or because they could be used as a source of inspiration.[41] In this way, his use of Mosaic law is similar to Luther's, who preferred the solutions in Mosaic law so often that Ernst Troeltsch could accuse him of forgetting his principal stand that Mosaic law was not binding and was secular legislation similar to the German *Sachsenspiegel*.[42] In some cases, however, Hemmingsen was very clear, and in a lengthy paragraph he refused the acceptance of polygamy in Mosaic law because it is contrary to Matthew 19 and nature.[43] In the present case, Hemmingsen stated that the prohibition of incest in Leviticus 18 did not cover the second degree and thus such marriage could be allowed.

Canon law is not binding on Christians because "the pope is the true Antichrist." This initial rejection of canon law was, however, softened in Hemmingsen's books, most clearly in the Danish version, where he immediately added, "But if there is something in the pope's law that is useful, then we follow it."[44] Hemmingsen thus referred explicitly and with approval to canon law and Gratian when defining incest and calculating the forbidden degrees.[45] His stand on canon law reflects the development in Denmark-Norway, where canon law principles often were adopted in the new secular legislation issued by king and council after the Reformation. In general, it was unproblematic to incorporate principles from canon law into the new secular legislation; should they conflict with the new Lutheran principles, they were quickly abandoned, as exemplified by the abolition of the prohibition of spiritual kinship, which was universally criticized by the reformers. The turn to canon law reflects a similar development in the German lands. The influence from canon law in the Danish realm was, however, clearly limited. It was only used as a source of inspiration; it was not used as a binding source of law, and as such it could not prevent a marriage in the second degree.[46]

Roman law was identified as the law of the emperor and probably included both *Corpus iuris civilis* and the later legislation of the Holy Roman Empire. Roman law was, however, only binding on the emperor's subjects and only so long as it was not contrary to the demands of God. Since Denmark-Norway was not a part of the Holy Roman Empire, the subjects were thus obliged to obey their own territorial secular authority—the king—and not the emperor. As with canon law, Roman law could be used as a source of inspiration, and it sometimes expressed natural law.[47] Hemmingsen's view is in accordance with the use of Roman law in Denmark-Norway: while it was part of the curriculum at the University of Copenhagen from its foundation in 1479 and continued to be so after the Reformation, Roman law was never used as a binding source of law.

National law is the last source of human law considered by Hemmingsen.[48] In the Latin book, national law was only shortly identified as *propriae nationum leges*, but in the Danish book Hemmingsen provided a much more thorough definition. The law (*loven*) consists of either custom that had been kept for a long time or legislation issued by the prince. This definition is identical to the classical definition of law (*ius*) provided by Gratian.[49] In *De lege naturae*'s dedicatory letter to Erik Krabbe (1510–65), a member of the council of the realm, Hemmingsen praised his patron for his effort to unite the Danish medieval provincial laws in a single code, a "just body"—which, however, was only realized with the 1683 Danish National Law and the 1687 Norwegian National Law of King Christian V (r. 1670–99)—stating that the "differences among the peoples" required "some laws here, others there." For without the law ("the norm of justice"), the commonwealth cannot use "its parts, its tendons, its bloods, and its limbs."[50] Hemmingsen did not explicitly include case law in the definition of law, but as a judge in the marital courts, he had firsthand knowledge of it, and he referred directly to case law from the marital court at Roskilde as an argument for the correct calculation of degrees of incest.[51] In contrast to the other sources of human law, Hemmingsen, as in *De lege naturae*, stressed that national law varies from each country, and thus in some countries marriage is prohibited in the first three degrees and in others in the first four. Because of the Lutheran teaching of obedience to the secular authority, the subjects of a country are bound to uphold the national law, and thus the subjects in Denmark-Norway have a religious duty to follow the national law of their realm. In Denmark-Norway the national law consisted of the prohibition of marriage within the first three degrees found in Bugenhagen's church ordinance. This law must be followed at the risk of "God's wrath" and "vengeance and punishment by the authority." The end of obedience was for Hemmingsen—following the general Reformation principle—the Word of God. If national law is contrary to "God's law," it is not binding. Hemmingsen, then, was a classical proponent of Christian natural law.[52]

Hemmingsen was also not shy about criticizing both national legislation and legal practice in Denmark-Norway, thus proving that even though books were censored, some criticism was allowed in the king's territories. This was particularly clear in his Danish book on marriage and was in accordance with his wish for more severe punishment for sexual offenses. In his foreword to the Danish book, he argued in favor of harsh penalties for both adulterers and violators of virgins. According to §60 in the 1558 Recess of Kolding, adultery, defined as unfaithfulness of a married man or woman, was punished with the loss of property the first time, local banishment the second time, and death the third time.[53] The first two sanctions, of course, were milder than the death penalty prescribed in Mosaic law. If a man seduced a virgin, he had to pay nine marks to her guardian and a small fine to the local authority. Hemmingsen directly compared the latter punishment with the far more severe punishment of thieves, who commonly were hanged:

> He who steals a sheep or a pig is hanged from the gallows, but he who steals the honor of poor parents' daughters, he is acquitted when he has given nine marks. Also, he brags about it, as if he had done well. God help that authority would reconsider this case.[54]

The death penalty for thieves was not found in Mosaic law but had been accepted by the reformers since Mosaic law in general was not binding, and thus the secular authority was allowed to punish more severely than prescribed by Mosaic law.[55] Since the secular authority was willing to use a harsher punishment for stealing than Mosaic law prescribed, Hemmingsen could argue for the similar punishment for what he believed were more severe crimes, such as fornication or adultery—cases in which national legislation was milder than Mosaic law.

Hemmingsen also criticized legal practice, especially when authorities pardoned criminals for offenses, like bigamy and incest, that should be punished with death. Capital punishment was directly prescribed by the law of God, and as a logical consequence of its status in Hemmingsen's legal hierarchy, he would not allow any dispensation from this punishment.[56]

The legal hierarchy Hemmingsen thus established in his discussion on incest in his two books on marriage can be systematized in the following order:

Legal hierarchy	*Latin terminology*	*Binding*	*Dispensations*	*Inspiration*
God's law	*Deus legem*[57]	Yes	–	–
National law	*Propriae nationum leges*	Subordinate to God's law	Yes	–
Canon law	*Pontificae leges*	–	–	Yes
Roman law	*Imperatoriae leges*	–	–	Yes

Based on this hierarchy Hemmingsen offered a solution to the question of marriages in the second degree—and, in particular, the prospect of the marriage of Frederik II.[58] A marriage in the second degree was not contrary to God's law but only to national law. While national law was entitled to impose a wider prohibition, it was possible to dispense with it. Such dispensation should be given only in limited cases and to princes. This dispensation could be granted since it was not against God's law or the well-being of the subjects, and since such marriages indeed could benefit the country. Ironically, this solution mirrored the practice in canon law, in which dispensations often were given to nobility or princes with the aim of securing peace. Such dispensations to princes were explicitly mentioned in the conclusions from the Council of Trent.[59] In a Danish-Norwegian context, Hemmingsen's solution and his legal hierarchy were clearly reflected in the 1582 Ordinance of Marriage II-1–2. After affirming the prohibition of marriage in the first three degrees in II-1, II-2 continues:

> This prohibition is necessary because of important reasons, however, with the exception of princes, who can be allowed to be married if they [the marital parties] both are [related] in the third or second degreed, because this is not contrary God's law, and it does not happen without special reasons.[60]

This paragraph is clearly based on Hemmingsen's work and leads us to the discussion of Hemmingsen's impact on the ordinance.

The 1582 Ordinance of Marriage

While Hemmingsen's book on marriage was an important and needed theological and juridical contribution at the time, his lasting legacy in Danish-Norwegian legal history lies in its result—that is, the 1582 Ordinance of Marriage. In that year, the king and council finally provided a clear and exhaustive legal framework for the new law of marriage with extensive rules on betrothal, marriage, and divorce. The work of formulating the ordinance began in 1579, when the superintendents with the theologians at the University of Copenhagen were asked to draft a law of marriage. That same year, they gathered in Copenhagen to prepare the draft. Unfortunately, neither the draft nor other sources of the preparatory work have been handed down to us. On June 19, 1582, the work was finished, and hence, king and council could issue the Ordinance of Marriage.[61]

While it is unknown to what extent Hemmingsen himself took part in the drafting of the ordinance, there is no doubt that the Ordinance of Marriage was based on Hemmingsen's Latin book on marriage. In his nineteenth-century edition of the Ordinance, V.A. Secher listed the source of its paragraphs and thus carefully showed which were based on Hemmingsen's book. Besides paragraphs lacking apparent sources, the Ordinance to a lesser degree uses foreign legislation, such as the 1573 *Visitations- und Consistorialordnung* of Brandenburg, Bugenhagen's 1542 Pomeranian church ordinance, and the 1561 *Les ordonnances ecclesiastiques de l'église de Geneve*. The Ordinance is divided into six parts, and the use of Hemmingsen's work in each part is systematized in the box below:

Chapter	*Paragraphs based on Hemmingsen*	*Total paragraphs*
I (on betrothal)	1	8
II (on betrothal—the rules of incest)	5	6
III (on betrothal—breaking betrothals)	5	8
IV (on fornication)	1	7
V (on divorce)	3	3
VI (special cases)	7	11
Total	22	43

That 22 out of 43 paragraphs of the Ordinance are based either directly or in part on Hemmingsen's Latin book shows his substantial influence on the law of marriage. Mind you, the fact that Hemmingsen was suspended from his chair in the Faculty of Theology did not hamper his influence.

Hemmingsen's influence is most obvious with regard to the rules on incest, breaking betrothals, divorce, and the final chapter on special cases. In contrast to the other chapters of the Ordinance, this chapter focuses on solving a number of particular and difficult cases that might arise in the marital court, and many of the paragraphs are extremely closely modeled on Hemmingsen's discussion of such special cases at the end of his book. By giving this list of special cases, Hemmingsen was most likely using his own experience as a judge in the marital court, an experience the Ordinance valued.[62] Even in cases where Hemmingsen's work was not directly used, other paragraphs show his influence. His wish for a more severe punishment for fornication was, for example, accommodated in IV.5, which prescribed that in the case of a man having seduced multiple virgins or widows of good reputation, a "God-fearing authority" should not let this go unpunished, and the man should be punished with the regular fine—and further sentenced to the mercy of the authority, which was authorized to punish him with a severe penalty, including death.

Article IV.7 also shows familiarity with Hemmingsen's work. If a man raped multiple women and did not marry one of them (cf. IV.6), he was to be executed "according to God's and natural law." This use of God's and natural law as an identical and binding source of law was a hallmark of Hemmingsen's legal writings.

The Ordinance of Marriage reflected many of the demands by Protestant reformers for changes in the old canon-law foundation of marriage. In accordance with the reformers' demands as well as Hemmingen's book, divorce was possible; and according to Chapter 3, the three primary reasons for divorce were adultery, desertion—the unwarranted abandoning of the spouse—and impotence.[63] The rules of incest in II.1–4 clearly reflected Hemmingsen's legal hierarchy. The prohibition of marriage within the first three degrees of affinity and consanguinity was kept, but as in Hemmingsen, articles II.2 and VI.1 stressed the difference between this prohibition in human, that is, national legislation and the prohibition in God's law. Unlike Hemmingsen, who defined in detail the prohibition of incest in God's law according to Leviticus 18, the ordinance did not include such a definition. The legislation only stressed that it did not cover relations in the second degree. It is unknown why an exhaustive definition was omitted, but perhaps the omission provided the authority with a wider margin of appreciation in legal practice going forward.[64] Unsurprisingly, canon law was not quoted as a legal source in the ordinance, but its principles were nevertheless applied to a great extent: even with many rules differing from canon law, such as the possibility of divorce, the continued prohibition of incest within the first three degrees as well as the rules of the calculation of degrees are clear examples of this.

The ordinance is not only a testimony to Hemmingsen's influence and the close relation between theology and law. We should not forget that in some ways the ordinance deliberately differed from Hemmingsen's views. While it accommodated his wish for harsher punishment for fornication, it did not change the punishment of adultery, which continued to be milder than in Mosaic law. The ordinance did not specify the punishment for either incest or bigamy, but among the list of special cases, VI.1 and VI.8 both presupposed the death penalty for incest only if it was contrary to God's law. Both paragraphs are based on Hemmingsen's work and deal with resolving marital problems if the authority decides to pardon the offender. While Hemmingsen in both cases argued in favor of the death penalty and rather polemically criticized the use of pardons, the corresponding paragraphs in the ordinance miss this critique and continue to rely on the fact that the authority can pardon, even if pardon—in the case of incest—would be contrary to God's law and in violence with legal hierarchy. In the end, there were still differences between theology and law, between the wishes of the theologian Niels Hemmingsen and the wishes of the legislating king and council.[65]

Conclusion

The Ordinance of Marriage can be viewed as a testimony to Hemmingsen's status as one of the great Christian jurists in the Nordic countries. At a time when theology and law were closely related—if not intertwined—it was only natural that he was a theologian. From his experiences in Wittenberg and the encounters with Luther and Melanchthon, he learned that it was possible to envision a Christian society, namely, one governed by natural law, where life flourished in God's three estates. Those of his students in Copenhagen who became authors of devotional literature themselves were active in disseminating their teacher's social thought to a broad readership.[66]

Nevertheless, during the following century his legacy was compartmentalized and in fact became more influential in jurisprudence than in theology proper, at least in national terms. As noted, Hemmingsen did not completely lose influence, even after the suspension in 1579, but when the theologians began to embrace Gnesio-Lutheranism in favor of Philippism, Hemmingsen was no longer a necessary authority. Preparing for the centenary of Luther's Reformation in 1617, the new rising star among the Danish divines, Bishop Hans Poulsen Resen (1561–1638) realized that Hemmingsen's unorthodox beliefs—for example, regarding the Eucharist and Christology—made it impossible to preserve the memory of the *preceptor Daniae* without damaging true Christianity.[67] Outside Denmark-Norway, however, Hemmingsen was still looked upon as a theological resource, though not primarily by those of his own confession. His liberal attitudes toward the Eucharist, and even predestination (he followed Melanchthon on this point rather than Luther and Calvin), apparently appealed more to Reformed Protestants than to his Lutheran brethren. In England, his works were immensely popular after the 1570s, and in the Dutch Republic the Remonstrant party defended themselves against their opponents by referring to the Danish professor. As late as 1651, English church historian Thomas Fuller (1608–61) praised Hemmingsen for his "wit and worthy parts."[68] However, none of these foreign interpreters took any interest in Hemmingsen's legal thought.

Things were otherwise in Denmark-Norway: when the prohibition of incest in God's law finally was defined in legislation with an ordinance of June 16, 1637, the definition was identical to what Hemmingsen had offered in his works, which were the likely source of inspiration for the ordinance. Some thirty years later, the final version of the legal dictionary *Glossarium juridicum Danico-Norvegicum* defined affinity with a reference to Hemmingsen.[69]

The Ordinance of Marriage had a lasting impact throughout Denmark-Norway. In 1587 it was issued in Iceland, and in 1589 in Norway.[70] It was, moreover, the primary source for the chapter on marriage in the 1683 Danish National Law and the 1687 Norwegian National Law. These national laws are a remarkable testimony to Hemmingsen's lasting impact on the legal history of the realm. The history of the law of marriage in early modern Denmark-Norway is also the history of Niels Hemmingsen.

Notes

1 Regarding Hemmingsen's biography, see Mattias Skat Sommer, "Hemmingsen, Niels," in *The Encyclopedia of Martin Luther and the Reformation*, vol. 1, ed. Mark A. Lamport (Lanham, MD: Rowman & Littlefield, 2017), 323–25; Trygve R. Skarsten, "Hemmingsen, Niels," in *The Oxford Encyclopedia of the Reformation*, vol. II, ed. Hans J. Hillerbrand (New York: Oxford University Press, 1996), 222–23; and Jens Glebe-Møller, "Niels Hemmingsen," in *Dansk Biografisk Leksikon online* (Copenhagen: Gyldendal, 1979–84), http://denstoredanske.dk/index.php?sideID=291107 (accessed 28 August 2017).

2 Martin Brecht, *Martin Luther, vol. 3: The Preservation of the Church 1532–1546* (Philadelphia, PA: Fortress Press, 1993), 134–41; regarding the chronology, see Peter Meinhold, *Die Genesisvorlesung Luthers und ihre Herausgeber* (Stuttgart: W. Kohlhammer, 1936), 132–37.

3 Martin Luther, *Enarratio in Genesin* (1535–45), in *Luther's Works: American Edition, vol. 5: Lectures on Genesis Chapters 26–30*, ed. Jaroslav Pelikan (Saint Louis, MO: Concordia Publishing House, 1968), 138–39; Gustaf Wingren, *Luthers lära om kallelsen*, 2nd ed. (Lund: C.W.K. Gleerup, 1948), 210–23.

4 Sachiko Kusukawa, "Melanchthon," in *The Cambridge Companion to Reformation Theology*, ed. David Bagchi and David C. Steinmetz (Cambridge: Cambridge University Press, 2004), 57–67, at 59–61; I. John Hesselink, *Calvin's Concept of the Law* (Allison Park, PA: Pickwick Publications, 1992), 217–76.

5 Philipp Melanchthon, *Loci Communes* (1535), in *Corpus Reformatorum: Philippi Melanthonis opera quae supersunt omnia, vol. 21: Loci Theologici*, ed. H.E. Bindseil (Braunschweig: Schwetschke, 1854), 405–06; cf. John Calvin, *Institutio Christianae Religionis* (1559), II.7.6–12, in *Joannis Calvini Opera Selecta*, vol. III, ed. Peter Barth and Wilhelm Niesel (Munich: Chr. Kaiser, 1928), 332–37.

6 Melanchthon, *Loci Communes* (1535), 398–99: "Lex naturae est notitia legis divinae, naturae hominis indita. Nec est quicquam in tota rerum natura melius ac pulchrius . . . quam quod Deus hanc suam effigiem et imaginem suae sapientiae humanis mentibus impressit."

7 Martin Luther, *Etliche Capitel S. Johannis* (1537), in *D. Martin Luthers Werke, Schriften*, vol. 46 (Weimar: Hermann Böhlaus Nachfolger, 1912), 669:

> Das ist das rechte und gruͤndliche erkentnis, weise und gedancke von Gott, welwchs genennet wird das erkentnis der Gnaden und warheit, die Evangelische erkentnis Gottes, aber sie wechst in unserm Garten nicht, die Vernunfft weis nicht

ein troffen davon, zur lincken hand kan sie Gott kennen nach dem Gesetz der natur und nach Mose, denn dass Gesetz ist uns ins hertz geschrieben.

8 James M. Estes, *Peace, Order and the Glory of God: Secular Authority and the Church in the Thought of Luther and Melanchthon 1518–1559* (Leiden: Brill, 2005). See also the article on Bugenhagen in this volume regarding the implications of the Lutheran-Melanchthonite social theology on the 1537/39 Danish church ordinance.
9 John Witte Jr., *Law and Protestantism: The Legal Teachings of the Lutheran Reformation* (Cambridge: Cambridge University Press, 2002), 200; cf. Luise Schorn-Schütte, *Evangelische Geistlichkeit in der Frühneuzeit* (Gütersloh: Gütersloher Verlagshaus Gerd Mohn, 1996), and Martin Heckel, *Staat und Kirche nach den Lehren der evangelischen Juristen in der ersten Hälfte des 17. Jahrhunderts* (Tübingen: Mohr Siebeck, 1968).
10 Regarding this, see the article on Bugenhagen in the present volume.
11 Ditlev Tamm,"Nolo falcem in alienam messem mittere: Der dänische Theologe Niels Hemmingsen (1513–1600) aus juristischer Sicht," in *Gerichtslauben–Vorträge*, ed. Karl Kroeschell (Sigmaringen: Jan Thorbecke, 1983), 47–56, at 48.
12 Bjørn Kornerup, ed., *Confessio et ordinatio ecclesiarum danicarum* (Copenhagen: G.E.C. Gad, 1953), 123.
13 Mattias Skat Sommer, "Niels Hemmingsen and the Construction of a Seventeenth-Century Protestant Memory," *Journal of Early Modern Christianity* 4/1 (2017): 135–60.
14 Niels Hemmingsen, *Enchiridion theologicvm præcipva veræ religionis capita breviter et simpliciter explicata continens* (Wittenberg: Johann Krafft, 1557), fol. Y6: "Ecclesiae unitas non consistit in cohabitationibus, necq. in externis ritibus aut ceremonijs, sed in doctrinae & fidei consensu . . . in doctrina Euangelij incorrupta, scilicet, in fundamento."
15 Martin Schwarz Lausten, ed., *Kirkeordinansen 1537/39* (Copenhagen: Akademisk Forlag, 1989), 231. See also Martin Schwarz Lausten, *Christian den 3. og kirken 1537–1559* (Copenhagen: Akademisk Forlag, 1987), 207–11.
16 Ole Peter Grell, "Intellectual Currents," in *The Cambridge History of Scandinavia, vol. 2: 1520–1870*, ed. E.I. Kouri and Jens E. Olesen (Cambridge: Cambridge University Press, 2016), 89–100.
17 Ole Peter Grell and Thorkild Lyby, "The Consolidation of Lutheranism in Denmark and Norway," in *The Scandinavian Reformation: From Evangelical Movement to Institutionalisation of Reform* (Cambridge: Cambridge University Press, 1995), 114–43, at 118–19.
18 Kornerup, ed., *Confessio et ordinatio*, xxxvii–xxxviii; Paul Douglas Lockhart, *Frederik II and the Protestant Cause: Denmark's Role in the Wars of Religion, 1559–1596* (Leiden: Brill, 2004), 66–67.
19 Articles VII, XII, and XXII of the *Confessio*, see Kornerup, *Confessio et ordinatio*, 15–18, 30–33, and 56–61.
20 See the royal preamble and the articles in Holger Frederik Rørdam, ed., *Danske Kirkelove samt Udvalg af andre Bestemmelser vedrørende Kirken, Skolen og de Fattiges Forsørgelse, 1536–1683*, vol. II (Copenhagen: Selskabet for Danmarks Kirkehistorie, 1886), 126–34.
21 Trygve R. Skarsten, "The Reception of the Augsburg Confession in Scandinavia," *The Sixteenth Century Journal* 11/3 (1980): 86–98. See also the study of the suspension case in minute detail by Jens Glebe-Møller, "Teologi og universitet i Danmark 1560–1700," in *Reformationen i dansk kirke og kultur, vol. 1: 1517–1700*, ed. Niels Henrik Gregersen and Carsten Bach-Nielsen (Odense: University Press of Southern Denmark, 2017), 246–48.
22 Sommer, "The Construction of a Seventeenth-century Protestant Memory," 149–58; Peder Winstrup, "D. Nicolai Hemmingii Vita" (Royal Library, Copenhagen, Langebeks Excerpter 222 Quarto).
23 Ute Lotz-Heumann, "Confessionalization," in *Reformation and Early Modern Europe: A Guide to Research*, ed. David M. Whitford (Kirksville, MO: Truman State University Press, 2008), 136–57 (151).

24 Melanchthon, *Loci Communes* (1521), in *Corpus Reformatorum, vol. 21*, 116: "De naturalibus legibus nondum vidi neque a Theologis, neque a Iurisconsultis aliquid digne scriptum." Regarding Hemmingsen's use of Melanchthon, see Tarald Rasmussen, "Skandinavien," in *Philipp Melanchthon. Der Reformator zwischen Glauben und Wissen. Ein Handbuch*, ed. Günter Frank (Berlin: De Gruyter, 2017), 647–58, at 649–52.

25 Niels Hemmingsen, *De lege naturae apodictica methodus* (Copenhagen: Forlaget Øresund, 1991), §§ 39 and 9: "Lex Naturae est divinitus impressa mentinus hominum notitia certa principiorum cognitionis atque conclusionum . . . ex principiis necessaria consequential ad humanae vitae gubernationem extruit ratio, ut homo ea quae recta sunt cognoscat, velit, eligat, agat, vitetque contrariis"; "autem omnes sani una nobiscum fatentur unam Justiciam esse, quae domos, quae civitates, quae provincias, quae regn conservat."

26 Niels Hemmingsen, preface to Niels Nielsen Kolding, *De Besynderligste Historier/ Sententzer oc Exempler/som findis i den hellige Scrifft/om Øffrigheds Kald/Regiment oc Bestilling* (Copenhagen: Laurentz Benedicht, 1567), fol. *4r: "Der fare er det raadeligt/at huer som er kaldet til nogen Bestilling/enten vdi Huss/eller i Kircke/eller vdi Verdslig Regimente/at hand veed sin Regel hand skal skicke sig effter/oc seer der hoss til Exempel/vdi huilcke Regelen malis oc vdtryckis/saa at mand icke alleniste forstaar aff Regelen huad man giøre skal/Men oc seer vdi Exempel/ huorlunde mand giøre skal. Thi Regelen giffuer *Sapientiam*, det er/ Forstand/paa huad som ræt oc wræt er. Exempel giffuer *Prudentiam*, det er/Forsictighed oc fornumftighed/at man acter/naar oc huor mand kand det som Ræt er bestille/ oc det som wræt er/affuerie"; cf. Max Weber, *The Protestant Ethic and the Spirit of Capitalism*, 2nd ed. (London: George Allen & Unwin, 1978), 81–92.

27 Niels Hemmingsen, *Liffsens Vey: Det er/ En vis oc Christelig Vnderuisning* (Copenhagen: Laurentz Benedicht, 1570), fol. Pv: "Disligist giøres Menniskens hierte bløt/ oc setter hen den naturlige gienstridighed/som kommer aff den oprindelige Synd/ oc tager sig for at være Gud lydig/effter den forstand som den hellig Aand haffuer indgiffuit vdi hiertet."

28 Niels Hemmingsen, *In epistolam divi Iacobi apostoli commentarivs* (Copenhagen: Johannes Xylander, 1563), fol. K4.

29 Ibid., fol. K7.

30 Ibid., fol. K7v–K8r.

31 Ibid., fol. K8v.

32 Hemmingsen, *Enchiridion*, fol. RR7v–TT1v.

33 Niels Hemmingsen, *Om Ecteskab At 1. Betencke. 2. Begynde. 3. Fuldkomme. 4. Leffue vdi. 1. Vislige. 2. ærlige. 3 Gudfryctige. 4. rolige. En Christelig Vnderuisning* (Copenhagen: Matz Vingaard, 1572), fol.):(2v–):(3v and 376–404).

34 Niels Hemmingsen, *Libellus de Coniugio, Repudio, & Diuovertio. In gratiam fratrum, qvi iudices causarum matrimonialium in Regnis Dania & Noruegia constitute sunt* (Leipzig: Hans Steinmann, 1572). The book, which is divided into paragraphs, has been digitalized with a parallel Danish translation at http://crassus.dk/Vejledning/vejledning_1.html, from which we hereafter quote (accessed 26 July 2017).

35 These editions may be traced by accessing the internet catalog *Early European Books* at http://eeb.chadwyck.co.uk/ (accessed 17 August 2017).

36 Hemmingsen, *Libellus*, §§ 5–6.

37 For a similar debate on incest and royal marriages in the wake of the Reformation, see the chapter on Laurentius Petri in this anthology.

38 Hemmingsen, *Om Ecteskab*, 107–22; Hemmingsen, *Libellus*, §§ 180–86, cf. §§ 156 and 170.

39 Hemmingsen, *Libellus*, §§ 148–51; Hemmingsen, *Om Ecteskab*, 91–4; cf. Hartwig Dieterich, *Das protestantische Eherecht in Deutschland bis zur Mitte des 17. Jahrhunderts* (Munich: Claudius Verlag, 1970), 51–52, 97–100, and 133–34.

40 E.g., Hemmingsen, *Om Ecteskab*, 91–94; Hemmingsen, *Libellus*, §§ 148–51; and, in general, Hemmingsen, *De lege naturae*, § 13. Regarding natural law reasoning in Lutheran jurisprudence, see John Witte Jr., "'The Law Written on the Heart': Natural

Law and Equity in Early Lutheran Thought," in *Law and Religion: The Legal Teachings of the Protestant and Catholic Reformations*, ed. Wim Decock et al. (Göttingen: Vandenhoeck & Ruprecht, 2014), 231–65.

41 E.g. Hemmingsen, *Om Ecteskab*, 385–87; Hemmingsen, *Libellus*, §§ 354, 398, and 409–10.

42 See Luther's position in *Instruction on How Christians Should Regard Moses* (1526), in *The Annotated Luther*, vol. 2: Word and Faith, ed. Kirsi Stjerna (Minneapolis, MN: Fortress Press, 2015), 136–43, and *Against the Heavenly Prophets* (1525), in *The Annotated Luther*, vol. 2, 59–65; cf. Ernst Troeltsch, *The Social Teachings of the Christian Churches*, vol. 2 (London: Macmillan, 1931), 534–35.

43 Hemmingsen, *Libellus*, §§ 74–83.

44 Hemmingsen, *Om Ecteskab*, 108–09: "Men om der findis noget vdi Paffuens Low som er til gaffns/ da holde wi det icke fordi at Paffuen haffuer det bødet/ eller wi ere hannem vndergiffne/men fordi det haffuer en anden sted sin grund"; cf. Hemmingsen, *Libellus*, §§ 182–84.

45 Hemmingsen, *Libellus*, §§ 5, 134–36, 186, and 194.

46 Morten Kjær and Helle Vogt: "Ret og reformation. Dansk retshistorisk status ved 500-året for Luthers 95 teser," *Ugeskrift for Retsvæsen* 36 (2017): 321–31; and the preceding chapter on Bugenhagen.

47 Hemmingsen, *Om Ecteskab*, 109–10; Hemmingsen, *Libellus*, § 185, and cf., e.g., §§ 92, 149, and 409.

48 Hemmingsen, *Om Ecteskab*, 110–12; Hemmingsen, *Libellus*, § 186.

49 D. 1, especially cc. 2–4, in Augustine Thompson and James Gordley, ed. and transl., *The Treatise on Laws with the Ordinary Gloss* (Washington, DC: The Catholic University of America Press, 1993), 3–8.

50 Hemmingsen, *De lege naturae*, §§ 22 and 1:

> Nam leges nostras Danicas (quae sunt Legis Naturae de qua nos agimus hypotheses quaedam) ut disjecta et veluti dissipata quaedam corporis membra (quod sane vitio legislatorum accidit, quorum alii aliis nationibus tulerunt leges, sed propter varietatem populorum, quibus aliae atque aliae leges ferendae erant) ad justum corpus revocare conaris, quo singula apto nexu cohaereant;

"Etenim ut corpora nostra sine mente, sic civitas sine Lege, Justiciae Norma, suis partibus et nervis et sanguine et membris (ut ait Cicero) uti non potest."

51 Hemmingsen, *Libellus*, § 136.

52 Hemmingsen, *Om Ecteskab*, 111–12: cf. Hemmingsen, *Libellus*, § 185, and Hemmingsen, *De lege naturae*, §§ 11 and 13.

53 After the edition in V.A. Secher, ed., *Corpus Constitutionum Daniæ: Forordninger, Recesser og andre kongelige Breve, Danmarks Lovgivning vedkommende 1558–1660*, vol. I (Copenhagen: Rudolph Klein, 1887), 40–41.

54 Hemmingsen, *Om Ecteskab*, fol): (4r: "Den som stiel it Faar eller it Suin/henger mand vdi Galien/men den som stiel fra fattige Forældre deris Barns ære/ hand bliffuer quit fra all tiltale/naar hand haffuer giffuet ix. Marck/oc der vdoffuer berymmer hand sig/lige som hand haffde vel giort. Gud giffue at Øffrighed her vdi vilde sig bedre betencke." In *Liffsens Vey* Hemmingsen used similar reasoning. The parents or guardians who keep their children away from religion ought to face the capital punishment. Their crime, Hemmingsen reasoned, is greater than that of those who steal livestock. Hemmingsen, *Liffsens Vey*, fol. D7.

55 Philipp Melanchthon et al., *Instructions for the Visitors of Parish Pastors in Electoral Saxony* (1528), in *Luther's Works: American Edition*, vol. 40: *Church and Ministry* II, ed. Conrad Bergendoff (Philadelphia, PA: Fortress Press, 1958), 285–86; and Philipp Melanchthon, *Commentary on Romans* (1540), ed. and transl. Fred Kraemer, 2nd ed. (Saint Louis, MO: Concordia Publishing House, 2010), 219–20.

56 Hemmingsen, *Libellus*, §§ 400 and 423–27.
57 E.g., ibid., § 148.
58 Hemmingsen, *Om Ecteskab*, 112–22; Hemmingsen, *Libellus*, §§ 187–93.
59 Helle Vogt, *Slægtens funktion i nordisk højmiddelalderret: Kanonisk retsideologi og fredsskabende lovgivning* (Copenhagen: Jurist- og Økonomforbundets Forlag, 2005), 300; and the decree on the reformation of marriage, chap. 5, in James Waterworth, ed., *The Canons and Decrees of the Sacred and Œcumenical Council of Trent* (London: Burns and Oates, 1848), 201.
60 "Dette forbud er fornøden at holdis for merkelige sager skyld, men dog førstelige personer undertagen, hvilke maa vel tilstedis at komme tilsammen, om de end bode ere i tredie eller andit led, fordi ded er icke mod guds loug och sker icke heller foruden synderlige aarsager." References to the Ordinance of Marriage are to the edition in V.A. Secher, ed., *Corpus Constitutionum Daniæ: Forordninger, Recesser og andre kongelige Breve, Danmarks Lovgivning vedkommende 1558–1660*, vol. II (Copenhagen: Rudolph Klein, 1889), 270–96.
61 Morten Kjær, *Guds og øvrigheds straf–centralmagt og sædelighed i Danmark-Norge 1536–1648* (Copenhagen: Ex Tuto Publishing, 2017), 177–78.
62 Hemmingsen, *Libellus*, §§ 400–402; cf. Martin Schwarz Lausten, *Niels Hemmingsen: Storhed og fald* (Copenhagen: Anis, 2013), 270.
63 Kjær and Vogt, "Ret og reformation," 326; and in general Witte, *Law and Protestantism*, chap. 6, and Dieterich, *Das Protestantische Eherecht*. For a minor fourth reason regarding serious crimes, see VI.6.
64 Hemmingsen, *Libellus*, §§ 148–71; Hemmingsen, *Om Ecteskab*, 90–129, cf. Kjær, *Guds og øvrigheds straf*, 182–87.
65 Hemmingsen, *Libellus*, §§ 400 and 427, cf. Kjær, *Guds og øvrigheds straf*, 188–89.
66 Mattias Skat Sommer, "Reformationen af dagligdagen," in Gregersen and Bach-Nielsen, *Reformationen i dansk kirke og kultur*, vol. 1, 331–66.
67 Sommer, "The Construction of a Seventeenth-Century Protestant Memory," 136–37.
68 Sommer, "The Construction of a Seventeenth-Century Protestant Memory," 139–41; Mattias Skat Sommer, "An Outsider's Voice? Dedications and Prefaces to Translations of Niels Hemmingsen in Elizabethan England," *Archiv für Reformationsgeschichte* 109 (2018): 261–94.
69 Kjær, *Guds og øvrigheds straf*, 277–78 and 351–52; Christen Osterssøn Veylle, *Glossarium juridicum Danico-Norvegicum* (Copenhagen: Gøde, 1665), 755.
70 Kjær, *Guds og øvrigheds straf*, 190.

Bibliography

Brecht, Martin. *Martin Luther, vol. 3: The Preservation of the Church 1532–1546* (Philadelphia, PA: Fortress Press, 1993).

Calvin, John. *Institutio Christianae Religionis* (1559), in *Joannis Calvini Opera Selecta*, ed. Peter Barth and Wilhelm Niesel, vol. III (Munich: Chr. Kaiser, 1928).

Dieterich, Hartwig. *Das protestantische Eherecht in Deutschland bis zur Mitte des 17. Jahrhunderts* (Munich: Claudius Verlag, 1970).

Estes, James M. *Peace, Order and the Glory of God: Secular Authority and the Church in the Thought of Luther and Melanchthon 1518–1559* (Leiden: Brill, 2005).

Glebe-Møller, Jens. "Niels Hemmingsen," in *Dansk Biografisk Leksikon online* (Copenhagen: Gyldendal, 1979–84), http://denstoredanske.dk/index.php?sideID=291107 (accessed 28 August 2017).

Glebe-Møller, Jens. "Teologi og universitet i Danmark 1560–1700," in *Reformationen i dansk kirke og kultur, vol. 1: 1517–1700*, ed. Niels Henrik Gregersen and Carsten Bach-Nielsen (Odense: University Press of Southern Denmark, 2017), 246–48.

Grell, Ole Peter. "Intellectual Currents," in *The Cambridge History of Scandinavia, vol. 2: 1520–1870*, ed. E.I. Kouri and Jens E. Olesen (Cambridge: Cambridge University Press, 2016), 89–100.

Grell, Ole Peter and Thorkild Lyby. "The Consolidation of Lutheranism in Denmark and Norway," in *The Scandinavian Reformation: From Evangelical Movement to Institutionalisation of Reform*, ed. Ole Peter Grell (Cambridge: Cambridge University Press, 1995), 114–43.

Heckel, Martin. *Staat und Kirche nach den Lehren der evangelischen Juristen in der ersten Hälfte des 17. Jahrhunderts* (Tübingen: Mohr Siebeck, 1968).

Hemmingsen, Niels. *De lege naturae apodictica methodus* (Copenhagen: Forlaget Øresund, 1991).

Hemmingsen, Niels. *Enchiridion theologicvm præcipva veræ religionis capita breviter et simpliciter explicata continens* (Wittenberg: Johann Krafft, 1557).

Hemmingsen, Niels. *In epistolam divi Iacobi apostoli commentarivs* (Copenhagen: Johannes Xylander, 1563).

Hemmingsen, Niels. *Libellus de Coniugio, Repudio, & Diuovertio. In gratiam fratrum, qvi iudices causarum matrimonialium in Regnis Dania & Noruegia constitute sunt* (Leipzig: Hans Steinmann, 1572).

Hemmingsen, Niels. *Liffsens Vey: Det er/En vis oc Christelig Vnderuisning* (Copenhagen: Laurentz Benedicht, 1570).

Hemmingsen, Niels. *Om Ecteskab At 1. Betencke. 2. Begynde. 3. Fuldkomme. 4. Leffue vdi. 1. Vislige. 2. ærlige. 3 Gudfryctige. 4. rolige. En Christelig Vnderuisning* (Copenhagen: Matz Vingaard, 1572).

Hemmingsen, Niels. Preface to Niels Nielsen Kolding, *De Besynderligste Historier/Sententzer oc Exempler/som findis i den hellige Scrifft/om Øffrigheds Kald/Regiment oc Bestilling* (Copenhagen: Laurentz Benedicht, 1567).

Hesselink, I. John. *Calvin's Concept of the Law* (Allison Park, PA: Pickwick Publications, 1992).

Kjær, Morten. *Guds og øvrigheds straf – Centralmagt og sædelighed i Danmark-Norge 1536–1648* (Copenhagen: Ex Tuto Publishing, 2017).

Kjær, Morten and Helle Vogt. "Ret og reformation. Dansk retshistorisk status ved 500-året for Luthers 95 teser," *Ugeskrift for Retsvæsen* 36 (2017): 321–31.

Kornerup, Bjørn, ed. *Confessio et ordinatio ecclesiarum danicarum* (Copenhagen: G.E.C. Gad, 1953).

Kusukawa, Sachiko. "Melanchthon," in *The Cambridge Companion to Reformation Theology*, ed. David Bagchi and David C. Steinmetz (Cambridge: Cambridge University Press, 2004), 57–67.

Lausten, Martin Schwarz. *Christian den 3. og kirken 1537–1559* (Copenhagen: Akademisk Forlag, 1987).

Lausten, Martin Schwarz, ed. *Kirkeordinansen 1537/39* (Copenhagen: Akademisk Forlag, 1989).

Lausten, Martin Schwarz. *Niels Hemmingsen: Storhed og fald* (Copenhagen: Anis, 2013).

Lockhart, Paul Douglas. *Frederik II and the Protestant Cause: Denmark's Role in the Wars of Religion, 1559–1596* (Leiden: Brill, 2004).

Lotz-Heumann, Ute. "Confessionalization," in *Reformation and Early Modern Europe: A Guide to Research*, ed. David M. Whitford (Kirksville, MO: Truman State University Press, 2008), 136–57.

Luther, Martin. *Against the Heavenly Prophets* (1525), *The Annotated Luther, vol. 2: Word and Faith*, ed. Kirsi Stjerna (Minneapolis, MN: Fortress Press, 2015), 59–65.

Luther, Martin. *Enarratio in Genesin* (1535–45), in *Luther's Works: American Edition*, vol. 5: *Lectures on Genesis chapters 26–30*, ed. Jaroslav Pelikan (Saint Louis, MO: Concordia Publishing House, 1968).

Luther, Martin. *Etliche Capitel S. Johannis* (1537), in *D. Martin Luthers Werke, Schriften*, vol. 46 (Weimar: Hermann Böhlaus Nachfolger, 1912).

Luther, Martin. *Instruction on How Christians Should Regard Moses* (1526), in *The Annotated Luther, vol. 2: Word and Faith*, ed. Kirsi Stjerna (Minneapolis, MN: Fortress Press, 2015), 136–43.

Meinhold, Peter. *Die Genesisvorlesung Luthers und ihre Herausgeber* (Stuttgart: W. Kohlhammer, 1936).

Melanchthon, Philipp. *Commentary on Romans* (1540), ed. and transl. Fred Kraemer, 2nd ed. (Saint Louis, MO: Concordia Publishing House, 2010).

Melanchthon, Philipp. *Loci Communes* (1535), in *Corpus Reformatorum: Philippi Melanthonis opera quae supersunt omnia, vol. 21: Loci Theologici*, ed. H.E. Bindseil (Braunschweig: Schwetschke, 1854).

Melanchthon, Philipp, et al. *Instructions for the Visitors of Parish Pastors in Electoral Saxony* (1528), in *Luther's Works: American Edition, vol. 40: Church and Ministry* II, ed. Conrad Bergendoff (Philadelphia, PA: Fortress Press, 1958), 285–86.

Rasmussen, Tarald. "Skandinavien," in *Philipp Melanchthon. Der Reformator zwischen Glauben und Wissen. Ein Handbuch*, ed. Günter Frank (Berlin: De Gruyter, 2017), 647–58.

Rørdam, Holger Frederik, ed. *Danske Kirkelove samt Udvalg af andre Bestemmelser vedrørende Kirken, Skolen og de Fattiges Forsørgelse, 1536–1683*, vol. II (Copenhagen: Selskabet for Danmarks Kirkehistorie, 1886).

Schorn-Schütte, Luise. *Evangelische Geistlichkeit in der Frühneuzeit* (Gütersloh: Gütersloher Verlagshaus Gerd Mohn, 1996).

Secher, V.A., ed. *Corpus Constitutionum Daniæ: Forordninger, Recesser og andre kongelige Breve, Danmarks Lovgivning vedkommende 1558–1660*, vol. I (Copenhagen: Rudolph Klein, 1887).

Secher, V.A., ed. *Corpus Constitutionum Daniæ: Forordninger, Recesser og andre kongelige Breve, Danmarks Lovgivning vedkommende 1558–1660*, vol. II (Copenhagen: Rudolph Klein, 1889).

Skarsten, Trygve R. "Hemmingsen, Niels," in *The Oxford Encyclopedia of the Reformation*, vol. II, ed. Hans J. Hillerbrand (New York: Oxford University Press, 1996), 222–23.

Skarsten, Trygve R. "The Reception of the Augsburg Confession in Scandinavia," *The Sixteenth Century Journal* 11/3 (1980): 86–98.

Sommer, Mattias Skat. "An Outsider's Voice? Dedications and Prefaces to Translations of Niels Hemmingsen in Elizabethan England," *Archiv für Reformationsgeschichte* 109 (2018): 261–94.

Sommer, Mattias Skat. "Hemmingsen, Niels," in *The Encyclopedia of Martin Luther and the Reformation*, vol. 1, ed. Mark A. Lamport (Lanham, MD: Rowman & Littlefield, 2017), 323–25.

Sommer, Mattias Skat. "Niels Hemmingsen and the Construction of a Seventeenth-Century Protestant Memory," *Journal of Early Modern Christianity* 4/1 (2017): 135–60.

Sommer, Mattias Skat. "Reformationen af dagligdagen," in *Reformationen i dansk kirke og kultur, vol. 1: 1517–1700*, ed. Niels Henrik Gregersen and Carsten Bach-Nielsen (Odense: University Press of Southern Denmark, 2017), 331–66.

Tamm, Ditlev. "Nolo falcem in alienam messem mittere: Der dänische Theologe Niels Hemmingsen (1513–1600) aus juristischer Sicht," in *Gerichtslauben–Vorträge*, ed. Karl Kroeschell (Sigmaringen: Jan Thorbecke, 1983), 47–56.
Thompson, Augustine and James Gordley, ed. and transl. *The Treatise on Laws with the Ordinary Gloss* (Washington, DC: The Catholic University of America Press, 1993).
Troeltsch, Ernst. *The Social Teachings of the Christian Churches*, vol. 2 (London: Macmillan, 1931).
Veylle, Christen Osterssøn. *Glossarium juridicum Danico-Norvegicum* (Copenhagen: Gøde, 1665).
Vogt, Helle. *Slægtens funktion i nordisk højmiddelalderret: Kanonisk retsideologi og fredsskabende lovgivning* (Copenhagen: Jurist- og Økonomforbundets Forlag, 2005).
Weber, Max. *The Protestant Ethic and the Spirit of Capitalism*, 2nd ed. (London: George Allen & Unwin, 1978).
Wingren, Gustaf. *Luthers lära om kallelsen*, 2nd ed. (Lund: C.W.K. Gleerup, 1948).
Winstrup, Peder. "D. Nicolai Hemmingii Vita" (Royal Library, Copenhagen, Langebeks Excerpter 222 Quarto).
Witte Jr., John. *Law and Protestantism: The Legal Teachings of the Lutheran Reformation* (Cambridge: Cambridge University Press, 2002).
Witte Jr., John. "'The Law Written on the Heart': Natural Law and Equity in Early Lutheran Thought," in *Law and Religion: The Legal Teachings of the Protestant and Catholic Reformations*, ed. Wim Decock et al. (Göttingen: Vandenhoeck & Ruprecht, 2014), 231–65.

Part 3

The enlightenment—secular law in Christian societies

9 Introduction

The enlightenment

Sören Koch and Kristian Mejrup

Introduction

The modern world began to emerge in Scandinavia in the eighteenth century. European Enlightenment movements influenced the intellectual foundations of all European legal cultures,[1] and the Nordic kingdoms were no exception.[2] Both religious reformers and Enlightenment thinkers contributed to the development that spurred new concepts about the natural world, society, citizenship, and the nature and science of humanity.[3] Educational reforms and the introduction of new forms of epistemology that facilitated more secular approaches to legal thinking also gave fresh impetus to the process of modernization. During the century, the separation of religion from law gradually increased. References to scripture and Christian metaphysics were gradually replaced with legal theories based on ethics, social mores, and rational thinking. Yet religious and enlightened ideas were part of the same intellectual discourse, debated and promoted by scholars, ministers, state officials, laypersons, and artisans, some more inclined to separatism than others. To introduce this section's selection of representative figures of great Christian jurists of the North, a few contextualizing remarks are warranted. We shall have a closer look at the intellectual, political, theological, and legal-institutional background relevant to developments in the eighteenth century.

Intellectual background

With the Thirty Years' War as a backdrop, it became clear that the confessional separation in Germany and Western Europe would remain permanent. Failing to provide universally applicable standards, theological doctrines were gradually replaced by secular rationalist thinking. In the writings of Hugo Grotius, Thomas Hobbes, Samuel Pufendorf, John Selden, and Christian Thomasius (in his earlier works),[4] biblical precepts were neither dispensed with nor automatically regarded as divinely mandated or universally valid. Grotius, in his major work, *De jure belli ac pacis* (1625), already had formulated that the rules of rational natural law would apply even if God did not exist. This gave rise to extensive debates about the relationships among law, moral philosophy, and religion. Samuel

Pufendorf, who developed a comprehensive system of natural law, became one of the most influential protagonists of secular natural law theory; in Germany, he was heralded as the father of enlightened thinking, and in the Nordic countries his natural law theory has left most significant traces in the legal literature of the early eighteenth century.[5]

For Pufendorf, the separation of moral theology and jurisprudence was a central topic.[6] In order to restrict the theological elements that pervaded natural law discourses, he distinguished religion as a matter pertaining to the afterlife, and natural law as a matter of social life. Religion was still a necessary precondition for social life.[7] But for him it was but one of three duties to which humankind was obligated: duty towards oneself, towards one's neighbor, and towards God. This distinction was supposed to further the overall purpose of natural law, which is to safeguard social peace despite confessional separation. In this he was followed by men such as Barbeyrac and Thomasius, who agreed on natural law's primary aim, but emphasized different ideas regarding its foundation.[8]

In the Nordic countries, the separation of law, morality, and religion was discussed by such thinkers as Ludvig Holberg, David Nehrman-Ehrenstråle, and Andreas Hojer. In their individual attempts to implement these ideas into the Danish-Norwegian and Swedish-Finnish contexts, these writers chose between more radical and more conservative theoretical approaches often based on their Continental role models.[9] Their contributions formed the intellectual framework for the next generation of Christian jurists, such as Ernst Gunnerus, Henrik Stampe, Anders Sandøe Ørsted, Johan Henrik Thomander, and Henrik Reuterdahl.

Political context

Another important contextual factor was the regional political framework. In Denmark and Norway, the absolute monarchy was introduced in 1660 and became manifest in a semi-constitutional document called *Lex Regia (Kongelov)* of 1665.[10] This new political ideology also shaped the Danish and Norwegian codes of 1683 and 1687. Absolutism prevailed throughout the long eighteenth century and was not officially dissolved before Norway was separated from Denmark as a consequence of the peace treaty of Kiel in 1814. In Denmark, the Danish Constitution of 1849 replaced the *Lex Regia* and thus abolished absolutism.

In Sweden, absolutism developed differently. It was introduced in 1680, interrupted by "the age of liberty" (1718–72), reinforced by King Gustavus III in 1772 and 1789, and finally dissolved with the Revolution of 1809. Even though political power during the age of liberty was vested in the hands of the estates, book censorship and the relationship between law and religion were organized in quite similar ways as in Denmark-Norway.[11] The eighteenth century thus sustained, cultivated, and eventually abolished different implementations of absolutism in the Nordics.

The Great Northern War (1700–21) had placed the Scandinavian countries on each side of an international conflict; it terminated Sweden's role as a European great power. This war marked the climax of the ancestral enmity between Sweden and Denmark-Norway that had prevailed from the sixteenth century. Even though the tensions between the two Scandinavian realms did not disappear immediately, armed conflicts became rarer. At the beginning of the nineteenth century, Sweden and Denmark-Norway ended up in opposing alliances one last time. After Napoleon's defeat, the Swedish king claimed Norway as compensation for having lost Finland to Russia. Norway had to enter into a personal union with Sweden. This time, however, the character of the union was quite different. Norway was recognized as a separate realm with its own national bank, university, and military, and, most importantly, its own parliament and constitution.[12]

Due to new trade routes to the new world and Asia, the Nordic realms became increasingly removed from the central political and economic stage in Europe.[13] Additionally, the constant wars of the seventeenth and early eighteenth centuries had exhausted their financial resources, and important reforms were suspended or canceled. Even though Sweden-Finland got a new code in 1734, important reforms of legislation failed, despite the fact that several commissions were assigned to the task. Neither Denmark, Norway, nor Sweden managed to adopt modern systematic codifications in the field of private law.[14] Instead, thousands of additional acts of legislation were issued, giving positive law in Scandinavia a fragmentary character. Also, in the early nineteenth century, attempts to systematically codify the law were basically unsuccessful.[15] This failure, in turn, had an enormous impact on the intellectual preconditions of producing and applying law, and especially on the institutional structures of the Nordic legal cultures, such as the system of courts and the professionalization of lawyers.[16]

Lutheran orthodoxy and Pietism

The two Scandinavian monarchies included remote regions and colonies inhabited by people of different nationalities, languages, and religions. The majority, however, adhered to the Lutheran faith, introduced in the beginning of the sixteenth century. In the seventeenth and eighteenth centuries, concurrently with the development and consolidation of Lutheran scholastic theology, a devotional theology flourished. While scholastic theology, represented by bishops and professors of theology, was concerned with doctrines and systems and maintaining and protecting the Lutheran faith against Calvinism and Catholicism, devotional theology focused on *praxis pietatis*, the inner life and transformation of the believer. These two sides of Lutheranism often collided. The devotional theology, advertised and promoted by Pietists, frequently included complaints about the present state of affairs. Such remarks could amount to unrestrained criticism of the official church, its ministers, and their liturgical practices, and could take radical forms. But here Pietism allied with promoters of secularized discourses on natural law. Christian Thomasius, for instance, would come to regard the Pietist theologian and pastor Gottfried Arnold (1666–1714), author of *Unparteyische Kirchen- und Ketzer-Historie* ("Impartial history of the church and heresy," 1700), as a "doughty comrade-in-arms."[17]

Both the more moderate and the more radical forms of Pietism entered and influenced the Nordic kingdoms in the eighteenth century.[18] The moderate version, associated with Halle, Philipp Jakob Spener (1635–1705), and August Hermann Francke (1663–1727), was particularly well received in Denmark and Norway. The more radical form, associated with Johann Conrad Dippel (1673–1734) and Count Nicolaus von Zinzendorf (1700–60), was, on the other hand, officially prohibited and regarded as a vehicle for separatism. Still, religious renewal and secularized discourses on natural law were part of the same Enlightenment campaign that shaped the modern world emerging in the Nordic kingdoms in the eighteenth century.[19] The perfect example of this is Andreas Hojer, who resided in the Royal Orphanage, the hub of Pietism, while working to renew the study of law at the University of Copenhagen.

Legal framework

The constantly growing administrations in Denmark-Norway and Sweden caused an increase in legal and nonlegal rules and thus contributed towards creating a multilayer normativity governing citizens' actions and behavior. This tendency could not be entirely stopped by the somewhat utopian pursuit of unifying all norms under royal legislation, which in the Nordic states became manifest in the enactment of the respective Danish Code (1683), Norwegian Code (1687), and Swedish Code (1734). Correspondingly, all attempts to reduce the variety of legal sources to just one, through the wording of the provisions in these codes, were doomed to fail when it came to the actual application of law.[20]

In addition, and in contrast to Continental Europe, the legal intellectual infrastructure in the Nordic kingdoms was still relatively weak in the eighteenth century.[21] Due to a lack of institutions providing a sufficient number of learned lawyers in all Nordic countries, Nordic jurists relied heavily on external developments. However, these new ideas were selected, adapted, and modified by Nordic jurists to match the needs and preconditions of the local legal cultures. This activity bears witness to the considerable impact individual writers and thinkers had on the local scientific discourse in this period. As long as orthodox protagonists such as Hans (Johannes) Vandal (1624–75) and influential court chaplain (*hofprest*) Hector Gottfried Masius (1653–1709) managed to carefully maintain a mutually beneficial relationship to the Danish monarch, theologians succeeded in exercising a decisive impact on norm production and the application of law.[22] By deliberately using the legal system to strictly censor all kinds of publications,[23] they tried to gain control over social and moral behavior.[24] In addition, they used their influence to severely regulate and actually limit the religious rights of members of other (than Lutheran) confessions, especially Jews in Denmark.[25] In Norway, based on legislation dating to 1569, both Jesuits (synonymous with all Catholics) and Jews were categorically banned from entering the realm—a rule that was maintained unaltered by the Norwegian constitution of 1814 and was not abandoned until 1851.[26] In Sweden, Jews were tolerated in some enumerated cities (Stockholm, Gothenburg, and Norrköping), owing to a regulation from 1782 (*judereglementet)* issued by the "enlightened absolutist king" Gustavus III.[27]

In Denmark-Norway, however, the impact of theologians on both law on the books and law in action gradually decreased after the death of the court chaplain Masius. This tendency was amplified by the increasing impact of Pietism.[28] Constantly increasing efforts to establish higher standards of general public education caused a demand for a higher degree of professionalization in society.[29] The establishment of mandatory legal examinations for all legal practitioners[30] facilitated the establishment of an independent legal science.[31] At the same time, legal professionalization contributed to a common intellectual framework for jurists beyond the faculty and the influence of theologians.[32] As a consequence, theologians eventually lost much of their influence in determining and authoritatively interpreting the law.

Professionalization also became the new ideal with regard to reformations of the court systems. Legal conflicts no longer would be solved by laymen or officials holding a degree in theology, but by professional lawyers. Both in Denmark-Norway and in Sweden-Finland, almost all judges toward the end of the eighteenth century held a law degree. In Denmark and Norway, this applied also to legal officers and advocates. As a consequence, in Denmark-Norway, the radical court reform of 1797 suspended all remaining elements of lay participation on the appellate and higher levels of the court hierarchy.[33] In Sweden, however, laymen were permitted to act as lawyers, and the professionalization of lawyers started first with the creation of the Swedish Bar Association in 1887.[34]

Despite the restrictions of the political system in Denmark-Norway, enlightened thinking eventually was promoted by leading state officials such as Henrik Stampe, the general prosecutor (*generalprokurator*) and the king's highest legal adviser, and thus became part of the self-conception of the absolutist state.[35] In his "statements" (*erklæringer*), we can find many examples of enlightened thinking, such as the promotion of the right of appeal, no conviction without legislative foundation, prohibition of administrative confinement, decriminalization of sex outside marriage, and establishment of a maintenance obligation for children born outside marriage. That theological objections against such developments become rare towards the end of the eighteenth century bears witness to the ongoing intellectual separation between law and religion.

Notes

1 We are applying an operationalize concept of 'legal culture'. This concept was defined by Jørn Øyrehagen Sunde as ideas and expectations to law made operational by institutional (-like) practice, cf. Jørn Ø. Sunde, "Champagne at the Funeral. An Introduction to Legal Culture" in Jørn Ø. Sunde and Knut Einar Skodvin (eds.), *Rendezvous of European Legal Cultures* (Oslo: Fagbokforlaget, 2010), 11 ff.

2 Regarding the term and content of Enlightenment in a Nordic context, see Nilsén, *Att "stoppa munnen till på bespottare,"* 53ff. See also Haakonssen, "Protestant Natural Law Theory." On the concept of "Enlightenment" and its relationship between philosophy and history, see Haakonssen, "History of Eighteenth-Century Philosophy."

On the relationship between Enlightenment and religion, see Haakonssen, "Enlightenments and Religions."

3 Gierl, "Pietism, Enlightenment, and Modernity." See also Haakonssen and Olden-Jørgensen, *Ludvig Holberg*.

4 On the topic in detail: Haakonssen, "Protestant Natural Law Theory."

5 Björne, *Patrioter og Institutionalister*, 39, 51. Nilsén, *Att "stoppa munnen till på bespottare,"* 38ff.

6 "Furthermore, that is by far the most important distinction whereby the end and aim of the natural law is included only in the circuit of this life, and therefore it moulds man accordingly as he ought to lead this life in society with others. But moral theology moulds a man into a Christian, [. . .] who especially hopes for the fruit of piety after this life [. . .]." Pufendorf, *De Officio*, Preface, p. vii; see also Chapter 4.

7 Pufendorf, *De officio*, Book 1, Chap. 3, para. 12. Religion was for Pufendorf crucial when it came "to promote the common Tranquillity and Sociability or reciprocal Union in this Life." See also comments by Hunter and Saunders in Pufendorf, *The Whole Duty of Man*, 59: "Pufendorf conceives of natural religion—that is, of the duties to God known through reason alone—as a subordinate part of natural law."

8 See, e.g., Hunter, *Secularisation of the Confessional State*.

9 Further examples are the first two lectures on natural law in Copenhagen by Weghorst and Reitzer, who had developed significantly different theories of natural law, disagreeing on such fundamental issues as the definition of law, the moral good, and the role of sociality in natural law. See, Jensen, "Contests about Natural Law," 1039–40.

10 *Lex Regia* was a *lex fundamentalis* and not a constitution in the modern sense. See Mohnhaupt, "On Verfassung."

11 See also paragraph 5 below.

12 Norges Grunnlov (Norway's constitution) of May 17, 1814, amended on November 4, 1814, resembling the union with Sweden.

13 Hodacs, *Silk and Tea*, 25ff.

14 On this issue, see Björne, "Konstitusjon och/eller Kodifikation."

15 That this was not caused by a lack of ambition to create modern codifications after continental European role models is evident by § 94 of the Norwegian Constitution commanding the legislature to issue both a civil and a criminal code. All plans to realize a civil code were finally abandoned in 1845; a criminal code was not enacted until 1864. For details consult Sandvik and Michalsen, *Kodifikasjon og konstitusjon*. Re. Sweden: Modéer, *Historiska rättskällor*.

16 Modéer, *Svenska domarkulturen*, C. For a more detailed analysis regarding Denmark, see Tamm, *Rettshistorie*, 205ff.; for Norway, see Sunde, *Speculum legale*, 197ff, especially 309ff. On the legal cultural effects of the fragmentary legislation in Sweden, see Modéer, *Svenska domarkulturen*; Modéer, "Det fria advokatyrket."

17 Mcintosh: "Pietists," 656.

18 Claesson, "Kris och kristnande."

19 Gierl gives a substantial account of the role of Pietism in relation to Enlightenment thinking and modernity. He states:

> The emergence of Pietism coincided with the evolution of our modern world. As *praxis pietatis*—as an expression of piety, church reform, creed, religious understanding, articulation of a world view, introspection, set of beliefs, disposition, self-confidence, role definition, discourse, communication, organisation, institution, social structure, and movement—it reacted to the modern age and helped shape it, whether it wanted to or not.

Gierl, "Pietism," 348. See also *Wege in den Norden*. Haakonssen and Horstbøll, *Northern Antiquities*. Nordbäck, "Conservative Pietism." Haakonssen and

Olden-Jørgensen, *Ludvig Holberg*. Pedersen, "Pietismens Tid 1699 –1746." See also Markussen, *Til Skaberens Ære, Statens Tjeneste og Vor Egen Nytte.*

20 The Danish Code (Danske Lov) contains in its first provisions the idea that all law is based on the will of the sovereign—alias the king—alone. Consequently, nobody but the king was allowed to modify, dispend, or even interpret the provisions of the code. (cf. Danish Code [*Danske Lov*] 1-1-1/4; Norwegian Code [*Norske Lov*] 1-1-1/4). Even Supreme Court judges were advised to follow the letter of the law (cf. Høiesteretts-fundats, April 15, 1667).

21 Compare the introductory chapter on the Reformation, with more details regarding the development of legal science. In the eighteenth century, legal science still had relatively limited impact on the practical application of law.

22 Tamm, "Rechtswissenschaft im Dienste der Theologie."

23 Regarding censorship in the Nordic countries, one example of the influence of orthodox theology was the public burning of Christian Thomasius's works in Copenhagen, initiated by Masius in 1686: see Grunert, "Zur aufgeklärten Kritik"; Grunert, *Händel mit Hector Gottfried Masio.*

24 Tamm, "Rechtswissenschaft im Dienste der Theologie," 186, holds that Nordic legal science in the seventeenth century was mainly serving theological means; Björne, *Patrioter och Institutionalister*, 19, confirms this notion for Sweden and Finland, even though the Swedish legal literature of this time "i högre grad producerade praktisk bruksjuridik."

25 Decree of July 30,1684, "Om Portugiser af den Ebraiske Religion."

26 Regarding the enforcement of the constitutional provision, see Ulvund, *Fridommens grenser.*

27 Valentin, *Judarnas historia.*

28 Tamm, "Rechtswissenschaft im Dienste der Theologie," 194.

29 At the beginning of the eighteenth century, formal education was not required for appointment as a judge, prosecutor, or advocate. Cf. chapter on the Reformation.

30 Introduced in Denmark-Norway in 1736 (Regulation of July 1, 1736) and in 1749 in Sweden (Regulation on Examen Juridicum. Kunglig Förordning 10.3.1749, Modéer Vol. 4), Modéer, *Historiska rättskällor*; Nilsén, *Att "stoppa munnen."*

31 Tamm, *Retsvitenskap i Danmark*, 108. Koch, "Consequences of Changing Expectations," 483f.

32 Sunde, *Speculum legale*, 222ff.

33 On the background and details of this reform, see Koch, "Changing Expectations," 487.

34 Modéer, "Det fria advokatyrket."

35 Tamm and Kjær, *Henrik Stampe*, 7ff.

Bibliography

Björne, Lars. "Konstitusjon och/eller Kodifikation- Finland, Sverige, Danmark och de Ryska Rike." In *Kodifikasjon og konstitusjon: Grunnlovens § 94s krav til lovbøker i norsk historie*, edited by Hilde Sandvik and Dag Michalsen, 66–84. Oslo: Pax, 2013.

Björne, Lars. *Patrioter og Institutionalister.* Lund: Institutet för rättshistorisk forskning, 1995.

Claesson, Urban. "Kris och kristnande: Olof Ekmans kamp för kristendomens återupprättende vid Stora Kopaberget 1689–1713: pietism, program och praktik." *Skrifter utgivna av Svenska kyrkohistoriska föreningen* 69, Forskning för Kyrkan 26. (Uppsala Svenska kyrkohistoriska föreningen, 2015).

Gierl, Martin. "Pietism, Enlightenment, and Modernity." In *A Companion to German Pietism 1660–1800*, edited by Douglas Shantz, 348–92. Leiden: Brill, 2014.

Grunert, Frank. "Händel mit Hector Gottfried Masio, Zur Pragmatik des Streits in der Kontroverse mit dem Kopenhagener Hofprediger." In *Appell an das Publikum: Die öffentliche Debatte in der deutschen Aufklärung 1687–1796*, edited by Ursula Goldenbaum, 119–74. Berlin: Akademie Verlag, 2004.

Grunert, Frank. "Zur aufgeklärten Kritik am theokratischen Absolutismus. Der Streit zwischen Hector Gottfried Masius und Christian Thomasius über den Ursprung und Begründung der summa potestas." In *Christian Thomasius (1655–1728). Neue Forschung im Kontext der Frühaufklärung*, edited by Friedrich Vollhardt, 55–77. Tübingen: Max Niemeyer Verlag, 1997.

Haakonssen, Knud. "Enlightenments and Religions." Pamphlet of the 14th Annual C. Th. Dimaras Lecture (2009). Athens: Institute for Neohellenic Research, 2010.

Haakonssen, Knud. "The History of Eighteenth-century Philosophy: History or Philosophy?" In *The Cambridge History of Eighteenth-century Philosophy*, edited by Knud Haakonssen, Vol. 1, 3ff. Cambridge: Cambridge University Press, 2006.

Haakonssen, Knud. "Protestant Natural Law Theory: A General Interpretation." In *New Essays on the History of Autonomy: A Collection Honoring J.B. Schneewind*, edited by Natalie Brender and Larry Krasnoff, 92–109. Cambridge: Cambridge University Press, 2004.

Haakonssen, Knud, and Henrik Horstbøll, eds. *Northern Antiquities and National Identities: Perceptions of Denmark and the North in the Eighteenth Century: Symposium Held in Copenhagen, August 2005.* Historisk-filosofiske Meddelelser 101. Copenhagen: The Royal Danish Academy of Sciences and Letters, 2008.

Haakonssen, Knud, and Sebastian Olden-Jørgensen. *Ludvig Holberg (1684–1754): Learning and Literature in the Nordic Enlightenment.* New York: Routledge, 2017.

Hodacs, Hanna. *Silk and Tea in the North: Scandinavian Trade and the Market for Asian Goods in Eighteenth-century Europe.* London: Palgrave Macmillan, 2016.

Hunter, Ian. *The Secularisation of the Confessional State: The Political Thought of Christian Thomasius.* Cambridge: Cambridge University Press, 2007.

Jakob, Lars. "Wege in den Norden. Der Hallische Pietismus in den Skandinavischen Ländern des 18. Jahrhunderts." *Kleine Schriftenreihe der Franckeschen Stiftungen* 14, 2014.

Jensen, Mads Langballe. "Contests about Natural Law in Early Enlightenment Copenhagen." *History of European Ideas* 42/8 (2016): 1027–41; available at http://dx.doi.org/10.1080/01916599.2016.1182045

Koch, Sören. "Consequences of Changing Expectations to Law and Its Institutions—Illustrated by the Role and Background of Judges in Norway." *The Legal History Review* 83 (2015): 461–86.

Markussen, Ingrid. *Til Skaberens Ære, Statens Tjeneste og Vor Egen Nytte. Pietistiske og kameralistiske idéer bag fremvæksten af en offentlig skole i landdistrikterne i 1700–tallet.* Odense: Universitetsforlag, 1995.

Mcintosh, Terence. "Pietists, Jurists, and the Early Enlightenment Critique of Private Confession in Lutheran Germany." *Modern Intellectual History* 12/3 (2015): 627–56.

Modéer, Kjell Å. *Den svenska domarkulturen: europeiska och nationella förebilder.* Lund: Corpus Iuris, 1994.

Modéer, Kjell Å. "Det fria advokatyrket: Kampen för en modern juridisk yrkesroll." In *Festskrift till Sveriges Advokatsamfund 1887–1987: rättsvetenskapliga studier*, edited by Mats Müllern, 11ff. Stockholm: Norstedts, 1987.

Modéer, Kjell Å. *Historiska rättskällor i konflikt: en introduktion i rättshistoria.* Stockholm: Santérus Förlag, 2010.

Mohnhaupt, Heinz. "On the Development of the Term 'Verfassung' from the Plurality of the Ancien Régime's 'Leges Fundamentales.'" In *Constitutionalism before 1789: Constitutional Arrangements from the High Middle Ages to the French Revolution*, edited by Jørn Øyrehagen Sunde, 147–64. Oslo: Pax Forlag, 2014.

Nilsén, Per. *Att "stoppa munnen till på bespottare": Den akademiska undervisningen i svensk statsrätt under frihetstiden*. Lund: Institutet för Rättshistorisk Forskning, 2001.

Nordbäck, Carola. "The Conservative Pietism and the Swedish Confessional State, 1720–1740." In *Confessionalism and Pietism: Religious Reform in Early Modern Europe*, edited by Fred van Lieburg, 213–30. Mainz: Philipp von Zabern, 2006.

Pedersen, Johannes. *Pietismens Tid 1699 –1746*. part of *Den Danske Kirkes Historie*, edited by Hal Koch and Bjørn Kornerup. Copenhagen: Gyldendal, 1951.

Pufendorf, Samuel. *De Officio hominis et civis juxta legem naturalem libri duo*. Lund, 1673.

Pufendorf, Samuel. *The Whole Duty of Man According to the Law of Nature*. Edited by Ian Hunter and David Saunders. Indianapolis, Liberty Fund, 2003.

Sunde, Jørn Øyrehagen. "Champagne at the Funeral." In *Rendezvous of Legal Cultures*, edited by Jørn Øyrehagen Sunde and Knut Einar Skodvin, 11–28. Bergen: Fagbokforlaget, 2010.

Sunde, Jørn Øyrehagen. "Managing the Unmanageable: An Essay Concerning Legal Culture as an Analytical Tool." In *Comparing Legal Cultures*, edited by Sören Koch et al., 23–40. Bergen: Fagbokforlaget, 2020, 2. edition.

Sunde, Jørn Øyrehagen. *Speculum legale—rettsspegelen: ein introduksjon til den norske rettskulturen si historie i eit europeisk perspektiv*. Bergen: Fagbokforlaget, 2010.

Tamm, Ditlev. "Rechtswissenschaft im Dienste der Theologie. Zur Stellung der Rechtswissenschaft an den nordischen Universitäten im 17. Jahrhundert." In *Med Lov skal Land bygges og andre rettshistoriske afhandlinger*, edited by Ditlev Tamm, 185ff. Copenhagen: Djof forlag, 1989.

Tamm, Ditlev. *Rettshistorie: Danmark, Europa, Globale Perspektiver*. Copenhagen: Jurist- og Økonomforbundets Forlag, 2002.

Tamm, Ditlev. *Retsvitenskap i Danmark: en historisk oversigt*. Copenhagen: Jurist- og Økonomforbundet, 1992.

Tamm, Ditlev, and Morten Kjær. *Henrik Stampe—Enevældens menneskelige ansigt*. Copenhagen: Jurist- og Økonomiforbundet, 2013.

Ulvund, Frode. *Fridommens grenser: 1814–1851. Handhevinga av den norske "jødeparagrafen."* Oslo: Scandinavian Academic Press, 2014.

Valentin, Hugo. *Judarnas historia i Sverige*. Stockholm: Bonniers, 1924.

10 Natural law and the struggle with pietism in eighteenth-century Denmark-Norway

Ludvig Holberg (1684–1751)

Sören Koch

Introduction

Ludvig Holberg was one of the leading intellectual figures of the Danish-Norwegian realm in the first half of the eighteenth century. He had studied at and graduated from the theological faculty in Copenhagen (1702–04) and produced thousands of pages of academic writing. Nevertheless, he later became famous for his fictional and poetic writings. Regardless of the genre, the relationship between society, religion, and law was a central topic for him. In his historical writings, Holberg was mainly concerned with presenting a broad overview of the legal sources and their influence on the development of Christianity in general and the realm in particular. Ecclesiastical and church law are only occasionally treated especially in his church history (1738)[1] and his account of the clerical and secular condition of the Danish and Norwegian kingdom (1749).[2] As in all his academic writings, his observations and conclusions were mainly compiled from other writers and often lack a source-critical methodological approach.[3] On the other hand, especially in his church history, he shows remarkable knowledge of the main sources of canon law, when frequently and precisely referring to and citing from *Decretum Gratiani*, the works of Gregory IX and Boniface VIII, as well as the supplements (*Clementinis*, *Extravaganti* and *Extravaganti Communi*). His contribution to ecclesiastical law may nevertheless be most aptly characterized as observations and historical presentations rather than a critical analysis of ecclesiastical law.

Against this background, one may even question whether Holberg was a jurist. He never earned a degree in law or even studied law systematically. In his autobiographical letters to an anonymous patron, he characterized himself to a certain extent as a lawyer (*ut inter Jurisperitos quodammodo referri possim*).[4] Consequently, some legal historians hold that Holberg was not an educated jurist or learned lawyer.[5] This seems convincing, especially when compared to many of his famous contemporaries who contributed to the development of law and legal theory on the Continent.[6] However, the lack of a profession in jurisprudence the Nordic countries and the permeability of borders between different scientific genres in the early eighteenth century make it almost impossible to differentiate jurists from other learned men.[7] Unquestionably, though, Holberg was a learned man. Moreover, Holberg's overly modest self-assessment can be regarded as characteristic of the genre of autobiography. Looking at the historical context, this becomes obvious. While Holberg remarks that he knows the theory but lacks the judicial experience of an advocate or judge,[8] this is an understatement. Between 1723 and 1729, Holberg was assigned an assessorship at a royal court dealing especially with university-related issues and matters of matrimonial law. The *Tamperett* was an institution established as a result of the abolishment of canon law after the Reformation had taken over some of the ecclesiastical jurisdiction held by the Catholic Church prior to 1537.[9] In addition to these tasks, the *Tamperett* advised the king on questions regarding the royal right of pardon. This right was frequently applied in cases of capital crimes, especially when it concerned severe breaches of legal norms pertaining to moral and religious conduct. Some of Holberg's votes have been preserved and show evidence of solid knowledge of the scriptures, one of the court's most important sources. Furthermore, he deftly applied theological sources in sophisticated legal argumentation to support his often conservative verdicts.[10]

The reason why Holberg is relevant in the context of this book is that his specific approach to natural law became highly influential among legal practitioners in the first half of the eighteenth century.[11] Holberg had multiple identities. As a Nordic contributor to the natural-law discourse in Europe, he was a part of a common European intellectual paradigm, but he was simultaneously a contributor to various national subcultures—*inter alia*, the legal culture. When introducing ideas of rational natural law to a rather orthodox legal and political national environment, he was forced to modify the message of his main sources to such an extent that they could pass through what I will call the legal cultural filter in order to be successfully distributed in Denmark and Norway.[12] This filter demands some basic preconditions like knowledge, incentive, applicability, and capability when implementing foreign ideas in specific legal cultures. In addition, a successful reception of foreign ideas demanded a certain degree of conformity with the official doctrine, not least in order to pass censorship. Highly influential religious movements, such as pietism, tightened the net of this filter for all ideas endangering the theological and political foundations of the realm and the interests of its ruling class. One of Holberg's tactics to pass the cultural filter was to reunite natural law with moral theology by stating the overall concordance between them. In plain contrast to his role model, the German philosopher Samuel Pufendorf, Holberg argues that divine revelation has been the most important source of natural law and natural reason.[13] This chapter aims to elaborate on the preconditions, methods, and impact of Holberg's Protestant version of natural-law theory. His struggle with Pietism in early eighteenth century Danmark-Norway is of crucial importance for a contextual understanding of highly popular treatise on this topic.

Holberg's background and ambitions

Ludvig Holberg was born in Bergen, Norway, on December 3, 1684 and died in Copenhagen, Denmark, on January 28, 1754. He attended the Cathedral

School in Bergen from 1698 to 1702. After studying theology at the University of Copenhagen from 1702 to 1704, he enjoyed a scholarship (*stipendium*) at Bourchs College from 1709 to 1714. Holberg started his academic career as a private lecturer in Oxford (1706–08) and in 1717 was appointed professor of metaphysics at the University of Copenhagen. He held this chair until 1720, when he was appointed professor of Latin literature. In 1730, he was appointed to the professorship of history, which he retained until his death. To the young and ambitious, though poor, Norwegian, writing a textbook on natural law appeared a logical step towards an academic career and economic security. However, due to the specific preconditions in Copenhagen, he encountered some serious obstacles in this endeavor. First, the strong Lutheran orthodoxy censored all new publications, especially those related to sensitive issues like secular ideas of natural law. Second, the absolutist regime had established strict rules governing interpretation of the law. Both the Danish and Norwegian Code (1683/1687) contained a prohibition against deviating from, modifying, or even interpreting its provisions.[14] In academia, there was an acknowledged, general prohibition against commenting on the national legislation, as this would necessarily entail an act of interpretation. Writing a treatise on natural law was at first glance less problematic. However, Holberg's textbook contains several detailed interpretations of both the Danish and the Norwegian codes. Consequently, he had to modify the content of his natural law to avoid coming into conflict with these special conditions in Denmark-Norway.

The result was a version of natural law mainly in accordance with the prevailing political and theological doctrines. Consequently, the first textbook on law written in Danish, despite natural law being regarded as a legal system of universal character, was a unique attempt to adjust universal legal principles to the special legal cultural environment still dominated by theologians and not lawyers.

Moral Cruxes or introduction to natural law and law of nations[15]

Holberg published the first edition of his textbook *Moralske Kierne eller Introduction til Naturens og Folkerettens Kundskab* [The Core of Morality or Introduction to Natural and International Law] in 1716. The textbook belongs to the Protestant-rationalistic, natural-law tradition established by Hugo Grotius and consolidated by Samuel Pufendorf and Christian Thomasius. In contrast to his predecessors writing in Latin, Holberg addressed a limited Scandinavian—mainly Danish and Norwegian—audience. Combining general principles of natural law with concise provisions in national legislation was one of the key factors in the textbook's success. Another contributing factor was its strong Lutheran-rooted anthropology. Holberg's textbook on natural law became a bestseller and was the most sold of his books during his lifetime. The book was published in several editions (1728, 1734, 1741, 1751, and—posthumously—1763).[16] However, just a couple of years after his death it lost popularity and was mainly forgotten until literary scholars like Billeskov Jansen and Kåre Foss discovered the enormous influence natural law-thinking had on Holberg's fiction and other prose writings.[17] In the twenty-first century, historians, philosophers, and legal historians also started to analyze Holberg's natural law. While older researchers of legal history had not devoted much attention to this book,[18] more recent studies indicate that *Moralske Kierne* was more than a mere compilation of Pufendorf's natural law translated into Danish.[19] When reinterpreting Holberg's impact on legal thinking, his views on the relationship between law, religion, and morality turned out to be decisive.[20]

Even though it is virtually impossible to demonstrate any direct impact the textbook may have had on contemporary legal science and legislation (*law in books*), the textbook was highly important to legal practitioners and their concept of law, in other words for *law in action*.[21] By reconstructing Holberg's particular version of natural law and its intended place in the Danish and Norwegian legal culture, it becomes possible to enhance the understanding of the legal reality the textbook addressed. This reality constituted the political, constitutional, and social framework that was the basis for legal practitioners in the first half of the eighteenth century. The basic hypothesis of this chapter is that Holberg modified several ideas, viewpoints, and rules held by his role models so as to make the content of his textbook more suitable to a Danish-Norwegian context and thus to the expectations of his audience. This audience, in contrast to Pufendorf's and Thomasius's, was almost exclusively Lutheran often impacted by pietism, making the clear distinction between law, morals, and theology not just dispensable but inexpedient. Not surprisingly, many aberrations from Holberg's sources of inspiration were caused by the desire to prove the concordance of Lutheran theology with natural-law theory. The importance of these adjustments becomes obvious when one takes into account that the popularity of Holberg's textbook was not significantly diminished even when a literal translation of Pufendorf's *De officio* into Danish was published in 1742.[22] This translation was never published in a second edition, whereas Holberg's *Introduction*, as mentioned earlier, came out in several new editions.

What makes Holberg's textbook more fitting to the pietistic environment in Denmark and Norway than Pufendorf's or Thomasius's treatises on natural law? To answer this question, one has to look at the differences between Holberg's text and his source texts.[23] This has been done in more detail elsewhere.[24] In this chapter, I focus on the specific theological aspects of the first textbook on natural law written in Danish.

Re-establishing a connection between natural law and Protestantism?

Until recently, the prevailing opinion among Holberg scholars was that the theological aspects in his textbook were disturbing debris in a treatise that—in the spirit of the Enlightenment—had the final aim of separating profane matters from theology.[25] However, a thorough reading of the textbook reveals that he had a quite different agenda than his role models Grotius, Pufendorf, and

Thomasius. Holberg's aim was to establish a framework of moral norms fitting the specific legal, cultural, and political circumstances and preconditions of the Danish-Norwegian realm. Jørgen Magnus Sejersted concludes in an article from 2012 that "one may even be inclined to say that re-establishing a connection between natural law and Christianity, especially Protestantism, is the core of Holberg's natural law."[26] This hypothesis seems convincing at least for some parts of the textbook. However, in other parts of the work, a specific Lutheran impact is more difficult to detect or entirely absent. In my opinion, it is therefore more correct to argue that statements containing a reference to specific elements of Christianity in general and Lutheran pietism more specifically are caused by Holberg's attempt to modify natural law to bring it into accordance with the experiences and expectations of his intended audience.[27] As those experiences and expectations were based in a homogeneous Lutheran culture where state power, law, religion, and morals had one common source, the royal authority, there was no point for Holberg in carefully distinguishing the different spheres. Somewhat oversimplifying, one can claim that Holberg's intention with his textbook was to create "a natural (legal) order for the Danish and Norwegian Realm(s)."[28] In this natural order, religious, moral, and legal norms are not conflicting entities but instead complementary.

In the following, I will give several specific examples supporting this argument. At the same time, I will demonstrate how Christian ideas had been re-established in the first textbook on (natural) law written in Danish.

The missing chapter on natural religion

A first interesting observation is that Holberg's textbook lacks a chapter regarding natural religion. This is remarkable because it had become common in the natural-law discourse in the late seventeenth and early eighteenth century to divide human duties into three main categories: duties towards oneself, our neighbors, and God.[29] The most prominent advocate for this division was the very man for whom Holberg had the highest regard among the natural philosophers,[30] his role model Samuel Pufendorf.[31] Nevertheless, Holberg does not refer to the natural religion, nor does he argue for a strict distinction between natural law and moral theology.[32] For Pufendorf, this was a central topic, which he treated at length both in his preface and again in Chapter 4 of the concise textbook *De Officio hominis et civis juxta legem naturalem libri duo*. The basic notion in Pufendorf's argumentation is to minimize the role of religion and especially moral theology when determining the content of natural law.[33]

Natural religion, for Pufendorf, was indeed a necessary precondition "to promote the common Tranquility and Sociability or reciprocal Union in this Life."[34] However, accepting the existence of an indefinitely perfect God who had created and governs the world was also the only requirement for the existence and application of natural law. Religion is hence necessary, but by reducing religion to its "natural" content, Pufendorf intends to eliminate all theological aspects from his concept of natural law. The reference to nature indicates here a limitation to aspects of religion that are (seemingly) in concordance with natural reason.[35] Indeed, Pufendorf defines natural religion as precepts according to natural reason without any (apparent) reference to or preference towards a particular denomination.

The separation between moral theology and natural law thus was a core element of Pufendorf's natural-law theory.[36] It was necessary not just to enable him to address a wider audience regardless of his readers' theological views, but also because natural law based on a rational rather than theological concept of religion would further the overall purpose of natural law, namely, to safeguard social peace and tolerance between Catholics and Protestants despite confessional separation. After the Thirty Years' War (1618–48), it eventually had become apparent that the confessional separation in Germany and Europe would remain permanent. Failing to provide universally acceptable standards for the coexistence of different religious groups in early modern society, theological theories of law were gradually replaced by secular natural-law theories in the seventeenth century. Consequently, a strict separation of moral theology and natural law became a common feature of the major contributions in this field by Hugo Grotius, Thomas Hobbes, Samuel Pufendorf, and the early Christian Thomasius.

In the early eighteenth century, the focus eventually started to change, as wars exclusively legitimized by denominational differences became fewer in Europe. Rational natural-law theories were no longer perceived as incommensurable with theological precepts.[37] This was particularly obvious in territories where the Lutheran doctrine was well established and consolidated, as it was in the Nordic countries and Prussia. Thomasius and Wolff's struggle with Lutheran orthodoxy in Leipzig were arguably the last major conflicts relating to different conceptions of natural law and moral theology. Halle had become the new center of intellectual development. After Thomasius's death in 1728, Johann Gottlieb Heineccius and later Wolff and his disciples were the leading figures of the natural-law movement in Germany. They were concerned with defining the primary principle of natural law and with refining the method used to deduce norms from their natural-law systems. Separation of law and morals was no longer on top of their agenda.

On the other hand, both Heineccius and Wolff would retain the traditional arrangement of natural duties: duties towards ourselves, our neighbors, and God.[38] With this background, Holberg's reluctance to present these duties in his textbook seems even more peculiar.

However, it would be wrong to conclude on the basis of this that Holberg was arguing for a radical secular theory of natural law. The opposite is true. In contrast to Heineccius, who published his natural law in a comparably less orthodox environment and at the height of his career and reputation, Holberg had to take precautions to pass the strict censorship of the theologians in Copenhagen. By avoiding any remarks on natural religion, he made his natural law less vulnerable to potential critics. That was particularly important in Denmark. Leading theologians there had severely criticized Pufendorf's idea of a natural religion aiming at separating moral theology and natural law. The two most prominent and influential protagonists of Protestant orthodoxy were theologians Hans (Johannes) Vandal (1624–75) and Hector Gottfried Masius (1653–1709).[39] The latter, especially, had openly accused both Pufendorf and Thomasius of promoting dangerous ideas that could enable the destruction of the Christian foundations of the Danish-Norwegian kingdom and society.[40] As priest at the royal court (*Hofprest*), he used his influence to get Thomasius's works banned and later even burned in public. Both Vandal and Masius strictly rejected any ideas of a social contract and remained strong advocates of the divine origin of absolute royal sovereignty.[41] It is no coincidence that the constitutional document establishing the absolutist regime in the realm from 1665 (*Lex regia* – Kongeloven) was first made public in the very year Masius died (1709). The *King's Law* is based on the narrative that the estates representing the people had willingly agreed to provide the crown with unlimited powers. The social-contractual basis of this narrative was obvious. If one takes this into account, it seems reasonable that Holberg did not start to work on his textbook on natural law before 1709.

However, the influence of the theologians at the royal court remained strong after Masius's death as well. As Holberg intended to use his textbook in natural law to promote his academic career and to gain a permanent position at the University of Copenhagen, it seems reasonable to assume that he tried to avoid provoking the theological establishment with radical secular ideas of natural law. Pufendorf's notion of natural religion was still regarded as dangerous and had even been labeled atheistic by leading theologians.

Furthermore, Calvinist authors, with Jean Barbeyrac in the lead, had been attracted to the idea of a natural religion for quite different reasons.[42] Their purpose was to establish an individual right to religious freedom, including the right of free conscience. As natural religion did not require a specific truth and a specific inner conscience, Pufendorf's natural law would not provide such individual rights.

In this context, leaving out a chapter regarding natural religion and the duties towards God probably seemed a good idea. To a certain extent, however, Holberg may have felt compelled to include it. There is convincing evidence that Holberg originally had written such a chapter and wanted it to be printed. Ten pages are missing in the first edition of the textbook, and Holberg wrote later that he once was forced to take out ten pages from a manuscript.[43] He is no more specific than that, but the exact number of pages missing in *Moralske Kierne* and the historical circumstances strongly indicate that Holberg was advised to remove the chapter.[44] The fact that his book was censored by professor Heinrich (Henrik) Weghorst (cf. imprimatur) supports this argument because Weghorst himself had criticized both Grotius's and Pufendorf's attempts to detach natural law from moral theology and Protestant doctrine.[45]

Nevertheless, while Holberg did not remove the chapter on natural religion entirely of his own will, he obviously did not regret his decision. After becoming a professor, he was exempted from any censorship and later even became his own publisher. Still, he never added a chapter on natural religion. Taking into account the relationship between natural law, morals, and religion in Holberg's natural-law theory more closely, this is not surprising.

Religion, morals, and law

The original title of the book was "Moral Cruxes" (*Moralske Kierne*).[46] This reference to morals indicates that Holberg himself regarded natural law as part of a bigger universe of moral norms.

Yet Holberg distinguishes between pure reason and moral considerations, including justice. Whenever these two come into conflict, he prefers moral considerations to reason. He even makes a fool of purely rational thinking. With reference to the French philosopher Pierre Bayle, he reminds the reader in his textbook on natural law that following pure reason and putting aside the Bible or God's precepts would lead to the absurd result that a man could lend his wife to another like a book.[47] For as a binding guideline for human actions, natural reason has thus to be in accordance with morality, especially Christian morality.[48] Natural-law norms are therefore binding only to the extent that their rationality is in concordance with Christian morals and not because they are in concordance with an objective, natural reason. It was obviously not a major concern for Holberg that this position is incompatible with the universal truth claim of rational natural-law theory.

Such a perception of natural law can also be identified in his later works. In the essay collection *Moral Thoughts*, from 1744, Holberg states:

> Nobody can doubt the benefit of making people used to read these [natural law] treatises, presenting human duties and natural laws in a lofty but dry style, even though they are generally not amusing but they are instructive.[49]

The underlying assumption is that norms of all kinds have to be learned. In concordance with the educational ideal of the Enlightenment, all humans are obliged to obey all norms that safeguard a peaceful and fruitful life in society. This principle applies not only for positive norms but for moral and natural ones as well. There are, however, different ways of learning. In addition, Holberg's comedies and other fictional writings are frequently constructed around a moral plot. Reading books on natural law is just another way of gaining the necessary insights. For Holberg, it was clear that studying the scripture is also to be regarded as necessary to achieve this goal.

For example, Holberg emphasizes the interconnection between religious morality and law when considering the duties of people in a civil state. He starts by claiming that citizens must obey the civil laws. However, he adds a restraint: this duty applies only to the extent that civil laws are in accordance with God's law (*Guds Lov*). He justifies this limitation by arguing that human beings must obey God more than humankind (*efterdi man maa adlyde Gud meere end Menneskene*).[50] Pufendorf's textbook on natural law does not contain a similar limitation. In contrast to Pufendorf, Holberg consequently argues that the obligation in natural law to obey civil laws applies only where those laws are in no violation of divine law.

Holberg emphasizes the importance of religion also when elaborating on the duties of the prince towards citizens.

> The Prince has especially to take care that the pure Christian Truth is to be taught, because this religion, besides promoting eternal salvation, facilitates civil society and live more than all positive precepts. This is especially true for the evangelical truth, as Doct. Masius has demonstrated in his treatise against Becman, *de Interesse Principum circa religionem Evangelicam.*[51]

The prince is obliged to ensure that the genuine (*uforfalsket*) Christian truth is taught, because religion, besides providing for eternal salvation, contributes more to civil society than do all civil laws. The reference to the pure teaching of Christian truth could also be found in Pufendorf's *De officio.*[52] Nevertheless, Holberg adds another sentence leaving no doubt that he refers to the Lutheran denomination when citing Masius's treatise against Becman.[53] In this writing, Masius had argued for the essential role of Lutheran doctrine to safeguard a stable government. All other Protestant denominations would contribute to undermining the absolute power of the sovereign. Supporting this point of view, Holberg concludes that Lutheran doctrine provides both the prince and the people with great certainty.

Modifications and additions in later editions

Holberg also worked on his textbook after the first edition and added several hundred pages of material to later editions. In many of these, he revised his position, and we can observe an even more critical attitude towards a separation of natural law and moral theological considerations. Concerning parents' authority over their children, he openly criticizes Pufendorf's point of view.

> Here in this point, however, I hold the opinion that due to certain considerations, Pufendorf's opinion should be narrowly interpreted. A father may by the rule of nature well possess great power over his offspring; however, he may not have the right to force them to things that will obviously cause them pain or damage, as such actions would displease God.[54]

Acknowledging the general authority of the father regarding his children, Holberg argues that this authority has some limitations. A father may not force a child to do something that would be harmful or destructive, because such a command would contradict the will of God. This statement refers to the question whether a father could force his daughter to marry a man she does not love.[55] In contrast to Pufendorf,[56] Holberg regards marriage as a divine institution[57] and not a mere civil contract based on both parties' consideration. In this context, more pragmatic considerations are applied to support Holberg's view against Pufendorf's opinion. Holberg argues that a marriage is a contract obliging the parties for the duration of their lives. With this principle in view, it has to be warranted that the spouses will be able to live a life based on mutual respect and affection. Consequently, God will find displeasure in a marriage that can be anticipated to end in hell [at least for one of the spouses].[58] God's pleasure (*Guds Behag*) in this context may be interpreted as sound reason, including both practical and moral considerations. Therefore, the marriage is void without the daughter's approval. The mutual consent of both spouses thus becomes necessary in Holberg's Nordic version of natural law. This view becomes predominant also in writings of other Scandinavian natural-law scholars.[59]

Holberg's critical attitude towards a natural law based purely on logical deductivism is reflected also in his struggle against a widespread opinion that natural law would allow a marriage between close relatives. Christian Thomasius was the most prominent advocate for this view.[60] His disciple Andreas Hojer had tried to defend Thomasius's radical ideas in his treatise *De nuptiis proprinquorum jure divino non prohibitis.*[61]

Hojer argues that there is no reasonable ground (*fornuftsgrund*) to prohibit a marriage between parents and children. Both the customs of many ancient and contemporary nations would allow such an alliance, and even the Bible contains no evidence in favor of the opposite.[62] Hojer attenuates his radical statement by emphasizing that such marriages would cause some disturbance in the social community and, more seriously, conflict with the ideas of Christian purification and perfection.[63] Nevertheless, this would not lead to a different outcome.

Holberg attacked this opinion in a separate writing. In the second edition of his textbook on natural law, he summarizes his main arguments. Once again, Holberg emphasizes that it is impossible to distinguish between natural reason and God's law, that is, Christian morality.[64] For Holberg, something that contradicts divine revelation and the Ten Commandments and at the same time conflicts with contemporary moral perception to such a degree that permitting it would cause civil disturbance cannot, under any circumstances, be regarded as in accordance to natural law.[65] Consequently, disobeying the moral law (*Moralske Lov*) and the Commandments is a sin not only against God but also against the natural order and ultimately natural law.

The Bible and ten commandments as sources of natural law

It becomes obvious that this position is more than a mere rhetorical reflex of Holberg, the former theology student,[66] when one looks at his argumentation regarding the grounds and sources of natural law. In this context, he re-establishes the Bible and the Ten Commandments as binding sources of natural law.

> And because God has commanded the natural law, and annealed it into the human heart, this law cannot be altered by anyone, but everyone is bound to

> abide by it; this law is labeled general law because it is issued to all and can be recognized and understood by natural reason; however, it is verbalized even more clearly and explicitly in the Scripture and the Ten Commandments.[67]

Building on Pufendorf's statement in his main work on natural law (*De Jure naturae et Gentium* 1672), Holberg converts the meaning almost to its opposite.[68] Without having consciously intended this, Holberg's view on natural law is more in concordance with the Christian natural law theories of Melanchton[69] and Hemmingsen[70] than the secular theories of his role models Pufendorf and Thomasius. Hemmingsen, especially, wrote in his book *De lege naturae apodictica methodus concinnata* [On the law of nature] that deduced natural- law duties form the Ten Commandments. Even though Holberg does not apply Hemmingsen's methodological approach, several other examples of Lutheran rhetoric and references to the Ten Commandments in his textbook on natural law bear evidence of a natural-law theory firmly based on religious morality.[71]

As mentioned earlier, Christian morality and natural law for Holberg are two sides of the same coin.[72] This perspective is also important for Holberg's view of the basis and function of positive law, as both morality and natural reason give positive law its legitimacy. At the same time, both are necessary to supplement or even correct legislation where it is fragmentary or leads to unjust results.[73] Assuming that all legislation is supposed to be in accordance with natural and divine law, these two sets of norms become the benchmark when interpreting secular legislation.

Conclusion

We have seen that the first textbook on basic legal principles written in Danish contains some remarkable traces of Protestant theology in a work that is supposed to explain the universal and secular principles of rational natural law. However, because of modifications intended to meet the expectations of Holberg's intended audience, precepts of moral theology merge here with sound reason to form a unique Nordic version of natural law showing traces of a pragmatic approach towards law, which is characteristic of the Nordic legal cultures even today.

Notes

1 Ludvig Holberg, *Almindelig Kirke-Historie – fra Christendommens første Begyndelse til Lutheri Reformation, med nogle Anmerkninger Over de udi Historien omtalte Cy-Clis og Aars-Beregninger, vol. 2* (Copenhagen: Johann Georg Høpffner, 1738), 485, 630ff., 774, 779, 856.

2 Ludvig Holberg, *Dannemarks og Norges Geistlige og Verdslige Staat*, 2nd ed. (Copenhagen, 1749), chap. 12–13, 425 ff., 569 ff. Rev. ed., with an introduction by Sebastian Olden-Jørgensen. Copenhagen: Vandkunsten, 2014.

3 Sebastian Olden-Jørgensen, *Introduction to Dannemarks og Norges Geistlige og Verdslige Staat*, in Ludvig Holberg, *Dannemarks og Norges Geistlige og Verdslige Staat*, 2nd ed. (Copenhagen, 1749) 14.

4 "*Paa retsvidenskaben har jeg anvendt saa megen tid og arbejde, at jeg paa en maade kan regnes med til de retskyndige. Jeg kender dens teori, men mangler praksis.*" Ludvig Holberg, *Tredje Levnedsbrev*, trans. A. Kragelund (Det Danske Sprog- og Litteraturselskab, 2014) 138, http://holbergsskrifter.no/holberg-public/view?docId=levnedsbreve%2FAdVir3_overs.page&chunk.id=part3&show.second=&toc.depth=1&toc.id=part3; cf. Erik Solems translation:

> Lovkyndighed har jeg anvendt så meget tid og flid på at jeg i visse måter kan regnes blant juristene. Jeg har tilegnet meg toerien, men praksis mangler, derfor er jeg litt rådvill med hensyn til juridiske formaliteter, som man kun lærer i praksis, og lar meg råde av andre.

Erik Solem, "Holberg som jurist," *Tidsskrift for rettsvitenskap* (1946): 381–433, 525–56; see also Erik Solem, *Holberg som jurist* (Oslo: Aschehoug & Co, 1947), 7ff.

5 Ditlev Tamm and Klaus Neiiendam, *Holberg og juristerne – et antologi med indledninger af Klaus Neiiendam and Ditlev Tamm* (Copenhagen: Jurist- og Økonomforbundets Forlag, 1982), 37, who translates the latin "*quodammodo*" to "almost/*nesten*."

6 Most prominently may be Johann Gottlieb Heineccius (1681–1741), who, having studied theology, turned to legal studies and became a law professor in 1720. Comparing these two writers is interesting also due to other remarkable parallels in their backgrounds and writings, not least their works on natural law, which were both heavily influenced by Samuel Pufendorf. See also Tamm and Neiiendam, *Holberg og Juristerne,* 37.

7 A prominent example is Christian Wolff, who, despite not being an educated lawyer, had an enormous impact on legal science and more indirect influence on law in action.

8 "Theoriam assecutus sum, sed deest praxis." Holberg, *Tredje Levnedsbrev*, 138.

9 See also the chapter on Hemmingsen in this volume.

10 Tyge Krogh, *Oplysningstiden og det magiske – henrettelser og korporlige straffe i 1700-tallets første halvdel* (Copenhagen: Samleren, 2000), 540–44, with an overview over some verdicts and their reasoning.

11 Sören Koch, *En naturlig rettsorden for det dansk-norske kongerike – en rettshistorisk analyse av Ludvig Holbergs lærebok i natur- og folkerett* (Ph.D. diss., University of Bergen, 2015), 16ff.

12 The concept of a legal cultural filter was introduced by Eirik Holmøyvik in the article "*A Little Bit of This and a Little Bit of That – The Complexity of Legal Reception,*" in *Rendezvous of European Legal Cultures,* Jørn Øyrehagen Sunde and Knut Einar Skodvin, eds. (Bergen: Fagbokforlaget, 2010), 45–59.

13 Ludvig Holberg, *Moralske Kierne eller Introduction til Naturens- og Folke-rettens Kundskab* (Copenhagen, 1716), book I, chap. 3, 81.

14 Danske Lov/Norske Lov 1-1-2 in conjunction with 1-1-1 states that the king possesses the exclusive authority to grant dispensation or even interpret the legislation that binds all citizens and judges (1-1-4).

15 Danish title: "Moralske Kierne eller Introduction til Naturens og Folkerettens Kundskab."

16 It was later translated into German (1748) and Swedish (1789), but was never distributed to a European audience on a wider scale.

17 *Ludvig Holberg: Værker i tolv bind*, F.J. Billeskov Jansen, ed., vol. 1, 1969 and vol. 12, 1971 (Copenhagen: Rosenkilde og Bagger, 1969–71); Kåre Foss, *Ludvig Holbergs naturrett. På idehistorisk bakgrunn* (Oslo: Gyldendal, 1934).

18 Solem, "*Holberg som jurist,*" 381–433, 525–56; Tamm and Neiiendam, *Holberg og juristerne.*

19 Koch, *En naturlig rettsorden*; Jørn Øyrehagen Sunde, "*Fornuft og Erfarenhed*" – *framveksten av metodisk medvit i dansknorsk rett på 1700-talet*" (PhD diss., University

of Bergen, 2007), 222; Jørn Øyrehagen Sunde, *Speculum legale – rettsspegelen – ein introduksjon til den norske rettskulturen si historie i eit europeisk perspektiv* (Bergen: Fagbokforlaget, 2010), 279.

20 Koch, *En naturlig rettsorden*, 184 ff.

21 Koch, *En naturlig rettsorden*, 16–29.

22 Samuel Pufendorf, *Menniskes og en Borgeres Plikter efter Naturens Lov, beskrevne i det Latinske Sprog af Baron Samuel Pufendorf, siden oversatte paa Fransk af Jean Barbeyrac, og nu efter samme franske Oversættelses 4de Edition, tillege med bemeldte Barbeyracs derhos giorte Anmerkninger, trykt til Amsterdam 1718. Fordanskede*, trans. Christian Homfred Brugman (Copenhagen: Gottmann Fridrich Kisel, 1742).

23 Regarding methodological challenges see Koch, *En naturlig rettsorden*, chap. 2.

24 Koch, *En naturlig rettsorden*.

25 Jansen, *Ludvig Holberg: Værker i tolv bind*, 44 ff.; Foss, *Ludvig Holbergs naturrett*, 473.

26 "Å knytte sammen naturrett og kristendommen, særlig protestantisme, er selve kjernen i Holbergs naturrett." Jørgen Magnus Sejersted, "Bibel og protestantisme i Holbergs naturrett," in *Ludvig Holbergs naturrett*, Jørgen Magnus Sejersted and Eiliv Vinje, eds. (Oslo: Gyldendal, 2012), 160.

27 Koch, *En naturlig rettsorden*, 199.

28 This is the title of my thesis. In Norwegian: "En naturlig rettsorden for det Dansk-Norske Kongerike."

29 Despite some reservations regarding details, this was also stated by Pufendorf's most prominent commentator Jean Barbeyrac, see note to Pufendorf's *De Jure Naturae et Gentium*, book II, chap. 3 § 15.

30 Despite the high esteem for Hugo Grotius in general, Holberg regarded Pufendorf's natural law system as perfect. See Holberg, foreword to *Moralske Kierne*, B4v: "Thus his system is regarded the most complete and best."

31 Samuel Pufendorf, *The Whole Duty of Man, According to the Law of Nature*, 5th ed., with the notes of Mr. Barbeyrac and many other additions and amendments, trans. Andrew Tooke, introd. Ian Hunter and David Saunders, eds. (Indianapolis: Liberty Fund, 1735 [2005]), chap. 3, para. 12, p. 59; chap. 4 with the title: "The Duty of Man towards God, or Concerning Natural Religion." See also Samuel Pufendorf, *The Law of Nature and Nations. Eight Books. Written in Latin by Baron Pufendorf, Counsellor of State to His late Swedish Majesty and the King of Prussia. Done into English by Basil Kenneth, to Which Are Added all the Large Notes of Mr. Barbeyrac, Translated from the Best Edition*, 4th ed. (London: J. Waltoe et al. 1729 [Reprint 2005]), book II, chap. 3, para. 24; furthermore, Samuel Pufendorf, *Of the Nature and Qualification of Religion in Reference to Civil Society*, trans. Jodocus Crull, ed. and introd. Simone Zurbuchen (Indianapolis: Liberty Fund, 1687 [2002]).

32 Koch, *En naturlig rettsorden*, 184 ff.

33 Sejersted, "Bibel og protestantisme i Holbergs naturrett," 161.

34 Pufendorf, *The Whole Duty of Man*, book I, chap. 3, para. 12.

35 "Pufendorf conceives of natural religion, that is—of the duties to God known through reason alone—as a subordinate part of natural law." Ian Hunter and David Saunders, *Comments on Samuel Pufendorf. The Whole Duty of Man According to the Law of Nature* (Indianapolis: Liberty Fund, 2003), 59.

36 "Furthermore, that is by far the most important distinction whereby the end and aim of the natural law is included only in the circuit of this life, and therefore it moulds man accordingly as he ought to lead this life in society with others. But moral theology moulds a man into a Christian, [. . .] who especially hopes for the fruit of piety after this life." Pufendorf, preface to *The Whole Duty of Man*, 7.

37 On this topic, Knud Haakonssen, "Protestant Natural Law Theory: A General Interpretation," in *New Essays on the History of Autonomy: A Collection Honoring*

J.B. Schneewind, Natalie Brender and Larry Krasnoff, eds. (Cambridge: Cambridge University Press, 2004) https://doi.org/10.1017/CBO9780511498039.005 92–109.

38 Johann Gottlieb Heineccius, *A Methodical System of Universal Law, with Supplements and a Discourse by George Turnbull*, edited with an introduction by Thomas Ahnert and Peter Schröder, ed. Knud Haakonssen, (Indianapolis: Liberty Fund, 1741 [2008]), book I, chap. 3, §§ 91 ff., who puts the duty towards God first.

39 Johannes Vandal, preface to *Juris regii ἀνυπευθύνον et solutissimi com potestate summa nulla nisi deo obnoxia libri VI*, [Six books on royal powers] (Copenhagen, 1663–68), 9, arguing for moral theology been a necessary precondition for the understanding of natural law and law in general.

40 Hector Gottfried Masius, *De Interesse Principum circa Religionem Evangelicam ad Serenissimum ac potentissimum Daniae Regem* (Copenhagen, 1687); Hector Gottfried Masius, *Ortodoxia Lutherana de origine imperii divina et immediate in Epist. Ad Rom. XIII v. 1, 2 fundata* (Copenhagen, 1688).

41 Masius, *Ortodoxia Lutherana*, 16ff.

42 Cf. *Barbeyrac*'s comments on Pufendorf, *The Whole Duty of Man*, book I, chap. 3, n. 15. See also Barbeyrac's answer to Leibniz's anonymous review of Pufendorfs *De Officio*: Jean Barbeyrac, "The Judgement of an Anonymus Writer on the Original of This Abridgement, with Reflections of the Translator, Intended to Clarify Certain of the Authors Principles," in *The Whole Duty of Man, According to the Law of Nature* (Indianapolis: Liberty Fund, 2005), 267–305, 274ff. §§ 6ff.; regarding this discourse J.B. Schneewind, "Barbeyrac and Leibniz on Pufendorf," in *Samuel Pufendorf und die deutsche Frühaufklärung*, Fiammetta Palladini and Gerald Hartung, eds. (Berlin, 1996), 181–89; Ian Hunter, "Conflicting Obligations: Pufendorf, Leibniz and Barbeyrac on Civil Authority," *History of Political Thought* 25 (4) (2004): 670–99.

43 Ludvig Holberg, *Ludvig Holbergs Tredje Brev Til En Højvelbaaren Herre* (Copenhagen, 1743), 108.

44 Koch, *En naturlig rettsorden*, 202ff.

45 "*Præcepta juris naturæ non dependant à voluntate humana, ut iis obligari pro suo arbitrio homo possit, vel non possit, sed à voluntate DEI, qui per rectam rationem homini indicat, quid ab eo fieri velit, aut omitti. Unde ante omnia Deum juris hujus autorem esse dicimus. Immò intellectus humanus non legislatoris, sed præconis duntaxat vicem obtinet, quem ad promulganda seu indicandam legem sua. Supremus Legum Arbiter adhibet. Unde facile apparet juris naturæ obligationem esse nullam, nisi præsupponatur DEus, quemadmodum jus voce præconis promulgatum non obligat, nisi sit Rex, aut Summa potestas, ex cujus Voluntate promulgetur.* **Non ergo affinimur Grotio**, *cujus hæc sunt verba Et hæc quidem, que jam diximus, locum aliquem haberent, etiam si daremus, quod sine summon scelere dari nequit, non esse DEum, aut non curari ab eo negotia humana: Tract. De jur. B. & P. Proleg. §. 11. Nec cum Thoma facimus in 1. 2. quest. 71 art. 6 sic loquentis. Tametsi Deus non esset, necmenadcium peccatum: Quam sententiam miror non carpi in notis Grotio novissime adjunctis,* **uti tamen allegatur Zieglerus, cujus contraria sententia silentio ibi involvitur.**" Henrik Weghorst, *Compendii Juris Naturæ, Dissertatio Prima, quam in Illustri Academia Equestri Regia Hafniensi, præside Henrico Wegehorst, defendet Nicolaus Trollehoeg ad diem 19 Martii An. 1696* (Copenhagen: Joachim Smetgen, 1696), chap. 1, § 14, 9 (my emphasis).

46 Cf. front page of volume 2 from the first edition, published 1716 [the first offprint was manufactured in 1715, but the entire book was not distributed in that year].

47 Holberg, *Moralske Kierne*, 2nd ed., book II, chap. 1, 4.

48 On this relationship, see Wim Decock, *Theologians and Cotract Law – The Moral Transformation of the Ius Commune* (Leiden/Boston, 2013).

49 Ludvig Holberg, *Moralske Tanker* (1744).

50 "Undersaattere ere forbundne til at være alle Borgerlige Love hørige, saa vidt de ikke stride mod Guds Lov, og det ikke saa meget af Frygt for Straf, som af indvortes

Forpligtelse, men ingen forbindes efter Øvrighedens Befalning at bedrive noget Ont, efterdi man maa adlyde Gud meere end Menneskene." Holberg, *Moralske Kierne,* book II chap. 10, 286.

51 "The Prince has to show special care for that the Christian Truth is tough unbiased, because it is the very Religion, which, besides leading to eternal salvation, also strengthens the civil society more than all civil laws; in particular, a Prince can find great security in the Lutheran truth, as Dr. Masius teaches us in his treatise against Beckman, *De Interesse Principum circa religionem Evangelicam.*" Holberg, *Moralske Kierne,* book II, chap. 9, 282. Transl. SK: For a rather different approach, see Christian Thomasius, *The Rights of Protestant Princes Regarding Indifferent Matters. I: Christian Thomasius. Esseys on Chruch, State and Politics,* eds., trans. and introd. Ian Hunter, Thomas Ahnert, and Frank Grunert (Indianapolis: Liberty Fund, 1695 [2007]), 27 ff.

52 Pufendorf, *The Whole Duty of Man,* book II, chap. 11, § 4.

53 Masius, *De Interesse Principum circa Religionem Evangelicam ad Serenissimum ac potentissimum Daniae Regem.*

54 "Here it seems to me that for different reasons that Pufendorf's opinion should be interpreted restrictively. A father for certain has naturally great power over his children, but can hardly force them to do things, which would obviously harm and deteriorate them, as this could not be approved by God." Holberg, *Moralske Kierne,* 2nd ed., book I, chap. 8, 116.

55 "If a daughter for fear of her father agrees to a marriage with a man against her will, is she still obliged to be truthful, because on the side of the bridgegroom no mistake has been made, therefore he is entitled to demand the promise fulfilled, and the daughter should complaisantly obey her father's command." Holberg, *Moralske Kierne,* book I chap. 9, 118 (my emphasis).

56 "Likewise, if we assume that a father can give a husband to his daughter even against her will, in case she has given her promise to the hated suitor out of fear of her Father's authority, she can by *no means* later break it. For *no defect attaches to the suitor,* whereby he cannot secure a right from the promise, while the daughter should have obeyed her father's orders of her own accord." Pufendorf (1729), book III chap. 6, § 11.

57 "Has the almighty God established the marriage." Holberg, *Moralske Kierne,* book II, chap. 1, 2.

58 "Thus, God has no delight in a marriage that is likely to end up in Hell." Holberg, *Moralske Kierne,* book I, chap. 9, 118.

59 Johann Frederik Vilhem Schlegel, *Naturrettens eller den almindelige Retslæres Grundsætninger,* vol. 2 (Copenhagen, 1798), chap. 2 § 187, 29, referring to the Nordic legal cultural preconditions for a valid marriage.

60 Christian Thomasius, *Institutes of Divine Juresprudence. With Selections from Foundations of the Law of Nature and Nations,* ed., trans., and introd. Thomas Ahnert (Indianapolis: Liberty Fund, 1688/1718 [2011]), book III, chap. 2 § 7; Christian Thomasius, *De crimine bigamiae* (Leipzig, 1685). Already in the first edition, Holberg criticized this view as "Thomasius's curious opinion" [Thomasii selsomme Meeninger], see Holberg, *Moralske Kierne,* book II, chap. 1, 4, 24 and 28; see also Thomasius, *Institutes of Divine Juresprudence,* book III chap. 2, §§ 6, 7 and 21 ff.

61 See page 85 in this volume.

62 "For nå samle de spredte udviklinger: da ekteskap mellom barn og foreldre hverken hos de antikke folk eller hos de nyere, moralske eller barbariske, har været fordømt, og der ikke kan fremføres noen solid fornuftsgrund mot dem, ikke heller findes spor hertil i skrifterne, men de snarere stemmer overens både med de gamles skikk før Moselovene og de fleste senere nasjoners og ekteskapets av naturen forskrevne formål, sees slike ekteskaper ikke å stride mod naturens rett og ikke å være usædelige og utillatelige på en sådan måte at om de finner sted, selve naturen foreskriver at de skal være ugyldige, skadelige og verdi til straff og vanære." Hojer, *De nuptiis proprinquorum jure divino non prohibitis* (Copenhagen, 1717), chap. 1, 34.

63 Ibid.

64 "Men der findes ogsaa de, som gaae end videre, og sige, at den Lov om Blodskam, som forbydes af GUD er ikke Moralsk, men alleene Borgerlig, nemlig skreven for det Jødiske Folk, og ikke for andre. De kand jo med samme Føye da ogsaa sige at Decalogus eller de 10 Guds Bud, ja at alt, hvad GUD har befalet i sin Lov, sigter alleene til det Jødiske Folk, og at vi synde hverken mod Naturen eller directe mod Gud, naar vi overtræde dem; thi der ere faa Bud udi den Moralske Lov, som man kand give fleere naturlige Raisons til end det Bud om Blodskam udi første Grad. Ved saadan Lærdom forarger man kun sin Næste, og lader see sin slette Forstand. Jeg har udføret dette Spørsmaal noget vitløftigen formedelst bekiendte Aarsager." Holberg, *Moralske Kierne*, 2nd ed., book II chap. 1, 34. In the last sentence, Holberg refers to his *Dissertatio Juridica De Nuptiis Proprinquorum*, a writing published anonymously in 1719 reviewing Hojer's *De Nuptiis* in a quite polemical way.

65 "[H]an [Hojer] nøjes ikke med ugudeligt og ublufærdigt at benægte, at et saadant ægteskab er forbudt efter naturretten, men ogsaa efter de positive guddommelige love." Further on p. 12 ff.:

> Alt det, som alle folkeslag har anset for afskyeligt, især naar det ikke ses at være nogen særlig grund, der kunde have ført i en gal retning, det strider mot naturen. [. . .] Enighet blandt alle folkeslag har jo saa stor vægt, at teologer og filosoffer ud derfra har bevist Guds existens, og romersk retskyndige har ment, at folkeret og naturret er to ord for det samme.

See also: p. 14: "Det vil sige, at den slags ægtesskaber har været utilstedelige ifølge den guddommelige almindelige *og* naturlige ret." Holberg, *Dissertatio Juridica De Nuptiis Proprinquorum*, 2.

66 As has been claimed by Foss: "Ubetydelig ryggemarksrefleks hos den unge teologen Holberg," *Ludvig Holbergs naturrett*, 460.

67 "Og effterdi GUD saaledes har forordnet den Naturlige Lov, og indprentet den udi Menneskenes Hierter, saa kand de udi ingen Maade forandre den, men ere stedse forbunden at leve derefter; den kaldes Allmindelig, effterdi den er given alle og kand forstaaes og kiendes af Naturens-Lys, hvorvel den klarligen, og meere udtrykkeligen er given udi den hellige Skrifft besynderlig udi de 10 Bud Ord." Holberg, *Moralske Kierne,* book I, chap. 3, 33.

68 "Though it be usually said, that we have the Knowledge of this Law from Nature itself, yet this is not so to be taken, as if there were implanted in the Minds of Men just new born, plain and distinct Notions concerning what is to be done or avoided." Pufendorf, *The Whole Duty of Man*, book I, chap. 3, §12, 58.

69 Philipp Melanchton, "Philosophiae moralis epitomes libri duo," in *Werke. Studienausgabe, vol. 3*, R. Stupperich, ed. (1546).

70 Niels Hemmingsen, *Om Naturens Lov*, 3 vol, trans., introd. and notes Richard Mott, foreword by Henrik Frandsen (Danmark: Forlaget Øresund, 1562). See in more detail the article on Hemmingsen in this volume, p. 70.

71 For more example see Koch, *En naturlig rettsorden*, 204ff.

72 This is not least indicated by the original title of the book: "*Moralske Kierne*"—Moral Cruxes.

73 Koch, *En naturlig rettsorden*, 143, 232ff., 253ff.

Bibliography

Barbeyrac, Jean "The Judgement of an Anonymus Writer on the Original of This Abridgement, With reflections of the translator, intended to clarify certain of the Author's principles," in Samuel von Pufendorf, *The Whole Duty of Man According to the Law of Nature* (Indianapolis 2005), 267–305.

Decock, Wim, *Theologians and Cotract Law – The Moral Transformation of the Ius Commune*, (Leiden/Boston 2013).

Haakonssen, Knud. "Protestant Natural Law Theory: A general interpretation," in *New Essays on the History of Autonomy: A Collection Honoring J.B. Schneewind*, Natalie Brender and Larry Krasnoff, eds. (Cambridge: Cambridge University Press, 2004).

Heineccius, Johann Gottlieb, *A Methodical System of Universal Law, with Supplements and a Discourse by George Turnbull*, edited with an introduction by Thomas Ahnert and Peter Schröder, ed. Knud Haakonssen, (Indianapolis: Liberty Fund, 1741 [2008]).

Hemmingsen, Niels, *Om Naturens Lov 1562*, 3 vol, trans., introd. and notes Richard Mott, forewords by Henrik Frandsen (Gentofte: Forlaget Øresund, 1993).

Hojer, Andreas, *De nuptiis proprinquorum jure divino non prohibitis* (Copenhagen: Gyldendal 1717).

Holberg, Ludvig, *Almindelig Kirke-Historie – fra Christendommens første Begyndelse til Lutheri Reformation, med nogle Anmerkninger Over de udi Historien omtalte CyClis og Aars-Beregninger*, vol. 2 (Copenhagen: Johann Georg Høpffner, 1738).

Holberg, Ludvig, *Dannemarks og Norges Geistlige og Verdslige Staat*, 2nd ed. (Copenhagen, 1749), Rev. ed., with an introduction by Sebastian Olden-Jørgensen. (Copenhagen: Vandkunsten, 2014).

Holberg, Ludvig, *Ludvig Holbergs Tredje Brev Til En Højvelbaaren Herre* (Copenhagen, 1743).

Holberg, Ludvig, *Moralske Kierne eller Introduction til Naturens- og Folke-rettens Kundskab*, (Copenhagen, 1716).

Holberg, Ludvig, *Moralske Tanker* (Copenhagen: Elias Caspar Reichard, 1744).

Holberg, Ludvig, "Tredje Levnedsbrev," trans. A. Kragelund (Det Danske Sprog- og Litteraturselskab, 2014), http://holbergsskrifter.no/holberg.

Hunter, Ian, *Conflicting Obligations: Pufendorf, Leibniz and Barbeyrac on Civil Authority. History of political Thought*, vol. 25 (4) (2004), 670–99.

Hunter, Ian and Saunders, David, *Comments on Samuel Pufendorf. The Whole Duty of Man according to the Law of Nature* (Indianapolis: Liberty Fund, 2003).

Jansen, F. J. Billeskov, *Ludvig Holberg: Værker i tolv bind*, vol. 1, 1969 and vol. 12, 1971 (Copenhagen: Rosenkilde og Bagger, 1969–71).

Koch, Sören, "En naturlig rettsorden for det dansk-norske kongerike – en rettshistorisk analyse av Ludvig Holbergs lærebok i natur- og folkerett." (Ph.D. diss., University of Bergen, 2015).

Krogh, Tyge, *Oplysningstiden og det magiske – henrettelser og korporlige straffe i 1700-tallets første halvdel* (Copenhagen: Samleren, 2000).

Masius, Hector Gottfried, *De Interesse Principum circa Religionem Evangelicam ad Serenissimum ac potentissimum Daniae Regem* (Copenhagen: Joh. Phil. Bockenhoffer, 1687).

Masius, Hector Gottfried, *Ortodoxia Lutherana de origine imperii divina et immediate in Epist. Ad Rom. XIII v. 1, 2 fundata* (Copenhagen: J.M. Liebe, 1688).

Melanchton, Philipp"Philosophiae moralis epitomes libri duo," in *Werke. Studienausgabe, vol. 3*, ed. R. Stupperich (1546).

Pufendorf, Samuel, *The Law of Nature and Nations. Eight Books. Written in Latin by Baron Pufendorf, Counsellor of State to his late Swedish Majesty and the King of Prussia. Done into English by Basil Kenneth, to which are added all the large Notes of Mr. Barbeyrac, translated from the best Edition*, 4th ed. (London: J. Waltoe et al. 1729 [Reprint 2005]).

Pufendorf, Samuel, *Menniskes og en Borgeres Plikter efter Naturens Lov, beskrevne i det Latinske Sprog af Baron Samuel Pufendorf, siden oversatte paa Fransk af Jean Barbeyrac, og nu efter samme franske Oversættelses 4de Edition, tillege med bemeldte Barbeyracs derhos giorte Anmerkninger, trykt til Amsterdam 1718. Fordanskede, trans.* Christian Homfred Brugman (Copenhagen: Gottmann Fridrich Kisel, 1742).

Pufendorf, Samuel, *Of the Nature and Qualification of Religion in Reference to Civil Society*, trans. Jodocus Crull, ed. and introd. Simone Zurbuchen (Indianapolis: Liberty Fund 1687 [2002]).

Pufendorf, Samuel. *The Whole Duty of Man, According to the Law of Nature*, 5th ed., with the notes of Mr. Barbeyrac and many other additions and amendments, trans. Andrew Tooke, introd. Ian Hunter and David Saunders, eds. (Indianapolis: Liberty Fund, 1735 [2005]).

Schlegel, Johann Frederik Vilhem, *Naturrettens eller den almindelige Retslæres Grundsætninger*, vol. 2 (J. F. Schulz: Copenhagen, 1798).

Thomasius, Christian, *De crimine bigamiae* (Leipzig: Martin Burgkaufmann, 1685).

Thomasius, Christian, *Institutes of Divine Juresprudence. With Selections from Foundations of the Law of Nature and Nations*, ed., trans., and introd. Thomas Ahnert (Indianapolis: Liberty Fund, 1688/1718 [2011]).

Thomasius, Christian, *The Rights of Protestant Princes Regarding Indifferent Matters. In Christian Thomasius. Esseys on Chruch, State and Politics*, eds., trans. and introd. Ian Hunter, Thomas Ahnert, and Frank Grunert (Indianapolis: Liberty Fund, 1695 [2007]).

Schneewind, J. B. "Barbeyrac and Leibniz on Pufendorf," in *Samuel Pufendorf und die deutsche Frühaufklärung*, Fiammetta Palladini and Gerald Hartung, eds., (Berlin: Akademie Verlag, 1996), 181–9.

Sejersted, Jørgen Magnus, "Bibel og protestantisme i Holbergs naturrett," in *Ludvig Holbergs naturrett*, Jørgen Magnus Sejersted and Eiliv Vinje, eds. (Oslo: Gyldendal, 2012), 159–76.

Solem, Erik, "Holberg som jurist," *Tidsskrift for rettsvitenskap* (1946), vol. 59, 381–433, 525–56.

Solem, Erik, *Holberg som jurist* (Oslo: Aschehoug & Co, 1947).

Sunde, Jørn Øyrehagen "Fornuft og Erfarenhed" – framveksten av metodisk medvit i dansknorsk rett på 1700-talet" (PhD diss., University of Bergen, 2007).

Sunde, Jørn Øyrehagen, *Speculum legale – rettsspegelen – ein introduksjon til den norske rettskulturen si historie i eit europeisk perspektiv* (Bergen: Fagbokforlaget, 2010).

Tamm, Ditlev and Neiiendam, Klaus, *Holberg og juristerne – et antologi med indledninger af Klaus Neiiendam and Ditlev Tamm* (Copenhagen: Jurist- og Økonomforbundets Forlag, 1982).

Vandal Johannes, *Juris regii ἀνυπευθύνου et solutissimi com potestate summa nulla nisi deo obnoxia libri VI*, [Six books on royal powers] (Copenhagen: Joh. Weissleb, 1663–68).

Weghorst, Henrik, *Compendii Juris Naturæ, Dissertatio Prima, quam in Illustri Academia Equestri Regia Hafniensi, præside Henrico Wegehorst, defendet Nicolaus Trolleboeg ad diem 19 Martii An. 1696* (Copenhagen: Joachim Smetgen, 1696).

11 Andreas Hojer (1690–1739)—the standard-bearer of Danish-Norwegian Pietism

Kristian Mejrup

Introduction

Andreas Hojer was a polymath and a promoter of legal, educational, and theological reforms. He served during the reign of two absolutist rulers of the Danish-Norwegian realm. In his work on jurisprudence, he elucidated trends in contemporary thinking about natural law, theology, and moral philosophy with an extensive historical and geopolitical knowledge. These contributions, along with his tireless effort in the state administration, at the university and in education and church-related matters, make him one of the great Christian jurists of the North.

Hojer is best known today as the initiator of standardized juridical examinations, introduced in 1736—the year celebrating the bicentennial of the Reformation in Denmark. This achievement denotes the "the birth certificate of lawyers."[1] The same year, he issued the *Ideal of a Danish Jurist*, a manual defining what was required of good lawyers. His work influenced and inspired not only future generations of lawyers and legal scholars but also historians.[2]

Hojer excelled in various disciplines. He was trained in medicine but was equally skilled in theology, philology, moral philosophy, history, and law. When he died at age forty-nine, he had produced books on medicine, history, law, and economy and had held positions as preceptor, doctor, royal historiographer, librarian, councilor, professor of natural law and moral philosophy, university rector, codirector of the royal orphanage, assessor at the supreme court, and chairman of various commissions.

Research into Andreas Hojer's life and work is primarily in Danish, although he composed most of his oeuvre in German and Latin.[3] The church historian Holger Frederik Rørdam (1830–1913) and the legal historian Troels Georg Jørgensen (1874–1970) have written most extensively on Hojer. Jørgensens's monograph of 1961 adds new material but mainly draws together the findings of Rørdam that were dispersed in sundry periodicals and collections from the late nineteenth century.[4] The following survey draws on the work of both scholars as well as consultation of Hojer's own writings.[5]

The religious side of Hojer's life and legal profile certainly merit attention. He was a key figure in promoting Pietism in Denmark and Norway, at first in the

1720s during the reign of Frederik IV and then again in the 1730s during that of Christian VI. He was inspired by legal thinkers as well as theologians: Hugo Grotius, Samuel Pufendorf, John Selden, and Christian Thomasius, as well as Philipp Jacob Spener, August Hermann Francke, and Johann Frantz Buddeus. The input from these thinkers informed the way Hojer strove to modernize the religious and intellectual climate of the eighteenth century. Like his contemporary Erik Pontoppidan, Hojer was both a subscriber to Pietism and a promoter of the enlightened ideas.

Appetite for knowledge

Hojer was born and raised in Karlum, a town in the Duchy of Schleswig, where the Danish-Norwegian king was duke. This region was, on one hand, far from the king's residence in Copenhagen; but at the same time, this area bordered the Holy Roman Empire of the German nation. From this region international, intellectual, and heterodox trends entered the north, and here also the Great Nordic War broke out at the turn of the century.

Hojer came from a family of Lutheran ministers. He was brought up in a religious and erudite environment and trained in Latin, Greek, French, Hebrew, geography, and history. In 1706 his father sent him to Halle, in Brandenburg, to continue his studies. Halle was an apt choice, since this was a new and flourishing center of education and religious reform.

At Halle, Hojer enrolled in the Pædagogium Regium, a school for sons of the nobility and boys of the middle class. The school was founded in the 1690s by the Lutheran minister and professor of theology August Hermann Francke and was one of the attractions of Halle Pietism.[6] This religious reform movement was centered on an orphanage building erected in 1698–1701, and included schools, a printing press, a pharmacy, charitable institutions, manufacturing, and trade businesses. Later in life Hojer administered a reform project in Copenhagen that was modeled after the one at Halle.[7]

At the Pædagogium, Hojer was placed in a top-level class with five others, all of whom continued their studies at the university. He signed up to study medicine and attended the lectures of Georg Ernst Stahl, Michael Alberti, and Friedrich Hoffmann. His unquenchable appetite for knowledge led him to lectures on moral philosophy, natural law, history, and international public law. He listened to the famous legal scholars Christian Thomasius, Nikolaus Hieronymus Gundling, and Jacob Friedrich Ludovici. Hojer reported this information in a letter of January 10, 1726, to Johann Fabricius, a former professor of theology at Helmstedt. The letter is an important source for his biography and therefore worth quoting.[8]

Like another Aladdin, Hojer had good fortune in becoming acquainted with the influential Holstein family, with whom he moved to Copenhagen in 1713. He was employed as a private teacher for the two youngest sons of Johan Georg Holstein,[9] who was one of Frederik IV's entrusted state executives. Johan's eldest son, Johan Ludvig Holstein, followed in his father's footsteps and became state minister and privy councilor to Christian VI. The close ties to the Holstein family were of paramount importance to Hojer's own career, first as a preceptor and a scholarly writer, and later in the state administration.[10]

In 1722, Hojer became royal historiographer for King Frederik IV, and from 1729 librarian at the Royal Library. In 1730 the king died, and the crown succeeded to Christian VI, who replaced his father's advisers and state executives. Hojer's career was thus suspended. Nonetheless, the first results of his effort as a historiographer were donated to the new king in 1732 and dedicated the work to Christian's son, the crown-prince Frederik V. This work, titled "The Glorious Life of Frederik IV," remained unpublished until 1829, but then was well received.[11]

Unburdening the religious authorities

Having frequented Francke's school of learned piety and Thomasius's of natural law, Hojer had first-hand experience with Halle's religious and educational reforms as well as the vigor of and tensions among the different scholars. He knew the pious entrepreneurs, the aspiring ministers working in Francke's schools as student teachers, as well as the famous scholars of the faculties of medicine and law. When Hojer later strove to reform the educational system in Denmark and Norway, his experience of and ongoing correspondence with Halle played a central role. In 1725, when the first initiatives occurred toward a reform of the University of Copenhagen, Hojer suggested to the queen that he be in charge of both the faculty of medicine and the faculty of law.[12] The reform of the university did not occur before 1732, however, during the reign of Christian VI, whose favor Hojer still had to win.

In 1734 the royal connections were reestablished, and Hojer resumed his career in Copenhagen. Together with a considerable collection of books and manuscripts, Hojer moved into the Royal Orphanage on Nytorv in Copenhagen and resided there until his death, in 1739. Frederik IV inaugurated this institution in 1727, and the model at Halle inspired it. The Royal Orphanage thus housed public schools, a printing press, and an apothecary shop. Open to visits, donations, support, and advice, the orphanage was to be a model for society with its own staff and jurisdiction, royal privileges, and exemption from taxes. In return, the institution took care of the social welfare and education, not only of the residing orphans, but also of children of the gentry and university students.[13] The Royal Orphanage also housed state administrative organs and lodged some of the king's best men. Both the Department for Promoting the Gospel (*Collegium de cursu Evangelii promovendo*, established in 1714) and the Department for Church Supervision (*Generalkirkeinspektionskollegiet*, established in 1737) were housed in and administered from the Royal Orphanage. Not only was Hojer a member of both committees, but he also soon was in charge of them and received the appointment of codirector of the orphanage.[14]

While the Department for Promoting the Gospel was in charge of missionary activities and foreign affairs, including translations of the *Bible* and edifying literature, the Department for Church Supervision focused on internal affairs. This new office was Hojer's invention, discreetly developed behind the backs of the bishops. The office was designed to monitor religious affairs and oversee book censorship to retain social order, which in those years was challenged by competing forms of Pietism entering the country.[15] This department also was in charge of improving educational standards and supplying churches and schools with affordable Bibles and edifying literature. To a large extent, the new department handled assignments that already were an integral part of the Royal Orphanage administration, but the power increased and the rhetoric sharpened. The legal charter, written by Hojer, spelled out that the new office should "unburden the religious authorities from their duties." This instruction inevitably meant that bishops and professors of theology lost power that traditionally had belonged to them. The Department for Church Supervision furthermore received the authority to overrule the censorship of the press imposed by theological professors and bishops.[16]

The Royal Orphanage, including its subsidiary departments, thus was at once a secular organization and a means for implementing educational and religious reforms. In addition, the orphanage was a publishing house, distributing Bibles, psalm books, edifying literature, and handbooks on law and religion. Here one could buy affordable books written by authors such as Thomas à Kempis, Spener, and Francke, as well as by Pufendorf, Buddeus, Jeremias Friedrich Reuss, and Hojer himself.

Many of the reforms instigated in the years 1734–39 relied on Hojer's effort as a knowledgeable and a skillful state executive. During the last five years of his life, he allegedly undertook the workload of four full-time officers.[17] His regular promotions from these years suggest his robust career advancement. He was appointed professor of law and moral philosophy (December 3, 1734); secretary of the Department for Promoting the Gospel (December 17, 1734); member of the Committee for Founding Charitable Schools (February 5, 1735); assessor at the Supreme Court (June 3, 1735); doctor of law by royal decree (January 20, 1736); procurator general and member of the chancellery (October 5, 1736); member of the Commission of Medicine (October 5, 1736); member of a Committee for Reforming Latin Schools (February 5, 1737); university rector (September 1, 1737); member of the Department for Church Supervision (October 1, 1737); member of the law committee (October 11, 1737); appointed with the honorary title of state councilor (*Etatsraad*) (November 28, 1738); and member of the Commission for Trade and Mission in Greenland (February 1738). On August 28, 1739, Hojer died on a business trip to Schleswig. He left behind a considerable book collection of 7,239 volumes, 590 manuscripts, 416 portraits, and 1156 charts, sold by the Royal Orphanage in 1740.[18]

Hojer and theology

Unlike the great Christian legal and political thinkers of the sixteenth and seventeenth centuries, Niels Hemmingsen, Jesper Brochmand, and Hans

Wandal—Hojer left no commentaries or sermons on the Bible, nor any treatise on Christian theology. He was largely content to work at the edges of theology and approach religious matters pragmatically. This characteristic meant, for instance, that he corresponded with learned ministers and engaged them to prepare a new revision of the Bible based on fresh study of the ancient sources. In addition, from the vantage point of his administrative posts, he promoted the Pietist way of reading scripture focused on individual devotion and edification. In 1735, together with colleagues from the Royal Orphanage administration, Hojer had one of August Hermann Francke's collections of sermons translated into Danish and dedicated to the king. In the dedication typically Pietist ideas found expression—that "all *true* Christian believers must prove their faith" and that scripture was a public means for education, edification, meditation, and discipline. Francke received praise as a "famed, respectable, evangelical teacher," and to have his words translated into Danish signified "fruit of the king's good institutions"—that is, the Royal Orphanage and its departments. The editors hoped that the book would help "the ungodly to change their hearts, be of comfort to the weary, an encouragement to repentant sinners, and a fortification of firm believers."[19]

Hojer had other and more confrontational experiences in working at the edges of theology. One of his early works, a juridical treatise on consanguine marriage (see below), first caused a scandal at the faculty of theology but eventually led to a reconsideration of the Old Testament as an authority for jurisdiction.

The early works

Hojer debuted as a scholarly author in 1717 and 1718 in three different disciplines—first with a medical thesis submitted to the faculty of medicine at Copenhagen University. The thesis that gave him the right to practice as a doctor was strongly influenced by Georg Ernst Stahl, a scholar of medicine at Halle.[20] The following year, he published a historical work, *Short History of Denmark*, written in German (*Kurtzgefasste Dännemärckische Geschichte*) and dedicated to King Frederik IV.

Similar to the structure of a catechism, the *Short History of Denmark* appeared as questions and answers intended as a schoolbook for the two young Holstein noblemen, whom Hojer was tutoring at that time.[21] In the preface he avers, with allusion to a work by Ludvig Holberg (see Chapter 8 in this volume), that no modern account of Danish history exists, and those he knows of are full of flaws.[22] This remark, although partly mitigated with disclaimers at the end of the book, offended Holberg, who under the pseudonym Paulus Ruter attacked Hojer and ridiculed his rural provenance and limited access to first-class source material. [23] Still, this work was not one that caused the most trouble and was critically received in Copenhagen. In 1718, he published a juridical thesis questioning the legal prohibition of incestuous marriages.

Together with the two young Holstein apprentices, Hojer embarked in 1717 on a journey to Helmstedt, the second renowned center of the study of law that he frequented. Both Helmstedt and Halle inspired his own legal thinking. In his *curriculum vitæ*, which appears in the letter of 1726 to Johannes Fabricius, Hojer reported that "meditations and friendly conferences with scholars at Helmstedt" inspired his juridical thesis.[24] The work was published in Germany and examined, as the title indicates, "the lack of prohibition of consanguineous marriage in divine law" (*Diagramma de Nuptiis Propinquorum Iure Divino non Prohibitis*).[25] News of this text received negative commentary in Copenhagen. Christen Worm, the bishop of Zealand and professor of theology, asked the king to expel Hojer from the country.[26]

Discourses on natural law

In the *Diagramma*, Hojer examined the philosophical, theological, and juridical arguments for prohibiting consanguineous marriages.[27] The erudite work comprises seven chapters, and Hojer dedicates the book to his patron, Johann Georg Holstein.[28] The questions this work raise were pertinent, and in fact a matter of life or death. In the eighteenth century, incest was a crime against nature, and the king—in accordance with the Danish Code (1683) (6.13.13–14) and on the advice of theologians and their reading of Leviticus 18 and 20—would punish the crime with banishment or death. Hojer clearly was not advocating incestuous marriage, but was theoretically engaging the question of the limited or universal impact of Mosaic law, and on which level prohibition should be sought. In that regard, he followed the footsteps of Grotius, Selden, Pufendorf, Thomasius, and Buddeus. He argued that the prohibition of consanguine marriages could not stem from natural law or universal divine positive law but derived from moral decency and Christian virtues. Hojer also specifies this idea in the letter of 1726 to Johann Fabricius.

> Indeed, in the main part of the work, I believe that I have firmly proven that neither natural law strictly speaking (*ius naturæ stricte sic dictum*) has anything to do with this; nor has the concept of universal positive law (*lex positiva universalis*) in its true sense. The question rather hinges on honesty and virtue (*doctrina honesti*), Christian precepts (*præceptis christianismi hypotheticis*), and public and private prudence (*doctrina prudentiæ publicæ et privatæ*).[29]

With this statement and these theoretical concepts, Hojer showed that he was engaging a major debate on legal pluralism vis-à-vis scripture as the basis of legislation and on the universal and the restricted impact of divine law.[30] In contradistinction to the medieval Christian natural-law tradition, the modern tradition had sought since the seventeenth century to separate religion from politics and theology from law. If, for instance, a law was based on scripture, that law was not automatically regarded as valid for all people at all times. The statutes and ordinances of Leviticus 18 and 20 prohibiting sexual relations were in the modern perspective interpreted as valid only for the particular group to whom they had once applied. If such prescripts, however, were resumed in the New Testament, then they would gain weight, impact, and perhaps universal application, not necessarily because they were determined by God or nature but because they were reasonable and honorable principles. Such considerations were part of a rich tradition that in Hojer's days scholars such as Thomasius and Buddeus discussed and revised.[31]

Ludvig Holberg's denigratory remark, that Hojer was only a mouthpiece for Thomasius's thoughts, ignores all the references to Buddeus, who emphasized passages in Pufendorf that Thomasius discarded.[32] Both scholars were integral to the discussion in which Hojer engaged, but researchers on Hojer hitherto have overlooked that fact.

Apart from the official condemnation pronounced by the clerical authorities in Copenhagen, the thesis also found less reserved readers. Søren Lintrup, one of the theological professors, sided with Hojer, as did the radical Pietist Johann Konrad Dippel (also known as Christianus Democritus, who at that time was imprisoned at Hammershus on Bornholm because of conflicts with the Danish authorities at Altona.[33] As Mads Langballe Jensen recently has argued, the reaction to the thesis showed two competing approaches to natural law thinking in Denmark. Henrik Weghorst and Ludvig Holberg represented the conservative camp and maintained that the universal positive divine law offered a prohibition of incestuous marriages, whereas the modern and eclectic camp, represented by Christian Reitzer and Hojer, were willing to question all arguments and keep only the best ones.[34] If Hojer's thesis had come out fifty years earlier, as the speculation goes, the reactions from the faculty of theology would have been far more severe.[35] As late as 1688, a debate between Christian Thomasius and the court preacher and professor of theology in Copenhagen, Hector Gottfried Masius, led to the public burning in Copenhagen of texts by Thomasius in 1691.[36]

Although Hojer's thesis caused a storm, he was neither expelled nor imprisoned. The protection afforded him by the influential Holstein family, to whom the work was dedicated, may have made the difference, or perhaps the times were changing. Although Hojer's thesis had no immediate impact on the public corporal punishment system, eventually it did challenge and affect the theologians' reading of Mosaic law.[37]

Recently scholars have taken renewed interest in Hojer's juridical thesis by pointing out that it reflects a more modern version of thinking on natural law than that of Ludvig Holberg.[38] Still, this version of natural law was not necessarily a campaign of secular enlightenment against religion but rather developed in critical and attentive engagement with sacred texts, moral philosophy, and Christian hermeneutics.

Celebrating the reformation

In 1734, Hojer was appointed professor of natural law and moral philosophy at the University of Copenhagen. Two years later, on January 20, 1736, he became a doctor of law. The occasion was the bicentennial of the Lutheran Reformation in Denmark, celebrated that year in the Danish-Norwegian kingdoms. On such occasions, the custom was to promote doctors at the university, and since no one at that time had a degree in law, and thus the authority to grant it to others, Hojer and his colleague Christian Bagger obtained the title by royal decree.[39]

A number of the statutes issued by the king in 1736 were aimed at raising theological, juridical, and educational standards at the university, as well as in churches and public schools. Both Hojer and the king's court preacher, Erik Pontoppidan, actively engaged in the reform program.[40] A statute of January 13, 1736, introduced mandatory confirmation of children between the ages of fourteen and nineteen. This initiative, which affected the entire youth of the nation, implied that new school buildings were built and more teachers and ministers trained to run them. The king appointed Pontoppidan to write a catechetical instruction and chose his version to be the standard in his kingdoms. Pontoppidan's *Truth to Godliness* (1737), which was an explanation of Luther's Small Catechism in 759 questions, thus obtained monopoly, and for centuries this treatise had a tremendous impact in Denmark and Norway, and even gained influence in North America.[41]

A statute of February 10, 1736, followed, and it instituted standardized examinations at the faculty of law. A suggestion sent to the king, written and signed December 21, 1735, by Hojer, formed the basis of the statute, which almost fully accorded with Hojer's suggestions.[42] He also wrote the *Ideal of a Danish Lawyer*—the first outline of professional standards for Nordic lawyers. This manual directly linked to the statute of February 10, 1736, and it served to define and implement the king's reforms of 1736. Lingering over these two contributions is worthwhile, since they demonstrate Hojer's design of and impact on the study of law.

Juridical examinations

The procedure and standards of the statute of February 10, 1736, that introduced standardized juridical examinations were not invented from scratch but followed those in force at the faculty of theology introduced in 1707. Instead of a probationary theological sermon, however, the aspiring lawyer had to deliberate on how to process a lawsuit.[43] The faculty of law was obligated to offer public examination once a month for up to eight candidates. Three grades were possible: the *haud contemnendus*, the *haud illaudabilis*, and the *laudabilis*.

To obtain the mark *haud contemnendus* (literally "by no means contemptible") required demonstrating knowledge of natural law, the Danish and Norwegian codes of 1683 and 1687, and juridical procedure and terminology. The second mark, *haud illaudabilis* ("not unworthy of note") required additional knowledge of international public law (*ius gentium*), and German-Roman law (*jurisprudentia romano-germanica*). The third degree, *laudabilis* ("worthy of praise") further implied insight into universal law (*ius universale*); differences between the Danish, Norwegian, and German law codes; and military law (*ius militare*).[44]

Prior to the examination, candidates had to render an account of their name, age, place of birth, graduation, parents' position, level of ambition, and the part of jurisprudence they expected to engage with. Candidates also had to disclose which courses they had attended and provide the faculty with letters of recommendation from their preceptors. Conversely, the faculty were required to take note of those candidates who demonstrated extracurricular knowledge. The juridical examination ended with a pledge, by which the candidate with a raised hand (*stipulata manu*) promised never to deviate from law and justice, nor to incite anyone to file needless lawsuits. The final test was to present a case and give suggestions on how to proceed with it.[45]

Not only students but everyone in juridical positions had to pass the exam. Doctors of law and licentiates, however, were excused. In fact, they were privileged. Doctors of law now had the right to be addressed as "noble" and "erudite" (*Velædle og Høilærd*), and to wear velvet and scarlet (*Frihed at bære Fløiel samt Skarlagen*), and only licentiates and doctors had permission to teach law. A new professional hierarchy thus was established. Licentiates were more likely to be hired as judges, and only candidates with the highest degree (*laudabilis*) could become judges of the supreme court.[46] Still not everyone had the resources or the intellectual capacity to pass the exam. Next to the official Latin exam, an inferior Danish version—supposedly impossible to fail—was established the following year. This version became the more frequent one. Despite the fact that Hojer took the first initiative towards modernizing the study of law, the road to establishing high standards was long.[47]

Ideals for Nordic lawyers

In 1736, Hojer lectured on the desirable qualities and requirements of Nordic lawyers. That same year, he published a Latin thesis pertaining to the topic, titled *Ideæ ICti Danici*. The thesis latched on to the new juridical and offered guidelines about how to undertake study of law. *The Ideal of a Danish Lawyer* soon was translated into Danish (*Forestilling på en Dansk Jurist*, 1737), supplemented with a synoptic outline of the Danish and the Norwegian codes,[48] and sold at the Royal Orphanage.

In the preliminary chapter, Hojer states that the scope of Nordic jurisprudence is to promote law, prudence, and piety (*ad promouendam Iuris & prudentiam & sanctitatem*). The discipline is not only for judges, lawyers, and advocates, but for everyone who desires to engage in public affaires.[49] Doctors of law therefore must become role models who guide the way for others.

> Doctors of law must carry the torch for those who vigorously will run through this course that is of uppermost necessity for the commonwealth, civil society, and the church. They must show the royal way, so that the outcome is not only good, but indeed respectable and fit citizens; citizens capable of being of use and delight to others.[50]

The sort of pastoral care that Hojer allots to doctors and professors of law is related to the claim that the study of law is of general benefit to society. The *Ideal* operates with a surprisingly broad definition of juridical objects in encouraging students to master all disciplines to be good lawyers. Since jurisprudence operates with divine, natural, and human laws, the study is essentially an infinite endeavor. The premises for studying law thus are presented in a paradox: no one has ever or will fully master jurisprudence. Everyone who fulfills his duties skillfully and rightly earns the title, however.[51] Character and sharp wits, a good education, or a bright mind are equally important preconditions for students of law. Mere finances do not suffice, although Hojer recounts a saying that all that is required to study law is "a head of iron, a bottom of lead, and a golden wallet."[52]

Linguistic skills are also preferable. A lawyer must master his mother tongue, German, Latin, and French. Aspiring lawyers, moreover, should acquaint themselves with (a) the Old Norse and Danish (*Antiquissima lingua Septentrionalis*), in which the old laws are written; (b) Swedish; (c) English—"relevant in regard to our laws and mores"; and (d) Greek and Hebrew—needed when consulting scripture, "the source of all divine law and religion," and "for settling religious disputes."[53] The series of demands continues. Relevant skills include decent handwriting, knowledge of geography, church history, genealogy, heraldry, moral philosophy, metaphysics, medicine, economics, and theology.[54]

The long list surely complements the image of Hojer as an erudite scholar and polymath. Still, Hojer's *Ideal* remained a torso without limbs. Of the 13 chapters listed in the table of contents, he realized only the first three (pp. 7–59). They elaborated on the topic of "Nordic jurisprudence," advertised in the preliminary introduction (pp. 1–7). Hojer never completed the following ten chapters, but the titles do indicate what he had in mind.[55] Although the work was unfinished, posthumous editions, based on manuscripts and notes from Hojer's lectures, suggest the full account. The editions of the *Juridical Lectures on Procedural Law* (1742, 1764, 1769) and *Public Law* (1783) are thus important testimony of Hojer's juridical work and his impact.[56]

Like other writings from Hojer's pen, the manual for students of law provoked Holberg's ridicule. With an allusion to the *Ideal of a Nordic Lawyer*, Holberg published his deliberation over the *Ideal of a Shoemaker*, in which he exhibited an endless list of lofty requirements necessary for this trade.[57]

Conclusions

Hojer's impact as an intellectual and religious jurisconsult is closely linked to his many roles as a scholar, reformer, and state executive. He was instrumental in initiating, defining, and implementing new standards for the church, the educational system, and the faculty of law. The natural-law tradition that he promoted shows the influence of Pietism and enlightened ideas developed in his close conversations with both legal scholars and Pietists. He introduced a modernized concept of natural law that provoked and challenged the religious establishment in Copenhagen. Legal pluralism and the religious and moral disposition of individuals were central features of his juridical thought. His definition of jurisprudence, launched in his manual for Nordic lawyers, was full of ambition for the future lawyer. The extensive list of requirements was put forward as a program of discipline and meditation. To complete the study of law is impossible, yet every proper attempt gradually makes the impossible possible. Law studies, as Hojer presents them, thus resemble an ongoing meditative praxis.

Notes

1 Tamm et al., *Juraen på Københavns Universitet 1479–2005*, 92.
2 Kofod, *Anviisning for en Dansk Jurist, angaaende Lovkyndigheds adskillige Deele, Nytte og* Hielpemidler, 66–68. Paludan-Müller, "Dansk Historiografi i det 18de Aarhundrede," 3–35.
3 Since I wrote this paper, Mads Langballe Jensen has published two articles in English on Andreas Hojer. Jensen sees Hojer as an intellectual legal thinker who together with Christian Reitzer (1665–1736) and Christoph Heinrich Amthor (1678–1721) represented a less conservative and a more modern and eclectic approach to natural law thinking than Henrik Weghorst and Ludvig Holberg. See Jensen, "*Libertas philosophandi* and Natural Law in Early Eighteenth-century Denmark-Norway" and "Serving Danish Foreign Policy."
4 Jørgensen, *Andreas Høјer*, and Rørdam, *Historiske Samlinger* vol. 1 (1891), 336–515; vol. 2 (1896), 313–84, 521–31; vol. 3 (1898), 144–86, 493–517; vol. 4 (1902), 133–247, 484–533. See also Rørdam "Andreas Hojer," 508–15.
5 I am indebted to professor Lisbet Christoffersen for inviting me to pursue studies on Hojer in the context of the research project *Protestant Legacies of Northern Law*, funded by HERA and hosted by the faculty of theology at Copenhagen University.
6 Whitmer, "Eclecticism and the Technologies of Discernment in Pietist Pedagogy."
7 For further reference about the reform movement at Halle, see Mejrup, "Grand Prospects of Halle Pietism."
8 The letter is published by Rørdam, *Historiske Samlinger* (1891), 395–408.
9 Hojer was a preceptor for Christian Frederik (1699–1722) and Carl Holstein (1700–1763). Jørgensen, *Andreas Høјer*, 14.
10 Jørgensen, *Andreas Høјer*, 14–15. On the Holsteins, see Bricka, *Dansk Biografisk Lexikon*, vol. 8 (1894), 35–43.
11 Hojer, *König Friedrich des IV.* Rørdam, *Historiske Samlinger* (1896) 376–81; (1898) 494–505). See also Ilsøe: "Status 1729–1730," 5–37.
12 Rørdam, *Historiske Samlinger* (1898), 145. Bruun et al., *Danske Samlinger.* See also Poul Johannes Jørgensen, "Retsundervisningen og Retsvidenskaben," 85.
13 The main documents concerning the founding of the Royal Orphanage are published in, *Kong Frederik d. Fjerdes Anordninger*, 1–33.
14 Rørdam, "Blade af Waisenhusets ældste Historie."
15 The negotiations concerning the new office were kept discreet in order to avoid the bishops' interference. Hojer's decisive part as an initiator is described by Rørdam, *Historiske Samlinger* (1902) 220, 222. See also Engelhardt, "Pietisme og krise. Den Halleske og Radikale Pietisme i den danske Helstat under Christian 6."
16 Patent XXI of October 1, 1737: "Anlangende at Hans Kongl- Majestæt Allernaadigst har funden for got [sic] at anordne en General Kirke=Inspektion, som bestandig skal have Opsigt med Kirken og Geistligheden," in *Kong Christian Den Siettes allernaadigste Forordninger og Aabne Breve*, Vol. 2 (1730–1746): Copenhagen 1946, 100–05. See also Rørdam, *Historiske Samlinger* (1902), 222–34 and Jakobsen, "Omorganiseringen af den teologiske censur. Generalkirkeinspektionskollegiets censurvirksomhed 1737–1747."
17 Rørdam, *Historiske Samlinger* (1902), 133–34.
18 Ibid., 524. See also Ildsøe, "Biblioteker til salg." Two editions of the *Bibliotheca Höjeriana, Catalogus Librorum*: Copenhagen 1740, are available at the Royal Danish Library.

19 Francke, *August Hermann Franckens Haand-Postill*, dedication to the king.
20 Höyer (sic), *Disputatio*. See Jørgensen, *Andreas Højer*, 16. Rørdam, *Historiske Samlinger* (1896), 314–15.
21 Jørgensen, *Andreas Højer*, 15–17.
22 Hojer, *Kurtzgefaßte Dänemarckische Geschichte*, Preface.
23 Jørgensen, *Andreas Højer*, 27–38, 38–47. Müller closely examines the rivalry between Holberg and Hojer by in *Den unge Ludvig Holberg*, 252–72. See Spang-Hanssen, *Fra Ludvig Holbergs Unge Dage, Hans Strid med Andreas Hojer*, 9–82. See also Harald Ilsøe's excellent review of these books in *Historisk Tidsskrift* 12/2 (1966–67): 469–78.
24 Letter to Johannes Fabricius 1726, Rørdam, *Historiske Samlinger* (1891) 403: "Diese Schrift war aus einigen meditationibus und freundlichen Conferenzien mit einem damals noch zu Helmstadt lebenden gelehrten Freunde erwachsen."
25 Hojer, *Diagramma*. Hereafter *Diagramma*. The text is available online via The Royal Danish Library, http://www.kb.dk/e-mat/dod/130021919951_color.pdf (accessed February 2018). Tamm et al., incorrectly state that this thesis was first published after Hojer's death. Tamm et al., *Juraen på Københavns Universitet 1479–2005*, 92.
26 Tamm et al., *Juraen på Københavns Universitet 1479–2005*, 66. Pedersen, "Pietismens Tid 1699–1746," 69.
27 See Jensen, "*Libertas philosophandi* and Natural Law in Early Eighteenth-century Denmark-Norway."
28 The *Diagramma* is structured as in the following seven chapters: 1: "Gradus Prohibiti Jure naturae nulli sunt"; 2: "Nullum datur Jus diuinum positivum vniversale"; 3: "Institutio Coniugii Genes[is] I. vtrum Legis instar sit?"; 4: "Legem Levit[icus] XVIII non esse vniversalem"; 5: "Rationes Legis XVIII. cap. Leviti exponit"; 6: "Consensus doctorum, Theologorum, & Jure consultorum"; and 7: "Finis vsusque dictorum."
29 Letter to Johannes Fabricius 1726, Rørdam, *Historiske Samlinger* (1891), 403: "Allein im Hauptwerk meine ich unwidertreiblich erwiesen zu haben, dass das Jus naturæ stricte sic dictum, so wenig als lex positiva universalis in sensu proprio hierin etwas disponiren, sondern die Gründe dieser Frage allein aus der doctrina honesti oder virtutis, den præceptis christianismi hypotheticis und der doctrina prudentiae publicæ et privatæ herzuleiten seyn."
30 Walch, "Gesetz," 1238–40.
31 Hojer, *Ideæ ICti Danici*, Chapter 2, §10, note f. In a work published in 1701, Jacob Friedrich Ludovici, whose lectures Hojer had attended at Halle, reported that both Thomasius and Buddeus were developing concepts to clarify the universal impact of divine law. See Ludovici, *Delineatio Historiae*, §108f. See also Walch, "Gesetz," 1238–41.
32 Grote, *The Emergence of Modern Aesthetic Theory*, 53–54.
33 Rørdam, *Historiske Samlinger* (1896), 355–59. See Büchsel, "Dippel Johann Konrad."
34 See Jensen, "*Libertas philosophandi* and Natural Law in Early Eighteenth-century Denmark-Norway."
35 See Glebe-Møller, "Det teologiske Fakultet 1597–1732," 205–206.
36 See Grunert, "Zur aufgeklärten Kritik am theokratischen Absolutismus."
37 Krogh, "Oplysningstiden og det magiske, henrettelser og korporlige straffe i 1700-tallets første halvdel," 158–90, 171.
38 Haakonssen, "The Law of Nature and Nations," 68–70. Jensen, "Contests about Natural Law in Early Enlightenment Copenhagen," 1039–1040.
39 Rørdam, *Historiske Samlinger* (1902), 147–77.
40 Horstbøll, "Pietism and the Politics of Catechisms," 145.
41 Ibid., 144, 151–53. See Olson, "Erik Ludvigsen Pontoppidan and the American Influence of His Catechism."
42 This proposition, including remarks on amendments made by J.L. Holstein, is printed in Rørdam, *Historiske Samlinger* (1902), 151–60.

43 The following paraphrase of the statute is based on the edition published by Schou, *Chronologisk Register*, 191–97. A German version of the statute was published in 1738: *Dänische Bibliothec oder Sammlung von alten und neuen gelehrten Sachen aus Dännemarck*, Vol 1. Copenhagen and Leipzig (1738), 360–72.

44 Schou, *Chronologisk Register*, 192. See also Tamm et al., *Juraen på Københavns Universitet 1479–2005*, 72. According to Jørgensen, "Retsundervisningen og Retsvidenskaben," 101, the mentioned universal law (*ius universale*) should be understood as the universal impact of divine law (*ius divinum positivum*).

45 Schou, *Chronologisk Register*, 191–97.

46 Ibid., 191–97.

47 Hammerich, "Juristerne og Embedslivet," 289.

48 Hojer's *Ideae ICti Danici* was translated by Peder Sommer in 1737: *Forestilling paa en Dansk Jurist*. A second edition was issued in 1744. The Latin version (1–43) is slightly shorter than the Danish translation (1–59) which includes a synoptic outline of the Danish and Norwegian codes (1–53). References are made to the Latin edition to make technical terms and concepts more transparent. All translations from the Latin are my own.

49 Hojer, *Ideae ICti Danici*, preface: "non futuri modo Iudices & Aduocati aut Procuratores ad legitimam scientiam rite sint formandi, sed cuius (. . .) qui recte & cum fructu in publicis regnorum negotiis cupiunt olim versari" ("Not only the future lawyers, advocates, or procurators, who will be formed by legitimate knowledge, but everyone . . . who at all times desires to be rightly and usefully versed in public affaires.")

50 Hojer, *Ideae ICti Danici*, preface: "[Iuris Doctoribus . . . mandatum est] in hoc stadio reipublicæ & Ciuili & Ecclesiasticæ summopere necessario decursuris facem pro virili præferre, viamque regiam ita monstrare, vt non ipsi modo boni ciues, sed & digni habilesque euadant, qui aliis ciuibus cum fructu præesse . . . possint."

51 Ibid., introduction §§ 1–5.

52 Ibid., introduction §7: "ferrum caput, plumbeus podex, & aurea crumena."

53 Ibid., Chapter 1, §§1–5.

54 Ibid., the remaining part of Chapter One, §§ 6–16.

55 The index of the *Idea ICti Danici* presents both the work Hojer realized and the one he imagined. The expounded chapters concern: (1) prerequisites for Danish and Norwegian jurisprudence; (2) divine law, natural law, and revealed law ("*de iure universali diuino, naturali et revelato*"); (3) present-day jurisprudence in Denmark and Norway ("*de iurisprudentia Dano-Norwagica moderna*"). The planned chapters were devoted to: (4) the origin and history of the Danish and Norwegian Laws—and differences between old and present laws; (5) the related old Germanic laws, especially Saxon, Salic, British, and Swedish law; (6) the present-day laws ("*de moderna iuribus*") in the Duchy of Schleswig, especially in regard to the *ius Iutico*; (7) the present-day laws in the Duchy of Holstein, especially in regard to the *ius Lubecense*; (8) the county law in Oldenburg and Delmenhorst; (9) the Roman law and its use in the king's countries; (10) canon law and its use in the king's countries; (11) ecclesiastical law; (12) public law (*ius publicum*) in Denmark, Norway, and Schleswig; and (13) German public law and its application in the Danish provinces.

56 Hans Hagerup first edited Andreas Hojer's *Juridisk Collegium over Processen* in 1742, followed by the enlarged edition of Christian Ditlev Hedegaard from 1764 and 1769. The *Jus Publicum* was translated and published by Peder Mortensen Bredsdorff in 1783. These editions are all available online at The Royal Danish Library.

57 Holberg, *Epistola 293*. Müller, *Holberg*, 270.

Bibliography

Ancher, Peder Kofod. *Anviisning for en Dansk Jurist, angaaende Lovkyndigheds adskillige Deele, Nytte og Hielpemidler*. [1752]. 2nd ed. Copenhagen: Gyldendal, 1777.

Bricka, C. F., ed. *Dansk Biografisk Lexikon*. Vols. 1–19. Copenhagen, 1887–1904.

Bruun, Christian, Oluf August Nielsen, and Anton Ludvig William Petersen, eds. *Danske Samlinger for Historie, Topographi, Personal- og Literaturhistorie* 3 (1867–68): 358–71.

Büchsel, Jürgen. "Dippel Johann Konrad." In *Theologische Realenzyklopädie*. Vol. 9, 9–10. Berlin/New York: De Gruyter, 1982.

Engelhardt, Juliane. "Pietisme og krise. Den Halleske og Radikale Pietisme i den danske Helstat under Christian 6." *Historisk Tidsskrift* 116/2 (2016): 281–308.

Francke, August Hermann. *August Hermann Franckens Haand-Postill, eller Korte Prædikener paa Søndage og Hell: Dage*. Copenhagen, 1735.

Glebe-Møller, Jens. "Det teologiske Fakultet 1597–1732." In *Københavns Universitet 1479–1979*. Vol. 5: *Det Teologiske Fakultet*, edited by Leif Grane, 93–211. Copenhagen: Gad, 1980.

Grote, Simon. *The Emergence of Modern Aesthetic Theory: Religion and Morality in Enlightenment Germany and Scotland*. Cambridge: Cambridge University Press, 2017.

Grunert, Frank. "Zur aufgeklärten Kritik am theokratischen Absolutismus. Der Streit zwischen Hector Gottfried Masius und Christian Thomasius über Ursprung und Begründung der summa potestas." In *Christian Thomasius (1655–1728): Neue Forschungen im Kontext der Frühaufklärung*, edited by Friedrich Vollhardt, 51–77. Tübingen: Max Niemeyer Verlag, 1997.

Haakonssen, Knud. "The Law of Nature and Nations." In *Ludvig Holberg (1684–1754): Learning and Literature in the Nordic Enlightenment*, edited by Knud Haakonssen and Sebastian Olden-Jørgensen, 59–79. New York: Routledge, 2017.

Hammerich, Kai Frederik. "Juristerne og Embedslivet." In *Festskrift i anledning af tohundrede Aars Dagen for Indførelsen af Juridisk Eksamen ved Københavns Universitet*, edited by Reitzel-Nielsen and Popp-Madsen, 259–307. Copenhagen: University of Copenhagen, 1936.

Hojer, Andreas. *Diagramma de nuptiis propinquorum iure divino non prohibitis*. Lemgow, 1718.

Hojer, Andreas. *Kurtzgefaßte Dänemarckische Geschichte Vom Anfang dieses mächtigen Reichs bis zum XVII Seculi, Aus den bewährtesten Scribenten zu mehrerer Deutlichkeit in Fragen und Antworten verfasset*. Flensburg, 1719.

Hojer, Andreas. *Ideæ ICti Danici. Disputatione Anniversaria Expositam Publico Eruditorum Examini*. Hafniae, 1736.

Hojer, Andreas. *Forestilling paa en Dansk Jurist*, translated by Peder Sommer. København, 1737.

Hojer, Andreas. *Juridisk Collegium over Processen*, edited by Hans Hagerup. København, 1742.

Hojer, Andreas. *Jus Publicum det er Stats-Ret eller Statsforfatning og Rettigheder for Danmark*, translated by Peder Mortensen Bredsdorff. Christiania, 1783.

Hojer, Andreas. *Salig Etats-Raad Høyers Juridiske Collegium saavidt den Danske og Norske Procesvedkommer*, edited by Christian Ditlev Hedegaard. København, [1764] 1769.

Hojer, Andreas. *König Friedrich des IV glorwürdigstes Leben*. 2 vols. Tondren: Niels Nicolaus Falck, 1829.

Holberg, Ludvig. *Epistola 293*. Copenhagen, 1750.

Horstbøll, Henrik. "Pietism and the Politics of Catechisms: The Case of Denmark and Norway in the Eighteenth and Nineteenth Centuries." *Scandinavian Journal of History* 29/2 (2004): 143–60.

Höyer (sic), Andreas. *Disputatio medico-practica de febre petrechizante epidemia*. Copenhagen, 1717.

Ildsøe, Harald. "Biblioteker til salg, om danske bogauktioner og kataloger 1661–1811." In *Danish Humanist Texts and Studies* 31, edited by Erland Kolding Nielsen, 131–33. Copenhagen: Det Kongelige Bibliotek, 2007.

Ilsøe, Harald. "Status 1729–1730, da Andreas Hojer satte skik på det Kongelige Bibliotek." *Bibliotekshistorie* 5 (1999): 5–37.

Ilsøe, Harald. "Review of books on Holberg." *Historisk Tidsskrift* 12/2 (1966–67): 469–78.

Jakobsen, Jesper. "Omorganiseringen af den teologiske censur. Generalkirkeinspektionskollegiets censurvirksomhed 1737–1747." *Historisk Tidsskrift* 111/1 (2011): 1–36.

Jensen, Mads Langballe. "Contests about Natural Law in Early Enlightenment Copenhagen." *History of European Ideas* 42/8 (2016): 1027–41. Available at http://dx.doi.org/10.1080/01916599.2016.1182045

Jensen, Mads Langballe. "*Libertas philosophandi* and Natural Law in Early Eighteenth-century Denmark-Norway." *Intellectual History Review* (2019), doi: 10.1080/17496977.2019.1643601

Jensen, Mads Langballe. "Serving Danish Foreign Policy: Andreas Hojer's De eo quod iure belli licet in minores (1735)." In *The Law of Nations and Natural Law 1625–1800.* Leiden, The Netherlands: Brill, 2019. doi: 10.1163/9789004384200_004

Jørgensen, Poul Johannes. "Retsundervisningen og Retsvidenskaben ved Københavns Universitet 1537–1736, Forordningen af 10. Februar 1736." In *Festskrift i anledning af tohundrede Aars Dagen for Indførelsen af Juridisk Eksamen ved Københavns Universitet*, edited by Reitzel-Nielsen and Popp-Madsen, 11–114.

Jørgensen, Troels G. *Andreas Højer jurist og historiker.* Copenhagen: A. Frost-Hansen, 1961.

Kong Frederik d. Fjerdes Anordninger, Instruks og Fundats m.m. af 21. Juli 1727. Copenhagen: 1914.

Krogh, Tyge. *Oplysningstiden og det magiske, henrettelser og korporlige straffe i 1700-tallets første halvdel.* Copenhagen: Samleren, 2000.

Ludovici, Jacob Friedrich. *Delineatio Historiae Iuris Divini Naturalis Et Positivi Universalis.* Halle, 1701.

Mejrup, Kristian. "Grand Prospects of Halle Pietism: The Acrobat, the Project-Maker, and the Shepherd." PhD thesis. Copenhagen, 2016.

Müller, Theodor Alfred. *Den unge Ludvig Holberg 1684–1722.* Copenhagen, 1943.

Olson, James B. "Erik Ludvigsen Pontoppidan and the American Influence of His Catechism." In *The Lutheran Historical Conference, Essays and Reports 1990.* Vol. 14: *Lutheranism and Pietism*, 20–39. St. Louis, MO: Lutheran Historical Conference, 1992.

Paludan-Müller, Caspar. "Dansk Historiografi i det 18de Aarhundrede." *Historisk Tidsskrift* 5/4 (1883–84): 1–188.

Patent XXI of October 1, 1737: "Anlangende at Hans Kongl- Majestæt Allernaadigst har funden for got [sic] at anordne en General Kirke=Inspektion, som bestandig skal have Opsigt med Kirken og Geistligheden." *Kong Christian Den Siettes allernaadigste Forordninger og Aabne Breve*, vol. 2 (1730–1746), 100–05. København, 1746.

Pedersen, Johannes. "Pietismens Tid 1699–1746." In *Den Danske Kirkes Historie*, edited by Hal Koch and Bjørn Kornerup, 11–227. Copenhagen: Gyldendal, 1951.

Reitzel-Nielsen, Erik, and Carl Popp-Madsen, eds. *Festskrift i anledning af tohundrede Aars Dagen for Indførelsen af Juridisk Eksamen ved Københavns Universitet.* Copenhagen: Nyt Nordisk forlag, 1936.

Rørdam, Holger. "Blade af Waisenhusets ældste Historie." In *Kirkehistoriske Samlinger* 4/3, edited by Holger Rørdam, 533–35, 1893.

Rørdam, Holger. "Andreas Hojer." In *Dansk Biografisk Lexikon*, edited by Carl Frederik Bricka, vol. 7, 508–15. Copnhagen, 1893.

Rørdam, Holger. *Historiske Samlinger og Studier vedrørende danske forhold og personligheder især i det 17. århundrede.* Copenhagen: Forlagt af Universitetsboghandler G.E.C. Gad, 1891–1902. vol. 1 (1891), 336–515; vol. 2 (1896), 313–84, 521–31; vol. 3 (1898), 144–86, 493–517; vol. 4 (1902), 133–247, 484–533.

Schou, Jacob Henric. *Chronologisk Register over de kongelige Forordninger og aabne Breve, samt andre trykte Anordninger, som fra Aar 1670 ere udkomne* (. . .), part three 1730–1746. Copenhagen, 1795.

Spang-Hanssen, Esbern. *Fra Ludvig Holbergs Unge Dage, Hans Strid med Andreas Hojer.* Copenhagen: Gad, 1963.

Tamm, Ditlev, Inger Dübeck, and Ejvind Slottved. *Juraen på Københavns Universitet 1479–2005.* Vol 4: *Københavns Universitet 1479–1979.* Copenhagen: Copenhagen University, 2005.

Walch, Johann Georg. "Gesetz." *Philosophisches Lexicon*, 1225–50. Leipzig, 1726.

Whitmer, Kelly J. "Eclecticism and the Technologies of Discernment in Pietist Pedagogy." *Journal of the History of Ideas* 70/4 (2009): 545–67.

Part 4

National romanticism and constitutionalism

12 Introduction

Anders Jarlert and Kjell Å Modéer

The "long nineteenth century" in European history, reaching from 1789 to 1914, is a chronological concept introduced by the British historian Eric Hobsbawm. The first part of this long century, described in his book *The Age of Revolution, 1790–1848*,[1] was marked in the Nordic countries by conflicts between reform-oriented liberal forces and recalcitrant conservatives. This conflict played out politically as the identity of the modern nation-state was constructed with the help of two legal and democratically adopted documents: the constitution and a codification. The American constitution of 1787 (effective since 1789) and the Napoleonic *les cinq codes* of 1804–11 became important models for constitutional and legal reforms. Culturally, Romanticism developed as a counterforce to the rational program of the Enlightenment and revolution. "Organism" and "evolution" became important keywords. During this Romantic era (1790–ca. 1850), Nordic theologians and jurists recognized that they had much in common—not only a common history but also a common Christian culture.

It has been argued that the German late Romantic movement appeared for the first time in Uppsala in 1800.[2] Scandinavian scholars, theologians, and jurists—many of whom had visited or studied in Germany—had good relations with their German colleagues. The Scandinavians encountered an especially inspiring scholarly environment at the new Reform University at Berlin, which opened in 1810. It was there that two of the icons of German Romanticism—the law professor Friedrich Carl von Savigny and the theologian and philosopher Friedrich Schleiermacher—were employed. Both of them contributed to the legacy of Johann Gottfried von Herder by advancing the imperative of a historical school of thought. Savigny was the father of the historical school of law, and Schleiermacher of the historical method in theology. There was also documented interaction between Savigny's students and Schleiermacher. The Romantic-era jurists in Scandinavia were to a great extent inspired by Schleiermacher, the father of modern liberal theology with its individualistic and nature-oriented approach to belief.

Theologians in the Nordic countries were well acquainted with the liberal theology of Schleiermacher, who made a noted journey to Scandinavia in the fall of 1833, during the last year of his life.[3] He first visited Lund University and met with the young theologian Henrik Reuterdahl[4]—later a Swedish archbishop, and at that time a lecturer in theology and the university librarian. Reuterdahl was one of Schleiermacher's devoted supporters and frequently quoted Schleiermacher's works in his *Jnledning till Theologien* (Introduction to theology, 1837).[5] At Uppsala Schleiermacher met two of the most representative of the Swedish Romantics, Eric Gustaf Geijer and Per Daniel Amadeus Atterbom, who appreciated Schleiermacher's Romantic philosophy and his criticism of the rationalism of the Enlightenment. In Christiania (now Oslo), he met with representatives of the university. On his way back to Berlin he stopped in Copenhagen, where he also had many supporters, among them the poet Adam Oehlenschläger and the professor of theology Henrik Nikolai Clausen, who had become enthusiastic about Schleiermacher's work during a study visit to Berlin.[6]

The aftermath of the French Revolution was introduced in the Nordic countries as a reaction to the orthodox rationalism of Lutheran thought. At Lund University, the orthodox perspectives were represented by a special conception of high church pietism advanced by the Swedish Lutheran priest Henrik Schartau and two of his supporters, the law professors Johan Holmbergson and his former student, the professor of legal history Carl Johan Schlyter.[7] Liberal theology, on the other hand, was represented by the law professor Christian Naumann and the professor of theology, later bishop in the Lund diocese, Johan Henrik Thomander.[8]

Others inspired by Schleiermacher were the German idealist philosopher Wilhelm Joseph Schelling (1775–1854) and the historically oriented legal philosopher and law professor Friedrich Carl von Savigny, along with his circle of students after 1815.[9] One of Savigny's special students, Moritz August von Bethmann-Hollweg (1795–1877), was affiliated with the revivalist movement. He regarded the historical courthouse as comparable to a Gothic cathedral, in which "the vaults seemed to hover."[10] This metaphysical metaphor was echoed by the Romantic law professor Carl Schildener at the Swedish Pomeranian University in Greifswald taphor.[11]

The conservatives in Scandinavia found their support in the old texts as sources—not only the Bible but also the historic laws—which fortified their argument for their belief in the organic relationship of God and law. The liberals, on the other hand, claimed the freedom found in the constitutions as fundamental to their belief in individual human rights, especially the freedom of religion. These issues were as important for the clergy as for the judiciary.

This conflict was carried out in private as well as publicly, and it revolved around the national constitutions and the concept of freedom of religion. In Sweden, the Instrument of Government of 1809 abolished absolutism and implemented the concept of constitutional monarchy. This instrument had no article on freedom of religion, however. Instead, constitutional freedom in Sweden developed with the help of the flexibility of customary law in interpreting Article 16 of the Instrument of Government. In Norway, on the other hand, the constitution of 1814 was characterized more by religious constraint than by religious freedom. Article 2 of that constitution upheld the Lutheran church as the state religion of Norway while prohibiting Jews and Jesuits as well as monastic orders.

The Swedish Instrument of Government also protected the freedom of religion, but only in an inward sense. Swedish citizens were assumed to participate in the services of the Swedish church, with exceptions for Jews and Catholics.

In Denmark, the development of theological thought in the nineteenth century was very much related to the constitutional discussions regarding freedom of religion, which resulted in the adoption of the liberal Danish constitution of 1849. The question had arisen whether this freedom should be articulated in the constitution or in the law. Two of the dominant figures in this debate were the jurist Anders Sandøe Ørsted and the theologian Nicolaj Severin Frederik Grundtvig, the founder of the Danish national folk church.[12] History was for both of them an important resource for supporting arguments—even though they came to different conclusions. Ørsted pleaded for legislative reforms to come, while Grundtvig wanted to enshrine the freedom within the constitution. The Danish constitution of 1849 was the first in the Nordic countries to articulate a freedom of religion clause.

Some basic divisions regarding law and religion developed between the countries in western Scandinavia and those in the east. One example is the establishment of a synod (*kyrkomöte*) in eastern Scandinavia, where Sweden and Finland created a synod in the 1860s. In western Scandinavia, no synods were established.

Although Finland came under Russian sovereignty in 1809, Finland maintained Swedish laws, including the ecclesiastical laws. A Russian commission for revising the Swedish church law was established in 1817, with Finnish archbishop Jacob Tengström as an active member. Although he drafted a revision, the commission under the leadership of professor and later bishop Frans Ludvig Schauman presented a new draft in 1863. Freedom of religion and the freedom of the Lutheran Evangelical church were priorities, and the commission proposed a synod to guarantee this legislative ecclesiastical autonomy. The draft was adopted as the new Finnish church law of 1869 and confirmed by the Tsar Alexander II the following year.[13] In Sweden, the synod had been introduced to give freedom to the church as a part of the representative reform a few years before, in 1866.

Ecclesiastically, however, Finland persisted after 1809 with a kind of dualism, maintaining two state churches, the Evangelical Lutheran and the Russian Orthodox. Religious argumentation also appeared in other Finnish legal reforms, such as the penal law adopted in 1866—two years after the Swedish penal law. The Christian (humanitarian) elements (e.g., in prison reform) were made visible in Finland by the jurist Karl Gustaf Ehrström.[14]

The revivalist movements of the nineteenth century developed quite different solutions in the Nordic countries than elsewhere, owing to different social and political contexts. In Denmark as well as in Norway, there was an aim more to include different theological movements (e.g., the Home Mission—*den Indre Mission*) as associations within the framework of the state church. Historically, Sweden—unlike the other Nordic countries—has excluded other religious communities from the state church.[15] Yet members of the Swedish Evangelical Mission (*Evangeliska Fosterlandsrörelsen*) and most of the members of the Mission

Covenant Church of Sweden (*Svenska Missionsförbundet*) were also registered as members of the Swedish church. The same held true in Finland.

Revolutionary change resulted in a new way of thinking geopolitically. The concept of nation was evaluated in a new way, and national identity became a way to find the Scandinavian citizens' position on the newly drawn European map. Sweden not only lost Finland in 1808–09 but also had to give up its old provinces in Pomerania and Wismar (Mecklenburg) in the Treaty of Kiel of 1815; in 1878, Sweden also lost the colony of Saint-Barthélemy in the Caribbean. Norway severed its long affiliation with Denmark in 1814 and reluctantly tried to find its new identity in a union with Sweden. Finland, on the other hand—also reluctantly—had to find its new national identity as a separate great duchy within the Russian jurisdiction.

A mass-media revolution in communication was introduced as pamphlets and dailies spread to the citizens: the folk/people.[16] Professional law journals, established in the Nordic countries at the beginning of the nineteenth century were made possible by a new technology (the industrial press) and contributed to the increasingly intense transnational legal discourses between the academic profession and the practitioners of law.[17] The German law professor Rudolph von Jhering emphasized the necessity for academic jurists to cooperate with practitioners and urged the interaction between theory and practice.[18]

In comparison with other European universities, the Nordic universities in the nineteenth century still were very small and few in number. The modern European idea of where to locate the university—in capital cities—was realized in Scandinavia already in 1479, when Denmark's university was located in the royal capital, Copenhagen. After separating from Denmark, Norway established a new university in 1811 in Christiania (now Oslo), the capital of Norway, using the new Humboldt University in Berlin as an important prototype. Mainland Sweden had only two universities, inaugurated in Uppsala (1477) and in Lund (1666).[19] But Sweden developed plans in the mid-nineteenth century to establish a university in Stockholm, an intention realized in 1907.[20] Finland had established its university in Turku in 1640, but two decades after the separation from Sweden, in 1809, the University in Turku was transferred during Russian sovereignty to the Finnish capital, Helsinki, in 1829. All of these universities held a faculty of theology as well as a law faculty.

In all the Nordic countries, the state churches in the nineteenth century held the position of majority churches. The church as well as the courts were state institutions, though still very much related to a lay culture. In the legal culture, the jurors (*nämndemän*) were laypeople, and in the religious culture, the laity was represented in the church by the church warden (*kyrkovärdar*). The officials of these different spheres of life—the vicar in the church and the professional judge in the courts —were still regarded because of their oaths to be bound to an idealistic and metaphysical calling in the state bureaucracy (*ämbetsmannastat*).

The Enlightenment had introduced freedom of religion for the citizen (freedom of belief and freedom of worship) as one of the important claims of the citizen within constitutional law. It also introduced a flexibility into the relation between church and state. The modern view held that religion was a private matter, publicly guaranteed by the state in the constitution. This view played out in different ways in the Nordic countries. For instance, they experienced the eighteenth-century Pietist movement, whose emphasis on private worship and biblical studies in the homes (conventicles) was a reaction to absolute and orthodox Lutheranism. Even though the conventicles (in Sweden) were explicitly prohibited after the 1720s, Pietists and radical evangelicals continued to hold them during the first part of the nineteenth century. The Swedish state's prohibition of the free exercise of religion endured until the late 1850s.[21]

In Denmark/Norway the Conventicle Act of 1741, repealed in 1842, was intended to encourage pious people to come together for worship, though under the strict control of the local priest. The act was used to harass and imprison the lay preacher and industrial entrepreneur Hans Nielsen Hauge (1771–1824), the most influential person in both religion and society in Norway until today.[22]

The Norwegian constitution of 1814 banned Jews, a provision abolished in 1851 thanks to many years of agitation by the poet Henrik Wergeland.[23] Christians of the Sàmi population in the nineteenth century also were oppressed by the state in the Scandinavian countries.

One central goal of nineteenth-century Scandinavian legal thought was to make a clear separation between constitutional, criminal, and regulatory (administrative) law on one hand—public law—and, on the other hand, the law of private transactions, such as torts, contracts, property, and commercial law.[24] Nineteenth-century jurists were to a great extent included in the dynamic discourse between public and private law. Due to increasingly secularization, family law also came under reform. The emancipation of women occupied much of the discourse in Scandinavian literature in the latter part of the nineteenth century and interacted with claims for reform of marriage law. New legal possibilities for divorce as well as the legal position of illegitimate children also became important elements of reform in the Nordic countries.

The question of civil marriages was related to issues of interfaith marriages and secularization in modern societies and resulted in the legal reform of civil marriage in Sweden in 1908. Within criminal law, blasphemy cases were frequent when state authorities perceived threats to their authority from radical authors and intellectuals. Important libel cases were decided beginning in the 1870s.

Scandinavism became an important movement among students beginning in 1840. In its first phase, it appeared as a student movement for liberal ideas, but in the late 1850s, it also became important to Scandinavian clergy and jurists. The first Scandinavian clergy meeting was held in Copenhagen, and the second in Lund, with subsequent synodal meetings. Nordic jurists' meetings were initiated with a first meeting in Copenhagen in 1872. From those meetings arose a movement to harmonize Nordic private law. The modern family law reform was based on harmonized Nordic laws on marriage, wills, and heritage.

The long nineteenth century endured up to the outbreak of World War I in 1914.

In the Nordic countries, the last decades of the century witnessed the turn from the idealistic, Christian, and historically oriented cognitive structure of an elitist society into a more social, pragmatic, and secular orientation. The Romantic and metaphysical concepts within the law and religion of the nineteenth century met the modern realistic and democratic "disenchantment of the world" (Max Weber) of the twentieth century.

Notes

1 Eric Hobsbawm, *The Age of Revolution, 1789–1848* (London: Weidenfeld & Nicolson, 1962).
2 Sten Lindroth, *Uppsala universitet 1477–1977* (Stockholm: Almqvist & Wiksell, 1976), 142.
3 Sigurd Hjelde, "Schleiermacher i Skandinavia (1833): En reiserapport med vekt på besøket i Christiania," *Teologisk Tidsskrift* 7/4 (2018): 263ff.
4 See Alexander Maurits's chapter on Henrik Reuterdahl in this volume.
5 Hjelde, "Schleiermacher i Skandinavia," 265.
6 Ibid., 269.
7 See Kjell Å Modéer's chapter on Carl Johan Schlyter in this volume.
8 See Alexander Maurits's chapter on Johan Henrik Thomander in this volume.
9 Hans Peter Haferkamp (2009), "Einflüsse der Erweckungsbewegung auf die 'historisch- christliche' Rechtschule zwischen 1815–1848," in *Konfession im Recht. Auf der Suche nach konfessionell geprägten Denkmuster und Argumentationsstrategien in Recht und Rechtwissenschaft des 19. und 20. Jahrhunderts*, ed. Pascale Cancik et al., Symposium zum 65. Geburtstag von Michael Stolleis (Frankfurt am Main: Klostermann, 2009), 71.
10 "Mit einem 'gotische Dome' vergleichbar, bei dem 'sein Gewölbe in der Luft zu schweben scheint.'": Haferkamp, "Einflüsse der Erweckungsbewegung auf die 'historisch- christliche' Rechtschule zwischen 1815–1848," 7.
11 Kjell Å Modéer, "Romanticism in Law & Art: German Romanticism, Creativity, and European Legal Culture," *NAVEIÑ REET: Nordic Journal of Law and Social Research (NNJLSR)* 5 (2014): 149f.
12 See Lisbet Christoffersen and Niels Henrik Gregersen's chapter on A.S. Ørsted and N.F.S. Grundtvig in this volume.
13 Christer Pahlmblad, "Kyrkomöte, läroämbete, demokrati: Kyrkomötets sammansättning i Evangelisk-lutherska kyrkan i Finland och i Svenska kyrkan," in *Svenskt i Finland—Finskt i Sverige*, ed. Gabriel Bladh and Christer Kuvaja (Helsinki: Svenska litteratursällskapet i Finland, 2005), 378ff.
14 See Jussi Sallila's chapter on Karl Gustaf Ehrström in this volume.
15 Kjell Å Modéer, "Internal Convergence—External Divergence: Religion in The Nordic Legal Culture and Tradition at the Treshold of the Third Millennium," in *Law & Religion in the 21st Century—Nordic Perspectives*, ed. Lisbet Christoffersen, Kjell Å Modéer, and Svend Andersen (Copenhagen: DJØF Publishing, 2010), 66ff.
16 Ruth Hemstad and Dag Michalsen, eds., *Frie ord i Norden? Offentlighet, ytringsfrihet og medborgerskap 1814–1914* (Oslo: Pax Forlag, 2019).
17 Kjell Å Modéer, *Historiska rättskällor i konflikt* (Stockholm: Sánterus Förlag, 2010).
18 Rudolf von Jhering, *The Struggle for Law*, trans. John J. Lalor (Charleston, SC: BiblioLife, 2008).
19 When Sweden was a great power in the seventeenth century, there were two more universities, in Greifswald in Pomerania (up to 1815) and in Tartu (Balticum).
20 Claes Peterson and Marie Sandström, "Kloster eller bordell? Om tillkomsten av Stockholms juridiska fakultet," in *Juridiska fakulteten 1907–2007: Juridiska fakulteten i Stockholm 100 år: en minnesskrift*, ed. Claes Peterson (Stockholm: Juridiska fakulteten, Stockholm University, 2007), 31ff.

21 Per Dahlman, *Kyrka och stat i 1860-talets svenska religionslagstiftning* [Church and state in the 1860 Swedish legislation on religion] (Skellefteå: Artos, 2009).
22 Andreas Aarflot, "Hans Nielsen Hauge," *Norsk Biografisk Leksikon*, vol.4 (Oslo: Kunnskapsforlaget, 2001).
23 Vigdis Ystad, "Henrik Wergeland," *Norsk Biografisk Leksikon*, vol. 9 (Oslo: Kunnskapsforlaget, 2005).
24 Morton J Horwitz, "The History of the Public/Private Distinction," *University of Pennsylvania Law Review*, 130 (1982): 1423–28.

Bibliography

Aarflot, Andreas. "Hans Nielsen Hauge." In Jon Gunnar Arntzen (ed.), *Norsk Biografisk Leksikon*. Vol. 4. Oslo: Kunnskapsforlaget, 2001.

Dahlman, Per. *Kyrka och stat i 1860-talets svenska religionslagstiftning* (Church and state in the 1860 Swedish legislation on religion). Skellefteå: Artos, 2009.

Haferkamp, Hans Peter. "Einflüsse der Erweckungsbewegung auf die 'historisch-christliche' Rechtschule zwischen 1815–1848." In *Konfession im Recht. Auf der Suche nach konfessionell geprägten Denkmuster und Argumentationsstrategien in Recht und Rechtwissenschaft des 19. und 20. Jahrhunderts*, ed. Pascale Cancik et al. Symposium zum 65. Geburtstag von Michael Stolleis. Frankfurt am Main: Klostermann, 2009.

Hemstad, Ruth, and Dag Michalsen, eds. *Frie ord i Norden? Offentlighet, ytringsfrihet og medborgerskap 1814–1914*. Oslo: Pax Forlag, 2019.

Hjelde, Sigurd. "Schleiermacher i Skandinavia (1833): En reiserapport med vekt på besøket i Christiania." *Teologisk Tidsskrift* 7/4 (2018): 263ff.

Hobsbawm, Eric. *The Age of Revolution, 1789–1848*. London: Weidenfeld & Nicolson, 1962.

Horwitz, Morton J. "The History of the Public/Private Distinction." *University of Pennsylvania Law Review* 130 (1982): 1423–28.

Jhering, Rudolf von. *The Struggle for Law*. Translated by John J. Lalor. Charleston, SC: BiblioLife, 2008.

Lindroth, Sten. *Uppsala universitet 1477–1977* [English-language version, *A History of Uppsala University, 1477–*1977]. Stockholm: Almqvist & Wiksell, 1976.

Modéer, Kjell Å. *Historiska rättskällor i konflikt*. Stockholm: Sánterus Förlag, 2010.

Modéer, Kjell Å. "Internal Convergence—External Divergence: Religion in The Nordic Legal Culture and Tradition at the Treshold of the Third Millennium." In *Law & Religion in the 21st Century: Nordic Perspectives*, ed. Lisbet Christoffersen, Kjell Å Modéer, and Svend Andersen, 66ff. Copenhagen: DJØF Publishing, 2010.

Modéer, Kjell Å. "Romanticism in Law & Art: German Romanticism, Creativity, and European Legal Culture." *NAVEIÑ REET: Nordic Journal of Law and Social Research (NJLSR)* 5 (2014): 149f.

Pahlmblad, Christer. "Kyrkomöte, läroämbete, demokrati: Kyrkomötets sammansättning i Evangelisk-lutherska kyrkan i Finland och i Svenska kyrkan." In *Svenskt i Finland—Finskt i Sverige*, ed. Gabriel Bladh and Christer Kuvaja, 378ff. Helsinki: Svenska litteratursällskapet i Finland, 2005.

Peterson, Claes, and Marie Sandström. "Kloster eller bordell? Om tillkomsten av Stockholms juridiska fakultet." In *Juridiska fakulteten 1907–2007: Juridiska fakulteten i Stockholm 100 år: en minnesskrift*, ed. Claes Peterson, 31ff. Stockholm: Juridiska fakulteten, Stockholm University, 2007.

Ystad, Vigdis. "Henrik Wergeland." In Jon Gunnar Arntzen (ed.), *Norsk Biografisk Leksikon*. Vol. 9. Oslo: Kunnskapsforlaget, 2005.

13 Shaping the Danish people's church in the context of freedom of religion

A.S. Ørsted (1778–1860) and N.F.S. Grundtvig (1783–1872)

Lisbet Christoffersen and Niels Henrik Gregersen

Introduction

This chapter brings together two leading figures of the Danish Golden Age central for understanding the legal and theological cultures behind the transition from a state church to the People's Church in the Danish Constitution of 1849. Anders Sandøe Ørsted is generally considered to be Denmark's leading jurist in the first half of the nineteenth century, as he laid the foundation for the subsequent generation of legal scholarship in Denmark. Alongside his own scholarship, he was head of the central legal office during the late absolutist period, and after the constitutional change, he was elected to serve as prime minister in 1853–54. His counterpart, the theologian Nikolaj Frederik Severin Grundtvig, was a prolific writer as historian and poet, theologian and educator, pastor and hymn writer, publishing more than thirty-seven thousand pages in his lifetime. Despite the many ups and downs of his life, he ended up as a towering cultural figure of the Danish church, and a member of the lower and upper houses of the Parliament as well.

Ørsted and Grundtvig had a long history with one another before they met as members of the constitutional assembly of 1848–49. The Constitution of June 5, 1849, still in force today, led to the installment of a representative democracy in Denmark.[1] In its own words, the Constitution is a constitutional monarchy, that is, "a monarchy limited by the parliamentary system" (article 1: *indskrænket-monarkisk*).

The constitutional rules on church and freedom of religion have undergone only very limited changes since 1849.[2] The preamble to the Constitution in article 3 (today article 4) defines the central national role of the Evangelical Lutheran Church: "The Evangelical Lutheran Church is the church of the Danish people, and is as such to be supported by the state."[3] This paragraph signaled the end of the absolutist royal state church and took its legal point of departure in the historical fact that the Evangelical Lutheran Church was the majority church of the Danish people, now dubbed the People's Church (*Folkekirke*). In 1849, more than 99 percent of the population were baptized members of the Evangelical Lutheran Church in Denmark (on January 1, 2020, 74.3 percent were members). The June Constitution refers to the Evangelical Lutheran Church as *a prior social fact*, as also stated in an earlier draft to the Constitution (article 1b): "The Lutheran church, being the church to which the majority of population confesses, is to be regarded as the Danish People's Church and is entitled to be supported by the state."[4] Article 3 is a concise abbreviation of this earlier draft.

The writers of the Constitution thus legitimized the central role of the Lutheran church by the de facto allegiance of the Danish people to this church, thereby avoiding confessionalist gestures on behalf of the legislators. Through legislation, the church should be given an internal legal structure, possibly independent from the state structure (article 80, now article 66), but despite several attempts, this so-called "promissory paragraph" (*Løfteparagraf*) was never fulfilled, much to the satisfaction of both Ørsted and Grundtvig.

At the same time, the Constitution secured the freedom of religion to all citizens (article 81, now article 67), changing the status of this right from a royal resolution (of June 21, 1848) to constitutional law. The legislative powers should organize the relations to other religious groups by law (article 82, now article 69). In addition, the Constitution gave full civil and political rights to all citizens regardless of their faith (article 84, since 1953 changed to "regardless of faith and race," article 70).

Only the king did not enjoy religious freedom, as stated in article 6: "The King must belong to the Evangelical Lutheran Church."[5] While the Constitution grants freedom of religion both to individuals (including members of the Parliament) and to religious groups (as long as they do not infringe the public order), the king cannot choose a religious community of his own will and discernment. This shows the particular profile of the Evangelical Lutheran Church as a national church rooted in the Danish people rather than in royal and parliamentary decisions. "People and King must be intertwined in order for the King to be really Danish, and this includes that he may not be of any other religion than the majority of the people."[6]

From a comparative perspective, some subtle differences come up here among the Scandinavian churches in the nineteenth century, which we may formulate as follows: in Denmark, the king had to be a member of the People's Church; in Norway, the people, according to the 1814 Constitution, had to belong to the king's church; in Sweden, both the people and the king belonged to the state church. Crude as this comparison is, it is interesting that the Danish version of a "People's Church" presupposes that the Parliament and the king are obliged to *acknowledge* the Evangelical Lutheran Church as the one shared by the majority of the Danish people, even though its practical affairs continued to be governed by royal decrees and parliamentary legislation.

In this chapter, we argue that A.S. Ørsted and N.F.S. Grundtvig were instrumental in shaping the legal and theological contours of the Danish People's Church and the freedom of religion. They had different ecclesiological ideals, however. While Ørsted preferred the continuation of a relaxed version of the old state church, Grundtvig ended up seeing the People's Church as a beneficial external framework for congregational life within the People's Church. And while Ørsted wanted to grant freedom of religion by law, as decided by

Parliament, Grundtvig argued strongly for the constitutional basis for that right. Nonetheless, they shared a fundamental distinction between the variegated religious life, on the one hand, and state organization, on the other hand; they also shared the social vision of common concerns between the national church and the national culture, given their long history of intertwinement. Eventually, many older structures of the state church survived in the People's Church, not least the territorial system of parishes and the common legislative, administrative, and judiciary rules decided by the Parliament and the minister for the church. Stable regulations were also maintained for the education of pastors (via the university), for the recruitment of pastors (via the bishops), and for organizing the church (since 1903, supplemented with congregational councils, and since 1922 with deanery councils), in addition to providing for a nationwide system of membership-based church taxes (introduced in 1903).

Ørsted and Grundtvig experienced quite a few controversies along the way to their later negotiations at the Constitutional Assembly in 1848–49. Differences between the two appear not only in their different educational backgrounds but also in relation to their place in the Danish establishment up to 1849. Together with his brother, H.C. Ørsted, A.S. Ørsted belonged to the inner circle of the Danish Golden Age, including literary figures such as the national poet Adam Oehlenschläger (Anders married his sister in 1802), the author Jens Baggesen, the Copenhagen and Zealand bishops Friederich Münther, J.P. Mynster, and H.L. Martensen, and others. By comparison, Grundtvig led a more solitary life as a free author and pastor until he began to attract ever more followers as well as support from the royal house. Whereas A.S. Ørsted was an early starter and held high positions in the Danish administration and government, Grundtvig was a late bloomer, living in insecure economic conditions until he was in his fifties, and even put under censorship between 1825 and 1837. While A.S. Ørsted had an overall smooth career, ending as prime minister in 1853–54, Grundtvig constantly involved himself in conflicts with his environments; only late in life did he gain the social recognition that he had been longing for since his youth. For a long period more infamous than famous, he began to receive greater recognition in the 1830s, and in 1861 he was given the title of "honorary bishop," an *ad hominem* title never used again in Danish history.

In what follows, we offer portraits of the two figures in which we show the contours of their work and their development as public discussants of the relationship between law and religion. We then follow their internal conflicts, sometimes by proxy, as when Anders's brother, the famous physicist H.C. Ørsted, entered into a debate on science and religion with Grundtvig in 1814–15. The major debate, however, took place between Grundtvig and the liberal theologian H.N. Clausen in 1825, a debate that also led to a significant intervention by A.S. Ørsted in 1826.

In the period between 1826 and 1849, we see Ørsted and Grundtvig coming closer to one another in their common wish to secure freedom of religion, though opting for different solutions. While Ørsted argued for retaining older Danish laws of religion and permitting administrative dispensations to relax the burden of uniformity, Grundtvig worked for new laws for church and religion in order to establish a law-based framework for the Danish people that promulgates freedom for individuals as well as for religious fractions and groups. In some detail, we follow their positions and interactions in the Constitutional Assembly, based on the rich sources in the official transcripts from the parliamentary negotiations. We round up our arguments for seeing Ørsted and Grundtvig as two concurrent shapers of the idea of the People's Church in Denmark (*Folkekirke*). We see Ørsted focusing on a relaxed administration, tolerant to internal differences within the church, and Grundtvig as a political promoter of the principle of religious freedom, both within and outside the People's Church in Denmark.

Anders Sandøe Ørsted: a biographical sketch

A.S. Ørsted was born in 1778 in a small town in rural Denmark (Rudkøbing on Langeland), one of two sons of a pharmacist. His older brother, H.C. Ørsted (1777–1851), was a pharmacist and physicist known for identifying the universal law of electromagnetism experimentally and for initiating and being the first director of the Polyteknisk Læreanstalt (1829), today the Technical University of Denmark.[7] While Hans Christian Ørsted was an internationally renowned name, the reputation of Anders Sandøe Ørsted has remained national and Nordic.[8]

The Ørsted brothers arrived at the University of Copenhagen in 1794, and both were initially strongly influenced by the philosophy of Immanuel Kant. H.C. Ørsted passed his examination in pharmacy in 1797, while A.S. Ørsted gained his law degree in 1799. Already as a student, he had earned his living as a private teacher of law, and he continued with this occupation until 1813, along with other obligations.[9]

In 1799, the twenty-year-old A.S. Ørsted applied for a position as assistant professor of law at Copenhagen University, but without success, and he never became a member of the faculty of law. Nonetheless, he continued on the academic path by his extensive scholarship, including editing important legal journals in Denmark (*Juridisk Maanedsskrift*, 1802–03; *Juridisk Arkiv*, 1804–12; *Nyt juridisk Arkiv*, 1812–20; *Juridisk Tidsskrift* 1820–30), to which he also contributed a great deal. He also published his collected essays in *Eunomia* (Good law-making), vols. 1–4 (1815–22), crowned by his main work, *Haandbog over den danske og norske Lovkyndighed* (Handbook on Danish and Norwegian Law) in six volumes, 1822–35. He produced all of these publications while carrying out his civil career. Intended for developing the juridical skills in the courts, Ørsted's contributions also laid the basis for the development of Danish and Norwegian legal thinking.[10]

Having not been accepted as a university teacher, Ørsted started his career in 1801 as an assessor in the city court of Copenhagen, followed by a promotion to the Supreme Court in 1810. In 1813, a calling to become a civil servant in the central administration changed his destiny. From 1825 to 1848 Ørsted worked as the chief person responsible for providing legal advice to the king and for formulating new legislation in the central administration (*Generalprokurør*). From

1842 he also worked as a leading member of the State Council, followed by his years as a politician during the new, more democratic era.

From 1809 to 1828, Ørsted supplemented his position in the court and in the central administration as a teacher of ecclesiastical law.[11] Ørsted thereby contributed to the development of the discipline of ecclesiastical law in Denmark, until he had to give up this function due to his intervention in the conflict between N.F.S. Grundtvig and the professor of theology H.N. Clausen in 1826. Much against Ørsted's will, the king forced Ørsted to make a choice between his academic legal writing and his central position in the state administration. Ørsted chose the latter path and was allowed to finish his ongoing publications until 1835.

From 1835 to 1844, Ørsted represented the government as royal commissary in two of the four advisory councils (*Stænderforsamlinger*) in Roskilde (Zealand, East Denmark) and Viborg (Jutland, West Denmark). Here he became acquainted with political realities before entering the Constitutional Assembly of 1848–49. After 1849, he was a member of the upper house, and from April 1853 until December 1854, he was prime minister as well as minister for church and education. This governmental period had to deal with the constitutional conflicts after the first wars against Prussia over Schleswig and Holstein in 1848. The governmental period ended in 1854 with a trial against Ørsted and the other ministers for high treason, a trial for which they were dismissed.

A.S. Ørsted dedicated his last years to writing his memoirs, *Af mit Livs og min Tids Historie* (Of the history of my life and my time, 4 vols., 1851–57), of which some parts carry a whiff of bitterness over having been one of the liberals within the government while being seen in his later years as one of the most conservative figures.

> Those who lived in those years knows that any young person was taken by the ideas of the French Revolution and wished the blossoming of religious and personal freedom in all countries. I have therefore always amused myself with the idea that we, the elders, according to the press of our times, should be seen as having grown up in days of slavery and darkness and that we, therefore, would not be able to understand the lures of freedom today. We learned about that already in our childhood.[12]

In Danish legal theory, Ørsted is seen primarily as a representative of a comparative legal method within private law and criminal law. He built on legal principles in legislative praxis but preferred a legal development that combined theoretical concepts with concrete case law, that is, a method focusing on administrative decisions and court decisions, or jurisprudence.[13] In his argumentation for new legal principles, Ørsted became what today may be called a pragmatic jurist by setting theoretical moral and legal questions in the context of real-life practical situations, in which the juridical problems appear.[14]

Ørsted, however, also discussed the theoretical foundations for the proposed solutions. He based his development of legal principles not only on particular cases and comparisons with foreign legal solutions but also on his detailed knowledge of the philosophy of law.[15] His 1798 Gold Medal thesis at Copenhagen University[16] dealt with the philosophy of Immanuel Kant and Johann Gottlieb Fichte. Looking back on his earliest writing, he recalled later that he was somehow disappointed with Kant's *Foundations on the Metaphysics of Virtue* from 1797; this led him to "a break with the admiring trust in the old wise man, which I [at that time] so lightly had given myself over to." [17] The problem in Kant, according to Ørsted, was that he could not derive positive laws from natural law, and much to the detriment of Ørsted's teacher in natural law (Prof. J. Fr. W. Schlegel), the young Ørsted opted in 1798 for Fichte's view of the role of the state. Fichte saw the task of the state to be using positive state laws as technical means for securing external peace and the domestic freedom for all citizens. The understanding of law-giving as an art not reducible to abstract morality continues in Ørsted's oeuvre, but he soon gave up on both Kant and Fichte. "After 1801, one cannot find any traces in my writings that smacks thereof,"[18] he wrote in his memoirs, thereby pointing to the beginnings of his civil career and of his own legal scholarship.

Moving away from the systems of natural law, both in the ontological tradition of Wolff and in the transcendental tradition of Kant, Ørsted integrated the idea of a normative impact on law from the moral and religious life of the people. Thus, already in 1804, he argued against the interpretation of the absolutist Royal Law of 1665 (article 1), as if the king single-handedly defines the people's religion.

In a lecture in 1807 titled "Is the state entitled to issue laws and make public initiatives to the benefit of religion?",[19] he answered emphatically in the positive. In relation to Kant, he conceded that morality is prior to religion but added that religion is more comprehensive than morality, and that morality cannot survive without religion.[20] In contrast to Fichte, he argued that his minimalist view of the role of the state as indifferent to religion and moral virtue is not tenable. "The goal of the state is the development of the force of reason in its fullness and glory."[21]

This goal, however, can be achieved only if the state is able to rely on the good will of its citizens; after all, laws can never be enforced in each and any particular circumstance.[22] The well-being of the heritage of virtue and religion is thus of central importance for a state that wants to care for the well-being of society. In the end, religion is the moral foundation of the law, and when jurists in court evaluate evidence, they should exercise their sense of justice (*Retsind*) and conscience (*Samvittighedsfuldhed*).[23] Ørsted thus emphasizes the positive role of moral and religious traditions for the state, the view that later carried the June Constitution of 1849, article 3 (today article 4).[24] Just as ecclesiastical legislation should take into account a nation's historical and religious culture, so the state has a positive interest in regulating the religion of the land.[25]

In a lecture introducing his teaching in ecclesiastical law at the Pastoral Seminary, published in 1811, Ørsted issued the proposal that ecclesiastical law should address three interrelated viewpoints: the principles of ecclesiastical law via the philosophy of law, a clarification of the historical uses of ecclesiastical law, and finally positive law. Here, already, Ørsted emphasizes how legal concepts, norms, and rules have developed in the life and legal traditions of a nation. Ørsted thus argued that a good knowledge of historical background serves the understanding of the legal situation in current society.[26]

How this program was carried out within ecclesiastical law, we do not know in detail, but normative issues were henceforth central to Ørsted. The aim of ecclesiastical law is thus to clarify "the relation between our church order as it stands, and how it should be."[27] One of the problems addressed in his opening lecture was the duty of pastors to follow their pastoral oath. Ørsted points to the continuous relevance of the Danish Law of 1683, which singles out the importance of the five confessions of the Evangelical Lutheran Church (the Apostles' Creed, the Nicene Creed of 381, the Athanasian Creed, Luther's Small Catechism, and the Augsburg Confession of 1530). However, he also refers to live theological options within the contemporary church.[28] Accordingly, nonallegiance to specific elements in the confessions should not automatically lead to a dismissal of a pastor.[29]

In general, Ørsted aimed to find practical solutions based on the existing laws in their historical and philosophical tradition, paired with an understanding of the concrete situation on which the legal decision should be made. This approach leads Ditlev Tamm to focus on Ørsted's development of Danish private law, based on the comparative method and German legal philosophy. It leads Jørgen Dalberg-Larsen to identify him as representing a realistic legal philosophy, namely a dialectic theory, which takes into account not only the formulation of the laws but also an interpretation of the concrete, factual situation. As highlighted in Sverre Blandhol's interpretation of Ørsted as a pragmatist, it is characteristic that Ørsted, in his concrete legal and scholarly work, did not apply a sharp distinction between law and context, between legal and moral argumentation, and between the current situation and the historical background.

In the broader perspective, A.S. Ørsted is a representative of Romanticism and the German historical school in legal science. Ørsted often referred to Savigny as one of his main inspirations. What he learned from Savigny was primarily that legal solutions should reflect the historical legal understandings in society. Law is based on, and derived from, natural feelings of justice and common sense with concerns for the needs of the state and the wider society at a given time. In this manner, Ørsted combined a cultural and historical awareness with a legal pragmatism—and with a focus on the learned jurist as the circumspective person responsible for interpreting the law.

Nicolai Frederik Severin Grundtvig: a biographical sketch

Unlike the writings of Ørsted, substantial parts of the works of N.F.S. Grundtvig (1783–1872) are available in German and English translations.[30] An extensive international research literature depicts various facets of his intellectual history as well. [31] For this reason, we will here focus on the aspects of Grundtvig's work of relevance for a comparison with Ørsted.

Like Ørsted, Grundtvig came to Copenhagen from the countryside. Born in a vicarage in Udby (southern Zealand), he received most of his schooling in Jutland and lived after his ninth year with friends and family until he graduated from Aarhus Cathedral School in 1800. In 1803, he passed his theological exams with excellence at the University of Copenhagen at the age of twenty.

While the Ørsted brothers belonged to the inner circles of the cultural elite of the Danish Golden Age, Grundtvig remained an outsider to the academic milieu in Copenhagen. As a young man, he left Copenhagen to become a teacher of small children at a manor house in the countryside (1805–08), where a platonic love affair opened his senses to a Romantic worldview. In his teenage years, like so many others, Grundtvig shared the Enlightenment ideals, and after his graduation in theology he decidedly did not want to become a pastor. Yet soon he was to take part in the Romantic turn in philosophy, history, and poetry. As early as 1802, Grundtvig heard the philosopher Henrich Steffens, a cousin of Grundtvig, give his nine lectures on the philosophy of nature, presented in the spirit of F.W.J. Schelling and published in Danish as *Indledning til philosophiske Forelæsninger* (Introduction to lectures on philosophy, 1803). Grundtvig later described Steffens as the "lightning-man" who appeared in Copenhagen "like an angel from the heavens," even though he admitted that he was not sure how much he actually understood as a young student.[32] Returning to Copenhagen from the manor house in 1808, he obtained a position as a teacher in history and geography at a high school until 1810, though he had hoped for a position as historian at the University of Copenhagen.

At this early stage, Grundtvig shared with the Ørsted brothers the longing for a deep, internal coherence between history and nature, as evidenced in his first book, *Om Religion og Liturgie* (On religion and liturgy, 1807). Soon after, however, he became convinced that life and death were opposing forces that could not be mediated within a natural philosophy based on the postulate of a deep-seated harmony of good and evil, nature and history. His translations and studies in Norse mythology (1808–10) convinced him of a more conflict-oriented view of good and evil. Giving up on the natural philosophy of Schelling and Steffens, Grundtvig aimed much more to find a bridge between Nordic mythology and Christian faith. In a poem from 1808, he refers to "High Odin" and "White Christ" as "sons of the All-Father," arguing that "settled is your former clash," for both have loved "our Father."[33] Compared to the Romanticism of the Ørsted brothers, Grundtvig's use of Romantic ideas was thus poetical and historical rather than scientific and legal in orientation.

In 1810, however, Grundtvig's father called upon him to become his vicar and help him out in his vicarage. His scholarly ambitions made Grundtvig reluctant to leave Copenhagen, but he felt obliged to do so, though to be ordained he had to pass a pastoral exam with a sermon. On April 11, 1810, Grundtvig published the sermon, titled "Why has the Word of the Lord disappeared from His House?" In this dimissory sermon, Grundtvig openly and sharply criticized the taste of rationalist theology and even accused his pastoral colleagues for not believing in the gospel that they were called to preach. A critical note from his examiners led to a rebuke of Grundtvig by the administration for attacking his fellow pastors. As a teacher in ecclesiastical law, Ørsted must have known of the sermon and the subsequent legal trial.[34]

With the official rebuke in his backpack, Grundtvig returned to the parish in Udby in a state of mental distress. A famous episode of mental breakdown on the way home led him further into a phase of biblicism and Lutheran piety. He no longer placed the figures of Norse mythology on a par with Christ but programmatically below "the holy Christians who follow the commandments of Christ and dare to receive the fruits of his death."[35] Soon after his recovery, Grundtvig wrote his first hymn, "Lovely Is the Midnight Sky,"[36] a retelling of the Christmas story, which already gives evidence of the world-affirming tone in the about 1,500 hymns that he would produce over his lifetime.

In 1813, when his father died, Grundtvig was able to return to Copenhagen. He was in the process of writing his *Kort Begreb af Verdens Krønike i Sammenhæng* (hereafter *World Chronicle*), published in 1812, 1814, and 1817. Writing in the 1812 volume on the early history of humanity up to his present day, Grundtvig appealed to revelation as the safest source of knowledge. He took for granted as historical facts what he read in the Old Testament, and criticized the secularism and pantheism of his own age. It was in this biblicist phase (1810–14) that the conflict between Grundtvig and H.C. Ørsted took place, as we will see in the next section.

Between 1813 and 1821, Grundtvig worked as an independent scholar. His strong views and fiery temperament caused annoyance in the leading cultural and ecclesiastical circles in Copenhagen and made it difficult for him to receive a calling as a pastor. Nonetheless, he wrote new versions of his *World Chronicle* inspired by the idea of universal history in Johann Gottfried Herder's *Ideas on the Philosophy of the History of Mankind* (1784–91). In particular, Grundtvig shared Herder's view that each nation has a particular "spirit," given with its history, language, and people.

He also produced the journal *Danne-Virke* (1816–19), singlehandedly written by the editor himself. These more philosophical articles show a broadening of Grundtvig's horizon. Alongside essays and poems on Danish history, he continued his earlier work on the Nordic spirit, but now within the framework of a Christian apologetics that appealed to common sense. Most importantly, Grundtvig criticized the view that human consciousness can be set apart from the outside world, as in Kant's and Fichte's idea of the transcendental Ego. Positively, Grundtvig argued for the view that all human understanding takes its point of departure in the human senses (in particular touching, hearing, and seeing), though always transformed within the specific human awareness of spiritual relations (beauty, truth, and goodness). God is the creator of a universe with both sensible and spiritual relations, but nowhere is divine creativity more visible than in the poetic activity of human beings, created as they are in the image and likeness of God.

In 1821–22, Grundtvig was finally given a position in Præstø, in southern Zealand, and in 1822–26, he served as a pastor in one of the centrally placed churches in Copenhagen, Our Savior's Church. Until then, his concept of the church had been relatively vague and even oscillating. Now Grundtvig began to discover the importance of the community as the people of God, whom he also warmly addressed in his sermons as "my friends" or "Christian friends." Grundtvig began to discover the importance of the congregational life as part of the historical church. He was no longer a lonely preacher: the church of Christ, even if small in number, was a reality based on the power of the Holy Spirit that had been at work in the preceding centuries.[37]

Grundtvig's main focus was now to identify the essentials of Christian faith aligned with the long tradition of a church that existed even prior to the writings of the New Testament. He began to develop what he called, after 1825, his "church view," arguing that baptism and the Holy Supper, "the font and the table," constitute the life of the church due to the personal presence of Christ. Baptism stands out as the beginning of the Christian life (faith), subsequently nourished by preaching (hope), in order to be fulfilled at the Lord's Supper (love). Since the Apostles' Creed is the condition for baptism, Grundtvig aired the contentious view that the Creed had been handed over to the apostles by Christ himself alongside the commandment of baptism and the invitation to join the table. With this new emphasis on the continuity of the church, he superseded his earlier biblicism while pointing to the presence of Christ in the midst of the faithful congregation. In this period, he also began to take seriously the revivalist movements of his day. He saw them as expressions of a vital Christian laypeople who were closer to the historical church than were the rationalist pastors of his day, even if he did not share their negative views of culture and their heated appeals to conversion.[38]

In 1825, Grundtvig's emotions were aroused again in his (in)famous conflict with the young promising professor of theology H.N. Clausen (1793–1877), who had just published a massive work on Catholic and Protestant church order, doctrine, and ritual.[39] Grundtvig immediately felt obliged to write a harsh response under the title, *Kirkens Gienmæle* (The Church's Retort), in which he attacked Clausen's version of Christianity as "completely false" and his idea of Protestantism as a "temple of idols," "a self-made castle-in-the-air."[40] Grundtvig even required that Clausen either apologize for his unchristian theology or resign his university chair and openly discard his name as a Christian.

This conflict established Grundtvig's entrance onto the public scene in Denmark, a scene he would not leave again until his death nearly fifty years later. The first printing of five hundred copies of *The Church's Retort* sold out within days. Clausen, however, did not respond to Grundtvig other than raising a libel case against him. It was during this legal process that A.S. Ørsted intervened in the debate, causing himself substantial troubles with the royal court, as we saw above. Soon after, Clausen won the case against Grundtvig, and Grundtvig was fined and put under lifelong censorship (lifted on December 27, 1837). In protest, Grundtvig stepped down from his position as pastor on the eve of Pentecost in 1826, in deep disillusion with the Danish church. How could he and other "old-fashioned Lutheran believers" live and express a Christian faith within the state church?

In a long period after 1826, Grundtvig again had nothing to support him for a living, except for what came in from his publications and his followers. In addition, the king gave him some subsidies, including financial support to make three trips to England during the summers of 1829, 1830, and 1831. Inspired by these English experiences, Grundtvig began to develop a new cultural vision for the relation between church and culture. Grundtvig now focused on what is common for human beings despite differences of faith.

In his famous introduction to a fully new version of *Nordisk Mythologi* (Nordic mythology, 1832), he laid out a new cultural agenda, based on a positive theological anthropology: a human being is a divine experiment of dust and spirit, "in whom divine powers through thousands of generations proclaim, develop, and enlighten themselves as a divine experiment, in order to show how spirit and dust can permeate one another and be transfigured into a common divine consciousness."[41] Based on this "Judeo-Christian" understanding of humanity and life, there should be a friendly collaboration between Christians and "naturalists of spirit." Grundtvig did not mention candidates for this designation, but who could qualify better as a naturalist of spirit than H.C. Ørsted, with whom he had twenty years earlier been in conflict?

Moreover, the travels to England convinced Grundtvig of the importance of dealing with practical and political affairs. "In all parliamentary matters, I think of the English," he declared in 1839, and he openly confessed his "Anglomania."[42] Grundtvig became a strong proponent of freedom of religion as a God-given human right, a right given not only to individuals but also to religious groups such as the Baptists, the Quakers, and other revivalists.[43] "Without every other freedom, religious freedom would be futile."[44] Grundtvig thus involved himself in many causes of freedom— freedom of expression, freedom of schools, freedom of trade—and was active in the cause for the liberation of slaves as well. Similarly, as early as 1831, he argued for freeing the German-speaking duchy of Holstein from its forced merger with the Danish kingdom, based on the rights of a people to decide for itself. "Self-done is well-done!"[45] In this spirit, Grundtvig and his collaborators established exam-free "people's high schools" beginning in 1844. These "schools for life" should enlighten the understanding of ordinary people in the Nordic countries and capacitate them for taking an active part in society. [46]

Aged sixty-five, Grundtvig offered himself as a candidate for the convention that would draft the new democratic constitution in 1848–49, and he became a member of the assembly after a couple of attempts.[47] Grundtvig was also a member of the lower house of the Parliament in 1849–52 and 1854–58. Rising frequently in the chamber, he spoke for freedom and against the involvement of the state in the internal affairs of religious communities. In 1848, Grundtvig was still hesitant about free electoral rights (and even refrained from voting for the new Constitution), since he believed in developing the union between "the hand of the king and the voice of the people."[48] In 1866, however, Grundtvig, now aged eighty-two, stood for the upper house of the Parliament in order to defend the very same free electoral rights, which he saw threatened by the constitutional change in 1866. This change from Romantic royalist to defender of representative democracy was based in his trust in state institutions, now redefined as institutions representing the people.

As late as 1839, Grundtvig was given an extraordinary vicarage in a hospital for elderly women, Vartov, in the Center of Copenhagen. There he stayed until his death, in 1872, and Vartov became (and still is) the center for present-day Grundtvigians.

Science and faith: the conflict between H.C. Ørsted and N.F.S. Grundtvig, 1814–15

Let us now return to the early clash between Grundtvig and the Ørsted brothers, occasioned by his *World Chronicle* of December 1812. A.S. Ørsted followed theological discussions closely, and his animosity toward Grundtvig was growing. This is witnessed in letters Ørsted exchanged with his brother in 1813. Ørsted found that Grundtvig's publication of a biblical world history was an example of "unreason and tastelessness," and his brother promised to take issue with "this man's animosity against reason" at the first given opportunity.[49] That opportunity came in 1814–15, when Grundtvig and H.C. Ørsted had a major intellectual debate concerning faith and science. H.C. Ørsted issued the booklet *Imod den store Anklager* (Against the big accuser) in August 1814, followed by Grundtvig's rejoinder, *Imod den lille Anklager* (Against the little accuser), in June 1815.[50]

H.C. Ørsted was a Christian natural philosopher who argued for a sympathetic harmony between faith and science while insisting on science as an independent inquiry within its own domains. Christian faith cannot and should not control empirical investigations and the search for laws of nature, he asserted. At the same time, Ørsted pursued an apologetic agenda when referring to contemporary trends that seek to "rediscover a renewed belief as well as a higher knowledge" after the Enlightenment period had driven reason beyond its proper domains. With this understanding, Ørsted presents Grundtvig as a "Don Quixote," out of tune with his time, who even had "a hideous character as author, fully devoid of love."[51]

Grundtvig, on his side, fought for what he understood at the time as the correct biblical worldview. In his *World Chronicle* from 1812, for example, he criticized the French Enlightenment with its emphasis on a chemistry that dissects the human body in disregard for the spiritual nature of humankind, and with an astronomy that only looks out for proximate causes while excluding divine providence as the deeper cause of things.[52] The kind of pantheism exemplified by Schelling and his Danish consorts was not any better.

The conflict could not be settled on the premises of the opponents. On the one hand, we have Grundtvig, who in this phase of his life judged history from a biblical perspective and wished to subsume the sciences under a theological worldview. On the other hand, we have H.C. Ørsted, who argued for a harmony of faith and knowledge mediated by a comprehensive Romantic philosophy. Beneath the debate, however, we see a battle for winning the audience. Which audience? H.C. Ørsted wrote for the cultural elite: "[B]y 'people,' I understand the more educated part of the people, the reading people, if I may say so."[53] Grundtvig had not yet found his audience, but his concept of "people" was decidedly broader, embracing in this early phase ordinary Christians, later extending to the Danish people at large.

State law as protector of true Christianity? Grundtvig and A.S. Ørsted 1825–26

In 1825–26, we see the first contours of a rapprochement between Grundvig and A.S. Ørsted, though still without their finding common cause. The occasion was the aforementioned conflict between Grundtvig and H.N. Clausen.

Clausen was a follower of the Berlin theologian Friedrich Schleiermacher (1768–1834), the main theological architect behind the establishment of the United Protestant Church in Prussia in 1822. Like Schleiermacher, Clausen saw a fundamental difference between the essence of Catholicism and the spirit of Protestantism. While the former rests on church authority (the Church being the mediator of Christ), the latter builds on the individual's relationship to Christ, as attested in the Bible. For the former, the Church is the precondition of the individual's relation to Christ; for the latter, the faithful relation to Christ is the precondition for being a member of the Christian church.[54] From Schleiermacher, Clausen took a combination of a contemporary interpretation of the Bible with an emphasis on Protestantism as based on personal piety and religious feeling. Accordingly, Clausen's voluminous book on *Catholicism and Protestantism: Their Constitution, Doctrine, and Ritual*[55] assumed only a minor difference between Calvinism and Lutheranism. Inspired by Calvinist tradition, Clausen argued for giving the Danish church a synodal order with its own internal legal structure.

With this background in view, the deeper theological reasons for Grundtvig's strong reaction in *The Church's Retort* are understandable. Grundtvig could not accept Clausen's attempt to divide the church into Catholics and Protestants, for all Christians are baptized with the same Apostles' Creed. Grundtvig's "Church View" of 1825 was thus an argument for the continuity of the "table and the font" in the long Christian tradition despite later theological and cultural divisions. Furthermore, the living Word of Christ in the community constitutes the Christian church through the ages. Grundtvig begins to see the Bible as a word of enlightenment, the "Light-Word" (*Lys-Ordet*), whereas baptism and the Eucharist bring the "Life-Word" (*Livs-Ordet*) of Christ, who constitutes the Christian church. Moreover, the scriptures are open to the use of all Christians. According to Grundtvig, the result of Clausen's view would be the erection of a new "exegetical papacy," in which any faithful reading of scripture would have to go through the interpretive filter of self-designated church teachers. If theologians at the university (and the rationalist pastors influenced by them) were given the right to interpret the Bible as they wanted, ordinary Christians would become slaves to such interpretations, and homeless in their own church. Grundtvig, who in this period insisted on the pastoral oath, wanted to protect congregations from "the exegetical papacy" of what he saw as unchristian teachers.

When Clausen sued Grundtvig for libel, Grundtvig refrained from appearing in court and continued his own writings. One of Clausen's supporters, Christian Paulsen, professor of Danish law at the University of Kiel, publicly called on A.S. Ørsted to stand on Clausen's side in the conflict.[56] Paulsen argued that the government (including Ørsted) had already supported a space for a charitable interpretation of the pastoral oath, based on a pastoral letter issued by the bishops in 1817. This letter said that even though the Bible was the final authority, it needed a pastoral interpretation of its essentials; pastors were free to interpret the Augsburg Confession or any of the old confessions in the same spirit as well. Paulsen therefore argued that Clausen, from a legal perspective, had to be vindicated against Grundtvig.

At this point, Ørsted decided to publish his understanding of the case, and he did so in two long articles in *Juridisk Tidsskrift* (Juridical Journal) under the title "Is the Danish Church Order in Need of a Thorough Revision?"[57] Ørsted's answer was in the negative, but he expressed his admiration for Clausen's book: "In this book the central tasks of ecclesiastical law are treated with insight, with a love for substance, and with a boldness that can only awaken the dormant interest in these important concerns."[58] He also praises Clausen's circumspect deliberations, and even though Clausen's view should be received with "much and warm criticism" in view of the hot topic, it should not have been "impeded by a bitter shouting war"[59]—no doubt an allusion to Grundtvig.

Ørsted thus sides with Clausen on the need for giving room for interpretations of the basic doctrines of scripture in general and the pastoral oath in particular. For even though any religious association must have "firm basic doctrines" (*faste Grundlærdomme*), the Lutheran confessions themselves state that only scripture has independent validity (*norma normans*), while the confessional documents are to be interpreted in light of scripture—hence, they are *norma normata*.[60] In this context, Ørsted is also referring with consent to Schleiermacher's work on the meaning of the symbolic books.[61] At the same time, Ørsted alludes positively to Grundtvig's position when referring to the Apostles' Creed as being used at baptism since the earliest days of the church, adding (against Grundtvig) that the Creed "as generally known, does not go back to the apostles themselves."[62]

Ørsted thus stands behind Clausen's emphasis on a liberal interpretation of the symbolic books—at least for pastors. On another matter, however, Ørsted took issue with Clausen. At some length, Ørsted points to the many practical problems of Clausen's proposal to develop the Danish church as an independent association within the state. If an internal church law were to be established, there could well be a lack of legal competence within the church, whereas the government, within the present order, always asks the bishops and others for theological advice. Clausen's idea of church government (*Kirkeregjering*), is not only legally unclear but potentially one of the most devastating (*fordærveligste*) steps to take. A moral and religious church government, led by pastors and presbyters, would easily infringe the innermost personal and social zones of church members. "Professor Clausen seems all too easy in allaying the fear that such a church regime could promote hypocrisy."[63] Referring to the experiences with Calvinist presbyters, Ørsted concludes that discipline in matters of faith rests better in the hands of professional lawyers.

Within the royal court, Ørsted's publication was seen as an interference in a pending court case. Moreover, Ørsted's superior in the royal government, Fr. Julius Kaas, wanted to enforce the strict allegiance of pastors to Lutheran orthodoxy, while Ørsted found that pastors should attend to the essentials of the Christian faith, particularly Christian love. Pastors should not be literalists but should "stay away from dogmatic conceptions that either are of no avail for the living Christian faith and the pious mind, or could even confuse their emotions."[64]

Ørsted's intervention was thus not only a plea for pastoral freedom but also a concern for the piety of everyday Christians. To Ørsted, the use of reason in religious life is not an enemy of the Christian faith. Rather, "the insight won by the effort of reason leads exactly to the awareness that all treasures of wisdom and higher understanding are contained within the Gospel."[65] Ørsted thus assumed a full congruence between the laws of universal reason and the fundamental commitments of the Christian faith. In a personal letter to Julius Kaas, Ørsted is particularly outspoken about the need to administer the church in a context-sensitive manner:

> If the idea of devilish influence on human beings, of eternal hellish punishment, and of the subtle definitions on the doctrine of the Trinity in the Athanasian symbol be as holy as the gospel of the eternal love revealed in Christ, the Son of God and the savior of the world, then there would not be ten orthodox pastors in the whole country.[66]

In his 1826 article, Ørsted was faithful to his general legal method: the inherited laws should be interpreted in the contemporary context, based on an understanding of the essential content of the confessional documents, the current situation, and the general opinion among leading public figures. In Ørsted's view, decisions on orthodoxy should not be made by over-eager theologians or courts but by a wise administrative government, which listens to the best advice of jurists and theologians. Ørsted thus suggested a third way between Clausen and Grundtvig: a historically informed, open-minded, and pragmatic state-governed interpretation of church laws.

Grundtvig was anything but a pragmatist in 1825–26. He believed that pastors in the Danish church should abide by their pastoral oath, his main concern being the full commitment to the Apostles' Creed. At this stage in his development, he understood the state church as a protector of the confessional nature of the Evangelical Lutheran Church. While he was in broad agreement with Ørsted on the protective role of the state vis-à-vis the Danish Church, Ørsted and Grundtvig disagreed about the method. Strict observation of the creedal commitment of pastors versus a more lenient practice with room for interpretations of the substance of the confessions—this was the dividing issue between Grundtvig and Ørsted in 1826.

Perhaps surprised by the legal aspects of the Clausen debate, Grundtvig replied with a new publication titled *Vigtige Spørgsmaal til Danmarks Lovkyndige* (Important questions for Denmark's jurists). In this rarely discussed booklet (published on September 2, 1826, that is, after the first part of Ørsted's 1826 article but before the verdict on Grundtvig on October 30, 1826), Grundtvig addressed Ørsted directly. Initially, he expressed his regret that Ørsted favored Clausen in (the first part of) his 1826 article. At the same time, he expressed the conviction that he and Ørsted in reality were "basically in juridical agreement, even though our tendencies, regarding the application of law, drive us to divergent sides."[67] As put by Grundtvig: a "theologizing jurist" who knows of the importance of religion in all spheres of life should be able to meet halfway with a "historicizing theologian" who knows of the importance of law for the life of a people.[68]

The critical question underlying Grundtvig's appeal to Ørsted can be rendered as follows: if Clausen were to be proven right at court, how then would the state ensure the freedom of religion for old-fashioned believers and orthodox pastors like Grundtvig himself? With this problem in mind, Grundtvig develops an early proposal for freedom of religion in the form of eight questions. (1) Can a civil servant be judged for libel when he is only performing his service? No! (2) In particular, can a pastor be sued for libel when he performs his proper task as a defender of true Christianity, a duty stated in his pastoral oath? If so, the state should change the oath![69] (3) Is it correct that the obligation for pastors to defend true Christianity has been central in Danish law since 1660? Yes! (4) Is it not the case that Lutherans following the Augsburg Confession have a right to religious freedom within the kingdom? Definitely so, and if they are not allowed to exist within the state church, such Lutherans should be tolerated outside of it! (5) Is it beneficial for any state that pastors are not obliged to follow a certain confession, and is it the case that pastors within the state church are their own lawgivers regarding church doctrine.[70] No! (6) In the given situation, is it foreseeable that the people of Denmark want to follow the Lutheran faith, or do they prefer another faith? This is a question for the state itself, since "no state can afford to resist the spirit of the people (*Folke-Aanden*) in matters of faith."[71] (7) If this is so, why can teachers of religion (that is, Clausen) be against the Lutheran confession and remain in their office? (8) In that case, at least, the state should by law open up for the possibility that old-fashioned Lutheran Christians separate themselves from the Danish church. In view of such impending "church divorce" (*kirkelig Skilsmisse*), Grundtvig argues for issuing "a general freedom of religion" (*en almindelig Religions-Frihed*) as the only possible political solution.[72]

Such a solution was unthinkable in 1826, however. Nobody wanted a church division, and freedom of religion was only later secured in the Constitution of 1849. We observe, however, a new social self-confidence in Grundtvig. He (not Clausen and his like) represents the Danish people. "The old faith was after the heart of the people," he writes, and if religious freedom was given, "I don't think I would miss any listeners even in an empty barn, but I really believe that the modernizing pastors would have an even smaller audience than they have now!"[73]

There is something contentious about Grundtvig hammering out his self-defense in juridical terms. Nonetheless, he has a greater agenda and really does seem to share two social understandings of public religion with the theologizing jurist A.S. Ørsted. The first is the need of the state to stay in contact with the cohesive force of popular religion. The second is Grundtvig's reference to the inherited Lutheran confessions, in contrast to Clausen's vision of a Protestant amalgam of Lutheranism and Calvinism. In these issues, Grundtvig wanted to persuade Ørsted that they were allies, and to some extent, they were.

This comes out in the second part of Ørsted's 1826 article, in which he gave a brief response to Grundtvig's booklet of September 2, 1826. He states that he of course could not interfere in a pending court case between Clausen and Grundtvig (only settled later, on October 30, 1826). This statement must have had some personal urgency for Ørsted since it was a delicate matter. For between the first and the second part of Ørsted's 1826 article, he had received the royal reprimand dated August 2, 1826, in which the king forced him to choose between his scholarship and his royal position.[74] This royal letter, painful as it was for Ørsted, was not publicly known beyond a very small circle, however. Ørsted therefore responds to Grundtvig that he has neither sided with Clausen in the court case nor harbored any personal reservations against Grundtvig. Rather, given the goodness and benevolence that Grundtvig showed him in the booklet, and on earlier occasions too, Ørsted expresses his goodwill for Grundtvig. Yet "*magis amica veritas*": truth is more than friendship.[75] Ørsted does not agree with Grundtvig's strict position on the pastoral oath, but he assures him that he takes the confessions very seriously, also from a legal point of view. In Ørsted's view, a teacher of religion would be in serious trouble if he did not teach about the Eucharist in accordance with the Augsburg Confession, article 10 (regarding the real presence of Christ). However, later Lutheran conflicts, such as the allegation against Melanchthon's students for being crypto-Calvinists, is not part of Danish church law. Ørsted is thus convinced that Niels Hemmingsen would not have been declared a heretic in the contemporary situation—probably an allusion to the parallel between the Calvinizing tendencies in Hemmingsen and Clausen. Another example is the doctrine of the Trinity, which belongs to the basic teachings of Christianity. Ørsted assures Grundtvig that he holds this doctrine in the highest regard, and emphasizes its simple and pious use in biblical references to the mystery of Father, Son, and Holy Spirit. What he has questioned is only the binding character of the philosophical subtleties of the Nicene and Athanasian Creeds in particular.[76] Ørsted's response to Grundtvig can certainly be read as a friendly and accommodating concession to Grundtvig. Yet it can also be read as a defense of Ørsted's stance in confessional matters vis-à-vis his critics within the royal court.

The "age of the people" and the freedom of religion

In the period from 1830 to 1850, Danish society was transformed from the age of segregated and hierarchical estates (clergy, nobility, peasantry, citizenry) to the age of the people. Grundtvig was particularly aware of this transformation: "The Age of the Estates is over, now is the Age of the People!" he exclaimed in 1849.[77] In Grundtvig's view, this transformation required a new education of the Danish people as well as a broadening of rights. In what follows, we focus on four aspects of freedom of religion.

Freedom within the Danish Church

After losing the libel case to Clausen in 1826, Grundtvig stepped down as pastor and gave up his hope that the state would protect a creedal "old-fashioned Christianity." He first focused on developing his ideas on freedom of religion, based on the English model of a state church alongside freedom of religion for others.[78] Grundtvig went further, though. In *Den Danske Stats-Kirke upartisk betragtet* (An impartial view of the Danish state church, 1834), he developed the idea of the state church as a roomy comprehensive church capable of accommodating both old-fashioned Christians and rationalists such as Clausen.[79] The established church was to be seen as a legal framework around local communities. Accordingly, members of the state church should have the right to follow the pastor they wanted outside the local parish. Grundtvig suggested this idea of loosening the parish tie in 1838 and already in 1855, after the Constitution had been adopted, the option of breaking with the parish tie was finally put into law. Ever since, this has been a central dimension of Danish ecclesiastical law.

Following this way of thinking, Grundtvig changed his earlier strategy and now argued for freedom for pastors to interpret Christianity according to their own Christian convictions, under the provision that they receive a calling from a significant number of congregational members. However, such a freedom from confessional commitment has never been established within the Danish church. On the contrary, the pastoral oath of committing to the Bible and the Lutheran confessions was renewed in 1872 and is still in force.

A less-known dimension of Grundtvig's views of freedom is his suggestion that pastors should be allowed to deny baptism and access to the Eucharist for church members whom the pastors found to be insincere. Such members should find another pastor to care for them; an exclusion from a local congregation should thus not imply an exclusion from the church. H.N. Clausen happened to agree with this view, based on his understanding of the church as an independent association. Ørsted, however, in collaboration with the bishops, rejected the idea entirely.[80] The state must protect the right of every citizen to belong to the church in his or her local parish. Rules on exclusion are not possible, either within the state church or within the People's Church. This has been the position of the Danish church ever since.

Conflicts with revivalist movements

In the years after the conflict of 1826, Ørsted remained the liberal voice within the state administration, even at times when a majority of members in the government wanted to strengthen Christian obligations in society.

Revivalist movements had long been under surveillance by the state. A regulation from 1741, *Konventikelplakaten* (Conventicle Edict), forbade lay people from meeting in private for Bible reading without pastoral attendance. Now revivalist groups wanted to meet on their own. They also wanted to use the old hymnbook from 1699 with pious addendums from 1740 instead of the later rationalist hymnbook authorized by the king in 1778 and 1798. Finally, they refused to replace Erik Pontoppidan's pietist catechism, *Truth into Piety* (1737), with bishop Balle's more rationalist catechism from 1791 in the school teaching of their children.[81]

As we saw above, Grundtvig supported the revivalist lay movements as early as 1825 on the understanding that they were fellow Christians. Ørsted, too, argued for more tolerance and freedom of religion, though in particular for foreigners. Ørsted had been a leading force behind offering the Jewish population in Denmark Danish citizenship in 1814,[82] and he now emphasized the privileges given to the Reformed congregations in 1685.[83] The new king, Christian VIII (r. 1839–48), ended the persecution of the revivalist movements in a royal letter of October 27, 1840, to the bishops; the priests should use only spiritual guidance, not enforcement, toward these groups. Eventually, the revivalist movements mostly remained within the Danish church, in some contrast to the situation in the Church of Sweden.

Enforcement of children's baptism

For a long period, however, the government underscored the obligation of all citizens (apart from Jews) to baptize their children. On the belief that a Christian state is responsible for taking care of religion, a regulation concerning infant baptism was issued in 1828 to establish deadlines for informing the priest and baptizing the infants.[84] Since 99.5 percent of the population belonged to the national church, this did not lead to immediate obstacles. Obstacles, however, appeared with the first rebaptism of a group of adults in Copenhagen on October 30, 1839. Over the next five years, 267 persons were rebaptized, and new Baptist congregations were formed in different parts of the country.[85] Using his position within the government, Ørsted suggested that Baptists be allowed to stay within the church and to postpone the baptism of their children until the age of fourteen.[86] He proposed, too, that they be allowed to come together for religious discussions (though without any proselytizing). Finally, Ørsted argued that legal solutions should be based on dispensations given by the government to individual Baptist groups. The government, however, did not allow the children of Baptists to remain unbaptized up to the age of adulthood. Instead, a new regulation of December 27, 1842, ordered vicars to enforce the baptism of children, and recalcitrant parents were sent to jail together with Baptist leaders. In his memoirs, Ørsted mentions the regulation on baptism from 1828 and the regulation against the Baptists from 1842 as two highly regrettable decisions during his time as a member of the central administration. He also reminds his readers that both regulations were issued during his absence in Norway and Schleswig. He would have decided differently.[87]

Grundtvig, in agreement with Ørsted on this matter, turned sharply against the religious persecution of the Baptists. After his travels to England, Grundtvig believed that the Danish people would remain united despite religious differences. Grundtvig took the principal position that any "religious persecution contradicts the Christian faith and Creed as well as the Augsburg Confession," adding that "persecution only increases division and disagreement in the kingdom."[88] Accordingly, he suggested that Baptists should remain within the state church and should be allowed to postpone the baptism of their children until their coming of age.

Grundtvig and Ørsted thus agreed concerning the result but differed in method. Grundtvig understood religious freedom as a right, whereas Ørsted preferred to build on dispensations, based on a tolerant interpretation of the old laws. Eventually, the regulation of 1842 was withdrawn in 1847, but the problem was solved only with the clauses on freedom of religion in the Constitution of 1849. The obligation for members of the People's Church to baptize their children was repealed by a law of 1857.

Catholic legislation in the country?

A final case regarding Catholicism shows the dilemmas in the late absolutist government between freedom of religion and the wish to keep unity within the laws of the country.[89] Ørsted's argument was that citizens in Denmark formed an Evangelical Lutheran people, unlike American citizens, who were a conglomerate of many different peoples, each with their own faith. In this context, Ørsted referred to the Norwegian constitution of 1814, in which the Evangelical Lutheran faith was identified as the public religion of the state. Ørsted suggested that people who confessed to other religions ought to have their religious freedom.

In 1839, the pope had installed a new bishop as the leader of Catholic missionary work in the Nordic countries, assuming an episcopal jurisdiction for Roman Catholics in Denmark as well. With Prussian support, Austria appealed to the Danish king to recognize this fact. From a Danish perspective, however, such recognition would imply that Danish Catholics should follow Catholic marriage laws, for example, rather than Danish law.[90] The king and the government strongly reacted against such a possibility, as they could not accept that a

Roman Catholic bishop had any jurisdiction over Danish citizens. Already in the regulation of Jewish citizenship in 1814, as well as in the discussion with the Baptists, freedom of religion did not provide an opening for independent religious laws in the country. The law of the land had to be followed. This had been Ørsted's view, too, when he discussed freedom of religion in 1826. Regarding the Catholic question, he therefore proposed to the king to accept the function of the Catholic bishop in Hamburg, but without acknowledging any Catholic jurisdiction in Denmark. Accordingly, the government ordered the Catholic bishop to follow the law of the land in his supervision of Danish congregations.[91]

Law and religion in the constitutional discussions 1848–49

Ørsted and Grundtvig met again, this time face to face, in the Constitutional Assembly of 1848–49. They were among the main participants in the discussions concerning the clauses on state, church, and religion in the Constitution.[92]

The first discussion concerning religion related to the role of the king in the new constitution.[93] All participants in the discussion, including Ørsted and Grundtvig, agreed with the government on the clause still in force, according to which the king must be a member of the Evangelical Lutheran Church.

It was generally agreed, too, that in these times of transition, freedom of religion was central. The chair of the constitutional committee, C.C. Hall, even suggested that there be no discussion concerning the freedom of religion clause (article 81, now article 67):

> It might politically be an advantage for a state if the citizens shared their religious conviction; it is, however, an even higher fortune if this shared conviction is based on persuasion, and not on force. It is therefore in the interest of neither the state nor the majority religion to enforce religious unity. Freedom of religion is the most holy principle of all.[94]

In the discussion on religious freedom, Grundtvig suggested that all clauses on church and religion should take their point of departure in the principle of freedom of religion.[95] The government, by contrast, argued that only the People's Church should be mentioned in the preamble of the new constitution, since it belongs to the founding elements of the nation.[96]

The constitutional committee proposed a confessional identification of the People's Church. Grundtvig initially argued that the church should be simply designated as the majority church, without any strict confessional identity, in order to ensure freedom for both priests and church members within the church. Rather early in the negotiations, however, Grundtvig accepted the Evangelical Lutheran identification of the People's Church.[97] In line with Grundtvig, a minority in the constitutional committee proposed a dissolution of the parish tie in the constitution itself, but the majority found that such concrete proposals should be decided by law, not by the Constitution.[98]

The consensual result was that the Evangelical Lutheran Church was dubbed the Danish People's Church, which as such was to be supported by the state (article 3, today article 4). Members of the assembly agreed that this support should be interpreted in both spiritual and economic terms. A major debate, however, concerned whether the content of this support should be decided in the Constitution itself. The representatives of the peasants (who paid for the church through tithes) proposed that no amount should be preset in the Constitution; rather, it should be left for the legislative powers to decide the extent to which, and how, the state should support the church in the future. A.S. Ørsted, on his side, proposed a rather strong bound to future legislative powers. According to his view, the Evangelical Lutheran religion, based on the Augsburg Confession, should be taught and practiced everywhere as the public religion of the country, supported by the existing church property, which should have constitutional protection.[99] Grundtvig, in opposition to Ørsted and in support of the peasants, found that "no such ideas as a constitutional protection of church property ought to be formulated."[100] Ørsted's proposal was rejected by a majority of eighty-seven to thirty-three.

The Constitution still includes the so-called "promissory paragraph" that a church order for the People's Church will be provided for by statute (article 80, today article 66). H.N. Clausen, Bishop Mynster, and D.G. Monrad were proponents of establishing an internal jurisdiction within the church. Grundtvig disagreed and supported the representatives of the peasants, who strongly opposed any such idea: "We do not want a double constitutional assembly in this country," argued A.F. Tscherning, and one of his fellow representatives from the peasant party, I.A. Hansen, added that "the proposal must be derived from a Catholic concept of the church"—not exactly a recommendation.[101] H.N. Clausen wanted a principal distinction between a political representation and a representation of the church, which would add a different kind of wisdom of which the farmers, according to him, had no real idea. It seemed as if these clarifications were anything but helpful for the governmental case since the proposal was rejected by sixty-eight votes to fifty-eight.[102] This is the only case in which the peasants' representatives had a clear success in voting against the church hierarchy at the assembly. They might have found it too provocative that they were found good enough to pay for the church, but not wise enough to make decisions about the church that they paid for. They wanted to establish ordinary legislative powers over the church, with no exemptions.

Regarding the issue whether to ensure religious freedom directly in the Constitution or leave that matter to future legislators, the positions were turned around. Ørsted proposed that all rules be left to future legislation, while Grundtvig took a strong stance for placing freedom of religion prominently in the Constitution. Ørsted delivered a long speech against placing freedom of religion directly in the Constitution. His concern was to retain a shared legal order for Danish citizens. What about marriage laws, registration of births, and funerals? He uttered, too, a concern for the moral and public order of the state. If there were no limitation to freedom of religion, any preacher could argue publicly for "treason, perjury, the infringement of private property, or any criminal act."[103] He therefore suggested that only one rule was to be formulated in the Constitution, namely that rules on religious bodies dissenting from the established church shall be laid down by law.[104]

Ørsted also argued against the view that freedom of religion implied no discrimination in relation to civic rights and duties.[105] Ørsted saw no problem in a full freedom of religion at private level, but "one should not allow a public exercise of any confessional doctrine, unless it was made known to the state beforehand, and placed under the supervision of the state."[106] New sects should be given rights only based on acknowledgment from the government. Ørsted even argued that it would be "scandalous if a Jew could become a judge," and that neither Jews nor Catholics should have access to becoming civil servants, such as teachers and religious instructors.[107] No, such rules should not be adopted in the Constitution.

In the status of freedom of religion, we see the starkest contrast between Ørsted and Grundtvig. The latter reacted immediately, as the next speaker. What Ørsted had just proposed was exactly as it had always been stated in the Danish state administration for the previous fifty years, Grundtvig rejoined: general arguments for formal freedom, but with no real freedom in the end. Grundtvig could allow distinctions with regard to foreigners but "[t]he Danish man must be equal in all matters."[108] Moreover, he said, it would always be arbitrary when civil servants who do not hold the same belief evaluate the religious teachings of others. Such administration would inevitably lead to unfair limitation of the freedom of religion.[109]

In the end, Ørsted gained the majority for a rule that sets limits to freedom of religion in relation to preaching as well as deeds against good morals and public order (article 81, today article 67). Grundtvig, however, gained the majority for placing the principle of freedom of religion in the Constitution itself. He also won the majority for the general rule on nondiscrimination based on religion (article 84, today article 70).

In constitutional thinking, one notices a general battle line between constitutionalism and a government that proceeds by continuous law-giving. It has been argued that Grundtvig represented a critical attitude towards constitutionalism as a formal political idea, insofar as he always argued that the heart of the people is more important than the written constitution.[110] In the constitutional debate, however, we have seen Grundtvig favor ensuring freedom of religion through constitutional clauses, whereas Ørsted preferred legislation. Regarding the legislation of the national church, the positions were somewhat different, as Grundtvig and the peasants' party did not want to inscribe a constitutional right to an independent church order. It had to be settled by subsequent law, as stated in the promissory paragraph of the Constitution, article 80 (today article 66): "The constitution of the People's Church will be ordered by law."[111] Such constitution has never been effected, however—much in line with Grundtvig's and Ørsted's views on the future of the People's Church in Denmark.

Grundtvig's and Ørsted's legislative positions after 1849

During the 1850s, the Parliament put into law central parts of Grundtvig's program for freedom of religion and freedom within the church. Already in 1850, a law was proposed which aimed at dissolving the parish ties to allow the people themselves to choose where to worship, where to have their children baptized and confirmed, and where to marry and be buried, while also allowing civil marriage.[112] Grundtvig, having supported a constitutional measure to this effect, naturally supported this proposal warmly. The idea was to dissolve any link between religious sacraments and services, on the one hand, and civil consequences, on the other hand. The first legal result was that couples who did not belong to any acknowledged religious community or belonged to different religious communities received the right to be married by a city mayor. The parish tie for members of the People's Church was dissolved by law in 1855. Finally, in 1857, the obligation of members of the People's Church to baptize their infants also was dissolved by law.[113]

In 1868, further legislation allowed for the establishment of free congregations associated with the People's Church. Even so, the question remained about the status of religious communities outside the Evangelical Lutheran Church. Thus, no legislation existed when the Methodist Church applied for and received state recognition in 1866. According to the constitutional thinking at that time,[114] such decisions might have been understood as a matter for parliamentary decision. Now, however, the chair of one of the parliamentary chambers, A.F. Tscherning, proposed that such cases be decided by the government, without any particular legislation—a path followed until recently.[115] Recognition of religious communities was not a matter for Parliament, but a case for the administration within the Church Department (*Kirkeministerium*) of the government.[116]

Grundtvig generally took a "rule-of-law" position as his basic approach to the function of the legislator. He did not argue for equality in all matters, apart from equal access to public functions in the democratic state. Rather, he focused on freedom in all spiritual matters, including not only religious affairs but also education, where he was a strong proponent of establishing free schools as an alternative to the schools established by municipalities.[117] Having himself suffered censorship, he worked for a free press and for a material, not just formal, freedom of expression.

Grundtvig also wanted to limit the influence of civil servants.[118] On the one hand, he wanted to ensure that the government could not lawfully discharge civil servants (or move their service to another part of the country) because of their political views. On the other hand, Grundtvig curiously did not support state-ensured pension rights for civil servants. As for judges, Grundtvig believed that their economic protection should not be higher than that for other citizens.

Grundtvig was among the first to suggest that members of the government should be legally bound by law, without immunity.[119] Public transparency should be extended to the administrators of justice so that no one is above the law.[120] In the same spirit, he strongly spoke for the right of the courts to ensure judicial review, that is, to ensure that a law is not in conflict with the Constitution.[121] Ørsted, on his side, was against any attempt to place the courts at a higher level than the government, and therefore voted against the constitutional rule (article 77, today article 63) that permits judicial review.[122]

Politically, Ørsted can be described as a liberal during absolutism and as a conservative during the early phase of democracy. Like Grundtvig, he focused on the long history and on the people as the spirit of the constitution.[123] In national politics, both before and after 1849, Ørsted was a strong defender of the monarchy and of keeping the kingdom together, including Schleswig-Holstein. The Constitution of 1849 was formulated and adopted during the 1848–50 war against Prussia and Austria regarding the duchies of Schleswig and Holstein.[124] The peace with Germany did not last long. Regarding the duchies, Ørsted tried his best to solve the problems as prime minister from April 1853 to December 1854, but without success. When the government was dismissed, Ørsted, now aged seventy-five, left public life, allowing himself time to publish the two remaining volumes of his memoirs, which appeared in 1855 and 1857.

We have seen how Grundtvig over time changed his views on the role of legislation, not least concerning religion and the confessional nature of the People's Church. He changed his views on democracy, too. In 1848–49 he was still hesitant about democracy, trusting the union between the king's decisions and the people's voice more than a formalized parliamentary system. However, he eagerly took part in the constitutional discussions, as we have seen, and in 1866 he stood up for the people's influence and the liberal orientation of the 1849 Constitution. His basic argument was that "experience teaches us that no government, especially in our day, can succeed and thrive without having the people's voice *behind* it."[125]

Conclusion: two roads toward convergent solutions

A.S. Ørsted and N.F.S. Grundtvig represent two different roads into and out of the Romantic turn in nineteenth-century Danish society. Parts of their disagreements had to do with different experiences of academic study in their youth as well as with different views on the legitimacy of law in wider society. Their agreements and disagreements are probably easier to track retrospectively than they might have been for their contemporaries. Already by 1826, Grundtvig had the impression that they were in deeper agreement than they seemed to be, insofar as both worked for a more liberal understanding of the use of law in the late epoch of absolutism. In *Important Questions to Denmark's Jurists*, Grundtvig appealed to a "later generation to find out, why the theologizing jurist and the historicizing theologian, who one would have thought could have met as friends halfway, instead had confrontations and then walked apart."[126] On the front page of the same publication, Grundtvig—in an opening appeal to Ørsted—included a saying by the German poet-philosopher Schiller: "The laws are still covered in the future. But this will be revealed before we depart from one another."[127]

Ørsted introduced a new legal method, pragmatically oriented, at once based on deep historical knowledge about the laws and their preparation, and extensive information about contemporary issues in life and society. A circumspect argumentation by the practicing jurist stands at the center of his method. Grundtvig, too, came to argue for a more pragmatic understanding of the laws of a nation related to the particular spirit of its people. Deeply inspired by his three visits to England in 1829–31, he learned to see the concept of common law as contrary to an externally imposed state authority. Arising out of these English experiences came his later conviction that the commoners—the people—should become the legislators, and that jurists should interpret and apply the laws accordingly.

Grundtvig has rightly been described as conservative who became a liberal.[128] For him, freedom should be put in the service of the common good, if it is not to be destructive, as happened in the French Revolution.[129] For Grundtvig, it was the responsibility of legislators to put freedom rights into the Constitution. However, it was up to the individual person and to social communities to ensure that freedom was materialized.

Ørsted, by contrast, was a liberal who became a conservative.[130] Already in his 1807/1813 article in *Eunomia* he realized that the revolutionary freedom of his youth needed to be revised in order to accommodate broader moral and religious concerns, and he was convinced that the coherence of the state depends on the religious norms articulated through the state church. Unlike Grundtvig, Ørsted did not change his basic views over time, but since the world had changed in the meantime, he appeared ever more as a conservative.

Despite their different ways through life, Ørsted and Grundtvig—sometimes in tandem, sometimes in conflict—contributed significantly to the legal contours of the People's Church in Denmark and of the religious freedom clauses in the Constitution of 1849—views and practical solutions still operative in the Danish regulation of law and religion.

Notes

1 The Danish Constitution was revised in 1855 and 1866, and again in 1915 (securing election rights for women) and 1953 (extending the Constitution to Greenland and securing equal female succession to the throne).

2 The clauses on the Evangelical Lutheran Church are unchanged. In the religion clauses, "race" is added in article 84 (now article 70) to ensure equal treatment of all citizens, regardless of faith *and race*. A rule that obliged citizens not belonging to any acknowledged religious community to pay the university an amount similar to the church taxes was deleted in 1915. Apart from these minor changes, the constitutional clauses on religion are unchanged since 1849. The religion clauses are now in articles 4, 6, and 66–70.

3 The Danish Constitution of June 5, 1849, article 3 (today article 4): "Den evangelisk-lutherske Kirke er den danske Folkekirke og understøttes som saadan af Staten." *Folkekirke* is sometimes rendered in English as "Folk Church."

4 Draft of June–July 1848 by the minister of culture and church (*Cultusminister*) D.G. Monrad: "§1b: Den lutherske Kirke er som den, hvortil den overvejende Deel af Befolkningen bekjender sig, at ansee som den danske Folkekirke og er berettiget at nyde Understøttelse af Staten," quoted from *Beretning fra Forhandlingerne paa Rigsdagen 1848–1849* (Transcript of the Negotiations in the Constitutional Assembly) (Copenhagen: Bianco Luno, 1849), vol. 2, col. 1529.

5 Article 6: "Kongen skal høre til den evangelisk-lutherske Kirke."

6 Ørsted, Grundtvig, and the government shared this position as expressed by Bishop Mynster, *Beretning*, col. 1599: "Folk og Konge maa være sammensmeltede, at Kongen er ægte dansk; men dertil hører, at han ikke maa bekjende sig til nogen anden Religion end den, til hvilken den langt overveiende Fleerhed af Folket bekjender sig."

7 H.A.M. Snelders, "Oersted's Discovery of Electromagnetism," in *Romanticism and the Sciences*, ed. Andrew Cunningham and Nicholas Jardine (Cambridge: Cambridge University Press 1990), 228–40. In his late work, *Aanden i Naturen* (1849–50), H.C. Ørsted spoke of a divine reason in nature exemplified in the laws of nature: "The laws of nature in the material world are laws of reason, revelations of a rational will. . . . Soul [Spirit] and nature are one, seen from two different sides: thus we cease to wonder at their harmony" (trans. *The Soul in Nature* (London, 1852), 384). We will find similar ideas in A.S. Ørsted regarding human laws and universal reason.

8 There is very little literature on A.S. Ørsted in other than Nordic languages. Frantz Dahl's biographical overview from 1927, written in order to rehabilitate his name, is published in English: Frantz Dahl, *Anders Sandøe Ørsted as a Jurist* (Copenhagen: Levin & Munksgaard, 1932). The central research monograph on A.S. Ørsted is Ditlev Tamm, *Fra 'Lovkyndighed' til 'Retsvidenskab'. Studier over betydningen af fremmed ret for Anders Sandøe Ørsteds forfatterskab* (Copenhagen: Juristforbundets forlag, 1976). Tamm focuses on the impact of foreign law in Ørsted's development of private law, with a general introduction to life and scholarship (13–41). Jørgen Dalberg-Larsen, *Retsvidenskaben som samfundsvidenskab* (Copenhagen: Juristforbundets Forlag, 1977), discusses Ørsted's development of legal research in general (219–50) in the context of English (Bentham) and German (Savigny) legal scholarship. Lars Björne, *Den nordiska rätsvetenskapens historia*, 4 vols. (Lund: Rättshistoriskt Bibliotek, 1995–2002), presents Ørsted in relation to Nordic legal scholarship in the context of natural law and Kant (vol. 1, 229–35), and in relation to Romanticism and Savigny (vol. 2). He concludes that 1815–70 is "the era of Ørsted and Savigny" (vol. 2, 427–34). Sverre Blandhol, *Nordisk Rettspragmatisme. Savigny, Ørsted og Scheweigaard om vitenskap og metode* (Copenhagen: DJØF Publishing, 2005) is the most recent analysis of Ørsted's influence on Nordic legal scholarship in general. Ditlev Tamm, ed., *Anders Sandøe Ørsted 1778–1978. Foredrag i anledning af 200-året for Anders Sandøe Ørsteds fødsel* (Copenhagen: Juristforbundets forlag, 1980), with summaries in German, 197–216, presents Ørsted's thinking in a broader philosophical context, including his contributions to ecclesiastical law. This is discussed in more detail in Per Kristian Aschim, "Herskende religion i den kristelige stat. Den statsteoretiske diskursen om religion og stat med henblikk på norsk religionspolitikk i 1840erne," (unpublished dissertation Menighetsfakultetet, Oslo, 2017), analyzing Ørsted's influence in Norwegian development of ecclesiastical law and politics in the first part of the nineteenth century.

9 Knud Waaben, *Jura på Frue Plads. Juridisk forskning og uddannelse ved Københavns Universitet gennem 500 år* (Copenhagen: GadJura, 2005), 167ff.

10 Tamm, *Fra 'Lovkyndighed' til 'Retsvidenskab'*, 13ff. and 331ff.

11 Leif Grane, "Ørsted og Kirkekampen i 1820erne," in D. Tamm, ed., *Anders Sandøe Ørsted 1778–1978*, 125–27.

12 A.S. Ørsted, *Af mit Livs og min Tids Historie*, vols. 1–4 (Copenhagen: Gyldendalske Boghandel, 1851; 1852; 1855; 1857). See vol. 1, 13–14:

Hvo som har levet på hiin Tid veed, at hele den yngre Verden sværmede for den religiøse og borgerlige Frihed, som ved Hjælp af den franske Revolution skulde udbrede sig trindt omkring i Landene. . . . Det har derfor altid moret mig, naar vor Tids Presse har forestilt sig os Ældre som opvoxede i Trældommens og Mørkets Dage, og deri fundet Undskyldning for, at vi ikke forstode de Frihedens Toner, som, efter hvad man meente, nu først kom os imøde. I Sandhed kunne vi om Meget af det, man nu vil lære os, sige, at vi 'det alt har med vore Barnesko slidt.'

13 Tamm, *Fra 'Lovkyndighed' til 'Retsvidenskab'*, 198ff. Dalberg-Larsen, *Retsvidenskaben som samfundsvidenskab*, 229–42, names this method "realistic," as it combines abstract theoretical approaches with concrete cases and solutions, as well as natural legal thinking and social circumstances.
14 Blandhol, *Nordisk Rettspragmatisme*, 172.
15 Tamm, *Fra 'Lovkyndighed' til 'Retsvidenskab'*, ch. 14.
16 A.S. Ørsted, *Over Sammenhængen mellem Dydelærens og Retslærens Princip* (On the relation between the principle of the doctrine of virtue and the doctrine of law), vols. 1–2 (Copenhagen, 1798).
17 Ørsted, *Af mit Livs og min Tids Historie*, vol. 1, 24: "dette Værk [Kant's Grundlegung der Metaphysik der Sitten] havde saadanne svage Sider, at det maatte gjøre Afbræk i den beundrende Tillid til den vise Olding, hvortil jeg saa gjerne overlod mig." On Ørsted's views on Kant's practical philosophy, see Mogens Blegvad, "Ørsted som moralfilosof 1796–1811," in ed. D. Tamm, *Anders Sandøe Ørsted 1778-1978*, 33–53.
18 Ørsted, *Af mit Livs and min Tids Historie*, vol. 1, 8: "Men det varede ikke mange Aar førend jeg frigjorde mig for, hvad der i min Forkjærlighed for disse Tydsklands philosophiske Choryphæer var blindt og slavisk, og man vil ikke fra 1801 finde noget i mine Skrifter, som smager deraf." See also Tamm, *Fra 'Lovkyndighed' til 'Retsvidenskab'*, 367ff.
19 The 1807 lecture is reprinted in A.S. Ørsted, *Eunomia,* vol. 1 (Copenhagen: Andreas Seidelin, 1815), 39–93, with the title, "Om Forholdet mellem Religion og Stat" [On the relation between religion and state].
20 Elegantly formulated in Ørsted, *Eunomia*, vol. 1, 47: "Moraliteten er *det første*, men Religionen *det største*." On the indispensability of religion for both morality and state governance, see 81.
21 Ørsted, *Eunomia*, vol. 1, 55: "Fornuftkraftens Udvikling i sin hele Fylde og Herlighed er dens [Statens] Øiemed."
22 Ørsted, *Eunomia*, vol. 1, 66.
23 Ørsted, *Eunomia*, vol. 1, 81. See also Björne, *Den nordiska rätsvetenskapens historia*, vol. 2, 427f.
24 See also the constitutional clauses on king and religion in the Norwegian Eidsvoll-constitution of 1814: Aschim, "Herskende religion i den kristelige stat," 195ff.
25 Blandhol, *Nordisk Rettspragmatisme*, 177–82, highlights the pragmatic dimension of Ørsted's acknowledgement of state interest in religion, based on Ørsted's argument that the state is responsible for organizing a good society; cf. Ørsted, *Af mit Livs og min Tids Historie*, vol. 1, 7ff.
26 Tamm, *Fra 'Lovkyndighed' til 'Retsvidenskab'*, 382–86, discusses how Ørsted interpreted and used the influence of the German historical school. According to Tamm, Ørsted argued that Savigny could sometimes overemphasize the historical understanding of the laws; Ørsted wanted to combine this understanding with the concrete situation.
27 A.S. Ørsted, "Indlednings Tale til Forelæsninger over Kirkeretten i det ved kongelig Resolution af 13. Januar 1809 stiftede Pastoral Seminarium," *Juridisk Archiv* 27–28 (1811), 1–17. See Grane, "Ørsted og kirkekampen i 1820'erne."
28 Ørsted himself did not write a text book on ecclesiastical law. Professor J.L.A. Kolderup-Rosenvinge wrote the first introduction to ecclesiastical law in Danish,

Grundrids af den danske Kirkeret. Til Brug ved Forelæsninger (Copenhagen: Gyldendalske Boghandlings Forlag, 1838). Kolderup-Rosenvinge was a disciple of Ørsted; see Björne, *Den nordiska rätsvetenskapens historia*, vol. 2, 31: "Till Ørsteds närmaste elever bland professorerna kan man råakna Janus Lauritz Andreas Kolderup-Rosenvinge (1792–1850)." In his introduction to *Grundrids af den danske Kirkeret*, Kolderup-Rosenvinge builds on Ørsted's legal thinking by including the theological foundational sources (the Bible, the church confessions, etc.) among the legal sources alongside legislation, etc., and by recommending a good knowledge of church history as the precondition for a deeper understanding of ecclesiastical law.

29 In his memoirs, Ørsted mentions that his legal philosophical program was generally acknowledged by legal authorities of the time; see Ørsted, *Af mit Livs og min Tids Historie*, vol. 1, 137–41. He also mentions that even Grundtvig commented positively on his introduction to the teaching of ecclesiastical law, referring to Grundtvig's World Chronicle of 1812, at 141.

30 A series of five volumes of N.F.S. Grundtvig's works has been published in recent years: (1) *The School for Life: N.F.S. Grundtvig on Education for the People*, eds. Edward Broadbridge (trans.), Clay Warren, and Uffe Jonas (Aarhus: Aarhus University Press, 2011); (2) *Living Wellsprings: The Hymns, Songs, and Poems of N.F.S. Grundtvig*, trans. and ed. Edward Broadbridge (Aarhus: Aarhus University Press, 2015); (3) *Human Comes First: The Christian Theology of N.F.S. Grundtvig*, trans. and ed. Edward Broadbridge (Aarhus: Aarhus University Press, 2018); (4) *The Common Good: N.F.S. Grundtvig as Politician and Contemporary Historian*, eds. Edward Broadbridge (trans.) and Ove Korsgaard (Aarhus: Aarhus University Press, 2019); and (5) *The Advance of Learning: N.F.S. Grundtvig's Philosophical Writings*, ed. and trans. Edward Broadbridge (Aarhus: Aarhus University Press, forthcoming 2020). See also the substantial volume N.F.S. Grundtvig, *Schriften in Auswahl*, eds. Knud Eyvind Bugge, Flemming Lundgreen-Nielsen, and Theodor Jørgensen (Göttingen: Vandenhoeck & Ruprecht, 2010). Autobiographical sketches in *N.F.S. Grundtvig—A Life Recalled: An Anthology of Biographical Source-Texts*, trans. and ed. S.A.J. Bradley (Aarhus: Aarhus University Press, 2008).

31 On Grundtvig's intellectual context and theological development, see A.M. Allchin, *Grundtvig: An Introduction to his Life and Work* (Aarhus: Aarhus University Press, 2015) and Niels Henrik Gregersen, "Church and Culture in Living Interaction—Grundtvig the Theologian," in N.F.S. Grundtvig, *Human Comes First: The Christian Theology of N.F.S. Grundtvig*, 22–54. On the development of Grundtvig's political thinking and career, see Ove Korsgaard, *N.F.S. Grundtvig—As a Political Thinker* (Copenhagen: DJØF Publishing, 2014). A good primer to Grundtvig's multifaceted biography with excerpts is Anders Holm, *The Essential N.F.S. Grundtvig* (Aarhus: Filo Forlag, 2019). Publications on Grundtvig's reception history include A.M. Allchin et al., eds., *Grundtvig in International Perspective: Studies in the Creativity of Interaction* (Aarhus: Aarhus University Press, 2000) and John A. Hall, Ove Korsgaard, and Ove K. Pedersen, eds., *Building the Nation: N.F.S. Grundtvig and Danish National Identity* (Copenhagen: DJØF Publishing, 2015).

32 See the poem "Henrik Steffens" (1845), translated in *Living Wellsprings*, 300–02.

33 The brief poem "High Odin, White Christ!" is translated in Grundtvig, *Living Wellsprings*, 225.

34 Grundtvig, *A Life Recalled*, 102ff. We have not found evidence suggesting that Ørsted played an active role in the 1810 case against Grundtvig.

35 The text of the dimissory sermon, with letters and poems to his parents, is printed in N.F.S. Grundtvig, *Værker i Udvalg*, eds. Georg Christensen and Hal Koch (Copenhagen: Gyldendal, 1944), vol. 1, 250–70, at 250.

36 "Dejlig er den Himmel blaa" is translated in *Living Wellsprings*, 82–83.

37 See Anders Pontoppidan Thyssen, "Grundtvig's Ideas on the Church and the People up to 1824," in eds. Christian Thodberg and Anders Pontoppidan Thyssen, *N.F.S. Grundtvig, Tradition and Renewal* (Copenhagen: The Danish Institute, 1983), 87–120, at 114ff.
38 Grundtvig, "On Godly Assemblies" (1825), translated in *Human Comes First*, 80–89.
39 Henrik Nikolai Clausen, *Catholicismens og Protestantismens Kirkeforfatning, Lære og Ritus* (Copenhagen: Andreas Seidelin, 1825).
40 Grundtvig, *The Church's Retort to Professor of Theology Dr. H.N. Clausen* (1825), translated in *Human Comes First*, 57–79 (73). Grundtvig shows no regret in "On the Clausen Libel Case" (1831), translated in *Human Comes First*, 105–13.
41 Grundtvig, *Nordic Mythology* (1832), translated in *The School for Life*, 42–75, at 66.
42 See Grundtvig's chapter on "England as a Model" (1838) in *Within Living Memory*, translated in *The Common Good*, 120–24.
43 See Grundtvig, "On Religious Persecution" (1842), translated in *Human Comes First*, 164–76.
44 Grundtvig, "Religious Freedom and Bodily Freedom" (1845), translated in *The Common Good*, 211–16, at 211.
45 See the excerpts on the freedom of people and slaves 1830–48, translated in *The Common Good*, 173–223.
46 See the texts translated in *The School for Life*, 173–351.
47 Tine Damsholt, "'Hand of King and Voice of People': Grundtvig on Democracy and the Responsibility of the Self," in ed. J. Hall et al., *Building the Nation: N.F.S. Grundtvig and Danish National Identity*, 151–67.
48 Grundtvig: "Against the Proposed Constitutional Revision" (1866), translated in *The Common Good*, 339–43.
49 A.S. Ørsted's letter to H.C. Ørsted of February 6, 1813, cited in Erland Jessen, "Striden mellem Grundtvig og H.C. Ørsted 1814–15," *Grundtvig Studier* (1971) 31–72, at 40.
50 H.C. Ørsted, *Imod den store Anklager* (Copenhagen, 1814); the title of Grundtvig's rejoinder can be translated as, *Against the Little Accuser, That Is, Prof. H.C. Ørsted, with Evidence that Schelling's Philosophy Is Unchristian, Ungodly, and Mendacious by N.F.S. Grundtvig, Pastor* (Copenhagen, 1815).
51 H.C. Ørsted, *Imod den store Anklager*, 9, 111, and 16.
52 Grundtvig, "Kort Begreb af Verdens Krønike i Sammenhæng," *Værker i Udvalg*, vol. 1, 417.
53 H.C. Ørsted, *Imod den store Anklager* (Copenhagen 1814), 37–38.
54 Friedrich Schleiermacher, *Der christliche Glaube nach den Grundsätzen der evangelischen Kirche im Zusammenhange dargestellt* [1821–22^1, 1830-31^2] (Berlin: De Gruyter, 1960), §24.
55 See note 40.
56 P.D. Christian Paulsen, *Betragtninger over den Danske Kirkes symboliske Bøger fra den kirkeretlige Synspunkt* (Considerations on the symbolic books of the Danish Church from the perspective of ecclesiastical law) (Copenhagen, 1826).
57 A.S. Ørsted, "Behøver den danske Kirkeforfating en omgribende Forandring?," *Juridisk Tidsskrift* 12/1–2, 213–88 and 250–304, cited from the reprint in Frantz Dahl, *Frederik VI og Anders Sandøe Ørsted i 1826. En aktmæssig Fremstilling* (Copenhagen: Gyldendal, 1929), 1–115.
58 Ibid., 5.
59 Ibid., 6–7: "hæmmet ved et forbittret Stridsraab."
60 Ibid., 23–35, at 25.
61 The symbolic books for Schleiermacher were those works that constituted the confessional basis of Protestantism, both Calvinist and Lutheran. In the Evangelical

Lutheran Church in denamrk, these included the ancient creeds, the Augsburg Confession, and Luther's Small Catechism only. See Friedrich Schleiermacher, *Über den eigenthümlichen Werth und das bindende Ansehen symbolischer Bücher* [On the proper value and binding authority of symbolic books] (Erfurt, 1819).

62 Ørsted, "Behøver den danske Kirkeforfatning en omgribende Forandring?," 33.

63 Ibid., 67–98, at 90 and 88: "saa synes Hr. Professor Clausen altfor let at have beroliget sig mod den Frygt, at en saadan Forfatning kunde fremkalde Hyklerie."

64 Ibid., 51 "Præster skal holde sig fra de dogmatiske Forestillinger, der enten er ufrugtbare for den levende kristelige Tro og det gudelige Sind eller endog forvirre Gemytterne."

65 Ibid., 51–52: "Thi langt fra at Kristendommen skulde staa i et fjendtligt Forhold til den Indsigt, der er erhvervet ved Fornuftens Anstrengelse, fører denne netop til den Erkendelse, at alle Visdommens og den højere Kundskabs Skatte indeholdes i Evangeliet."

66 Letter to Julius Kaas, August 11, 1826:

> Skal Læren om Djævelens indvirkninger paa Mennesket og om evige Helvedsstraffe samt det athanasianske Symbols subtile Bestemmelser om Treenighedslæren være lige saa hellige som Læren om den evige Kærligheds Aabenbaring i Kristus, Guds Søn og Verdens Frelser, saa gives der ikke 10 rettroende Præster i hele Landet.

quoted in Dahl, *Frederik VI og Anders Sandøe Ørsted i 1826*, 122. See further Hans Jensen, "Fr. Juul Kaas og A.S. Ørsted i 1826," *Historisk tidsskrift* (1931): 51–77.

67 N.F.S. Grundtvig, *Vigtige Spørgsmaal til Danmarks Lovkyndige fra Nik. Fred. Sev. Grundtvig, Præst* (Copenhagen: Madvigske Boghandel, 1826), 6: "Hr. Etatsraaden og jeg [er] i Grunden juridisk enige, skjøndt vore Tilbøieligheder, under Anvendelsen, drage os til modsatte Sider."

68 Ibid., 7.

69 Ibid., 19.

70 Ibid., 32.

71 Ibid., 33.

72 Ibid., 31 and 50.

73 Ibid., 36.

74 Dahl, *Frederik VI og Anders Sandøe Ørsted i 1826*, xxxiv.

75 Ørsted, in Dahl, *Frederik VI og Anders Sandøe Ørsted i 1826*, 100.

76 Ibid., 98–107.

77 Grundtvig, "A Time of Transition in Denmark" (1849), translated in *The Common Good*, 289–304, at 297.

78 Ole Vind, "'The Gordian Knot': Grundtvig and British Liberalism," in ed. J. Hall et al., *Building the Nation*, 254–66.

79 Grundtvig, "An Impartial View of the Danish State Church" (1834), translated in *Human Comes First*, 114–155.

80 Jens Rasmussen, *Religionstolerance og religionsfrihed. Forudsætninger og Grundloven i 1849* (Religious tolerance and freedom of religion: Presuppositions for the Constitution of 1849) (Odense: Syddansk Universitetsforlag, 2009), 155–59.

81 Hanne Sanders, "Religious Revivalism in Sweden and Denmark," in ed. J. Hall et al., *Building the Nation*, 95–109.

82 Ørsted, *Af mit Livs og min Tids Historie*, vol. 3, 296–98. In spite of the Lutheran absolutism (1660–1849), Jews were from 1683 acknowledged to settle in the kingdom as "foreign believers." Their situation as "foreigners" was clarified with the introduction of Danish citizenship in 1776. Riots against the Jewish population after the state bankruptcy in 1813 and the loss of Norway at the peace in Kiel in 1814 led the state to offer Jews citizenship. Again in 1819, the king issued a public statement on "my Jewish citizens" to settle peace. Ørsted was a leading force in the strategy of making Jews citizens rather than sending them out of the country.

83 Ørsted, in Dahl, *Frederik VI og Anders Sandøe Ørsted i 1826*, 102–03.
84 On this regulation, see Kolderup-Rosenvinge, *Grundrids af den danske Kirkeret*, 102–08.
85 On the Baptists, see Rasmussen, *Religionstolerance og religionsfrihed*, 169–94.
86 Ibid., 180ff.
87 Ørsted, *Af mit Livs og min Tids Historie*, vol. 3, 177.
88 Grundtvig, "On Religious Persecution" (1842), in *Human Comes First*, 164–76, at 166.
89 See Jes Fabricius Møller, "Katolikkernes stilling og antikatolicisme i Danmark 1800–1849" (The position of Catholics and anti-Catholic views in Denmark 1800–1849), *Kirkehistoriske Samlinger* (2012): 113–36; Rasmussen, *Religionstolerance og religionsfrihed*, 110–34.
90 Rasmussen, Ibid., 121ff.
91 Ibid., 127–28.
92 The debates at the assembly are transcribed in *Beretning fra Forhandlingerne paa Rigsdagen 1849*. The negotiations concerning the clauses on religion and church took up more than a tenth of the negotiations. H.N. Clausen was a member of the government and J.N. Madvig the responsible minister in the government. C.C. Hall represented the committee that had prepared the discussion. Together with these three officials, Grundtvig and Ørsted were among those who participated most eagerly in the debate. See H.J.H. Glædemark, *Kirkeforfatningsspørgsmaalet i Danmark* (Copenhagen: Ejnar Munksgaard, 1948), 242.
93 See *Beretning*, cols. 1597–1605.
94 C.C. Hall, *Beretning*, col. 2165:

> Ihvorvel det nemlig vistnok ogsaa i politisk Henseende maa betragtes som en Lykke for en Stat, naar der er Enhed i Borgernes religiøse Bekiendelse, saa er det dog klart, at Eenheden kun da i Sandhed er en Lykke, naar den er grundet paa Frihed, og at Staten derfor ikke giør Ret i—enten i sin egen eller i en privilegeret Kirkes Interesse—at ville sikre Eenheden ved Lovens Tvang, hvorved den ikke kan undgaae at besvære Manges Samvittighed og at krænke en Ret, som for Enhver maa regnes til de helligste blandt Alle.

95 Grundtvig, *Beretning*, col. 2513: "Jeg skulde derfor ogsaa have ønsket, at den Paragraph i Grundloven som fastsætter en saadan Gudsdyrkelsesfrihed, at den var ved denne Leilighed kommen til at staae i Spidsen."
96 *Beretning*, col 36.
97 *Beretning*, cols. 2513, 2517, and 3037.
98 *Beretning*, col. 2514.
99 A.S. Ørsted, *Beretning*, col. 2526.
100 Grundtvig, *Beretning*, col. 3101."Der burde efter mine Tanker slet ikke være nogen Grundlovsbestemmelse om saadanne foranderlige og omtvistelige Ting som Kirkegods, Klostergods og alt andet beneficeret Gods."
101 A.F. Tscherning, *Beretning*, col. 3055: "[Vi ønsker ikke] en dobbelt Rigsforsamling her i landet"; I.A. Hansen, *Beretning fra Forhandlingerne*, col. 3111: "Forslaget . . . maa være udgaaet fra et katholsk Begreb om Kirken."
102 H.N. Clausen, *Beretning*, col. 2526: "en Folkerepræsentation, som kunde siges at være Folkets politiske Repræsentation, [kan] derfor ikke siges at være dets kirkelige Repræsentation. Det er forskellige Kundskaber og Indsigter, en forskjellig Aandsretning og Interesse." In his argumentation, Clausen incidentally uses a distinction between "inner and external affairs of the church" (col. 2532), which still plays a central role in discussions of the relations between state and church in Denmark.
103 A.S. Ørsted, *Beretning*, col. 3072: "det [kan] virkelig ikke tilstedes i en velordnet Stat, at der kan føres de allerfordærveligste Lærdomme . . . , som aabenbart tillode Forræderi, Meened, at krænke Eiendomsretten eller hvilken som helst Udaad."

104 A.S. Ørsted, *Beretning*, col. 3073: "Alt hvad der er nødvendigt for at forberede større Religionsfrihed, som vistnok bør indføres, det er, at der optages en saadan Bestemmelse som den, at de fra Folkekirken afvigende Religioners Forhold skulle ordnes ved Lov." This sentence is almost verbatim what is today stated in article 69 of the Constitution, referring back to the rules on freedom of religion in article 67.

105 Now the Danish Constitution article 70: "No person shall by reason of his creed or descent be deprived of access to the full enjoyment of civic and political rights, nor shall he escape compliance with any common civic duty for such reasons."

106 A.S. Ørsted, *Beretning*, col. 2546: "man [kan] dog ikke vilde tillade en offentlig Øvelse af nogen Troesbekjendelse, uden den iforveien var Staten bekjendt og undergiven Statens Tilsyn."

107 A.S. Ørsted, *Beretning*, col. 5547: "forargeligt, om en Jøde skulde være Dommer"; "Visse Stillinger . . . kunde falde i hænderne paa Katholiker eller Jøder."

108 Grundtvig, *Beretning*, col 5548, cf. 5549: "Den danske Mand maa være ligeberettiget til Alt."

109 Grundtvig, *Beretning*, col 2170: "[Når] de, som skulle bedømme Lærdommen, vare af en anden Troesbekiendelse, ville de ved tusinde Leiligheder kunne finde Noget, som muligen kunde blive skadeligt for Sædeligheden og den offentlige Orden, hvilket altsaa maatte skille hine Troesbekiendere igjen ved deres frie Gudsdyrkelse."

110 Korsgaard, *N.F.S. Grundtvig—As a Political Thinker*, 68–69.

111 Today article 66: "Folkekirkens forfatning ordnes ved lov."

112 Grundtvig, "The People, the People's Church, and Popular Belief in Denmark" (1851), translated in *Human Comes first*, 197–230. See also Poul Andersen, *Grundtvig som Rigsdagsmand* (Copenhagen: Gyldendal, 1940), 32ff. Poul Andersen was a professor of public administrative law at the University of Copenhagen.

113 Andersen, *Grundtvig som Rigsdagsmand*, 32.

114 See Henning Koch and Kristian Hvidt, *Danmarks riges Grundlove 1849, 1866, 1915, 1953* (Copenhagen: Chr. Ejlers' Forlag, 1999), article 68, second sentence.

115 A law on religious communities was not introduced until December 2017.

116 Lisbet Christoffersen, "Ved Lov," *Ugeskrift for Retsvæsen* (1998): 505–10.

117 Andersen, *Grundtvig som Rigsdagsmand*, 34. It should be noted, however, that Grundtvig did not support the general obligation for municipalities to organize schools for all children; according to him, education should be in the hands of the parents.

118 Andersen, *Grundtvig som Rigsdagsmand*, 43–47.

119 Ibid., 43.

120 Ibid., 49–51.

121 Ibid., 51–52.

122 Povl Bagge, "Ørsted som politiker," in ed. Ditlev Tamm, *Anders Sandøe Ørsted 1778-1978*, 139–48, at 144.

123 Ibid., 141 and 147.

124 Initially, Grundtvig was even against discussing a new constitution during wartime; see Andersen, *Grundtvig som Rigsdagsmand*, 18.

125 Grundtvig, "For the General Franchise," speech in the upper house, July 16, 1866, translated in *The Common Good*, 344–45, at 345; italics in original.

126 Grundtvig, *Vigtige Spørgsmål til Danmarks Lovkyndige*, 7.

127 Schiller, "Noch Liegen die Lofve Dunkel verhüllt in der Zukunft Schovfe! Doch es wird sich noch eh wir uns trennen entscheiden."

128 Ove Korsgaard, "N.F.S. Grundtvig and His Time," in ed. N.F.S. Grundtvig, *The Common Good*, 21–40, at 31.

129 Grundtvig, "The Danish and the French Revolutions" (1838), translated in *The Common Good*, 63–71.

130 Bagge, "Ørsted som politiker," 147.

Bibliography

Allchin, A.M. *Grundtvig: An Introduction to his Life and Work*. Aarhus: Aarhus University Press, 2015.

Allchin, A.M., S.A.J. Bradley, N.A. Hjelm, and J.H. Schiørring, eds. *Grundtvig in International Perspective: Studies in the Creativity of Interaction*. Aarhus: Aarhus University Press, 2000.

Andersen, Poul. *Grundtvig som Rigsdagsmand*. Gyldendal: Copenhagen, 1940.

Aschim, Per Kristian. "Herskende religion i den kristelige stat. Den statsteoretiske diskursen om religion og stat med henblikk på norsk religionspolitikk i 1840erne." Oslo: Unpublished dissertation, Menighedsfakultetet, 2017.

Bagge, Povl. "Ørsted som politiker." In Ditlev Tamm, ed., *Anders Sandøe Ørsted 1778–1978. Foredrag i anledning af 200-året for Anders Sandøe Ørsteds fødsel*, 139–48. Copenhagen: Juristforbundets Forlag, 1980.

Beretning fra Forhandlingerne paa Rigsdagen 1848–49 (Transcript of the Negotiations in the Constitutional Assembly), Vols. 1–2. Copenhagen: Bianco Luno, 1849.

Björne, Lars. *Den nordiska rätsvetenskapens historia*. 4 vols. Lund: Rättshistoriskt Bibliotek, 1995–2000.

Blandhol, Sverre. *Nordisk Rettspragmatisme. Savingy, Ørsted, og Scheweigaard om vitenskap og metode*. Copenhagen: DJØF, 2005.

Blegvad, Mogens. "Ørsted som moralfilosof 1796–1811." In Ditlev Tamm, ed., *Anders Sandøe Ørsted 1778–1978. Foredrag i anledning af 200-året for Anders Sandøe Ørsteds-fødsel*, 33–53. Copenhagen: Juristforbundets Forlag, 1980.

Christoffersen, Lisbet. "Ved Lov." *Ugeskrift for Retsvæsen* (1998), vol. 132: 505–10.

Clausen, Henrik Nikolai. *Catholicismens og Protestantismens Kirkeforfatning, Lære og Ritus*. Copenhagen: Andreas Seidelin, 1825.

Dahl, Frantz. *Anders Sandøe Ørsted as a Jurist*. Copenhagen: Levin & Munksgaard, 1943.

Dahl, Frantz. *Frederik VI og Anders Sandøe Ørsted i 1826. En aktmæssig Fremstilling*. Copenhagen: Gyldendal, 1929.

Dalberg-Larsen, Jørgen. *Retsvidenskaben som samfundsvidenskab*. Copenhagen: Juristforbundets Forlag, 1977.

Damsholt, Tine. "'Hand of King and Voice of People': Grundtvig on Democracy and the Responsibility of the Self." In Hall et al. (eds.), *Building the Nation*, 151–67.

Glædemark, H.J.H. *Kirkeforfatningsspørgsmaalet i Danmark*. Copenhagen: Ejnar Munksgaard, 1948.

Grane, Leif. "Ørsted og Kirkekampen i 1820erne." In D. Tamm (ed.), *Anders Sandøe Ørsted 1778–1978. Foredrag i anledning af 200-året for Anders Sandøe Ørsteds fødsel*, 122–47 Copenhagen: Juristforbundets Forlag, 1980.

Gregersen, Niels Henrik. "Church and Culture in Living Interaction—Grundtvig the Theologian." In N.F.S. Grundtvig, *Human Comes First*, 22–54.

Grundtvig, N.F.S. *The Advance of Learning: N.F.S. Grundtvig's Philosophical Writings*. Translated by Edward Broadbridge. Aarhus: Aarhus University Press, 2020 (forthcoming).

Grundtvig, N.F.S. *The Common Good: N.F.S. Grundtvig as Politician and Contemporary Historian*. Edited by Edward Broadbridge and Ove Korsgaard. Translated by Edward Broadbridge. Aarhus: Aarhus University Press, 2019.

Grundtvig, N.F.S. *Human Comes First: The Christian Theology of N.F.S. Grundtvig*. Translated and edited by Edward Broadbridge. Aarhus: Aarhus University Press, 2018.

Grundtvig, N.F.S. *Imod den lille Anklager, det er Prof H.C. Ørsted, med Bevis for at Schellings Philosophie er uchristelig, ugudelig og løgnagtig* (Against the little accuser, that is, Prof. H.C. Ørsted, with evidence that Schelling's philosophy is unchristian, ungodly, and mendacious). Copenhagen: Andreas Seidelin, 1815.

Grundtvig, N.F.S. *Living Wellsprings: The Hymns, Songs, and Poems of N.F.S. Grundtvig.* Translated and edited by Edward Broadbridge. Aarhus: Aarhus University Press, 2015.

Grundtvig, N.F.S. *N.F.S. Grundtvig—A Life Recalled: An Anthology of Biographical Source-Texts.* Translated and edited by S.A.J. Bradley. Aarhus: Aarhus University Press, 2008.

Grundtvig, N.F.S. *The School for Life: N.F.S. Grundtvig on Education for the People.* Edited by Edward Broadbridge, Clay Warren, and Uffe Jonas. Translated by Edward Broadbridge. Aarhus: Aarhus University Press, 2011.

Grundtvig, N.F.S. *Schriften in Auswahl.* Edited by Knud Eyvind Bugge, Flemming Lundgreen-Nielsen, and Theodor Jørgensen. Göttingen: Vandenhoeck & Ruprecht, 2010.

Grundtvig, N.F.S. *Værker i Udvalg.* Vol. 1. Edited by Georg Christensen and Hal Koch. Copenhagen: Gyldendal, 1940.

Grundtvig, N.F.S. *Vigtige Spørgsmaal til Danmarks Lovkyndige fra Nik. Fred. Sev. Grundtvig, Præst.* Copenhagen: Madvigske Boghandel, 1826.

Hall, John A., Ove Korsgaard, and Ove K. Pedersen, eds. *Building the Nation: N.F.S. Grundtvig and Danish National Identity.* Copenhagen: DJØF Publishing, 2015.

Holm, Anders. *The Essential N.F.S. Grundtvig.* Aarhus: Filo Forlag, 2019.

Jensen, Hans. "Fr. Juul Kaas og A.S. Ørsted i 1826." *Historisk tidsskrift* (1931): 51–77.

Jessen, Erland. "Striden mellem Grundtvig og H.C. Ørsted 1814-15." *Grundtvig Studier* (1971): 31–72.

Koch, Henning, and Kristian Hvidt. *Danmarks riges Grundlove 1849, 1866, 1915, 1953.* Copenhagen: Chr. Ejlers' Forlag, 1999.

Kolderup-Rosenvinge, J.L.A. *Grundrids af den danske Kirkeret. Til Brug ved Forelæsninger.* Copenhagen: Gyldendalske Boghandlings Forlag, 1838.

Korsgaard, Ove. "N.F.S. Grundtvig and his Time." In Grundtvig, *The Common Good*, 21–40.

Korsgaard, Ove. *N.F.S. Grundtvig—As a Political Thinker.* Copenhagen: DJØF Publishing, 2014.

Møller, Jes Fabricius. "Katolikkernes stilling og antikatolicisme i Danmark 1800–1849." *Kirkehistoriske Samlinger* (2012), 113–36. Syddansk Universitetsforlag, 2012.

Ørsted, A.S. *Af mit Livs og min Tids Historie.* 4 vols. Copenhagen: Gyldendalske Boghandel, 1851; 1852; 1855; 1857.

Ørsted, A.S. "Behøver den danske Kirkeforfating en omgribende Forandring?" In F. Dahl (ed.), *Frederik VI og Anders Sandøe Ørsted i 1826*, 1–115.

Ørsted, A.S. *Eunomia. Første Deel.* Copenhagen: Andreas Seidelin, 1815.

Ørsted, A.S. "Indlednings Tale til Forelæsninger over Kirkeretten i det ved kongelig Resolution af 13. Januar 1809 stiftede Pastoral Seminarium." *Juridisk Archiv* 27–28 (1811): 1–17.

Ørsted, A.S. *Over Sammenhængen mellem Dydelærens og Retslærens Princip.* 2 vols. Copenhagen, 1798.

Ørsted, H.C. *Imod den store Anklager.* Copenhagen, 1814.

Ørsted, H.C. *The Soul in Nature.* London, 1852.

Paulsen, P.D. Christian. *Betragtninger over den Danske Kirkes symboliske Bøger fra den kirkeretlige Synspunkt.* Copenhagen, 1826.

Pontoppidan Thyssen, Anders. "Grundtvig's Ideas on the Church and the People up to 1824." In Christian Thodberg and Anders Pontoppidan Thyssen (eds.), *N.F.S. Grundtvig, Tradition and Renewal*, 87–120. Copenhagen: The Danish Institute, 1983.

Rasmussen, Jens. *Religionstolerance og religionsfrihed. Forudsætninger og Grundloven i 1849.* Odense: Syddansk Universitetsforlag, 2009.

Sanders, Hanne. "Religious Revivalism in Sweden and Denmark." In Hall et al. (eds.), *Building the Nation*, 95–109.

Schleiermacher, Friedrich. *Der christliche Glaube nach den Grundsätzen der evangelischen Kirche im Zusammenhange dargestellt.* Berlin: De Gruyter, 1960.

Schleiermacher, Friedrich. *Über den eigenthümlichen Werth und das bindende Ansehen symbolischer Bücher.* Erfurt, 1819.

Snelders, H.A.M. "Oersted's Discovery of Electromagnetism." In Andrew Cunning and Nicholas Jardine (eds.), *Romanticism and the Sciences.* Cambridge: Cambridge University Press, 1990, 228–240.

Steffens, Henrich. *Indledning til philosophiske Forelæsninger.* Copenhagen: Andreas Seidelin, 1803.

Tamm, Ditlev, ed. *Anders Sandøe Ørsted 1778–1978. Foredrag i anledning af 200-året for Anders Sandøe Ørsteds fødsel.* Copenhagen: Juristforbundets Forlag, 1980.

Tamm, Ditlev. *Fra 'Lovkyndighed' til 'Retsvidenskab'. Studier over betydningen af fremmed ret for Anders Sandøe Ørsteds forfatterskab.* Copenhagen: Juristforbundets Forlag, 1976.

Vind, Ole. "'The Gordian Knot': Grundtvig and British Liberalism." In Hall et al., *Building the Nation*, 254–66.

Waaben, Knud. *Jura på Frue Plads. Juridisk forskning og uddannelse ved Københavns Universitet gennem 500 år.* Copenhagen: Forlaget Thomson, GadJura, 2005.

14 Christian legal historian and intermediary of Henric Schartau's religious heritage

Carl Johan Schlyter (1795–1888)

Kjell Å Modéer

Introduction

Romanticism played a substantial role in European academic confessional discourses in the nineteenth century—among jurists and theologians. At the newly founded reform university in Berlin (1810), the jurist Friedrich Carl von Savigny and his students established the historical school of law in the early 1810s, and they interacted closely with the most famous theologian of their time, Friedrich D.E. Schleiermacher.[1] as well as among cultural circles i In Germany the revival movement engaged the participants of the historical school. The jurist Moritz August von Bethmann-Hollweg has been pointed out as an example of this "historical Christian" link between jurists and theologians.[2] At the same time, at Greifswald University, in the Swedish province of Pomerania in Germany, jurists such as Karl Schildener and theologians such as Ludwig Gotthard Kosegarten represented this form of Romanticism in theology as well as in law.[3]

Swedish religious life also reflected similar discourses, including between more orthodox and conservative members of the academy, on one hand, and more liberal and reform-oriented thinkers on the other.[4] Carl Johan Schlyter, the first professor of legal history in the Lund law faculty and the editor of the classical edition of Swedish medieval laws,[5] was the main representative of the historical school of law in Sweden. On the basis of his Christian faith, he contributed not only to legal science but also to the theological discourses of his time.[6]

Schlyter was born in Karlskrona, a marine base in southern Sweden, in 1795. Already by the end of his student time at Lund, in the 1810s, he was observed as a religious person. He was inspired by the German nature historian Gotthilf Heinrich von Schubert, and in 1820 he published a translation of Schubert's provocative work *Altes und neues aus dem Gebiete der inneren Seelenkunde.*

The sister of Schlyter's mother was married to the bishop of the Lund Diocese, Vilhelm Faxe, and the bishop's house became the young Schlyter's home during his time as a student at Lund University. Schlyter received his first education in foreign languages from the professor of Greek, Esaias Tegnér, and in algebra from Carl Adolph Agardh—both of them belonging to the dominant intellectual elite at Lund University (identified as the contemporary "hostel circuit,"

Härbärgeskretsen). In 1811 Schlyter took his preliminary exam (*kameralexamen*)) and then began his studies in law. Within two years he had taken two law degrees—the *examen juridicum* (1812) and the chancellery exam (*kansliexamen*, 1813). In 1814, he made a study trip to Greifswald, Berlin, and Rostock and received a master's degree in mathematics. During this *peregrinatio academica*, he was influenced by the idealism among German philosophers, mainly by Friedrich Schelling. Together with his colleague at the law faculty, Ebbe Samuel Bring,[7] Schlyter was especially influenced by Schelling's work on the freedom of the human being.[8] Schlyter and Bring belonged to those at Lund who, with "persistent assertiveness," upheld Schelling's "absolute." Tegnér ironically and with arrogance called Lund, the university city, an "academic farmers' village" and the junior Schlyter the "village sheriff of the phosphorists" (*fosforisternas byfogde*).[9] "The beldams side with the boy, but I will scourge him in front of their eyes."[10]

Schlyter and the historical school of law at Lund

Schlyter's teacher in law and mentor was Johan Holmbergson, a son of a vicar in Härnösand, a diocese in northern Sweden. After graduating in law from Uppsala University in 1790, Holmbergson worked there as a teacher in law and served in Stockholm as secretary of the standing committee on the law in 1809–10, when the new instrument of government was adopted in 1809. In 1811 he was appointed professor of law at Lund, where he arrived as the only law professor on the faculty; when he passed away in 1842, however, the faculty had expanded to four law professors. Holmbergson is referred to as the founder of the modern Lund law faculty. After his death, his move from Uppsala to Lund in 1811 was described metaphorically as "the candle of legal science being extinguished in Uppsala and ignited in Lund." [11] He was a very popular teacher and served during the formative period of the historical school in Sweden. As an admired and diligent law professor, Holmbergson attracted many admiring and talented students. Among those to whom he became a mentor, Schlyter would become the most important representative of this legal historical movement in Sweden.

In 1816 Schlyter defended a dissertation on the principles for the revision of the penal law legislation (*De principiis legislationis poenalis*), a work that opened the door for him to attain a position as docent at the law faculty the same year. When he graduated two years later (1818) with a *juris utriusque candidate* degree, he received the very rare grade of *egregie laudatur*. In 1820 he defended the dissertation *Tentamina ad illustrandam historiam juris Scandinavici*, in which he commented on some obscure matters in the laws of Uppland (1296) for the *jur.lic.* exam. He received the same extraordinary grading once again, and that same year, together with his contemporary Hans Samuel Collin, he was promoted in the cathedral to be the first *juris doctor*. Their proud teacher, Johan Holmbergson, said that those two doctoral students "more honored the hat than the hat honored them." Schlyter was offered a position at the law faculty without salary, an offer he declined. He had to find a position outside the university, but doing so was not at all easy. He was rejected as inappropriate for the position as a notary in the newly established Court of Appeal for Southern Sweden,[12] as well as in the Lower Justice Audit (*Nedre justitierevisionen*) at the Supreme Court in Stockholm. Schlyter left Lund and landed a couple of positions, one of them as a clerk at the Svea Court of Appeal in Stockholm.

Law and religion: Johan Holmbergson, Schlyter, and Henrik Schartau

Holmbergson and Schlyter not only shared the scholarly fields of law and legal history but also had in common a warm religiosity based on Christian Lutheran faith. Both of them were rooted in religious families. Holmbergson was a close friend to the chaplain (*komminister*) in the Lund Cathedral, Henric Schartau. As chaplain, Schartau also served as vicar in a congregation (Stora Råby) south of Lund. In his theological views, Schartau was critical of the new Romantic renewal tendencies of his time. Instead, he interpreted his mission to be fighting against almost all religious books but the Bible, the collections of homilies by Luther and Anders Nohrborg, and the publications of the German theologian Magnus Friedrich Roos. The court chaplain Nohrborg's publications were characterized by a "rapt Lutheranism" (*fördjupad lutherdom*), identified as an old Swedish tradition influenced by Pietism and the Moravians' (Herrnhuters') frankness in faith.[13] Schartau's didactic sermons were renowned to be harsh and strict.[14] Holmbergson listened to Schartau's sermons every Sunday that he preached in the Lund Cathedral, and Holmbergson became one of Schartau's devoted supporters and a close friend. Schlyter, too, had held from his childhood a warm and deep religious attitude; at the end of his student years, he found a strong religious view very close to that of Henric Schartau.

Schlyter left Lund University after receiving his doctoral law degree in 1820. There was no place for him either in academia or in legal practice. From this period on, he actively searched for and found his faith. Among Schartau's letters, some might have been written directly to Schlyter. He learned that it was by "asking the right teacher" that his faith in God would be activated with the help of "the Word, the sacraments and the preaching office."[15] Even if Schlyter in the 1820s was open to more liberal preaching meetings (*konventiklar*), he changed his mind when Schartau's letters were published, and he turned to a more fundamental faith and became one of the founders of a "Schartau party" in Lund.

Schlyter and the edition of Swedish medieval laws

In 1822, Schlyter received a charge that would occupy him for the rest of his life. Together with Henrik Samuel Collin, he was commissioned by the law committee—the reformers of the Swedish code—to produce an edition of the medieval laws of Sweden based on the original sources. The project was to a great extent financed by a grant from King Charles XIV. The context of this mission was, of course, a part of the implementation of the ideas of the historical school in Sweden. The parliament—the legislature—had to have knowledge of the original historical legal sources before they decided on modern legal reforms. Collin and Schlyter started this work in 1822, and the first volume, the Västgöta Code (*Västgötalagen*) was published in 1827. Although Collin died in the early 1830s, Schlyter fulfilled their mission, editing and publishing thirteen volumes on all the Swedish medieval laws (*Sveriges gamla lagar*) based on about eight hundred manuscripts in libraries not only in Sweden but all over Europe. He concluded the project after fifty-five years, in 1877. In the preface to the last volume, the dictionary, he noted: "If the question has to be raised whether somebody should be honored for this work, the honor belongs to Him, Him alone, who is mighty in the weak and who has given courage and force to its realization."[16]

Henrik Samuel Collin's contributions to the project must be mentioned. Collin was weak and unhealthy from childhood and passed away in 1833. Schlyter and Collin had totally different temperaments. Schlyter was categorical, blunt, and repellently straightforward. He liked to judge the clergy. Collin, on the other hand, was well known for his "mild and meek being." Collin included in his religion more humility and tolerance for different thinking rather than emphasizing strict orthodoxy. Schlyter, on the other hand, regarded Collin as not having the ability to judge humans and above all missing the spiritual insight to be able to judge their inner condition.[17] Yet while their piety was essentially different, both of them admired Schartau.

Schartau and Holmbergson were contemporary and met regularly in an open and warm atmosphere, developing a warm friendship. Due to their close friendship, Schartau donated all of his handwritten material to Holmbergson shortly before his death in 1825 and gave Holmbergson permission to publish in the future "what he found useful." In his will, Schartau also appointed Holmbergson administrator of his estate. Holmbergson soon began to publish Schartau's letters on spiritual matters (1828). Holmbergson, in turn, shortly before his own death, in 1842, donated Schartau's papers to the vicar Hans Fredrik Cedergren in St. Peter's congregation in Lund. During the latter part of his life, Holmbergson became increasingly devoted to theology, especially to that of Schartau and his literary heritage. After Holmbergson passed away in 1842, Schlyter became Schartau's most important apostle.

Up to the mid-1830s, Schlyter had his workplace in the royal library in the royal castle in Stockholm. During his stay in the capital, he increasingly distanced himself from conventicles, while Collin became their great authority. "The conventicle has to be free regarding access and freedom of expression," Collin said.

In Lund, Holmbergson's position was more complex. It combined two lines: "orthodoxy in Christian dogma and liberalism in his Enlightenment thought regarding politics." Collin's position was close to Holmbergson's, but Holmbergson was critical of conventicles. He was one of the first Swedes who quoted the Danish clergyman N.F.S. Grundtvig's position when one of his pamphlets was discussed in Lund. Holmbergson eloquently argued for "a legally protected entity of conventicles within the Swedish church." The Moravians enjoyed such a freedom. [18]

Schlyter as the first professor of legal history in Sweden

In 1835 Schlyter returned to the university when he became a member of the Uppsala law faculty as the faculty's first professor of legal history. From that position he published his lectures, in which he demonstrated his close affiliation to Savigny and the historical school of law. In Uppsala, he also married Carolina Christina Liljesköld.

In 1838 he left Uppsala and returned to Lund as a law professor, first in penal law but after 1842 in a personal chair in legal history, which gave him the opportunity to continue full-time with his impressive editorship. It is from this time that he also anonymously published Schartau's writings, mostly his sermons. Thanks to Schlyter, Schartau's theology was implemented in the works of several generations of Swedish clergy, especially on the Swedish west coast.

Schlyter's marriage was also characterized by the commitment of his deep religiosity; he combined his faith in Old Testament law with that of the grace in the New Testament. He wrote an article "On the dominium of the husband over his wife regarding her person,"[19] in which he argued for the right of the husband to discipline his wife. Schlyter argued that the rule in the medieval laws (Christoffer's Law Iniquity Beam 1442) still was valid law, even if there was no rule regarding the admissible discipline of the wife in the-then valid law, the code of misdeed in the national code of 1734. The legislature had excluded only flogging, as "it [the legislature] regarded it as precarious to, by an expressive consent of such a right, seem to encourage its use."[20] Schlyter's biographer made the comment that Schlyter regarded the husband's right to discipline the wife only from a legal point of view, and "it would have been a gross error if anybody thought that, concerning the husband's relation to his wife, he favored brutality, which nobody could detest more than he."[21]

Schlyter's private cathechism 1880

At the end of his life, Schlyter also published a catechism, which he had used for his daily evening education of his children on Sundays and holy days. In this private book, published in 1880,[22] he often quoted Schartau and returned to the importance of reconciliation. The explanations of the Fourth Commandment ("Honor thy father and mother," according to the Augustinian enumeration used by Catholics and Lutherans) dominate his presentation and confirm his patriarchal view of life.

In his comments on the Eighth Commandment, against bearing false witness, he quoted Schartau's *Draft to public examination*:[23] Christians "ought to remember what they often forget, that each vain word they speak they have to reckon for on doomsday." Thus, reconciliation became the concluding message for Schlyter. "It's love for God and, from this, fluent love for your neighbor, which makes one willing to obey this [the Tenth Commandment] as well as God's other commandments." A good Christian avoids, if possible, conflicts regarding his or her real rights. A Christian never provokes a neighbor to sue for what the Christian is obliged to give. On the contrary, a Christian should be "disposed to avoid conflict by satisfying the neighbor's claims, even if they are unreasonable, when this can be made without too great damage." [24]

If humanity regards the teachings of God's law, Schlyter argued, "humanity, with help of the law, will know sin and, consequently, the need for repentance." He identified the close and indissoluble connection between the teachings of the law and the gospel. His messages ended with the conclusion: "The Law is given to us by Moses, but grace and truth come to us through Jesus Christ."[25]

Schlyter's conflicts with the representatives of liberal theology

Schlyter's conflicts with liberal theology and its representatives at Lund University are an important part of this story. When Schlyter received his first professorship at Lund in 1838, another of Holmbergson's then newly graduated students, Christian Naumann, entered the academic scene. Contrary to Schlyter, Naumann's religious position was inspired by the German Herrnhut tradition. Naumann married into the family of a Stockholm merchant, Gustaf Theodor Keyser, who importantly inspired his religiosity, the tenets of which included "sobriety, music, and missionary work."[26] At Lund, Naumann became one of the founders of the Lund Missionary Society, in which one faction (called the *mouvement*) regarded missionary work as a private matter, and in which the theologian Johan Henrik Thomander[27] and the jurist Christian Naumann held important positions. Naumann's religious position was provocative in relation to that of Schartau's supporters—among them Carl Johan Schlyter. Moravians (Herrnhuters) and Pietists were regarded as enemies to the conservatives in the Schartau party. So in the religious life in Lund in the 1840s and 1850s, Schlyter and Naumann took diametrically opposite positions. This disagreement had consequences for Naumann's academic career. Due to critical views of Naumann's research in Swedish constitutional law, Holmbergson and increasingly Schlyter regarded Naumann as incompetent for a professorship in this field of law.[28] Nevertheless the king, Oscar I, appointed him as a professor in 1851. Naumann held this position until 1860, when he was appointed justice of the Swedish Supreme Court, but those years in the 1850s at the law faculty were very conflicted. The split had its context in those religious oppositions between conservatives and liberal law professors and theologians.

Schlyter's conservative and text-oriented religiosity explains his legal cognitive structure within the historical school of law. It also explains the role of religiosity for the jurists during the premodern history of the nineteenth century. His contributions to the heritage of Schartau through the end of the nineteenth century made Schlyter instrumental in the religious discourses in Sweden up to modern times.

Summary

For two centuries Schlyter has been an icon within legal history thanks to his magnum opus of Swedish medieval laws. Internationally, he traditionally has had a good reputation owing to his scientific method in identifying the chronology of medieval legal sources by their errors and differences in relation to the original code. His religious belief and his productivity in ecclesiastical law, however, have been much less studied. Nonetheless, he is an important example of the Scandinavian Christian jurists who devoted themselves to theological discourses in the nineteenth century—a period when conservative and liberal thought clashed over questions of religious freedom.

Notes

1 Rückert, "Religiöses und Unreligiöses."
2 Haferkamp, "Einflüsse der Erweckungsbewegung."
3 Modéer, "Unter dem gemeinsamen."
4 Modéer, "Christian Naumann."
5 Schlyter, *Sveriges Gamla Lagar.*
6 This article is mainly based on Modéer, "Schartau och juristerna" (2005).
7 Möller, "Ebbe Samuel Bring."
8 Schelling, *Philosophische Untersuchungen.*
9 The phosphorists, "so called from *Phosphorus*, [their]at Uppsala published literary review, inclined substantially to . . . the imitation of foreign [literary] models, especially those of Germany, and clamored loudly for the exclusion of Gothic subjects as smacking too much of an outlived age of coarseness": Tegnér, *Frithiof's Saga*, introduction, "Bishop Tegnér, His Life and Work," xi.
10 "In the Bishop's house there is now a terrible clatter. The beldams side with the boy, but I will scourge him in front of their eyes." ["I Biskopshuset är nu ett grufligt väsende. Käringarna tar pojkens parti men jag skall hudflänga honom inför deras ögon.") Letter from E. Tegnér to C.P. Hagberg, Lund, January 21,1819: *Esaias Tegnérs brev*, Vol, 2, 87.
11 Modéer, *Det förpliktande minnet*, 92.
12 Modéer, *Hovrätten över Skåne och Blekinge*, 95.
13 Brohed, "Anders Nohrborg."
14 Modéer, "Schartau och juristerna," 62f.
15 Ibid., 73.
16 Schlyter, *Sveriges Gamla Lagar*, Vol. 13, xxx.
17 Gladh, *Lars Vilhelm Henschen*, 58f.
18 Schlyter, *Sveriges Gamla Lagar*, Vol. 13, "Kristoffers landslag 1442, Missgärningsbalken," 66f.
19 Schlyter, "Om mannens välde," 169ff.
20 Ibid., 170.
21 Wisén, *Minnesteckning*, 207.
22 Schlyter, *Betraktelser till grund för cathechetisk underwisning.*
23 Schartau, *Utkast till offentliga förhör.*
24 Schlyter, *Betraktelser*, 287.
25 Ibid., 288f.
26 Ahnfelt, *Studentminnen*, 126.
27 See Alexander Mauritz's chapter about Thomander in this volume.
28 Modéer, "Christian Naumann," 154.

Bibliography

Ahnfelt, P.G. *Studentminnen*. Stockholm: Natur och Kultur, 1964.
Brohed, Ingmar. "Anders Nohrborg." *Svenskt Biografiskt Lexikon*, vol. 27, p. 118. Stockholm: Bonnier, 1990–91.

Cancik, Pascale, et al., eds. *Konfession im Recht. Auf der Suche nach konfessionell geprägten Denkmustern und Argumentationsstrategien in Recht und Rechtswissenschaft des 19. und 20. Jahrhunderts.* Frankfurt am Main: Klostermann, 2009.

Gladh, Henrik. *Lars Vilhelm Henschen och religionsfrihetsfrågan till 1853.* Uppsala: Almqvist & Wicksell, 1953.

Haferkamp, Hans-Peter. "Einflüsse der Erweckungsbewegung auf die historisch-christliche Rechtsschule zwischen 1815 und 1848." In Cancik et al., *Konfession im Recht. Auf der Suche nach konfessionell geprägten Denkmustern und Argumentationsstrategien in Recht und Rechtswissenschaft des 19. und 20. Jahrhunderts*, 71 ff. Frankfurt am Main: Klostermann, 2009.

Modéer, Kjell Å. "Christian Naumann—Redivivus: En juristbiografisk essay." In *Festskrift till Rune Lavin*, edited by Marianne Eliason et al., 143–95. Lund: Juristförlaget, 2005.

Modéer, Kjell Å. *Det förpliktande minnet: Juridiska fakulteten i Lund 1666–2016.* Stockholm: Santérus Förlag, 2017.

Modéer, Kjell Å. *Hovrätten över Skåne och Blekinge: En överrätts tillkomsthistoria.* Stockholm: Norstedts Förlag, 1971.

Modéer, Kjell Å. "Schartau och juristerna." In *Henric Schartau 1757–1825: Syfte, Samtid, Samhälle*, edited by Anders Jarlert, 52–85. Skellefteå: Artos Bokförlag, 2005.

Modéer, Kjell Å. "Unter dem gemeinsamen gotischen Gewölbe. Das Verhältnis von Theologie und Recht bei schwedisch-pommerschen Juristen." In *Die Universität Greifswald in der Bildungslandschaft des Ostseeraums*, edited by Dirk Alvermann et al., 231ff. Berlin: LIT Verlag, 2007.

Möller, Bert. "Ebbe Samuel Bring." *Svenskt Biografiskt Lexikon*, vol. 6, p. 247. Stockholm: Bonnier, 1926.

Rückert, J. "Religiöses und Unreligiöses bei Savigny." In Cancik et al., *Konfession im Recht. Auf der Suche nach konfessionell geprägten Denkmustern und Argumentationsstrategien in Recht und Rechtswissenschaft des 19. und 20*, 49ff. Jahrhunderts. Frankfurt am Main: Klostermann, 2009.

Schartau, Henric. *Utkast till offentliga förhör, tillika med afhandlingar i frågor och swar öfwer några stycken af Christendomskunskapen.* Lund: Gleerup, 1850.

Schelling, Friedrich. *Philosophische Untersuchungen über das Wesen der menschlichen Freiheit.* 1809.

Schlyter, Carl Johan. *Betraktelser till grund för cathechetisk underwisning i Guds lags lära med ledning af första hufwudstycket i Luthers lilla cateches*, edited by Waldermar Cederberg. Lund: Gleerup, 1880.

Schlyter, Carl Johan. "Om mannens välde öfver hustrun i afseende på hennes person." In id., *Juridiska afhandlingar*, 169ff. Uppsala: Leffler och Sebell, 1836.

Schlyter, Carl Johan. *Sveriges Gamla Lagar.* 13 vols. Lund, 1827–77.

Tegnér, Esaias. *Esaias Tegnérs brev* [Utgivna av Tegnérsamfundet], edited by Nils Palmborg, Vol. 2 (1818–23). Malmö: Allhems Förlag, 1954.

Tegnér, Esaias. *Frithiof's Saga: Legend of Norway*, translated by L. A. Sherman. Boston: Osgood, 1878.

Wisén, Theodor. *Minnesteckning öfver Carl Johan Schlyter.* Stockholm: Norstedt, 1890.

15 The Theological Battle for Freedom of Religion in Sweden

Henrik Reuterdahl (1795–1870) and Johan Henrik Thomander (1798–1865)

Alexander Maurits

Introduction

For Sweden, the first part of the nineteenth century was a period marked by incipient societal changes. In 1810, the French general, Jean Baptiste Bernadotte (1763–1844) was elected crown prince. Bernadotte succeeded to the throne in 1818. With the support of the nobility, the king was able to hold back and to modify the increasing demands for reforms. During his last decade as king, the urge for reform increased and the liberal opposition gained influence in Parliament. This development was a result of a widespread eagerness for reform in all of Europe. Even though the course of events in Sweden was not as intense and uncontrolled as in Eugène Delacroix's allegorical painting of the July Revolution in Paris in 1830 ("Liberty Leading the People"), the situation was tense and minor riots caused actual casualties.[1] The decades that followed were also marked by commotion, and the events in Paris in February 1848 gave rise to demonstrations in Stockholm. On March 18–19, 1848, the Swedish king, Oscar I (1799–1859), decided to stop the protest by force, causing several causalities including the death of 18 demonstrators.

The changes that occurred in Sweden during the first half of the nineteenth century should not be underestimated. Agricultural reforms, for example in 1827, resulted in more effective farming with larger crops. This, together with a continued state of peace and various medical advances, stimulated a major growth in population. From 2.3 million inhabitants in 1800, the population had increased to 3.5 million at the turn of the century. Among the ruling elite, this rapid growth caused anxiety. Officially, the Swedish king was positively inclined to public opinion, but in practice, he tried to counter the liberalization of society. With rather strict censorship, the government tried to outmaneuver publicists and debaters who held ideas that were considered a threat to the societal order. As a consequence of this censorship, "liberalism" became the code word of the day. However, it must be emphasized that "liberalism" had a rather different meaning from the one we are used to today. In this context, "liberalism" denoted the right to speak one's mind without the risk of reprisal.[2]

During this period of great unrest between an authoritarian form of government with loyal subjects and an emerging liberal form of government based on the idea of citizenship, various associations gained in importance.[3] The ecclesiastical scene of the nineteenth-century was marked by "tremendously broadened associational activity." All over Europe, pious associations were organized in a previously unseen number. There were Christian associations in Sweden as well, mainly with the purpose of fostering temperance and supporting different kinds of missions at home and abroad. In Catholic countries, the associations became church-oriented, while the associations in Protestant countries like Sweden often had a critical attitude to the Established churches, thus fueling religious antagonism and reinforcing an urge for separation.[4]

Since the Reformation Sweden had been a mono-confessional country, with close collaboration between the state and the Lutheran Church of Sweden. Swedish citizens were obliged to submit to the Lutheran confession according to the *Cuius regio, eius religio* principle of the Peace of Augsburg in 1555 and subsequent Swedish laws. The religious homogeneity of Sweden was codified with a standardized national hymnbook (1695), a catechism (1689), and a comprehensive ecclesiastical law (1686). As regards the ecclesiastical law of 1686, it has been emphasized that it was ratified in order to secure the absolute rule of the monarch and to make matters concerning religion more homogeneous.[5] The ecclesiastical law was a mix of formal law and prescriptive liturgical instructions.[6] Of course, the law of 1686 was supplemented and revised over time; in formal terms, however, a different law did not replace it before 1992.

Because of the changes and the turmoil that marked the nineteenth century, the role of the Church of Sweden of course changed as well—at least, to some extent. During the course of the century, the religious homogeneity and the privileged role of the Church of Sweden were contested. However, this was not a period of secularization, but rather a period marked by increasing activity among religious groups. The period has even been depicted as a second confessional age or as a period of rechristianization. Thus, awakening movements within the Church and revivalist Free Church movements played an important role during the century.[7]

Due to the influence of the emerging Free Churches and of liberal politics, the privilege of the Church of Sweden and its clergy was severely scrutinized.[8] Anticlericalism was one important component of the sometimes fierce debates that took place during the nineteenth century. Since theological conviction was considered as a part of the private domain, liberal debaters argued that clergymen who took part in parliamentary affairs neglected their pastoral duties and that the bishops were too occupied with worldly power.[9] Representatives of both the state and the Church of Sweden monitored the events and tried to adapt to the new situation.

However, the opinions among the leading clergy to a large part reflected the different opinions held by Members of Parliament or the public. Among the bishops, there were proponents of more liberal views as well as advocates with a more conservative and reactionary approach. This also became evident in the vivid discussions during the 1830s, 1840s, 1850s, and 1860s about the need to update the ecclesiastical laws in keeping with the new situation.

"I cannot rejoice in transformations that interrupt the historical progress of an ancient people"[10]

Perhaps the most ardent defender of the established order and the historically strong bonds between church and state in Swedish society was Henrik Reuterdahl (1795–1870). Reuterdahl's childhood was characterized by poverty and hardship. His father, who earned his living as a wigmaker, died of tuberculosis when Reuterdahl was barely nine years old. At this point, the family was in debt, but Reuterdahl's mother was able to persuade the debtors to postpone collecting payments that were due. At the end of 1807, however, Reuterdahl's mother died too. An orphan from the age of twelve, it is not surprising that Reuterdahl's memories of his childhood years are rather dreary. In his autobiography, Reuterdahl has emphasized how, as a poor orphan, he was dependent on the goodwill of different benefactors in Malmö. It was these benefactors, some of them previous customers of Reuterdahl's father, who enabled him to attend secondary grammar school in Malmö and then to be enrolled as a student in Lund.[11]

As an intermittent student in Lund between 1811 and 1817, Reuterdahl spent a considerable amount of time as a private tutor in prosperous families on the Swedish west coast. It was also during this period that Reuterdahl had an affair with a married woman ten years his senior. In his autobiography, compiled at the end of the 1850s, Reuterdahl reproached himself for this grave sin and concluded that this deeply immoral act had been agonizing him for a long time and that it was the main reason why he had remained unmarried.[12]

During his first years as a student, Reuterdahl studied philology and Greek. Eventually, in accordance with the curriculum of the period, he would continue with theology, becoming first a reader at the theological seminary in 1817 and then a lecturer at the same seminary in 1824. In 1828–33, he co-edited the *Theological Quarterly* (*Theologisk Quartalskrift*) with J.H. Thomander (1798–1865). In 1844, he was appointed Professor of Dogmatics and Moral Theology, and in 1845, he became Professor of Church History, both positions in Lund. Reuterdahl was Minister of Education and Ecclesiastical Affairs 1852–55, elected Bishop of the diocese of Lund in 1855 and a year later elected Archbishop of Uppsala. Reuterdahl was a Member of Parliament during seven sessions of the Riksdag (1844–45, 1847–48, 1850–51, 1856–58, 1859–60, 1862–63, and 1865–66), and he was speaker of the clergy during the last four sessions of the four-estates-Parliament.[13]

As a church historian inspired by rationalism, Reuterdahl came to be one of the first Swedish scholars applying a rigorous method for criticism of the sources. Contemporaneous with the influential German historian Leopold von Ranke (1795–1886), Reuterdahl strove to apply a similar scholarly method, i.e. to perform an objective analysis of the historical source material using different scientific criteria. Being perhaps the first Swedish scholar to adopt this historical-critical method strictly, Reuterdahl is considered the pioneer of modern Swedish church historiography.

As for his theological standpoint, Reuterdahl was highly influenced by romanticism and he found the German theologian Friedrich Schleiermacher (1768–1834) an important inspiration. Through different articles, Reuterdahl introduced Schleiermacher to a Swedish audience and he was highly influenced by Schleiermacher's systematization of theology into distinct academic disciplines.[14] At this point in his career, Reuterdahl seems to have been theologically liberal. However, when it came to politics and social ethics his political standpoint must be regarded as strictly conservative.

Reuterdahl was influenced by romanticism, but instead of adopting a liberal political viewpoint, Reuterdahl, owing to his historical perspective, was strictly conservative. As a leading representative of the Lutheran neo-orthodoxy that was gradually introduced in Sweden from the 1850s, Reuterdahl did his utmost to counteract the pluralization and liberalization of Swedish society. In contrast to for example J.H. Thomander, Reuterdahl regarded state and church as organically intertwined. This established societal order "was sanctioned and sanctified by religion and embraced by the national Church."[15] The ideal that Reuterdahl tried to uphold was rooted in the Lutheran doctrine of the three estates and the Lutheran Catechism's Table of Duties. However, these ideas also corresponded to the philosophical ideas about the nature of society that were expressed by the influential German philosopher Friedrich Hegel (1770–1831), even though Reuterdahl could not be considered an ardent follower of Hegel's world of ideas.[16]

According to Reuterdahl, church and state had been closely united during the course of history. The close bond between church and state was manifested on all levels of society—in the family, in the church, and in the relation between the ruler and his subjects. From this understanding of society, Reuterdahl objected to the emerging liberal movement's individualistic understanding of freedom and to the Free Church revival with its lay preachers, whose activities he saw as a threat to a divinely ordained social and religious order.

As a consequence, it may not come as a surprise that the liberal reforms introduced during the period to a large extent were counteracted by Reuterdahl. In opposition to a liberal position regarding dissenters and lay preachers, Reuterdahl as Minister of Education and Ecclesiastical Affairs prohibited the abolition of the strict laws regarding conventicles, and he even introduced more rigid laws regarding worship (1855). According to this law, which had Reuterdahl as its key architect, any layman who administered the sacraments should be punished and forced to pay a large fine. His critics argued that Reuterdahl was too strict—even using the police—in counteracting illegal expressions of religious diversity.[17]

With this law, and other measures, Reuterdahl tried to counteract the religious revival, religious deviance, and pluralism that were gaining in importance.

From Reuterdahl's point of view, it was essential to promote unity in religion, and thus to penalize any deviation from the established order and the traditional church service. As for the revival movement, the right for laymen to gather for religious purposes without the supervision of a pastor was strictly prohibited. According to the law on conventicles from 1726, all types of religious worship except public worship and the hour of devotion led by the father of the household was forbidden. Although few people were prosecuted for breaching the conventicle law, it became an important symbol for liberals and an effective weapon in the public debate.[18] This law and the laws on religious unity that strictly limited the individual religious freedom of Swedish citizens were highly contested. To some extent, the strict laws in Sweden even attracted international attention. This was the case in 1858 when six women who had converted to the Roman Catholic Church were expatriated. This event gave fuel to the debate on extended freedom of religion, and Reuterdahl and like-minded people were considered, by both Swedish and foreign liberal press, as inhuman retrogrades.[19]

In the subsequent parliamentary discussion on extended freedom of religion, Reuterdahl and the Lund High Church fraction among the leading clergy tried to uphold the strong connection between state and church. They were critical to King Oscar I's initiative for an increased freedom of religion. Eventually Reuterdahl and like-minded realized the need for minor reforms, i.e. an alleviation of the different forms of penalties, such as expatriation. However, it was impossible to compromise with the unity of religion that, to Reuterdahl, had strong historical roots and characterized Swedish society. To be religiously indifferent was furthermore an absurd idea to Reuterdahl, and it was of great importance that a person that left the Church of Sweden belonged to another denomination that could take responsibility for the pastoral care of that person.[20] Having this in mind, the legislation of freedom of religion that was introduced in 1860—the Decree on Foreign Religious Adherents, also known as the Dissenter Act—was certainly a departure, but a minor one, from Reuterdahl's program. However, more drastic changes were underway.[21]

The young Reuterdahl may be characterized as politically conservative and theologically liberal. It must be emphasized, however, that Reuterdahl's orthodox views developed and deepened over time. When he was at the height of his power during the 1850s and 1860s he did his utmost to counter what he perceived a violent process of change in order to safeguard what he thought of as a God-given societal order.[22] As speaker of the clergy during the last session of the four-estates-Parliament (1865–66), he of course deplored the development that was at hand. In his opinion, it was regrettable if the new social order meant protecting the state from "the direct influence of positive Christian faith." At the same time, he also emphasized God as an agent in history and that the new order was introduced with "God's" permission and perhaps with a special purpose in mind.[23]

"In order not to founder, one must follow one's time"[24]

The most noticeable representative of liberal reforms of the Church of Sweden was Johan Henrik Thomander (1798–1865). Historians have regarded Thomander as one of the most influential and forward-looking theologians of the Swedish nineteenth century.[25]

Thomander had a remarkable career; a career that to a large extent resembled that of Reuterdahl. Thomander was appointed Professor of Practical Theology at Lund University in 1833, Member of Parliament during six consecutive sessions of the Riksdag (1840–41, 1844–45, 1847–48, 1850–51, 1853–54, and 1856–58), Dean in Gothenburg in 1850, and finally Bishop of the diocese of Lund in 1856. In 1855, he was elected to the Swedish Academy. Thomander's was exceptionally productive and his bibliography comprises a remarkable 780 items, including not only theological texts but also translations of various English dramas, e.g. Shakespeare (whom Thomander was the first to translate into Swedish).[26]

Thomander had a difficult upbringing in the rural parts of Scania and Blekinge. He was the result of a short love affair between the daughter of a vicar and his curate. The affair was a scandal, and his mother and father never married. Raised by his widowed maternal grandmother, resources were strictly limited. These rough conditions seem to have had a severe effect on Thomander's personality and nature, being the foundation of an inferiority complex that resulted in a haughty attitude as an adult. It has even been claimed that his rapid social advancement and his prolific academic writing was a result of his eagerness to compensate for a modest background.[27]

During a few decades, Thomander introduced several ecclesiastical reforms, his proposal for a new Church Law in 1837 being the most notable example.[28] For this article, this proposal is of major interest since it could be said to comprise all the main ideas for reforms of the Church of Sweden suggested by Thomander.

In 1823—when Thomander was twenty-five years old—the Swedish Parliament had initiated a revision of the Church Law from 1686, and thus the government had appointed a drafting committee. The committee consisted of several high-ranking vicars, some of whom were later to become bishops. Right from the start, Thomander took a keen interest in the undertakings of the committee, and in 1826, having not yet even received tenure at the university; he tried to use his contacts in the Swedish capital in order to have the committee assign him the task of making a comprehensive proposal for a new law. However, these efforts failed.

All those who have tried to make biographical sketches of Thomander have noticed this ambitiousness and eagerness to take on major tasks. Thomander's main biographer—Lars Österlin (1923–2006)—has concluded that this must be seen as a result of Thomander's enormous capacity for work, but also a result of ambitions to retain a social status and a high ranking position. As emphasized above, these ambitions were a result of Thomander's upbringing under harsh economic circumstances, accompanied by a feeling of inferiority. His eagerness to participate in the revision of the ecclesiastical law should be seen in this context and his efforts in this matter actually also seem to have helped him to get tenure at the Faculty of Theology in Lund. However, his hard work was of course also based on a conviction that this task was a way to initiate important reforms for the Church of Sweden in a broader sense.[29]

As the drafting committee published a proposal for a new church statute in 1828, Thomander rapidly published a review of it in the *Theological Quarterly*.[30] In the preamble to the review—which is lengthy—Thomander legitimizes the need for a revision of the current church statute. To him it was urgent to introduce a statute that was more up to date; to revise it in concordance with the newly revised hymnbook and service-book of the church and in concordance with other laws in Swedish society. In the review, it became clear that Thomander, unlike several of his contemporaries, was of the opinion that there must be a strict demarcation between secular and ecclesiastical matters. From Thomander's point of view, the church statute should merely include regulations strictly referring to the Church, which he considered a separate sphere from other parts of society. Additionally, he stressed the importance of excluding liturgical and spiritual matters from the church statutes, only including issues that belonged to a strict juridical-administrative domain. Edifying advice to the priesthood and regulations concerning the secular tasks performed by pastors thus should be left out of the new church statutes. Thus, Thomander proposed a distinction between ecclesiastical law and other ecclesiastical regulations that had previously been unheard of in Sweden. Eventually, the responsible Undersecretary of State, August von Hartmansdorff (1792–1856), also ratified this distinction. At the end of the review, Thomander expressed the necessity of revising the proposal and he overtly expressed his interest in undertaking this work himself. In 1836, von Hartmansdorff yielded to Thomander's recurrent lobbying and assigned him the task of writing a comprehensive proposal for a new Church Law.[31]

Thomander's proposal was published in the *Theological Quarterly* the following year.[32] In the proposal, he had used the guiding principles mentioned above. In the preamble to his proposal, Thomander stated the following:

> In the Codex of the Church Laws there should be nothing but that which is of a purely or predominantly ecclesiastical nature and has the characteristics of a legal text; thus nothing parenetic, nothing liturgical, although this is all pertaining to the church; nothing that is integrated in the constitution, privileges, civil law, or criminal law, since the constitution and privileges are regulated in other laws, but civil and criminal law should retain what belongs to them. It must be possible to separate these alien constituents from the church law, and through such a procedure the law should not lose but win in context as much as it wins in unity.[33]

Thus, in comparison with the Church Law of 1686 and subsequent additions, large parts of what was previously considered as part of the Church Law had thus been excluded. There were even parts that Thomander considered alien to ecclesiastical jurisdiction; for example, Thomander considered laws concerning marriage as part of civil law. His ideas about marriage were rooted in a liberal understanding of natural law. This was something novel in the Swedish context, and the proposal was severely criticized.[34]

As the drafting committee continued its work, important parts of Thomander's proposal were included. At the end of the 1830s, von Hartmansdorff was replaced by the more conservative C. I. Heurlin (1786–1860). This, together with the personal animosity displayed towards Thomander by newly appointed members of the committee, severely reduced the influence that Thomander was to exert in the committee.[35] Even so, the final proposal for new church statutes that were presented to the government in 1846 mainly rested on Thomander's work. Due to the harsh criticism leveled against the proposal, mainly from influential cathedral chapters, it was not accepted.[36]

In retrospect, the liberal jurisdictional position introduced by Thomander symbolized a kind of paradigmatic shift, which implied a new ecclesiology for an emerging modernized and individualized society. The preamble of the proposal stated that the church statutes concerned citizens who belonged to the Church of Sweden, thus implicitly saying that state and church were two different entities. Grounded in the idea of natural law, Thomander saw the Church of Sweden as a legal entity in its own right. Theoretically, Thomander thus made no effort to maintain the privileged role that the established church previously had held in the national legislation. However, on a practical level, the Church of Sweden could have a privileged position since it was the task of the state to see to the well-being and benefit of its citizen, and a vast majority of these belonged to the Church of Sweden.[37] Thus, Thomander's proposal deviated from the above-mentioned principle of the Reformation that the ruler of a nation should decide the confession of the country. In contrast to this, the faith of the majority of the citizens should settle the religion of the state. By emphasizing this Thomander also justified that not all citizens had to belong to the Church of Sweden. Here Thomander's liberal position and the legacy from the Enlightenment became obvious.

The conviction that there could be other denominations alongside the established church also had other consequences for the reform program put forward by Thomander. As one of the few figureheads of the church, Thomander held an obliging attitude towards the awakening movements. It is from this perspective that we should see his eagerness to suspend the so-called parish bond (i.e. the law that prohibited people from going to general confession and communion in a different parish from the one they belonged to geographically), to increase the power of the laity, and to abolish the Conventicle Act that restricted lay-organized worship.[38]

However, there were some limitations to Thomander's benevolent attitude towards religious lay movements. As far as possible, awakening and revivalist movements should conform to the Church of Sweden since unity of religion was beneficial to the state and the majority of its citizens. When trying to adopt these ideas in practice, Thomander met with unforeseen problems. As a dean in

Gothenburg, he took measures against Baptists and Mormons. Baptists were to be instructed by the local pastor regarding their apostasy before being handed over to the secular authorities, and the Mormons should be questioned and warned by the Cathedral Chapter and they were to be excluded from the church. Thus, it is clear that Thomander did not advocate complete freedom of religion.[39]

Lacking formal legal training it might seem striking that Thomander engage so full heartedly in the process of revising the ecclesiastical law. However, it must be emphasized that Church Law was an important discipline at theological faculties at the time and the boundaries between theology and law was not strict. To take Lund as an example, there were strong links between the two faculties and prominent figures of the Faculty of Law had a pronounced Lutheran conviction, often with conformist profile. Conservative theologians as Reuterdahl had close contacts with teachers at the Faculty of Law, as for example Carl Johan Schlyter (1795–1888), and for theologians as Thomander it was natural to interact with and promote liberal members of the faculty of law as for example Christian Naumann (1810–1888). Being close friends, it is also reasonable to think that Naumann influenced Thomander with his interest in natural law and the question of religious freedom.[40]

Of course, Thomander's proposal had its prototypes, the initiative for reforms in the Lutheran churches in Germany and in Denmark being the most notable example. Already in 1815, a proposal for ecclesiastical reforms and renewal was debated in Prussia. This proposal included several aspects of ecclesiastical life, but an important part was stressing the Church as a legal entity, distinctively separate from the state. When it comes to Denmark, the ecclesiastical aspects were also discussed in a way that had characteristics similar to the debate that was to take place in Sweden a few years later. In 1825, the Danish pastor H. N. Clausen (1793–1877) published an influential book in which he compared Catholic and Protestant ecclesiastical statutes from a rationalistic point of view. Influenced by the German debate, Clausen urged the introduction of a synod through which the Danish Church could act as a judicial person in its own right. These international influences were important to Thomander when he proposed a synod—a general convocation of clergy—to legislate on matters concerning spiritual books and ecclesiastical ordinances.[41]

On the national level, Thomander argued that the church should be ruled by a synod, and not (as was the case) by the Parliament. In opposition to influential parts of the clergy, Thomander emphasized the importance of lay representation, both in the synod and in the local parish. In this respect, he was in stark opposition to his former friend Henrik Reuterdahl. In a pamphlet-like book, Thomander responded in 1853 to Reuterdahl's conservative ideas and underscored the problems that arose as a consequence of the close connection between state and church in Swedish society. Thomander was eager to safeguard an ecclesiastical domain, in which the Swedish parliament and government could not interfere. The rationale behind this was the fact that the church was ruled and governed by people who were not theologically equipped to make wise decisions.

Furthermore, the representatives of civic society often lacked interest and/or were too busy with governing other parts of Swedish society.[42]

In the book, which was a direct response to a publication by Reuterdahl, Thomander also urged for other liberal reforms. For example, he promoted a changed role for the clergy, having pastors as representatives of the state to engage less in matters of a worldly nature and allocate more time to spiritual matters. He also advocated new forms of pastoral care due to increased industrialization and proletarianization in the larger cities; in this sense, his farsightedness forestalled the social upheaval that would mark the (ecclesiastical) debates during the 1870s and the 1880s. Thomander also stressed the importance of freedom of religious practice amongst members of the church. However, it is important to note that Thomander did not support unrestricted freedom of religion.[43]

Also at the local level, where the parish meeting had ruled in both secular and ecclesiastical affairs, Thomander urged for a separation between church and state. In 1862 this separation eventually took place. As for the national level, Thomander's idea was materialized in part with the Parliament reform in 1865, which also entailed the creation of the General Synod of the Church of Sweden.

With his different reform proposals, one could argue that Thomander tried to make the Church of Sweden more up to date. Throughout his career, Thomander politically embraced a liberal view, while at the same time being theologically conservative. This standpoint was, to say the least, somewhat strange for a leading theologian within the Church of Sweden during this period. While other contemporary theologians adhered to what could be regarded as a Lutheran neo-Orthodoxy, Thomander with his bourgeois upbringing was of the opinion that spiritual and secular matters should be strictly separated.

Of course, Thomander's proposal for new church statutes must be seen as his most impressive jurisprudential contribution. As a Member of Parliament, he was nevertheless engaged in the debates concerning several new laws: for example, the proposal for a new criminal law in 1844–1845.

Conclusion

It is often said that different types of debates, whether political, theological, or others, lack nuances. Eagerness to win a polemical discussion makes arguments more brutal than they were intended to be and valid points made by opponents are disregarded. Perhaps it could also be said that bystanders, for example historians, monitoring a debate are easily misled and thus facilitate the process of reproducing oversimplified arguments. Anton Niklas Sundberg (1818–1900), colleague to both Reuterdahl and Thomander, and successor to the former as archbishop, has emphasized that the conflicts between the two have been exaggerated, and the different positions they held were compatible.[44] Nineteenth-century Swedish church history is often depicted, and perhaps most accurately so, as a gradually evolving and increasing struggle, in which an established order gave way to a pluralistic religious landscape marked by liberalism.

Perhaps it is reasonable to regard Reuterdahl and Thomander as personifications of these tensions.

Starting off as friends, academic colleagues, and co-editors of the *Theological Quarterly*, Thomander and Reuterdahl were to move along rather opposite ideological and theological trajectories and end up as ecclesiastical adversaries. During the 1850s and 1860s, they took different stands on all important societal and ecclesiastical issues that were debated.[45] In contrast to Thomander, Reuterdahl was a conservative and reactionary representative of the Church of Sweden. In the short run, Reuterdahl was the one who drew the longest straw since he was able to counteract and to postpone several of the liberal reforms suggested by Thomander and others. In the long run, however, his ideas would not prevail, and, as aptly expressed by Lars Österlin, "Reuterdahl lived to see almost all the reforms he had opposed being adopted."[46]

For Thomander it was the other way around. During his lifetime, he was only able to see some of his reform proposals materialized. In the end, however, his efforts to make the Church of Sweden an independent church would come to fruition, but it was to take quite some time. As of January 1, 2000, the relations between the Swedish state and the Church of Sweden changed. The Ecclesiastical Act was abrogated and replaced by an act on the Church of Sweden and an act on other religious communities. With the act on the Church of Sweden, the church ceased to be a part of the public sector. With this change, the influence of the secular authorities over the church has been minimized, and the status of the Church of Sweden resembles the status of other religious denominations and communities in Swedish society.[47]

Notes

1 Jakob Christensson, "Inledning": Jakob Christensson (ed.), *Signums svenska kulturhistoria: Karl Johantiden*. Stockholm: Bokförlaget Signum, 2008, pp. 9–11; Bo Stråth, *Sveriges historia 1830–1920*. Stockholm: Norstedts, 2012, pp. 45–57.

2 Torkel Jansson, "Mellan öst och väst": Jakob Christensson (ed.), *Signums svenska kulturhistoria: Karl Johantiden*. Stockholm: Bokförlaget, Signum, 2008, pp. 19–26; Bo Stråth, *Sveriges historia 1830–1920*, pp. 249–51.

3 Torkel Jansson, *Adertonhundratalets associationer: forskning och problem kring ett sprängfullt tomrum eller sammanslutningsprinciper och föreningsformer mellan två samhällsformationer c:a 1800–1870*. Univ., Uppsala, 1985.

4 Anders Jarlert, "Introduction": Anders Jarlert (ed.), *The Dynamics of Religious Reform in Northern Europe, 1780–1920: Piety and Modernity*. Leuven: Leuven University Press, 2012, pp. 7–24 (quotation from p. 21); Anders Jarlert, *Sveriges kyrkohistoria, 6: Romantikens och liberalismens tid*. Stockholm: Verbum, 2001, pp. 107–23.

5 Göran Inger, "Kyrkolagstiftningen under 1600-talet": Ingun Montgomery , *Sveriges kyrkohistoria, 4: Enhetskyrkans tid*. Stockholm: Verbum, 2002, pp. 204–13.

6 *1686 års kyrkolag*, utgiven av Samfundet Pro Fide et Christianismo med inledning av Gabriel Thulin. Stockholm: Svenska kyrkans diakonistyrelses bokförlag, 1936, pp. ix–xxvi.

7 For an introduction to the nineteenth century as a second confessional age or an age of rechristianization, see Olaf Blaschke, "Das 19. Jahrhundert: Ein Zweites Konfessionelles Zeitalter?": Hans-Peter Ullmann (ed.), *Geschichte und Gesellschaft* (26:1). Göttingen, 2000; Hartmut Lehmann, "Von der Erforschung der Säkularisierung

zur Erforschung von Prozessen der Dechristianisierung und der Rechristianisierung im neuzeitlichen Europa": Hartmut Lehmann (ed.), *Säkularisierung, Dechristianisierung, Rechristianisierung im neuzeitlichen Europa: Bilanz und Perspektiven der Forschung*. Göttingen: Vandenhoeck und Ruprecht, 1997. On the Scandinavian context, and Sweden in particular, see Anders Jarlert, "Reform in Sweden: From Confessional Provincialism towards World Ecumenism": Anders Jarlert (ed.), *The Dynamics of Religious Reform in Northern Europe, 1780–1920: Piety and Modernity*. Leuven: Leuven University Press, 2012, pp. 286–306; Anders Jarlert, "Det 'långa' 1800-talet som en andra konfessionell tidsålder": Rune Imberg and Torbjörn Johansson (eds.), *Nåd och sanning: Församlingsfakulteten 10 år*. Göteborg: Församlingsförl., 2003; Anders Jarlert, "State Churches and Diversified Confessionalization in Scandinavia": Nigel Yates (ed.), *Bishop Burgess and His World: Culture, Religion and Society in Britain, Europe and North America in the Eighteenth and Nineteenth Centuries*. Cardiff: University of Wales Press, 2007.

8 Alexander Maurits, *Den vackra och erkända patriarchalismen: Prästmannaideal och manlighet i den tidiga lundensiska högkyrkligheten* [Splendid Establishment patriarchalism: Lund High Church ideals of clerical manliness]. Lund: Universus Academic Press, 2013, pp. 42–50.

9 Jakob Evertsson, *Bishops, Politics and Anti-clericalism in Nineteenth Century England and Sweden: An Analysis of the Debate on the Political Role of the Anglican Bishops during the 1830s Parliamentary Reform Debate*. Falun: Högskolan Dalarna, 2005, pp. 64–77; Jakob Evertsson, *"En dam mot tidens ström": Kritiken mot biskoparna i det svenska stånds- och enhetssamhället vid mitten av 1800-talet*. Åbo: Åbo akademis förlag, 2002, pp. 47–154.

10 *Högvördiga preste-ståndets protocoll vid lagtima riksdagen i Stockholm åren 1865 & 1866*. Femte bandet. Stockholm: Typografiska föreningens boktryckeri, 1867, p. 409. The quotation in Swedish: "Fröjda mig kan jag icke över förändringar, som avbryta ett gammalt folks hela utvecklingshistoria och för detsamma påbörja en ny."

11 Oloph Bexell, "Henrik Reuterdahl": *Svenskt biografiskt lexikon*, 1998–2000, vol. 30, p. 26, Henrik Reuterdahl, *Ärkebiskop Henrik Reuterdahls memoarer*. Lund: C.W.K. Gleerups förlag, 1920, pp. 3–30.

12 Reuterdahl, *Ärkebiskop Henrik Reuterdahls memoarer*, 1920, pp. 40–41.

13 Bexell, "Henrik Reuterdahl," p. 26.

14 Bexell, "Henrik Reuterdahl," pp. 28–29.

15 Lars Österlin, *Churches of Northern Europe in Profile: A Thousand Years of Anglo-Nordic Relations*. Norwich: The Canterbury Press, 1995, pp. 170–73.

16 Hilding Pleijel, *Hustavlans värld: Kyrkligt folkliv i äldre tiders Sverige*. Stockholm: Verbum, 1970, pp. 30–44; John Witte, *Law and Protestantism: The Legal Teachings of the Lutheran Reformation*. Cambridge: Cambridge University Press, 2002, pp. 7, 93, 100–01, and 109–10; Svante Nordin, *Romantikens filosofi: Svensk idealism från Höijer till hegelianerna*. Lund: Bokförlaget Doxa, 1987, pp. 378, 389–90. For an introduction to Hegel's ideas on society, see Frederick Beiser, *Hegel*. New York: Routledge, 2005, pp. 80–109.

17 Jarlert, *Sveriges kyrkohistoria*, pp. 177–78, 200–04.

18 Jarlert, *Sveriges kyrkohistoria*, pp. 200–04.

19 Erik Sidenvall, "Tolkningen av 'katolikmålet' 1858 i ett internationellt perspektiv": *Kyrkohistorisk årsskrift* 2002, pp. 97–101; Per Dahlman, *Kyrka och stat i 1860 års svenska religionslagstiftning* [Bibliotheca Theologiae Practicae, 87]. Skellefteå: Artos & Norma bokförlag, 2009, pp. 33–36.

20 Dahlman, *Kyrka och stat i 1860 års svenska religionslagstiftning*, pp. 111–13, 235–41 and 257–58.

21 See Martin Nykvist, "A Superfluous Legislation? Historical and Contemporary Perspectives on Religious Freedom in Sweden": *Religion – Staat – Gesellschaft* 18 (2017), pp. 95–108.

22 A brief comparison between Thomander and Reuterdahl can be found in Jarlert, *Sveriges kyrkohistoria*, pp. 177–79.

23 *Högvördiga preste-ståndets protocoll vid lagtima riksdagen i Stockholm åren 1865 & 1866*, p. 409.

24 Quotation from J. H. Thomander from 1828 on the need for a new Church Law. The quotation in Swedish: "Sin tid måste man följa, om man icke vill gå i qvaf..." in J.H. Thomander, "Förslag till Kyrkolag och Ordning för Swenska Församlingen, på Konungens befallning, af dertill särskildt utsedde Comiterade, författadt och af trycket utgifvet": *Theologisk Quartalskrift*, utgifven av H. Reuterdahl och J.H. Thomander, 4:e häftet 1928. Lund: Bokhandlaren G.W.K. Gleerups förlag, 1828, p. 60.

25 See for example, Karl Ragnar Gierow, *Johan Henrik Thomander. Fysionomi i tre belysningar.* [Svenska Akademiens minnesteckningar]. Stockholm: Norstedts, 1975; P.G. Ahnfeldt, *Studentminnen: Anteckningar och tidsbilder från hemmet, skolan, universitetet och församlingen.* Stockholm 1882. However, the most important work on Thomander is Lars Österlin, *Thomanders kyrkogärning* [Samlingar och studier till Svenska kyrkan historia, 37]. Stockholm: Svenska kyrkans diakonistyrelses bokförlag 1960. Österlin's work on Thomander is very comprehensive, and it does not feel outdated even though almost sixty years have passed since its publication.

26 Selma Colliander, *Joh. Henr. Thomanders skrifter.* Lund: C.W.K. Gleerups förlag, 1942.

27 Lars Österlin, "'Själv en hel kommitté i en person'. J.H. Thomander och hans program för Svenska kyrkan": Anders Jarlert, *Sveriges kyrkohistoria, 6: Romantikens och liberalismens tid.* Stockholm: Verbum, 2001, pp. 288–97.

28 J.H. Thomander, *Förslag till Kyrko-ordning.* Lund, 1837; J.H. Thomander, "Förslag till Kyrkoordning," *Theologisk Quartalskrift*, utgifven af H. Reuterdahl och J.H. Thomander. Ny följd. Andra bandet 1837. (Lund: Bokhandlaren G.W.K. Gleerups förlag, 1837), pp. 332–400.

29 Österlin, *Thomanders kyrkogärning*, pp. 164–66.

30 J.H. Thomander, "Förslag till Kyrkolag och Ordning för Swenska Församlingen, på Konungens befallning, af dertill särskildt utsedde Comiterade, författadt och af trycket utgifvet," *Theologisk Quartalskrift*, utgifven av H. Reuterdahl och J.H. Thomander, 4:e häftet 1928, pp. 57–94.

31 J.H. Thomander, "Förslag till Kyrkolag och Ordning för Swenska Församlingen, på Konungens befallning, af dertill särskildt utsedde Comiterade, författadt och af trycket utgifvet," *Theologisk Quartalskrift*, utgifven av H. Reuterdahl och J.H. Thomander, 4:e häftet 1928, pp. 59–63, 93–94; Österlin, *Thomanders kyrkogärning*, 1960, pp. 166–74; Jarlert, *Sveriges kyrkohistoria*, pp. 126–30.

32 Thomander, *Forslag till Kyrko-ordning*, 1837; J.H. Thomander, "Förslag till Kyrkoordning," *Theologisk Quartalskrift*, utgifven af H. Reuterdahl och J.H. Thomander. Ny följd. Andra bandet 1837. Lund: Bokhandlaren G.W.K. Gleerups förlag, 1837, pp. 332–400.

33 Thomander, "Förslag till Kyrkoordning," p. 10; in: J.H. Thomander, "Förslag till Kyrkoordning," *Theologisk Quartalskrift*, utgifven af H. Reuterdahl och J.H. Thomander. Ny följd. Andra bandet 1837. Lund: Bokhandlaren G.W.K. Gleerups förlag, 1837, pp. 338–39. The quotation in Swedish:

> I kyrkolagens codex bör intet annat förekomma än det som är af rent eller öfvervägande kyrklig beskaffenhet och har lags egenskap; således intet parenetiskt, intet liturgiskt, ehuru detta allt är kyrkligt; intet som integrerar i grundlag, privilegier, civillag eller brottslag, emedan grundlag och privilegier stiftas i annan ordning, men civil- och brottslag böra behålla hvad dem tillhörer. Det måste låta sig göra att ifrån kyrkolagen afskilja dessa främmande beståndsdelar, och genom ett sådant förfarande bör lagen icke förlora utan vinna i sammanhang lika visst som den vinner i enhet.

34 On the question of Thomander and civil marriage, see Jan Janson, *Debatten om civiläktenskapets införande i Sverige*. Stockholm: Natur och Kultur, 1964, pp. 15–17,
35 Österlin, *Thomanders kyrkogärning*, pp. 166–74; Jarlert, *Sveriges kyrkohistoria*, pp. 126–30.
36 Österlin, *Thomanders kyrkogärning*, pp. 247–54, 310–21.
37 Österlin, *Thomanders kyrkogärning*, pp. 174–88.
38 Österlin, *Thomanders kyrkogärning*, pp. 463–69; Österlin, "'Själv en hel kommitté...", pp. 295–97.
39 Anders Jarlert, *Göteborgs stifts herdaminne 1620–1999. I: Domprosteriets kontrakt*. Göteborg: Tre Böcker Förlag AB & Göteborgs stiftshistoriska sällskap, 2009, pp. 55–56. For an account of Thomander's attitude toward Baptists as bishop in the diocease of Lund, see Owe Samuelsson, *Sydsvenska baptister inför myndigheter: Tillämpning av religionsbestämmelser i Lunds och Växjö stift 1857–1862*. Lund: Lund University Press, 1998.
40 Kjell Å. Modéer, Carl Johan Schlyter, in this vol. pp. 242–249; and Modéer, *Det förpliktande minnet. Juridiska fakulteten i Lund 1666-2016*. Stockholm 2017, pp. 105-106, 120-128.
41 Österlin, *Thomanders kyrkogärning*, pp. 188–92; Per-Olov Ahrén, *Kyrkomöte och synodalförfattning. En studie i svensk kyrkoförfattningsdebatt 1827–1865*. Lund, 1956, pp. 23–38; Helge Larsen & Michael Neiiendam, "H.N. Clausen": *Dansk Biografisk Leksikon*, 3rd ed., Gyldendal, Copenhagen: 1979–84. Retrieved 1 July 2018 from http://denstoredanske.dk/index.php?sideId=288444.
42 J.H. Thomander, *Om svenska kyrkans och skolans angelägenheter*. Stockholm, 1853, pp. 4–17. Reuterdahl's work was published the same year, see Henrik Reuterdahl, *Svenska kyrkans och skolans ifrågavarande angelägenheter*. Stockholm: P.A. Norstedt & söner, 1853.
43 Thomander, *Om svenska kyrkans och skolans angelägenheter*, pp. 17–42.
44 Anton Niklas, Sundberg, *Henrik Reuterdahl: Minnesteckning*. Stockholm: P.A. Norstedt & söner, 1883 pp. 49–53.
45 *Svenskt biografiskt lexikon*, vol. 30, p. 28.
46 Österlin, *Churches of Northern Europe in Profile*, p. 172.
47 *Lag om Svenska kyrkan*, Swedish Code of Statutes SFS, 1998:1591.

Bibliography

1686 års kyrkolag, utgiven av Samfundet Pro Fide et Christianismo med inledning av Gabriel Thulin. Stockholm: Svenska kyrkans diakonistyrelses bokförlag, 1936.

Ahnfeldt, P.G., *Studentminnen. Anteckningar och tidsbilder från hemmet, skolan, universitetet och församlingen*. Stockholm: Lamm, 1882.

Ahrén, Per-Olov, *Kyrkomöte och synodalförfattning. En studie i svensk kyrkoförfattningsdebatt 1827–1865*. Lund 1956.

Beiser, Frederick, *Hegel*. New York: Routledge. 2005.

Bexell, Oloph, "Henrik Reuterdahl", *Svenskt biografiskt lexikon, 1998–2000*, vol. 30. 1998, 26–33.

Blaschke, Olaf, "Das 19. Jahrhundert. Ein Zweites Konfessionelles Zeitalter?". In: Hans-Peter Ullmann (ed.), *Geschichte und Gesellschaft* (26:1). Lower Saxony: Göttingen, 2000, 38–75.

Christensson, Jakob, "Inledning". In: Jakob Christensson (ed.), *Signums svenska kulturhistoria. Karl Johantiden*. Stockholm: Bokförlaget Signum, 2008, 9–17.

Colliander, Selma, *Joh. Henr. Thomanders skrifter*. Lund: C.W.K. Gleerups förlag, 1942.

Dahlman, Per, *Kyrka och stat i 1860 års svenska religionslagstiftning* [Bibliotheca Theologiae Practicae, 87]. Skellefteå: Artos & Norma bokförlag, 2009.

Evertsson, Jakob, *Bishops, Politics and Anti-clericalism in Nineteenth Century England and Sweden. An Analysis of the Debate on the Political Role of the Anglican Bishops during the 1830s Parliamentary Reform Debate.* Falun: Högskolan Dalarna, 2005.

Evertsson, Jakob, *"En dam mot tidens ström". Kritiken mot biskoparna i det svenska stånds och enhetssamhället vid mitten av 1800-talet.* Åbo: Åbo akademis förlag, 2002.

Gierow, Karl Ragnar, *Johan Henrik Thomander. Fysionomi i tre belysningar* [Svenska Akademiens minnesteckningar]. Stockholm: Norstedts, 1975.

Högvördiga preste-ståndets protocoll vid lagtima riksdagen i Stockholm åren 1865 & 1866. Femte bandet. Stockholm: Typografiska föreningens boktryckeri, 1867.

Inger, Göran, "Kyrkolagstiftningen under 1600-talet". In: Ingun Montgomery (ed.), *Sveriges kyrkohistoria, 4: Enhetskyrkans tid.* Stockholm: Verbum, 2002, 204–213.

Janson, Jan, *Debatten om civiläktenskapets införande i Sverige.* Stockholm: Natur & Kultur, 1964.

Jansson, Torkel, *Adertonhundratalets associationer: forskning och problem kring ett sprängfullt tomrum eller sammanslutningsprinciper och föreningsformer mellan två samhällsformationer c:a 1800–1870.* Uppsala: Uppsala universitet, 1985.

Jansson, Torkel, "Mellan öst och väst". In: Jakob Christensson (ed.), *Signums svenska kulturhistoria. Karl Johantiden.* Stockholm. Bokförlaget Signum, 2008, 19–47.

Jarlert, Anders, "Det 'långa' 1800-talet som en andra konfessionell tidsålder". In: Rune Imberg & Torbjörn Johansson (eds.), *Nåd och sanning. Församlingsfakulteten 10 år.* Göteborg: Församlingsförl., 2003, 87–98.

Jarlert, Anders, *Göteborgs stifts herdaminne 1620–1999. I. Domprosteriets kontrakt.* Göteborg: Tre Böcker Förlag AB & Göteborgs stiftshistoriska sällskap, 2009.

Jarlert, Anders, "Introduction". In: Anders Jarlert (ed.), *The Dynamics of Religious Reform in Northern Europe, 1780–1920. Piety and Modernity.* Leuven: Leuven University Press, 2012, 7–29.

Jarlert, Anders, "Reform in Sweden. From Confessional Provincialism towards World Ecumenism". In: Anders Jarlert (ed.), *The Dynamics of Religious Reform in Northern Europe, 1780–1920. Piety and Modernity.* Leuven: Leuven University Press, 2012, 286–306.

Jarlert, Anders, "State Churches and Diversified Confessionalization in Scandinavia". In: Nigel Yates (ed.), *Bishop Burgess and his World. Culture, Religion and Society in Britain, Europe and North America in the Eighteenth and Nineteenth Centuries.* Cardiff: University of Wales Press, 2007, 171–197.

Jarlert, Anders, *Sveriges kyrkohistoria, 6: Romantikens och liberalismens tid.* Stockholm: Verbum, 2001.

Lag om Svenska kyrkan, Swedish Code of Statutes SFS 1998:1591.

Larsen, Helge & Neiiendam, Michael, "H.N. Clausen", *Dansk Biografisk Leksikon*, 3rd ed., Gyldendal: Copenhagen, 1979–1984. Retrieved July 1 2018 from http://denstoredanske.dk/index.php?sideId=288444.

Lehmann, Hartmut, "Von der Erforschung der Säkularisierung zur Erforschung von Prozessen der Dechristianisierung und der Rechristianisierung im neuzeitlichen Europa". In: Hartmut Lehmann (ed.), *Säkularisierung, Dechristianisierung, Rechristianisierung im neuzeitlichen Europa: Bilanz und Perspektiven der Forschung.* Göttingen: Vandenhoeck und Ruprecht, 1997, 9–16.

Maurits, Alexander, *Den vackra och erkända patriarchalismen. Prästmannaideal och manlighet i den tidiga lundensiska högkyrkligheten* [Splendid Establishment patriarchalism. Lund High Church ideals of clerical manliness]. Lund: Universus Academic Press, 2013.

Modéer, Kjell Å., *Det förpliktandet minnet. Juridiska fakulteten i Lund 1666–2016.* Stockholm: Santérus förlag, 2017.

Nordin, Svante, *Romantikens filosofi. Svensk idealism från Höijer till hegelianerna*. Lund: Bokförlaget Doxa, 1987.

Nykvist, Martin, "A Superfluous Legislation? Historical and Contemporary Perspectives on Religious Freedom in Sweden". *Religion – Staat – Gesellschaft* vol. 18 (2017), 95–108.

Österlin, Lars, *Churches of Northern Europe in Profile. A thousand years of Anglo-Nordic relations*. Norwich: The Canterbury Press, 1995.

Österlin, Lars, "'Själv en hel kommitté i en person'. J.H. Thomander och hans program för Svenska kyrkan". In: Anders Jarlert, *Sveriges kyrkohistoria, 6: Romantikens och liberalismens tid*. Stockholm: Verbum, 2001, 288–297.

Österlin, Lars, *Thomanders kyrkogärning* [Samlingar och studier till Svenska kyrkan historia, 37]. Stockholm: Svenska kyrkans diakonistyrelses bokförlag, 1960.

Pleijel, Hilding, *Hustavlans värld. Kyrkligt folkliv i äldre tiders Sverige*. Stockholm: Verbum, 1970.

Reuterdahl, Henrik, *Ärkebiskop Henrik Reuterdahls memoarer*. Lund: C.W.K. Gleerups förlag, 1920.

Reuterdahl, Henrik, *Svenska kyrkans och skolans ifrågavarande angelägenheter*. Stockholm: P.A. Norstedt & söner, 1853.

Samuelsson, Owe, *Sydsvenska baptister inför myndigheter. Tillämpning av religionsbestämmelser i Lunds och Växjö stift 1857–1862*. Lund: Lund University Press, 1998.

Sidenvall, Erik, "Tolkningen av 'katolikmålet' 1858 i ett internationellt perspektiv". *Kyrkohistorisk årsskrift*, 2002, 97–101.

Stråth, Bo, *Sveriges historia 1830–1920*. Stockholm: Norstedts, 2012.

Sundberg, Anton Niklas, *Henrik Reuterdahl: Minnesteckning*. Stockholm: P.A. Norstedt & söner, 1883.

Thomander, Johan Henrik, "Förslag till Kyrkolag och Ordning för Swenska Församlingen, på Konungens befallning, af dertill särskildt utsedde Comiterade, författadt och af trycket utgifvet". In: H. Reuterdahl and J.H. Thomander (eds.) *Theologisk Quartalskrift*, 4:e häftet 1928. Lund: Bokhandlaren G.W.K. Gleerups förlag, 1828.

Thomander, Johan Henrik, "Förslag till Kyrkoordning". In: H. Reuterdahl and J.H. Thomander (eds.) *Theologisk Quartalskrift*, Ny följd. Andra bandet 1837. Lund: Bokhandlaren G.W.K. Gleerups förlag, 1837.

Thomander, Johan Henrik, *Om svenska kyrkans och skolans angelägenheter*. Stockholm 1853.

Witte, John, *Law and Protestantism. The Legal Teachings of the Lutheran Reformation*. Cambridge: Cambridge University Press, 2002.

16 Karl Gustaf Ehrström (1822–1886)

Humanity, the Christian spirit, and criminal law in Finland in the nineteenth century

Jussi Sallila[1]

Introduction

Karl Gustaf Ehrström (1822–86) was one of the most prominent jurists of nineteenth-century Finland. From the 1850s on, he played a key role in the modernization of Finnish legal scholarship and was appointed as professor of criminal law at the Imperial Alexander University in 1860. Ehrström left the university in 1877 to serve in senior positions of the judiciary and as a legal adviser to the Finnish government.[2] He was the leading figure in the early phases of the reform of Finnish criminal law initiated in the early 1860s. Although he did not see the project completed, as the Finnish Criminal Code of 1889 was enacted a few years after his death, his ideas about modern criminal law had a notable influence on the codification project.[3] Interestingly, Ehrström saw the spirit of Christianity as the guiding principle of modern criminal law.

Ehrström's career coincided with a period of great reform in Finnish society. Finland had become an autonomous country within the Russian Empire after the Russo-Swedish War of 1808–09 and the Finnish Diet (*Lantdag*) of Porvoo/Borgå in 1809, while retaining the old Swedish legal and constitutional system and the Lutheran state church. After the meeting at Porvoo, the Finnish Diet did not convene again for more than fifty years. The situation in Finland changed dramatically after Russia was defeated in the Crimean War and Tsar Alexander II (r. 1855–81) began to modernize the empire. In Russia proper, the reforms of the period included the abolition of serfdom and reform of the judicial system. In Finland, the era of regular activity of the Diet began in 1863, and in the following decades, major reform legislation was enacted in many different areas, of which criminal law was among the most important.[4]

In most cases, the Finnish law reformers of the late nineteenth century could follow the example of Sweden and other European countries and could implement reforms in accordance with the "standards of the civilized world." After all, the long inactivity of the legislature meant that Finland had fallen behind in many respects. In criminal law, too, the law proposals drafted in Sweden some years earlier were used as a model in Finland. Yet the estates at the Finnish Diet of 1863–64 endorsed radical changes in criminal law, including the abolition of capital punishment, even though most civilized nations had not ventured so far. The work of Karl Gustaf Ehrström was a vital inspiration for such calls for reform.

Ehrström's radical proposals were not fully implemented in the nineteenth century. Finland retained the death penalty partly because imperial interests required such punishment for high treason and other severe political offenses in the entire Russian Empire. More generally, the final stages of the drafting of the Finnish Criminal Code of 1889, following a proposal drafted in 1879 under Ehrström's leadership, were dominated by scholars with more conservative views than Ehrström's. Indeed, in many ways, the vision of Ehrström would not be realized until a century later.

Karl Gustaf Ehrström regarded the spirit of Christianity as an essential foundation of modern criminal law. In his view, true Christian spirit required that rehabilitation rather than retribution be the goal of criminal punishment. James Whitman has underscored the importance of Christianity in criminal law reform of the late eighteenth and early nineteenth centuries. In his view, "the transition to modernity in criminal justice" from about 1750 to 1830 was a "de facto Christianization of secular justice" as "the states of the Atlantic world embraced a practice of criminal justice that had historically been associated with one of the great rivals to state power, the Church."[5] For Ehrström, too, the reforms of criminal law were an important part of the Christianization of secular justice, but he emphasized change rather than continuity. He saw the reform efforts as part of the new religious revival of the nineteenth century that manifested itself both in overseas missionary work and in new forms of activity in old Christian countries, bringing previously marginalized groups such as the blind and the deaf to the attention of churches. In a public lecture on the history of incarceration in 1858, Ehrström welcomed such new forms of activity as signs of living Christian faith. His conclusion, however, was dramatic. Pointing to the contrast between the humane prison reforms of other countries and the harsh reality of contemporary Finnish prisons, he ended his lecture with a question: "Is Finland a Christian country?"[6]

Ehrström and Christianity: notes on historiography

This chapter builds on a large body of scholarship in Finnish legal history and criminal law. Karl Gustaf Ehrström's reputation as a modernizer of Finnish legal scholarship makes him one of the most significant figures in nineteenth-century legal history. As Heikki Pihlajamäki has shown, Ehrström's scholarly authority played a central role in the adoption of free evaluation of evidence in nineteenth-century judicial practice, even though statutory law on the legal theory of evidence was not abolished before 1948.[7] Ehrström's contributions in criminal procedure were linked to criminal law, where his reputation as a progressive for whom rehabilitation rather than retribution was the goal of punishment is significant from a historiographical perspective. Finnish criminal law scholars and legal historians have studied the nineteenth-century development of criminal law in considerable detail. Given that the final stages of the drafting of the

Finnish criminal code of 1889 were dominated by scholars with more conservative views, progressive scholars of later times have regarded Ehrström as a "kindred spirit" and pioneer. These scholars, however, usually have focused on either the political context of law reform or criminal law doctrine and its philosophical foundations.[8] Both of these perspectives are mainly secular; however, a religious perspective can bring new light on Ehrström's philanthropic and humanitarian activities.

Currently, the leading authority on Ehrström is the criminal law scholar Markus Wahlberg. He has shown how Ehrström adopted ideas of Hegelian philosophy and nineteenth-century German criminal law doctrine and developed them further in his own work. Wahlberg's earlier research focused on theoretical aspects of criminal law and the grand sweep of the history of philosophy.[9] In recent years, he has investigated Ehrström's life in detail, and the first volume of a planned two-volume biography was published in 2017. [10] Using unpublished sources such as private correspondence, diary notes, and lecture manuscripts, Wahlberg places Ehrström in the social and cultural context of nineteenth-century Finland. Wahlberg has pointed to the importance of religious faith in Ehrström's criminal law thought and argues that this original religious perspective explains some important differences between Ehrström and the Hegelian thought he usually followed. Yet Wahlberg does not analyze this aspect in great depth, and the specifically Christian aspects of Ehrström's thought have not been investigated in detail by other scholars either.

Another historiographical aspect worth noting concerns the traditional narrative of church-state relationship, which may obscure some of the ways in which the Evangelical Lutheran Church of Finland influenced social reforms in the late nineteenth century.[11] In 1869, a new church law was enacted. The new legislation accepted the principle of religious freedom (with practical limitations) and gave the church more independence vis-à-vis the state than most of its Lutheran sister churches had at the time, even though the emperor and the Senate retained a significant role in the executive administration of the church.[12] Other reforms of the late 1860s secularized local government in rural areas and the administration of schools, both previously areas of church jurisdiction.[13] For the period after 1869, ecclesiastical history often focuses on internal church affairs, such as the activities of the newly established General Synod or the relationship between the clergy and popular revivalist movements within the church. Contemporary observers, however, did not necessarily view the changes of the 1860s as secularization. On the contrary, it was generally agreed that the Christian mission of the clergy had been hampered by the mundane tasks of local government of the countryside. While these responsibilities had earlier been a part of the pastoral ideal, both liberals and members of revivalist movements saw them as a burden in the nineteenth century.[14] According to an author of an elementary textbook of Finnish ecclesiastical history published in 1875, the improvement of popular education through the establishment of folk schools and teacher seminaries was necessary for the advance of Christianity in Finland. The establishment of schools for missionaries, a prison association, special schools for the blind and deaf, and several new charity organizations in mid-nineteenth-century Finland were evidence of new ways of advancing Christianity and practicing Christian love.[15]

It is worth noting that in the 1860s, clergy associated with revivalist movements tended to approach criminal law from a more conservative, retributive perspective. If their view is considered as the genuinely Christian opinion in nineteenth-century Finland, advocates of criminal law reform may appear more secular than they were. Similarly, as Whitman points out, contemporary American Christian revivalism tends to emphasize the harshness of criminal law by supporting "offense egalitarianism"—equal sentences that do not leave room for individual differences. Whitman notes that harsh punishment is not a necessary consequence of Christian ideals; indeed, Christian arguments have also been used to support more lenient sanctions.[16]

Biographical sketch

Karl Gustaf Ehrström belonged to a family of clergy, and several of his family members were prominent in academic and artistic circles. His mother, Ulrika Lovisa née Ahlstedt (1797–1831), was a daughter of an assistant vicar. His father, Erik Gustaf Ehrström (1791–1835), is known as one of the "Turku Romantics," intellectuals supporting the development of Finnish language, even if many of them (including Ehrström) were themselves Swedish-speaking. Erik Gustaf Ehrström was also a specialist in the Russian language, having studied at Moscow University after the war of 1808–09. He was appointed as lecturer of Russian at the Imperial Alexander University in 1816. Erik Gustaf Ehrström switched to a clerical career in 1824, both because of religious conviction and for political and economic reasons; his energetic promotion of teaching Russian — not an official language in Finland — was seen by many as a threat to Finnish autonomy. After serving briefly as a vicar in Finland, he moved to Russia, where he made his career as the vicar of the Swedish-language Lutheran congregation of St. Petersburg.[17]

After the early death of his parents, Karl Gustaf Ehrström returned to Finland and lived in Helsinki with his uncle Fredrik August Ehrström (1801–50), a music teacher and church organist whose choral compositions made him a central figure in the budding musical life of the Finnish capital.[18] Karl Gustaf Ehrström attended the Helsingfors Lyceum, a private secondary school established in 1831 by a group of young academics after the university had been moved from Turku to Helsinki in 1828. Several luminaries of mid-nineteenth-century Finnish intellectual life were among Ehrström's teachers. The school was also distinguished by its use of modern pedagogical methods and the restriction of physical punishment. Unlike traditional schools, the lyceum was not administered by church authorities. The founding headmaster of the school, philosopher and theologian Axel Adolf Laurell (1801–52), thought that education should be detached from the church organization. This secularization of education was not antireligious in character, however. Laurell saw faith, justice, and science as the highest goals of humanity, and education as a means of serving these interests.[19]

Ehrström began his studies at the university in 1840. He was a gifted student with good family connections in academic and intellectual circles, but his relative poverty required him to earn his living as a private tutor.[20] In addition, he worked as a journalist, standing in for the editor of the *Helsingfors Tidningar* newspaper in the summer of 1846. He was also interested in politics and poetry, and his studies progressed slowly.

In the student politics of the 1840s, Ehrström became known as a radical liberal. Wahlberg has pointed to an interesting speech Ehrström made in his Ostrobothnian student nation, on the occasion of the 1848 February revolution in France. Following Hegel, Ehrström gave an account of the history of Western civilization as progress. Although Hegel had emphasized the genealogy of the modern state and the role of great historical statesmen, Ehrström was more interested in the rise of human rights. Christ in his teachings had evoked the human rights of all persons, but the realization of this idea was slow. The Reformation and the French Revolution of 1789 were major steps forward. While Hegel had been largely satisfied with the status quo that followed the revolutions of 1789 and 1830, Ehrström argued that these events had only meant the realization of human rights for the middle class. After the events of 1848, it was clear that the principle of equality required a right to work and a right to education for everyone. As Wahlberg points out, one may discern a modern conception of social human rights in embryonic form in this argument.[21]

After graduating from the Faculty of Philosophy in 1846, Ehrström toyed with the idea of establishing a book shop or a publishing company, but friends and family members advised him to abandon the idea. Philosopher Johan Vilhelm Snellman (1806–81) thought that Ehrström had no business acumen and should stick to his earlier plan and focus on legal studies.[22] Ehrström followed Snellman's advice and studied law in the late 1840s and early 1850s. His progress was relatively slow, as he had to earn a living as a teacher at the Helsingfors Lyceum and as editor of the *Morgonbladet* in 1850 and for shorter periods at *Helsingfors Tidningar*. After graduating in law in 1852, Ehrström served as clerk in the town court of Helsinki. His journalistic work in the *Helsingfors Tidningar* shows an increasing interest in criminal law and criminal procedure. Accordingly, Ehrström wrote his theses for higher law degrees about these topics. The 1854 licentiate thesis compared the inquisitorial and adversarial forms of criminal procedure, concluding that the adversarial form was superior.[23] In 1856, Ehrström made what seems to have been his only visit outside of Finland and Russia, traveling to Germany via Sweden. The doctoral thesis he defended in 1859 was concerned with principles of incarceration as a method of punishment.[24]

Ehrström was not the only scholar investigating criminal law in Finland. His licentiate thesis was sharply criticized by another young scholar, Knut Ferdinand Lagus (1824–59), and a newspaper polemic followed.[25] When the chair of criminal law and legal history became open, Lagus and Ehrström were rivals in a bitter contest with a lot of intrigue within the small circle of professors of the Imperial Alexander University. A narrow majority of professors opted for Lagus, but when he died some months later, Ehrström was appointed professor in January 1860.[26] As professor of criminal law and legal history, he worked to bring Finnish legal scholarship up to the standards of the "civilized world." His lectures on criminal law combined ideas of German legal scholarship with his deep knowledge of Swedish-Finnish statutory law. Ehrström did not publish major research works as a professor, largely because of the increasing demands for his legal expertise by the government.

After the meetings of the Finnish Diet resumed in 1863, following a hiatus of more than fifty years, Ehrström's expertise was regularly called upon in law reform projects. He played an important role in drafting legislative reforms both as a politician and as an academic expert, particularly in the early stages of the comprehensive reform of Finnish criminal law. Ehrström's activity in law reform was not limited to criminal law, as he also championed legislation protecting the intellectual property of artists and writers as member of the diet representing the Imperial Alexander University in the Estate of the Clergy.[27] Although Ehrström's time as professor was dominated by teaching and law reform duties, he contributed to the development of legal scholarship as chair of the Finnish Legal Association (established in 1862) and editor of the journal of the association, the only Finnish law review (established in 1865). In 1877, Ehrström switched from his university career to judicial and governmental service as he was made senator of the Judicial Department of the Senate (the highest court). In 1886, he was appointed procurator, or senior legal adviser of the Senate who functioned as, among other things, the chief prosecutor, but he died soon after the appointment.

Liberalism, nationalism, and Christian humanitarianism

Ehrström was known as a moderate supporter of liberalism and Finnish nationalism. Like many of his friends and family members, he spoke Swedish as his first language and had limited proficiency in Finnish, but he was sympathetic toward the promotion of the Finnish language in official life. The liberal activities of his youth made him politically suspect in the view of some and complicated his appointment as professor as the decision ultimately rested with the emperor. Unlike many of his liberal contemporaries, however, Ehrström had a realist and loyalist attitude towards the Russian Empire. In this respect, he followed the example of his mentor Johan Vilhelm Snellman.[28] Ehrström's childhood years in St. Petersburg, along with other imperial connections, may have strengthened such an outlook; his uncle Otto Wilhelm Ehrström (1806–71) and brother-in-law Claes Gustaf Beyrath (1812–73) served as clergymen both in the Finnish church and in Russian military congregations.[29]

Christianity was also an important part of Ehrström's personality. He came from a religious family, and although family correspondence from his student years showed doubts about religious faith,[30] it seems that Ehrström soon overcame this crisis. As he was not a theologian, it is rather difficult to classify his views in detail. It seems probable, however, that his humanitarian, reform-minded Christian thinking was to some degree influenced by the theological currents of the time.

Christianity and prison reform in mid-nineteenth century

When Ehrström would speak about reform of criminal law to a general audience, he explicitly would invoke religious arguments.[31] This practice was not merely a strategy of persuasion. On the contrary, it reflected the personal convictions Ehrström wrote about in his private notebook in 1855 (*God's will is not the death of the sinner, but his conversion and repentance*).[32] He saw the reform of criminal law and the penal system as a religious question. Embracing rehabilitation or moral improvement (*bättring*, *Besserung*) as the goal of punishment was the Christian thing to do. For Ehrström, such reform was part of the religious revival of the nineteenth century that manifested itself both in overseas missionary work and in new forms of social work in old Christian countries.

In his journalism, Ehrström often wrote about punitive systems in other countries. During his period as the editor of *Morgonbladet* in 1850, the newspaper published an article comparing prisons operating according to the Philadelphia system and the Auburn system, concluding that the Philadelphia model was preferable because statistics pointed to better results for prisoners' mental health.[33] In the same year, Stepan Baranovski, a Ukrainian professor of Russian literature at the University of Helsinki, had published a survey of Finnish criminal statistics for 1842–47. In Baranovski's view, the major cause of crime in Finland was vagrancy, which he blamed, in turn, on idleness caused by alcohol and tobacco. Ehrström admitted that alcohol was involved with many criminal cases, but he did not take the tobacco argument seriously. Following Baranovski's logic, all small luxuries like coffee or sugar could be seen as detrimental to public health and waste of money. There was no evidence that a Spartan lifestyle would be beneficial for social progress. And even in the case of alcohol, the root cause was not the substance itself but, rather, inadequate education.[34]

What, then was education or "self-formation" (*bildning*[35])? Ehrström argued that true self-formation was not a matter of school knowledge about history, languages, or mathematics. Instead, it was awareness of one's duties and willingness to fulfill them. From this perspective, even the poorest could develop themselves, and education and religious upbringing were the most important supports of such development. While reform of popular education was necessary, religious education had to be transformed as well. For too long, the fear of punishment and the wrath of God had dominated the thinking about criminal offenders. Focusing on the love and charity of God supported a more rehabilitation-oriented modern criminal policy.

Yet religious education alone was not enough. Finland also had to overcome the challenge of pauperism. For Ehrström, the prospects of the country were promising, as Finland did not suffer from overpopulation. On the contrary, the country had great potential if the people were educated in practical skills such as handicraft and agriculture. Finland could be a "golden country" like California, then in international news because of the Gold Rush. Ehrström showed his Protestant colors, pointing out that Spaniards had lived in California for centuries without benefit, whereas Americans, with their vitality and resourcefulness, made gold useful immediately.

Ehrström's reference to California points to the American inspiration for his reformist activities. In his academic writings, he seldom referred to English-language sources that were generally not accessible in Finland; for information on the United Kingdom and the United States, he relied on German and Swedish publications, such as those of K. J. A. Mittermaier and Carl Schmidt.[36] However, his period as the editor of *Morgonbladet* in 1850 provides some evidence of his interest in America. The newspaper published extracts of the 1845–46 travelogue of the British lawyer-geologist Charles Lyell (1797–1875), previously published in the Swedish magazine *Bore*. Lyell was a well-known natural scientist and friend of Charles Darwin, even though he struggled with reconciling evolution and his religious faith. The passages Ehrström published in his newspaper included geological information but concentrated even more on social reform activities of states on the American East Coast. Lyell was an optimist who believed former slaves could be empowered by education in abolitionist-founded colleges, while some of his contemporaries believed biological racial differences would frustrate such attempts. Lyell also reported on progress in education of deaf and blind children, nonsectarian Christian social work and educational efforts, and the development of American public schools and teacher training colleges, where the role of women was often very important.[37]

I believe this reporting about American reform is significant when one investigates Ehrström's vision of prison reform and modern criminal law. It is a commonplace that American models such as the Auburn system and the Philadelphia system inspired European prison reform in the nineteenth century. It seems, however, that the American models are often approached in legal history as "legal transplants" or "best practices" that could be easily detached from their original social and cultural background. Of course, it can safely be assumed that few reformers in the Nordic countries or Continental Europe would have been inspired by the religion of Quakers in the strict sense of the word, even if many prison reform campaigners belonged to the Religious Society of Friends. Yet in a more general way, their influence ought to be studied as part of trans-Atlantic general Protestantism of the nineteenth century. This perspective ought to be investigated at least as seriously as the influence of Bentham's Panopticon, which Foucault and his followers have focused on rather obsessively.

In November 1858, Ehrström developed his ideas about prison reform in his public lecture on the history of incarceration. Although the "literary soirée" in Helsinki did not attract many listeners, the text was printed in the leading intellectual magazine of Finland, *Litteraturblad för allmän medborgerlig bildning*, and thus reached a nationwide audience.[38] Ehrström gave an account of the history of penal punishments until the modern reform projects of the eighteenth and nineteenth centuries. He assessed the Philadelphia and Auburn prison systems but was not satisfied with either of them. Instead, he was greatly impressed by the ideas of the eighteenth-century English prison reformer John Howard (1726–90) about the humane treatment of prisoners. According to Wahlberg, this ideology included the essential characteristics of the so-called Irish system, in which the prisoner could be granted release after completing progressive stages of imprisonment with good behavior. Wahlberg argues, however, that Ehrström could not have been aware of the works that made the system internationally famous, as they were published after 1858.[39]

Christianity and the foundations of criminal law

In 1859, Ehrström defended a professorial thesis on the theoretical foundations of imprisonment. The structure of the book reflects a Protestant reading of universal history, reminiscent of Ehrström's 1848 speech on the progress of human rights. While Roman Catholic influence in late antiquity and the medieval period represented an improvement of the morality guiding criminal punishment, it was only after the Protestant Reformation that the true meaning of free will had been understood.[40] As in other aspects of social life, however, there was no immediate change. Corporal punishments remained part of the prison regime for a long time. In the legislation of German states, "especially Catholic ones," many corporal sanctions remained in use. Ehrström mentions the 1852 Austrian criminal code, which retained many cruel punishments, such as fasting on bread and water, flogging, hard beds, and dark cells. By contrast, the new legislation of Protestant Prussia had abolished these cruel forms of punishment.[41]

Nevertheless, Ehrström's discussion of German criminal law doctrine and philosophy was not based on questions of confessional identity. Rather, he reviewed different theories of punishment presented in nineteenth-century German scholarship by jurists and philosophers. As Wahlberg notes, Ehrström sought to reconcile contrasting views in a new synthesis; in true Hegelian fashion, he rejected relative theories of punishments which saw utility through deterrence as the basis of criminal law.[42] State legislation had to rest on an absolute foundation of justice, and this applied to criminal law as well. Punishment had to follow the criminal act. But punishment was not only about retribution. The state had to make sure that the punishment actively facilitated the repentance of the criminal, not merely that it did not obstruct such change. In comparison with corporal sanctions, and naturally capital punishment, imprisonment was better suited to facilitate repentance and improvement. Even here, early forms of incarceration had been too cruel to awaken the good genius of the offender and let Christian gravity and leniency lead him to seek reconciliation with his own conscience. The organization of the prison and the mental and physical work (*sysselsättning*) expected of the offender should awaken him to self-control (*väcka honom till besinning*) and help him accustom himself to lawful ways of life (*vänja sig till rättslig vandel*).[43]

According to Wahlberg, Ehrström's insistence on rehabilitation as the main object of punishment was based on an idealistic Christian understanding of the necessity of true repentance of the criminal. In this respect, Ehrström did not accept the Hegelian approach, which regarded retribution as the main object.[44] As Whitman has noted, authors of the early German Protestant Enlightenment in the late seventeenth and early eighteenth centuries saw a link between religious toleration and the idea of moral improvement.[45] The Christian argumentation of Ehrström was significant for the future of Finnish criminal law reform. As Pihlajamäki has pointed out, in a small country like Finland, the sole expert of a specific subject, such as Ehrström in criminal procedure, could easily assume practically uncontested authority on law reform.[46] On a more general level, however, the Christian spirit that sustained Ehrström's vision of reform was of central importance in building a new consensus on criminal policy.

Law, religion, and the reform of criminal law: a new consensus

In the early 1860s, Ehrström belonged to a small group of criminal law reformers who managed to shift public opinion significantly in a few years. When Emperor Alexander II ordered the Imperial Senate of Finland to draft a legislative reform agenda for the Diet, the majority of the senators did not see a pressing need for major reforms of criminal law. Senator Johan Fredrik Bergbom (1796–1869) dissented from the majority. He had embraced the reformist ideas Ehrström had written about in newspaper articles in the 1850s. In 1860, Ehrström wrote several articles concerning the same theme, focusing on criticism of capital punishment, in *Helsingfors Tidningar*.[47]

Although Bergbom had no support from his colleagues in the Senate, his dissenting opinion was given to the members of the so-called January Committee, a consultative body elected by the Finnish estates to discuss the reform agenda in 1862. At the meeting of the January Committee, professor and later bishop Frans Ludvig Schauman (1810–77), a theologian best known as the drafter of the Church Act of 1869, endorsed Bergbom's proposals without reservations, and the cautious proposals of the Senate received little support. After the January Committee had classified criminal law reform as one of the most urgent issues for the upcoming Diet, Senator Bergbom was appointed chair of the drafting committee. Professor Ehrström was one of the committee members.[48]

That criminal law reformers could build a new consensus in a short period is significant. In contrast, as I have shown elsewhere, the reform of Finnish bankruptcy legislation in the 1860s was more difficult and controversial. The new legislation differed from contemporary foreign models in that it was not possible to limit the liability of the insolvent debtor by a composition accepted by the majority of the creditors. Critics of the legislation argued that the possibility of a fresh start for the insolvent debtor was important for the needs of commerce and industry and limiting such relief to cases where all creditors were unanimous stood in conflict to the standards of the civilized world. However, the legislation was defended with arguments underlining the impeccably modern and liberal principles of sanctity of property rights and individual freedom. Supporters of majority compositions realized that mere utility was not a sufficient argument in legal policy.[49]

In the case of bankruptcy reform, the "strictly legal" principles of sanctity of property rights and individual freedom were supported by jurists serving in the

Senate and appellate courts in particular. Thus, it was no small accomplishment for the criminal law reformers to change the course of legal policy making. They were aided by the fact that in criminal law, they could build on the foundations of the legal scholarship of Ehrström and other jurists, who had discussed the principles underlying modern forms of punishment from the 1850s onward. The support of theological authorities such as Schauman probably was also significant in building a new consensus that challenged the majority view of the old legal elites.

True Christianity or sloppy philanthropy? Reform of criminal law and the Finnish diet

Although the criminal law reform project took more than twenty-five years to be completed, several key reforms occurred already in the mid-1860s. At the Diet of 1863–64, the Finnish estates debated a government proposal on the leading principles of the reform project. At the Diet, Ehrström served as the secretary of the Legal Committee of the Diet, which coordinated the legislative work of the four estates. The proposal prepared by the committee advocated total abolition of capital punishment. The committee report admitted that most civilized nations had not yet taken such a step, possibly fearing the adverse effects of abolition. In Finland, however, where capital punishment had been commuted to transportation to Siberia since 1826, experience supported abolition.

The Estate of Clergy debated the proposal for criminal law reform at great length on February 15, 1864.[50] Many members were highly learned theologians, well-versed in exegetic analysis and systematic thought. The opinions of the clergy varied considerably, and there was no consensus about fundamental questions, such as the desirability of abolishing capital punishment or the main object of punishment. It seems that the clergy associated with revivalist movements tended to support a more traditional approach, focusing on retribution and accepting capital punishment for most serious offenses. Brothers Julius Immanuel Bergh (1810–78) and Johan Fredrik Bergh (1795–1866), important authorities within the Awakening revivalist movement, represented this view.[51] They also referred to Swedish political debate and the arguments of Bishop Gustav Daniel Björck (1806–88) in defense of capital punishment. In their view, rehabilitation could only be a secondary aim of criminal punishment. Principles of justice and the fundamental truths of Christianity required that retribution be the guiding principle.[52] This fundamental criticism of the reform proposals was countered by leading members of the estate, such as Frans Ludvig Schauman, who supported the progressive reform proposals, but there were also many other critics of reform.

The progressive proposals of Ehrström were defended by his uncle, the Reverend Otto Vilhelm Ehrström. He argued that the new proposal should not be regarded as reflecting "sloppy philanthropy," without any Christian principles, as some representatives had claimed. He argued that new legislation would represent a step from the Old Testament to the New, the love of Christ replacing the strict *ius talionis* of earlier times. He also quoted the parable of the barren fig tree (Luke 13:6–9) as an argument for giving the criminal a chance for true repentance.[53] Rev. Ehrström thus popularized the learned argument of his nephew for a more general audience.

The Estate of Peasants did not debate the proposal in such great detail, but religious arguments were an important part of their approach as well.[54] Some of the representatives with a background in religious revivalist groups were critical of proposals that increased the latitude for judges in sentencing criminals—the same problem that interests many contemporary American Christians.[55] Yet some of the peasant representatives also invoked the liberal arguments supporting values of the New Testament, and the majority of the estate supported the total abolition of capital punishment.

In the debates at the Estate of Nobility and the Estate of Burghers, the presence of many of the leading jurists of the country shaped the debate and gave less room for religious arguments in the strict sense. Tension existed in the Estate of Nobility between the conservative views of older members and the progressive criminal policy of the younger members. The leading voice for reform was Adolf Grotenfelt (1822–92), the university secretary, who had been a member of the drafting committee chaired by Bergbom.[56] When one of the leading conservatives, Baron Karl Johan Carpelan (1811–93), had invoked the Bible in support of capital punishment, Grotenfelt argued that Christianity had surpassed the punishments of the Mosaic Law.[57] In the following years, Grotenfelt continued his cooperation with Ehrström in criminal law and prison reform. At the Estate of Burghers, the discussion was dominated by judicial burgomasters and other town court judges. The merchant members who made up the majority of the estate trusted the judgment of the judiciary in legal policy. The estate endorsed the abolition of capital punishment unanimously. As Blomstedt argues, it seems the town court judges had embraced the reformist views of Ehrström.[58]

Implementing the criminal law reforms—the Finnish prison association between church, state, and civil society

The partial reforms of criminal law enacted in 1866 came into force in 1870. This change was accompanied by reforms of prison administration and an ambitious program to build modern prisons. Ehrström was much involved in these projects and cooperated with the first inspector of prisons, Adolf Grotenfelt, who later headed the Prison Administration Board established in 1881. Both men were also active in the Prison Association (*Fängelseföreningen*), a semiofficial organization founded in 1870. The association cooperated with prison authorities in the religious education of prisoners and tried to facilitate their reintegration into society. This nongovernmental social work was meant to implement the ideals of the criminal law reforms, as the authorities did not have sufficient resources.

The association did not receive any state subsidies; however, when the emperor confirmed its charter, it was given the right to collect Sunday collections twice a year in churches around the country. This is an illuminating example of how misleading it is to say the Church Law of 1869 would have "separated" church and state in Finland. The annual meetings of the association were organized in the Old Church of Helsinki, and the program always included religious elements.[59] The Prison Association took much guidance from Germany, where the Lutheran minister Theodor Fliedner (1800–64) had been active in prison reform through more general social work and home-missionary efforts (*innere Mission*). Board members of the Prison Association included influential Finnish theologians known as active proponents of home-missionary work, among them Gabriel Mauritz Waenerberg (1818–87), a senior education official in the Senate, and Herman Råbergh (1838–1920), professor and later bishop.[60]

Conclusion

The reform of Finnish criminal law and prisons during the late nineteenth century is an interesting phenomenon. The practical work of the Prison Association was often a disappointment for its more idealistic members. Recruiting volunteers for social work in prisons proved difficult, and the results of the efforts toward reintegration of prisoners into society were often disappointing. On the other hand, the efforts themselves are worth noting. The Finnish state invested heavily in building modern prisons, and Finnish experts participated actively in international cooperation in the field. For a small and poor country that experienced a devastating famine in the late 1860s, none of this was predictable. The reformers and activists of the period were living in a period of transition, when the moral leadership of the church was increasingly questioned, but when the church could still play an important role in shaping and implementing social reforms.

Among scholars of comparative criminal justice, Nordic countries have a "reputation for humane prisons."[61] In his analysis of this "Scandinavian exceptionalism," John Pratt points to two key characteristics of penal policy in the region. First, the imprisonment rate is relatively low. Second, because prison restricts freedom, "it is recognized that going to prison is itself the punishment for crime; prison conditions can then approximate to life outside as far as possible, rather than being allowed to degrade and debase all within."[62] Pratt argues that the roots of this exceptional approach can be found in more general features of Scandinavian/Nordic societies, such as strong state bureaucracies, high levels of social capital, and the egalitarian and homogeneous origin of the nation.[63] One of the historical factors behind homogenous societies is the religious uniformity of the Lutheran countries

While the characteristic features of Nordic societies are generally associated with the dominant cultural role of Lutheran "folk churches," the connection between confessional culture and modern criminal law is not obvious. After all, the modern punitive systems of Nordic countries emerged in the nineteenth and twentieth centuries and might be analyzed in the context of modernization and secularization. Yet historians and social scientists increasingly underscore the importance of the Lutheran tradition in modern Nordic societies. As American economist Robert Nelson argues in his recent comparative analysis of the topic, "a Lutheran ethic provided a powerful normative foundation" that underlay the rise of Nordic welfare states in the twentieth century, even if twentieth-century scholars mostly ignored the religious factor. [64] While Nelson does not focus on criminal policy and prison management, his arguments point to intriguing questions for future research. The Christian and specifically Lutheran spirit that Karl Gustaf Ehrström saw as the guiding principle of criminal law reform may live on in the Nordic penal policies of the twenty-first century.

Notes

1 I would like to thank Sofia Söderholm for her research assistance.
2 Lars-Folke Landgrén, "Ehrström, Karl Gustaf (1822–1886)," *Suomen kansallisbiografia 2*, ed. Matti Klinge et al., Studia biographica 3:2 (Helsinki: Suomalaisen Kirjallisuuden Seura, 2003), 496–97.
3 For an overview of the making of the Criminal Code of 1889, see Raimo Lahti, "Criminal Sanctions in Finland: A System in Transition," *Scandinavian Studies in Law* 21 (1977): 119–57, 122–27.
4 David Kirby, *A Concise History of Finland* (Cambridge: Cambridge University Press, 2006), 67–121. On the Finnish law reforms during the period, see Jukka Kekkonen, "The 'Golden Age of Legislation' in Finland 1863–79: Judicial Reforms in a Societal Context," *Russian Law Journal* 2 (2014): 63–77.
5 James Q. Whitman, "The Transition to Modernity," in *The Oxford Handbook of Criminal Law*, eds. Markus D. Dubber and Tatjana Hörnle (Oxford: Oxford University Press, 2014), 84–110, 84–86.
6 G[ustaf]. E[hrström],"Några blad ur fängelsernas historia," *Litteraturblad för allmän medborgerlig bildning* 12/1858: 536–55.
7 Heikki Pihlajamäki, *Evidence, Crime, and the Legal Profession: The Emergence of Free Evaluation of Evidence in the Finnish Nineteenth-century Criminal Procedure*, Rättshistoriskt bibliotek 54 (Lund: Institutet för rättshistorisk forskning, 1997), 215–30.
8 For the political developments, see Yrjö Blomstedt, "Rikoslakireformin ensimmäiset vaiheet vuoden 1866 osittaisuudistuksiin saakka," *Historiallinen arkisto* 59 (Turku: Suomen Historiallinen Seura, 1964): 422–517.
9 Markus Wahlberg, "Punishment as Ideal Reconciliation and Real Regeneration: Karl Gustaf Ehrström's Interpretation and Criticism of Hegel's Theory of Punishment." In *Right, Morality, Ethical Life. Studies in G. W. F. Hegel's Philosophy of Right*, ed. Jussi Kotkavirta (Jyväskylä: University of Jyväskylä, 1997), 5–29.
10 Markus Wahlberg, *Kaikki rangaistus pitää olla parannukseksi. Professori, senaattori ja Suomen rikosoikeuden uudistaja Karl Gustaf Ehrströmin elämä ja tuotanto. Ensimmäinen osa.* (Helsinki: Oikeustieteellinen tiedekunta, Helsingin yliopisto, 2017). The Swedish-language publication *Den finska straffrättsvetenskapens födelse I. Calonius, Ehrström och den finska straffrättsvetenskapens födelse* (Helsingfors: Juridiska fakulteten vid Helsingfors universitet, 2003) includes an edition of Ehrström's lectures as well as an extensive biographical introduction.
11 For an English-language survey, see Markku Heikkilä and Simo Heininen, *A History of the Finnish Church* (Helsinki: Suomalaisen Kirjallisuuden Seura, 2016).
12 Eino Murtorinne, *Suomen kirkon historia 3: Autonomian kausi 1809–1899* (Helsinki: WSOY, 1992), 218–20.
13 Heikkilä and Heininen, *A History of the Finnish Church*, 127–29.

14 Eino Murtorinne, *Suomen kirkon historia 3*, 206–09. Erkki Kansanaho, *Sisälähetys ja diakonia Suomen kirkossa 1800–luvulla* (Pieksämäki: Suomen kirkon sisälähetysseura, 1960), 69–71.
15 L. L. Laurén, *Sammanställning af de viktigaste kyrkohistoriska fakta i Finland : ett försök att framställa finska kyrkans öden* (Helsingfors: K.E. Holm, 1875), 108. Murtorinne, *Suomen kirkon historia 3*, 254–69.
16 James Q. Whitman, 'Equality in Criminal Law: The Two Divergent Western Roads," *The Journal of Legal Analysis* 1 (2009): 119–65, 147–50.
17 Johanna Wassholm, *Svenskt, finskt och ryskt. Nationens, språkets och historiens dimensioner hos E. G. Ehrström 1808–1835*, Skrifter utgivna av Svenska litteratursällskapet i Finland 731 (Helsingfors: Svenska litteratursällskapet i Finland, 2014). Wahlberg, *Kaikki rangaistus*, 20–37.
18 Seija Lappalainen, "Ehrström, Fredrik August (1801–1850)," *Suomen kansallisbiografia 2*, eds. Matti Klinge et al., Studia biographica 3:2 (Helsinki: Suomalaisen Kirjallisuuden Seura, 2003), 494–96. Wahlberg, *Kaikki rangaistus*, 37–39.
19 Tarja-Liisa Luukkanen, *Axel Adolf Laurell ja Oikean teologian myytti* (Oulu: Oulun yliopisto, 2016), 127–29.
20 Wahlberg, *Kaikki rangaistus*, 46–58.
21 Wahlberg, *Kaikki rangaistus*, 73–75.
22 Wahlberg, *Kaikki rangaistus*, 63–64.
23 Karl Gustaf Ehrström, *Om företrädet emellan ackusations- och inqvisitionsförfarandet i brottmålsprocessen* (Helsingfors: Frenckell, 1854).
24 Karl Gustaf Ehrström, *Om principen för fängelsestraffets ordnande* (Helsingfors: Frenckell, 1859).
25 Wahlberg, *Kaikki rangaistus*, 114–20.
26 Wahlberg, *Den finska straffrättsvetenskapens födelse*, Lars Björne, *Brytningstiden. Den nordiska rättsvetenskapens historia II. 1815-1870* (Rättshistoriskt bibliotek, band 58, Lund: Institutet för rättshistorisk forskning, 1998), 214–17.
27 Landgrén, "Ehrström, Karl Gustaf."
28 Kirby, *A Concise History of Finland*, 117–18.
29 See the entries in the register of students at the Royal Academy of Turku, later Imperial Alexander University (1640–1852). Yrjö Kotivuori, *Ylioppilasmatrikkeli 1640–1852*. Internet publication, 2005. https://ylioppilasmatrikkeli.helsinki.fi [Accessed September 16, 2018.]
30 Wahlberg, *Kaikki rangaistus*, 49–51.
31 Ehrström,"Några blad."
32 "Gud vill icke syndares död, utan att han sig omvänder och bättrar." Cited in Markus Wahlberg, "Karl Gustaf Ehrström – en biografisk skiss." In Karl Gustaf Ehrström, *Föreläsningar över straffrättens allmänna läror*, ed. Markus Wahlberg (Helsingfors: Helsingfors universitet, 1994), 1–45, 27–28.
33 "Om olika fängelsesystemer," *Morgonbladet* November 25, November 28, and December 2, 1850.
34 "Om brott och uppfostran." *Morgonbladet* October 7, October 10, and October 17, 1850.
35 The Swedish word *bildning*, equivalent to the German *Bildung*, is difficult to translate into English.
36 See Kjell Å. Modéer, "Transatlantic Intercultural Legal Communication in the 19th Century: K.J.A. Mittermaier and the Schmidt Brothers, Carl and Gustavus," *Journal of Civil Law Studies* 8:2 (2015): 409–41. On the influence of Mittermaier in Finland – often channeled through Swedish law reviews – see Blomstedt, "Rikoslakireformin ensimmäiset vaiheet," 436–37.
37 "Charles Lyell's besök i Amerika åren 1845, 46," *Morgonbladet* (August 8, 12, 19, 22, 26, and 29, 1850).

38 Ehrström, "Några blad." (Information about the low attendance is given by Wahlberg, *Kaikki rangaistus*, 148.)
39 Wahlberg, *Kaikki rangaistus*, 148–53.
40 Ehrström, *Om principen för fängelsestraffets ordnande*, 17–18. "Det var den utaf protestantismen framkallade bättre insigten uti menniskans vilja, som sålunda gjorde sig gällande samt sedermera också förskaffade sig inflytande på lagstiftningen." (18).
41 Ehrström, *Om principen för fängelsestraffets ordnande*, 18.
42 See the much more sophisticated discussion in Wahlberg, *Kaikki rangaistus*, 163–77.
43 Ehrström, *Om principen för fängelsestraffets ordnande*, 78.
44 Markus Wahlberg, "G.W.F. Hegelin ja K.G. Ehrströmin rangaistusteorian ykseydestä eroavuudessaan," in *Rikosoikeudellisia kirjoitelmia VI: Rikosoikeuden juhlavuonna 1989*, ed. Raimo Lahti (Helsinki: Suomalainen Lakimiesyhdistys, 1989), 493–522.
45 James Q. Whitman, "The Opposition to Public Punishment in Germany: At the Christian Sources," in *Grundlagen des Rechts. Festschrift für Peter Landau zum 65. Geburtstag*, eds. Richard H. Helmholz, Paul Mikat, Jörg Müller, and Michael Stolleis, Rechts- und Staatswissenschaftliche Veröffentlichungen der Görres-Gesellschaft, n. F., Bd. 91 (Paderborn: Schöningh, 2000), 759–76, 768–73.
46 Pihlajamäki, *Evidence*, 230.
47 "Dödsstraffets vanmakt," *Helsingfors Tidningar* (March 31, 1860); Om straf till lifvet och straff för bättring," *Helsingfors Tidningar* (April 28, 1860); "Ännu om straff och bättring," *Helsingfors Tidningar* (May 29, 1860).
48 Blomstedt, "Rikoslakireformin ensimmäiset vaiheet," 447–58.
49 Jussi Sallila, "Insolvency, Commercial Utility and Principles of Justice: The Making of Bankruptcy Law in Sweden and Finland, ca. 1680-1868," PhD dissertation, University of Helsinki, 2015.
50 The debate takes up eighty-eight pages in book form. *Prestesståndets protokoll vid Landtdagen i Helsingfors* 1863–1864 II, 471–559.
51 Blomstedt, *Rikoslakireformin ensimmäiset vaiheet*, 486.
52 *Högvördiga Prestesståndets Pleni-protokoll vid Landtdagen i Helsingfors 1863–1864 II*, Helsingfors 1865, xx.
53 *Prestesståndets protokoll 1863–1864 II.*
54 Estate of Peasants, session of February 22, 1864. *Suomen Talonpoikaissäädyn keskustelupöytäkirjat. 1863–1864*, 285–89.
55 Whitman, "Equality in Criminal Law."
56 Estates of Nobility, session of February 15, 1864. *Protokoll förda hos Finlands Ridderskap och adel vid Landtdagen i Helsingfors åren 1863–1864 III* (), 594–656. Blomstedt, *Rikoslakireformin ensimmäiset vaiheet*, 484–85.
57 *Protokoll förda hos Finlands Ridderskap och adel vid Landtdagen*, 635–36.
58 Estate of Burghers, session of February 17, 1864. *Protokoll fördt hos välloffliga borgareståndetl å Landtdagen i Helsingfors 1863–1864 II*, 506–33. Blomstedt, *Rikoslakireformin ensimmäiset vaiheet*, 487.
59 Axel af Forselles, *Fängelseföreningen i Finland 1870–1920: en kort redogörelse för dess tillkomst, utveckling och verksamhet* (Helsingfors: Fängelseföreningen, 1920), [3]-11.
60 Kansanaho, *Sisälähetys ja diakonia*, 74–78, 132–36.
61 Doran Larson, "Why Scandinavian Prisons Are Superior," *The Atlantic* (September 23, 2013). https://www.theatlantic.com/international/archive/2013/09/why-scandinavian-prisons-are-superior/279949/ [Accessed on August 4, 2020]
62 John Pratt, "Scandinavian Exceptionalism in an Era of Penal Excess: Part I: The Nature and Roots of Scandinavian Exceptionalism," *The British Journal of Criminology* 48, Issue 2 (March 2008): 119–37.

63 Pratt, "Scandinavian Exceptionalism," 137.
64 Robert H. Nelson, *Lutheranism and the Nordic Spirit of Social Democracy: A Different Protestant Ethic* (Aarhus: Aarhus University Press, 2017), 23.

Bibliography

Björne, Lars, *Brytningstiden. Den nordiska rättsvetenskapens historia II. 1815–1870.* Rättshistoriskt bibliotek, 58, [Institutet för rättshistorisk forskning] Lund, 1998.

Blomstedt, Yrjö, "Rikoslakireformin ensimmäiset vaiheet vuoden 1866 osittaisuudistuksiin saakka," *Historiallinen arkisto* 59, Suomen Historiallinen Seura: Turku (1964), 422–517.

E[hrström] G[ustaf], "Några blad ur fängelsernas historia," *Litteraturblad för allmän borgerlig bildning* (12/1858), 536–55.

Ehrström, Karl Gustaf, *Om företrädet emellan ackusations- och inqvisitions-förfarandet i brottmålsprocessen,* Helsingfors: Frenckell, 1854.

Ehrström, Karl Gustaf, *Om principen för fängelsestraffets ordnande,* Helsingfors: Frenckell 1859.

Forselles, Axel af, *Fängelseföreningen i Finland 1870–1920 En kort redogörelse för dess tillkomst, utveckling och verksamhet.* Helsingfors: Fängelseföreningen, 1920.

Heikkilä, Markku and Heininen, Simo, *A History of the Finnish Church,* Helsinki; Suomalaisen Kirjallisuuden Seura, 2016.

Helsingfors Tidningar, "Dödsstraffets vanmakt," March 31, 1860.

Helsingfors Tidningar, "Om straf till lifvet och straff för bättring," April 28, 1860.

Helsingfors Tidningar, "Ännu om straff och bättring," May 29, 1860.

Högvördiga Prestesståndets Pleni-protokoll vid Landtdagen i Helsingfors 1863–1864, vol. 2, Helsingfors, 1865.

Kansanaho, Erkki, *Sisälähetys ja diakonia Suomen kirkossa 1800 – luvulla.* Pieksämäki: Suomen kirkon sisälähetysseura (1960), 69–71.

Kekkonen, Jukka, "The Golden Age of Legislation" in Finland 1863–79: Judicial Reforms in a Societal Context, *Russian Law Journal* 2 (2014), 63–77.

Kirby, David, *A Concise History of Finland,* Cambridge: Cambridge University Press 2006, 67–121.

Kotivuori, Yrjö, *Ylioppilasmatrikkeli 1640 – 1852.* [Register of students at the Royal Academy of Turku, later Imperial Alexander University (1640–1852). Internet publication, 2005. https://ylioppilasmatrikkeli.helsinki.fi [Accessed on August 4, 2020]

Lahti, Raimo, "Criminal Sanctions in Finland: A System in Transition," *Scandinavian Studies in Law* 21 (1977), 119–57.

Landgrén, Lars Folke, "Ehrström, Karl Gustaf (1822–1886)," *Sumen kansallisbiografia 2,* Matti Klinge et al., (eds.), Studia biographica 3:2, Helsinki: Suomalaisen Kirjallisuuden Seura, 2003, 496-497.

Lappalainen, Seija, "Ehrström, Fredrik August (1801–1850)," Klinge, Matti et al. (eds.), *Suomen kansallisbiografia 2, Studia biographica* 3:2, Helsinki: Suomalaisen Kirjallisuuden Seura 2003, 494–96.

Larson Doran, "Why Scandinavian Prisons Are Superior," *The Atlantic,* September 23, 2013. https://www.theatlantic.com/international/archive/2013/09/why-scandinavian-prisons-are-superior/279949 [Accessed on August 4, 2020]

Laurén, L.L., *Sammanställning af de viktigaste kyrkohistoriska fakta i Finland: Ett försök att framställa finska kyrkans öden,* Helsingfors: K.E. Holm, 1875.

Luukkanen, Tarja-Liisa, *Axel Adolf Laurell ja Oikean teologian myytti*, Oulu: Oulun yliopisto, 2016.

Modéer, Kjell Å, "Transatlantic Intercultural Legal Communication in the 19th Century: K.J.A. Mittermaier and the Schmidt Brothers, Carl and Gustavus," *Journal of Civil Law studies* 8:2 (2015), 409–41.

Morgonbladet, [Helsingfors Morgonblad], "Carles Lyell's besök i Amerika åren 1845, 46," August 8, 12, 19, 22, 26, and 29, 1850.

Morgonbladet, [Helsingfors Morgonblad], "Om brott och uppfostran," October 7, 10, and 17, 1850.

Morgonbladet, [Helsingfors Morgonblad], "Om olika fängelsesystemer," November 25 and 28, and December 2, 1850.

Murtorinne, Eino, *Suomen kirkon historia 3: Autonomian kausi 1809 – 1899*, Helsinki: WSOY 1992.

Nelson, Robert H., *Lutheranism and the Nordic Spirit of Social Democracy: A Different Protestant Ethic*, Aarhus: Aarhus University Press, 2017.

Pihlajamäki, Heikki, *Evidence, Crime, and the Legal Profession: The Emergence of Free Evaluation of Evidence in Finnish Nineteenth-century Criminal Procedure,* Rättshistoriskt bibliotek 54, [Institutet för rättshistorisk forskning] Lund, 1997.

Pratt, John, "Scandinavian Exceptionalism in an Era of Penal Excess: Part I: The Nature and Roots of Scandinavian Exceptionalism," *The British Journal of Criminology* 48:2 (March 1, 2008), 119–37.

Protokoll förda hos Finlands Ridderskap och adel vid Landtdagen i Helsingfors 1863–1864. III, [Estates of Nobility] Session of February 15, Helsingfors 1864

Protokoll fördt hos välloffliga borgareståndet å Landtdagen i Helsingfors, 1863–1864. II. [Estate of Burghers] Session of February 17, 1864, Helsingfors 1864.

Sallila, Jussi, "Insolvency, Commercial Utility, and Principles of Justice: The Making of Bankruptcy Lawin Sweden and Finland, ca 1680–1868." [Ph.D. dissertation] University of Helsinki, 2015.

Suomen Talonpoikaissäädyn keskustelupöytäkirjat. 1863–1864, [Estates of Peasants, Session of February, 1864.]

Wahlberg, Markus, *Den finska straffrättsvetenskapens födelse I. Calonius, Ehrström och den finska straffrättsvetenskapens födelse,* Helsingfors: Juridiska fakulteten vid Helsingfors universitet, 2003.

Wahlberg, Markus, "G.W.F. Hegelin ja K.G. Ehrströmin rangaistusteorian ykseydestä eroavuudessaan". In: Raimo Lahti (ed.), *Rikosoikeudellisia kirjoitelmia VI: Rikosoikeuden juhlavuonna 1989*, Helsinki: Suomalainen Lakimiesyhdistys, 1989, 493–522.

Wahlberg, Markus, *Kaikki rangaistus pitää olla parannukseksi, Professori, senaattori ja Suomen rikosoikeuden uudistaja Karl Gustaf Ehrströmin elämä ja tuotanto. Ensimmäinen osa.* Helsinki: Oikeustieteellinen tiedekunta, Helsingin yliopisto, 2017.

Wahlberg, Markus, "Punishment as Ideal Reconciliation and Real Regeneration: Karl Gustaf Ehrström's Interpretation and Criticism of Hegel's Theory of Punishment," in Jussi Kotkavirta (ed.), *Right, Morality, Ethical Life. Studies in G.W.F. Hegel's Philosophy of Right,* Jyväskylä: University of Jyväskylä 1997, 5–29.

Wassholm, Johanna, *Svenskt, finskt och ryskt. Nationens, språkets och historiens dimensioner hos E.G. Ehrström 1808–1835.* [Skrifter utgivna av Svenska litteratursällskapet i Finland 731], Helsingfors: Svenska litteratursällskapet i Finland, 2014.

Wahlberg, Markus, "Karl Gustaf Ehrström – en biografisk skiss," in Wahlberg, Markus (ed.), Karl Gustaf Ehrström, *Föreläsningar över straffrättens allmänna läror.* Helsingfors: Helsingfors universitet, 1994, 1–45.

Whitman, James Q, "The Opposition to Public Punishment in Germany: At the Christian Sources," in Richard H. Helmholz, Paul Mikat, Jörg Müller and MichaelStolleis (eds.), *Grundlagen des Rechts. Festschrift für Peter Landau zum 65. Geburtstag,* Rechts- und Staatswissenschaftliche Veröffentlichungen der Görres-Gesellschaft, n.F., vol. 91, Paderborn Schöningh 2000, 759–76.

Whitman, James Q., "Equality in Criminal Law: The Two Divergent Western Roads," *The Journal of Legal Analysis* 1 (2009), 119–65.

Whitman, James Q., "The Transition to Modernity," in Markus D. Dubber and Tatjana Hörnle (eds.), *The Oxford Handbook of Criminal Law*, Oxford: Oxford University Press 2014, 84 110.

Part 5

Modernity

Secularism and positivism/ legal realism

17 Introduction

Anders Jarlert and Kjell Å Modéer

As the nineteenth century turned to the twentieth, the relation between the law and the Christian church became increasingly challenged in Europe. Social claims from political forces and increasingly strong labor unions formed the introduction to the modern social welfare state. In Germany of the Second Empire, a *Kulturkampf* (culture struggle) developed between the state and the Roman Catholic Church, as the state aimed to adopt laws designed to bring education and marriage under the control of the state.[1] German Chancellor Otto von Bismarck and his "white revolution"—in contrast to the red revolution of socialism—often spoke of the obligation of the state to take care of "the little poor man," *der kleine arme Mann.* In 1891, Pope Leo XIII, in the encyclica *Rerum Novarum*, or the Rights and Duties of Capital and Labor, addressed the condition of the working classes. This fundamental source of Catholic social teaching not only talked about the mutual duties between labor and capital but also rejected both socialism and unrestricted capitalism, while accepting the right to private property.

Beginning around 1890, there also emerged a common view on developing the concept of diaconia in Protestant churches. It turned from charity from the individual and communities, *sällskapsdiakoni* to a more commonly organized care for the needy. Now there was a common approach within the religious communities (*församlingsdiakoni*). On the local level, philanthropy became an important instrument, though now organized in a more public way. In the increasingly secularized Nordic societies, Christian philanthropy was replaced by social legal reforms in the early welfare state.[2]

Within theology as well as within law, the twentieth century introduced separation between theology and church, between idealistic, metaphysical legal constructs and positive law, and between law and politics. Torgny Segerstedts's doctoral disputation on the rise of polytheism at Lund[3] and Vilhelm Hägerström's inaugural lecture for his professorship in philosophy at Uppsala, in 1911,[4] are two examples of this new paradigm regarding modern antimetaphysical perspectives on law and religion before World War I.

As a consequence of modernity and its transformation of society (urbanism, industrialization, democracy) at the secular turn of 1900, the reform to harmonize Nordic family law was initiated in 1909. This reform resulted in similar legislation within family law in all of the Nordic countries from the end of the 1910s.[5] In Sweden, it was the last time the Church of Sweden had an impact on family law reform, with the proposal for compulsory mediation by the church before application to the courts for divorce.[6]

Nathan Söderblom (1866–1931), the Swedish archbishop from 1914 to 1931 and an international ecumenist, was a dominant representative of Swedish theology during the first decades of the twentieth century.[7] He was considered to be "quite old and quite new" at the same time. During his tenure, the church acquired a very national identity while at the same time opening to internationalism—especially towards the Baltic region, which in the midwar period became a part of the Swedish sphere of interest. At the same time, some regarded him as a cultural imperialist.[8] Söderblom's ecumenical movement, with its famous meeting in Stockholm in 1925, initiated the "Life and Work" movement and became a divine/sacral alternative to the League of Nations.[9]

In the realm of international public law, a quite new interpretation grew with modernity.[10] At the Uppsala School of Law, the law professors Vilhelm Lundstedt and Östen Undén were the most outspoken representatives in this discipline. Law and politics were regarded as related. Treaties had to be observed as positive law. Only bilateral—not universal—rights had to be observed.[11]

The democratic breakthrough around 1920 did not change anything related to the clerical and the legal professions in the Nordic countries. The Swedish Competence Act (*Behörighetslagen*) of 1923 still prohibited women from serving as church ministers as well as judges. In Sweden in the midwar period, the welfare-state concept was introduced in a positive way as the societal "folk home," including the persistence of equity and equality as "almost tedious themes" in social democratic propaganda.[12] Simultaneously, the spiritual "folk church" was established. In Denmark, this concept (*Folkekirken*) had greater significance, having been legally founded on the freedom of the local congregations since the 1840s. In Sweden, the concept emphasized the national church, whose ideas regarding society, people, and culture were reflected in the social events and tensions of modernity.[13]

The Uppsala school of legal realism within modern Swedish jurisprudence—represented principally by the professors Vilhelm Lundstedt, Östen Undén, and Karl Olivecrona—had its parallel within Lundensian theology, represented by the professors and bishops Anders Nygren and Gustaf Aulén. Both of them, however, claimed Söderblom especially as a source of the Lundensian system. This is because, in spite of the many differences between them, they shared many emphases: "the typological approach to religions, the uniqueness of God's revelation in Jesus Christ, the view of history as continuous and dramatic revelation, the rejection of the possibility of metaphysics, and the centrality of ecclesiology, among others."[14]

The democratic breakthrough in the Nordic countries appeared after the Great War. In Sweden, however, the Act of Eligibility (*Behörighetslagen*) of 1923, which granted men and women equal access to all professions in society, made two important exceptions regarding female judges and priests. Not until

1944 did female lawyers have the possibility of making a career in the Swedish judiciary. In Denmark, Bodil Dybdal (1901–92) pioneered as a female judge in the Copenhagen city court (1940) and on a court of appeal (1949), and she was appointed the first female justice on the Danish Supreme Court in 1953 (serving until 1970). The first female justice on the Norwegian Supreme Court, Lilly Bølviken, was appointed in 1968. In that same year, Ingrid Gärde Widemar pioneered as the first female justice on the Swedish Supreme Court, and Anna Greta Winberg was appointed as the first Swedish female chief district judge.[15]

Even though interest in ordaining female priests arose in the Scandinavian countries in the midwar period, this reform was not adopted until after World War II. In Sweden, professor Lydia Wahlström, an active suffragist, unsuccessfully had demanded this reform already in the 1910s. Denmark ordained its first female priest in 1948, while Sweden opened the way for this reform in 1958; the first female priests there were ordained in 1960. One year later, the first female priest in Norway was ordained. In Finland, the first female priest was not ordained until 1987, and the first female bishop was elected in 1993.

The Nuremberg Laws of 1935 in the German Third Reich brought the Scandinavian countries into a special relationship with Nazi Germany because of the Hague Convention of 1907. Sweden had ratified the convention, which bound signatories to recognize each other's internal laws, so Swedish clergy had to apply Nazi laws regarding marriages of German citizens. Denmark and Norway had not ratified the Hague Convention and felt free not to apply those laws before the German occupation in 1940.[16] The German-inspired intellectual climate, which since the late nineteenth century had dominated intellectual and cultural discourse, including that of the clergy and the judiciary, was the important context for this period in Nordic history.

During World War II, all the Nordic countries but Sweden were involved in hostilities. The clergy as well as the judiciary in those countries were brought into conflict with the state. Individual clergymen were engaged in political activities, and individual jurists demonstrated the autonomy of the judiciary or the legal profession. In Norway, the totalitarian political occupation resulted in clashes over interpretation of the constitution. The members of the Norwegian Supreme Court in 1940 refused to apply the laws of the occupier. They laid down their offices, as did the Norwegian bishops and most clergymen one year later, as far as duties toward the state. The judiciary in the commissarial Supreme Court of this period has recently been studied and given a more nuanced view, which holds that some justices on the court at this time upheld traditional legal principles adopted and implemented before the occupation.[17]

In Sweden, Bishop Gustaf Aulén[18] belonged to those Swedes who supported the Norwegian resistance against the Nazi occupation. He maintained close connections with the Norwegian bishop Eivind Berggrav—the Norwegian icon for the resistance movement among theologians.[19] Denmark also had individuals in the resistance—for example, the priest Kaj Munk (1899–1944). He was initially friendly to National Socialism, but turned to the resistance movement and was murdered by the Germans in 1944.[20]

After the war, legal purging became the rite of passage in many countries for the return to a democratic society and the rule of law. Such court proceedings took place in all the Nordic countries except Sweden, which, as a neutral country, never was involved in hostilities and had been the asylum for resisters in the other Nordic countries. These different experiences had a great impact on the development of the legal cultures and the secularization processes in the Nordic countries.

The institutionalized Meetings of Nordic Jurists (*Nordiska Juristmöten*) resumed after the war, and Nordic church leaders regained their status immediately after the war, in August 1945.[21] Nordic Lutheranism contrasted with the compromised German church. Several Nordic theologians (Eivind Berggrav, Regin Prenter, Gustaf Aulén, and Anders Nygren) expressed a distinct theological position for the need for a purge of the burdened Lutheranism in Germany.[22]

The Lundensian school of theology dominated the theological discourses of the 1930s and 1940s. Idealistic and positivistic movements clashed. The Lund professor of theology and later bishop Anders Nygren (1890–1978) published in 1930–36 his most-read work, *Agape and Eros.* In this classic of modern theology, Nygren delivered an analysis and evaluation of the most influential ideas about the essential meaning of the atonement and the sharp contrast between the two concepts of love: agape and eros. Nygren commented that numerous books had been written on the doctrinal details of Christianity, but few had tackled the idea at its heart—love. A parallel discourse was to be found within the law. The Swedish jurist Ivar Strahl in 1941 published an essay in which he questioned the strict positivistic Uppsala school of legal realism.[23]

In the spring of 1941, the Roman Catholic bishop of Sweden for the first time took part in a national conference of the Church of Sweden. In the fall of 1941, the Swedish archbishop Erling Eidem (1880–1972) and the Social Democratic speaker in the second chamber of the Parliament, August Säfström (1879–1960), met under the national slogan "The Swedish Line is the Christian Line."[24] The meeting included Swedish lawyers and clergy in a cultural Christianity which presumed loyalty not only to the state but also to the church. This double loyalty remained after the war. One example is the judges' oath included in the new procedural law, *Rättegångsbalken*, Chapter 4, section 11,[25] which was brought into force in 1948. This oath was principally identical to the oath in the Code of 1734, requiring the judge to serve "before God and his holy gospel" (*inför Gud och hans heliga evangelium*).

Nordic cooperation between the church and state law continued during the war, though in different forms. The Sweden-based Nordic Ecumenical Institute (Nordiska Ekumeniska Institutet) maintained important contacts with the resistance. Immediately after the war, this cooperation reached its peak. In West Germany, the construction of church buildings also reached a peak in the post-war period. In Scandinavia, there was a counterpart in the "small church movement." This movement had started in Copenhagen as early as the turn of the century but was realized on a broad scale in the Nordic countries when suburban areas grew after World War II. The churches in the city centers added supplementary venues in small churches close to community members in the suburbs.

On the other hand, after World War II international engagement was growing. The Lutheran World Federation was created in Lund in 1947, and the World Council of Churches was established in Amsterdam in 1948 with substantial Scandinavian participation.[26] The European Council was founded the same year and adopted its European Convention on Human Rights in 1950, which the following year was ratified by all the Nordic countries. The ecclesiastical Swedish jurist Göran Göransson is an important representative of the postwar generation who regarded the deep structures of ecclesiastical law as a requisite for the reform of the Swedish Church Law, adopted in 1992.[27]

Sweden, however, could not ratify the ECHR without adopting an act of religious freedom. This act was realized in 1951.[28] The most important paragraph for the modern Swedish citizen in this legislation regarded the negative freedom of religion, that is, the right not to have a religion—then, as now, a legislation of exception.

In Sweden, there were interesting discourses regarding the role of the church in modern society[29] as well as on belief and knowledge.[30] Archbishop Yngve Brillioth (1891–1959) argued that it was the jurists who should deal with the ecclesiastical law, not the theologians. Ecclesiastical law, however, was abolished in the curriculum of the Swedish law faculties and had to be studied at the faculties of theology.

In the aftermath of World War II, the Danish professor of constitutional law Alf Ross published his most-read book, *Why Democracy?*, in 1946.[31] It originated from the author's experiences of and reflections on the German occupation of Denmark, but it resulted in important discourses throughout the postwar decades. Ross was the most important representative of the Uppsala school of legal realism in Denmark. When his innovative but premature dissertation was declined in 1926 at Copenhagen University, he went to Uppsala, where Axel Hägerström inspired him. In 1929 Ross defended his dissertation in law successfully at Uppsala. He returned to Copenhagen and made an outstanding career at the Faculty of Law, where he was professor of international public law beginning in 1938 and was appointed professor of constitutional law in 1958.[32]

As a counterpoint to the influential legal realists and their antimetaphysical legal concepts, which dominated modern legal science in the Nordic countries after World War II, the professor of constitutional law Frede Castberg was the main figure. During and after the war, he related his scientific position to the concept of natural law and human rights in relation to positive law.[33]

The results of the Second Vatican Council of the Roman Catholic Church (1962–65) were important also for the Lutheran churches, as the liturgy was democratized—the altar often placed in the middle of the church. This democratization was also translated into the Nordic court systems, which abolished podiums in the courtrooms. The members of the court were placed on the floor, the better to conciliate the parties in private law cases.

In Europe, the 1960s have been called a decade of secularization. In Sweden, however, it was more the following decade that brought significant secularization of society. In the Swedish court system, oaths taken by witnesses were made on the Bible until 1970. After that, the Bibles were brought from the courtroom into the court's library and placed in the section of *Varia*.

Legal modernity also reached its peak in the 1970s. New democratic legislation was adopted in the Scandinavian countries within labor law, consumer law, and tenants' law for the common citizen. From the United States, legislation on affirmative action became an important influence on equality between the sexes.

Denmark got its first female Minister for Ecclesiastical Affairs in 1950, Bodil Koch (1903–1972). She worked not only for the modernization of the Danish church but also for the introduction of female clergy.[34] In Norway, a new church law was adopted in 1953.[35] In the same year, a dispute between Frede Castberg[36] and Eivind Berggrav[37] about the state's authority to decide on the teachings and internal integrity of the state church evolved. Berggrav claimed that his opponent's reasoning would have made impossible the church resistance to the National Socialist government during World War II.

Scandinavian postwar theology had an international reputation. Anders Nygren and Gustaf Aulén, the best-known representatives of Lundensian theology, also played a central role in implementing the transnational World Council of Churches, a part of Nathan Söderbolm's ecumenical heritage. Nygren held the first chair in the Lutheran World Federation, established in Lund in 1947. In Denmark, it was the theologians at Aarhus University who gained international renown, foremost among them K.E. Løgstrup, with his deep roots in Grundtvigianism, who also inspired Gustaf Wingren, in Lund, to his theology of creation. In a period when most Protestants adjusted to secularization, Løgstrup and Wingren both were regarded as theologians adjusting their creation theology to Luther and Grundtvig. [38] Løgstrup consequently was called "the theologian of the welfare state."[39]

The new church law in Sweden, adopted in 1992,[40] replaced the one from 1686. The old church law had been valid for more than three centuries, but the new one was abolished already in 1998, due to the new relation between the state and the Church of Sweden.[41] Legislation in 1996 had made membership in the church related to baptism (and no longer to citizenship). In Norway, church membership is connected to baptism, according to the church law of 1996, and in Denmark, baptism has been strongly emphasized in congregational life since the nineteenth century, and was confirmed as the basis of church membership in 1991/92.

Another aspect of secularization and the growing autonomy of the church became the extensive discourse on separation between church and state. In Sweden, this project was initiated in the 1950s and, after decades of governmental and synodal investigations, reached its conclusion in 1998[42] with the adoption of a new relationship in 1998[43] and brought into practice in 2000. A special law of the Swedish church stated that the church should be democratic and nationwide. This means that the state still makes claims regarding the majority church in Sweden.

After the fall of the Iron Wall, the Maastricht Treaty of 1992 opened the way for the foundation of the European Union. Referenda in the Nordic countries in 1994 resulted in membership for Finland, Sweden, and Denmark, while Norway decided to stay outside the union. The Nordic countries also incorporated the ECHR as national law. The jurisdictions of the national supreme courts in the Nordic countries have been replaced by those of the transnational European Court of Justice in Luxemburg and the European Court of Human Rights in Strasbourg. The court in Strasbourg has been especially important for its decisions regarding freedom of religion—a problem of increasing importance in the Norwegian multireligious society.

The changes in the relationship between church and state in Sweden resulted in an investigation of this matter in Norway as well, and later also in Denmark. The result in Norway was a constitutional change in 2008. The church is still a state church, but the church has great internal autonomy and is today appointing its bishops and clergy. In Denmark, however, the study of this matter in 2014 led to no changes.

For historical reasons, Finland has two state churches—the Lutheran majority church and the Orthodox minority church. Here, too, legislation has changed the influence of the state, and the president of the country no longer appoints bishops in the Finnish Evangelical Lutheran Church.

The positions of free churches and revival movements differ extensively among the Nordic countries. In Denmark, the Lutheran folk church dominates the scene, with its different movements (Grundtvigians, Inner Mission, etc.). In Norway, the mission organizations are very strong, most of them within the national church. In Sweden, the very strong revival movements form an active component of the Lutheran church, although they have their own meetings as well. In Sweden, the free churches are much stronger than in the other Nordic countries, due to the split of the Evangelical movement in the nineteenth century.

Europe after 1989 has become a postsecular entity: religion is back in the public sphere. This is true to a great extent also in the Nordic countries. The visits of Pope John Paul II to Uppsala in 1989 and of Pope Francis to Lund in 2016, which aimed to strengthen relations between the Roman Catholic Church and the Protestant countries, are one example of the new trends. The attitudes toward the pope and the Reformation jubilees differ, however, with Denmark nurturing its special form of Danish Lutheranism, and a more ecumenical attitude prevailing in Sweden. The Porvoo Communion, created in 1992 by mainly northern European Anglican and Lutheran churches, establishes full communion among the 15 church bodies. All of the Nordic churches joined the Porvoo Communion from the start, with the exception of the Danish church, which signed the Porvoo declaration in 2010.

In the new millennium, and especially after the migration wave from Eritrea, Somalia, Afghanistan, and the Middle East, the societies in the Nordic countries can be identified as multicultural and multireligious. The state Lutheran churches and the Church of Sweden are still majority churches, with church membership in Sweden numbering 5.9 million (57.7 percent of the population), in Norway 3.75 million members (ca. 71 percent), in Denmark (the Danish Folk Church) 4.3 million members (74.7 percent), and the Evangelical Lutheran Church of Finland 3.8 million members (69.7 percent).

Notes

1 Stefan Ruppert, *Kirchenrecht und Kulturkampf: Historische Legitimation, politische Mitwirkung und wissenschaftliche Begleitung durch die Schule Emil Ludwig Richters* [Ecclesiastical Law and the Struggle between Church and State. Historical Legitimation, Political Cooperation and the Influence of the Emil Ludwig Richter School] (Mohr Siebeck: Tübingen, 2000).
2 Jørn Henrik Petersen, "Staten, kirken og velfærden," in *Reformationen i dansk kirke og kultur*, eds. Niels Henrik Gregersen and Carsten Back Nielsen, Vol. 3 (Odense: Syddansk Universitetsforlag, 2017), 163ff.
3 Eva Stohlander Axelsson, *Ett brännglas för tidens strålar: Striden om Torgny Segerstedts docentur 1903 (Lund: Arcus, 2001).*
4 Max Lyles, *A Call for Scientific Purity: Axel Hägerström's Critique of Legal Science (Stockholm: Rättshistoriskt forskning, 2006).*
5 Henrik Tamm, *De nordiske juristmøder 1872–1972: Nordisk Retssamvirke gennem 100 År* (Copenhagen: Nyt Nordisk Forlag Arnold Busck, 1972), 165ff.
6 Olof Sundby, *Luthersk äktenskapsuppfattning. En studie i den kyrkliga äktenskapsdebatten i Sverige efter 1900* (Stockholm: Svenska Kyrkans Diakonistyrelses Bokförlag, 1959).
7 Jonas Jonson, *Jag är bara Nathan Söderblom, satt till tjänst: En biografi* (Stockholm: Verbum, 2014).
8 Lars Österlin, *Korstågen till Kina. Linjer i protestantisk kinamission* (Malmö: Sekel, 2005); Kjell Blüchert, *The Church as Nation: A Study in Ecclesiology and Nationhood* (Frankfurt am Main: P. Lang, 2000).
9 Sara Gehlin, "Nathan Söderblom, freden och ekumeniken. En analys av Nathan Söderbloms definition av begreppen fred och ekumenik, med utgångspunkt från fredsuppropet För fred och kristlig gemenskap," *Kyrkohistorisk årsskrift* 108 (2008): 59ff.
10 The Uppsala school of legal realism; see below.
11 Kjell Å Modéer, "Transparens och djupstruktur: Folkrätten i rättshistorien," in *Rätten och rättsfamiljer i ett föränderligt samhälle—rättshistoriskt och komparativt. Vänbok till Rolf Nygren*, ed. Maarit Jänterä Jareborg and Mats Kumlien (Uppsala: Iustus Förlag, 2011), 305 ff.
12 David Bradley, "Women's Right to Work: Social and Private Security in the Nordic Countries and in the European Union," in *The Nordic Countries and Europe: 3, Evaluations,* ed. Krister Ståhlberg (Copenhagen: Nordic Council of Ministers, n.d.), 59f.
13 Urban Claesson, "Folkhemmets kyrka: Harald Hallén och folkkyrkans genombrott. En studie av socialdemokrati, kyrka och nationsbygge med särskild hänsyn till perioden 1905–1933" [A Church for a Social Democratic Nation: Harald Hallén and the emergence of the Swedish Folk Church. A study in Social Democracy, Church and Nation-building with specific interest in the period 1905–1933], Thesis, Uppsala University, 2004; Sven Thidevall, *Folkkyrkan, vision och verklighet. Ett folkkyrkligt reformprograms öden 1928–1932* (Stockholm: Verbum, 2000).
14 Lundensian theology, http://people.bu.edu/wwildman/bce/mwt_themes_720_lund.htm.
15 Kjell Å Modéer, *Den svenska domarkulturen: Europeiska och nationella förebilder* (Lund: Corpus Iuris, 1994).
16 Anders Jarlert, *Judisk "ras" som äktenskapshinder i Sverige: effekten av Nürnberglagarna i Svenska kyrkans statliga funktion som lysningsförrättare 1935–1945* (Malmö: Sekel, 2006).
17 Hans Petter Graver, *Okkupasjionstidens Høyesterett* (Pax Forlag: Oslo, 2019).
18 See Anders Jarlert's chapter on Gustaf Aulén in this volume.
19 See Egil Morland's chapter on Eivind Berggrav in this volume.
20 Per Stig Møller, *Munk* (Copenhagen: Gyldendal, 2000).

21 Jens Holger Schjørring, "Introduktion," in *Nordiske folkekirker i opbrud: National identitet og international nyorientering efter 1945*, ed. Jens Holger Schjørring (Århus: Aarhus Universitetsforlag, 2001), 11ff.
22 Ibid., 29.
23 Ivar Strahl, "Idealism och realism i rättsvetenskapen," *Svensk Juristtidning* (1941): 302ff.
24 Sverker Oredsson, *Jönköpingsperspektiv på världen: JP 1935–1970* (Stockholm: Atlantis, 2015).
25 The Swedish Code of Judicial Procedure (1942:740).
26 See Kjell Å Modéer's chapter on Göran Göransson in this volume.
27 Ibid.
28 Religious Freedom Act (1951:680).
29 Ruben Josefson and Per Stjernquist, *Rättens ursprung och grund* (Stockholm: Svenska Bokförlaget, 1961).
30 Ingemar Hedenius, *Tro och vetande* [Belief and Knowledge] (Stockholm, 1949).
31 Alf Ross, *Hvorfor Demokrati?* (Copenhagen: Munksgaard, 1946).
32 Knud Waaben, "Alf Ross," in *Dansk Biografisk Leksikon*, 3rd ed. (Copenhagen: Gyldendal, 1979–84).
33 See Kjell Å Modéer's chapter on Frede Castberg in this volume.
34 Birgitte Possing, "Bodil Koch, 1903–1970," *Dansk kvindehistorisk Leksikon*, https://www.kvinfo.dk/side/170/bio/573/
35 Lov av den 29. april 1953 om den norske kirkes ordning.
36 Modéer, chapter on Castberg in this volume.
37 Morland, chapter on Berggrav in this volume.
38 Bengt Kristensson Uggla, "Gustaf Wingren and Scandinavian Creation Theology," in *Reformation Theology for a Post-secular Age: Løgstrup, Prenter, Wingren, and the Future of Scandinavian Creation Theology*, ed. Niels Henrik Gregersen, Bengt Kristensson Uggla, and Tryggve Wyller (Göttingen: Vandenhoeck & Ruprecht, 2017), 94.
39 Niels Henrik Gregersen, "K.E. Løgstrup and Scandinavian Creation Theology," in Gregersen et al., *Reformation Theology for a Post-Secular Age*, 46f.
40 Kyrkolag (1992:300).
41 Lag (1998:1592) om införande av lagen (1998:1591) om Svenska kyrkan.
42 Sören Ekström, *Makten över kyrkan. Om Svenska kyrkan, folket och staten* (Stockholm: Verbum Förlag, Stockholm, 2003).
43 Lag (1998:1591) om Svenska kyrkan.

Bibliography

Axelsson, Eva Stohlander. *Ett brännglas för tidens strålar: Striden om Torgny Segerstedts docentur 1903*. Lund: Arcus, 2001.

Blüchert, Kjell. *The Church as Nation: A Study in Ecclesiology and Nationhood*. Frankfurt am Main: P. Lang, 2000.

Bradley, David. "Women's Right to Work: Social and Private Security in the Nordic Countries and in the European Union." In *The Nordic Countries and Europe: 3, Evaluations*. Edited by Krister Ståhlberg. Copenhagen: Nordic Council of Ministers, n.d.

Claesson, Urban. "Folkhemmets kyrka: Harald Hallén och folkkyrkans genombrott. En studie av socialdemokrati, kyrka och nationsbygge med särskild hänsyn till perioden 1905–1933." Thesis, Uppsala University, 2004.

Ekström, Sören. *Makten över kyrkan. Om Svenska kyrkan, folket och staten*. Stockholm: Verbum Förlag, Stockholm, 2003.

Gehlin, Sara. "Nathan Söderblom, freden och ekumeniken. En analys av Nathan Söderbloms definition av begreppen fred och ekumenik, med utgångspunkt från fredsuppropet För fred och kristlig gemenskap." *Kyrkohistorisk årsskrift* 108 (2008): 59ff.

Graver, Hans Petter. *Okkupasjonstidens Høyesterett.* Pax Forlag: Oslo, 2019.

Gregersen, Niels Henrik. "K.E. Løgstrup and Scandinavian Creation Theology." In Gregersen et al., *Reformation Theology for a Post-Secular Age: Løgstrup, Prenter, Wingren, and the Future of Scandinavian Creation Theology.* Göttingen: Vandenhoeck & Ruprecht, 2017.

Gregersen, Niels Henrik, Bengt Kristensson Uggla, and Tryggve Wyller, eds. *Reformation Theology for a Post-Secular Age: Løgstrup, Prenter, Wingren, and the Future of Scandinavian Creation Theology.* Göttingen: Vandenhoeck & Ruprecht, 2017.

Hedenius, Ingemar. *Tro och vetande.* Bonniers: Stockholm, 1949.

Jarlert, Anders. *Judisk "ras" som äktenskapshinder i Sverige: effekten av Nürnberglagarna i Svenska kyrkans statliga funktion som lysningsförrättare 1935–1945.* Malmö: Sekel, 2006.

Jonson, Jonas. *Jag är bara Nathan Söderblom, satt till tjänst: En biografi.* Stockholm: Verbum, 2014.

Josefson, Ruben, and Per Stjernquist. *Rättens ursprung och grund.* Stockholm: Svenska Bokförlaget, 1961.

Lyles, Max. *A Call for Scientific Purity: Axel Hägerström's Critique of Legal Science.* Rättshistoriskt bibliotek, vol. 65. Stockholm: Institutet för Rättshistorisk forskning, 2006.

Modéer, Kjell Å. *Den svenska domarkulturen: Europeiska och nationella förebilder.* Lund: Corpus Iuris, 1994.

Modéer, Kjell Å. "Transparens och djupstruktur: Folkrätten i rättshistorien." In *Rätten och rättsfamiljer i ett föränderligt samhälle—rättshistoriskt och komparativt. Vänbok till Rolf Nygren.* Edited by Maarit Jänterä Jareborg and Mats Kumlien. Uppsala: Iustus Förlag, 2011.

Møller, Per Stig. *Munk.* Copenhagen: Gyldendal, 2000.

Oredsson, Sverker. *Jönköpingsperspektiv på världen: JP 1935–1970.* Stockholm: Atlantis, 2015.

Österlin, Lars. *Korstågen till Kina. Linjer i protestantisk kinamission.* Malmö: Sekel, 2005.

Petersen, Jørn Henrik. "Staten, kirken og velfærden." In *Reformationen i dansk kirke og kultur.* Edited by Niels Henrik Gregersen and Carsten Back Nielsen. Vol. 3. Odense: Syddansk Universitetsforlag, 2017.

Possing, Birgitte. "Bodil Koch, 1903–1970." In *Dansk kvindehistorisk Leksikon*, https://www.kvinfo.dk/side/170/bio/573/.

Ross, Alf. *Hvorfor Demokrati?* Copenhagen: Munksgaard, 1946.

Ruppert, Stefan. *Kirchenrecht und Kulturkampf: Historische Legitimation, politische Mitwirkung und wissenschaftliche Begleitung durch die Schule Emil Ludwig Richters.* Tubingen: Mohr Siebeck, 2000.

Schjørring, Jens Holger, ed. *Nordiske folkekirker i opbrud: National identitet og international nyorientering efter 1945.* Århus: Aarhus Universitetsforlag, 2001.

Strahl, Ivar. "Idealism och realism i rättsvetenskapen." *Svensk Juristtidning* , vol. 26 (1941): 302ff.

Sundby, Olof. *Luthersk äktenskapsuppfattning. En studie i den kyrkliga äktenskapsdebatten i Sverige efter 1900.* Stockholm: Svenska Kyrkans Diakonistyrelses Bokförlag, 1959.

Tamm, Henrik. *De nordiske juristmøder 1872–1972: Nordisk Retssamvirke gennem 100 År*. Copenhagen: Nyt Nordisk Forlag Arnold Busck, 1972.

Thidevall, Sven. *Folkkyrkan, vision och verklighet. Ett folkkyrkligt reformprograms öden 1928–1932*. Stockholm: Verbum, 2000.

Uggla, Bengt Kristensson. "Gustaf Wingren and Scandinavian Creation Theology." In Gregersen et al., *Reformation Theology for a Post-Secular Age: Løgstrup, Prenter, Wingren, and the Future of Scandinavian Creation Theology*. Göttingen: Vandenhoeck & Ruprecht, 2017.

Waaben, Knud. "Alf Ross." In *Dansk Biografisk Leksikon*. 3rd ed, Svend Cedergreen Bech (ed.). Copenhagen: Gyldendal, 1979–84.

18 Absalon Taranger (1858–1930)

Legal historian and church politician in Norway around 1900

Egil Morland and Torgeir Landro

Introduction

Absalon Taranger (1858–1930) was called "the first strile professor."[1] "Stril" is a local term with a slightly negative ring, used to designate the rural and rude population living in the countryside surrounding the city of Bergen, in the southwest of Norway.[2] As the tension embedded in the term implies, Taranger made an enormous improvement of his social status, climbing from a community consisting mostly of small-scale fishermen and farmers, to a professional life among the intellectual elite in the capital of Norway.

Taranger was a legal historian and made his academic breakthrough on a thesis at Kristiania (Oslo) University on the origin of the medieval Norwegian church. It is, however, not only his academic accomplishments that make his name stand out. As important for his posthumous reputation was his engagement as a church politician in the beginning of the twentieth century and his efforts to sort out the relationship between church and state in his struggle for an independent Norwegian church.

Biography[3]

Absalon Taranger was born in the countryside near the city of Bergen in 1858. His father, Anders Absalonsen Taranger, was a baker and a village shopkeeper, born at Austevoll, south of Bergen, while his mother, Inga Oldereide, grew up on a farm at Bømlo, farther south along the coast. Thus, the young Taranger grew up in a nonacademic environment; he initially prepared for a professional career as a carpenter. But the encounter with Johannes Kierland, described by Taranger later on as a "farmer-genius,"[4] spurred his scholarly and academic aspirations and motivated him to study theology. Supported financially by private loans from nine neighbors, Taranger finally managed through self-directed studies and private lessons to qualify for theological studies.[5]

Move to Kristiania

In the early 1890s, Taranger entered a new stage of his life, both privately and professionally. In 1891 he married Alfhild Scheel, and the couple became parents to six children during the 1890s.[6] But his professional career also took a new direction. His study in theology was interrupted, partly due to illness and partly because Taranger's interests turned to historical and legal topics. While he was employed as an assistant at the National Archives, a part-time position he held while studying theology, an academic competition was advertised. The research question for the assignment was given in advance: to examine the influence of the Anglo-Saxon church on the process of Norwegian conversion and Christianization during the Middle Ages.[7] Taranger embarked on the task and submitted a thesis of more than 450 pages when published, and he won first prize.[8]

This achievement was a turning point in his professional life and career. He was awarded a scholarship, completed a law degree, and went abroad to study legal history, Roman law, and canon law under professors Heinrich Brunner (1840-1915), Karl Zeumer (1849-1914), and Paul Hinschius (1835-1898) in Berlin. In 1887, he defended his doctoral thesis and was hired at the university in Kristiania as a professor and lecturer in legal history and ecclesiastical law. The position was newly established, and Taranger had to develop the study from the ground up, writing instructional books in both legal history and ecclesiastical law.[9]

Taranger's list of publications is impressive. He published a large number of articles in different journals[10] and was engaged in the publication of the medieval Norwegian laws—an ongoing project instigated by the first generation of Norwegian historians, Rudolf Keyser (1803–64) and P. A. Munch (1810–63). He also translated King Magnus the Law-mender's national law of 1274 into modern Norwegian.[11] Despite Taranger's impressive scholarly production, however, it was his early work—his thesis on the Anglo-Saxon church and its influence on the Norwegian church, which initiated his academic career—that has made a lasting impact on Norwegian historiography.

The Anglo-Saxon church and the Christianization of Norway

The circumstances that led to the advertisement of the contest that would change Taranger's professional life involved an ongoing dispute about the origin of the medieval Norwegian church. The key question was: which foreign influences had made the greatest impact on the Norwegian Christianization process. Rudolf Keyser had declared the Norwegian church to be a daughter of the Anglo-Saxon church,[12] while his contemporary colleague P. A. Munch assumed that the southeastern part of Norway, the area around the Oslo fjord, had been influenced by Danish and German missionaries.[13] The German legal historian Konrad Maurer, an established authority in the field, pointed to the mission from the archbishopric of Hamburg-Bremen as a source of inspiration.[14]

A further essential part of the context of the debate was the break of the Norwegian kingdom in 1814 from a four-century-long union with Denmark and the forging of Norway's identity as a young nation state through the nineteenth century. There was an urgent need to establish an origin of the national church distinct from that of Denmark.[15] The opposing views held by Keyser and Munch were, however, nothing but presumptions and assumptions, and there was a general recognition that a systematic examination was needed, which, in turn, led to the advertisement of the competition.

Taranger, in contrast to Keyser and Munch, made a thorough comparison of Anglo-Saxon and Norwegian conditions and used a wide array of ecclesiastical sources. He compared the church organizations, the ecclesiastical languages, the sacraments, and liturgical years, and made thorough use of the Norwegian Christian laws (*kristenrett*) as a point of departure. Although there admittedly were signs of adaptations to Norwegian conditions, indicating interaction and compromises between the native farmers and the missionaries, Taranger allegedly found traces of borrowings and inspiration from the Anglo-Saxon church in the source material. He therefore concluded that there was no doubt that English missionaries had been the dominant force during the foundation of the Norwegian church, which in terms of liturgy, ecclesiastical language, and laws relied heavily on the Anglo-Saxon.[16]

The striking resemblance was explained by a coherent and convincing chain of events. The key figure and driving force behind the process was St. Olaf (r. 1015–28), who, after being converted abroad, returned home from England accompanied by an entourage of English clergymen, most prominently Bishop Grimkell. Their plans for the Norwegian church were discussed and sanctioned at the preliminary Mosterthing around 1024, and thereafter at the four regional *things*, resulting in four different Christian laws. These regional laws had a common core, which allegedly pointed back to St. Olaf's original program. This was the starting-point of the official phase of the Christianization of Norway, subsequently followed up by new generations of English missionaries in the following decades.[17]

Taranger's theory has proven to be surprisingly resilient and is still the standard scholarly view more than a century later. That said, there has been criticism and debate. Taranger's thesis has met with criticism on methodological grounds, first by Konrad Maurer and later by other scholars,[18] for "limiting his comparisons to English and Norwegian sources and for taking parallels as proof of influence."[19] Marit Myking (1953–2013), who has written a survey on the reception of Taranger's contribution and how "Taranger's theory has stood the test of time," nevertheless concludes that "his theory is still generally accepted."[20] More recent scholarly works confirm Myking's assessment. Knut Helle (1930–2015), one of the leading Norwegian medievalists of the postwar generation, refers to Taranger's conclusions without reservation.[21] Furthermore, the historian Olav Tveito (b.1951), author of a doctoral thesis on the Norwegian Christianization process, published an article in 2007 positively appraising Taranger's contribution. Tveito claims that Taranger's study leaves the impression of a thorough comparison of Norwegian and English provisions, and that Taranger argues convincingly for Anglo-Saxon influence, and, in certain matters, even literary dependence.[22]

But Taranger did not spend all of his time on academic studies. In the beginning of the twentieth century, he combined the role of a professional academic with church politics and fought for an independent Norwegian church.

The controversy between church and state—historical background

Absalon Taranger was an engaged and committed person, both within academia and in society in general. The professor of history Oscar Albert Johnsen (1876–1954) pointed out in his postmortem tribute to Taranger that his social, religious, and political commitments made his long list of publications even more impressive.[23] He was a dean of the law faculty, engaged in the process of formulating new rules for governing the university in 1905, and was a board member in the Norwegian Historical Association, to mention just one of the many religious and nonprofit organizations he led.[24] The issue that would occupy much of his time in the first two decades of the twentieth century was the growing disturbance and conflict within the Church of Norway, the state church. These circumstances turned Taranger into the political leader of the Norwegian Church Party and a proponent of quite controversial ideas.[25]

The relationship between church and state had been at issue since the late nineteenth century, with a growing movement arguing for a more independent church. The question was put on hold, however, during the escalating tension between Norway and Sweden, which finally led to the dissolution of their union at the turn of the century.[26]

Nevertheless, a couple of events in the early 1900s put the question back on the agenda. The administration of Christian Michelsen, who was prime minister of Norway when the Swedish-Norwegian union was dissolved in 1905, was also responsible for the appointment of Johannes Ording (1869–1929), a liberal theologian, as professor of theology at the Royal Frederick University. This specific appointment revealed that the organizational arrangement of the national church implied that secular government had the power to determine the outcome even in ecclesiastical matters. The conservative faction of the church, to which Taranger belonged, was shaken, and the situation led to the foundation of the Norwegian Church Party.[27]

Church polity and ecclesiology

Absalon Taranger had already achieved his greatest academic contribution (1889) before he left theology and began his career in jurisprudence. He soon managed to combine insights from both academic fields. This equipped him with the necessary tools to take a leading role in the debates on the church's need to organize itself, within or outside of the state church system. These debates reached a peak around the turn of the century.

From about 1850, in all fields of public life, whether in politics, art, literature, or the shaping of a written language of its own—distinctively different from Danish, until then the only written language in Norway for four hundred years—Norway experienced a time of national romanticism and national awakening without parallel in its history. What, then, about the church? The question arose whether it should continue to structure its life within the strict formal boundaries of a royal autocracy of the seventeenth century. Taranger threw himself into a powerful work for the church's legal freedom. The task, and the man to handle it, met. The time was ripe.

Teacher of church law

For several years, Taranger taught church law to the candidates at the practical theological seminary in Oslo. Like his predecessors, Ulrich A. Motzfeldt (1807–65) and Henrik S. Broch (1819–1905), Taranger presented his view on the history of church law in a book titled *Norwegian Church Law*.[28] Like them, too, he "anchored" his understanding of the law in theology—or, rather, in ecclesiology. The first part of the book deals with the development and changes in church law and church order, from apostolic times to the Roman church law and its sources, and then to German church law and the rivalry between the king's or emperor's power and the church's striving for autonomy from—and sometimes supremacy over—the state. He gave a rather thorough presentation of canon law and its written sources, as well as of Protestant church law, rooted in the Reformation. Taranger thus demonstrated profound insight into the theoretical reasoning behind the Lutheran church order. He gave ecclesiology a legitimate place in the understanding of the need for churches—any church—to shape their own order.

Taranger characterized one of the many ways the churches of the Reformation had organized themselves by the slogan *a free church in a free state*.[29] He regarded the Free Church of Scotland, which had withdrawn from the national church in the 1840s, as the very prototype for this model. This church became a tremendous inspirational resource for him when, as a member of a governmentally appointed commission, he had the opportunity to propose reforms of the Norwegian church—as we will see later. Taranger regarded this work as a way of restoring what went wrong after the Reformation due to political circumstances in the sixteenth century and afterward.

The political concessions' bitter fruits—the state church

Regarding church law and church order, Taranger described the history of the early Reformation as an unwanted deterioration of Lutheran ideas and principles. During that period, the concept of an invisible church led by true believers devolved into an organized church that had partially retained elements of the Catholic Church. The origin of this development stemmed from the *Reichstag* at Speier in 1529, which—due to political circumstances—recognized the Lutheran princes' right to reform the church (*jus reformandi*).[30] This right was not limited to external matters alone (*jus reformandi disciplinae*) but included even the inner church order, i.e., confessional matters and church order (*jus reformandi cultus*). The often-quoted expression that links the religion of the prince (or king) and the people of the realm (*cujus regio, eius religio*) also originates from this eventful meeting in Speier.

The decisions at Speier laid the theoretical foundation for the German system of recognized confessional churches. Although the Lutheran princes were regarded as a kind of emergency bishops in times of need, their role in this capacity became the norm in the enlightened autocracy a hundred years later. By then, this understanding had developed further into a notion of the king as the supreme bishop (*summus episcopus*) of the church. Luther experienced "the political concessions' bitter fruits" when, in 1540, he had to accept that his friend and protector, count Friedrich of Hessen, married a second wife, while the first one, from whom he was divorced, was still alive.

The Reformers soon learned not to be naïve in their ecclesiology, though. The first Lutheran church orders surfaced very early,[31] and in his German Mass (1526), Luther envisaged that every congregation could organize itself according to New Testament examples. Even further, the concept of evangelical freedom led the Reformers to regard it as a good thing that congregations should not all be coerced into the same form.[32] According to Taranger, events of a different kind, namely the excesses of the revolutionary peasants (the Peasants' War of 1525), also forced him to acknowledge the need to establish a church order for the congregations.

Through all this, the true, invisible church became a visible society, too. The parochial system, the ministerial office, and the patronage all were adopted from the Catholic Church. Superintendents (replacing bishops) and consistory boards became established. In this way, the originally Catholic notion of the church as an institution of salvation re-emerged: "The evangelical church body gradually became the same as the geographical state (the territories). The visible church comprised, factually and practically, the state—in the hope, however, that the state would be led by the doctrines of the Reformation. To their own disappointment, that did not happen." Taranger thus quotes Luther's exclamation from 1543: "Satan is still Satan: Through the pope he mixed the church into the state; now he wants to mix the state into the church."[33] The peace of Augsburg (1555) resulted in the acceptance of *two* religions instead of one, both monolithic within their different domains, and binding for their followers.

Based on the concept and teaching of the three orders (the political, the ecclesiastical, and the economic), the churches of the Reformation developed three different—very different!—systems for the relation between church and state: the episcopal, the territorial, and the collegial systems. The first of these—the territorial system—represents the principle of the autocracy's church order. The spokesperson for this system, the German jurist Christian Thomasius (1655–1728), rejected the idea that the church represents a legal society of its own kind, and that it possesses a regimen in itself. The church is merely a societal union under the state, even in religious matters. In this way, Thomasius laid a theoretical foundation for the state-church system as such, which, since then, has been the church order of the Nordic countries until the turn of the twenty-first century.

The "guilty" party here is not only the autocracy, according to Taranger. The theoretical basis for the state church also stems from Thomasius's ideas of *natural law*, which are clearly rooted in the Enlightenment, and not in scripture.

In the middle and south of Europe, however, the ideology behind the state-church system was broken by the February Revolution of 1848. After this, the ideas of the reformed churches also penetrated the Lutheran state churches.[34] It is along these lines that we can trace Absalon Taranger's own journey towards his program for the future church of Norway—from a territorial to a collegial system.

The collegial system

The collegial system bears a concern for the common members of the church and for their legal right to have a say in the decision making of the church. The Pietistic movement of the eighteenth century is the first such system—inside the evangelical church family—which quite directly rejects the state church and claims the congregation's right to autonomy. The Pietists regarded the early church's congregational structure order as an ideal, and the ecclesial "fall" therefore happened in the era of Constantine and the following secularization of the church. The church is a community of equals (a *collegium equale*), and the real church authority lies in the community (in a *jura collegiala in sacra* or *jus in sacra*). The political authorities should have only a supervisory right in external church matters (*jus circa sacra*).[35]

Taranger honors the Reformed churches of the Calvinist tradition for their great contribution to creating an evangelical church order and an evangelical church law. According to him, Calvin gave up the medieval perception that Christianity represented a unity governed by two powers, one worldly and one clerical, each of which either entrusts the worldly society to the church (canon law) or, quite the opposite, delivers the church to the worldly authorities (Lutheranism). Neither is right, in Calvin's perception. The church is a society which *organizationally* shall exist as distinct from the world.

It is therefore, Taranger argues—in what we may call a stimulating hypothesis—no coincidence that it was the Calvinist church which brought Protestantism to the world, and not the Lutheran church, chained as it was to the state. In all countries of the Reformed tradition, apart from England, the relation between state and church is organized in accordance with the principle of *a free church in a free state*. In many of these countries, however, the church's contribution to society is, nonetheless, highly appreciated, and the state may therefore support the churches, and even impose the taxation for the benefit of the churches.

It is important, though, to understand that the meaning of the slogan "a free church in a free state" does not describe a free-church *system*, because such a system would denote a full separation between state and church. Taranger names four different categories of the existing relation between state and church in Europe: (1) the state-church system, (2) the autonomous churches controlled by the state, (3) the free church in the free state, and (4) the separation between the two parties—which is another name of the free-church system.[36] In this system, the state will not support the churches, and, as in France (and in some parts of Switzerland), religion is treated as a private matter entirely—in effect, however, combined with an anticlerical policy enforced since 1880.

Confessional commitment

From the Reformation until 1878, all state officials in Norway were required to commit themselves to the official religion. In 1878, the obligation was limited to ministers of the government and to judges, the latter group being exempted in 1892. In 1955, the Storting decided that professors at theological faculties, teachers of religion in high schools and teacher seminaries, and even officials in public schools and their administration were still obliged to adhere to the Lutheran faith. The confessional claim naturally applied to the king and—after 1919—to "only" half of the government members. The other half, consequently, were not allowed to deal with state church matters.[37] Even after the separation between church and state in 2012, the commitment still applies to the king, according to the present monarch's personal wish. The Lutheran religion thus comprised the whole society.

Reform efforts

The history of reform efforts in Norway prior to Taranger's work with the church order is rather meager. In the turmoil of national awakening around 1850, the clergy in particular engaged in the work for church autonomy. In response, the government appointed an official commission in 1859. Its task was to "deal with the issue of church reforms." Nine years later, the commission proposed that a synod be established and given a rather comprehensive mandate—for instance, to decide on new church laws within the state church. In modern eyes, this may seem like a rather radical proposition—and it was. But this was at exactly the time when synods were being established in the Swedish and Finnish state churches. Obviously, those events influenced the proposals.[38]

By this time, however, the Parliament was divided into multiple factions on the issue of reforms of the state church, and it was impossible to reach a unified outcome. Besides, although the government wanted to invite an advisory church synod to vote on the commission's proposals, an ongoing—and rising—debate on the relations among king, government, and Parliament (resulting in the definite introduction of a constitutional monarchy and parliamentary rule in the 1880s) meant that all reform efforts were effectively stopped.

Fifty years later, Taranger entered the stage. His role in the drama all started with a few popular articles he published under the title "State Religion or Free Folk Church" in a newspaper in Kristiania in the spring of 1906. To Taranger this was an "either-or" matter. By this time the Church of Norway did not have a single representative board on any level, local or national, or even on the diocesan level, apart from the old Norwegian tradition of parochial meetings, which, among other local businesses, were entitled to vote on the introduction of approved new liturgies and hymn books.

Into this "black hole" of church democracy, Taranger proposed that king, government, and all other state authorities should be released from their duties in the field of *religion*. Taranger was troubled by the negative side effects of the current state-church arrangement. It made no sense that the king and the members of the governing body of the state were required to confess the Lutheran faith. Likewise, it was unfortunate that the national assembly, the Storting, where no confession was required, had legislative authority in ecclesiastical matters.[39] His vision was of an autonomous *folk* (people's) church, and in describing the situation that then prevailed, he did not hesitate to use harsh words or kowtow to any secular, cultural, or radical critic. From the perspective of religion, he claimed that "the state church system is, has been, and will always be a lie, a public hypocrisy, which is the exact opposite and greatest enemy of true religion – a scandal."[40] Likewise, when seeing the matter from a secular perspective, he deemed this system to conflict with two fundamental tenets in modern times, namely, the principles of tolerance and of democracy.

Surprisingly enough—despite of or because of the harsh words?—those articles ignited a frenzy of debate, but also of constructive initiatives. Besides, the time was full of unrest, both politically and culturally. A deep divide between liberal and conservative theology had existed for some time, culminating with the establishment of a new, private, and free theological faculty in Oslo, which soon captured the majority of students.

Very soon a multitude of "tools" became available for Taranger's ideas. In autumn 1906 the fifth voluntary church council—simply a forum for discussions, begun in the late 1870s—placed the issue on the agenda. This time the most important question was whether to request a law concerning parochial counsels. Taranger, *in absentia* because he was a guest at a university jubilee in Scotland (!), intervened. He proposed that a resolution should be passed, asking Parliament and the government to appoint an official commission whose mandate would be to study all aspects of a separation between state and church, and even to prepare a constitution for the Norwegian folk church.

The meeting found a middle way by appointing such a commission on its own authority and asking Taranger to be a member of it. Now things were set in motion. Soon, the Norwegian Church Party saw daylight.[41] This party had a single purpose, namely, to influence politicians in all parties to sympathize with the idea of a free folk church and, in the coming elections, to promote those candidates who did so. An influential strategist, Hartvig Halvorsen (1854–1910), the editor of a church periodical, now became Taranger's ally.[42] Halvorsen's periodical thus also became an organ for the Church Party and for the reform movement as a whole. When Halvorsen died all too soon, at the age of 56 in 1910, Taranger was elected chair of the Church Party.

In 1908, the church's own commission finished its work, unanimously concluding in agreement with Taranger's slogan of a free church in a free state, even in recommending the Scottish church as its ideal. The commission's proposals were followed by discussions on diocesan "synods" in the spring of 1908. Finally, at the sixth voluntary church council in the fall of 1908, a vast majority voted to work for a free folk church. So far, it was a full victory for Taranger's strategy and for his ultimate goal.

Prior to the elections in 1909, Taranger traveled and lectured in almost all the coastal cities of Norway. The commission's draft outlined a democratic, synodically governed folk church, whose autonomy would be based on local boards in the congregations and, further, on a board at the middle (diocesan) level, and finally on a church synod and church council (the latter consisting of just three members) at the national level. The council would decide all important church matters.

The concept of a "democratic folk church" did not entirely connote the modern idea we have of it, as expressed in the latest reforms of the Nordic state churches around 2000. To Taranger, "democratic" meant that all nominal members who asked to be registered in the church census and, in addition, declared their approval of the church's belief and confession, would be allowed to vote. There were also profound differences from our current understanding of church economy. At that time, fortunately, church economy was almost entirely local and thus did not essentially affect the state/church relation. This difference increased the probability of getting the proposals passed on the political level, and that is what happened—the politicians finally took the baton.

Politics and church polity

In his inaugural speech to the Parliament in February 1908, Prime Minister Jørgen Løvland (1848–1922) commented on the unrest and changeability in the people concerning religion and church autonomy. He announced a public commission to deliberate on the strong demands for changes in church legislation, and within a couple of weeks, the commission was appointed.[43]

It proved more difficult to agree on the commission's mandate, however. In reality, the friends of reform believed, in view of the respectable and comprehensive job already done by the church's "voluntary" commission, that the one important remaining issue was to create a new *constitution* for the church. That task would be sufficient.

Whether due to tactical reasons or not, the commission was given a variety of matters to discuss, such as guidelines for visitations, confirmation, marriage, communion, lay preachers in the churches—the list was long before the hot issue of a new church constitution could be debated. Again, Absalon Taranger was a key person and driving force. Appointed by the government as one of the nine (later eight) members of the commission, he—and two other reformers—fought for the proposals from the church synod.[44]

In many important issues, though, the whole commission was surprisingly unanimous. Apart from the disagreements on the main question—a new church constitution and, consequently, the necessary changes in the constitutional law of Norway—they all agreed in strengthening the local congregations' influence on the appointment of pastors and on the possibility to erect "free" parishes within the framework of the Norwegian church. They even agreed on the right of individuals to change parish membership, which was a breach of the territorial concept.[45] Some of this had been unheard of in Norway but was already established practice in Denmark (since 1868).

The commission also agreed on the recommendation to establish parish councils, which in themselves are of importance in Lutheran churches. What the commission really disagreed on was whether these changes should take place within or outside of the state-church system. The majority wanted to hold on to the system and saw no need for radical changes in Norway's constitutional law. But the minority wanted to discard the whole system.

Religious freedom, tolerance, and dissidents

In a long and reasoned discourse, Taranger and his allies presented historical evidence which proved that—all the way back to the Reformation—worldly authorities always had recognized the inner core of church autonomy, also called God's ordinance. Even the Constitution of 1814, and the customary practice that followed, treated church matters differently from all other areas of civil life.[46] The minority on the commission also referred to Denmark and claimed—from historical sources—that synods and bishops there had been entitled to discuss reforms and church matters before they were adopted. It was mainly owing to geography and logistics that these customs were not implemented in Norway.

On behalf of the commission's minority, Taranger also presented a complete draft for a new law regarding religious freedom and religion societies outside the Church of Norway. The aim was a revision of the *Dissenter law:* "It is really an anomaly, that a state, which commits itself to the principle of religious freedom, gives a law concerning 'dissenters'," he wrote, adding, with merely hidden irony: "already in the name itself there is a characterization of certain religious standpoints as deviating from normality. That is not something a state should involve itself in.[47]

By this initiative, Taranger proved to be sixty years ahead of his time. The actual law, first passed in 1845, lasted until 1969, when a new "law concerning religious societies and other issues" was adopted.[48]

Almost there, and yet ....

Compared to the old reform strategy fifty years previously, the proposals from the commission did indeed represent new and radical ideas. They were still, however, deemed realistic, partly because of the development in other countries, and partly because the ideas of *freedom* of many kinds were so alive in public life. Besides, the Church Party worked persistently in influencing politicians.

All the efforts stalled, though. In the elections of 1912, the liberal party (*Venstre*) won. They feared that a "free" church would become an intolerant church. On the other side, the lay movement guarded its own freedom within the old system, a freedom it had won by political victories. A strong church, free from the state, could disturb the balance. By now, even the commission's majority reform proposals seemed to be too radical. The case became a political liability

31 Gerda Scharffenorth, *Kirchenordnungen der Reformation* [The Order of the Reformation], in a study group in the Lutheran World Federation, 1976. Also see: Egil Morland, Confessio Augustana, art. 28 i kyrkjeordningsdebatten, in *Ung Teologi*, 1/1978, Oslo, 1–14.
32 Egil Morland, "Fritt og fast. Gudstenesta sin ordo" [The Order of the Service] in *Guds rikes skatt* [The Treasure of God's Kingdom], ed. Morland, Johnsen & Haavik (Bergen: Fagbokforlaget, 2013), 111.
33 Taranger, *Norsk kirkeret* [Norwegian Ecclesial Law], 37.
34 Ibid., 40.
35 Ibid., 39.
36 Ibid., 48.
37 Kristian Hansson, *Norsk kirkerett,* [Norwegian Ecclesial Law] 2nd ed. (Oslo: Aschehoug & Co., 1957), 29–31.
38 Ellingsen, 11.
39 Ellingsen, 30, 42.
40 Carl Fredrik, Wisløff, *Norsk Kirkehistorie III* [The Norwegian Church History III], (Oslo: Lutherstiftelsen Forlag, 1971), 175; Terje Ellingsen, *Kirkestyre i historisk lys* [Church Governing in the Perspective of History] (Stavanger: Nomi Forlag, 1969).
41 Ellingsen, 21.
42 Ibid., 22.
43 Wisløff, 188.
44 Kirkekommissionen av 1908, *Den norske kirkes organisation* [The Church Commission on the Organization of the Church of Norway] (Kristiania, 1911).
45 Ibid., 80.
46 Ibid., 203.
47 Ibid., 441.
48 Lov om trudomssamfunn og ymist anna [Law concerning belief societies].
49 Ellingsen, 27.
50 Myking, 64.
51 Ellingsen, 31ff., 45ff., 60ff.; Myking, 64.
52 Changes made on 21 May 2012, in §§ 2, 4, 12, 16, 21, 22, and 27 in the Norwegian Constitutional Law.

Bibliography

Bade, L, et al. (ed.), *Studenterne fra 1883. Biografiske meddelelser samlede i anledning af deres 25-aars studenterjubilæum* (Kristiania: Det Mallingske Bogtrykkeri, 1908), 380–87.

Bull, Edvard, "Norsk historisk forskning 1869–1919," in Halvdan Koht et al. (ed.), *Norsk historisk videnskap i femti år*, 1869–1919 (Kristiania: Den Norske Historiske Forening, 1920), 52–129.

Ellingsen, Terje, *Fri folkekirke. Den norske kirkes forfatning under debatt 1906–1916* [Free Folk Church], (Oslo; Bergen; Tromsø: Universitetsforlaget, 1973).

Ellingsen, Terje, *Kirkestyre i historisk lys* [Church Governing in the Perspective of History] (Stavanger: Nomi Forlag, 1969).

Frølich, Thorbjørn, *Fjon eller Masfjorden i Hordaland fylke* (Kristiania: Det Mallingske Bogtrykkeri, 1924).

Hansson, Kristian, *Norsk kirkerett,* [Norwegian Ecclesial Law] 2nd ed. (Oslo: Aschehoug & Co., 1957).

Helle, Knut, *Gulatinget og Gulatingslova* (Leikanger: Skald, 2001).

Johnsen, Oscar Albert, "Minnetale over Professor Dr. Absalon Taranger holdt i den hist.-fil. Klasses møte den 13de november 1931," in *Det norske videnskapsakademi i Oslo, Årbok 1931* (Oslo: A.W. Brøggers boktrykkeri, 1932), 57–62

Kirkekommissionen av 1908, Den norske kirkes organisation [The Church Commission on the Organization of the Church of Norway] (Kristiania, 1911).

Landro, Torgeir, "Absalon Taranger – Strileprofessoren frå Sund," in *Havstrilen – Kulturhistorisk årbok for Sund, Fjell og Øygarden* (Straume: Bodoni, 2012), 15–23.

Landro, Torgeir, *Kristenrett og kyrkjerett. Borgartingskristenretten i eit komparativt perspektiv*, unpublished PhD thesis, University of Bergen (2010).

Lov om trudomssamfunn og ymist anna [Law concerning belief societies], Oslo, 1969.

Maurer, Konrad, "Nogle Bemærkninger til Norges Kirkehistorie," [Commentaries on the Church History of Norway], *Historisk Tidsskrift* (Kristiania, 1895), 1–113.

Morland, Egil, Confessio Augustana, art. 28 i kyrkjeordningsdebatten, in *Ung Teologi*, 1/1978, Oslo.

Morland, Egil, "Fritt og fast. Gudstenesta sin ordo" [The Order of the Service], in Morland, Johnsen & Haavik (eds.), *Guds rikes skatt* [The Treasure of God's Kingdom], (Bergen: Fagbokforlaget, 2013), 111.

Myking, Marit, *Vart Noreg kristna frå England? Ein gjennomgang av norsk forsking med utgangspunkt i Absalon Tarangers avhandling Den angelsaksiske kirkes indflydelse paa den norske (1890)* (Oslo: Senter for studier i vikingtid og middelalder, 2001.

Scharffenorth, Gerda, *Kirchenordnungen der Reformation* [The Order of the Reformation], in a study group in the Lutheran World Federation, 1976.

Taranger, Absalon, "Barndomsminner fra Sunds kirke og prestegård," in Salmund Djuvik (ed.), *Festskrift – Sund kirke gjennem 600 år: 1327–1877–1927* (Sund menighetsråd, 1927), 34–42.

Taranger, Absalon, *Den angelsaksiske kirkes indflydelse paa den norske* [The Anglo-Saxon Church's Influence on The Norwegian Church»], (Kristiania: Den norske historiske forening, 1890).

Taranger, Absalon, *Norsk kirkeret: forelæsninger ved det praktisk-teologiske seminar* [The Norwegian Church Law], (Kristiania: Cammermeyers boghandel, 1917).

Taranger, Absalon, *Tillegg til norsk kirkerett: forelesninger ved de praktisk-teologiske seminarer* (Kristiania: Cammermeyers boghandel, 1928).

Taranger, Absalon, *Udsigt over den norske rets historie: forelæsninger [Perspectives on Norwegian Law]*, vol. 1–4 (Kristiania: Cammermeyers boghandel, 1898–1907).

Tveito, Olav, "Erkebiskop Wulfstan av York og de eldste norske kristenrettene," *Norsk Teologisk Tidsskrift* (2007), 170–186.

Wisløff, Carl Fredrik, *Norsk Kirkehistorie III* [The Norwegian Church History III], (Oslo: Lutherstiftelsen Forlag, 1971).

concept.[45] Some of this had been unheard of in Norway but was already established practice in Denmark (since 1868).

The commission also agreed on the recommendation to establish parish councils, which in themselves are of importance in Lutheran churches. What the commission really disagreed on was whether these changes should take place within or outside of the state-church system. The majority wanted to hold on to the system and saw no need for radical changes in Norway's constitutional law. But the minority wanted to discard the whole system.

Religious freedom, tolerance, and dissidents

In a long and reasoned discourse, Taranger and his allies presented historical evidence which proved that—all the way back to the Reformation—worldly authorities always had recognized the inner core of church autonomy, also called God's ordinance. Even the Constitution of 1814, and the customary practice that followed, treated church matters differently from all other areas of civil life.[46] The minority on the commission also referred to Denmark and claimed—from historical sources—that synods and bishops there had been entitled to discuss reforms and church matters before they were adopted. It was mainly owing to geography and logistics that these customs were not implemented in Norway.

On behalf of the commission's minority, Taranger also presented a complete draft for a new law regarding religious freedom and religion societies outside the Church of Norway. The aim was a revision of the *Dissenter law:* "It is really an anomaly, that a state, which commits itself to the principle of religious freedom, gives a law concerning 'dissenters'," he wrote, adding, with merely hidden irony: "already in the name itself there is a characterization of certain religious standpoints as deviating from normality. That is not something a state should involve itself in.[47]

By this initiative, Taranger proved to be sixty years ahead of his time. The actual law, first passed in 1845, lasted until 1969, when a new "law concerning religious societies and other issues" was adopted.[48]

Almost there, and yet ....

Compared to the old reform strategy fifty years previously, the proposals from the commission did indeed represent new and radical ideas. They were still, however, deemed realistic, partly because of the development in other countries, and partly because the ideas of *freedom* of many kinds were so alive in public life. Besides, the Church Party worked persistently in influencing politicians.

All the efforts stalled, though. In the elections of 1912, the liberal party (*Venstre*) won. They feared that a "free" church would become an intolerant church. On the other side, the lay movement guarded its own freedom within the old system, a freedom it had won by political victories. A strong church, free from the state, could disturb the balance. By now, even the commission's majority reform proposals seemed to be too radical. The case became a political liability

Prior to the elections in 1909, Taranger traveled and lectured in almost all the coastal cities of Norway. The commission's draft outlined a democratic, synodically governed folk church, whose autonomy would be based on local boards in the congregations and, further, on a board at the middle (diocesan) level, and finally on a church synod and church council (the latter consisting of just three members) at the national level. The council would decide all important church matters.

The concept of a "democratic folk church" did not entirely connote the modern idea we have of it, as expressed in the latest reforms of the Nordic state churches around 2000. To Taranger, "democratic" meant that all nominal members who asked to be registered in the church census and, in addition, declared their approval of the church's belief and confession, would be allowed to vote. There were also profound differences from our current understanding of church economy. At that time, fortunately, church economy was almost entirely local and thus did not essentially affect the state/church relation. This difference increased the probability of getting the proposals passed on the political level, and that is what happened—the politicians finally took the baton.

Politics and church polity

In his inaugural speech to the Parliament in February 1908, Prime Minister Jørgen Løvland (1848–1922) commented on the unrest and changeability in the people concerning religion and church autonomy. He announced a public commission to deliberate on the strong demands for changes in church legislation, and within a couple of weeks, the commission was appointed.[43]

It proved more difficult to agree on the commission's mandate, however. In reality, the friends of reform believed, in view of the respectable and comprehensive job already done by the church's "voluntary" commission, that the one important remaining issue was to create a new *constitution* for the church. That task would be sufficient.

Whether due to tactical reasons or not, the commission was given a variety of matters to discuss, such as guidelines for visitations, confirmation, marriage, communion, lay preachers in the churches—the list was long before the hot issue of a new church constitution could be debated. Again, Absalon Taranger was a key person and driving force. Appointed by the government as one of the nine (later eight) members of the commission, he—and two other reformers—fought for the proposals from the church synod.[44]

In many important issues, though, the whole commission was surprisingly unanimous. Apart from the disagreements on the main question—a new church constitution and, consequently, the necessary changes in the constitutional law of Norway—they all agreed in strengthening the local congregations' influence on the appointment of pastors and on the possibility to erect "free" parishes within the framework of the Norwegian church. They even agreed on the right of individuals to change parish membership, which was a breach of the territorial

19 Swedish modernity in transition within law and theology

Halvar G F Sundberg (1894–1973) and Gustaf Aulén (1879–1977)

Anders Jarlert

Introduction

The idealist position to the law

The Scandinavian legal heritage has been described as a fusion of German Law and Canon Law. Medieval provincial laws could state that 'Christ is first in our law'. The so-called Rules for Judges by the Swedish reformer, Olavus Petri,[1] are still being printed in modern annual editions of the Swedish law (originally from 1734).

To an older, idealistic understanding of the sense of justice as one of the most important foundations of state and society, its meaning was self-evident, and not in need of any explanation or problematization. When questioned by new, positivist theories of legal realism, these traditional arguments did not work any longer.

Traditional, conservative ideas of guilt as the presupposition for punishment, and the connection between punishment and its justice, were placed in the same idealist position as the philosopher Locke's 'liberal' theories of Natural law, and thus severely criticized by its modern critics.

The positivist idea of legal realism

In the 1930s, the *sense of justice* was hardly disputed in academic Swedish legal discourse. It was commonly refused. By professor Vilhelm Lundstedt (1882–1955) and other jurists in the tradition of Legal realism,[2] who all were inspired by the value-neutral philosophy of Axel Hägerström (1868–1939), the so-called *nihilism of values* was described as the only possible, scientific position. Natural sense of justice was exposed as being unscientific. The study of Law had to be liberated from 'metaphysics' and 'superstition,' and changed into something like natural science.[3]

The starting-point for the criticism of natural sense of justice was the assumption that our ideas about rights and obligations do not have any correspondence in the reality of time and space. While the old versions of Law positivism (Austin, Bentham, Kelsen, and others) had understood justice as an expression of the will of the sovereign or the state, the philosopher Hägerström rejected this theory as a sort of anthropomorphism, since the state could not be treated like an individual person. He emphasized that ideas of rights and obligations did not have any parallel in everyday reality. When understood as power, the rights were only of mystical or magical nature. This so-called realism of law tried to dissolve the connections between justice as norm and justice as fact. Hägerström's solution was that justice was nothing more than a social machinery, with human beings as its gearwheels.

Hägerström's pupil the law professor Vilhelm Lundstedt even found that the state and the individuals were inseparable, and, consequently, that the individual could not have any rights of his or her own against the state. Lundstedt introduced *social welfare,* a sort of public utility, as the determining concept for the meaning and understanding of Law. His influence was wide, not least in political circles, since Lundstedt also was a member of Parliament (Social Democrat), 1929–48. It has even been stated that the so-called Scandinavian Legal realism has been more internationally influential than any other effort by Swedish twentieth-century philosophy.[4] One of Lundstedt's most famous publications was *Die Unwissenschaftlichkeit der Rechtswissenschaft* (1936).

To Lundstedt, the so-called ideology of justice was a hindrance to social welfare. During the second world war, theological criticism (Ruben Josefson, *Rätten och den kristna moralen.* 1941) emphasized that if the social welfare was recognized as decisive for justice, also morals must be given priority in relation to the law. Josefson (1907–72) pointed out that the Christian faith found social welfare in other places and values than the current and powerful religion of races.

In one area, the ideas of Legal realism were not accepted in Sweden, and that was in Law of Nations or International law. In the concept of the Legal realists, rights and obligations were pure illusions. Thus, Law of Nations was still more 'superstitious' since it did not relate to any distinct, social machinery of law. Lundstedt severely criticized the League of Nations and the political sanctions against Italy after the occupation of Abyssinia. As a member of Parliament for the Social Democrats, Lundstedt was influential, though not in his views on International Law, where other politicians, such as the later Foreign minister Östen Undén, himself a professor of Law, distanced themselves from Lundstedt. International law was also to become the crucial point where the Lundensian theologians created their independent position in criticism of the Legal realists.

In the other Scandinavian countries, the ideas of Legal realism were least influential in Finland, more so in Norway, mostly in Denmark. A Danish example of Legal realism is Alf Ross (1889–1977). Significant for the Danish mentality, he followed a more independent road, inspired also by Hans Kelsen in Vienna. He presented his doctoral thesis for Hägerström in Uppsala, and he was obviously dependent on Upsaliensan philosophy, for example, in his *Kritik der sogenannten praktischen Erkenntnis* (1933). But Ross did not follow Lundstedt in his concept of social welfare as the necessary foundation of a so-called scientific practice of law. Ross would rather talk about Law as a technical science, that is a sort of social engineering. But the practical result was similar.[5]

Halvar G. F. Sundberg

One of the most severe critics of Legal realism was Halvar G.F. Sundberg (1894–1973), professor of Constitutional law, Administrative law, and International law at Uppsala University. Sundberg was born in a bourgeois milieu without legal interests and studied with the support of his family. His father died shortly before his matriculation. He studied in Uppsala, starting with Theology, but continuing with Law. His younger years were marked by severe Tuberculosis, which forced him to several stays in sanatoria.[6] For twenty years, Sundberg served in the city administration of the capital, Stockholm, from 1929 as its first City jurist. Sundberg wrote his dissertation on Law of the staple towns, and in 1935 he was the first professor with Administrative law as his main subject. The following year, he returned to Stockholm as Chief administrator of the economy of the capital. He was elected as a Conservative, remaining in service until 1940, when this post passed to the Socialist majority.

In his broad overview of Ecclesiastical law (1948), Sundberg returned to the theological interest of his youth. He also took part in the General Church Synods of 1948 and 1951. An important contribution was his development of the general principles of law. His approach came to be regarded as outdated when a softer approach was applied. However, in the 1990s this changed with the European changes after the fall of the Berlin wall and the creation of the European Union and its legal consequences. Much of his views on jurisprudential and legal policy issues are nowadays mainstream, and reforms that he wanted have been implemented. The importance of an objective interpretation of law, and common principles of law are in line with European law, an expanded use of judicial review has been accepted, the European Convention on Human Rights has been implemented into Swedish law, etc.[7]

In his magisterial exposition of contemporary Ecclesiastical law (*Kyrkorätt.* Helsinki 1948; 438 pages), Sundberg defined Ecclesiastical law as the part of the legal order that deals with the Church of Sweden as an active, public organization in society. It contains the organizational conditions of the Church, regulates the Public law relationship between Church and State or between the Church and its members, and determines the legal forms and contents of Church activities.[8]

Sundberg described the Reformation as breaking off the Swedish Church province from Rome, simultaneously supporting the national strivings for liberation from the union with Denmark-Norway. The ties that in temporal respect had bound the Church to Rome, were now instead bound to the new, national state power.[9]

Sundberg was very keen on demarcating Ecclesiastical law from Theology. For example, pastoral or other instructions of purely religious, personal nature belonged to Theology, and not to Ecclesiastical law as a legal discipline.[10] Thus, "Church" here denoted an organization, not the Church in its religious or theological sense, but only a legal or judicial term. However, that this latter concept had been designed with the support of the former was given.[11] The Church was primarily a real phenomenon, not a legal one. It had been created by the spiritual reality that constituted the Creed. Thus, the Church was not created by the State or its legal order, but the State and the legal order only recognized the factual, existing Church as being *also* a legal institution.[12]

The best illustration of Sundberg's double or twofold view of "Church" is what he writes on membership, where he starts noting that the legal definition of "Church member" was something else than "Church member" according to the Confession of the Church. Since membership in *Confessio Augustana* was constituted by Baptism, an unbaptized person could not be a member of the Church "as a Christian denomination" (*trossamfund*). The legal definition had a different meaning, as the Swedish citizen, who did not belong to any other Christian denomination, the Mosaic creed, or had formally left the Church of Sweden. In the legal sense, it was an indifferent matter if the person in question confessed the Creed or was baptized—the legal membership was of a formal nature only. Still, Sundberg recognized inclusion in the Church also through Baptism alone, since this was a consequence of the ecclesiastical confession to which the registration had to adjust.[13]

When the Church of Sweden was described as a National Church, this referred to the fact that the state exercised ecclesiastical rule, but in cooperation with ecclesiastical agencies. The State had no right to deal with the spiritual regiment, while the State, in cooperation with the Church, should devote itself to the supervision, care and defense of the Church for the promotion of its important work to the people.[14]

Since the ministry of the Word and the sacrament was necessary for the forgiveness of sins, the spiritual power or *potestas magisterii* could not be exercised by any worldly institution. Every function of *summus episcopus* in the government must therefore be excluded. The King was never a "Notbischof" and, thus, never was in possession of any *jus reformandi*.[15]

In one of his motions to the Church synod 1948, Sundberg rejected the proposed change of proportions between clergy and laymen in the synod and wanted to keep their previous parity.[16] In the discussions, he searched guarantees for lay members as consciously church-minded, thus counteracting the complained politicization of the General Synod. Sundberg even accused the Church Law committee in the Synod for representing a State Church ideal of the old German nature, which was criticized by Bishop Yngve Brilioth (1891–1959) and Sundberg's jurist colleague, Professor Åke Hassler (1893–1980).[17]

In his great book, Sundberg exemplified such non-church-minded laymen with Baptists or Communists, who both were legally selectable for ecclesiastical duties. Sundberg writes that this application was against the law, at least in the former case.[18] This was not an abstract example, but a very real one, since the professor of Church history at Uppsala University at the time, Gunnar Westin (1890–1967), was an active Baptist, even president of the Swedish Baptist Community 1956–60.

In 1951, Sundberg submitted a motion in the General Synod about the minister's duty to perform marriages, where he wanted such measures to be taken that the minister would not risk prosecution "because he follows the doctrine of the Church." In another motion, Sundberg wanted the compulsory examination of impediments to marriage to be restructured to a compulsory civil marriage, i.e. a civil registration of marriages.[19] In this, he was far ahead of his time, and his proposal has not yet been implemented in Sweden, where all marriages still are performed either by a religious or a civil ceremony, never by registration only.

In a private letter after the General Synod of 1948, Sundberg described his impressions of the synod, which roughly corresponded to his beliefs about "that illustrious gathering," and the contradictions between the "vegetating State Church" and the "independent and fighting, living Church."[20] It is obvious that Sundberg, in emphasizing Ecclesiastical law as an issue of the Faculty of Law, and not a theological one, tried to frame his own rather conservative understanding of the Church, and to protect the Church of Sweden from her more or less liberal theologians.

In a later article on State and Church under current Swedish Law (1961), Sundberg compared the legal position of the Church of Sweden to that of the Norwegian State Church. While Norwegian constitutional law was based on a principled identity between State and Church, so that the King had supreme power in the Church in the same way as in the military forces, the situation in Sweden was different. The designation "State Church" did not appear here until 1846 and was never made legal.[21] The fact that the Church of Sweden had a public law status did not make her a State Church. She was both protected and controlled by the State, she was both recognized and dependent.[22] Here, Sundberg described the new situation after the Law on Religious freedom (1951).[23] He also made an interesting comparison with the Mosaic congregations and their (before 1952) compulsory membership for those who belonged to the Mosaic confession.[24]

However, he wrote, the later development had shown that the Church of Sweden had become more and more dependent on the State, in the direction of her transformation to a State Church in the strict sense. While the ideal ties between Church and State had been loosened, the economic ones had been tightened, and the suborder of the Church under the State had also in other ways increased.[25] Sundberg very clearly saw that while individual, religious freedom was granted by the new law in 1951, the claims of the state on the Church of Sweden were simultaneously strengthened.

Despite this and other updates, it was a tragedy that Sundberg's great work on Ecclesiastical law had been published only three years before the new regulation of individual religious freedom. He built his teaching on the historical fact that all Swedish citizens—with only a few, specially mentioned exceptions—were members of the Church of Sweden, and that leaving this Church should be combined with the entrance into another church or denomination. From 1952 these fundamental presuppositions were changed due to the new legislation.

Sundberg did not himself develop an argument on the theological concept of Law, but in a review 1963 of Hans Dombois's *Das Recht der Gnade. Oekumenische Kirchenrecht*, he commented on it. According to Dombois, the task of

Ecclesiastical Law was threefold: to answer the question about the legitimacy of religious functions, to form a platform for judgments on the actions of the Church, and to help theology to understand the historical figure and problems of the Church. He notes the difference between Dombois's perspectives and the current, positivistic Swedish ones. Dombois's understanding of Ecclesiastical Law as "Liturgy tested for their legitimacy" is only being mentioned, while he agrees on the emphasis on a public legal regulation of the position of the Church as necessary.[26]

Sundberg is the founder of modern administrative law in Sweden. He possessed the overview and the historical knowledge needed to formulate general principles based on Swedish legal traditions. He regarded the possibilities of the individual to appeal against the decisions of the authorities as central to the legal system.[27]

Gustaf Aulén

Gustaf Aulén (1879–1977) was professor of Systematic Theology at Lund University, and Bishop of Strängnäs diocese 1933–52. In contrast to Sundberg, he was, together with the other "Lundensian theologians," i.e. Anders Nygren (1890–1978), and Ragnar Bring (1895–1988), dependent on the Uppsala School of philosophy.

Aulén was the son of a clergyman in the South East of Sweden. He started his academic career at Uppsala University with a dissertation on the theology of Archbishop Henrik Reuterdahl (1795–1870) and his position to Schleiermacher (1906), continuing with a study of the Lutheran concept of the Church, its history and value (1912). He was appointed professor of dogmatics at Lund University in 1913 and became Bishop of Strängnäs diocese in 1933. Aulén's first major theologian work was *Den allmänneliga kristna tron* (1923; English: *The Faith of the Christian Church*, 1948), followed by his most famous work, *Christus Victor* (1930, English translation 1931).

The negative understanding of law in Lundensian theology

The theologians of Lund University of the early twentieth century shared with the tradition of Legal realism its critical attitude towards metaphysics as well as its search for a so-called realistic position, but their connection to Uppsaliensian philosophy was much more complicated than the connection of the jurists.

Something like an opening to the problem was made by Anders Nygren (1890–1978), professor of Ethics at Lund University, as early as in 1923, in his work on Philosophical and Christian Ethics, where he explained that the philosopher Hägerström was perfectly right in emphasizing that it is hardly possible to speak about the *truth* of moral ideas. However, this did not imply that it would not be possible to speak about the *validity* of these ideas.[28] In his book on Ethical fundamental questions, 1926, Nygren, in emphasizing the importance of the immediate, ethical judgment, created a certain space for endeavors that in other words could be connected to the traditional sense of justice.[29]

To the Lundensian theologian Gustaf Aulén, the German Luther renaissance and its reaction against Liberal theology had been most influential. However, while Aulén rejected the understanding of Luther in the liberal theology of the German theologian Albrecht Ritschl, he continued Ritschl's interpretation of Lutheran orthodoxy as a petrification of Luther's theology and a backlash into Medieval ideas of satisfaction and justice. In consequence, Aulén up to 1935 showed a negative attitude towards 'justice' and 'legal' as theological categories. In the third edition of his dogmatic teaching, *The Faith of the Christian Church*, 1931, Aulén stressed that in the so-called classic Christian idea of atonement, emphasizing the victory of Christ over his enemies instead of the *satisfactio vicaria*, the order of justice had been broken through. As an especially negative example, he mentioned that in scholastic theology, divine love was subjected in the framework of legal order, 'regulated by *iustitia*'.[30] In the subject index of his book, words like 'order of justice' or 'legal relation' do not have the slightest connotation to social matters but are restricted only to soteriological ones. He still did not make any ethical application of these terms.

This is in accordance also with the views of Anders Nygren at that time. In the first volume of his famous *Eros and Agape*, Nygren explained the order of justice to be incapable to express divine fellowship. In the second volume, 1936, he tried to show that when *agape* was changed from actual revaluation into a new, remaining order of values, this was basically identical to abolishing the tension so necessary to overcome *nomos*. Even Marcion (dead 160) had understood that the Christian fellowship with God was not a fellowship of justice, but a fellowship of love.[31]

Changing positions influenced by world politics

A beginning change came at a manifestation in the Stockholm Concert Hall on September 17, 1935, when Manfred Björkquist (1884–1985) and Gustaf Aulén were the main speakers. In his later published speech on the Christian religion and the world situation, Aulén described the Italian assault on Abyssinia as 'nothing else than a direct sabotage of all strivings to erect a lawfully ordered relationship between peoples'. He found that 'justice lost its cause, when it got into conflict with the will of power'. Aulén emphasized the importance of obeying God more than men, but this struggle was not as still in 1934 described only as a struggle of love. The Church of Christ was to speak for *both* justice *and* love, and to pray to the Almighty, that He in His grace would turn away misfortune and constrain the hearts of human beings with the love that does not seek its own[32]. This implies, that in the struggle of injustice against justice, the Church must speak for both justice and love, but the victory is still the victory of *agape* alone.

Aulén's theological publications during World War II are to a great extent related to the contemporary Swedish political context and its theologian discourses. In 1939, the lundensian professor of Law, Karl Olivecrona (1897–1980)—a student of Vilhelm Lundstedt—published his famous book on the law and the state.[33] He tried to create a 'realistic' position, and to remove what he called 'diverse metaphysical obscurities'. As a reply, bishop Gustaf Aulén asked already in the title of his small book if any Christian demand could be put on public life. He shared Olivecrona's criticism of metaphysics but found it unsatisfying that the jurist had found the origin of legal ideas only in the *feelings* of human beings since these legal ideas were still of direct and concrete importance to legislation. The strange ethos of the Christian religion was a principal, historical factor of importance in this context. Natural law was still rejected as being strongly loaded with metaphysics, and as a fiction without correspondence to reality. Instead, Aulén presented his new idea of the law of creation, *lex creationis:* the Christian belief in God's creation of the world gave the Christian view on justice its universal direction.[34]

Here, Aulén tried to define a third position between Olivecrona's realism of law and the alleged metaphysical Natural law. A remaining problem was how to apply the law of love on public life, and the bishop's positive effort for a solution is an objective care for one's neighbor, in German 'sachliche Fürsorge um den Nächsten'.[35] This third position of Aulén seems to have been constructed in conscious opposition to the German *Ordnungstheologie,* its emphasis on the orders of creation, and its connections to National Socialism, but also in opposition to Karl Barth, who in his struggle against National Socialism motivated the Law from the Gospel. In his struggle with concrete problems in Social Ethics, Aulén emphasized the importance of a theology of Creation. The revelation of the Law in the Bible through Christ was needed to interpret *lex creationis,* which had been darkened by sin.[36]

In his article on the Church and the order of Law, published in a well-known anthology, *A Book on the Church,* 1942, Aulén further explained his thoughts. He explicitly criticized the persecutions of the Jews but found that this criticism could not be founded on objections such as that 'we feel our sense of justice being violated', or that such actions 'are contrary to the simplest demands of humanity'. These motivations would be answered by the concerned, that it was a matter of two different forms of legal order. Aulén still rejected Natural Law but emphasized that only such an opinion of Law that did not violate the demands of the Law of God could be recognized from a Christian position as an opinion of Law.[37]

In the fourth edition of *The Faith of the Christian Church,* 1943, Gustaf Aulén added a new paragraph 21, the Law of Creation, where the characteristics of the creation's order of justice are defined as 'that everything basically is determined by the demands of the divine will of love'. The order of justice is regarded as something positive, and as determined by *agape.* This is done in a polemical attitude towards the German *Ordnungstheologie.* Simultaneously, Aulén confesses that 'it is undeniable, that the will of God here can be realized within the framework of the Law, even if this realization takes place under force and does not bear the character of spontaneity'. To maintain the order of justice, the state must use its organized power, that does not hesitate to use violence, when that is necessary, and power is a requirement for the function of the state as a state of justice. However, if the state would place power into the service of selfish interests, the perspective of justice would be set aside, and the state would miss its purpose.[38]

The clearest formulation of these new perspectives is presented in Bishop Aulén's article on the foundation of the sense of justice, published in Norway (after the War) in 1945. Here he states that the universal demand of justice that is inseparably united with a Christian view of life is immediately anchored in the Christian belief in God, more precisely in the belief in creation. The sense of justice has its starting-point in this demand. A theory emanating from fixed, human rights does not present any effective protection against the relativization of justice, neither does any abstract theory of equality, built on the foundation of human dignity. Justice cannot be constructed from below, from distinct, human prerogatives. Then it could too easily be relativized. But the demands emanating from the belief in the creation are unshakeable. This universal sense of justice is no exclusive Christian phenomenon, no Christian monopoly. It exists also among people who do not want to build on Christian foundations. The Christian religion has not created the sense of justice but has revealed and elucidated the real content of the law of creation. This qualified sense of justice has its strong and unshakeable fortress in the Christian belief in God.[39]

In his continuing explanation of the creation and the law, Aulén emphasized the importance of the guarding service of the Church around the Law of God. The Church has the possibility to listen to and to implement the divine Law in concrete situations. This was made clear especially in Aulén's book on the Church and National Socialism, 1944, translated into both Danish and Dutch. Important to his resistance towards National Socialism was also Aulén's marriage (from 1907 to her death in 1959) to a Norwegian lady, Kristine Bjørnstad, and his close relation to Bishop Eivind Berggrav in Oslo during the Nazi occupation of Norway.

Law of Creation and/or Ecclesiastical Law

Despite his great interest in theological law, and his own concept of the Law of Creation, Gustaf Aulén was not concerned about Ecclesiastical Law, but rather uninterested in all temporal and practical law. As a professor of Systematic theology, his responsibility was the Church as a theological concept, not as its legal. As a bishop, he was very active for the renewal of worship, including Church buildings, liturgy, singing, and preaching, but he did not devote himself to organizational matters.[40] When his doctrinal, or sometimes even political understanding of a problem collided with Ecclesiastical law, Aulén sometimes did not even pay attention to the collision. So was the case, for example, when Aulén on Midsummer's Day, 1935, ordained the American Eric Ringenhjelm as a minister, though not for any special diocese. Acting on his own, Ringenhjelm tried to organize an American Episcopal congregation in Stockholm. As Aulén's biographer, Bishop Jonas Jonson, concludes, this ordination clearly violated both the English, the American, and the Swedish ecclesiastical orders.[41] Halvar Sundberg, on the other hand, emphasized that Ecclesiastical Law belonged to the Faculty of Law, and was not a theological matter. In this, they both seem to agree in a way.

Epilogue

In Lund, Sven Kjöllerström (1901–81) was professor of Practical Theology and Ecclesiastical Law, but his interest was mostly historical, and he changed the emphasis of the theological study of Ecclesiastical Law into Ecclesiastical History. In a review of Sundberg's Ecclesiastical Law, Kjöllerström explained that already the distinguished Lund professor of law David Nehrman Ehrenstråle (1695–1769) had emphasized that Ecclesiastical Law belonged to the Faculty of Law, and not to the theologians.[42]

The only modern effort to combine Theology and Law had been made by Kjöllerström's predecessor in Lund, the later Archbishop Yngve Brilioth, in his *Svensk kyrkokunskap* (1933, 2.ed. 1946), aiming partly at a description of Ecclesiastical law as the norms of the living Ecclesiastical life, and partly to let Ecclesiastical law as a theological science comprehend the throughout the history of the Church ongoing struggle of the Gospel to master and design the refractory materials of constitutional and legal forms.[43]

Brilioth was in most ways an idealist of the old school, interested in British theology and conservative historiography. He found that Martin Luther did not see any absolute state of opposition between the Church and the Law. On the contrary, he regarded the Law as part of God's common or natural revelation. All since the Reformation, Lutheran tradition had been tormented by theologians like Rudolph Sohm, the German theologian of law, who tried to be more Lutheran than Luther himself. In Sohm's view, the idea of Ecclesiastical Law was contradictory to the essence of the Church. Brilioth's comment was that Sohm had failed—Luther never saw any absolute contradiction between the essence of the Church and the essence of the Law.[44]

Brilioth's words may serve as a comment to the words of *Confessio Augustana*, where justification by faith, in Article IV, is stated as the main principle of the Church. But in Article V, the ministry is motivated by this faith, not only as a practical, human order, but, in the German version, 'hat Gott das Predigtamt eingesetzt'. However, this and other orders do not have to be alike everywhere in time and space (Article VII).[45]

In Brilioth's theology, the spiritual Church needs a lawful form for its work in this world. But this lawful form must serve the spiritual Church, guard its life, and create a useful form for the personal fellowship around the Word of God and the Sacraments. Therefore, the concrete, lawful forms of the Church have only a relative importance, they must relate in a 'plastic' way to the dynamic life of the Spirit, and no special organization of the Church can be given absolute authority.[46]

Since Brilioth's position in many ways represented the old idealistic one, uninfluenced by nihilistic philosophy and Legal realism, his aspects were neglected at an early stage, but revived after the Second World War.

In their methodical approach, Sundberg and Aulén differed widely. While Aulén was a visionary man, sometimes rather airy in his concepts, tending towards a High Church position especially in liturgy, Sundberg was a positivist in his method, always exact, rather "High and dry" in his attitude, while strongly emphasizing "the living Church" in a High Church understanding.

However, in their views on the Church as a special category in its own, instituted by God, Sundberg and Aulén converged, though they both suffered from the sharp division between theology and law in contemporary Swedish academic life.

Biographies

Gustaf Aulén (1879–1977) was Professor in Systematic theology at the Lund University from 1913, and from 1933 Bishop of Strängnäs. Together with Anders Nygren and Ragnar Bring he formed the "Lundensian theology." Married to a Norwegian woman, he engaged himself in the resistance against the German occupation of Norway during World War II. He is well known for his theological concept of the Law of Creation. He became Honorary Doctor in Erlangen, Saint Andrews, Oslo, Glasgow, and at the Augustana College.

Halvar G. F. Sundberg (1894–1973) was Professor in State law at the Uppsala University from 1935. He was the first Swedish Professor to regard Administrative law as a major subject and is regarded as the founder of modern Administrative law in Sweden. His textbook in Ecclesiastical law (1948) became very influential. Sundberg emphasized the special character of the Christian Church even as a State Church. He was also active as a politician (Conservative).

Notes

1 Heikki Pihlajamäki in this volume.
2 E.g. Karl Olivecrona and Östen Undén.
3 Svante Nordin, Från Hägerström till Hedenius. Den moderna svenska filosofin. Bodafors 1983, 120, 28, 133; Staffan Källström, Värdenihilism och vetenskap. Uppsalafilosofin i forskning och samhällsdebatt under 1920- och 30-talen. Göteborg 1984, 30, 63; Max Lyles, A Call for Scientific Purity: Axel Hägerström's Critique of Legal Science, Rättshistoriskt bibliotek Vol. 65, Stockholm 2006.
4 Nordin 1983, 118.
5 Jens Evald, Alf Ross - a life, DJØF: Copenhagen 2014.
6 Fredrik Sterzel, art. Sundberg, Halvar Gustaf Fredrik., in: Svenskt Biografiskt Lexikon 34. Stockholm 2014, 206.
7 Sterzel 2014, 207f.
8 Halvar G.F. Sundberg, Kyrkorätt. Helsingfors 1948, 1.
9 Sundberg, 1948, 25.
10 Sundberg, 1948, 1.
11 Sundberg, 1948, 36.
12 Sundberg, 1948, 37.
13 Sundberg, 1948, 90f., 93.
14 Sundberg. 1948, 59.
15 Sundberg, 1948, 61.
16 Motioner vid allmänna kyrkomötet 1948, nr 20.
17 Carl F. Hallencreutz, Yngve Brilioth. Svensk medeltidsforskare och internationell kyrkoledare. Uppsala 2002, 168.

18 Sundberg, 1948, 99. The situation was soon changed with the Law on Religious freedom, 1951.
19 Motioner vid allmänna kyrkomötet 1951, nr 30, 31.
20 LUB, Collection Bo Giertz, Sundberg to Giertz 1948, Dec. 21.
21 Halvar G.F. Sundberg, Stat och kyrka enligt gällande svensk rätt (AUU, SIU 3). Stockholm 1961, 6.
22 Sundberg, 1961, 11.
23 Religionsfrihetslag (1951:680)
24 Sundberg, 1961, 14.
25 Sundberg, 1961, 36f.
26 Halvar G.F. Sundberg, "Kyrkorättslig problematik" in: Förvaltningsrättslig tidskrift 1963, 7–9.
27 Sterzel, 2014, 207.
28 Anders Nygren, Filosofisk och kristen etik. Lund 1923, 139.
29 Anders Jarlert, Nygren, Aulén och nationalsocialismen – omvärderingar av historiska positioner in: Samuel Rubenson & Anders Jarlert, Kyrkohistoriska omvärderingar. Lund 2004, 65f.
30 Gustaf Aulén, Den allmänneliga kristna tron. 3rd edition, Stockholm 1931, 156.
31 Anders Nygren, Den kristna kärlekstanken genom tiderna. Eros och Agape II. Stockholm 1936, 123.
32 Gustaf Aulén, "Kristendomen och världsläget," in: Gustaf Aulén & Manfred Björkquist, Rätt och frihet. Stockholm 1935, 20, 24f., 27.
33 Karl Olivecrona, *Law as Fact* (London: Oxford University Press, 1939). Swedish translation: Om lagen och staten, Ejnar Munksgaard, Copenhagen 1940.
34 Gustaf Aulén, Kan något kristet krav ställas på statslivet? Stockholm 1940, 37, 39f., 42.
35 Aulén, 1940, 49, 54.
36 Gustaf Aulén, Den allmänneliga kristna tron. 4th edition. Stockholm 1943, 212–213.
37 Gustaf Aulén, Kyrkan och rättsordningen in: En bok om kyrkan. Stockholm 1942, 414f., 417f.
38 Aulén, 1943, 211, 213, 342, 454.
39 Gustaf Aulén, "Rättsmedvetandets grundval," in: Kirke og Kultur 51. 1945, 190f., 195, 196.
40 Jonas Jonson, Gustaf Aulén. Biskop och motståndsman. Skellefteå 2011, 208, 217.
41 Jonson, 2011, 187–90.
42 Sven Kjöllerström, Review of Sundberg 1948, in: Statsvetenskaplig tidskrift 1949, 201.
43 Yngve Brilioth, Svensk kyrkokunskap, preface to the first edition. Uppsala 1946, 5.
44 Brilioth, 1964, 61–63.
45 Brilioth, 1946, 62f.
46 Brilioth, 1946, 63.

Bibliography

Aulén, Gustaf, Den allmänneliga kristna tron. 3rd edition: Svenska kyrkans diakonistyrelses bokförlag, Stockholm 1931.

Aulén, Gustaf, *Den allnmänneliga kristna tron*. 4th edition. Stockholm: Svenska kyrkans diakonistyrelses bokförlag, 1943.

Aulén, Gustaf, Kan något kristet krav ställas på statslivet? Stockholm 1940.

Aulén, Gustaf, "Kristendomen och världsläget" in: Aulén, Gustaf & Björkquist, Manfred, Rätt och frihet. Stockholm: Svenska kyrkans diakonistyrelses bokförlag, 1935.

Aulén, Gustaf, Kyrkan och rättsordningen, in: En bok om kyrkan. Stockholm 1942.

Aulén, Gustaf, "Rättsmedvetandets grundval," in: Kirke og Kultur 51. 1945.
Brilioth, Yngve, Svensk kyrkokunskap. Svenska kyrkans diakonistyrelses bokförlag: Uppsala 1946.
Evald, Jens, Alf Ross - a life, DJØF: Copenhagen 2014.
Hallencreutz, Carl F., Yngve Brilioth. Svensk medeltidsforskare och internationell kyrkoledare. Swedish Institute of Mission Research: Uppsala 2002.
Jarlert, Anders, Nygren, Aulén och nationalsocialismen – omvärderingar av historiska positioner in: Rubenson, Samuel & Jarlert, Anders, Kyrkohistoriska omvärderingar. Lund: Lunds universitets kyrkohistoriska arkiv, 2004.
Jonson, Jonas, Gustaf Aulén, Biskop och motståndsman. Artos: Skellefteå 2011.
Källström, Staffan, Värdenihilism och vetenskap. Uppsalafilosofin i forskning och samhällsdebatt under 1920- och 30-talen. Göteborg: Acta Universitatis Gothoburgensis, 1984.
Kjöllerström, Sven, Review of Sundberg 1948, in: Statsvetenskaplig tidskrift, vol. 52: 1949. 201–204.
Lunds universitetsbibliotek (LUB), (Lund University Library), Collection Bo Giertz.
Lyles, Max, A Call for Scientific Purity: Axel Hägerström's Critique of Legal Science, Rättshistoriskt bibliotek Vol. 65, Institutet för rättshistorisk forskning: Stockholm 2006.
Motioner vid allmänna kyrkomötet 1948.
Motioner vid allmänna kyrkomötet 1951.
Nordin, Svante, Från Hägerström till Hedenius. Den moderna svenska filosofin. Doxa: Bodafors 1983.
Nygren, Anders, Den kristna kärlekstanken genom tiderna. Eros och Agape II. Svenska Kyrkans Diakonistyrelses Bokförlag: Stockholm 1936.
Nygren, Anders, Filosofisk och kristen etik. Lund: Lunds universitets årsskrift, 1923.
Olivecrona, Karl, Law as Fact. Humphrey Milford: London 1939.
Olivecrona, Karl, Om lagen och staten. Munksgaard: Copenhagen 1940.
Religionsfrihetslag (Svensk Författningssamling, 1951:680)
Sterzel, Fredrik, art. Sundberg, Halvar Gustaf Fredrik., in: Svenskt Biografiskt Lexikon 34. Stockholm 2014.
Sundberg, Halvar G.F., Kyrkorätt. Institutet för offentlig och internationell rätt: Helsingfors 1948.
Sundberg, Halvar G.F., "Kyrkorättslig problematik" in: Förvaltningsrättslig tidskrift, Issue 1, 1963, 1 ff.
Sundberg, Halvar G.F., Stat och kyrka enligt gällande svensk rätt (AUU, SIU 3). Stockholm 1961.

20 Church leader in times of trouble

Eivind Josef Berggrav (1884–1959)

Egil Morland

A brief biography

Bishop of Oslo and prelate of the Church of Norway, Dr. Eivind Josef Berggrav, unquestionably the most important church leader in Norway in his lifetime, laid the foundation for this leadership role during World War II. In those turbulent years, he became famous for his and the church's resistance to the Nazi occupation.

Berggrav was born in Stavanger, where his father, Otto Jensen, served as a parish priest. Jensen also became Minister of Church and Education and shortly before his death was appointed bishop to the diocese of Hamar. Eivind, who later changed his surname to Berggrav after his grandmother, started his studies of theology in 1903. On graduating from the university in 1908, in a turmoil of thoughts and doubts about life in general and the Christian belief in particular, Berggrav taught school for a decade. He also started writing for the journal *Kirke og Kultur* [*Church and Culture*], of which he later became owner and editor.

Overcoming his religious crisis, Berggrav answered the call to serve as a parish priest in eastern Norway (1918) and at the same time continued his studies for a doctorate in religious psychology. For three years, after receiving this degree in 1925, Berggrav also served as a chaplain of the national prison in Oslo. In 1928, he was appointed bishop to the northernmost diocese in Norway, Hålogaland, where he served until 1937. That year, Berggrav was appointed bishop to the diocese of Oslo, then the highest position in the national Church of Norway ("*the state church*").

In 1910, Eivind Berggrav married Kathrine Seip and became happily involved in a family that held positions in many important areas of public life. One of her brothers was Didrik Arup Seip, rector of the University of Oslo (deposed in 1941 and sent to the concentration camp at Sachsenhausen). Another brother, Hans Seip, was a member of parliament (the Storting), and a third was a famous rural dean in the area where Nazi Norwegian *Ministerpresident* Quisling had his roots. Henrik Aubert Seip became a close friend and counselor to Berggrav, but also a strong opponent in his debates on the state church before the war. Clearly, Berggrav honed his positions in these arguments between equal intellectual minds.[1]

As most theologians of his time, Berggrav had ties to Germany, and he spent several periods at German universities. During World War I, he also worked in Germany as a war correspondent for an Oslo newspaper. When World War II broke out, Berggrav was already famous in the Nordic countries as a great public speaker. While working on his doctorate, he found a refuge in Lund, Sweden, and developed a deep, personal friendship with Gustav Aulén, a professor in Lund and later bishop of Strängnäs. During the war, Aulén became "the voice of Norway" in Sweden.[2]

Eivind Berggrav was a Lutheran, and like most of the theologians in Norway, he never embraced the Barthian paradigm. His, and the church's, ideological resistance to Nazism reflects this view. Unlike the German Barmen Declaration, rooted in Christology, the Norwegian equivalent, *The Foundation of the Church*, has a base in the moral implications of God's law.[3] Through his involvement in ecumenical work, Berggrav became one of the leaders of the peacekeeping work within the World Alliance of Churches. He personally conducted peace travels between the foreign ministers of Germany and Great Britain in 1939.[4]

In 1942, the *New York Times* chose Berggrav as one of the six religious leaders profiled in a series titled "Churchmen Who Defy Hitler." *Time Magazine* put him on its cover in its Christmas 1944 edition, and this publicity was one of many indications of his reputation as a leader in occupied Europe. Berggrav was one of the speakers when the United Bible Societies (UBS) was established in 1946, and he later became its first president. He resigned from office as bishop in 1950 but continued his work as an international church leader. Eivind Josef Berggrav died in 1959, at the age of seventy-five.

World War II: the epicenter of Berggrav's life

Recent studies underline the key role Berggrav played in the spiritual battle of Norway during the war. These studies also tend to restore his reputation regarding the more dubious incidents from the first confusing days of the German occupation.[5] For example, an American researcher values Berggrav's "exceptional leadership": his "intellect, flexibility of mind, force of personality, persuasive power, ecumenical exposure, political acumen, rhetorical flair, foresight, capacity for work, strategic thinking, or tactical brilliance" surpassed that of all of his bishop colleagues and other leaders of his time.[6]

The war represented a *kairos* for the Norwegian church. The judicial controversies in which Berggrav was involved warrant attention, especially concerning the legal status of the church in a state-church system.[7] The war experiences also had a tremendous impact on Berggrav's view of the state's basis and mandate. The state's inclination to trespass its legitimate authority became one of the important tendencies that concerned him.

The relevant works

Eivind Berggrav was a public speaker, journalist, writer, preacher—and a master of cleverly crafted slogans. In punchlines, he communicated much more than the mere words, and he conveyed new insights in an instant. Famous is his comment on the hot issue of the attitude of the church to the "situation" in June 1940: "Let it first of all be clear, that the most important fact in the situation is that 'the situation' is not the most important, but God, who is the Lord of the situation!"[8]

In addition to his extensive oral communication, Berggrav steadily wrote books and lengthy articles. Relevant to the focus on church jurisdiction and the moral leadership of the church, the following written material is of importance: in 1930 he debated, and in 1932 released, a booklet on the balance between state and church.[9] The controversy with the director general in the Department for Ecclesiastical Affairs, Søren Oftenæs, resulted in a new article, "Church and Department,"[10] followed by "Episcopal and Royal Power."[11] In this debate, Berggrav also met a formidable adversary in his brother-in-law, Henrik A. Seip, who in two articles revealed a more symbiotic view of the relation between state and church and claimed that in matters of conflict, the king (and the government) had the final word.[12] An important document, *On the Church's Order*, written in December 1941, dealt with the obligation of the department to involve the bishops in church matters. Berggrav played a key role in the conception of *The Foundation of the Church: A Confession and a Declaration* [Kirkens Grunn], which laid the ideological basis for the mass resignation of the clergy on Easter Day, 1942.

In 1945, Eivind Berggrav published *Man and State*, probably his most famous book, translated into English in 1951.[13] He wrote a major part of this book in 1943–44 when he was in solitary confinement outside Oslo. The book included a lecture, "Religion and Law," delivered at the Bar Association in Oslo on February 5, 1941. The address "When the Driver Is Out of his Mind," first delivered in the spring of 1941, was also included.[14]

In his confinement, Berggrav also wrote a book about his expectations for the future church order in Norway.[15] In this book, he boldly claimed that what happened in 1942, when the church became an independent free folk church, restored what was broken in 1537, when the church, by the introduction of the Reformation, lost its independence: "The period that started in 1537 lasted until 1942." Berggrav wrote this book in the summer of 1943, "in the hope that it would soon be possible to work for an *inner liberation* of the church," he says in the foreword.

Three postwar writings about the legal status of the church are noteworthy. The first is a book titled *The Norwegian Church in Its International Setting*.[16] The second is an address on the Lutheran World Federation's General Assembly in Hannover, in 1952, titled "State and Church Today in a Lutheran Perspective," which led to a heated debate on the understanding of the Lutheran doctrine of the two kingdoms. Finally, in a booklet, *Contra Castberg*, he fought the last battle in his lifelong struggle for the (relative) independence of the church.[17] He claimed that Castberg, the leading jurist on constitutional law in Norway, challenged the principal thinking in the *Foundation*. Bishop Berggrav, now retired, stated that the *Foundation of the Church* should be quoted in the *present* tense, "because it is still valid words."

The church resistance: a brief introduction

The German invasion of Norway on April 9, 1940, led to a period of confusion and a need for time to strategize. The king and the government fled the capital and retreated to the north and eventually to London in June 1940. An administrative council was established in an effort to maintain regular civil life and affairs, and not in the least to overturn the coup d'état of Vidkun Quisling. Eivind Berggrav was central in establishing this council.

Since the church was a state church, formally led by the king, but in the parliamentary system more realistically by the government and its church cabinet, the church had to maneuver through murky waters. Formally hoping that Germany would respect the international law for occupied nations, churchgoers had the opportunity to adjust to the new authorities.[18] The bishops gave in to the demands of omitting the prayer for King Haakon in the intercessions in Sunday services. In the wording of the new prayer, however, they avoided using the former words of "upholding all authority" in society.[19]

Along with the occupants' abuse of power and the arbitrary use of violence and disrespect of civil rights, a firmer and more consequent strategy of resistance by the church developed. Berggrav was the strategist in this work, and he possessed the ability and personality to be the integral force therein. In establishing the Christian Consultative Council in October 1940, including the leaders of the lay movement within the Church of Norway, he laid the foundation for a unified Christian front.

In this and other ways, The Norwegian Church resistance avoided some of the failures of the German *Kirchenkampf*, and one had quite another basis—and willingness—for discussing and confronting the heathen traits of Nazi ideology. The readiness to confront injustice, rather than waiting until the unjust directly reached the church, seems to have been the gracious touch that the church needed to restore its position as a moral leader of the nation. Shortly after the Supreme Court laid down its office in December 1940, the bishops addressed the parishes (practically all the people of Norway) in a pastoral letter, which disclosed to the public the whole process of arguments with the government.

The authorities were furious, ordered the documents confiscated—successfully for maybe half of the copies—and forbade the clergy to read them in services, but to no avail. The pastoral letter questioned the legitimacy of the Nazi state by a reference to the Augsburg Confession (CA):

"According to the church's confession, the church stands in a relation to a just state, insofar as the state through its agencies is presumed to uphold the God-given order of law and justice." Consequently, the other side of this matter is that the obligation to obey (cf. Romans 13) is restricted to a *just* state.

From then, the path turned towards the final break between the two parties, which took place on Easter Day, 1942. The immediately previous event was the installation of Vidkun Quisling as Minister President in an act of state at the Castle of Akershus, on February 1. The National Socialist government wanted to celebrate this occasion with a service in the Nidaros Cathedral in Trondheim and thus overruled the local minister's right to serve. This action also denied him, with the help of police, the right to arrange an extra afternoon service, and eventually he was relieved from office. Quisling's frenetic verbal attacks on Berggrav, and the introduction of new laws concerning an obligatory program for indoctrinating all children and youth in the National Socialist worldview, made the final confrontation unavoidable. Now the bishops approached the clergy. The bishops had already on February 24 resigned from their stately offices, and thus prepared the mass resignation of the clergy on Easter Day. It was important to Berggrav that this resignation resulted from their initiative, instead of their waiting for the government to fire them.

With World War II at the center, Eivind Berggrav's theological, legal, and political interests revolved around several key ideas during most of his life, such as (I) State and Church and the preconditions for their coexistence; (II) Religion and Law and the transcendence of both of them; and (III) Humanity and State and the corruptibility of power.

I State and church: preconditions for their coexistence

Eivind Berggrav was the coauthor of and the most influential contributor to the document *Kirkens Grunn* (*The Foundation of the Church: A Confession and a Declaration*, hereafter: the *Foundation*). When most of the parish priests in the church resigned from their state offices, and at the same time proclaimed that they intended to continue their parish duties, they did so on the basis of this confession. Under severe threats of high treason, more than 92 percent of the clergy still defied and held their ground. The two last articles of the *Foundation* concern the judicial status and role of the church in society: "On the Proper Relation of the Christians and the Church's to the Authorities" (Article V) and "On the State Church" (Article VI). According to Article V, the proclamation of the Word addresses all realms of life. Three topics are important.

The "clear distinguishing," but not separation, between the two kingdoms, orders or realms

Article V very strongly underscores that the authority of the church, as well as that of the state, rests in a mandate from God. They shall not intervene in each other's responsibility: "It is the *church's* calling to … let the light of God's Word fall on all human relationships." The calling of the state is to "defend the body and material things against manifest wrongs, and hold the people in check in order to maintain civil justice and peace" (a reference to CA 28).

Limitation of the state's authority

The article identifies, in principal formulations, the trespassing of this authority in Norway: "[I]t is a sin against God if the state begins to tyrannize souls." A state which tries to "coerce" souls comes under the judgment of God's law: "It is no longer God's instrument, but a demonic power" (Luke 4,6; John 14,30; Revelation 12-13). The article aims to show the "proper obedience that Christians should show to the state, but also the limits of that obedience." Possibly the most famous sentence in the *Foundation* reads: "[W]here the State forsakes justice, it is no longer God's instrument but a demonical power."[20]

The implications of a conditional understanding of the state

The *Foundation* therefore has to cope with Romans 13. What the authorities *are*, according to Paul, is here understood not as a mere fact, but rather as a precondition: "The apostle has clarified how this authority is to be recognized ... *by its not being a terror to good conduct,* but to bad." If the authorities do not conform to this understanding, "then they are no longer an authority according to God's will," which in that case also invokes the responsibility of the church to "let such an authority hear the word of truth." Article V in the *Foundation* thus anchors the conscience in the belief in and responsibility to God, and rejects, by a quotation from a letter from the Ministry of Church affairs, the idea that the earthly power shall have "the highest authority and the greatest right over every single citizen." Such an assumption is in conflict with God's command.

The last article in *The Foundation of the Church* is about the state church:

> According to Norway's constitution and laws, the state's organs have certain directing and regulatory authority in church affairs. This does not mean that the state shall rule the church through outward power... The state church arrangement has come about simply because the state has declared that it will serve the church's cause and protect the Christian faith. Therefore, according to the constitution, the aforementioned state organs are also pledged to scripture and the confession.

The connection to the state does not change the fact that the church is "supreme and spiritually free in all affairs pertaining to God. The state can never become a church." The nature of the relation between church and state will then be an important issue. The answer to that depends on the starting-point, whether it is in the historical origins of the Christian church, in the introduction of the Reformation in Norway (1537), in the absolute monarchy (1660), in the Constitution (1814), or in customary law, which gradually developed the concept of a church as an institution per se in the apparatus of the state.[21]

Preliminary debates

Rather surprisingly, a debate about the necessity of the bishops' recommendation letter (Latin *collatio*) to the appointed parish priests arose in 1930.[22] One of the bishops denied giving his recommendation letter in a particular matter. The ministry then decided that the priest could install himself. Berggrav protested, and the Bishops' Conference confirmed his view.[23]

In 1932, in *The Balance between State and Church,* Berggrav gave his reasons for this position. The key question is whether the bishops play an independent role within the state church system. He considered that the consequence of the ministry's reasoning in the actual case would mean that the recommendation letter (as prescribed in the Altar Book) was "without any reality, although it could have a moral one." The Bishops' Conference deemed such a position to lack any legal basis."[24]

Berggrav engaged on two fronts in this argument: on one side with the director general of the church ministry, and on the other side with his brother-in-law, Henrik Seip. Berggrav argued that Seip, whom the spokesman of the departmental ministry took to his heart, was reducing the role of the church in the process as merely automatic-ecclesial consequences of an act of the state. A conflict between the parties, however, is not within the purview of the constitution, Berggrav claims. The arrangement between church and state rests on mutual trust and unconditional respect, and the king represented both sovereignties. An eventual conflict will not end in the Parliament, because it is excluded by the constitution from deciding internal religious matters. All church jurists agree on this principle, he adds.

Berggrav naturally agrees, as Seip asserts, that the king has appointed the bishops, too. Whether they are therefore subordinate to the king in religious matters is a viable question. The answer is that no, the bishops' duty is to ensure that the king fulfills his commitments, according to the constitution. To achieve this goal, the king has delegated to the bishops' office a strong factual authority. A *ius in sacris* exists, by virtue of which the king executes a direct authority, not by virtue of the elected assembly.

On this point, Berggrav relates his words to Luther's teaching of the two kingdoms. The path to serve as a priest in the church therefore consists of two acts: appointment and ordination. Ordination is decreed by the king on the basis of a commitment, which rests with him as well as with the church. Consequently, Berggrav asks, using Seip's words, whether ordination is possible merely as "a ceremonious act of installation." Not even for civilian law is ordination merely ceremonious, because ordination includes civil law obligations. The Altar Book is simply a part of Norwegian law.

Berggrav does not discard the system but rather aims to find a balance in it, which gives the church space to be a society of faith within the system.[25] Nobody could even imagine how soon the following situation would come to a test: "What if it comes to conflict?" Berggrav's answer—in 1932—is: "If the king in a matter of central ecclesial importance acts against all the (theological) experts …, this would be … a constitutional violation and revolution… [W]e will have to discuss that when we have more than our fantasy to build on."

From fantasy to reality—and beyond

The Church of Norway became an autonomous church at Easter, 1942, and functioned—for more than three years—as a self-governed folk church.

A provisional church leadership came to life in the summer of 1942. Leading to these events, a number of controversies about the legal aspects of the state church system came under discussion. In their pastoral letter, the bishops said that if "the state …apparatus … restricts our obedience to Christ, we will involuntarily become engaged." The letter further states that "the Church *is* not the State. And the State *is* not the Church."

The latent tension between the bishops and the ministry was nourished by the fact that tradition and common customs were the basis for the relation between these two entities, rather than laws and regulations. The Nazi government systematically tried to take advantage of this distinction by, for instance, addressing its information directly to the parish priests and ignoring the bishops as mediators.[26] This tactic resulted in a rather comprehensive letter, the "Order of the Church," signed by all the bishops, in December 1941. They wrote that "our church's relation to the state is possible only on the condition that the state … submit all important matters to declaration by the bishops." The bishops gave a number of legal, customary, and theological reasons for this practice: "The spiritual authority of the bishops is derived, but also limited, by Scripture and by the Church as the assembly of believers. [T]his authority cannot be derived or limited by any other authority."[27]

Berggrav contra Castberg

A new controversy arose after the war, in 1953, which also included deliberations about law, or right. In the aftermath of a speech broadcast by Professor Ole Hallesby, in which he urged people to repent to escape hell, the bishop of Hamar, Kristian Schjelderup, said that the doctrine of eternal damnation does not belong to the religion of love (Cf. CA, Art. 17). A harsh debate followed. Schjelderup then asked the Ministry of Church Affairs to decide whether, by this view, he had placed himself outside of the church's confession. The ministry followed procedure and asked the theological experts (the two theological faculties and the bishops) about their views on this matter, and the discussion revealed a rather deep disagreement about the understanding of the biblical texts and about the commitment to the confession, theological as well as legal.

Nothing of this caused Berggrav to become involved. Once again, however, he found the opportunity to fight for his ideas. He did not intervene because the king ruled in favor of Schjelderup, but rather because the ministry also sent the case to Frede Castberg, the professor of constitutional law at Oslo University. Castberg's commentaries made it clear that what started the process was far less important than the professor's view on church and church law.[28] This moment was a defining one for truth: "If this thesis [read: Castberg's commentaries] had been available before the occupation took place, the Norwegian church resistance in that period would have been impossible," Berggrav writes in his booklet.[29]

His main objection is that Castberg limits the case to legal formalities. Berggrav recalls the question he had asked in his book on the future order of the church: whether it will fall back on the old system and thus prevent the birth that had begun. The key question is whether the church needs an external independence at all. Because the situation for the church after the war was so clean; unmarred by selfish motivation or political ambition, the church now had a rare opportunity to realize the ideas being born from that struggle.

Berggrav claimed that all real authority needs a certain shape, a form, or a way to assert itself (Norw.: *hevdelsesform*). Every church must alone decide the way it expresses its faith, whether in the confession, in the service (liturgy), or in the (church) order. "The freedom the church must possess"—one chapter headline in the book—is the freedom of preaching, of confession, and of calling. He deemed all of these freedoms possible in a state-church system, but this system must presuppose that a disruption between the parties, however hypothetical, might be a possible result: "The break up is and remains our *ultima ratio*," he states.

Berggrav considered his lifelong battle about this issue threatened by Castberg's interpretations of the law. Castberg's nine points were as follows: 1. The Constitutional law stipulates that the state religion shall remain Evangelical Lutheran, but it does not imply anything about the confessional documents. 2. Scripture and confession must be interpreted in the "spirit of the time," and should not be taken too literally. 3. The confessional obligation for the "public teachers of religion [to] follow the norms prescribed for them" (§ 16 in the Constitutional Law) is not a legal commitment to preach what a person considers to be untrue or incorrect. 4. The king is not legally committed to ask the bishops for advice, nor to follow their advice. 5. An eventual change of the church's confessional writings can be done by a royal resolution alone. 6. A bishop's unwillingness to ordain or give his letter of recommendation is no obstacle for the priest to accede to his office. The business of the bishop is not to judge whether the appointed person fulfills the legal preconditions. The decision to alter or repeal the prescriptions for ordination and collation can be made by a royal resolution alone. 7. The king's authority in important church matters is executed in the government, submitted to ordinary parliamentary control. 8. The state religion has no other legal protection than any other acknowledged faith society. 9. The church has no rights of its own towards the state but is a spiritual community. Above all in importance is securing wide boundaries for the freedom of belief within The Norwegian Church, Castberg concluded.

Berggrav argued that none of these assumptions is acceptable for the church, for reasons I will offer below.

The church order commission

After the war, Eivind Berggrav was appointed leader of the Church Order Commission of the government, which proposed the legal foundation for the church for the next fifty years. The report was presented in 1948.[30] In this, Berggrav tried to make use of the war experiences. To a certain degree, he did succeed in the commission, although even there he was in the minority. To his great disappointment, however, Parliament discarded almost all of the proposals.

Berggrav even had to endure accusations from politicians who claimed that the church had developed a taste for power during the war, and now was hungry for more! The final report resulted in only modest adjustments of the church law in 1953. The relations between state and church returned to the prewar system, based on the assumption of a mutual confidence that the church polity would be executed in an atmosphere of good will.[31]

Einar Molland, the leading Norwegian church historian of his time, also a member of the commission, thought highly of the church resistance and of the *Foundation*, as he did of Berggrav. To Molland, however, these years had not changed much fundamentally. When the parish priests resumed their offices in 1945—by pledging loyalty to the *Foundation*—that did "not imply any change in the relations between church and state which is now restored," Molland claimed.[32] The reform expert Terje Ellingsen drew the same conclusions, albeit from a different perspective: "The church reforms, which were supposed to exploit the experiences and the thinking from the fateful 1940s, showed to be rather meager."[33]

II Religion and law and the transcendence of both of them

The relation between the formal, codified law and the ideas from which it emanates is a central question. In his pamphlet *Contra Castberg*, Berggrav's aim is to show the unreasonable characteristics in all of Castberg's nine paragraphs. He quotes the *Foundation*, which in its second article reads—"not *read*, because it is to this day valid!"—: "For nine hundred years, ordination in our Norwegian church has been a scripturally authorized and regulated consecration. It is an independent and immutable component of a proper call to serve in the church." Berggrav also hints that "a very competent church jurist" assisted the church leaders when they wrote these lines.[34]

The root of the problem is that Castberg has taken into consideration only the formal character rather than the complexity of the material. Berggrav accuses Castberg of promoting "law without reasonableness," which in itself represents a violation of the idea that a law should promote. Even today, the Roman *ius* gives guidance to jurists of the world, Berggrav claims. The strict, formal *ius* needs a counterbalance in *aequitas—reasonableness.* A Latin proverb warns, *summum ius, summa iniuria*: the greatest law is the greatest injury. Injustice may be the result of a strict judicial interpretation and practice. Because of this cautionary note, our daily language says that a case must be "right and reasonable." Even if Castberg were right in his legal deliberations, that is, in the formalities, he is in no way reasonable because the subject in question stands above the codification of the jurisdiction concerning that same subject.

Ten years after the war, Berggrav quoted a decree from Quisling's church ministry in 1941: "The state alone is, according to §16 of the Constitutional Law, entitled to make decisions regarding the Altar Book. It *alone* possesses the right to repeal former as well as current regulations of this kind."[35] These words did fit completely Castberg's principal position. Berggrav notes the possibility that Castberg will dismiss everything from the occupation period as no more than manifestations of abnormal conditions.

The church does not regard the matter this way. Because "it has all too much been overlooked and concealed, that when the Norwegian priests and bishops after the liberation took [up] their office duties anew, they added that this happened by declaring that they were still standing on *the Foundation*."

Finally, Berggrav commented on Castberg's words about the importance "above all" to secure freedom of belief within The Norwegian Church. This is straight-out unconstitutional: "The government is *above all* bound by the Constitution and by the therein instituted Evangelical Lutheran religion."[36]

"Right" and "law": The nature of the law

Berggrav's arguments in 1954 had been presented in an even more philosophical approach in his famous lecture on "Religion and Law." The Norwegian word he used, "*right*," connotes right, law, natural law, justice, and a few other words. The lecture occurred in a tense situation. The same day, Berggrav had been summoned to a lengthy hearing before the Gestapo, regarding rumors about the release of the bishops' pastoral letter, which he in fact had sent to press the same day. In this interrogation, he learned that Paal Berg, the chief justice of the Norwegian Supreme Court, had been arrested. A more appropriate day to give such a lecture is hardly imaginable.

In both law and religion, certain principles and ineffable qualities transcend humanity, Berggrav says in his lecture. They do not "necessarily" have a common origin, but "there is a similarity in their nature," namely "the transcendent before which we *prostrate ourselves*." The law needs to maintain the right unless it will be unstable and fluid: "Law that is ignorant of grace can never *create* law."[37]

The origin of our Western culture is in the Hebrew, Greek, and Roman cultures. "[I]n all of them law and religion have originally come from one and the same source, namely, from [...] "the divine will."[38] The progressive codification of the law had a historically great upside, but at the expense of the nature of the law, "of... the eternal source of the sense of justice." The sentence *ubi societas, ibi jus*—"where there is society, there is law," meaning that society creates the law—mirrors this downside. This idea is contrary to the Germanic system, where "conception of law is built on *freedom*, or the dignity of man, as one of its foundation pillars."[39]

The definite separation between religion and law regards the latter simply as an expression of power by the state, an idea which also appears in Marxism. The law has two archenemies: one is external brute force; another is enslavement to alien purposes. Recognizing values higher than those we can manage as we please is important, and that especially includes values that acknowledge the absolute: "*the law must be regarded as inherently sovereign* or else it is no longer law."

Human dignity belongs to the noblest part of a human being and involves a person's conscience and conviction: "In other words, there is a sense of obligation from which no one can release himself, an obligation to something transcendent which both binds and sets free." Berggrav seeks a better term for the word "transcendent," and he suggests that "holy" might cover it. He highlights this sentence: "*It is when truth becomes something sacred that it creates martyrs.*" Towards the end of his lecture, he states that the church has at least two roles in which it interacts with the law: "as the maintainer of morality in society and as asserter of the dignity of man." The law is *holy*, as God is holy.[40] In the foreword to the English edition, Berggrav writes that the last sentence of his lecture—quoted from the church prayer—is a tribute to the imprisoned chief justice: "Be Thou the strength of those who suffer persecution for righteousness' sake."

Natural law

One of Berggrav's theological interests before and especially during World War II was political ethics.[41] Now he benefited greatly from this enthusiasm. The law, according to Berggrav, has metaphysical roots and consequently is universal and stands above all. The law is majestic and holy and therefore has a godly authority. In these lectures, he refrained from using the concept of natural law, although he already had included this matter in his ideological reasoning. In *Man and State*, however, he promoted the idea of a Christian natural law (cf. Romans 2:14).[42] Here, he rejects the idea of an autonomous law which, apart from God, could be a source of law and justice. The impulses for this idea probably came from Berggrav's engagement in ecumenical work. He accentuated the common, human character of ethics. His interest in religious psychology, too, led to an anchoring of concrete ethical guidance in a transcendent reality.[43]

Berggrav never shared the hesitance of Protestant and dialectic theology toward the idea of natural law. The Swedish theologians Gustav Aulén and Anders Nygren inspired him. Aulén talked about a universal Christian perspective of law and suggested that "the law of creation," *lex creationis*, could replace the concept of natural law, *lex naturae*.[44] Expressions similar to these occur in *Man and State*. A state of justice is, in his thinking, based on a theological understanding of natural law. For Berggrav, as well as for Aulén, this idea mirrored their principal reflections on the relation between power and justice that developed in the 1930s.[45]

Berggrav explains the Protestant reluctance as a fear for a natural law conception founded on *nature*. "If the natural *condition* is to constitute the norm, then the days of law are numbered," he eloquently asserts. The Protestant church, broadly speaking, fought this nature-based thinking. Inside the Roman church, however, there was a fifth column, as long as "the natural" constituted the basis. Natural law cannot, however, be rooted in fallen humanity. The later separation between natural law and God therefore was inevitable.[46]

One of Berggrav's memorable sentences is that "the law can never find release in statutes."[47] His point is that certain mandates must take a higher position above the codified laws, as illustrated in *Man and State*: "Agreements that are made in no higher name than one's own are always in a class with the fox's promise not to touch the chickens."[48] By a reference to Ephesians 6 about "the full armor," Berggrav admits that "Christianity regards the struggle with a somewhat pessimistically tinged sobriety," but it is on the same time realistic.[49] The idea of natural law must be built on the belief that the Creator has laid down the universal prerequisites to acknowledge his will.

III Man and state: The corruptibility of power

The title *Man and State* refers to an even wider subject, namely Berggrav's lifelong engagement in the relation between the individual and society.[50] His view of the transcendence of law, and his conviction of the existence of a common, universal moral law for all of humanity, has significant implications for the principles of the relation between humanity and the state.[51]

Article V of the *Foundation* says, "[I]t becomes the church's duty to let such an [unjust] authority hear the word of truth and... warn them." Christians shall obey the authorities in all temporal matters, but limits to this obedience do occur, and "we must therefore obey God more than man." This means that obedience to God is more than a *right*; it is also a spiritual *duty*. Is the end of this road silence and martyrdom? And what about active resistance?

In a series of meetings in 1941, Berggrav had been lecturing about "the duty of disobedience." In "When the Driver is Out of his Mind," Berggrav stated, "[w]herever God is concerned it is never a matter of right only, but also of duty." The "common task" of the two kingdoms to do good can occur only if Christians are prepared "[t]o oppose Satan and his rule in every form and manner, to ward off the attacks of evil, to beat down violence and unrighteousness."[52]

The key to understanding this principle is that because God is above both kingdoms, whoever preaches must preach God's word to both. This conviction is so fundamental to Berggrav that he ridicules those who misuse Jesus's words about giving to Caesar what is Caesar's. Rhetorically he lashed out: "Try substituting another word for 'Caesar' in Jesus's sentence—e.g., give to the world what belongs to the world, or give to Satan what is Satan's, and at once lightning flashes from Sinai!"[53] This way of thinking would elevate worldly obedience above obedience to God.

Therefore, a requirement is that "one of God's offices is to speak to the other of God's offices."[54]

The church must use nonviolent methods of resistance appropriate to the kingdom of "the right hand," the hand of mercy and salvation: "If the church takes to worldly means, then it goes over to the camp of the enemy. The church's domain and existence is *the Word*, God's Word, the word of conscience." Words are never mere words, however: words are action, contribution, courage, the willingness to accept consequences, and finally the willingness to suffer. The one who resists must prepare fully to accept those consequences.[55] The willingness to suffer is a way of knowing that one is disobeying for the right reasons. Suffering is as much a Christian "weapon" against evil as is the Word.

What the next step is and what role active resistance plays are the next questions to consider. Certainly, the Christian has only two weapons, the Word and the suffering—as long as he is behaving on behalf of his office or the church. That said, Berggrav took a further step. He did not completely rule out a kind of resistance, and he referred to Luther, who taught that traitors and rebels would have a free hand to do as they pleased if the citizens of a land had to submit to the moral law of avoiding resisting violence.

In such a situation, a Christian citizen is not different from any other citizen. He must act in the name of the law. Just as one is under no obligation to the murderer whom he meets on a highway, so a Christian citizen is released from the duty of obedience to nonviolence. In such a situation, weapons must be used in the name of the law: "His responsibility is to the law."[56] Berggrav quoted the Augsburg Confession's emphasis on *lawful* authority, and he claims that all "that the worldly power calls upon us to acknowledge and obey has to be *de iure*."

The church's resistance to the Nazi occupation stemmed from the assumption that all authorities, regardless of how they came to power, have to uphold the right. From this position The Norwegian Church contributed to a renewal of the Lutheran "doctrine of the two kingdoms." Leading theologians in Germany had argued that the behavior of the state in ethical issues had to follow its own legality (German*: Eigengesetzlichkeit*). Berggrav challenged and discarded German Lutheranism on this point. To the question of what to do "when the driver is out of his mind," which sounds like a rhetorical question, the answer is obvious: you grasp the reins. The ancient church did not "condemn the murder of a tyrant. It continued to be a praiseworthy deed if a man sacrificed his own life to rid his fatherland of a tyrant," Berggrav wrote without reservation.[57]

The insights from the occupation, as formulated in the *Foundation*, became the standard Lutheran position after the war. A legitimate question is whether this position represented a new insight, or simply was a calling into life of an inherent Lutheran theological position, for a long time neglected in practice as well as in theory.

The state's moral fundament and corruptibility of power

During his three years of confinement, family and couriers managed to smuggle books on religion, philosophy, and politics to Eivind Berggrav. He used them as resources and references for books and articles, which he hid in devious ways. His extensive reading also meant that Berggrav was better prepared for peace than most of those who were struggling with their daily duties during these years. He thus could develop the premises for the necessary initiatives in May 1945, such as the immediate removal of priests who had been loyal to the National Socialist government.

The most comprehensive work from this time is the book *Man and State*. Berggrav's mission is to unmask the roots of the ideology behind much political thought, with its inherent potential to create atrocities like Nazism and Communism. The first chapter bears the title "The Demon of Politics." The expression is from Max Weber, who once said: "Between the demon of politics and the God of love, there is an inner tension which can break out into horrible conflict at a moment's notice." Weber said this after World War I. Now, Berggrav stated that this prophesy had come to full realization.

Berggrav found the roots of the demon in the time of the Reformation, "at the very point which we designate as the birthday of modern times."[58] He did not, however, find it in Wittenberg but in Florence! By subtle analogies and illustrative quotations from a number of philosophers and politicians, he demonstrated how the cynicism of Machiavelli easily permeates how we think about the authority of the state over the lives of individuals.

Berggrav took a particular interest in two of Machiavelli's principles: the first is the exalted character of the state; the second is the relation of the state to the divine. According to Machiavelli, the state is absolute sovereign in its own realm and also is beyond morality. The state not only can break with morality but must do so, if its welfare is at stake. In this self-preservation, the state needs to conceal its conflict with the moral law.

The translation of Machiavelli's book title *Il Principe* is *The Prince*. Berggrav argued, in alluding to *der Führer,* that a better translation would be "The Leader," who has "to play the role of the lion but also that of the fox, and even of the lamb, if need be."[59]

God, his substitute, and its camouflage: reason

Berggrav asserts that morality is "inextricably" related to God, but as time has passed, God has been replaced by "the welfare of the community." When the people and their leaders no longer accepted that the natural law is God's law, they elevated reason to his place and "made it the mysterious incarnation of the divinity of state." Reason proved to be an excellent camouflage, Berggrav said.[60]

This effect, the camouflage of what the ideologies might lead to, was never the original intention. The obverse is that the ideas that formed Europe in the late eighteenth century (inspired by the French Revolution), "intended that the state should embrace the whole life and that it should gradually permeate all the areas of daily and private life." No end to this permeation is apparent, but the consequence is that even people's attitude is a concern of the state and punishable if necessary.[61] This kind of interference can happen only because the claim of the state to be sovereign is not about a relative sovereignty; it craves sovereignty in an absolute sense. Consequently, the modern state will inevitably become demonic if it does not humanize.

Whether Eivind Berggrav had nothing but criticism against the modern state and whether healing exists anywhere for the state are pertinent questions. First, in Berggrav's sharp analysis of the development of the modern state, at any given time the opportunity was present for state leaders to think and act differently about the state's reason to exist. This reason is owing to obligation and duty rather than to power and force. Second, Berggrav wanted concepts like reciprocity to be the key to what society is about, with the biblical ideas of commonality and reciprocity as the ideal.[62] Reciprocity is a prerequisite for a qualitative equality, he claimed, which also should guide the way the political powers act towards their citizens. He contrasted the concepts of power (force) and authority and asserted that force is a substitute because authority is the real entity.

Berggrav's understanding of the mandate of the state and the dangers of the state's tendency to penetrate the private sphere, and thus usurp illegitimate authority, seems to have a lasting validity. His main thesis in his Hannover lecture was that the welfare state put at risk the practical application of the doctrine of two kingdoms. The consequence may be that the church will have no role to play in society. Consequently, the radical question arises whether the doctrine of two kingdoms can be sustained under such circumstances.[63]

Despite all contrary evidence, Berggrav had a profound belief in creating an international law. If this law placed the majesty of God (or of Natural Law) above the legal consciousness of the world, it would deliver humanity from its curse, which he described in his presentation of the Machiavellian way of thinking.

Berggrav lived to witness not only the Nuremberg Trials but also the establishment of the United Nations Declaration of Human Rights and the European Convention on Human Rights. He thus became a catalyst to the human rights revolution of our time.

Notes

1 Morland, Egil, *Widerstand und Verkündigung* [Resistance and Preaching], Arbeiten zur Historischen und Systematischen Theologie, Band 22 (Münster: LIT Verlag, 2018), 73.
2 Jonson, Jonas, *Gustaf Aulén, biskop och motståndsman* [Gustaf Aulén, Bishop and Resistance Man] (Skellefteå: Artos & Norma bokförlag, 2011), 297–306.
3 Heiene, Gunnar, *Eivind Berggrav* (Oslo, Universitetsforlaget, 1992), 291.
4 Berggrav, Eivind, *Forgjeves for fred* [In Vain for Peace] (Oslo, Land og Kirke, 1960), and *Da kampen kom* [When the Battle began] (Oslo, Land og Kirke, 1945).
5 Bauer, Joanna, "Eivind Berggravs motivasjon for å endre kirkebønnen under okkupasjonstiden" [Eivind Berggrav's motivation for changing the church prayer during the occupation], *Teologisk tidsskrift* 2 (2017), 129–45.
6 Hassing, Arne, *Church Resistance to Nazism in Norway 1940–1945* (Seattle and London, University of Washington Press, 2014), 272–73.
7 Morland, *Widerstand*, 133f.
8 From a letter to the priests and congregations in Oslo in June 1940. Berggrav presented similar formulations in a letter to the entire church in July, titled *The Temporal and the Eternal.*
9 Berggrav, Eivind, Balansen mellom stat og kirke. Illustrert ved betydningen av ordinasjon og kollats [The Balance between State and Church. Illustrated by the Significance of Ordination and Collatio], (*Kirke og Kultur 39*, Oslo, 1932), 82–113.
10 Berggrav, Eivind, "Kirke og Departement" [Church and State Ministry], (*Kirke og Kultur 39*, Oslo, 1932), 211–25.
11 Berggrav, Eivind, "Bispemakt og kongemakt" [Episcopal and Royal Power], (*Kirke og Kultur*, Oslo), 312f.
12 Seip, Henrik, "Det rette kall og de kristelige garantier" [The Right Calling and the Christian Warranties], (*Norsk Kirkeblad*, Oslo, 1930), and Seip, Henrik, "Biskopenes kompetanse innenfor statskirkens ramme" [The Competence of the Bishops within the Framework of the State Church System], (*Norsk Kirkeblad*, Oslo, 1932).
13 Berggrav, Eivind, *Staten og mennesket: Oppgjør og framblikk* (Oslo, Land og Kirke, 1945). Trans., George Aus, *Man and State* (Philadelphia, 1951).
14 Berggrav, Eivind, "Når kusken er gal. Luther om motstand mot øvrigheten" [When the Driver is out of his mind. Luther on the Duty of Disobedience], in *Man and State*, 300–19.

15 Berggrav, Eivind, *Kirkens ordning i Norge* [The Church Order of Norway] (Land og Kirke, Oslo, 1945).
16 Berggrav, Eivind, *The Church of Norway in Its International Setting* (London, S.C.M. Press, 1946).
17 Berggrav, Eivind, *Contra Castberg. Om Kirkens Grunn* [Contra Castberg. On the Foundation of the Church] (Oslo, Land og Kirke, 1954).
18 The Hague Convention of 1907.
19 Morland, *Widerstand,* 120.
20 *Kirchliche Zeitgeschichte/Contemporary Church History*, Vandenhoeck & Ruprecht, 2 (2015), 294–99.
21 Motzfeldt, U.A., *Den norske Kirkeret* [The Norwegian Church Law] (Christiania, J. Dahl, 1844), 20.
22 Until 1989, all pastors in the Church of Norway were appointed by the state church department.
23 Aarflot, Andreas, *Bispemakt og kirkestyre* [The Bishops' Authority and Church Governance] (Bergen, Eide Forlag, 2011), 54.
24 Berggrav, *The Balance*, 82.
25 Morland, Egil, "New Relations between Church and State in Norway," *European Journal of Theology*, 27/2 (2018).
26 Austad, Torleiv, *Kirkelig motstand* [Church Resistance], (Høyskoleforlaget, Kristiansand, 2005), 101.
27 The Order of The Church, par. 2.
28 Castberg, Frede, *Statsreligion og kirkestyre* [State Religion and Church Governance] (Oslo, Land og Kirke, 1953).
29 Berggrav, Eivind, *Contra Castberg* (Oslo, 1954), 5.
30 *Innstilling om Den norske kirkes ordning* [Proposal for the Order of The Norwegian Church] (Oslo, 1948).
31 Løvlie, Birger, *Kirke, stat og politikk i en etterkrigstid* [Church, State and Politics in Post War Time] (Oslo, Luther Forlag, 1996).
32 Molland, Einar, *Statskirke og Jesu Kristi kirke*, [State Church and the Church of Jesus Christ] (Oslo, Land og Kirke, 1954), 48.
33 Ellingsen, Terje, *Kirkelig visjon – politisk dragkamp* [Church Visions – Political Combat] (Stavanger, Nomi Forlag, 1973), 86.
34 Hansson, Kristian, *Norsk Kirkerett* [The Norwegian Church Law] (Oslo, Aschehoug & Co., 1935).
35 Berggrav, *Contra Castberg*, 16.
36 Ibid., 30.
37 Berggrav, *Religion and Law*, in *Man and State*, 289.
38 Ibid., 290.
39 Ibid., 291.
40 Ibid., 297.
41 Austad, Torleiv, "Eivind Berggrav and the Church of Norway's Resistance against Nazism, 1940–1945," *Mid-Stream* 26/1 (1987), 52.
42 Austad, Torleiv, *Kirkens Grunn* [The Foundation of the Church] (Oslo, Luther Forlag, 1974), 103.
43 Heiene, Gunnar, *Den menneskelige stat* [The Human State] (Oslo, 1991), 122.
44 Aulén, Gustav, *Kan något kristet krav ställas på statslivet* [Can There Be Any Christian Demands on the State's Life?] (Stockholm, 1940), 42.
45 Jonson, *Gustaf Aulén*, 195.
46 Berggrav, *Man and State*, 45.
47 Berggrav, *Religion and Law*, 290.
48 Berggrav, *Man and State*, 40.
49 Ibid., 67.

50 Cf. Reinhold Niebuhr's famous book *Moral Man and Immoral Society: A Study in Ethics and Politics*, (Philadelphia, PA, Westminster John Knox Press, 1932/1960).
51 Morland, Egil, "Love and Justice. Individual Man and Society and the Respective Parties' Moral Obligations: A Comparison of Two Different Approaches in Times of Turbulence," *Theophilos* 9/2 (2017), 158–68.
52 Berggrav, "When the Driver."
53 Ibid., 301.
54 Ibid., 313.
55 Ibid., 307.
56 Ibid., 315.
57 Berggrav, *Man and State*, 278.
58 Ibid., 5.
59 Ibid., 10.
60 Ibid., 19.
61 Ibid., 25.
62 This paragraph and the next have their references in part 2 of the Norwegian edition of *Man and State*.
63 Tønnessen, Aud V., Eivind Berggrav og velferdsstaten [Eivind Berggrav and the Welfare State], in Christoffersen and Wyller, eds., *Arv og utfordring* [Heritage and Challenge] (Oslo, Universitetsforlaget, 1995), 181.

Bibliography

Aarflot, Andreas, *Bispemakt og kirkestyre* [The Bishops Authority and Church Governance] (Bergen, Eide Forlag, 2011).

Aulén, Gustav, *Kan något kristet krav ställas på statslivet* [Can There Be Any Christian Demands on the State's Life?] (Svenska Kyrkans Diakonistyrelses Bokförlag: Stockholm, 1940).

Austad, Torleiv, "Eivind Berggrav and the Church of Norway's Resistance against Nazism, 1940–1945," *Mid-Stream* 26/1 (1987).

Austad, Torleiv, *Kirkens Grunn* [The Foundation of the Church] (Oslo, Luther Forlag, 1974).

Austad, Torleiv, *Kirkelig motstand* [Church Resistance] (Høyskoleforlaget, Kristiansand, 2005).

Bauer, Joanna, "Eivind Berggravs motivasjon for å endre kirkebønnen under okkupasjonstiden" [Eivind Berggrav's Motivation for Changing the Church Prayer during the Occupation], *Teologisk tidsskrift* 2 (2017), 129–145.

Berggrav, Eivind, *Balansen mellom stat og kirke*. Illustrert ved betydningen av ordinasjon og kollats [The Balance between State and Church. Illustrated by the Significance of Ordination and Collatio] (*Kirke og Kultur 39*, Oslo: Steenske Boktrykkeri, 1932).

Berggrav, Eivind, *Contra Castberg. Om Kirkens Grunn*. [Contra Castberg. On the Foundation of the Church] (Oslo, Land og Kirke, 1954).

Berggrav, Eivind, *Da kampen kom* [When the Battle Began] (Oslo, Land og Kirke, 1945).

Berggrav, Eivind, *Forgjeves for fred* [In Vain for Peace] (Oslo, Land og Kirke, 1960).

Berggrav, Eivind, "Kirke og Departement" [Church and State Ministry] (*Kirke og Kultur 39*, Oslo, 1932).

Berggrav, Eivind, *Kirkens ordning i Norge* [The Church Order of Norway] (Oslo, Land og Kirke, 1945).

Berggrav, Eivind, "Når kusken er gal. Luther om motstand mot øvrigheten" [When the Driver is out of his Mind. Luther on the Duty of Disobedience], in *Man and State*, (Philadelphia, Muhlenberg Press, 1951).

Berggrav, Eivind, *Religion and Law*, in *Man and* State, (Philadelphia, Muhlenberg Press, 1951).

Berggrav, Eivind, *Staten og mennesket: Oppgjør og framblikk* (Oslo, Land og Kirke, 1945). Trans., George Aus, *Man and State* (Philadelphia, Muhlenberg Press, 1951).

Castberg, Frede, *Statsreligion og kirkestyre* [State Religion and Church Governance] (Oslo, Land og Kirke, 1953).

Ellingsen, Terje, *Kirkelig visjon – politisk dragkamp* [Church Visions – Political Combat] (Stavanger, Nomi Forlag, 1973).

Hansson, Kristian, *Norsk Kirkerett* [The Norwegian Church Law] (Oslo, Aschehoug & Co., 1935).

Hassing, Arne, *Church Resistance to Nazism in Norway 1940–1945* (Seattle and London, University of Washington Press, 2014).

Heiene, Gunnar, *Den menneskelige stat* [The Human State] (Oslo, Det teologiske menighetsfakultet, 1991).

Heiene, Gunnar, *Eivind Berggrav* (Oslo, Universitetsforlaget, 1992).

Innstilling om Den norske kirkes ordning [Proposal for the Order of The Norwegian Church] (Oslo, Committee (appointed by Kirke- og utdanningsdepartementet (KUD) report, 1948).

Kirchliche Zeitgeschichte /Contemporary Church History, Vandenhoeck & Ruprecht, (Göttingen, 2015).

Løvlie, Birger, *Kirke, stat og politikk i en etterkrigstid* [Church, State and Politics in Post War Time] (Oslo, Luther Forlag, 1996).

Molland, Einar, *Statskirke og Jesu Kristi kirke* [State Church and the Church of Jesus Christ] (Oslo, Land og Kirke, 1954).

Morland, Egil, "Love and Justice. Individual Man and Society and the Respective Parties' Moral Obligations: A Comparison of Two Different Approaches in Times of Turbulence," *Theophilos* 9/2 (2017).

Morland, Egil, "New Relations between Church and State in Norway," *European Journal of Theology* 27/2 (2018).

Morland, Egil, *Widerstand und Verkündigung* [Resistance and Preaching], Arbeiten zur Historischen und Systematischen Theologie, Band 22 (Münster, LIT Verlag, 2018).

Motzfeldt, U.A., *Den norske Kirkeret* [The Norwegian Church Law] (Christiania, J. Dahl, 1844).

Niebuhr, Reinhold, *Moral Man and Immoral Society: A Study in Ethics and Politics* (Philadelphia, PA, Westminster John Knox Press, 1932/60).

Seip, Henrik, "Biskopenes kompetanse innenfor statskirkens ramme" [The Competence of the Bishops within the Framework of the State Church System] (*Norsk Kirkeblad,* Oslo, 1932).

Seip, Henrik, "Det rette kall og de kristelige garantier" [The Right Calling and the Christian Warranties] (*Norsk Kirkeblad,* Oslo, 1930).

Tønnessen, Aud V., Eivind Berggrav og velferdsstaten [Eivind Berggrav and the Welfare State], in Christoffersen and Wyller, eds., *Arv og utfordring* [Heritage and Challenge] (Oslo Universitetsforlaget, 1995).

21 Frede Castberg (1893–1977)

A counterpoint in modern Nordic legal culture

Kjell Å Modéer

Frede Castberg, professor of public law (constitutional law and administrative law) at Oslo University between 1928 and 1963, was an important representative of the modern Norwegian legal and societal culture of the twentieth century.[1] He experienced two world wars, the creation of the European social welfare-state, and became—also in a European context—a catalyst for the Human Rights paradigm after World War II. His fields of research were international public law, constitutional law and administrative law as well as legal philosophy. Due to his support for natural law perspectives he also became an idealistic counterpoint in the strong positivistic legal culture of the Nordic countries in the postwar times, characterized by Scandinavian legal realism and Kelsian value neutrality within the law.

His important contribution to law and religion in Norway came in the post-World War II period when he as a well-established law professor and as a constitutional expert gave his position regarding the constitutional position of the Norwegian Church in relation to its Church law. His complex position in this *Schul-Streit* had three perspectives, that of the law professor within constitutional law, that of the politician regarding the Norwegian Church, and that of the believing member in this Church.

Castberg was a catalyst in the post-World War II reaction to the un-law of the totalitarian Nazi regime. His strong liberal position was not only related to his professional authority but also to a great extent to his human abilities. Due to a contemporary colleague of his, his "breadth of vision, humanity and tolerance" were fundamental traits of his personality.[2]

Frede Castberg's father, Johan Castberg (1862–1926), was a lawyer and a civil servant, and member of the Norwegian parliament at the time for the dissolution of the personal union with Sweden in 1905. Johan Castberg belonged to the Norwegian political aristocracy, and in this social position also Frede Castberg was included. His constitutional views regarding the ecclesiastical law were of importance for his son.[3] "Politics was the air we breathed," Frede Castberg remembered, "the national, union-hostile view was certainly the right one—valid as a religious belief."[4] He admired his father, but he never involved in politics himself. To a great extent the father and son were contrasts, "the pugnacious and dominating politician and the peaceable and much beloved university professor."[5]

After graduation as a *cand.iur.* from the University of Oslo in 1914, Frede Castberg went into practice, and he made his *grand European tour* during the Great war. He studied law in France and England 1916-1917, and later in Germany 1919 and in Austria 1921.

In that dynamic mid-war period, starting with the Versailles Treaty 1919 and the creation of League of Nations 1920, he developed his interest in international public law. In 1921 he defended his legal dissertation on the prohibition of the Norwegian constitution to adopt retroactive legislation (*Grunnlovens forbud mot å gi lover tilbakevirkende kraft*)[6] and entered the academic world.

The German occupation of Norway during World War II became a formative period for Castberg and his *Rechtsstaat*-based views. He shared this period of time between Norway and Sweden. In Sweden, he was affiliated to Uppsala University and gave several polemically public talks and lectures at Swedish universities, in which he demonstrated his idealistic and human rights-oriented legal position in relation to that of the increasingly dominating realistic Uppsala School. He articulated his polemical attitude to the philosophy of the Uppsala School of Law in his lecture, "*Law and Metaphysics*," also published in the leading Swedish law journal.[7] The last months of the war Castberg spent together with the Norwegian exile government in London.

Castberg's views on constitutional law from the war years 1940–45 have to be put into its context. He found it necessary to search for an ethical anchoring of the law, for which the Norwegian people struggled throughout the war.[8] This historical argumentation within the constitutional law became an important element also when he studied the role of religion and the Norwegian Church in relation to the 1814 Constitution.

Castberg was one of the few Scandinavian jurists who declared himself a supporter of natural law, which he understood as "fundamental legal principles which the social order have to respect."[9] After World War II, this was a logical postulate for him for the idea of human rights and their renaissance on the European continent.[10] Human rights became for him a focus theoretically as well as in his practical work. His position was a defense against the dominating Scandinavian realism he met not only in Sweden and Denmark (Axel Hägerström in Sweden and Alf Ross in Denmark) but also to some extent in Norway (Ragnar Knoph, Vilhelm Aubert and Torstein Eckhoff). [11] For ten years from 1960, he was the Norwegian representative in the *European Commission of Human Rights*, and from the same year he for ten years chaired the *Hague Academy of International Law*. He also wrote a book on the European Convention on Human Rights (*Den europeiske konvensjon om menneskerettighetene*).[12] His early "subjectivistic—and individualistic—idealism" turned into a more objective one close to the belief in the human rights. The reference to the human rights and constitutional order (democracy and *Rechtsstaat*) materialized his concept of the natural law. In his own words, he believed in a "natural law with a fluid content" (*naturrett med vekslende innhold*). Natural law therefore played an important role in Castberg's legal philosophy, where he argued that "some stances seemed to be anchored in the human nature" and that there was an increasing recognition of a "natural law minimum" for "all legal order in the human society."[13]

In 1945 during the Norwegian reconciliation of its German past, a revision of the Norwegian ecclesiastical law became an important topic due to the conflicts of the Church with the Quisling-regime during the war. The Oslo bishop Eivind Berggrav[14] published a pamphlet on his visions regarding the Norwegian Church order already in 1945[15] and the same year a commission was established to revise the Church law. It got the directive to revise the church legislation within the tradition: "The Norwegian Church shall be kept as a state church and within this frame satisfactory organs should secure the life of the Church."[16] The aim for the commission was to create terms for a "state church with spiritual freedom" by a participation of the Church in the government's authority in internal Church matters. The proposal—to a great extent Berggrav's work—was published in 1948. It met great support from the Church but in the parliamentarian operation, the proposal was changed. The proposed autonomy of the Church, however, was to a great extent reduced in the new Church Law 1953.[17]

In summer 1953 Frede Castberg was asked by the Norwegian government to write an opinion in a conflict in which the Bishop in the Hamar diocese Kristian Schelderup was accused of having used expressions regarding the eternal perdition in conflict with the confession. Castberg's investigation in this case, "*State Religion and Church government*," published in the fall this year resulted in an inflamed discourse in which Bishop Berggrav in a polemical writing, *Contra Castberg* (1954),[18] demonstrated his ecclesiastical arguments in relation to the constitutional ones in Church matters in conflict with Castberg.[19] Castberg's publication changed the focus in the debate from the extraordinary relation between the Church and the un-legal government during the war to the constitutional position of the Church Order related to the system of the State church.[20] Castberg avoided to enter the theological debate. Berggrav's views on the other hand resulted in a political defeat. The last battle was a debate arranged by the Students' Law Association (*Juristforeningen*) at Oslo University in spring 1954. In his speech, Berggrav polemically attacked Castberg, who, however, more looked like the "Bull Ferdinand" and neglected Berggrav's attacks. It became a "duel" between "the Church and the University about the position of the Church in the state religion."[21] Even if the debate continued within theological media, for Castberg the struggle was over. The tendency, which for decades had upheld the position of the Church regarding itself as an autonomous entity within the State, and that the ecclesiastical organs chaired by the bishops should have the jurisdiction over the Norwegian clergy and implement an austere Lutheran orthodoxy within the clergy itself, was now defeated.[22]

Castberg's constitutional position in Church law

As the Church and the State in Norway was one entity, and the constitution regulated state as well as church authorities, Castberg stated the same principles were valid to govern both Church and State. His focus became the individuals' freedom in relation to the central governmental organs of the Church. It was a task of the *Rechtsstaat* to protect not only economical values but also natural law values as codified within the Human Rights. For Castberg this particularly was focused on the clergy's freedom to preach in relation to the bishops' caring for the learning (*læreomsorg*).[23] Interestingly enough Castberg lacked confidence in the bishops and their position in the Church's government. In his view, they lacked legal education and legal thinking, and it was the task for the State to assume the bishops' functions to secure the freedom of the individual member of the clergy. The space of freedom within natural law had a central position in his concept of the *Rechtsstaat*. It was also relevant for his views regarding freedom of religion.[24]

In postwar social-democratically ruled Norway the strong governmental role legitimated the State to govern differently from Castberg's liberal views on the *Rechtsstaat*. He regarded the development towards a "total welfare-state" as a challenge for the *Rechtsstaat*. The Church-government in his view should guarantee an open and tolerant Church. The most important task for the State in this respect was "to secure wide limits for the freedom of belief within the Norwegian Church."[25] He was pragmatically threatened to get a dominium of the bishops. He didn't want the experts, the theologians, to govern the Church. He wanted specialists in "folk-religiosity" (*folkereligiøsitet*). So the government was as a well-suited governmental organ for the Church—as they were no specialists.[26]

Castberg acted in "the modern state" which transferred the traditional *Rechtsstaat*-model into that of the democratic and corporative welfare-state. This legal transition also included the ecclesiastical law. Castberg anchored the *Rechtsstaat*-ideology and the constitutionalism within his natural law-concept. The upcoming "modern" democracy and the Social state for him had negative connotations. They challenged the traditional *Rechtsstaat*-concept. He looked upon the modern welfare-state as a threat to the legality principle, which for him was of great importance.[27] Castberg's concept of the *Rechtsstaat* was heterogeneous and complex. For him, it was normative *and* descriptive. It referred to the classical liberal understanding of the *Rechtsstaat* and its importance of the individual human rights affiliated to the state *and* new elements as democracy and welfare. There were also formal as well as material parts within his concept. He didn't only regard the State from a legal perspective; he also took the view of a political scientist.[28]

The Norwegian Church law of the twentieth century had during Frede Castberg's lifetime an unclear and controversial, debatable position. His description of the Church as the "public essence of religion of the State" (*statens offentlige religionsväsen*) more or less explicitly based the position as valid law from the post-war period up to the current times.[29] The Norwegian Church has traditionally had a positive relationship with the state, but the legal framework based on Castberg's interpretations has within the Church cast a shadow on the practice of the Church law. The Norwegian Church has never fully accepted the "Castberg understanding of the Church law."[30]

Especially the period after World War II the national fellowship became an important part of the Norwegian identity. Castberg took part in an international United Nation-project on the terms of "interpersonal understanding." It resulted in a book 1949, "Norwegian Spirituality and Community" (*Norsk Livssyn og samfunnsliv),* in which he anchored the state church system in the religious setting of the public majority.[31]

The Norwegian State and Church had traditionally been fundamental and common entities including and serving all the people. With the help of state control of the Church, the state church system secured the best conditions for a church supported by the people. "The Church serves the State's affair. "[32] Its "nation-sacral" identity collected the people to a unity. For Castberg this concept may have been important. The problem, however, is that the close relation to the nation contradicts the character of the Church as universal and transnational. His views were national, related to the Norwegian constitution. But it has to be underlined that Castberg by no means can be characterized as a nationalist. His international engagement and his fundamentally open and tolerant attitude contradict such an allegation.[33] For Eivind Berggrav, however, the international and ecumenical contexts were essential. Their different views on the relation between State and Church give an explanation to their inflamed discourse.

Castberg's works within constitutional law deal with the relation power and law in the nation-state. His general view on power was, that it's based on law, but he also included non-legal elements of power. He opened for an exercise of power outside the system, and it gives his concept of the *Rechtsstaat* a touch of realism. The most important in his interpretation of this concept was the qualitative aspects of the exercise of power, not the formal ones. Again, he didn't find the leading figures within the Church (especially the bishops) suited to uphold this power. They were regarded as conservative and represented adverse attitudes in the contemporary society.[34] His views in that respect were a part of the *Zeitgeist.* The skepticism of the folk-church to the power of the "Clerics" was demonstrated in the parliamentarian discourse regarding the church law 1953 and also the discourses related to Castberg's investigation in the fall that year. The internal freedom could, in Castberg's view, scarcely be combined with the freedom of the church in relation to the State.[35]

Interestingly enough, Castberg never gave the Church institutions such an autonomous position. In his view, the power of the Church given by the constitution was consumed by the State. His position as far as the Church is concerned was based on the contexts in the post-war Norwegian society. The organizations became increasingly important collaborators with the state in the construct of the modern corporate society. Castberg didn't regard the Church as a corporation *outside* the modern state. Even if he wanted to develop the legal traits in the corporative state, he didn't use those instruments in his concept of the ecclesiastical law. The Church in his view didn't have the right to be heard, neither in "pure" Church cases nor in value questions in a wider sense.[36] Even if Castberg's principal perception of the *Rechtsstaat* identified important material hallmarks, they were of less importance in his concept of the perception of the State church.

The Norwegian church was a foreign element in his concept of the *Rechtsstaat* as an ideal type—even if the Church constitutionally was closely related to the organization of the state.[37]

Castberg certainly was conscious of the conflicts related to the cleric civil servant, his legal obligations, and the duties he believed he had within the church due to his religious conviction.[38] As a jurist Castberg only related to the concept the Church articulated in the text of the constitution, *the state church.* From a cultural policy perspective, however, Castberg was committed to the concept of the *"folk-church"* (folkekirken). His "theology" in this respect was upheld by a humanistic basic view. This can be identified in his analysis in 1953 *(Statsreligion og kirkestyre)* even if the general concept *folk-church* never was used as a designation of his own personal views. Instead it was characterized by prestige words like: "tolerance, openness, diversity and freedom."[39]

Castberg argued that tolerance within the state church order represented better conditions for an open and including *folk-church* than an eventual free-church order would do. The state guaranteed tolerance through its participating in the governing of the Church—and secured "space limits for the freedom of belief" in the Church. His legal interpretation of the jurisdiction of the Church placed comprehensive warrants to the members of the government.[40]

Throughout the years Castberg argued, that the confession had to be interpreted liberally and in the spirit of its time. He regarded this as a culture politically ideal and a legal position. The orthodox interpretation of the texts and confession the Church had implemented, in his view had created an unfortunate separation between the official learning of the Church and folk-religiosity.[41] The "official religion" had to reflect the "religion of the people." If the Church had to be a Church *for* the people, not *by* the people Castberg's ideal of an open and including Church for most of the population had to be balanced with that of a confessional Church legally founded.[42]

Backer Hjorthaug has noticed, that Castberg's concept of the state church to some extent is parallel to some elements of the concept *civil religion* as described by Robert N. Bellah[43] and Inger Furseth.[44] Like Forseth identified the civil religion as a "set of religious beliefs, symbols and rituals, which legitimize the nation with reference to an exceeding reality," Castberg looked upon the religion as a "common national identity-building and integrating factor.[45] Castberg seemed to look upon the public religion something like "the least common multiple of the religious perception of the people"—some few central dogmas. It will prepare the religion to function more integrating, he argued. In his works (1949 and 1974) Castberg may have argued with sociological thoughts regarding "civil religion" as legitimating factors for the state. Even if so, for Castberg, however, the state was mainly secularly legitimized through its legal basis.[46]

On the other hand, in Castberg's time, the legal use of the concept *folk-church* was rare. This concept had no official status within Church law. "The principle of *folk-church* is not derived from the Church law. On the other hand, the *folk-church* presupposes a Church law of a certain content."[47] Castberg's understanding of the Church within the *folk-church* had no theological but a fundamental secular-humanistic base. His cultural political ideal was an open *folk-church*. The task of the state was to create space so different theological views were regarded as "the life of the law" within the Norwegian church. The understanding of the Church—the "state church" as an open *folk church*—played a role as a (value) premise for his legal interpretation of the state church order.[48]

Another important perspective was Castberg's views on individual freedom and private religion. He underscored, that the teachers in the Church must have a sphere for freedom and consciousness without intervention from the Church government. The common Norwegian citizen was in possession of such an individual space of freedom—based on natural law.[49] His thinking in this part was parallel to his *Rechtsstaat*-thinking and its private sphere, where the citizens have a freedom from engagement by the state. This principle can also be viewed from the natural law principle on freedom of religion, protected by the *Rechtsstaat*. Castberg used this legal argument to give the clergy a high degree of personal freedom in their preaching.[50]

Backer Hjorthaug also argues, that Castberg's position can be regarded as an individually centered understanding of Christianity, in which the personal Christianity of the individual is privatized, decoupled from a central administration of preaching. Instead of a strong official religion, he wanted to open up for diversity, tolerance, and freedom for the single member of the Norwegian church. Within the consisting relation between Church and State, he might have wanted to relieve the historically given public religion in the constitution and substitute it with a private and individual religion. Such an understanding of his interpretation regarding the Christianity is fitting well with his liberal political ideology, rather than the social-democratic steering model, which related religion to welfare.[51]

When Castberg after the war supported a "liberal idealistic tradition" many looked upon his view as obsolete. In 1953 Castberg was elected vice-chancellor of Oslo University, a position he held for five years. Castberg emphasized the particularity of legal thought, but also had an open gaze for social and political realities, in his research emphasized in legal sociology and political science. During his years as vice-chancellor, he initiated studies in political science at the University of Oslo. It became his way to construct a bridge between theory and praxis, between law and politics.[52]

In 1955 Castberg was invited by the US Embassy to visit American universities. Among others, he visited the University of Chicago Law School,[53] where he gave a lecture on "*The Legal Philosophy in the Scandinavian Countries*" with professor Karl Llewellyn—the nestor of American Legal Realism—in the audience.[54] In his lecture, Castberg emphasized the ideas of his opponents (Axel Hägerström, Ingmar Hedenius, Alf Ross) more than his own, and Llewellyn complemented him for having in such a short period of time given the audience "an understanding of the Nordic legal philosophical realism." Castberg's well-established international position was demonstrated by the several honorary degrees he received from international universities.

Epilogue

Frede Castberg was primarily a jurist when he was solving problems within the ecclesiastical law. He used the term "constitutionally determined Church law" to underline that the central part of the Church law was authorized by the constitution, and other parts of the Church law was not (the confessional statutes in the Norwegian law 2-1).[55] As a constitutional lawyer, he constructed a method, in which the constitution was superior and the Church law was absorbed by the Constitutional law. Consequently, he separated the law from religion and Church. He found it obvious that e.g. the ordination was an act "which had its basis in valid positive law, but also—and foremost—had a special spiritual understanding, outside the norms of the positive law."[56]

It was not only Eivind Bergrav who criticized Castberg. Due to the critics among the theologians, his legal interpretations missed important and necessary parts within the Church law discussion. His picture of the Church law had no connection to reality, they argued. The Church expected from jurists and political rulers that "they accept and respect the spirit of the Church, and that the Christian-theological prerequisites, which always have to underline all thinking on the Church, not are substituted by timebound reasonings alien to the Church."[57]

The Norwegian *Schul-Streit* within the church law in the 1950s between jurists and theologians, between Castberg and Berggrav, between idealists and realists, is exemplary in the contemporary discourses on Scandinavian modernity. Interestingly enough Castberg with his natural law perception problematized the discourse and made it more complex.

Frede Castberg was a distinguished scholar within the Scandinavian legal academy. His scholarly ideological context was characterized by dichotomies: democratic law and totalitarian un-law. During World War II, one of his main interests was constitutional law in relation to international public law and its customary natural law principles.[58] In the post-war law faculty of Oslo several of his colleagues (Johs. Andenæs, Carl Jacob Arnholm, Torstein Eckhoff) had belonged to the resistance men and together with them, he upheld a passionate relationship to the law, to the civil religion of the historical constitution, to the rule of law and to the *Rechtsstaat.* The post-war Norwegian legal academy and judiciary in this respect upheld an intellectual high profile, different from the Swedish one, which to a great extent was characterized by its outsiders' perspective due to its neutrality during the war.[59]

In contrast to the Scandinavian realists of the Uppsala school, Castberg can be regarded as a legal *naturalist,* who took a pragmatic position finding the solution in the practical case.

In Norway Frede Castberg in the post-war era got a status of a cultural celebrity, he was active up to his last day in life. He died in Oslo the age of eighty-four years in 1977.

As an old man Castberg summed up his position to Christianity in belief and culture.[60] "*What can we keep of Christianity in the modern society?*" Castberg put the question in a talk in Norwegian Public Service Radio in July 1974.[61] His position was that the fundamental dogma of the Christianity could be rejected. They run counter to our understanding and ethical emotions, he stated. Nor could Castberg accept all dogmas in Jesus' ethical preaching. Jesus was just one of the wise men, who throughout the centuries had proclaimed: do well to your enemies. Treat evil with good. What will remain in the belief in Jesus? The human greatness of the figure of Jesus gives the gospels value for us who don't believe in the dogma. But do we believe in God? Castberg asked. The development has reached the idea of one God, God as a human being in the Old Testament. The belief in a personal God in heaven, however, is absurd related to our knowledge of the universe. But we, who are alien also to a mechanic and materialistic view on world and life, feel that life is a marvel. But the nature is not perfect. But we experience moments of joy and impressions of beauty in the nature, so Castberg.

From the Christianity stays a deep respect for the shape of Christ and the idea of a God as the reason for the spiritual and ethical life. Castberg, however, didn't identify himself with such a belief. He didn't dispute the great transcendent values Christianity has brought. Some of the elevated spiritual works are created from a Christian belief or to its honor. The development of our culture is inspired by the Christian faith. To its honor Gothic cathedrals, the music of Bach and Rembrandt's paintings on the narratives of the Bible are created. For sure, he/she who tries to find a life orientation for his/her part, can't escape to take a stance to the belief of our fathers.

Castberg regarded God as the Soul, the spirit in the existence. He condensed and related his own searching relation to Christianity into a poem by the then young Norwegian author and journalist Tore Jonsson (1916–51), *Who should I thank?*, (Kven skal eg takke)[62]

Who should I thank
for I could see
the sun set
and the mountains be blue?
Who should I thank
for this great honor
just to walk here
and be and be?

Notes

1 This article is to a great extent based on *Torbjørn Backer Hjorthaug*, Frede Castbergs statskirkeoppfatning, (Rettshistoriske studier nr 4), Institutt for offentlig retts skriftserie nr.4/1998, Oslo 1998. I thank Torbjørn Backer and Karen Danbolt, law librarian at the Oslo Law Faculty, for their support.

2 *Johs. Andenæs*, [Art.] Frede Castberg, Norsk Biografisk Leksikon (NBL) Bd 2, Oslo, 2000. https://nbl.snl.no/Frede_Castberg

3 *Torbjørn Backer Hjorthaug*, Frede Castbergs statskirkeoppfatning, [Rettshistoriske studier nr. 4], Institutt for offentlig retts skriftserie nr4/1998, Oslo, 1998, Fotnot.
4 *Frede Castberg*, Minner om politikk og vitenskap fra årene 1900–1970, Universitetsforlaget: Oslo, 1971, 13.
5 *Johs. Andenæs*, [Art.] Frede Castberg, in: Norsk Biografisk Lexikon, Vol.2. (2000).
6 *Frede Castberg*, *Grunnlovens forbud mot å gi lover tilbakevirkende kraft*, (Dissertation), Kristiania, 1919.
7 *Frede Castberg*, Rett og metafysikk, Svensk Juristtidning, 1945, 19 ff.
8 *Frede Castberg*, (1971), 204.
9 *Johs.Andenæs*, (2000).
10 Re. the renaissance of natural law in post-war Germany: *Stanley L. Paulson*, On the Background and Significance of Gustav Radbruch's Post-war Papers, *Oxford Journal of Legal Studies*, Vol. 26, No. 1 (2006), 17–40. —*Karl Acham, Knut Wolfgang Nörr, Bertram Schefold* (eds.), Erkenntnisgewinne, Erkenntnisver-luste: Kontinuitäten und Diskontinuitäten in den Wirtschafts-, Rechts- und Sozialwissenschaften zwischen den 20er und 50er Jahren, Franz Steiner Verlag: Stuttgart, 1998, 621 ff., *Lena Foljanty*, Recht oder Gesetz: juristische Identität und Autorität in den Naturrechtsdebatten der Nachkriegszeit, Mohr Siebeck,: Tübingen, 2013.
11 *Torbjørn Backer Hjorthaug*, (1999), 28.
12 *Frede Castberg*, Den europeiske konvensjon om menneskerettighetene. Universitetsforlaget: Oslo, 1971.
13 *Frede Castberg*, Forelesninger over rettsfilosofi, Universitetsforlaget: Oslo, 1965, 132.
14 *Egil Morland*, Eivind Berggrav in this volume.
15 *Eivind Berggrav*, Kirkens ordning i Norge, Land og Kirke: Oslo, 1945.
16 *Torbjørn Backer Hjorthaug*, (1998), 18.
17 Lov om den norske kirkes ordning 29.4.1953.
18 *Eivind Berggrav*, Contra Castberg: Om kirkens grunn, Land og Kirke, Oslo, 1954.
19 *Frede Castberg*, (1971), 260 ff.
20 *Torbjørn Backer Hjorthaug*, (1998), 18 f.
21 *Frede Castberg*, (1971), 263.
22 *Frede Castberg*, (1971), 263.
23 *Torbjørn Backer Hjorthaug*, (1998), 37 f.
24 *Torbjørn Backer Hjorthaug*, (1998), 39.
25 *Frede Castberg*, Statsreligion og folkestyre (1953), 64.
26 *Torbjørn Backer Hjorthaug*, (1998), 40.
27 *Torbjørn Backer Hjorthaug*, (1998), 34.
28 *Torbjørn Backer Hjorthaug*, (1998), 35 f.
29 *Torbjørn Backer Hjorthaug*, (1998), 3.
30 *Andreas Aarflot*, Jus in sacris. Noen bemerkninger til dommen i Hålogaland lagmannsrett i avskjedssaken mot sogneprest Børre Knudsen. Lov og Rett 1983, 205. –*Torbjørn Backer Hjorthaug* (1998), 4.
31 *Frede Castberg*, Norsk livssyn og samfunnsliv. H. Aschehoug & C:o: Oslo 1949, 61 f. –*Torbjørn Backer Hjorthaug* (1998), 40 f.
32 *Torbjørn Backer Hjorthaug*, (1998), 41.
33 *Torbjørn Backer Hjorthaug*, (1998), 53. – Frede Castberg (1971), 207.
34 *Frede Castberg*, (1971), 263.
35 *Frede Castberg* (1971), 263. –*Torbjørn Backer Hjorthaug*, (1998), 49.
36 *Torbjørn Backer Hjorthaug*, (1998), 43.
37 *Torbjørn Backer Hjorthaug*, (1998), 44.
38 *Frede Castberg*, Statsreligion og kirkestyre, 1954, 64. –*Torbjørn Backer Hjorthaug*, (1998), 45.
39 "toleranse, åpenhet, mangfold og frihet." *Torbjørn Backer Hjorthaug*, (1998), 47.
40 *Torbjørn Backer Hjorthaug*, (1998) 47 f.
41 *Frede Castberg*, Kristendommen og dens dogmer. – In: Samtiden. Årg. 83 nr. 8 (1974), 457. –*Torbjørn Backer Hjorthaug*, (1998), 51.

42 *Torbjørn Backer Hjorthaug*, (1998), 52.
43 *Robert N. Bellah*, Civil Religion in America, Dædalus, *Journal of the American Academy of Arts and Sciences*, issue entitled, "Religion in America," Winter 1967, Vol. 96, No. 1, 1–21.
44 *Inger Furseth*, Samfunnsreligion i Norge. En sosiologisk analyse av nasjonal legitimering 1905–1980. Institutt for sosiologi ved Universitetet i Oslo 1986. –*Inger Furseth*, Civil Religion in a low Key: The Case of Norway. *Acta Sociologica* (1994), Vol. 37, 39–54.
45 *Inger Furseth* (1986), 4. –*Torbjørn Backer Hjorthaug* (1998), 54.
46 *Torbjørn Backer Hjorthaug*, (1998), 54 f.
47 *Ole Herman Fisknes*, Kirkerett og folkekirke, med særlig henblikk på Grunnlovens § 2. Kirke og Kultur 9/1984, 530. –*Torbjørn Backer Hjorthaug*, (1998), 56.
48 *Torbjørn Backer Hjorthaug* (1998), 56 f.
49 "The confessional duty is by no means a legal duty to preach what you personally regard as false or incorrect." *Frede Castberg*, Statsreligion og kirkestyre (1953), 31. –*Torbjørn Backer Hjorthaug* (1998), 57 f.
50 *Torbjørn Backer Hjorthaug* (1998), 58.
51 *Torbjøn Backer Hjorthaug* (1998), 58 f.
52 *Torbjørn Backer Hjorthaug* (1998), 23.
53 *Frede Castberg*, (1971), 270.
54 The lecture was published: *Frede Castberg*, Philosophy of Law in the Scandinavian Countries, *The American Journal of Comparative Law*, Volume 4, Issue 3, 1 July 1955, 388–400.
55 *Torbjørn Backer Hjorthaug*, (1998), 66.
56 *Frede Castberg*, Statsreligion og kirkestyre (1953), 63. –*Torbjørn Backer Hjorthaug*, (1998), 69.
57 *Johs. Smemo*, Kirkesituasjonen: omkring spørsmålet bekjennelsekirke of statskirke, Oslo 1954, 12 f.
58 *Frede Castberg*, Norges statsrett under krigen med Tyskland, *Statsvetenskaplig tidskrift för politik, statistik, ekonomi* 3 (1946): 243 ff.
59 This position was also demonstrated after the war, when Swedish law professors participated with Norwegian colleagues in an International Lawyers' Conference in Berlin in July 1952. –*Kjell Å Modéer*, "Den kulan visste var den tog!": Om svenska juristers omvärldssyn 1935-1955, in: Andersson, Torbjörn & Lindell, Bengt (eds.), Festskrift till Per Henrik Lindblom, Jure: Uppsala 2004, 443 ff.
60 "Bestrider ikke de veldige åndsverdier kristendommen har ført med seg. Noen av de mest opphøyde åndsverk er skapt ut fra den kristne tro eller til dens ære. Sikkert at den som søker livsorientering for sin egen del, ikke kan unngå å ta standpunkt til våre fedres tro." –*Frede Castberg*, Hva kan vi beholde av kristendommen? Siste foredrag av Frede Castberg om kristendommen og dens dogmer. [Speech in Norwegian Broadcasting Corporation 1974. https://urn.nb.no/URN:NBN:no-nb_dra_1994-26538P
61 *Frede Castberg*, Hva kan vi beholde av kristendommen? Siste foredrag av Frede Castberg om kristendommen og dens dogmer. Sent NRK Sept. 27, 1974. http://www.nb.no/nbsok/nb/a17777450ed08e5666ff7fc9c4aaca68?index=17
62 "Kven skal eg takke/for det eg fekk sjå/sola gå under/og berga bli blå? Kven skal eg takke/for all denne æra/i dette å gå her/å vera og vera—*Tore Jonsson*, Dikt i samling, Noregs Boklag: Oslo 1967, 187.

Bibliography

Aarflot, Andreas, Jus in sacris. Noen bemerkninger til dommen i Hålogaland lagmannsrett i avskjedssaken mot sogneprest Børre Knudsen. Lov og Rett, 1983, 205.

Acham, Karl, Knut Wolfgang Nörr, Bertram Schefold (eds.), Erkenntnisgewinne, Erkenntnisver-luste: Kontinuitäten und Diskontinuitäten in den Wirtschafts-,

Rechts- und Sozialwissenschaften zwischen den 20er und 50er Jahren, Franz Steiner, Verlag: Stuttgart, 1998, 621 ff.

Andenæs, Johs [Art.] Frede Castberg, Norsk Biografisk Leksikon (NBL) Bd 2, Oslo, 2000. https://nbl.snl.no/Frede_Castberg

Hjorthaug, Torbjørn Backer, Frede Castbergs statskirkeoppfatning, (Rettshistoriske studier nr 4), Institutt for offentlig retts skriftserie nr.4/1998, Oslo, 1998.

Bellah, Robert N, Civil Religion in America, Dædalus, *Journal of the American Academy of Arts and Sciences*, issue entitled, "Religion in America," Winter 1967, Vol. 96, No. 1, 1–21.

Berggrav, Eivind, Contra Castberg: Om kirkens grunn, Land og Kirke: Oslo, 1954.

Berggrav, Eivind, Kirkens ordning i Norge, Land og Kirke: Oslo, 1945.

Castberg, Frede, Den europeiske konvensjon om menneskerettighetene, Universitetsforlaget: Oslo, 1971.

Castberg, Frede, Forelesninger over rettsfilosofi, Universitetsforlaget: Oslo, 1965, 132.

Castberg, Frede, *Grunnlovens forbud mot å gi lover tilbakevirkende kraft,* (Dissertation) Kristiania, 1919.

Castberg, Frede, Hva kan vi beholde av kristendommen? Siste foredrag av Frede Castberg om kristendommen og dens dogmer. [Speech in Norwegian Broadcasting Corporation], 1974. https://urn.nb.no/URN:NBN:no-nb_dra_1994-26538P

Castberg, Frede, Kristendommen og dens dogmer. – In: Samtiden. Årg. 83 nr. 8 (1974), 457.

Castberg, Frede, Minner om politikk og vitenskap fra årene 1900-1970, Universitetsforlaget: Oslo, 1971.

Castberg, Frede, Norges statsrett under krigen med Tyskland, *Statsvetenskaplig tidskrift för politik, statistik, ekonomi*, Vol. 3, 1946, 243 ff.

Castberg, Frede, Norsk livssyn og samfunnsliv. H. Aschehoug & Co: Oslo, 1949.

Castberg, Frede, Philosophy of Law in the Scandinavian Countries, *The American Journal of Comparative Law*, Vol. 4, No. 3, 1 July 1955, 388–400.

Castberg, Frede, Rett og metafysikk, Svensk Juristtidning, 1945, 19–31.

Fisknes, Ole Herman, Kirkerett og folkekirke, med særlig henblikk på Grunnlovens § 2. Kirke og Kultur 9/1984, 530.

Foljanty, Lena, Recht oder Gesetz: juristische Identität und Autorität in den Naturrechtsdebatten der Nachkriegszeit. Mohr Siebeck: Tübingen, 2013.

Furseth, Inger, Civil Religion in a Low Key: The Case of Norway. Acta sociologica (1994), Vol. 37, 39–54.

Furseth, Inger, Samfunnsreligion i Norge. En sosiologisk analyse av nasjonal legitimering 1905–1980. Institutt for sosiologi ved Universitetet i Oslo, 1986.

Jonsson, Tore, Dikt i samling, Noregs Boklag: Oslo, 1967, 187.

Lov om den norske kirkes ordning 29.4.1953.

Modéer, Kjell Å,"Den kulan visste var den tog!": Om svenska juristers omvärldssyn 1935-1955, in Andersson, Torbjörn & Lindell, Bengt (eds.), Festskrift till Per Henrik Lindblom, Jure: Uppsala, 2004, 443 ff.

Paulson, Stanley L, On the Background and Significance of Gustav Radbruch's Post-war Papers, *Oxford Journal of Legal Studies*, Vol. 26, No. 1, 2006, 17–40.

Smemo, Johs, Kirkesituasjonen: omkring spørsmålet bekjennelsekirke of statskirke, Oslo, 1954, 12 f.

22 A late-modern catalyst in Swedish ecclesiastical law

Göran Göransson (1925–1998)[1]

Kjell Å Modéer

Introduction

In the postwar era (1945–75) Swedish ecclesiastical law was transformed into the category of mainstream secular administrative law for the Swedish state-church. Consequently, ecclesiastical law no longer appeared in the curriculum of Swedish legal education, of which it had been a part for centuries. Instead, theological faculties monopolized this field, while law faculties no longer offered classes in church law. Postwar Swedish legal scholars belonged to the Hans Kelsen-inspired and value-neutral-oriented scholars of the Uppsala school of legal realism.[2] They dominated the cognitive structures of the representatives of Swedish public law—a discipline that experienced its heyday during the construction of the modern Swedish welfare-state from 1945 to 1975. These jurists were metaphorically described as "social engineers." Philosophy professor Axel Hägerström, the founder of the Uppsala school, argued that the concept of basic rights and duties in Roman law had its foundation in atavistic superstition, and the contemporary common legal thinking had its roots in "confused metaphysic," which had to be purged once for all.

Background and early career

Göran Göransson was the most knowledgeable and influential Swedish jurist in ecclesiastical law during the second half of the twentieth century and a catalyst for late-modern ecclesiastical law in Sweden. He was born and raised in Gothenburg as the son of the city statistician Werner Göransson and his wife, Jane, née Wester.[3]

After receiving his baccalaureate in 1943, Göran started his career with plans to be a diplomat. During World War II he studied foreign languages at Gothenburg University, where he received a BA degree (in English, French, and practical philosophy) in 1946. He then continued with law studies at Uppsala University, from which he graduated in 1951.[4]

From childhood he was educated into Christian belief. His father was an old childhood friend of one of the most important Swedish theologians of his generation, Torsten Bohlin, professor at Turku and Uppsala and bishop at Härnösand diocese in northern Sweden, and an admirer of archbishop Nathan Söderblom and his ecumenical theology.[5] In the summer of 1940, Bohlin confirmed his son Torgny together with one of his friends from Uppsala and Göran Göransson. The preparation for the confirmation during some summer weeks in Antjärn, outside Härnösand, became important not only for Göransson, who recalled his confirmation as a "fabulous period of time in his life,"[6] but also for Torsten Bohlin, who based his confirmation class on a manuscript which he published in 1941.[7] "Uncle Torsten" became Göransson's older friend and comrade, "whom young people approach with religious questions." The bishop talked with them about the difficulties and richness regarding Christian belief "from his own experiences and with a vocabulary we understood," Göransson later remarked."[8] Bohlin facilitated Göransson's seeing "the essential in Christianity and dar[e]ing to *start* to believe." "He helped us with the first steps, the most difficult ones and those that one mostly hesitates to take."[9]

In high school (*Gymnasium*) Göransson was active in the Society of Christian High-School Students (*Sveriges Kristliga Gymnasiströrelse*), and his Christian commitment continued in the Swedish Christian Student Union (*Sveriges Kristliga Studentförbund*) at Gothenburg and later at Uppsala University.[10] Ecclesiastical commitment and interests in theology became an important part of his life during those of his formative years.

Law studies at Uppsala coined by secularism and legal realism

The intellectual life at Uppsala University in the years after World War II was, in Göransson's own word, "frustrating," especially regarding the position of the law in the social welfare state. Philosophers, law professors, and theologians all contributed to inflamed discourses related to the spirit of the law and its foundations. The increasingly old-fashioned, idealistic, and metaphysically oriented legal perspectives were replaced by more positivistic, pragmatic, and realistic concepts of the law. Especially prominent among the representatives of the Uppsala school was the professor of private law at Uppsala, Vilhelm Lundstedt, who found no satisfactory answers to those older questions. Göransson remembered that Lundstedt, in his lectures in tort law, "chased metaphysical inconsistencies" in case law from the Swedish Supreme Court. "With a body language showing evident disgust, he pushed from the rostrum the volume of Swedish case law from which he had quoted. But when he turned to his own social welfare theory of law to construct a reason for how to resolve a specific case, the final result generally speaking was the same as that of the members of the court." Göransson posed the question whether the aim of the rather vaguely defined "social welfare" as an expression of the real values of a people was a more certain basis for judicial practice than hereditary ideas about some "'rights,' which without further ado could be violated."[11]

The representative of the Uppsala school at Lund University at this time was Karl Olivecrona, the professor of legal procedure. He formulated a theory of free-standing imperatives in a generally accepted basic law (constitution). which gained respect from the people because of a common moral code.[12]

From a theological perspective, a parallel modern discourse took place in the years after the war. In 1946, the Social Democratic parliamentarian Stellan Arvidson together with the bishop (and professor of theology) Torsten Bohlin, published a much-read and -discussed book, *Christianity—Against and For* (Kristendomen. Mot—för). When, in 1949, Ingemar Hedenius, the professor of philosophy at Uppsala, published his classical work *Belief and Knowledge* (Tro och vetande), the book initiated an extensive debate on contemporary religion and a critical view regarding the role of the church in the modern Swedish folk-home. During his years at Uppsala, Göransson took part intensively in the discussions regarding secularization and Christian belief. His commitment to Christian students brought him and his then-wife, Gudrun, in close connection with influential theologians, e.g., Krister Stendahl, the high-profile student pastor (1948–50), whose position politically was highly controversial in Uppsala in the late 1940s.[13]

The professor for public law at the Uppsala Law Faculty was Halvar G. F. Sundberg, who had engaged since his youth in ecclesiastical matters.[14] In 1948 he published an extensive commentary on Swedish ecclesiastical law, *Kyrkorätt*, which for decades became the main reference book in this field.[15] Sundberg also participated in the important discourses within the Swedish state-church in the 1950s.[16]

International church law relations in postwar Europe

In contrast to the Swedish national legal culture, the international context of the intellectual debates in Uppsala in the late 1940s was much more colorful, rich, and engaged regarding the foundations of law that were left "in ruins after a perverted legal system … had raised an abomination, against which one wanted to create guarantees for the future."[17] The European postwar legal and constitutional discourses were connected to the concepts of human dignity and natural law, especially in the canon law of the Roman Catholic Church. The modern Swedish jurists, trained in the Uppsala School of Law, were extremely reluctant to accept this revival of natural law.[18] Göransson, however, belonged to those students who publicly stood up for Christian belief. "I believe in Christ. For his message—even the 'foul words' from His mouth—open a streak of forgiveness and hopefulness, hoc est: glory, in the middle of darkness in the barbarian wood."[19]

After World War II, the churches became important institutions to restore belief in human dignity. The concept engaged theologians as well as jurists. Already in 1942, Bishop Bohlin had published an article on "The Struggle for Human Dignity" (*Kampen för människovärdet*), in which he formulated Christ as our incomparably best spiritual asset. "He is the only great hope for our ill-fated generation. In that sign, the struggle for human dignity once will be turned into victory."[20]

Immediately after the war, international Christian organizations reorganized. In the Lutheran World Foundation as well as the in World Council of the Churches (WCC), the Nordic representation was significant. At a conference in Lund, Sweden, from June 30 to July 6, 1947, the Lutheran World Federation was founded,[21] and under the theme "The Lutheran Church in the World Today," two hundred delegates from twenty-six countries participated and elected professor Anders Nygren, of Lund, to the first presidency of the federation. This conference was saluted as a new start after the war, even if no debate occurred in the media about this event in the Swedish church.[22]

From July 22 to 31, 1947, the World Student Christian Federation (WSCF) met in Oslo, and the twenty-two-year-old law student Göran Göransson participated together with about fifty internationally engaged Swedish students, among them Olof Sundby, later archbishop of Sweden. For many of them, including Göransson, this meeting with young Christians from all over the world became of "vital importance."[23] Students during the war had not had the possibility of traveling abroad. When the borders opened in the summer of 1945, they compensated for this lack of experience. Many of them now became internationalists. The Christians among them also became involved in ecumenical Christian work, which had started before the war with a conference in Amsterdam in 1939 and resulted in an "emergency committee" for international Christian organizations.

Göransson became involved in the work of the WSCF, originally founded in Vadstena (Sweden) in 1895. During World War I, this organization had played an important role in the ecumenical debate. After World War II, this international organization, together with the Young Men's Christian Association (YMCA) and the Young Women's Christian Association (YWCA), met in Oslo in July 1947, at a World Conference of Christian Youth.[24] Some twelve hundred young Christians from seventy-five countries participated in the conference under the motto "Jesus Christ is Lord." For the Nordic participants, this conference became the starting-point for a comprehensive ecumenical engagement in the years to come.[25]

The Norwegian bishop Eivind Berggrav took the initiative at this conference, to which famous Christian church leaders were invited, including Reinhold Niebuhr from New York and Martin Niemöller from Frankfurt am Main. Niebuhr stated that this conference had impressed him: "The usual differences between American and European Christians were not nearly as wide as in previous years."[26] The Oslo meeting became a catalyst for the young generation. Göransson wrote an article on this important event for a Swedish daily, in which he referred to the speeches given by Niebuhr and Niemöller.[27] He explained that Niebuhr had underlined how "God had used human institutions, movements, or nations to claim justice and law to crush the Nazi regime." The difficulties "to claim justice but avoid oppression, to abolish or punish obvious injustice within social and international life, but not revert into self-righteousness," had become a new postwar problem. "Only by being permanently open to repentance and a will to change for the better a human institution could avoid this danger."[28]

Fifty years after the Oslo meeting, Göransson recalled its importance for contemporary young Christians. The law student from Uppsala in 1947 had experienced how "the dominion of Christ in each area of individual and societal life is the road to the solution of the problems of its time." Each of the participants had a sense of how it would be to live in a world under the dominion of Christ. "It's a matter for us in thoughts and life to give witness to that dominion, for only in this do we see the possibility of a more blessed future for this world, which seems to be doomed to chaos so long as it's serving other masters."[29] The quotation demonstrates the frustration of the young, idealistic, postwar generation, who dreamed of a future in human rights and human dignity and at the same time felt surrounded by the real world with its Iron Curtain and the threat of a nuclear war.

The Oslo meeting became a prologue for the establishment of the World Council of Churches, organized in Amsterdam in August 1948. Several of the leading theologians who participated at Oslo were instrumental for the Amsterdam conference. Because of his language skills, Göransson also attended as a youth delegate at this meeting. His participation in this ecumenical event became for him an important experience. The foundation of this world organization had come about before the war. The motto of the meeting was "Man's Disorder and God's Design." Göransson was part of the active Youth Department, with the task to be the liaison for all the youth organizations participating in the WCC. In Amsterdam, the saying was that "the youth can be the most explosive power in the WCC."[30]

Back in Sweden, Göransson published a dedicated report on his experiences in Amsterdam. In the discussions he observed fragmentation as well as unity. He was a member of a World Council of Churches in which every church had to make its walk to Canossa. The plural form of *Churches* became a memento for all: that this organization was an emergency solution to "the sin of fragmentation." He also got the strong impression that each church was aligned with a distinct group, class, race, or nation. He observed, however, that in that respect, a recent improvement had occurred, perhaps related to the advance of secularization. "When you less and less (without an undertone of irony) can talk about the West, the middle class, and the people of Sweden as carriers of Christian belief and ethos, the consequence will be that the church increasingly is aware of its single task to be the salt and light in a neopagan world."[31]

Göransson's strongest experience from the Amsterdam conference, however, was his encounter with a "penitent Christendom." "We intend to stay together," was the message to all Christians and to "those who want to listen." Despite the presence of historical organizations, national prejudices, racial antagonism, "denying the unity of the Christian, or a self-satisfied patronized attitude to 'young' churches and 'colored' people," he realized that all of these were false. The only true position, he stated, was "the one and only loyalty," to the Lord. He felt the existence of unity—"deep under the confessional barriers." He recalled meeting with one of the many youth delegates, a young student from Ceylon who was in Europe for the first time. In the conversations with him, Göransson realized, "he had more common in belief and ethos" with this stranger from another corner of the world than he had with "most of [his] friends in [his] boarding house in Uppsala."[32]

Göransson's involvement in the WCC brought him twice (in 1952 and 1964) to legal conferences at the Château Bossey ecumenical institute, close to Geneva, Switzerland. He also seems to have participated in the important conference of the WCC in Treysa in 1950.[33]

His meetings with international Christian students affected him strongly, and they meant a lot for his professional work in ecclesiastical law in postwar Europe.[34] Consequently, he strengthened his skills in international public law and made study trips to war-torn European countries—to the Hague in 1948 and to Bonn in 1950.

In 1950, he received a grant to study in West Germany at the University of Bonn, a partner university with Uppsala. Five years after the war, he experienced how reconstruction successfully occurred in a ruined city. Bonn was the capital of West Germany; he found the task "hardly grownup to fulfill." The university had temporary facilities in several locations. He found that the responsibility for the political student work was more articulated among the liberal or evangelical students at this university dominated by Catholics. "Academic citizenship is an asset in the Western world which we ought to diligently make use of," he stated after his time in Bonn. "As a student you self-evidently belong to each university in our cultural hemisphere. Unfortunately, later in life you seldom are more then a tourist or at the most a guest lecturer."[35]

A strong political engagement occurred at those meetings. The topic of Christians and power politics stirred a strong discourse within the WSCF during those years.[36] For Göransson, Karl Barth's works became an important source of inspiration. In Amsterdam, in 1948, he purchased Barth's booklet *Rechtfertigung und Recht,* (Justification and Justice/Law) from 1938, which he read extensively.[37] In this chapter, Barth articulated his opposition to Hitler's politicized church, which divided German Christians, who supported the Hitler regime and its "fundamental anti-Christian antichurch" (*grundsätzlich antichristliche Gegenkirche*) from the Confessing Church.[38] Worldly law is the ordinance that secures the church's teaching, Barth argued. The church therefore may not refuse the ecclesiastical law but must secure it by "proclaiming divine justification."[39]

After World War II, the reconstruction of the relationship between an autonomous church and the democratic state made Barth's position regarding the New Testament important. The renaissance of natural law in the early postwar period contributed to this rapprochement. Moreover, in the late 1940s, the justification of human sin became a counterpoint to the most important discourse regarding human dignity.[40] Several other European jurists and theologians contributed to this discourse, among them the Calvinist theologian Erik Wolf, who in a 1947 work (*Rechtsgedanke und biblische Weisung*) demonstrated an easier way to formulate a Christian basis for the law. In the Bible, Wolf argued, directives and instructions apply to the societal and legal framework. Those ideas were not to be interpreted as legal rules but as directives and guidelines for legislators, judges, and administrators.[41] Karl Barth's concept of *Rechtstheologie* became a keyword for the Swedish Christian jurist.

European Convention on Human Rights and freedom of religion

An international counterforce developed with roots in the reaction to the "unlaw" in totalitarian and authoritarian countries in the 1930s and early 1940s. During the years of war, the later Swedish archbishop Ruben Josefson urged the church to transplant Christian life values into modern citizenship.[42] The project, however, was an uphill battle. The secularization of society steadily increased. In 1951, more or less obliged to ratify the European Convention on Human Rights (ECHR), the Swedish government first had to adopt (for the first time in Swedish history) a Freedom of Religion Act.[43] For the modern Swedish citizen, the most important issue with this statute, however, was not establishing a positive freedom of religion or the right to worship, but instead the opposite—the right to abjure religion.

For Christian jurists like Göransson, the Freedom of Religion Act of 1951 was not meant to be a radical change but rather a part of a long tradition and process. The church was obliged to carry out its work without the support of coercion by the state. "The unrestrained right of the individual to withdraw from the church is for the church herself a religious necessity, for the church cannot be exclusively a function of the state," he pointed out.[44] By 1929, the synod already had underlined the role of the church in a modern state and proposed legislation which aimed to broaden the right to withdraw. In a 1951 bill to the parliament asking for the liberty of religious freedom, the Swedish government also made a statement regarding the nature of the Swedish Church. The Church of Sweden had not been established as a part of the functions of the state. "The church is a spiritual community, a religious community (*trossamfund*)—and its character and activities were defined by its confession." For Göransson, the Swedish state church, like the free churches and the Roman Catholic Church, should have the right to "design and shape its own work." He argued for a quite new platform for the church in Sweden.[45] Together with the theologian Carl Strandberg, Göransson's friend and contemporary in Uppsala,[46] he argued for the reform that baptism and not birth should constitute membership in the Swedish Church.[47]

The Swedish ratification of the ECHR in 1952, however, was to a great extent a quasi-political event. Few in Sweden felt included in the idealistic pan-European perspectives of that time. After World War II, Sweden as a neutral country uniquely had a position of exclusion when the reconstruction of Europe took place and traditional European values were reconsidered.

Göransson identified as a professional Christian lawyer

After graduation from Uppsala in December 1951,[48] Göransson practiced law at a highly esteemed law firm in Gothenburg (Johan Rambergs Advokatbyrå) and served as a law clerk at a local court in Gothenburg (Askims, Vättle och Sävedals häradsrätt) from 1952 to 1954. In the fall of 1951, the Social Democratic Party formed a new government together with the Agrarians (Bondeförbundet), and Ivar Persson, its parliamentarian, was appointed minister of education and religion.

The Freedom of Religion Act also emphasized that the Church of Sweden was a unique state institution. "It had its own tasks and another character than other institutions," the Minister of justice Herman Zetterberg stated. The religious communities as ecclesiastical entities were to be regarded as autonomous entities within the state system.[49]

When Ivar Persson recruited new staff to the Ministry of Education and Religion, the bishop in Gothenburg, Bo Giertz, a friend of his, "tried to get him to understand how necessary it was to recruit civil servants who had some sense for what the church is and wants."[50] Persson needed to hire "a couple of good men" to the Ministry. Giertz wrote Halvar Sundberg and asked him to keep his eyes open for suitable candidates at the Law Faculty at Uppsala.[51]

Sundberg replied that he had two "particularly qualified names." One of them was Göran Göransson.[52] After his clerkship, Göransson was recruited in August 1954 to Persson's ministry, where he served for ten years. He wanted to take a more active part in matters related to ecclesiastical law but was rejected because of his publicly demonstrated faith. In the Social Democratic political environment, he was regarded as too ecclesiastical ("*kyrklig*"). For him this situation was annoying and irritating. During all his years in the department, Göransson demonstrated his engagement as an active participant in Christian youth organizations.[53]

Göransson's career in ecclesiastic law in postwar Sweden paralleled the period of increased secularization of the society. In 1956, just a few years after the Freedom of Religion Act, the parliament initiated the separation between the state and the church. That action resulted in an expert investigation (1958), which delivered several proposals and in 1968 concluded its work.[54] The Swedish Church appointed another committee in 1956 and worked parallel to the state committee, the Church Organization Committee (*Kyrkoorganisationskommittén* 1956–64), chaired by Bishop Giertz of Gothenburg.[55] Göransson was recruited to this committee from its beginning.[56]

Göransson was well aware of the important discourses on human dignity and human rights that dominated West European Christianity after World War II. In a 1965 article, he underlined the paucity of thought given to the question of human dignity because of the secularization in Sweden. "It's not indifferent which view of man in the long run will prevail in our country—Christian or pagan."[57] Even if Sweden ratified the ECHR, the convention's concrete role in postwar Swedish legal culture was nonexistent. Nonetheless, because of his demonstrated international perspectives and participation in Christian networks, Göransson experienced how important the convention was in the reconstruction of the *Rechtsstaat*, especially for Christian jurists. Twenty-five years after the UN declaration, the WCC arranged a conference in Vienna on "Human Rights and Christian Responsibility." In preparation for this conference, a meeting took place at the WCC ecumenical center at Chateau Bossey on the theme of

"The Struggle for Human Rights." Christian jurists and social scientists from twenty-five countries participated, including Göransson from Sweden. After the conference he explained for his Swedish readers the position of human rights in the newly adopted postcolonial constitutions in Asia and Africa. At Bossey, discussion focused on the responsibility of Christian jurists for introducing and implementing the concept of the rule of law. In an article in 1974, he put the question, "Do the Human Rights concern us?" His answer was: "Due to its supranational character, universal Christianity has its given responsibility."[58]

The legal profession had a particular responsibility as opinion formers, he stated, but they often were blind to the problems, since they were recruited from socially privileged environments"

> But we Christians have a special reason to be perceptive to those questions and create an opinion in favor of those who are the weakest in society, who experience humiliation, and whose dignity is violated or disregarded, and who perhaps themselves lack funds and possibilities to claim their rights. Still, it ought to be one of the keenest tasks of the church to speak out on their behalf in inhumane situations. It was good during some days abroad to get the experience that some parts of Christianity recognize this.[59]

Göransson evidently used his international experiences to take a stand against Swedish public opinion—and within the legal profession—regarding the concepts of justice and human rights.

Move to Lund as secretary of the Lund diocese 1963–78

In 1963, Göransson left Stockholm to take up his position at the Chapter for Lund, where he was appointed secretary of the Lund diocese, a position he held for fifteen years. During his active years at Lund, Göransson became an established specialist in Swedish church law.[60] From 1968 to 1972 he also served as an expert on the State Church Council (*Beredningen om Stat-Kyrka*), chaired by Alva Myrdal, a member of the Social Democratic government.[61] Göransson also served as an expert for the church in the task force of the Bishops' Council (chaired by Bishop Arne Palmqvist), related to this governmental investigation from 1972 to 1977. Finally, he belonged to the study group for questions related to church organization chaired by his bishop in the Lund diocese, Martin Lindström. During this period Göransson also extended his international networks and participated in several international seminars and conferences in West Germany. Because of his skills in church law and church history—he always argued with the help of history—he also regularly published the talks he gave at national and international arenas.

Göransson as expert in church law at the ministry of civil affairs, 1978–96

In 1979 Göransson moved back to Stockholm to become assistant undersecretary at the church department at the Ministry of Civil Affairs, with primary responsibility for the church law reform in progress. Swedish church law at that time had to be adapted (and adjusted) to the new Instrument of Government (*Regeringsformen*) of 1974, which in its opening and its first paragraph emphasized the democratic imperative that all public power emanates from the state. The statutory power (*normgivningskompetens*) in the relationship between church and state especially had to be reformed. Whether the Swedish state church would be reformed and conform to the new constitutional principles was an important question.

Göransson returned to Stockholm at a time when the reform of the Swedish Church had been stymied. The synod had declined to accept the suggested reforms, stating that it accepted the role of the parliament as an interpreter of the confession of the Swedish church. The new Instrument of Government had made popular sovereignty its key principle, for the church had moved far beyond matters of confession and legal theology. The secularization of the society also was the dominant context.[62] "Opponents to a fundamental change in the relations between state and church had, due to the decision by the synod, prevented the further development in the discussions between government and church."[63]

The first step in the autonomy of the Swedish Church was a legal reform in 1982, which established an autonomous synod and also adapted the church law to the Instrument of Government. (SFS 1982:942–3). Göransson wrote and published the commentary for this new legislation. [64] He also was an expert in the subsequent church committee of 1982 (*1982 års kyrkokommitté*),[65] which prepared for the separation between state and church.[66] During his legislative work for the reformation of Swedish ecclesiastical law, he participated regularly in international conferences and published extensively in international law journals.

As a member of a theological commission to the Swedish Bishops Conference, regarding how to organize the membership in the Swedish Church, Göransson forcefully and logically argued in 1983 for baptism as the basis for membership in the Swedish Church.[67] He was strongly criticized by Arne Palmqvist, one of the bishops, who argued that membership in the Swedish Church organization did not pertain to the Church of Christ as an eschatological entity.[68] In the new legislation, Göransson's position prevailed.

Göransson's combinations of skills in law in general and church law in particular became essential for him as a Christian jurist. He appeared from then on as one of the foremost experts in Swedish church law. He cooperated in ecclesiastical matters with Carl Strandberg, his friend from Uppsala who was now dean of Strängnäs diocese, and an important representative among those who argued for a separation between the Swedish church and state. As a member of the ongoing legal reform within the Swedish state church in the 1990s, Göransson also published frequently in this field of law.

Göransson not only was instrumental when the new church law was prepared and adopted in 1992,[69] but also wrote the necessary commentary to this legislation[70] in the first handbook in Swedish ecclesiastical law since Halvar Sundberg's in 1948. This handbook marked a new trend in the post-positivistic Swedish legal culture. In *Svensk kyrkorätt* (Swedish Church Law) he also made his great reverence for theological features visible. In the chapter on the essence of the understanding of ecclesiastical law, he wrote:

> But if one limits the field of view to solely the state acquis [the accumulated body of law], one risks losing sight of the specific essence of ecclesiastical law. With such a view, the church would become an institution which would be wholly a creation of the Swedish legal framework and would depend only on the existence of state church legislation.[71]

Göransson as a European Christian legal jurist

After his experience in Amsterdam in 1948, Göransson increasingly used his international networks among European Christian jurists, and he became the communicator to Lutheran scholars and networks on Swedish church-state relations from the 1950s to the late 1990s.

When the committee presented its results in 1968, Göransson became the expert who introduced them to international audiences. Several times he was invited by the United Evangelical Lutheran Church of Germany (VELKD) to participate in its seminars for theologians at Pullach, close to Munich. In 1969 he presented the state of the art of current state-church reform,[72] and four years later he presented there the Swedish concept of freedom of religion as well as the ongoing state-church reform.[73] When the 1979 synod had made its decision in 1979, he returned to a VELKD seminar in Liebfrauenberg (Alsace) to continue his presentations on Swedish church law reforms.[74] He also wrote a substantial historical survey of Swedish ecclesiastical law and its relationship between state and church.[75]

Göransson's international experiences also were important in presenting the state of the art of church law in Germany in relation to the Swedish situation, where church law since the early 1950s had been abolished in the curriculum of Swedish law schools.[76] He also reviewed books on German church law for his Swedish audience.[77] His credo was that Swedish church law should receive the status given to the subject among German Christian jurists.

Göransson and the concept of theology of law (*Rechtstheologie*)

During his career, Göransson had a European Lutheran view of the concept of ecclesiastical law that he based on theological grounds. In Germany, the theology of law (*Rechtstheologie*) had been an enduring discourse. In the 1990s—when the reform in Sweden was adopted and implemented—he repeatedly returned to the theological context.

When his Turku colleague Gunnar Träskman, in an article regarding the Finnish church law reform of 1993, emphasized that church law had to be attached to divine law—that is, to the constitutive elements of the church, evangelism, and the sacraments—Göransson totally agreed. Confession defined the commitment.[78] He referred to this article and related it to the new church law to be adopted in 1992. He also published an article on the necessity of the theological dimension of church law.[79]

In the continuous work on changing the relation between the Swedish state and church, Carl Axel Petri, the president of the Göta Court of Appeal, chaired a commission that resulted in an opening for the new relation adopted in 1998. Göransson took part in this commission regarding the investigation related to the property of the church.[80] He was generally critical of the development of this field of law after 1974.[81] In a festschrift article honoring Andreas Aarflot, the Norwegian bishop, he completely agreed with Aarflot's imperative statement, "Let the church be church" (*La kirken være kirke*).[82] The possibilities of influencing state legislation and judicature had to occur in the preaching of the gospel and participation in Christian organizations and congregations. In postwar Sweden, a secularized—and, from a religious perspective, neutral—welfare state, the possibilities to reach this form of idealistic Christian community were small. Göransson quoted an anonymous German theologian: "How should theology help at the foundation of legal science, when the jurist does not participate in the decline of its last bond, that to God?"[83] An Evangelical Lutheran "folkchurch" (*Folkkyrka*) cannot live in a constant tension between the constitutional sovereignty principle and the society of baptized members with constitutional principles, administrations, and jurisdictions of its own.

With his internationally oriented background since the late 1940s, Göransson developed an extensive international network. He also took part in several postwar legal and theological discourses in the Protestant world, especially in Germany, and that work gave him important contextual perspectives on the intersection between law and religion.

Göran Göransson's contributions to ecclesiastical law from an academic as well as more pragmatic and realistic perspective resulted in a 1995 honorary degree given to him by the Theological Faculty at Lund University. The faculty emphasized in its justification that Göransson "in his practical deed and in his theoretical work with ecclesiastical law acquired deep insights and reported knowledge characterized by qualified analytical overview and valuable educational ability."[84] In connection with this event, Göransson delivered a lecture in which he referenced Ruben Josefson's statement 1941, and continued:

> Today the task for *Rechtstheologie* might be to investigate how such [life values] have to be formulated for citizens of our time, and how they have to be implemented into a legal framework for a multicultural society. From my point of view, there are in this case tasks for a theological study on which fundamental values we share and can uphold together with other religious communities represented in our country.[85]

He also returned to the importance of legal theology within church law.

Göransson quoted Josefson in 1995, the same year in which Sweden became a member of the European Union and incorporated the ECHR into Swedish law. He wanted to regard the church law from a more contextual perspective and uphold the contextual, deep structures of ecclesiastical law. The theological principles, so special for ecclesiastical law, had to be observed, he said: "Church law is not only a set of administrative legal rules, *Verwaltungsrecht*, it has also an underlying theology, a *Rechtstheologie*, that belongs to the transnational, borderless deep structures of European law." In that sense, he connected to the concept of Barth and the debates he had met on the spirit and fundamental common values in the early 1950s.

Göransson became the Swedish interpreter of the intertwining of law and theology in secularized, modern Swedish society, and his theological positions became of great importance for the new role of the Swedish church after 2000, even in relation to an international audience.[86]

After the signing of the Maastricht treaty in 1992, the initiated discussions with the churches in the future member-states on the relation between church and state within the European Community. Because of his good international relations, especially with the German Lutheran Church, Göran Göransson was appointed to be the observer of the Nordic Ecumenical Council (NEC) for the initial consultations in Brussels in April 1993.[87] Göransson reported to the NEC at its meeting in Turku in May of that year.[88] He noted with urgency that the Nordic countries should closely monitor the interests of the Nordic churches because of their close relations to the state. The conflicts between ecclesial legislation and its future changes and the norms within the coming European Union were yet to be seen.[89] Göransson announced he was a "lively supporter" of the European concept and looked at the European communities as a conceivable instrument for the realization of a close community. His visit to Brussels, however, confirmed his objections regarding the working models of the European Communities.

Göransson's last mission was as an expert when, in 1996, the Legal, Financial and Administrative Services Agency (*Kammarkollegiet*) investigated the basis/presumptions for the property of the church because of the new relations between the state and the church implemented in 2000.[90]

Conclusion

Göransson passed away in 1998, the same year that the Swedish parliament decided the legislation regarding the new relationship between the state and the autonomous Swedish Church.[91] During his lifetime, he became an important catalyst for the transformation of Swedish church law. In a time dominated by secularization, with the help of a historical argumentation throughout the decades, he consistently upheld the deep structures related to European Christian theology and law.

In the new millennium, his work and thought have resulted in new perspectives on this field of law, as a result of a desecularization of the modern concept of administrative church law. One example of this transition is the new Swedish Church Order of 1999, which took effect after the change of relations between the state and church in 2000. In this order for the Swedish Church as an autonomous entity in relation to the state, each chapter has a preamble containing the theological arguments for the administrative legal rules to follow.[92]

This example demonstrates not only a new relationship between state and church but also an example of a postsecular time, to which Göran Göransson contributed to a great extent from its inception. His views on *Rechtstheologie* and law and religion come into distinct focus within contemporary Swedish interdisciplinary legal research.[93]

Notes

1 My warm thanks to G. Göransson's widow, Gudrun Göransson, and their daughters, Birgitta Stymme Göransson and Annika Mörner for their valuable information and support for this article.

2 Max Lyles, "A Call for Scientific Purity: Axel Hägerström's Critique of Legal Science," Vol. 65 of Skrifter/Institutet för Rättshistorisk Forskning: Ser. I, Rättshistoriskt bibliotek (Stockholm, 2006).

3 Paul Harnesk (red.), Vem är vem? Vol. 3 Götalandsdelen utom Skåne, Stockholm 1948, 364.

4 Juridiska examina höstterminen 1951, Svensk Juristtidning (1952), 334.

5 Gert Borgenstierna, Nils Karlström & Gustaf Risberg (eds.), En minnes- och vänbok, (Stockholm: Svenska Kyrkans Diakonistyrelses Bokförlag, 1950). Bo Bengtson & Gunnar Åkerstedt, En bok om Torsten Bohlin av 40 författare. (Uppsala: J.A. Lindblads Förlag, 1950). I thank Harald Bohlin of Uppsala for important information about his father, Torsten Bohlin.

6 Göran Göransson, "Min konfirmationslärare," in: *Bo Bengtson & Gunnar Åkerstedt*, (1950), 307 ff.

7 Torsten Bohlin, *Kristen livssyn: Frågor och svar*, (Stockholm: Svenska kyrkans diakonistyrelse, 1941). This book was based on Bohlin's major work, *Evangelisk troslära* (Stockholm: SKD, 1937) and based on his lectures at Uppsala from 1932 to 1935.

8 Göran Göransson, (1950), 307.

9 "[H]an underlättade för andra att se till det väsentliga i kristendomen och att våga *börja* tro. Så hjälpte han oss de första stegen, de som är de svåraste och som man tvekar mest inför." Göransson (1950), 310.

10 Chairman in the Swedish Christian Student Union in Gothenburg (1945) and in Student Christian Movement of Sweden in Uppsala (1949–50).

11 Göransson, Göran. "Om rätten och rättsteologin," *Svensk Teologisk Kvartaltidskrift* 71, no. 3 (1995): 115.

12 Jarl Hemberg, Etik och lagstiftning: *En studie av rättsfilosofisk teoribildning och konkret lagstiftningsarbete*, (Uppsala: Verbum-Dialog, 1975).

13 Håkan Hagwall, "Dagens namn: Krister Stendahl," *Svensk Tidskrift* (1984): 563 f.

14 See Anders Jarlert's article on Halvar G. F. Sundberg in this volume.

15 Halvar G F Sundberg, *Kyrkorätt* [Institutet för offentlig och internationell rätt] (Uppsala: Helsingfors, 1948).

16 Fredrik Sterzel, "Halvar G. F. Sundberg," *SBL* 34: 205 ff.

17 Göran Göransson, "Om rätten och rättsteologin," *STK* 71 (1995): 112.

18 Kjell Å Modéer, "Den kulan visste var den tog," in Torbjörn Andersson & Bengt Lindell (eds.), *Festskrift till Per-Henrik Lindblom* (Uppsala: Iustus förlag, 2004), 443 ff.

19 Göran Göransson, "Självförsvar av en barbar," *Ergo* [Organ för Uppsala studentkår] 2 (1950): 23.

20 Torsten Bohlin, "Kampen för människovärdet," in Natanael Beskow (ed.), *En bok om människan.* Av tjugofem författare (Stockholm: P.A. Norstedt & Söners Förlag, 1942), 25. This article was given by the author to Göran Göransson as an off-print.
21 Jens Holger Schjørring et al. (eds.), *From Federation to Communion: The History of the Lutheran World Federation* (Minneapolis, MN: Fortress Press, 1997).
22 Jens Holger Schjørring (ed.), *Nordiske folkekirker i opbrud. National identitet og internationell nyorientering efter 1945* (Århus: Aarhus Universitetsforlag, 2001), 417.
23 Göran Göransson, Kristna världsungdomsmötet i Oslo – ett femtioårsminne. Ärkestiftet [*En hälsning till församlingarna i ärkestiftet*] 1998–99, 89–92.
24 Oslo 1947: World Conference of Christian Youth. Conference papers and programmes (1947). At the private boarding-school Lundsberg in Sweden, the WSCF also held a summer school August 1–9, 1947. Yale Divinity Library, YMCA Student Division Records: RG 58, Delegate list and morning prayer service for WSCF Lundsberg Conference, August 1–9, 1947.
25 Gunnar Heiene, "Den norske kirke og økumenikken i etterkrigstiden," in Holger Schjørring (ed.), *Nordiske Folkekirker i Opbrud* (2001), 392.
26 Charles C. Brown, *Niebuhr and His Age: Reinhold Niebuhr's Prophetic Role and Legacy* (Harrisburg, PA: Trinity Press, 2002), 142.
27 Göran Göransson, "Oslo 1947," Göteborgs-Posten nr 243 (9.9.1947), 2.
28 Charles C. Brown, Niebuhr (2002), 142.
29 Göran Göransson, "Oslo 1947," *Göteborgs-Posten,* nr 243, (1947), 2.
30 Göran Göransson, Amsterdam – splittring eller enhet? SKS – Organ för Sveriges Kristliga Studentrörelse, (Nr 4 – oktober, 1948), 50 ff.
31 Göran Göransson, Amsterdam, SKS (1948), 52.
32 Göran Göransson, Amsterdam, SKS (1948), 53.
33 Göran Göransson, STK (1995), 113.
34 Carl Gustaf Andrén to KÅM, e-mail 03/24/17.
35 Göran Göransson, "Sommartermin vid Rhen," *Ergo* [Organ för Uppsala Studentkår] 9 (1950):144, 147.
36 "Christians and Power-Politics," *The Student World* [Special issue] 41/3, Third Quarter (1948).
37 Karl Barth, *Rechtfertigung und Recht*, 2. Ed. Theologische Studien. Eine Schriftenreihe hrggn. von Karl Barth (Zollikon-Zürich: Evangelischer Verlag A.G., 1944).
38 Andreas Pangritz, *Politischer Gottesdienst: Zur theologischen Begründung des Widerstands* bei Karl Barth, https://www.ev-theol.uni-bonn.de/.../politischer-gottesdienst.pdf, 12.
39 Alice Lorber, "Divine Power and Human Politics: Karl Barths understanding of Church and State in His Writings from 1926 – 1946. An Investigation of the Consistency of his Thought," in Heather M Morgan, Jerner Letnar Černič, and Lindsay Milligan (eds.), *Perspectives on Power: An Inter-Disciplinary Approach* (Newcastle: Cambridge Scholars, 2010), 175.
40 Cfr Torsten Bohlin, Kampen för människovärdet. In: Stellan Arvidsson/Torsten Bohlin, Kristendomen: mot – för, (Stockholm: Natur och Kultur, 1947).
41 Göran Göransson, *Om rätten och rättsteologien*, STK (1995), 115.
42 Ruben Josefson, Rätten och den kristna moralen, Svenska Kyrkans Diakonistyrelses Bokförlag 1941.
43 Religionsfrihetslag, SFS (1951):680.
44 Göran Göransson, *On Religious Liberty in Sweden, Lutheran World* [Publication of the Lutheran World Federation] 3/1(June, 1956): 81.
45 Göran Göransson, Riksdag och kyrkomöte, Kristen student [Sveriges kristliga studentrörelse] nr 5: (1951), 3 ff (6).
46 Oloph Bexell, "Carl Strandberg 1926-2013," *Svensk Pastoraltidskrift* (2013): 593 ff.

47 Carl Strandberg, Andra kinden – eller väktarns lur. Inför höstens kyrkomötesfrågor, Kristen student, nr 5:(1951), 11.
48 (14.12.1951) – Juridiska examina höstterminen 1951, SvJT 1952, 334.
49 Sören Ekström, 3.
50 Giertz Archiv, University Library Lund.
51 Bo Giertz to Halvar Sundberg 1952 4/7.

> Jag har vid flera tillfällen talat med Persson /=Skabersjö/ om Departementets nyrekryteringsfråga och försökt få honom förstå, att det är nödvändigt att få in tjänstemän som har något sinne för vad kyrkan är och vill.—Det vore verkligen mycket vunnet, om man kunde få in ett par bra karlar i Departementet. Som universitetslärare kanske Du får en eller annan kontakt eller får ögonen på någon, som möjligen kunde vara lämplig.

52 The other was Ivar Nylander [1915–2012], later associate professor in legal history. Halvar Sundberg to Bo Giertz, Letter 1952 7/7.

> jag har två synnerligen kompetenta namn att föreslå omedelbart. Den ena är jur. och fil. kand. Göran Göransson, som jag tror son till statistikern i Göteborg, den andre teol. och jur.kand. V.D.M. Ivar Nylander. Huruvida de stå att få är mig däremot icke bekant. Jag tror, att Göransson har för avsikt att fortsätta sina studier, och Nylander håller sedan flera år tillbaka på med en avhandling om episkopatet under medeltiden.

Bo Giertz archive, LUB. I thank Prof. Anders Jarlert for this reference.
53 Riksförbundet kyrklig ungdom (Chair), Kristliga studentförbundet i Göteborg resp. Uppsala (Chair), Ekumeniska nämnden (Member).
54 SOU 1968:11 Svenska kyrkan och staten—Slutbetänkande.
55 Sören Ekström, Kyrkan och staten: Förteckning omfattande utredningarnas sammansättning 1956–1999, 9. Latest review: (March 27, 2011). https://www.yumpu.com/sv/document/read/4347063/staten-utredningarnas-soren-ekstrom.
56 Sören Ekström, Makten över kyrkan. Om svenska kyrkan folket och staten, Verbum: (Stockholm, 2003, 328.
57 Göran Göransson, "Skapelse –människovärde – frihet," *Kyrkans ungdom*, nr 3 (1965), 67.
58 Göran Göransson, "Angår oss de mänskliga rättigheterna?" *Vår Kyrka*, Nr 46, (1974), 3.
59 Göran Göransson, *Vår Kyrka* (1974), 3.
60 Sören Ekström, Makten över kyrkan.(2003), 206.
61 SOU 1971:29, 1972:36 (Samhälle och trossamfund). Fredrik Sterzel, Staten och kyrkan, Svensk Juristtidning (1974), 269–294.
62 Sören Ekström, Makten över kyrkan (2003), 136 ff.
63 Sören Ekström, Makten över kyrkan (2003), 138.
64 Göran Göransson, Kyrkolagarna, del 6, Kyrkans egendom, Älvsjö: Verbum 2 uppl. 1983.
65 Framtid i samverkan : 1982 års kyrkokommittés slutförslag till lokal och regional organisation i Svenska kyrkan, Liber: (Stockholm, 1986).
66 Sören Ekström, Makten över kyrkan (2003), 158 ff, 169 ff.
67 Dopet. Teologiskt, kyrkorättsligt, pastoralt. Rapport från Biskopsmötets teologiska kommission 1983 om dop och kyrkotillhörighet (1984).
68 Palmqvist's position may have been an expression of an obsolete theology from the 1950s and 1960s, during which "the open folk church" was emphasized as a sign of God's grace. (R. Bring, R. Josefsson m.fl.). Gunnar Träskman (review.) Göran Göransson, Svensk kyrkorätt (1993), Preben Espersen, Kirkeret, Almindelig del (1993).

69 Church law 1992: Kyrkolag (SFS 1992:300).

70 Göran Göransson, Svensk kyrkorätt: en översikt, (Stockholm: Norstedt, 1993).

71 "Men begränsar man synfältet till enbart det statliga regelverket, riskerar man att förlora blicken för vad som utgör kyrkorättens specifika väsen. Kyrkan skulle med ett sådant synsätt vara en institution som helt och hållet vore en skapelse av den svenska rättsordningen och som står och faller med förekomsten av en statlig kyrkolagstiftning." Göransson, Svensk kyrkorätt (1993), 18.

72 Göran Göransson, "Reform des Staatskirchenrechts in Schweden?" Zeitschrift für evangelisches Kirchenrecht, Vol 15 (1970), 60 ff.

73 Erich Ruppel, "Dritter Studienkurs für Kirchenjuristen in Pullach," *Zeitschrift für evangelisches Kirchenrecht*, 18 (1973): 270 f.—Göran Göransson, "Religion und Staatskirchenreform," *Zeitschrift für evangelisches Kirchenrecht*, 19 (1974): 106 ff.

74 Göran Göransson, "1979–1984, fünf Jahre staatkirchlicher Entwicklung in Schweden," *Zeitschrift für evangelisches Kirchenrecht*, 29 (1984): 578 ff.

75 Göran Göransson, "Die Majestät des Vaterlandes und die Kirche Gottes, die darin ruht." "Die Entwicklung des Kirchenrechtes in Schweden in 1000 Jahren," *Zeitschrift der Savigny-Stiftung für Rechtsgeschichte Kanonistische Abteilung* (ZRG KA) 66 (1980): 421–53 . Göran Göransson, "Neuere Entwicklungen im Verhältnis von Staat und Kirche in Schweden," *Zeitschrift der Savigny-Stiftung für Rechtsgeschichte Kanonistische Abteilung* (ZRG KA) 81 (1995): 372–80.

76 Göran Göransson, Kyrkorätt – något att lära i Tyskland, Juristnytt, våren (1969).

77 [Rev.] E Friesenhahn & U.Scheuner, Handbuch des Staatkirchenrechts der Bundesrepublik Deutschland [Berlin 1974-75]: Göran Göransson, Problemet kyrka-stat i tysk belysning, [Under strecket], SvD (1975-10-24).

78 Gunnar Träskman, "Kyrkorätten som teologi," *Svensk Pastoraltidskrift* 16, (1991): 269–273.

79 Göran Göransson, "Kyrkolag och rättsteologi," *Svensk Kyrkotidning*, sommaren (1991).

80 Göran Göransson & Robert Schött, *Kyrklig egendom: en kommentar.* (Stockholm: Norstedts Juridik, 1996).

81 Göran Göransson, "Normgivningskompetens och kyrka-stat-relation i svenskt perspektiv," In Per-Otto Gullaksen (ed.), *Reform og embete: Festskrift til Andreas Aarflot på 65-årsdagen den 1.* (juli, 1993), (Oslo: Universitetsforlaget, 1993).

82 Andreas Aarflot, *Let the Church Be the Church. The Voice and Mission of the People of God* (Minneapolis, MN: 1988); Norwegian edition: *La kirken være kirke*, 1990).

83 "Wie soll die Theologie bei der Grundlegung der Rechtswissenschaft helfen, wenn der Jurist den Rückgang auf die letzte Bindung, auf Gott nicht mitmacht?" Göransson, "Om rätten och rättsteologin," *Svensk Teologisk Kvartalstidskrift* (STK) 71 (1995): 115.

84 Lunds universitet: Doktorspromotionen 24.5.1995. Hedersdoktorer (1995) Teologiska fakulteten. "Göransson har i sin praktiska gärning och i sitt teoretiska arbete med kyrkorättsproblem förvärvat djupa insikter och redovisat kunskaper präglade av kvalificerad analytisk överblick och värdefull pedagogisk förmåga."

85 Göran Göransson, "Om rätten och rättsteologin," *STK*, årgång 71 (1995): 117. "I dag skulle . . . uppgiften för rättsteologin kunna vara att finna ut, hur sådana värderingar skall formuleras för vår tids människor för att kunna omsättas i ett regelverk för ett mångkulturellt samhälle. Här finns då, enligt min mening, också uppgifter för ett teologiskt studium av vilka grundläggande värderingar vi delar och kan hävda tillsammans med andra religionssamfund som är företrädda i vårt land."

86 Kjell Å Modéer, "Religionens plats i det offentliga rummet: Rättshistoriska och rättskulturella perspektiv," *STK* (2005): 2ff.

87 Letter from Virpi Pakkanen-Wiberg (NEC) to Göran Göransson, Uppsala (March 3, 1993).

88 Manuscript report of NEC meeting in Turku (May 22, 1993).
89 Göran Göransson, Manuscript report from a EECCS-consultation on Church-State relations and the EC. [Rapport från en EECCS-konsultation om kyrka-stat-relationerna och EG.)
90 SOU (1997:47). Experts: F.d. departementsrådet Göran Göransson, direktorn Lennart Stolt, kyrkojuristen Anders Karlberg, lantmätaren Thomas Linder och professorn Bertil Bengtsson.
91 Law re. the Swedish Church: Lag om Svenska kyrkan, SFS (1998):1591.
92 Preambles in the Church Order to safeguard the confession was recommended by Göransson in a talk "The Belief of the Folk-Church" [Folkkyrkans tro] at a church law seminar in Lund (October 11, 1996).
93 Kjell Å Modéer, "Religionens plats i det offentliga rummet. Rättshistoriska och rättskulturella perspektiv," *STK* (2005): 1ff.

Bibliography

Literature

Aarflot, Andreas, *Let the Church Be the Church. The Voice and Mission of the People of God* (Minneapolis, MN: Augsburg Publishing House, 1988).

Barth, Karl, *Rechtfertigung und Recht*, 2. Ed. Theologische Studien. Eine Schriftenreihe hrggn. von Karl Barth (Zollikon-Zürich: Evangelischer Verlag A.G., 1944).

Bengtson, Bo & Åkerstedt, Gunnar (eds.), *En bok om Torsten Bohlin av 40 författare.* (Uppsala: J.A. Lindblads Förlag, 1950).

Oloph, Bexell, "Carl Strandberg 1926–2013." *Svensk Pastoraltidskrift Nr 20, 55* (2013): 593–601.

Bohlin, Torsten, "Kampen för människovärdet." In Natanael Beskow (ed.), *En bok om människan.* Av tjugofem författare (Stockholm: P.A. Norstedt & Söners Förlag, 1942), 19–25.

Bohlin, Torsten, *Kristen livssyn: Frågor och svar*, Svenska kyrkans diakonistyrelse (Stockholm, 1941).

Borgenstierna, Gert, Karlström, Nils & Risberg, Gustaf (eds.), *En minnes- och vänbok* (Stockholm: Svenska Kyrkans Diakonistyrelses Bokförlag, 1950).

Brown, Charles C, *Niebuhr and His Age: Reinhold Niebuhr's Prophetic Role and Legacy* (Harrisburg, PA: Trinity Press, 2002).

"Christians and Power-Politics." *The Student World* [Special issue] 41/3, Third Quarter (1948).

Ekström, Sören, *Makten över kyrkan. Om svenska kyrkan folket och staten* (Stockholm: Verbum, 2003).

Ekström, Sören, *Kyrkan och staten: Förteckning omfattande utredningarnas sammansättning 1956–1999*, 9. Latest review: (March 27, 2011). https://www.yumpu.com/sv/document/read/4347063/staten-utredningarnas-soren-ekstrom

Göransson, Göran, "Amsterdam – splittring eller enhet?" *SKS – Organ för Sveriges Kristliga Studentrörelse*, (Nr 4 – oktober, 1948), 50–53.

Göransson, Göran, "Angår oss de mänskliga rättigheterna?" *Vår Kyrka*, Nr 46, (1974), 3.

Göransson, Göran, "Die Majestät des Vaterlandes und die Kirche Gottes, die darin ruht." "Die Entwicklung des Kirchenrechtes in Schweden in 1000 Jahren." *Zeitschrift der Savigny-Stiftung für Rechtsgeschichte Kanonistische Abteilung* (ZRG KA) 66 (1980), 421–53.

Göransson, Göran, "Kristna världsungdomsmötet i Oslo – ett femtioårsminne." *Ärkestiftet* [En hälsning till församlingarna i ärkestiftet] (1998–99), 89–92.
Göransson, Göran, Kyrkolagarna, del 6, Kyrkans egendom, Älvsjö: Verbum 2 uppl. 1983.
Göransson, Göran, "Kyrkolag och rättsteologi." *Svensk Kyrkotidning*, sommaren (1991).
Göransson, Göran, "Kyrkorätt – något att lära i Tyskland." *Juristnytt*, våren 1969.
Göransson, Göran, "Neuere Entwicklungen im Verhältnis von Staat und Kirche in Schweden." *Zeitschrift der Savigny-Stiftung für Rechtsgeschichte Kanonistische Abteilung* (ZRG KA) 81 (1995), 372–80.
Göransson, Göran, "Normgivningskompetens och kyrka-stat-relation i svenskt perspektiv." In: Gullaksen, Per-Otto (ed.), *Reform og embete: Festskrift til Andreas Aarflot på 65-årsdagen den 1.* (juli, 1993), (Oslo: Universitetsforlaget, 1993).
Göransson, Göran, "Om rätten och rättsteologin." *Svensk Teologisk Kvartaltidskrift* (STK) 71, no. 3 (1995), 111–18.
Göransson, Göran, *On Religious Liberty in Sweden, Lutheran World* [Publication of the Lutheran World Federation] 3/1(June, 1956), 78–84.
Göransson, Göran, "Oslo 1947." *Göteborgs-Posten*, nr 243, (September 9, 1947), 2.
Göransson, Göran, "Problemet kyrka-stat i tysk belysning." [Under strecket], *Svenska Dagbladet* (October 24, 1975).
Göransson, Göran, "Reform des Staatskirchenrechts in Schweden?" *Zeitschrift für evangelisches Kirchenrecht*, 15 (1970), 60–76.
Göransson, Göran, "Religion und Staatskirchenreform." *Zeitschrift für evangelisches Kirchenrech*t, 19 (1974), 106–24.
Göransson, Göran, "Riksdag och kyrkomöte." *Kristen student* [Sveriges kristliga studentrörelse], no. 5 (1951), 3–6.
Göransson, Göran, "Självförsvar av en barbar." *Ergo* [Organ för Uppsala studentkår] 2 (1950), 23.
Göransson, Göran, "Skapelse –människovärde – frihet." *Kyrkans ungdom*, nr 3 (1965), 66–69.
Göransson, Göran, "Sommartermin vid Rhen." *Ergo* [Organ för Uppsala Studentkår] 9. (1950), 144–47.
Göransson, Göran, *Svensk kyrkorätt: en översikt.* (Stockholm: Norstedt, 1993).
Göransson, Göran, "1979–1984, fünf Jahre staatkirchlicher Entwicklung in Schweden." *Zeitschrift für evangelisches Kirchenrecht*, 29 (1984), 578–85.
Göransson, Göran &Schött, Robert, *Kyrklig egendom: en kommentar.* (Stockholm: Norstedts Juridik, 1996).
Hagwall, Håkan, "Dagens namn: Krister Stendahl." *Svensk Tidskrift* (1984), 563 f.
Hemberg, Jarl, *Etik och lagstiftning: En studie av rättsfilosofisk teoribildning och konkret lagstiftningsarbete.* Uppsala: Verbum-Dialog, 1975).
Harnesk, Paul (ed.), Vem är vem? D. 3 Götalandsdelen utom Skåne (Stockholm, 1948).
Heiene, Gunnar, "Den norske kirke og økumenikken i etterkrigstiden," in Schjørring, Holger (ed.), *Nordiske Folkekirker i Opbrud* (Aarhus Universitetsforlag: Aarhus, 2001), 385–98.
Josefson, Ruben, *Rätten och den kristna moralen.* Stockholm, Svenska Kyrkans Diakonistyrelses Bokförlag, 1941.
"Juridiska examina höstterminen 1951," *Svensk Juristtidning* (1952), 334.
Lorber, Alice, "Divine Power and Human Politics: Karl Barths Understanding of Church and State in His Writings from 1926–1946. An Investigation of the Consistency of His Thought," in Morgan, Heather M, Černič, Jerner Letnar, and Milligan, Lindsay

(eds.), *Perspectives on Power: An Inter-Disciplinary Approach* (Newcastle: Cambridge Scholars, 2010), 172–88.
Lyles, Max, "A Call for Scientific Purity: Axel Hägerström's Critique of Legal Science," Vol. 65 Institutet för Rättshistorisk Forskning: Ser. I, Rättshistoriskt bibliotek (Stockholm, 2006).
Modéer, Kjell Å, "Den kulan visste var den tog," in Andersson, Torbjörn & Lindell, Bengt (eds.), *Festskrift till Per-Henrik Lindblom* (Uppsala: Iustus förlag, 2004), 443–68.
Modéer, Kjell Å "Religionens plats i det offentliga rummet: Rättshistoriska och rättskulturella perspektiv," *Svensk Teologisk Kvartaltidskrift* 81, no. 1 (2005), 2–13.
Pangritz, Andreas, *Politischer Gottesdienst: Zur theologischen Begründung des Widerstands* bei Karl Barth, https://www.ev-theol.uni-bonn.de/.../politischer-gottesdienst.pdf, 12.
Ruppel, Erich, "Dritter Studienkurs für Kirchenjuristen in Pullach," *Zeitschrift für evangelisches Kirchenrecht*, 18 (1973), 270–71.
Schjørring, Jens Holger, et al. (eds.), *From Federation to Communion: The History of the Lutheran World Federation* (Minneapolis, MN: Fortress Press, 1997).
Schjørring, Jens Holger (ed.), *Nordiske folkekirker i opbrud. National identitet og internationell nyorientering efter 1945* (Århus: Aarhus Universitetsforlag, 2001).
Sterzel, Fredrik, "Halvar G. F. Sundberg," *Svenskt Biografiskt Lexikon, Vol.* 34 (Stockholm 2013–2019), 205–207.
Sterzel, Fredrik, "Staten och kyrkan," *Svensk Juristtidning* (1974), 269–294.
Strandberg, Carl, "Andra kinden – eller väktarns lur. Inför höstens kyrkomötesfrågor," *Kristen student,* nr 5 (1951), 10–14.
Sundberg, Halvar G F, *Kyrkorätt* [Institutet för offentlig och internationell rätt] (Uppsala: Helsingfors, 1948).

Unprinted and printed sources

Göran Göransson's Archive Stockholm

Träskman, Gunnar (review.) Göran Göransson, Svensk kyrkorätt (1993), Preben Espersen, Kirkeret, Almindelig del (1993). [Manuscript].
Letter from Virpi Pakkanen-Wiberg (NEC) to Göran Göransson, Uppsala (March 3, 1993).
Manuscript report of Nordic Ecumenical Council's meeting in Turku (May 22, 1993).
Manuscript report from a EECCS-consultation on Church-State relations and the EC. [Rapport från en EECCS-konsultation om kyrka-stat-relationerna och EG.)
Manuscript "The Belief of the Folk-Church" [Folkkyrkans tro] at a church law seminar in Lund (October 11, 1996).

Lund University Library (LUB):

Bo Giertz' Archive

Letters: Halvar Sundberg to Bo Giertz 1952.
Lunds universitet: Doktorspromotionen 24.5.1995. Hedersdoktorer (1995) Teologiska fakulteten.

Printed sources

Act on Freedom of Religion 1951: *Religionsfrihetslag*, SFS (1951):680.
Swedish Church law 1992: *Kyrkolag* SFS (1992):300).
Law re. the Swedish Church: *Lag om Svenska kyrkan*, SFS (1998):1591.
SOU 1968:11 Svenska kyrkan och staten – Slutbetänkande.
SOU 1971:29, 1972:36 (Samhälle och trossamfund).
SOU (1997:47). Kyrklig egendom – Slutbetänkande.
Dopet. Teologiskt, kyrkorättsligt, pastoralt. Rapport från Biskopsmötets teologiska kommission 1983 om dop och kyrkotillhörighet (1984).
Framtid i samverkan : 1982 års kyrkokommittés slutförslag till lokal och regional organisation i Svenska kyrkan, Liber: (Stockholm, 1986).
Oslo-1947: World Conference of Christian Youth. Conference papers and programmes (1947) (Unpublished material: Google books).
Yale Divinity Library, YMCA Student Division Records: RG 58, Delegate list and morning prayer service for WSCF Lundsberg Conference, August 1–9, 1947.

Names and Places Index

General Index

For Product Safety Concerns and Information please contact our EU
representative GPSR@taylorandfrancis.com
Taylor & Francis Verlag GmbH, Kaufingerstraße 24, 80331 München, Germany

www.ingramcontent.com/pod-product-compliance
Ingram Content Group UK Ltd.
Pitfield, Milton Keynes, MK11 3LW, UK
UKHW020023200926
475702UK00014B/2027

* 9 7 8 0 3 6 7 5 6 3 5 7 8 *